JUSTICE UNBOUND

JUSTICE UNBOUND
VOICES OF JUSTICE FOR THE 21ST CENTURY

Patrizia Longo

ROWMAN &
LITTLEFIELD
———INTERNATIONAL———
London • New York

Published by Rowman & Littlefield International Ltd

6 Tinworth Street, London SE11 5AL
www.rowmaninternational.com
Rowman & Littlefield International Ltd is an affiliate of Rowman & Littlefield
4501 Forbes Boulevard, Suite 200, Lanham, Maryland 20706, USA
With additional offices in Boulder, New York, Toronto (Canada), and Plymouth (UK)
www.rowman.com

Copyright © 2019 by Patrizia Longo

All rights reserved. No part of this book may be reproduced in any form or by any electronic or mechanical means, including information storage and retrieval systems, without written permission from the publisher, except by a reviewer who may quote passages in a review.

British Library Cataloguing in Publication Data
A catalogue record for this book is available from the British Library

ISBN: HB 978-1-7866-0813-0
PB 978-1-7866-0814-7

Library of Congress Cataloging-in-Publication Data
Names: Longo, Patrizia, author.
Title: Justice unbound : voices of justice for the 21st century / Patrizia
   Longo.
Description: London ; New York : Rowman & Littlefield International, Ltd.,
   [2018] | Includes bibliographical references and index.
Identifiers: LCCN 2018041039 (print) | LCCN 2018050970 (ebook) |
   ISBN 9781786608154 (electronic) | ISBN 9781786608130 (cloth : alk. paper) |
   ISBN 9781786608147 (pbk. : alk. paper)
Subjects: LCSH: Justice. | Social justice. | Environmental justice. |
   Transitional justice.
Classification: LCC JC578 (ebook) | LCC JC578 .L67 2018 (print) | DDC
   320.01/1—dc23
LC record available at https://lccn.loc.gov/2018041039

∞™ The paper used in this publication meets the minimum requirements of American National Standard for Information Sciences—Permanence of Paper for Printed Library Materials, ANSI/NISO Z39.48-1992.

Printed in the United States of America

Dedication

For Anthony Kortens for his unwavering commitment to justice

Contents

Preface by Charles W Mills xi

Acknowledgements xv

Permissions xvii

INTRODUCTION 1

SECTION I From the State of Nature to Society: The Social Contract and Its Critics 5

John Locke, 'Freedom and Property' 10

Jean-Jacques Rousseau, 'Freedom and Equality' 17

Jean-Jacques Rousseau, 'The Social Contract' 20

John Rawls, 'Two Principles of Justice' 25

Carole Pateman, 'The Sexual Contract' 32

Carole Pateman, 'Consent' 34

Charles W Mills, 'The Racial Contract and Ideal Theory' 40

CASE STUDY: J M Dieterle, 'Food Deserts and Lockean Property' 46

CASE STUDY: Ronald M Green, 'Health Care and Justice in Contract Theory Perspective' 58

SECTION II Racial and Gender Justice: The Quest for Civil Rights 69

Maria Stewart, 'Lecture at Franklin Hall' 77

Frederick Douglass, 'What to the Slave Is the Fourth of July'? 80

Ida B Wells, 'A Red Record' 84

Ida B Wells, 'Lynch Law in America' 86

W E B Du Bois, 'How Does It Feel to Be a Problem'? 91

W E B Du Bois, 'The Souls of White Folk' 97

James Baldwin, 'Letter to My Nephew' 106

Ella Baker, 'Address at the Hattiesburg Freedom Day Rally' 108

CASE STUDY: Eduardo Bonilla-Silva, '"Keeping Them in Their Place": The Social Control of Blacks since the 1960s' 110

CASE STUDY: Edwidge Danticat, 'Message to My Daughters' 127

SECTION III Economic Justice and Social Welfare 131

Karl Marx, 'The Power of Money' 135

Karl Marx and Friedrich Engels, 'Communism' 138

Karl Marx, 'Capitalism and Exploitation' 139

Edward Bellamy, 'Looking Backward' 146

Jane Addams, 'Democracy and Charity' 150

Eduardo Bonilla-Silva, 'Racial Economic Inequality' 156

CASE STUDY: Barry Estabrook, 'Politics of the Plate: The Price of Tomatoes' 162

CASE STUDY: Eric Schlosser, 'The Most Dangerous Job' 166

CASE STUDY: Josiah Heyman and Merlyn Heyman, 'Occupy in a Border City: El Paso, Texas, U.S.A.' 170

SECTION IV Environmental Justice: Confronting Racism and Imperialism 183

Robert D Bullard, 'Anatomy of Environmental Racism and the Environmental Justice Movement' 187

James Cone, 'Whose Earth Is It Anyway'? 195

Peter S Wenz, 'Just Garbage' 203

CASE STUDY: Diane-Michele Prindeville, 'For the People: American Indian and Hispanic Women in New Mexico's Environmental Justice Movement' 212

CASE STUDY: Robert Melchior Figueroa, 'Other Faces: Latinos and Environmental Justice' 226

CASE STUDY: Elizabeth Hoover et al. 'Indigenous Peoples of North America: Environmental Exposures and Reproductive Justice' 234

SECTION V Global Justice: Confronting Colonialism and Imperialism 245

Walter D Mignolo, 'Philosophy and the Colonial Difference' 249

Dipesh Chakrabarty, 'The Idea of Provincializing Europe' 254

Aimé Césaire, 'Discourse on Colonialism' 258

Frantz Fanon, 'The Black Man and Language' 261

Frantz Fanon, 'On National Culture' 264

Edward Said, 'Orientalism' 266

Oyèrónkẹ́ Oyěwùmí, 'Colonizing Bodies and Minds: Gender and Colonialism'   276

Rajeev Bhargava, 'Reparations for Cultural Injustice'   293

CASE STUDY: Kinhide Mushakoji, 'The Case of the "Comfort Women": Sexual Slavery by the Japanese Military'   298

CASE STUDY: Ofelia Schutte, 'Resistance to Colonialism: The Latin American Legacy of José Martí'   308

SECTION VI Transitional and Restorative Justice: Working towards a Just World   319

Jennifer Llewellyn, 'Truth Commissions through a Restorative Lens'   323

Louise Mallinder, 'Amnesties in the Pursuit of Reconciliation, Peacebuilding and Restorative Justice'   331

CASE STUDY: Chris Cuneen, 'When Does Transitional Justice Begin and End? Colonised Peoples, Liberal Democracies and Restorative Justice'   339

CASE STUDY: Hon Joan Gottschall and Molly Armour, Rethinking the War on Drugs: What Insights Does Restorative Justice Offer?   355

Glossary   363

Index   367

Preface

Charles W Mills

I am deeply honoured by Patrizia Longo's shout-out to me in her introduction, and delighted to think that I could have played a role in motivating her to do all the hard work necessary to put together this valuable and innovative anthology on justice, *Justice Unbound*.

Some personal history might be useful. As I have described in more than one autobiographical essay – most recently in my 2016 Dewey Lecture at the American Philosophical Association's Central Division annual meeting – I left my native Jamaica in the 1970s to go to graduate school in philosophy.[1] I was hoping to find an illuminating intellectual framework for making sense of the debates then raging in the nation about imperialism, socialism, slavery, race, neo-colonialism, Third World underdevelopment and enduring poverty. Admittedly, I had very little background in the subject. My undergraduate degree at the University of the West Indies had been in physics, though I subsequently did a course (the only one available) with the professor who constituted the one-person philosophy unit on the Mona (Jamaica) campus. But still, I assumed that – as the discipline whose boast it was to provide the Big Picture, the answers to the foundational questions we all had about the world – philosophy was the natural choice.

How profoundly mistaken I was! So disillusioning, so 'white' and unhelpful did I find the field, that more than once I considered dropping out. Imagine a Third World/Global South subject opening a book titled *A Theory of Justice* and being told that our starting point would be to think of society as 'a cooperative venture for mutual advantage', governed by rules 'designed to advance the good of those taking part in it'.[2] How could such a framework possibly make sense of the history of Western domination of the rest of the planet in modernity, as manifest in conquest, expropriation, genocide, colonial rule and racial slavery? And if the reply was that we supposedly needed to start with 'ideal' theory so as to eventually move on, suitably equipped, to 'non-ideal' theory, then why was it – despite the conceded 'pressing and urgent' nature of these matters – that there was no indication (either then or now) that such a transition was actually in progress?[3] Not to mention that the concepts needed to grasp these non-ideal realities would obviously need to be significantly different than those generated from such an idealised starting point.

Yet I decided to persevere, telling myself that perhaps I could establish a space in the discipline, a beachhead, from which, along with other malcontents, I could expand the room to explore what seemed to me (and still seem all these years later) the really important issues. And though the battle is by no means over – as illustrated by the ongoing rarity of anthologies like Longo's – it is clear that progress has been made in recent decades, if one considers the range of topics being discussed in philosophy today and compares it to the far more tightly circumscribed curricula of the 1970s.

So, what historically has the problem been? Why has philosophy been so reluctant to take up these topics? One standard answer is that the abstractness of philosophy as a discipline itself constitutes an obstacle to dealing with real-world issues of social oppression. These are empirical matters best investigated with the tools of history, sociology, political science and so forth, not a discipline committed to the investigation of ontology and being, epistemology and truth, justice and the normative.

But I have come to believe that this answer, plausible as it may initially seem, is wrong. For its tacit assumption is that abstraction cannot illuminate the structures of social oppression, and their impact on people's social being, the actual and ideal cognitive practices of the social order, and the radical deviation of existing societies from the ideal of a just *polis*. If this were true, abstraction as a cognitive enterprise would then be intrinsically limited to the mapping of the ideal, not the non-ideal. And once one extracts this hidden assumption and exposes it to a critical light, it should be obvious how absurd it is. Abstraction as an investigative method can be fruitfully applied both to the realm of the optimal and the realm of the sub-optimal. And since we are almost always in the latter, it is precisely here that our analytical and diagnostic efforts need to be focussed, so that we can improve our understanding of the obstacles to, and thus enhance our chances of, moving closer to the former.[4] As Onora O'Neill pointed out a quarter-century ago – in an essay that I have quoted repeatedly ever since first reading it – the problem in the profession is not abstraction as such, but *idealising* abstractions that abstract away from social oppression and its workings.[5]

Once we reframe the issue in this way, the natural question then raised is: But why should philosophers historically have been so prone to abstractions of this kind? And the answer, I believe, lies in what historically in the Western tradition has been its hugely *unrepresentative* demographic base: class privileged, male, and (from modernity onwards, when race comes into existence) overwhelmingly white. In other words, the sub-section of the population least vulnerable to social oppression. It is the *combination* of demography and the discipline's abstract orientation that has led to such a deeply problematic conceptual array and correspondingly flawed repertoire of investigative practices.

I would contend that we can trace this negative material influence on the ideational across most of the sub-areas of the discipline, but let us concentrate on justice, the theme of this anthology. In the Western tradition, justice as a key subject of philosophical inquiry seems, on the terminological face of it, to go all the way back to Athens of the 5th century BCE. But in fact this appearance is misleading for both Plato and Aristotle. Justice (the standard translation of *dikaiosune*) in Plato, as explored in the *Republic*, is not about the distribution of goods – our contemporary sense – but about the achievement of a particular pattern of harmony in the individual and in the *polis*. Justice in Aristotle, on the other hand, as in the *Nicomachean Ethics*, which might seem unequivocally to fit the description – after all, this is the text that gives us the classic distinction between distributive and rectificatory justice still in use today – turns out to be crucially different from its standard representations in the secondary literature. As the path-breaking work of Samuel Fleischacker has demonstrated, justice for Aristotle is tied to social status, not simple humanity, and does not extend to property rights.[6] The concept of justice with which Rawls and other contemporary philosophers are working is *not* traceable back to antiquity, as is standardly assumed in the profession (including by Rawls himself). Rather, it is first put forward by the French revolutionary François-Nöel ('Gracchus') Babeuf, guillotined in 1797 for his membership in the 'Conspiracy of the Equals'. And even then, of course, it is really 'universal' only over the sub-population of white men. *Their* social status becomes irrelevant; the social status of white women and people of colour does not.

Think about this for a moment. What has become, since Rawls, the central concept of Western normative political philosophy – the distributive justice of society's 'basic structure', and how it affects the rights and opportunities of all members of society, in virtue of their common humanity – is only slightly more than two hundred years old even for white men. For white women and people of colour, the substantive (as against nominal) extension of this concept to their own situation is still being fought over. And rectificatory justice for subordinated groups is even more under-theorised since, of course, they weren't considered worthy of distributive justice in the first place, so what need would there have been to work out the principles of the correction of wrongdoing against them, when it was not even seen *as* wrongdoing? Could there be a clearer illustration of how seemingly neutral and all-encompassing philosophical abstractions, stratospherically removed in ideal Platonic space from our vulgar material bodies, have in fact been deeply shaped from the start by illicit social privilege, by class and gender and racial domination? 'Justice' very much bound!

Once one understands the development of the profession in this historical and material context, its elisions, evasions and moral shirkings immediately become un-mysterious. Social justice as a concept has not been theorised in a way sensitive to the situation of the subordinated because its theorisers have for the most part not been drawn from their ranks. To put it bluntly (but not, I believe, unfairly), social justice as a *concept* has been in the hands of the people not merely with the least experience of social injustice, but with the most to lose from social justice as a *reality*. Is it any wonder that its conceptual genesis and subsequent trajectory has been so problematic, so unresponsive to the actual problems of the majority of the population?

And that brings me back to Rawls and my introduction to his work in graduate school. As I write this preface in the summer of 2018 – only three years away from the fiftieth anniversary of the 1971 publication of the book – the promised segue to non-ideal theory and corrective justice, that never took place in his own work, has not manifested itself in the vast body of secondary literature produced by his disciples, interlocutors and exegetes either. Historical injustice, above all the racial injustice of an American polity originally founded as a white supremacist state, is simply ignored, as is the broader colonial legacy of the Western-imposed polities of modernity, despite the fact that the later Rawls explicitly made them his normative reference point.[7]

For any undergraduates considering grad school in political philosophy, or, for that matter, any grad students already in school surveying the field, who are shocked to find the sub-discipline so removed from the discussions of social justice in the real world, be reassured. There *is* an alternative, as this anthology will make clear to you. It could be said (to modify a phrase from recent American electoral politics) to represent the social justice wing of the American social justice philosophical community. It is an anthology that takes as its starting point the *actual* non-ideal reality of social injustice, whether of class, race, gender or colonial domination, and then asks what social justice demands of us under such circumstances. It is an anthology, in sum, that is serious about guiding us towards creating a better world. Had I been introduced to political philosophy with such a book, I would not have been tempted to drop out in the first place – and, I believe, neither will you.

Notes

1. Charles W Mills, 'The Red and the Black', *Proceedings and Addresses of the American Philosophical Association* 90 (November 2016): 90–113.
2. John Rawls, *A Theory of Justice*, rev ed (Cambridge, MA: Harvard University Press, 1999), p 4.
3. Rawls, *Theory of Justice*, p. 8.
4. Charles W Mills, '"Ideal Theory" as Ideology' (2004), rpt in Mills, *Black Rights/White Wrongs: The Critique of Racial Liberalism* (New York: Oxford University Press, 2017).
5. Onora O'Neill, 'Justice, Gender, and International Relations', in *The Quality of Life*, eds Martha C Nussbaum and Amartya Sen (Oxford: Clarendon Press, 1993).
6. Samuel Fleischacker, *A Short History of Distributive Justice* (Cambridge, MA: Harvard University Press, 2004).
7. John Rawls, *Political Liberalism*, exp ed (New York: Columbia University Press, 1996).

Acknowledgements

There are many people who deserve my deepest gratitude and without whom this book would have never come to be.

Thanks to Charles Mills, who gave me the inspiration for this anthology, for 'decolonising political philosophy', and for being the model of an engaged scholar.

Thanks to my editor, Dhara Snowden, at Rowman & Littlefield International, for her recognition of the importance of my project and encouragement throughout the process. And to my publisher, Rowman & Littlefield International, for the financial contribution to copyright permissions.

Thanks to my friend Wendy Sarvasy for her intellectually nurturing friendship, and her enthusiasm and encouragement for my project.

Thanks to my student assistant, Megan Crain, for her invaluable help with obtaining copyright permissions and work on formatting the manuscript.

Thanks to Saint Mary's College of California, its Faculty Development Fund and the Department of Politics for the financial support of my research.

Thanks to my colleagues in the Department of Politics at Saint Mary's College for their support and friendship, and special thanks to my friend and colleague, Hisham H. Ahmed, for encouraging me and supporting me to apply for a scholarly workshop in Amman, Jordan, where I had the opportunity to discuss some of the authors and readings that are included in this anthology. And thanks to our administrative assistant, Cathy Huston, for her indefatigable secretarial help.

Thanks to my friend, Tom R. Muyunga-Mukasa, for reinforcing through example my belief in *Ubuntu*, the universal bond that connects humanity.

Thanks to my students in my Theories of Justice course in the fall of 2017 for allowing me to explore unconventional readings and ideas with them and for providing feedback; and thanks to all the students I have taught through the years for their engagement, suggestions and constructive criticism.

Thanks to all my friends and my mentors in different countries and continents who have enriched my life, without whom I would not be who I am. A special thanks to Sara Ababneh, whom I met at a seminar in Amman, and with whom I had enlightening conversations about gender and colonialism while floating on the Dead Sea or sharing delicious Middle Eastern food. Thank you, Sara, for your friendship, affection and inspiration.

Thanks to Cheri Cook, my friend and neighbor with a heart of gold, with whom I shared walks and ideas, who listened to me and always provided support, compassion and insightful comments.

My deepest thanks to my mother, Maria Grazia Tramma, who died in 2015; she was my model of strength, humility, courage, perseverance and dedication to others. *Grazie*.

Thanks to my son, David, who buoys my spirit and allows me to believe that we can make the world better. Thank you, David, for your love, affection and positive attitude.

At the risk of sounding silly, I want also to acknowledge my beloved dogs, Annie and Lucio, for their unconditional love, which was the most effective therapy in moments of crisis and self-doubt. Our hikes together cleared my mind and renewed my energy.

Last but not least, this book would have not been possible without the encouragement, patience, support, love and friendship of my husband and life companion, Anthony Kortens, to whom this book is dedicated. Thank you for believing in me.

—P.L.

Permissions

The following extracts were reproduced with kind permission. The publishers have made every effort to trace copyright holders and to obtain permission to reproduce extracts. Any omissions brought to our attention will be remedied in future editions.

'Freedom and Property', by John Locke, from *Two Treatises of Government* (London: C and Rivington, 1824). Chapter II: § 4, 6–9, 11–14; Chapter V: § 25–34; Chapter VIII: § 95–99, 119; pp 131–38, 144–49, 186–88, 201.

'Freedom and Equality', by Jean-Jacques Rousseau, in *The Social Contract and Discourses* (London: J M Dent & Sons, 1913), pp 175, 182–83, 185–86, 195–98, 203, 207.

'The Social Contract', by Jean-Jacques Rousseau, in *The Social Contract and Discourses* (London: J M Dent & Sons, 1913). Book I: Chapters I, VI–VIII; Book II: Chapter III; Book III: Chapter IV; pp 5–6, 14–19, 25–26, 57–59.

'Two Principles of Justice', by John Rawls, from *A Theory of Justice* (Cambridge, MA: The Belknap Press of Harvard University Press, 1971), pp 11–16, 60–65. Reprinted by permission of the president and fellows of Harvard College.

'The Sexual Contract', by Carole Pateman, from *The Sexual Contract* (California: Stanford University Press and Polity Press, 1988), pp 1–4, 219–21. Reprinted by permission of Stanford University Press and Polity Press.

'Women and Consent', by Carole Pateman, in *Political Theory* 8, no 2 (May 1980): 150–56, 158, 162–63, 164. Reprinted by permission of Sage Publications, Inc.

'The Racial Contract and Ideal Theory', by Charles W Mills, from *Black Rights, White Wrongs: The Critique of Racial Liberalism* (Oxford: Oxford University Press, 2017), pp 29–32, 139–41. Reprinted by permission of Oxford University Press, USA.

'Food Deserts and Lockean Property', by J M Dieterle, in *Just Food: Philosophy, Justice and Food*, edited by J M Dieterle (Lanham, MD: Rowman & Littlefield, 2015), pp 39–54. Reprinted by permission of Rowman & Littlefield.

'Health Care and Justice in Contract Theory Perspective', by Ronald M Green, in *Ethics and Health Policy*, edited by R Veatch and R Branson (Pensacola, FL: Ballinger, 1976), pp 111–26. Reprinted by permission of Ronald M Green.

'Lecture at Franklin Hall', by Maria Miller Stewart, 21 September 1832, Boston, Massachusetts. Available online http://voicesofdemocracy.umd.edu/stewart-lecture-delivered-speech-text/.

'What to the Slave Is the Fourth of July'? by Frederick Douglass, in *The North Star*, July 5, 1852.

'A Red Record', by Ida B Wells, in *A Red Record*, 1895. Available online http://instruct.westvalley.edu/kelly/Distance_Learning/Online_Readings/Wells_Barnett.htm.

'Lynch Law in America', by Ida B Wells, Chicago, IL, January 1900. Available online http://www.sojust.net/speeches/ida_wells_lynch_law.html.

'How Does It Feel to Be a Problem'? by W E B Du Bois, from *The Souls of Black Folk* (Chicago: A C McClurg & Co, 1903), pp 1–14.

'The Souls of White Folk', by W E B Du Bois, from *Darkwater* (New York: Harcourt, Brace and Company, 1920), Chapter II. Available online https://www.gutenberg.org/files/15210/15210-h/15210-h.htm.

'Letter to My Nephew', by James Baldwin, from *The Fire Next Time* (New York: Vintage Books, 1993), p 310. Reprinted by permission of the James Baldwin Estate.

'Address at the Hattiesburg Freedom Day Rally', by Ella Baker, 21 January 1964, Hattiesburg, Mississippi. Available online http://voicesofdemocracy.umd.edu/ella-baker-freedom-day-rally-speech-text/.

'Keeping Them in Their Place: The Social Control of Blacks since the 1960s', by Eduardo Bonilla-Silva, from *Racism without Racists. Color-Blind Racism and the Persistence of Racial Inequality in America* (Lanham, MD: Rowman & Littlefield, 2018), pp 32–42, 204–5, 232–37. Reprinted by permission of Rowman & Littlefield.

'Message to My Daughters', by Edwidge Danticat, in *The Fire This Time: A New Generation Speaks about Race*, edited by Jesmyn Ward (New York: Scribner, 2016), pp 205–16. Reprinted by permission of Edwidge Danticat.

'The Power of Money', by Karl Marx, from *Economic and Philosophical Manuscripts of 1844*, in *The Marx-Engels Reader*, 2nd edition, edited by Robert C Tucker, pp 102–5. (New York: W W Norton & Company, 1978, 1972). Reprinted by permission of W W Norton & Company, Inc.

'Communism', by Karl Marx and Friedrich Engels, from *The Communist Manifesto*, in *The Marx-Engels Reader*, 2nd edition, edited by Robert C Tucker, pp 486, 489–91. (New York: W W Norton & Company, 1978, 1972). Reprinted by permission of W W Norton & Company, Inc.

'Commodities' and 'Wages', by Karl Marx, from *Karl Marx: Capital: An Abridged Edition*, with Introduction and Notes by David McLlellan (Oxford: Oxford World's Classics, 1995–2008), pp 13–17, 309–14. Reprinted by permission of Oxford University Press, USA.

'Looking Backward', by Edward Bellamy, from *Looking Backward: 2000–1887* (Toronto: William Bryce, 1890), pp 62–66, 89–91.

'Democracy and Charity', by Jane Addams, from *Democracy and Social Ethics* (1902) (Chicago: University of Illinois Press, 2001), pp 13–70 (selections). Reprinted by permission of the University of Illinois Press.

'Racial Economic Inequality', by Eduardo Bonilla-Silva, from *Racism without Racists: Color-Blind Racism and the Persistence of Racial Inequality in America* (Lanham, MD: Rowman & Littlefield, 2018), pp 44–49. Copyrights by Rowman & Littlefield.

'Politics of the Plate: The Price of Tomatoes', by Barry Estabrook, in *Gourmet*, March 2009. Available online http//www.gourmet.com/magazine/2000s/2009/03/politics-of-the-plate-the-price-of-tomatoes.html.

'The Most Dangerous Job', by Eric Schlosser, from *Fast Food Nation* (New York: Houghton Mifflin Harcourt Publishing Company, 2001), pp 176–78, 186–90. Copyright 2001 by Eric Schlosser. Reprinted by permission of Houghton Mifflin Harcourt Publishing Company. All rights reserved.

'Occupy in a Border City: El Paso, Texas, U.S.A.', by Josiah Heyman and Merlyn Heyman, in *What Comes After Occupy? The Regional Politics of Resistance*, edited by Todd A Comer (London: Cambridge Scholars Publishing, 2015), pp 104–23. Reprinted by permission of Josiah Heyman and Merlyn Heyman.

'Anatomy of Environmental Racism and the Environmental Justice Movement', by Robert D Bullard, in *Confronting Environmental Racism*, edited by Robert D Bullard (Cambridge, MA: South End Press, 1993), pp 15–22. Reprinted by permission of Robert D Bullard.

'Whose Earth Is It Anyway'? by James H Cone, from *Risks of Faith: The Emergence of a Black Theology of Liberation, 1968–1998* (Boston: Beacon Press, 1999), pp 138–45. Reprinted by permission of James H Cone.

'Just Garbage', by Peter S Wenz, in *Faces of Environmental Racism: Confronting Issues of Global Justice*, edited by Laura Westra and Bill E Lawson (Lanham: Rowman & Littlefield, 1995), pp 57–71. Reprinted by permission of Rowman & Littlefield.

'For the People: American Indian and Hispanic Women in New Mexico's Environmental Justice Movement', by Diane-Michelle Prindeville, in *Our Backyard: A Quest for Environmental Justice*, edited by Gerald R Visgilio and Diana M Whitelaw (Lanham: Rowman & Littlefield, 2003), pp 139–57. Reprinted by permission of Rowman & Littlefield.

'Other Faces: Latinos and Environmental Justice', by Robert Melchior Figueroa, in *Faces of Environmental Racism: Confronting Issues of Global Justice*, edited by Laura Westra and Bill E Lawson (Lanham: Rowman & Littlefield, 1995), pp 167–75, 177–80, 182–84. Reprinted by permission of Rowman & Littlefield.

'Indigenous People of North America: Environmental Exposure and Reproductive Justice', by Elizabeth Hoover et al. in *Environmental Health Perspectives* 120, no 12 (December 2012): 1645–49. Available online https://ehpniehs.nih.gov/1205422/.

'Philosophy and the Colonial Difference', by Walter D Mignolo, in *Latin American Philosophy: Currents, Issues, Debates*, edited by Eduardo Mendieta (Bloomington: Indiana University Press, 2003), pp 80–86. Reprinted by permission of *Philosophy Today*.

'The Idea of Provincializing Europe', by Dipesh Chakrabarty, from *Provincializing Europe: Postcolonial Thought and Historical Difference* (Princeton: Princeton University Press, 2000), pp 3–6. Reprinted by permission of Princeton University Press.

'Discourse on Colonialism', by Aimé Césaire, from *Discourse on Colonialism* (New York City: Monthly Review Press, 1972), pp 9–12, 20–25. Reprinted by permission of Monthly Review Press.

'The Black Man and Language', by Frantz Fanon, from *Black Skin, White Masks* (New York: Grove Press, Inc., 2008), pp 17–23. Reprinted by permission of Grove Press.

'On National Culture', by Frantz Fanon, from *The Wretched of the Earth* (New York: Grove Press, 2004), pp 146–49, 168, 173–75. Reprinted by permission of Grove Press.

'Orientalism', by Edward Said, from *Orientalism* (New York: Penguin, 1978), pp 1–14. Used by permission of Pantheon Books, an imprint of the Knopf Doubleday Publishing Group, a subdivision of Penguin Random House LLC. All rights reserved.

'Colonizing Bodies and Minds: Gender and Colonialism', by Oyèrónkẹ́ Oyěwùmí, from *The Invention of Women: Making an African Sense of Western Gender Discourses* (Minneapolis: University of Minnesota Press, 1997), pp 121–27, 128–31, 133–34, 135–38, 140, 141–42, 144–46, 149–54. Reprinted by permission of the Regents of University of Minnesota.

'Reparations for Cultural Injustice', by Rajeev Bhargava, in *Reparations*, edited by Jon Miller and Rahul Kumar (Oxford: Oxford University Press, 2007), pp 241–51. Reprinted by permission of Oxford University Press.

'The Case of the "Comfort Women": Sexual Slavery by the Japanese Military', by Kinhide Mushakoji, from 'Engendering the Japanese "Double Standard" Patriarchal Democracy: The Case of the "Comfort Women" and Military Sexual Slavery', in *Gender, Globalization, and Democratization*, edited by Rita Mae Kelly, Jane H Bayes, Mary E Hawkesworth and Brigitte Young (Rowman & Littlefield, 2001), pp 211–22. Reprinted by permission of Rowman & Littlefield.

'Resistance to Colonialism: The Latin American Legacy of Jose Marti', by Ofelia Schutte, in *Colonialism and Its Legacies*, edited by Jaco Levy (with Iris Marion Young) (Lanham: Lexington Books, 2011), pp 181–204. Reprinted by permission of Rowman & Littlefield.

'Truth Commissions through a Restorative Lens', by Jennifer Llewellyn, from 'Truth Commissions and Restorative Justice', in *Handbook of Restorative Justice*, edited by Gerry Johnstone and Daniel W Van Ness (London: Routledge, 2011), pp 357–58, 361–66. Reproduced by permission of Taylor & Francis Books UK.

'Amnesties in the Pursuit of Reconciliation, Peacebuilding, and Restorative Justice', by Louise Mallinder, in *Restorative Justice, Reconciliation and Peacebuilding*, edited by Jennifer Llewellyn and Daniel Philpott (Oxford: Oxford University Press, 2014), pp 138–40, 141–42, 151–52, 164. Reprinted by permission of Oxford University Press, USA.

'When Does Transitional Justice Begin and End? Colonized Peoples, Liberal Democracies and Restorative Justice', by Chris Cunneen, in *Restorative Justice in Transitional Settings*, edited by Kerry Clamp (London: Routledge, 2016), pp 190–210. Reproduced by permission of Taylor & Francis Books UK.

'Rethinking the War on Drugs: What Insights Does Restorative Justice Offer'? by the Hon Joan Gottschall and Molly Armour, in *Restorative Justice in Practice: A Holistic Approach*, edited by Sheila M Murphy and Michael P Seng (Lake Mary, FL: Vandeplas Publishing, 2015), pp 89–101. Reprinted by permission of the Hon Joan Gottschall.

INTRODUCTION

This book is intended to meet an increasing need for a comprehensive volume on modern and contemporary theories of justice. Since the publication in 1971 of John Rawls's *A Theory of Justice* there has been much debate on his views both from the right and the left of the political spectrum; political theorists, especially in the United States, delved into Rawls's ideas and arguments, neglecting other, especially non-Western, traditions. As a result, there is a lack of textbooks that provide not only a compilation of substantial selections on challenges to Rawls's theory from feminist and postcolonial scholars but that also include writings by non-white and non-Western authors on different aspects of justice that go beyond Rawls's contractual model. This book tries to fill that gap and brings together many influential writings on the topic of justice that are often omitted in philosophy and political theory collections and that address complex issues in an increasingly diverse society. As its title, *Justice Unbound*, suggests, this anthology attempts to break the 'chains' that have tied political theory to the dominant Rawlsian approaches to the meaning of justice and to introduce many voices and insights that have been neglected in the traditional canon or ghettoised in specific areas such as 'African-American political theory' or 'postcolonial theory'. My hope is that by engaging with the work of these thinkers it will open new horizons by imagining different ways of political theorising and open the doors to insights from other disciplines. Following Edward Said's advice to dig into the past to recover what has been left out of historical accounts told by those in power, this anthology introduces challenging readings that 'will not allow conscience to look away or fall asleep'.[1]

Although each reading reflects the context and the demands and constraints of the time in which it was written, all the authors challenge the liberal paradigm and orthodoxy in political theory and reject its individualistic outlook. They focus instead on collective categories like class, race, gender and coloniality, and on related concepts like identity and recognition in addition to more traditional issues of just distribution of social goods and resources. Since they start from the common assumption that injustices are structural and the product of social institutions and laws rather than of individual acts and mindsets, it follows that the solutions must address the historical legacies of racism, sexism and colonialism.

This anthology is not meant to be another multicultural reader, but rather is intended to provide its readers with a change in perspective that is necessary for future political theorising. Political theory has been chained to its neatly contained Western canon for too long: it is time to break the 'chains' of the discipline by investigating lost voices that will allow us to expand our horizons for the study of the contemporary world.

The anthology is divided into six sections, and each section addresses one aspect of justice. Although it will become clear through the readings that forms of oppressions cannot be compartmentalised and are often correlated, for pedagogical reasons each category of injustice is examined in a separate section. As intersectionality has taught us, markers of difference do not act independent of one another, and our social identities interrelate to negate the possibility of a unitary experience of any one manifestation of injustice and oppression. It follows that each section contains readings that could likely fit into another; for instance, Du Bois's writings could belong to both sections on civil rights and colonialism, and Ella Baker's speech could fit in both sections on civil rights and economic rights. Therefore, I have tried to link the sections together so the authors 'engage in a conversation', and the readings in the last section can relate back to those in the first, coming full circle.

The first section starts with selections from Locke's *Second Treatise* and Rousseau's *Discourse on Inequality* and *Social Contract* on the hypothetical beginning of society through a social contract and highlights the tension in liberalism between freedom and equality, exemplified by Rawls's attempt to address it with his two principles of justice. It also includes contemporary critiques of the social contract as a 'sexual contract' (Carole Pateman) and a 'racial contract' (Charles Mills), challenging John Rawls's 'original position' and 'veil of ignorance' as excluding the voices of women and racial minorities. The section ends with two case studies that apply Locke's theory of property to food justice and Rawls's principles of justice to the discussion on universal health care.

The second section includes excerpts of speeches by Maria Stewart, Frederick Douglass, and Ella Baker, and writings by Ida B Wells, W E B Du Bois and James Baldwin that address the lack of freedom and civil rights for African Americans. These readings show that intersectionality is fundamental in understanding the issues confronted by African American women. One of the several ways of keeping Blacks oppressed was by accusing them of the rape of a white woman, and then lynching them. The case studies in this section show that lynching has become newly 'legalised' into police brutality and that Black males are disproportionately targeted and incarcerated.

The third section addresses the connection between political rights and economic rights, and the importance of a foundation of economic equality to achieve 'real' freedom and democracy. The section includes selections from Marx's writings and Bellamy's *Looking Backward*, from Jane Addams's *Democracy and Social Ethics*, and three case studies: one on the treatment of farmworkers in Florida's tomato fields, one on the conditions of workers in the meatpacking industry, and the last on the Occupy movement in El Paso and its denunciation of economic inequalities.

The fourth section shows how racism and poverty are directly correlated to environmental injustice and how the burden of pollution and toxic waste falls primarily on minorities and the poor. Gender, class and race intersect to mediate people's lives. Essays on the beginning of the environmental justice movement and its critique of (the mainly white) mainstream environmentalist groups are included in this section, as are two case studies that portray the grassroots activism in the communities of colour affected by the consequences of environmental racism, and one case study on the struggle of Indigenous women in North America for the survival of their tribes and cultures.

The fifth and sixth sections move to global justice issues and the legacy of colonialism. In section 5 classic works by Césaire, Fanon and Said are followed by an essay by Oyèrónkẹ́ Oyèwùmí questioning the portrayal of the colonised as male and the neglect of women's experience of colonialism in the work of both Fanon and Memmi. The first case study in this section focuses on the Korean 'Comfort Women' during World War II and Japan's responsibility for reparations. The second looks at the influence of José Martí's thought on the critique of the political, cultural and economic conditions of post-coloniality in the Global South. The discussion by Bhargava of cultural reparations for colonialism leads to the sixth section on transitional and restorative justice.

The sixth and final section provides contemporary readings on transitional justice, amnesty and reparations as well as case studies on the implementation of both transitional and restorative justice at the global and local levels. The hope is that perhaps a new approach to justice would be more effective in dealing with past horrors and in preventing their repetition in the future.

The selection of readings is always subjective to an extent and not everything can be included, but I believe that the students who will read the excerpts in this volume will gain an understanding and appreciation of the different meanings and aspects of justice. My hope is that they will appreciate the art of political thinking and its fundamental role in maintaining justice and democracy.

'No problem can withstand the assault of sustained thinking'.

—Voltaire

Note

1. Edward Said, *Humanism and Democratic Criticism* (New York: Columbia University Press, 2004), 142.

SECTION I

From the State of Nature to Society
The Social Contract and Its Critics

In truth, laws are always useful to those with possessions and harmful to those who have nothing; from which it follows that the social state is advantageous to men only when all possess something and none has too much.
—Jean-Jacques Rousseau, *The Social Contract*

The 'social contract', in the only sense in which it is not completely mythical, is a contract among conquerors, which loses its raison d'être if they are deprived of the benefits of conquest.
—Bertrand Russell, *Power: A New Social Analysis*

In the liberal tradition, justice has been linked to private property and the importance of the social contract to protect it. Thomas Hobbes (1588–1679) described a hypothetical state of nature where lawlessness and violence reign and where life is 'solitary, poor, nasty, brutish and short'.[1] Since there are no laws nor civil authority to enforce them in the state of nature, it is a 'war of all against all'.[2] In such a situation, justice is not possible, and thus Hobbes recommends that humans create a social contract that turns all the authority to an all-powerful 'Leviathan' in exchange for peace and the protection from violent death.[3] An important reason that justice is not possible in the state of nature is that humans have rights to everything; the social contract thus establishes the right to private property as a guarantee of peace.

John Locke (1632–1704) agreed with Hobbes on the connection between justice and private property established by the social contract. Although Locke's state of nature seems quite idyllic in many ways, a state of 'perfect freedom', and thus very different from Hobbes's 'war of all against all', it has some 'inconveniences' that lead individuals to form a social contract to protect their property rights.[4] Locke's contract thus institutionalises the inequalities of property that were present in the state of nature as 'just'. Locke's ideas exerted extensive influence on the American Founders and subsequent liberal thinkers, who placed a high value on property rights and negative freedom and a low value on equality. Arguably, Locke's theory of land appropriation was employed in the justification of colonialism and the expropriation of Native Americans from their lands.[5]

Jean-Jacques Rousseau (1712–1778) regarded the social contract as institutionalising inequality by giving political power to those who possessed economic power, thus enabling them to protect and maintain their privilege. According to Rousseau, the founding of society 'gave new fetters to the weak and new powers to the rich'.[6] The establishing of property is the turning point in Rousseau's account of human history. Since natural talents are unequal, he argues, property is bound to become unequal, and this inequality become institutionalised when property becomes a social or political convention. Dismissing Locke's claim that private property is a natural right, Rousseau argued that it is only a matter of convention and that the right of an individual to his own piece of land is always subordinate to the common good. Rousseau defended equality based on his belief in the corrupting influence of inequality on the moral character of both rich and poor, and on the civic body. He also defended equality because 'liberty cannot continue to exist without it'.[7] Liberty, he argued, requires at least rough economic and political equality. Economic inequality erodes liberty, according to Rousseau, by creating economic and psychological dependence, and by forcing the relatively powerless to live by rules and laws created by the relatively powerful in their own interest. Finally, Rousseau argued that democracy requires not just freedom but both political equality and a measure of economic equality. In *The Social Contract* he writes:

> If one investigates in what precisely consists the greatest good of all – which should be the end of every system of legislation – one will find that it comes down to the following two principal objects: *freedom* and *equality*. Freedom, because any particular dependence is that much force taken away from the body of the state. Equality, because freedom cannot endure without it.[8]

John Rawls (1921–2002) addresses the need for both freedom and equality in a social contract that is just. His work follows in the contract tradition of liberalism that shaped the US Constitution, and is concerned with questions of justice, equality and freedom. Rawls argues that the principles of justice that should regulate the basic institutions of society are those that would be agreed to by persons reasoning in what he terms 'the original position'. The agreement reached in the original position, Rawls admits, is both hypothetical and ahistorical.[9] Rawls wants us to think about how we would design society if we didn't know what place we would have in it: 'The idea of the original position is to set up a fair procedure, so that any principles agreed to will be just'.[10] We are to imagine a group of individuals in the original position who are rational, mutually disinterested, and who deliberate behind a thick veil of ignorance. While there are no limits on what general information is available to the parties in the original position, a thick veil of ignorance obtains that denies each person knowledge of what their conception of the good actually is, and of their particular circumstances – their social and economic status, their race, gender or their endowment of 'natural assets' such as talents, skills and abilities.[11] Since everyone in the original position is ignorant of the position he or she would occupy in the alternative social arrangements proposed, then one must allow for the possibility of occupying any position. How would you like your society to be if your enemy was going to assign you your place in it? You would not want any really bad positions and would want to make sure the worst thing that can happen to you is as good as it could be. That is Rawls's big idea – that if you were to design society not knowing your place in it, you'd want to make sure the worst positions in society were as good as they could be, therefore – and it's a big therefore which needs lots of intermediate steps – a just society is one that makes the worst off as well off as possible.

By removing sources of bias and requiring unanimity, Rawls hopes to find a solution that is acceptable to everyone from a position of equality; that is, that respects each person's claim to be treated as a free and equal being. Such arrangement, according to Rawls, would establish a system of 'justice as fairness'.[12] In this conception of justice, 'all social primary goods – liberty and opportunity, income and wealth, and the bases of self-respect – are to be distributed equally unless an unequal distribution of any or all of these good is to the advantage of the least favored'.[13] It is important to note that in Rawls's theory of justice, liberty has priority over other social good and thus cannot be restricted for the sake of another good. Basic civil and political liberties, according to Rawls, are essential to a decent life, so people in the original position will not trade their basic civil and political liberties in order to promote increasing social wealth and efficiency. Rawls also claims that not all inequalities must be removed, but only those that disadvantage someone. If some inequalities benefit everyone, they will be acceptable to everyone.

What Rawls calls the liberty principle (we should all have equal and extensive basic liberty), the fair opportunity principle, and the so-called difference principle, which says we should make the worst off as well off as possible, prompt three questions: Are these principles just? Would these principles actually be chosen from the original position? And is the original position a good way of doing political philosophy? Even though *A Theory of Justice* was written in 1971, Rawls created the world of contemporary political philosophy that we still live in now.

Rawls is addressing specifically 'basic liberties', the civil and political rights recognised by liberal democracies, such as the right to vote, free speech, and more, which are fundamental to liberalism and whose importance is widely recognised in our society.[14] Protections for individual rights in Rawls's first principle of justice resonate with the US individual rights tradition that is embodied in the Constitution's Bill of Rights. Rawls's main innovation concerned inequality. Before the publication of his book, politicians on the Left maintained that if inequalities exist then they have to benefit everyone. We can allow inequalities but only if everyone is made better off. Rawls modified that and said it's not good enough that they make everyone better off, they've got to make the worst off as well off as possible. For Rawls, some social and economic inequalities are inevitable; but we can demand, in the name of justice as fairness, that the inequalities that do exist are to the benefit of the most disadvantaged.

The hypothetical contract, however, is not just about the terms of the agreement but also about who has the power to freely consent to them. Most of the well-known contract theories, with the notable exception of Rousseau's, do not address the actual power inequalities of the participants in the moment of consent. John Rawls adopts contract theory in his attempt to establish the principles of justice that are to regulate the basic structure of society. And he 'assumes' the equality of the participants who consent to the contract in the original position, an assumption contested by critics such as Carole Pateman, Susan Okin, and Charles Mills. The 'fair agreement' in the original position on the principles of justice is between 'free and equal persons' even if in society they are neither free nor equal. Although Rawls admits the need to continue to readjust the distribution of resources to achieve justice as fairness, he fails to address the historical grievances that have given rise to the unequal power of certain groups and institutions and thus limits the possibility of democratising society.

Rawls's vision of 'free and equal citizens' is starkly at odds with contemporary US society where inequalities have increased exponentially. The solution proposed by the 'Difference Principle', that social and economic inequalities are to be to the benefit of the least advantaged members of society, resembles charity more than democracy (or a trickle-down economic approach): the wealthy are justified if they improve the situation of those who have less. Thus, the primacy Rawls gives to individual rights (the First Principle) justifies inequality. However, the historical experiences of African Americans and other people of colour of discrimination, exclusion, slavery, nativism and colonialism are not addressed by the liberal values of freedom and equality precisely because they ignore those historical legacies.

The main question raised by the critics of the social contract, therefore, is how society must be rethought and reconfigured so that all can participate in public life and its goals can be met for everyone.

Carole Pateman in her 1988 classic work, *The Sexual Contract*, responded to theorists of the liberal social contract by pointing to their foundation on Kantian individualism and their neglect of the social and political context, and particularly of gender. Pateman reminds us that feminists have been challenging the social contract since the seventeenth century. Pateman's work had a profound impact in political theory and feminist theory, particularly her argument that 'the specific purpose of the contract is to consolidate "the law of male sex-right" which gives men access to women's bodies'.[15] She writes that 'women are not party to the original contract through which men transform their natural freedom into the security of civil freedom. Women are the subject of the contract. The (sexual) contract is the vehicle through which men transform their natural right over women into the security of civil patriarchal right'.[16]

In agreement with Pateman, Charles Mills insists that, whereas Rawls is operating with a conceptual framework that makes equality and consent the norm, inequality and domination are the principles governing modern civil society. Therefore, the recognition of inequality and domination must be the starting point for any theory to be relevant to today's unjust society. Mills argues that, by employing a colour-blind approach in the original position, Rawls, in effect, ignores the material reality of white supremacy and how it has shaped modern liberal democratic societies. In *The Racial Contract*, Mills proposes a literal, historical contract that 'has the best claim to being a historical fact' in contrast to Rawls's hypothetical and idealised contract.[17] The origin of the Racial Contract, Mills writes, is 'clearly historically locatable in the series of events marking the creation of the modern world by European colonialism and the voyages of "discovery" now increasingly and more appropriately called expeditions of conquest'.[18] The Racial Contract, according to Mills, is a domination or exclusionary contract that provides a conceptual framework for understanding the reality of group domination, particularly white supremacy. Contrary to the claims of Rawls and other contract theorists, both Pateman and Mills claim that it is not a contract in which all citizens are free and equal persons. Rather, it is a contract in which white men as a group are dominant over the subordinate women and nonwhite population. Nonwhites and women are thus the objects rather than the subjects of the agreement. Mills concludes: 'If we see the racial contract as establishing the racial polity, white supremacy, then the task of the ideal contract should be how to dismantle white supremacy and realize justice'.[19]

The questions Carole Pateman and Charles Mills raise point us in an important direction. As they suggest, the issue is not so much that Rawls himself ignored race and gender as it is the ways in which Rawlsian 'ideal theory' has reinforced a kind of blindness to issues of racial and sexual justice that have pervaded mainstream academic political philosophy. Mills and Pateman introduce the concept of 'domination contract' to capture this kind of non-ideal theorising, and contrast it with a mainstream, ideal contract. While ideal theory asks what justice requires in a perfectly just society, nonideal theory asks what justice requires in a society with a history of injustice and is concerned with corrective measures (rectificatory justice). By focussing on ideal theory, Rawls and other white political philosophers have avoided dealing with the legacy of sexism, racism and white supremacy in our present society.

The section ends with two case studies. The first addresses the injustice of food deserts through an analysis of Locke's theory of property. Dieterle argues that any theory of justice that relies on a Lockean theory of property must come to the conclusion that, in order to correct the injustice of food deserts, limitations on property rights must be imposed. The second case study, Ronald M. Green's 'Health Care and Justice in Contract Theory Perspective', discusses Rawls's theory of justice in relation to the right to health care. He asks whether health care should or could be included among the basic liberties included in the first principle of justice without changing Rawls's theoretical framework and concludes that rational individuals under the 'veil of ignorance' would choose a fair distribution of health care to all.

Notes

1. Thomas Hobbes, *Leviathan* (Harmondsworth: Penguin, 1985), 186.
2. Hobbes, *Leviathan*, 185.
3. Hobbes, *Leviathan*, 188, 190.
4. John Locke, *Two Treatises of Government* (London, 1824), 137.
5. See John Douglas Bishop, 'Locke's Theory of Original Appropriation and the Right of Settlement in Iroquois Territory', *Canadian Journal of Philosophy* 27, no. 3 (September 1997): 311–37.
6. Jean-Jacques Rousseau, *First and Second Discourses*, ed Roger D Masters, trans by Roger D and Judith R Masters (New York: St Martin's Press, 1964), 160.
7. Jean-Jacques Rousseau, *The Social Contract*, trans by Maurice Cranston (London and New York: Penguin, 1968), 96.
8. Rousseau, *The Social Contract*, 96.
9. John Rawls, *A Theory of Justice* (Cambridge, MA: Harvard University Press, 1971), 12.
10. Rawls, *A Theory of Justice*, 119.
11. Rawls, *A Theory of Justice*, 12.
12. Rawls, *A Theory of Justice*, 11.
13. Rawls, *A Theory of Justice*, 303.
14. Rawls, *A Theory of Justice*, 61.
15. Carole Pateman, *The Sexual Contract* (Stanford: Stanford University Press; Oxford: Polity Press, 1988), 22.
16. Pateman, *The Sexual Contract*, 6.
17. Charles W Mills, *The Racial Contract* (Ithaca: Cornell University Press, 1997), 20.
18. Mills, *The Racial Contract*, 20.
19. Charles W Mills, 'Race and the Social Contract Tradition', *Social Identities* 6, no. 4 (2000): 456.

Suggested Readings

Armitage, David. 'John Locke, Carolina, and The Two Treatises on Government'. *Political Theory* 32, no. 5 (2004): 602–27.
Mills, Charles W. *The Racial Contract*. Ithaca: Cornell University Press, 1997.
———. 'Rawls on Race/Race in Rawls'. In *Race, Racism, and Liberalism in the 21st Century*, ed. Bill E Lawson. Supplement, *Southern Journal of Philosophy* XLVII (2009), 161–84.
———. *Black Rights, White Wrongs: The Critique of Racial Liberalism*. Oxford: Oxford University Press, 2017.
Okin, Susan Moller. *Justice, Gender, and the Family*. New York: Basic Books, 1989.
Pateman, Carole. *The Sexual Contract*. Stanford, CA: Stanford University Press, 1988.

———. *The Disorder of Women*. Stanford, CA: Stanford University Press, 1989.
Pateman, Carole, and Charles W Mills. *The Contract and Domination*. Malden, MA: Polity, 2007.
Rawls, John. *Political Liberalism*. New York: Columbia University Press, 1993.
Sandel, Michael. *Liberalism and the Limits of Justice*. Cambridge, UK: Cambridge University Press, 1982.
Shklar, Judith N. 'Jean-Jacques Rousseau and Equality'. *Daedalus* 107, no. 3 (1978): 13–25.

John Locke*, 'Freedom and Property'
Chapter II. Of the State of Nature

§ 4. To understand political power right, and derive it from its original, we must consider what state all men are naturally in, and that is, a state of perfect freedom to order their actions and dispose of their possessions and persons, as they think fit, within the bounds of the law of nature; without asking leave or depending upon the will of any other man.

A state also of equality, wherein all the jurisdiction is reciprocal, having more than another; there being nothing more evident, than that creatures of the same species and rank, promiscuously born to all the same advantages of nature, and the use of the same faculties, should also be equal one amongst another without subordination or subjection; unless the lord and master of them all should, by any manifest declaration of his will, set one above another, and confer on him, by an evident and clear appointment, an undoubted right to dominion and sovereignty. . . .

§ 6. But though this be a state of liberty, yet it is not a state of license: though man in that state have an uncontrollable liberty to dispose of his person or possessions, yet he has not liberty to destroy himself, or so much as any creature in his possession, but where some nobler use than its bare preservation calls for it. The state of nature has a law of nature to govern it, which obliges every one: and reason, which is that law, teaches all mankind, who will but consult it, that being all equal and independent, no one ought to harm another in his life, health, liberty, or possessions: for men being all the workmanship of one omnipotent and infinitely wise Maker; all the servants of one sovereign master, sent into the world by his order, and about his business; they are his property, whose workmanship they are, made to last during his, not another's pleasure: and being furnished with like faculties, sharing all in one community of nature, there cannot be supposed any such subordination among us, that may authorize us to destroy another, as if we were made for one another's uses, as the inferior ranks of creatures are for ours. Everyone, as he is bound to preserve himself, and not to quit his station wilfully, so by the like reason, when his own preservation comes not in competition, ought he, as much as he can, to preserve the rest of mankind, and may not, unless it be to do justice to an offender, take away or impair the life, or what tends to the preservation of life, the liberty, health, limb, or goods of another.

§ 7. And that all men may be restrained from invading others rights, and from doing hurt to one another, and the law of nature be observed, which willeth the peace and preservation of all mankind, the execution of the law of nature is, in that state, put into every man's hands, whereby everyone has a right to punish the transgressors of that law to such a degree as may hinder its violation: for the law of nature would, as all other laws that concern men in

* John Locke, *Two Treatises of Government*. London: C. and Rivington, 1824 (selections).

this world, be in vain, if there were nobody that in the state of nature had a power to execute that law, and thereby preserve the innocent and restrain offenders. And if anyone in the state of nature may punish another for any evil he has done, every one may do so: for in that state of perfect equality, where naturally there is no superiority or jurisdiction of one over another, what any may do in prosecution of that law, everyone must needs have a right to do.

§ 8. And thus, in the state of nature, 'one man comes by a power over another'; but yet no absolute or arbitrary power, to use a criminal, when he has got him in his hands, according to the passionate heats, or boundless extravagancy of his own will; but only to retribute to him, so far as calm reason and conscience dictate, what is proportionate to his transgression; which is so much as may serve for reparation and restraint: for these two are the only reasons, why one man may lawfully do harm to another, which is that we call punishment. In transgressing the law of nature, the offender declares himself to live by another rule than that of reason and common equity, which is that measure God has set to the actions of men, for their mutual security; and so he becomes dangerous to mankind, the tye, which is to secure them from injury and violence, being slighted and broken by him. Which being a trespass against the whole species, and the peace and safety of it, provided for by the law of nature; every man upon this score, by the right he hath to preserve mankind in general, may restrain, or, where it is necessary, destroy things noxious to them, and so may bring such evil on any one, who hath transgressed that law, as may make him repent the doing of it, and thereby deter him, and by his example others, from doing the like mischief. And in this case, and upon this ground, 'every man hath a right to punish the offender, and be executioner of the law of nature'.

§ 9. I doubt not but this will seem a very strange doctrine to some men: but before they condemn it, I desire them to resolve me, by what right any prince or state can put to death, or punish any alien, for any crime he commits in their country. It is certain their laws, by virtue of any sanction they receive from the promulgated will of the legislative, reach not a stranger: they speak not to him, nor, if they did, is he bound to hearken to them. The legislative authority, by which they are in force over the subjects of that commonwealth, hath no power over him. Those who have the supreme power of making laws in England, France, er Holland, are to an Indian but like the rest of the world, men without authority: and therefore, if by the law of nature every man hath not a power to punish offences against it, as he soberly judges the case to require, I see not how the magistrates of any community can punish an alien of another country; since, in reference to him, they can have no more power than what every man naturally may have over another. . . .

§ 11. From these two distinct rights, the one of punishing the crime for restraint, and preventing the like offence, which right of punishing is in every body; the other of taking reparation, which belongs only to the injured party; comes it to pass that the magistrate, who by being magistrate hath the common right of punishing put into his hands, can often, where the public good demands not the execution of the law, remit the punishment of criminal offences by his own authority, but yet cannot remit the satisfaction due to any private man for the damage he has received. That, he who has suffered the damage has a right to demand in his own name, and he alone can remit: the damnified person has this power of appropriating to himself the goods or service of the offender, by right of self-preservation, as every man has a power to punish the crime, to prevent its being committed again, 'by the right he has of preserving all mankind'; and doing all reasonable things he can in order to that end: and thus it is, that every man, in the state of nature, has a power to kill a murderer, both to deter others from doing the like injury, which no reparation can compensate, by the example of the punishment that attends it from everybody; and also to secure men from the attempts of a criminal, who having renounced reason, the common rule and measure God hath given to mankind, hath, by the unjust violence and slaughter he hath committed upon one, declared war against all mankind; and therefore may be destroyed as a lion or a tiger, one of those wild savage beasts, with whom men can have no society nor security: and upon this is grounded that great law of nature, 'Whoso sheddeth man's blood, by man shall his blood be shed'. And Cain was so fully convinced, that everyone had a right to destroy such a criminal, that after the murder of his brother, he cries out, 'Every one that findeth me, shall slay me'; so plain was it writ in the hearts of mankind.

§ 12. By the same reason may a man in the state of nature punish the lesser breaches of that law. It will perhaps be demanded, with death? I answer, each transgression may be punished to that degree, and with so much severity, as will suffice to make it an ill bargain to the offender, give him cause to repent, and terrify others from doing the like. Every offence, that can be committed in the state of nature, may in the state of nature be also punished equally, and as far forth, as it may in a commonwealth: for though it would be beside my present purpose, to enter here into the particulars of the law of nature, or its measures of punishment, yet it is certain there is such a law, and that too as intelligible and plain to a rational creature, and a studier of that law, as the positive laws of commonwealths: nay, possibly plainer, as much as reason is easier to be understood, than the fancies and intricate contrivances of men, following contrary and hidden interests put into words; for so truly are a great part of the municipal laws of countries, which are only so far right, as they are founded on the law of nature, by which they are to be regulated and interpreted.

§ 13. To this strange doctrine, viz. That 'in the state of nature everyone has the executive power' of the law of nature, I doubt not but it will be objected, that it is unreasonable for men to be judges in their own cases, that self-love will make men partial to themselves and their friends; and on the other side, that ill-nature, passion, and revenge will carry them too far in punishing others; and hence nothing but confusion and disorder will follow: and that therefore God hath certainly appointed government to restrain the partiality and violence of men. I easily grant, that civil government is the proper remedy for the inconveniencies of the state of nature, which must certainly be great, where men may be judges in their own case; since it is easy to be imagined, that he who was so unjust as to do his brother an injury, will scarce be so just as to condemn himself for it: but I shall desire those who make this objection, to remember, that absolute monarchs are but men; and if government is to be the remedy of those evils, which necessarily follow from men's being judges in their own cases, and the state of nature is therefore not to be endured; I desire to know what kind of government that is, and how much better it is, than the state of nature, where one man commanding a multitude, has the liberty to be judge in his own case, and may do to all his subjects whatever he pleases, without the least liberty to anyone to question or control those who execute his pleasure? and in whatsoever he doth, whether led by reason, mistake or passion, must be submitted to? much better it is in the state of nature, wherein men are not bound to submit to the unjust will of another: and if he that judges, judges amiss in his own, or any other case, he is answerable for it to the rest of mankind.

§ 14. It is often asked as a mighty objection, 'where are, or ever were there any men in such a state of nature'? To which it may suffice as an answer at present, that since all princes and rulers of independent governments, all through the world, are in a state of nature, it is plain the world never was, nor ever will be, without numbers of men in that state. I have named all governors of independent communities, whether they are, or are not, in league with others: for it is not every compact that puts an end to the state of nature between men, but only this one of agreeing together mutually to enter into one community, and make one body politic; other promises and compacts men may make one with another, and yet still be in the state of nature. The promises and bargains for truck, &c. between the two men in the desert island, mentioned by Garcilasso de la Vega, in his history of Peru; or between a Swiss and an Indian, in the woods of America; are binding to them, though they are perfectly in a state of nature, in reference to one another: for truth and keeping of faith belongs to men as men, and not as members of society. . . .

Chapter V. Of Property

§ 25. Whether we consider natural reason, which tells us, that men, being once born, have a right to their preservation, and consequently to meat and drink, and such other things as nature affords for their subsistence; or revelation, which gives us an account of those grants God made of the world to Adam, and to Noah, and his sons; it is very clear that God, as king David says, Psal. cxv. 16, 'has given the earth to the children of men'; given it to mankind in common. But this being supposed, it seems to some a very great difficulty how anyone should ever come to have a property in anything; I will not content myself to answer that if it be difficult to make out property, upon a supposition, that God gave the world to Adam, and his posterity in common, it is impossible that any man, but one universal monarch, should have any property upon a supposition, that God gave the world to Adam, and his heirs in succession, exclusive of all the rest of his posterity. But I shall endeavour to show, how men might come to have a property in several parts of that which God gave to mankind in common, and that without any express compact of all the commoners.

§ 26. God, who hath given the world to men in common, hath also given them reason to make use of it to the best advantage of life, and convenience. The earth, and all that is therein, is given to men for the support and comfort of their being. And though all the fruits it naturally produces, and beasts it feeds, belong to mankind in common, as they are produced by the spontaneous hand of nature; and nobody has originally a private dominion exclusive of the rest of mankind, in any of them, as they are thus in their natural state; yet being given for the use of men, there must of necessity be a means to appropriate them some way or other, before they can be of any use, or at all beneficial to any particular man. The fruit, or venison, which nourishes the wild Indian, who knows no enclosure, and is still a tenant in common, must be his, and so his, i.e., a part of him, that another can no longer have any right to it, before it can do him any good for the support of his life.

§ 27. Though the earth, and all inferior creatures, be common to all men, yet every man has a property in his own person: this nobody has any right to but himself. The labour of his body, and the work of his hands, we may say, are properly his. Whatsoever then he removes out of the state that nature hath provided, and left it in, he hath mixed his labour with, and joined to it something that is his own, and thereby makes it his property. It being by him removed from the common state nature hath placed it in, it hath by this labour something annexed to it, that excludes the common right of other men. For this labour being the unquestionable property of the labourer, no man but he can have a right to what that is once joined to, at least where there is enough, and as good, left in common for others.

§ 28. He that is nourished by the acorns he picked up under an oak, or the apples he gathered from the trees in the wood, has certainly appropriated them to himself. Nobody can deny but the nourishment is his. I ask then, when did they begin to be his? when he digested? or when he eat? or when he boiled? or when he brought them home? or when he picked them up? and it is plain, if the first gathering made them not his, nothing else could. That labour put a distinction between them and common: that added something to them more than nature, the common mother of all, had done; and so they became his private right. And will anyone say he had no right to those acorns or apples he thus appropriated, because he had not the consent of all mankind to make them his? was it a robbery thus to assume to himself what belonged to all in common? If such a consent as that was necessary, man had starved, notwithstanding the plenty God had given him. We see in commons, which remain so by compact, that it is the taking any part of what is common and removing it out of the state nature leaves it in, which begins the property; without which the common is of no use. And the taking of this or that part does not depend on the express consent of all the commoners. Thus the grass my horse has bit; the turfs my servant has cut; and the ore I have digged in any place, where I have a right to them in common with others; become my property, without the assignation or consent of any body. The labour that was mine, removing them out of that common state they were in, hath fixed my property in them.

§ 29. By making an explicit consent of every commoner necessary to any one's appropriating to himself any part of what is given in common, children or servants could not cut the meat, which their father or master had provided for them in common, without assigning to everyone his peculiar part. Though the water running in the fountain be every one's, yet who can doubt, but that in the pitcher is his only who drew it out? His labour hath taken it out of the hands of nature, where it was common, and belonged equally to all her children, and hath thereby appropriated it to himself.

§ 30. Thus this law of reason makes the deer that Indian's who hath killed it; it is allowed to be his goods, who hath bestowed his labour upon it, though before it was the common right of every one. And amongst those who are counted the civilized part of mankind, who have made and multiplied positive laws to determine property, this original law of nature, for the beginning of property, in what was before common, still takes place; and by virtue thereof, what fish any one catches in the ocean, that great and still remaining common of mankind: or what ambergris any one takes up here, is by the labour that removes it out of that common state nature left it in, made his property, who takes that pains about it. And even amongst us, the hare that any one is hunting, is thought his who pursues her during the chase: for being a beast that is still looked upon as common, and no man's private possession; whoever has employed so much labour about any of that kind, as to find and pursue her, has thereby removed her from the state of nature, wherein she was common, and hath begun a property.

§ 31. It will perhaps be objected to this, that 'if gathering the acorns, or other fruits of the earth, &c. makes a right to them, then any one may engross as much as he will'. To which I answer, Not so. The same law of nature, that does by this means give us property, does also bound that property too. 'God has given us all things richly', 1 Tim. vi. 17, is the voice of reason confirmed by inspiration. But how far has he given it us? To enjoy. As much as anyone can make use of to any advantage of life before it spoils, so much he may by his labour fix a property in: whatever is beyond this, is more than his share, and belongs to others. Nothing was made by God for man to spoil or destroy. And thus, considering the plenty of natural provisions there was a long time in the world, and the few spenders; and to how small a part of that provision the industry of one man could extend itself, and engross it to the prejudice of others; especially keeping within the bounds, set by reason, of what might serve for his use; there could be then little room for quarrels or contentions about property so established.

§ 32. But the chief matter of property being now not the fruits of the earth, and the beasts that subsist on it, but the earth itself; as that which takes in and carries with it all the rest; I think it is plain, that property in that too is acquired as the former. As much land as a man tills, plants, improves, cultivates, and can use the product of, so much is his property. He by his labour does, as it were, enclose it from the common. Nor will it invalidate his right, to say every body else has an equal title to it, and therefore he cannot appropriate, he cannot enclose, without the consent of all his fellow commoners, all mankind. God, when he gave the world in common to all mankind, commanded man also to labour, and the penury of his condition required it of him. God and his reason commanded him to subdue the earth, i.e., improve it for the benefit of life, and therein lay out something upon it that was his own, his labour. He that, in obedience to this command of God, subdued, tilled, and sowed any part of it, thereby annexed to it something that was his property, which another had no title to, nor could without injury take from him.

§ 33. Nor was this appropriation of any parcel of land, by improving it, any prejudice to any other man, since there was still enough, and as good left; and more than the yet unprovided could use. So that, in effect, there was never the less left for others because of his enclosure for himself: for he that leaves as much as another can make use of, does as good as take nothing at all. Nobody could think himself injured by the drinking of another man, though he took a good draught, who had a whole river of the same water left him to quench his thirst; and the case of land and water, where there is enough for both, is perfectly the same.

§ 34. God gave the world to men in common; but since he gave it them for their benefit, and the greatest conveniences of life they were capable to draw from it, it cannot be supposed he meant it should always remain common and uncultivated. He gave it to the use of the industrious and rational, (and labour was to be his title to it) not to the fancy or covetousness of the quarrelsome and contentious. He that had as good left for his improvement, as was already taken up, needed not complain, ought not to meddle with what was already improved by another's labour: if he did, it is plain he desired the benefit of another's pains, which he had no right to, and not the ground which God had given him in common with others to labour on, and whereof there was as good left, as that already possessed, and more than he knew what to do with, or his industry could reach to. . . .

Chapter VIII. Of the Beginning of Political Societies

§ 95. Men being, as has been said, by nature, all free, equal, and independent, no one can be put out of this estate, and subjected to the political power of another, without his own consent. The only way, whereby any one divests himself of his natural liberty, and puts on the bonds, of civil society, is by agreeing with other men to join and unite into a community, for their comfortable, safe, and peaceable living one amongst another, in a secure enjoyment of their properties, and a greater security against any, that are not of it. This any number of men may do, because it injures not the freedom of the rest; they are left as they were in the liberty of the state of nature. When any number of men have so consented to make one community or government, they are thereby presently incorporated, and make one body politic, wherein the majority have a right to act and conclude the rest.

§ 96. For when any number of men have, by the consent of every individual, made a community, they have thereby made that community one body, with a power to act as one body, which is only by the will and determination of the majority: for that which acts any community, being only the consent of the individuals of it, and it being necessary to that which is one body to move one way; it is necessary the body should move that way whither the greater force carries it, which is the consent of the majority: or else it is impossible it should act or continue one body, one community, which the consent of every individual that united into it, agreed that it should; and so everyone is bound by that consent to be concluded by the majority. And therefore we see, that in assemblies, impowered to act by positive laws, where no number is set by that positive law which impowers them, the act of the majority passes for the act of the whole, and of course determines; as having, by the law of nature and reason, the power of the whole.

§ 97. And thus every man, by consenting with others to make one body politic under one government, puts himself under an obligation, to every one of that society, to submit to the determination of the majority, and to be concluded by it; or else this original compact, whereby he with others incorporate into one society, would signify nothing, and be no compact, if he be left free, and under no other ties than he was in before in the state of nature. For what appearance would there be of any compact? what new engagement if he were no farther tied by any decrees of the society, than he himself thought fit, and did actually consent to? This would be still as great a liberty, as he himself had before his compact, or anyone else in the state of nature hath, who may submit himself, and consent to any acts of it if he thinks fit.

§ 98. For if the consent of the majority shall not, in reason, be received as the act of the whole, and conclude every individual; nothing but the consent of every individual can make anything to be the act of the whole but such a consent is next to impossible ever to be had, if we consider the infirmities of health, and avocations of business, which in a number, though much less than that of a commonwealth, will necessarily keep many away from the public assembly. To which if we add the variety of opinions, and contrariety of interest, which unavoidably happen in all collections of men, the coming into society upon such terms would be only like Cato's coming into the theatre, only to go out again. Such a constitution as this would make the mighty leviathan of a shorter duration, than the feeblest creatures, and not let it outlast the day it was born in: which cannot be supposed, till we can think, that rational creatures should desire and constitute societies only to be dissolved; for where the majority cannot conclude the rest, there they cannot act as one body, and consequently will be immediately dissolved again.

§ 99. Whosoever therefore out of a state of nature unite into a community, must be understood to give up all the power, necessary to the ends for which they unite into society, to the majority of the community, unless they expressly agreed in any number greater than the majority. And this is done by barely agreeing to unite into one political society, which is all the compact that is, or needs be, between the individuals, that enter into, or make up a commonwealth. And thus that, which begins and actually constitutes any political society, is nothing, but the consent of any number of freemen capable of a majority, to unite and incorporate into such a society. And this is that, and that only, which did, or could give beginning to any lawful government in the world. . . .

§ 119. Every man being, as has been showed, naturally free, and nothing being able to put him into subjection to any earthly power, but only his own consent; it is to be considered, what shall be understood to be a sufficient declaration of a man's consent, to make him subject to the laws of any government. There is a common distinction of an express and a tacit consent, which will concern our present case. Nobody doubts but an express consent, of any man entering into any society, makes him a perfect member of that society, a subject of that government. The difficulty is, what ought to be looked upon as a tacit consent, and how far it binds, i.e., how far any one shall be looked upon to have consented, and thereby submitted to any government, where he has made no expressions of it at all. And to this I say, that every man, that hath any possessions, or enjoyment of any part of the dominions of any government, doth thereby give his tacit consent, and is as far forth obliged to obedience to the laws of that government, during such enjoyment, as anyone under it; whether this his possession be of land, to him and his heirs forever, or a lodging only for a week; or whether it be barely travelling freely on the highway: and, in effect, it reaches as far as the very being of anyone within the territories of that government. . . .

Jean-Jacques Rosseau*, 'Freedom and Equality'

The subject of the present discourse, therefore, is more precisely this. To mark, in the progress of things, the moment at which right took the place of violence and nature became subject to law, and to explain by what sequence of miracles the strong came to submit to serve the weak, and the people to purchase imaginary repose at the expense of real felicity.

The philosophers, who have inquired into the foundations of society, have all felt the necessity of going back to a state of nature; but not one of them has got there. Some of them have not hesitated to ascribe to man, in such a state, the idea of just and unjust, without troubling themselves to show that he must be possessed of such an idea, or that it could be of any use to him. Others have spoken of the natural right of every man to keep what belongs to him, without explaining what they meant by *belongs*. Others again, beginning by giving the strong authority over the weak, proceeded directly to the birth of government, without regard to the time that must have elapsed before the meaning of the words authority and government could have existed among men. Every one of them, in short, constantly dwelling on wants, avidity, oppression, desires and pride, has transferred to the state of nature ideas which were acquired in society; so that, in speaking of the savage, they described the social man. It has not even entered into the heads of most of our writers to doubt whether the state of nature ever existed; but it is clear from the Holy Scriptures that the first man, having received his understanding and commandments immediately from God, was not himself in such a state; and that, if we give such credit to the writings of Moses as every Christian philosopher ought to give, we must deny that, even before the deluge, men were ever in the pure state of nature; unless, indeed, they fell back into it from some very extraordinary circumstance; a paradox which it would be very embarrassing to defend, and quite impossible to prove....

We should beware, therefore, of confounding the savage man with the men we have daily before our eyes. Nature treats all the animals left to her care with a predilection that seems to show how jealous she is of that right. The horse, the cat, the bull, and even the ass are generally of greater stature, and always more robust, and have more vigour, strength and courage, when they run wild in the forests than when bred in the stall. By becoming domesticated, they lose half these advantages; and it seems as if all our care to feed and treat them well serves only to deprave them. It is thus with man also: as he becomes sociable and a slave, he grows weak, timid and servile; his effeminate way of life totally enervates his strength and courage. To this it may be added that there is still a greater difference between savage and civilised man, than between wild and tame beasts: for men and brutes having been treated alike by nature, the several conveniences in which men indulge themselves still more than they do their beasts, are so many additional causes of their deeper degeneracy.

It is not therefore so great a misfortune to these primitive men, nor so great an obstacle to their preservation, that they go naked, have no dwellings and lack all the superfluities which we think so necessary. If their skins are not covered with hair, they have no need of such covering in warm climates; and, in cold countries, they soon learn to appropriate the skins of the beasts they have overcome. If they have but two legs to run with, they have two arms to defend themselves with, and provide for their wants. Their children are slowly and with difficulty taught to walk; but their mothers are able to carry them with ease; an advantage which other animals lack, as the mother, if pursued, is forced either to abandon her young, or to regulate her pace by theirs. Unless, in short, we suppose a singular and fortuitous concurrence of circumstances of which I shall speak later, and which would be unlikely to exist, it is plain

---

* Jean-Jacques Rousseau, *The Social Contract and Discourses*. London: JM Dent, 1913 (selections from *The Discourse on Inequality*).

in every state of the case, that the man who first made himself clothes or a dwelling was furnishing himself with things not at all necessary; for he had till then done without them, and there is no reason why he should not have been able to put up in manhood with the same kind of life as had been his in infancy. . . .

Whatever moralists may hold, the human understanding is greatly indebted to the passions, which, it is universally allowed, are also much indebted to the understanding. It is by the activity of the passions that our reason is improved; for we desire knowledge only because we wish to enjoy; and it is impossible to conceive any reason why a person who has neither fears nor desires should give himself the trouble of reasoning. The passions, again, originate in our wants, and their progress depends on that of our knowledge; for we cannot desire or fear anything, except from the idea we have of it, or from the simple impulse of nature. Now savage man, being destitute of every species of intelligence, can have no passions save those of the latter kind: his desires never go beyond his physical wants. The only goods he recognises in the universe are food, a female, and sleep: the only evils he fears are pain and hunger. I say pain, and not death: for no animal can know what it is to die; the knowledge of death and its terrors being one of the first acquisitions made by man in departing from an animal state. . . .

It appears, at first view, that men in a state of nature, having no moral relations or determinate obligations one with another, could not be either good or bad, virtuous or vicious; unless we take these terms in a physical sense, and call, in an individual, those qualities vices which may be injurious to his preservation, and those virtues which contribute to it; in which case, he would have to be accounted most virtuous, who put least check on the pure impulses of nature. But without deviating from the ordinary sense of the words, it will be proper to suspend the judgment we might be led to form on such a state, and be on our guard against our prejudices, till we have weighed the matter in the scales of impartiality, and seen whether virtues or vices preponderate among civilised men; and whether their virtues do them more good than their vices do harm; till we have discovered, whether the progress of the sciences sufficiently indemnifies them for the mischiefs they do one another, in proportion as they are better informed of the good, they ought to do; or whether they would not be, on the whole, in a much happier condition if they had nothing to fear or to hope from any one, than as they are, subjected to universal dependence, and obliged to take everything from those who engage to give them nothing in return.

Above all, let us not conclude, with Hobbes, that because man has no idea of goodness, he must be naturally wicked; that he is vicious because he does not know virtue; that he always refuses to do his fellow-creatures services which he does not think they have a right to demand; or that by virtue of the right he truly claims to everything he needs, he foolishly imagines himself the sole proprietor of the whole universe. Hobbes had seen clearly the defects of all the modern definitions of natural right: but the consequences which he deduces from his own show that he understands it in an equally false sense. In reasoning on the principles he lays down, he ought to have said that the state of nature, being that in which the care for our own preservation is the least prejudicial to that of others, was consequently the best calculated to promote peace, and the most suitable for mankind. He does say the exact opposite, in consequence of having improperly admitted, as a part of savage man's care for self-preservation, the gratification of a multitude of passions which are the work of society, and have made laws necessary. A bad man, he says, is a robust child. But it remains to be proved whether man in a state of nature is this robust child: and, should we grant that he is, what would he infer? Why truly, that if this man, when robust and strong, were dependent on others as he is when feeble, there is no extravagance he would not be guilty of; that he would beat his mother when she was too slow in giving him her breast; that he would strangle one of his younger brothers, if he should be troublesome to him, or bite the arm of another, if he put him to any inconvenience. But that man in the state of nature is both strong and dependent involves two contrary suppositions. Man is weak when he is dependent, and is his own master before he comes to be strong. Hobbes did not reflect that the same cause, which prevents a savage from making use of his reason, as our jurists hold, prevents him also from abusing his faculties, as Hobbes himself allows: so that it may be justly said that savages are not bad merely because they do not know what it is to be good: for it is neither the development of the understanding nor the restraint of law that hinders them from doing ill; but the peacefulness of their passions, and their ignorance of vice: *tanto plus in illis proficit vitiorum ignoratio, quam in his cognitio virtutis.*[1] There is another principle which has escaped Hobbes; which, having been bestowed on mankind, to moderate, on certain occasions, the impetuosity of egoism, or, before its birth, the desire of self-preservation, tempers the ardour with which he pursues his own welfare, by an innate repugnance at seeing a fellow-creature suffer,[2] which could not be denied him by the most violent detractor of human virtue. I am speaking of compassion, which is a disposition suitable to creatures so weak and subject to so many evils as we certainly are: by so much the more universal and useful to mankind, as it comes before any kind of reflection; and at the same time so natural, that the very brutes themselves sometimes give evident proofs of it. Not to mention the tenderness of mothers for their offspring and the perils they encounter to save them from danger, it is well known that horses show a reluctance to trample on living bodies. One animal never passes by the dead body of another of its species: there are even some which give their fellows a sort of burial; while the mournful lowings of the cattle when they enter the slaughter-house show the impressions made on them by the horrible spectacle which meets them. We find, with pleasure, the author of the Fable of the Bees obliged to own that man is a compassionate and sensible being, and laying aside his cold subtlety of style, in the example he gives, to present us with the pathetic description of a man who, from a place of confinement, is compelled to behold a wild beast tear a child from the arms of its mother, grinding its tender limbs with its murderous teeth, and tearing its palpitating entrails with its claws. What horrid agitation must not the eye-witness of such a scene experience, although he would not be personally concerned! What anxiety would he not suffer at not being able to give any assistance to the fainting mother and the dying infant!

Such is the pure emotion of nature, prior to all kinds of reflection! Such is the force of natural compassion, which the greatest depravity of morals has as yet hardly been able to destroy! . . .

Let us conclude then that man in a state of nature, wandering up and down the forests, without industry, without speech, and without home, an equal stranger to war and to all ties, neither standing in need of his fellow-creatures nor having any desire to hurt them, and perhaps even not distinguishing them one from another; let us conclude that, being self-sufficient and subject to so few passions, he could have no feelings or knowledge but such as befitted his situation; that he felt only his actual necessities, and disregarded everything he did not think himself immediately concerned to notice, and that his understanding made no greater progress than his vanity. If by accident he made any discovery, he was the less able to communicate it to others, as he did not know even his own children. Every art would necessarily perish with its inventor, where there was no kind of education among men, and generations succeeded generations without the least advance; when, all setting out from the same point, centuries must have elapsed in the barbarism of the first ages; when the race was already old, and man remained a child.

The first man who, having enclosed a piece of ground, bethought himself of saying *This is mine*, and found people simple enough to believe him, was the real founder of civil society.

From how many crimes, wars and murders, from how many horrors and misfortunes might not any one have saved mankind, by pulling up the stakes, or filling up the ditch, and crying to his fellows, 'Beware of listening to this impostor; you are undone if you once forget that the fruits of the earth belong to us all and the earth itself to nobody'.

Notes

1. Justin Hist ii, 2. So much more does the ignorance of vice profit the one sort than the knowledge of virtue the other.
2. Egoism must not be confused with self-respect: for they differ both in themselves and in their effects. Self-respect is a natural feeling which leads every animal to look to its own preservation, and which, guided in man by reason and modified by compassion, creates humanity and virtue. Egoism is a purely relative and factitious feeling, which arises in the state of society, leads each individual to make more of himself than of any other, causes all the mutual damage men inflict one on another, and is the real source of the 'sense of honour'. This being understood, I maintain that, in our primitive condition, in the true state of nature, egoism did not exist; for as each man regarded himself as the only observer of his actions, the only being in the universe who took any interest in him, and the sole judge of his deserts, no feeling arising from comparisons he could not be led to make could take root in his soul; and for the same reason, he could know neither hatred nor the desire for revenge, since these passions can spring only from a sense of injury: and as it is the contempt or the intention to hurt, and not the harm done, which constitutes the injury, men who neither valued nor compared themselves could do one another much violence, when it suited them, without feeling any sense of injury. In a word, each man, regarding his fellows almost as he regarded animals of different species, might seize the prey of a weaker or yield up his own to a stronger, and yet consider these acts of violence as mere natural occurrences, without the slightest emotion of insolence or despite, or any other feeling than the joy or grief of success or failure.

Jean-Jacques Rousseau*, 'The Social Contract'
Book I

1. Subject of the First Book Man is born free; and everywhere he is in chains. One thinks himself the master of others, and still remains a greater slave than they. How did this change come about? I do not know. What can make it legitimate? That question I think I can answer.

If I took into account only force, and the effects derived from it, I should say: 'As long as a people is compelled to obey, and obeys, it does well; as soon as it can shake off the yoke, and shakes it off, it does still better; for, regaining its liberty by the same right as took it away, either it is justified in resuming it, or there was no justification for those who took it away'. But the social order is a sacred right which is the basis of all other rights. Nevertheless, this right does not come from nature, and must therefore be founded on conventions. Before coming to that, I have to prove what I have just asserted.

6. The Social Compact I suppose men to have reached the point at which the obstacles in the way of their preservation in the state of nature show their power of resistance to be greater

---

* Jean-Jacques Rousseau, *The Social Contract and Discourses*. London: JM Dent, 1913 (selections from *The Social Contract*).

than the resources at the disposal of each individual for his maintenance in that state. That primitive condition can then subsist no longer; and the human race would perish unless it changed its manner of existence.

But, as men cannot engender new forces, but only unite and direct existing ones, they have no other means of preserving themselves than the formation, by aggregation, of a sum of forces great enough to overcome the resistance. These they have to bring into play by means of a single motive power, and cause to act in concert.

This sum of forces can arise only where several persons come together: but, as the force and liberty of each man are the chief instruments of his self-preservation, how can he pledge them without harming his own interests, and neglecting the care he owes to himself? This difficulty, in its bearing on my present subject, may be stated in the following terms:

'The problem is to find a form of association which will defend and protect with the whole common force the person and goods of each associate, and in which each, while uniting himself with all, may still obey himself alone, and remain as free as before'. This is the fundamental problem of which the Social Contract provides the solution.

The clauses of this contract are so determined by the nature of the act that the slightest modification would make them vain and ineffective; so that, although they have perhaps never been formally set forth, they are everywhere the same and everywhere tacitly admitted and recognised, until, on the violation of the social compact, each regains his original rights and resumes his natural liberty, while losing the conventional liberty in favour of which he renounced it.

These clauses, properly understood, may be reduced to one – the total alienation of each associate, together with all his rights, to the whole community; for, in the first place, as each gives himself absolutely, the conditions are the same for all; and, this being so, no one has any interest in making them burdensome to others.

Moreover, the alienation being without reserve, the union is as perfect as it can be, and no associate has anything more to demand: for, if the individuals retained certain rights, as there would be no common superior to decide between them and the public, each, being on one point his own judge, would ask to be so on all; the state of nature would thus continue, and the association would necessarily become inoperative or tyrannical.

Finally, each man, in giving himself to all, gives himself to nobody; and as there is no associate over whom he does not acquire the same right as he yields others over himself, he gains an equivalent for everything he loses, and an increase of force for the preservation of what he has.

If then we discard from the social compact what is not of its essence, we shall find that it reduces itself to the following terms:

> 'Each of us puts his person and all his power in common under the supreme direction of the general will, and, in our corporate capacity, we receive each member as an indivisible part of the whole'.

At once, in place of the individual personality of each contracting party, this act of association creates a moral and collective body, composed of as many members as the assembly contains votes, and receiving from this act its unity, its common identity, its life and its will. This public person, so formed by the union of all other persons formerly took the name of city, and now takes that of Republic or body politic; it is called by its members State when passive. Sovereign when active, and Power when compared with others like itself. Those who are associated in it take collectively the name of people, and severally are called citizens, as sharing in the sovereign power, and subjects, as being under the laws of the State. But these terms are often confused and taken one for another: it is enough to know how to distinguish them when they are being used with precision.

7. The Sovereign This formula shows us that the act of association comprises a mutual undertaking between the public and the individuals, and that each individual, in making a contract, as we may say, with himself, is bound in a double capacity; as a member of the Sovereign he is bound to the individuals, and as a member of the State to the Sovereign. But the maxim of civil right, that no one is bound by undertakings made to himself, does not apply in this case; for there is a great difference between incurring an obligation to yourself and incurring one to a whole of which you form a part.

Attention must further be called to the fact that public deliberation, while competent to bind all the subjects to the Sovereign, because of the two different capacities in which each of them may be regarded, cannot, for the opposite reason, bind the Sovereign to itself; and that it is consequently against the nature of the body politic for the Sovereign to impose on itself a law which it cannot infringe. Being able to regard itself in only one capacity, it is in the position of an individual who makes a contract with himself; and this makes it clear that there neither is nor can be any kind of fundamental law binding on the body of the people – not even the social contract itself. This does not mean that the body politic cannot enter into undertakings with others, provided the contract is not infringed by them; for in relation to what is external to it, it becomes a simple being, an individual.

But the body politic or the Sovereign, drawing its being wholly from the sanctity of the contract, can never bind itself, even to an outsider, to do anything derogatory to the original act, for instance, to alienate any part of itself, or to submit to another Sovereign. Violation of the act by which it exists would be self-annihilation; and that which is itself nothing can create nothing.

As soon as this multitude is so united in one body, it is impossible to offend against one of the members without attacking the body, and still more to offend against the body without the members resenting it. Duty and interest therefore equally oblige the two contracting parties to give each other help; and the same men should seek to combine, in their double capacity, all the advantages dependent upon that capacity.

Again, the Sovereign, being formed wholly of the individuals who compose it, neither has nor can have any interest contrary to theirs; and consequently the sovereign power need give no guarantee to its subjects, because it is impossible for the body to wish to hurt all its members. We shall also see later on that it cannot hurt any in particular. The Sovereign, merely by virtue of what it is, is always what it should be.

This, however, is not the case with the relation of the subjects to the Sovereign, which, despite the common interest, would have no security that they would fulfil their undertakings, unless it found means to assure itself of their fidelity.

In fact, each individual, as a man, may have a particular will contrary or dissimilar to the general will which he has as a citizen. His particular interest may speak to him quite differently from the common interest: his absolute and naturally independent existence may make him look upon what he owes to the common cause as a gratuitous contribution, the loss of which will do less harm to others than the payment of it is burdensome to himself; and, regarding the moral person which constitutes the State as a *persona ficta*[1] because not a man, he may wish to enjoy the rights of citizenship without being ready to fulfil the duties of a subject. The continuance of such an injustice could not but prove the undoing of the body politic.

In order then that the social compact may not be an empty formula, it tacitly includes the undertaking, which alone can give force to the rest, that whoever refuses to obey the general will shall be compelled to do so by the whole body. This means nothing less than that he will be forced to be free; for this is the condition which, by giving each citizen to his country, secures him against all personal dependence. In this lies the key to the working of the political machine; this alone legitimises civil undertakings, which, without it, would be absurd, tyrannical, and liable to the most frightful abuses.

8. The Civil State The passage from the state of nature to the civil state produces a very remarkable change in man, by substituting justice for instinct in his conduct, and giving his actions the morality they had formerly lacked. Then only, when the voice of duty takes the place of physical impulses and right of appetite, does man, who so far had considered only himself, find that he is forced to act on different principles, and to consult his reason before listening to his inclinations. Although, in this state, he deprives himself of some advantages which he got from nature, he gains in return others so great, his faculties are so stimulated and developed, his ideas so extended, his feelings so ennobled, and his whole soul so uplifted, that, did not the abuses of this new condition often degrade him below that which he left, he would be bound to bless continually the happy moment which took him from it forever, and, instead of a stupid and unimaginative animal, made him an intelligent being and a man.

Let us draw up the whole account in terms easily commensurable. What man loses by the social contract is his natural liberty and an unlimited right to everything he tries to get and succeeds in getting; what he gains is civil liberty and the proprietorship of all he possesses. If we are to avoid mistake in weighing one against the other, we must clearly distinguish natural liberty, which is bounded only by the strength of the individual, from civil liberty, which is limited by the general will; and possession, which is merely the effect of force or the right of the first occupier, from property, which can be founded only on a positive title.

We might, over and above all this, add, to what man acquires in the civil state, moral liberty, which alone makes him truly master of himself; for the mere impulse of appetite is slavery, while obedience to a law which we prescribe to ourselves is liberty. But I have already said too much on this head, and the philosophical meaning of the word liberty does not now concern us.

Book II

3. Whether the General Will Is Fallible It follows from what has gone before that the general will is always right and tends to the public advantage; but it does not follow that the deliberations of the people are always equally correct. Our will is always for our own good, but we do not always see what that is; the people is never corrupted, but it is often deceived, and on such occasions only does it seem to will what is bad.

There is often a great deal of difference between the will of all and the general will; the latter considers only the common interest, while the former takes private interest into account, and is no more than a sum of particular wills: but take away from these same wills the pluses and minuses that cancel one another, and the general will remains as the sum of the differences.

If, when the people, being furnished with adequate information, held its deliberations, the citizens had no communication one with another, the grand total of the small differences would always give the general will, and the decision would always be good. But when factions arise, and partial associations are formed at the expense of the great association, the will of each of these associations becomes general in relation to its members, while it remains particular in relation to the State: it may then be said that there are no longer as many votes as there are men, but only as many as there are associations. The differences become less numerous and give a less general result. Lastly, when one of these associations is so great as to prevail over all the rest, the result is no longer a sum of small differences, but a single difference; in this case there is no longer a general will, and the opinion which prevails is purely particular. . . .

It is therefore essential, if the general will is to be able to express itself, that there should be no partial society within the State, and that each citizen should think only his own thoughts: which was indeed the sublime and unique system established by the great Lycurgus. But if there are partial societies, it is best to have as many as possible and to prevent them from being unequal, as was done by Solon, Numa and Servius. These precautions are the only ones that can guarantee that the general will shall be always enlightened, and that the people shall in no way deceive itself.

Book III

4. Democracy He who makes the law knows better than anyone else how it should be executed and interpreted. It seems then impossible to have a better constitution than that in which the executive and legislative powers are united; but this very fact renders the government in certain respects inadequate, because things which should be distinguished are confounded, and the prince and the Sovereign, being the same person, form, so to speak, no more than a government without government.

It is not good for him who makes the laws to execute them, or for the body of the people to turn its attention away from a general standpoint and devote it to particular objects. Nothing is more dangerous than the influence of private interests in public affairs, and the abuse of the laws by the government is a less evil than the corruption of the legislator, which is the inevitable sequel to a particular standpoint. In such a case, the State being altered in substance, all reformation becomes impossible. A people that would never misuse governmental powers would never misuse independence; a people that would always govern well would not need to be governed.

If we take the term in the strict sense, there never has been a real democracy, and there never will be. It is against the natural order for the many to govern and the few to be governed. It is unimaginable that the people should remain continually assembled to devote their time to public affairs, and it is clear that they cannot set up commissions for that purpose without the form of administration being changed.

In fact, I can confidently lay down as a principle that, when the functions of government are shared by several tribunals, the less numerous sooner or later acquire the greatest authority, if only because they are in a position to expedite affairs, and power thus naturally comes into their hands.

Besides, how many conditions that are difficult to unite does such a government presuppose! First, a very small State, where the people can readily be got together and where each citizen can with ease know all the rest; secondly, great simplicity of manners, to prevent business from multiplying and raising thorny problems; next, a large measure of equality in rank and fortune, without which equality of rights and authority cannot long subsist; lastly, little or no luxury – for luxury either comes of riches or makes them necessary; it corrupts at once rich and poor, the rich by possession and the poor by covetousness; it sells the country to softness and vanity, and takes away from the State all its citizens, to make them slaves one to another, and one and all to public opinion.

This is why a famous writer has made virtue the fundamental principle of Republics; for all these conditions could not exist without virtue. But, for want of the necessary distinctions, that great thinker was often inexact, and sometimes obscure, and did not see that, the sovereign authority being everywhere the same, the same principle should be found in every well-constituted State, in a greater or less degree, it is true, according to the form of the government.

It may be added that there is no government so subject to civil wars and intestine agitations as democratic or popular government because there is none which has so strong and continual a tendency to change to another form, or which demands more vigilance and courage for its maintenance as it is.

Under such a constitution above all, the citizen should arm himself with strength and constancy, and say, every day of his life, what a virtuous Count Palatine[1] said in the Diet of Poland: *Malo periculosam libertatem quam quietum servitium.*[2]

Were there a people of gods, their government would be democratic. So perfect a government is not for men.

Notes

1. A fictitious person created under law; juridical or artificial person.
2. 'I prefer liberty with danger to peace with slavery'.

John Rawls*, 'Two Principles of Justice'
The Main Idea of the Theory of Justice

My aim is to present a conception of justice which generalizes and carries to a higher level of abstraction the familiar theory of the social contract as found, say, in Locke, Rousseau, and Kant.[1] In order to do this we are not to think of the original contract as one to enter a particular society or to set up a particular form of government. Rather, the guiding idea is that the principles of justice for the basic structure of society are the object of the original agreement. They are the principles that free and rational persons concerned to further their own interests would accept in an initial position of equality as defining the fundamental terms of their association. These principles are to regulate all further agreements; they specify the kinds of social cooperation that can be entered into and the forms of government that can be established. This way of regarding the principles of justice I shall call justice as fairness.

Thus we are to imagine that those who engage in social cooperation choose together, in one joint act, the principles which are to assign basic rights and duties and to determine the division of social benefits. Men are to decide, in advance how they are to regulate their claims against one another and what is to be the foundation charter of their society. Just as each person must decide by rational reflection what constitutes his good, that is, the system of ends which it is rational for him to pursue, so a group of persons must decide once and for all what is to count among them as just and unjust. The choice which rational men would make in this hypothetical situation of equal liberty, assuming for the present that this choice problem has a solution, determines the principles of justice.

* John Rawls, *A Theory of Justice*. Cambridge, MA: The Belknap Press of Harvard University Press, pp. 11–6, 60–5. Copyright © 1971 by the President and Fellows of Harvard College.

In justice as fairness the original position of equality corresponds to the state of nature in the traditional theory of the social contract. This original position is not, of course, thought of as an actual historical state of affairs, much less as a primitive condition of culture. It is understood as a purely hypothetical situation characterized so as to lead to a certain conception of justice.[2] Among the essential features of this situation is that no one knows his place in society, his class position or social status, nor does anyone know his fortune in the distribution of natural assets and abilities, his intelligence, strength, and the like. I shall even assume that the parties do not know their conceptions of the good or their special psychological propensities. The principles of justice are chosen behind a veil of ignorance. This ensures that no one is advantaged or disadvantaged in the choice of principles by the outcome of natural chance or the contingency of social circumstances. Since all are similarly situated and no one is able to design principles to favor his particular condition, the principles of justice are the result of a fair agreement or bargain. For given the circumstances of the original position, the symmetry of everyone's relations to each other, this initial situation is fair between individuals as moral persons, that is, as rational beings with their own ends and capable, I shall assume, of a sense of justice. The original position is, one might say, the appropriate initial status quo, and thus the fundamental agreements reached in it are fair. This explains the propriety of the name 'justice as fairness': it conveys the idea that the principles of justice are agreed to in an initial situation that is fair. The name does not mean that the concepts of justice and fairness are the same, any more than the phrase 'poetry as metaphor' means that the concepts of poetry and metaphor are the same.

Justice as fairness begins, as I have said, with one of the most general of all choices which persons might make together, namely, with the choice of the first principles of a conception of justice which is to regulate all subsequent criticism and reform of institutions. Then, having chosen a conception of justice, we can suppose that they are to choose a constitution and a legislature to enact laws, and so on, all in accordance with the principles of justice initially agreed upon. Our social situation is just if it is such that by this sequence of hypothetical agreements we would have contracted into the general system of rules which defines it. Moreover, assuming that the original position does determine a set of principles (that is, that a particular conception of justice would be chosen), it will then be true that whenever social institutions satisfy these principles those engaged in them can say to one another that they are cooperating on terms to which they would agree if they were free and equal persons whose relations with respect to one another were fair. They could all view their arrangements as meeting the stipulations which they would acknowledge in an initial situation that embodies widely accepted and reasonable constraints on the choice of principles. The general recognition of this fact would provide the basis for a public acceptance of the corresponding principles of justice. No society can, of course, be a scheme of cooperation which men enter voluntarily in a literal sense; each person finds himself placed at birth in some particular position in some particular society, and the nature of this position materially affects his life prospects. Yet a society satisfying the principles of justice as fairness comes as close as a society can to being a voluntary scheme, for it meets the principles which free and equal persons would assent to under circumstances that are fair. In this sense its members are autonomous and the obligations they recognize self-imposed.

One feature of justice as fairness is to think of the parties in the initial situation as rational and mutually disinterested. This does not mean that the parties are egoists, that is, individuals with only certain kinds of interests, say in wealth, prestige, and domination. But they are conceived as not taking an interest in one another's interests.

They are to presume that even their spiritual aims may be opposed, in the way that the aims of those of different religions may be opposed. Moreover, the concept of rationality must be interpreted as far as possible in the narrow sense, standard in economic theory, of taking the most effective means to given ends. I shall modify this concept to some extent, as explained later, but one must try to avoid introducing into it any controversial ethical elements. The initial situation must be characterized by stipulations that are widely accepted.

In working out the conception of justice as fairness one main task clearly is to determine which principles of justice would be chosen in the original position. To do this we must describe this situation in some detail and formulate with care the problem of choice which it presents. These matters I shall take up in the immediately succeeding chapters. It may be observed, however, that once the principles of justice are thought of as arising from an original agreement in a situation of equality, it is an open question whether the principle of utility would be acknowledged. Offhand it hardly seems likely that persons who view themselves as equals, entitled to press their claims upon one another, would agree to a principle which may require lesser life prospects for some simply for the sake of a greater sum of advantages enjoyed by others. Since each desires to protect his interests, his capacity to advance his conception of the good, no one has a reason to acquiesce in an enduring loss for himself in order to bring about a greater net balance of satisfaction. In the absence of strong and lasting benevolent impulses, a rational man would not accept a basic structure merely because it maximized the algebraic sum of advantages irrespective of its permanent effects on his own basic rights and interests. Thus it seems that the principle of utility is incompatible with the conception of social cooperation among equals for mutual advantage. It appears to be inconsistent with the idea of reciprocity implicit in the notion of a well-ordered society. Or, at any rate, so I shall argue.

I shall maintain instead that the persons in the initial situation would choose two rather different principles: the first requires equality in the assignment of basic rights and duties, while the second holds that social and economic inequalities, for example inequalities of wealth and authority, are just only if they result in compensating benefits for everyone, and in particular for the least advantaged members of society. These principles rule out justifying institutions on the grounds that the hardships of some are offset by a greater good in the aggregate. It may be expedient but it is not just that some should have less in order that others may prosper. But there is no injustice in the greater benefits earned by a few provided that the situation of persons not so fortunate is thereby improved. The intuitive idea is that since everyone's well-being depends upon a scheme of cooperation without which no one could have a satisfactory life, the division of advantages should be such as to draw forth the willing cooperation of everyone taking part in it, including those less well situated. Yet this can be expected only if reasonable terms are proposed. The two principles mentioned seem to be a fair agreement on the basis of which those better endowed, or more fortunate in their social position, neither of which we can be said to deserve, could expect the willing cooperation of others when some workable scheme is a necessary condition of the welfare of all.[3] Once we decide to look for a conception of justice that nullifies the accidents of natural endowment and the contingencies of social circumstance as counters in quest for political and economic advantage, we are led to these principles. They express the result of leaving aside those aspects of the social world that seem arbitrary from a moral point of view.

The problem of the choice of principles, however, is extremely difficult. I do not expect the answer I shall suggest to be convincing to everyone. It is, therefore, worth noting from the outset that justice as fairness, like other contract views, consists of two parts: (1) an interpretation of the initial situation and of the problem of choice posed there, and (2) a set of principles which, it is argued, would be agreed to. One may accept the first part of the theory (or some variant thereof), but not the other, and conversely. The concept of the initial contractual situation may seem reasonable although the particular principles proposed are rejected. To be sure, I want to maintain that the most appropriate conception of this situation does lead to principles of justice contrary to utilitarianism and perfectionism, and therefore that the contract doctrine provides an alternative to these views. Still, one may dispute this contention even though one grants that the contractarian method is a useful way of studying ethical theories and of setting forth their underlying assumptions.

Justice as fairness is an example of what I have called a contract theory. Now there may be an objection to the term 'contract' and related expressions, but I think it will serve reasonably well. Many words have misleading connotations which at first are likely to confuse. The terms 'utility' and 'utilitarianism' are surely no exception. They too have unfortunate suggestions which hostile critics have been willing to exploit; yet they are clear enough for those prepared to study utilitarian doctrine. The same should be true of the term 'contract' applied to moral theories. As I have mentioned, to understand it one has to keep in mind that it implies a certain level of abstraction. In particular, the content of the relevant agreement is not to enter a given society or to adopt a given form of government, but to accept certain moral principles. Moreover, the undertakings referred to are purely hypothetical: a contract view holds that certain principles would be accepted in a well-defined initial situation.

The merit of the contract terminology is that it conveys the idea that principles of justice may be conceived as principles that would be chosen by rational persons, and that in this way conceptions of justice may be explained and justified. The theory of justice is a part, perhaps the most significant part, of the theory of rational choice. Furthermore, principles of justice deal with conflicting claims upon the advantages won by social cooperation; they apply to the relations among several persons or groups. The word 'contract' suggests this plurality as well as the condition that the appropriate division of advantages must be in accordance with principles acceptable to all parties. The condition of publicity for principles of justice is also connoted by the contract phraseology. Thus, if these principles are the outcome of an agreement, citizens have a knowledge of the principles that others follow. It is characteristic of contract theories to stress the public nature of political principles. Finally, there is the long tradition of the contract doctrine. Expressing the tie with this line of thought helps to define ideas and accords with natural piety. There are then several advantages in the use of the term 'contract'. With due precautions taken, it should not be misleading.

Two Principles of Justice

I shall now state in a provisional form the two principles of justice that I believe would be chosen in the original position. In this section I wish to make only the most general comments, and therefore the first formulation of these principles is tentative. As we go on I shall run through several formulations and approximate step by step the final statement to be given much later. I believe that doing this allows the exposition to proceed in a natural way.

The first statement of the two principles reads as follows.

> First: each person is to have an equal right to the most extensive basic liberty compatible with a similar liberty for others.
> Second: social and economic inequalities are to be arranged so that they are both (a) reasonably expected to be to everyone's advantage, and (b) attached to positions and offices open to all.

By way of general comment, these principles primarily apply, as I have said, to the basic structure of society. They are to govern the assignment of rights and duties and to regulate the distribution of social and economic advantages. As their formulation suggests, these principles presuppose that the social structure can be divided into two more or less distinct parts, the first principle applying to the one, the second to the other. They distinguish between those aspects of the social system that define and secure the equal liberties of citizenship and those that specify and establish social and economic inequalities. The basic liberties of citizens are, roughly speaking, political liberty (the right to vote and to be eligible for public office) together with freedom of speech and assembly; liberty of conscience and freedom of thought; freedom of the person along with the right to hold (personal) property; and freedom from arbitrary arrest and seizure as defined by the concept of the rule of law. These liberties are all required to be equal by the first principle since citizens of a just society are to have the same basic rights.

The second principle applies, in the first approximation, to the distribution of income and wealth and to the design of organizations that make use of differences in authority and responsibility, or chains of command. While the distribution of wealth and income need not be equal, it must be to everyone's advantage, and at the same time, positions of authority and offices of command must be accessible to all. One applies the second principle by holding positions open, and then, subject to this constraint, arranges social and economic inequalities so that everyone benefits.

These principles are to be arranged in a serial order with the first principle prior to the second. This ordering means that a departure from the institutions of equal liberty required by the first principle cannot be justified by, or compensated for, by greater social and economic advantages. The distribution of wealth and income, and the hierarchies of authority, must be consistent with both the liberties of equal citizenship and equality of opportunity.

It is clear that these principles are rather specific in their content, and their acceptance rests on certain assumptions that I must eventually try to explain and justify. A theory of justice depends upon a theory of society in ways that will become evident as we proceed. For the present, it should be observed that the two principles (and this holds for all formulations) are a special case of a more general conception of justice that can be expressed as follows.

> All social values – liberty and opportunity, income and wealth, and the bases of self-respect – are to be distributed equally unless an unequal distribution of any, or all, of these values is to everyone's advantage.

Injustice, then, is simply inequalities that are not to the benefit of all. Of course, this conception is extremely vague and requires interpretation.

As a first step, suppose that the basic structure of society distributes certain primary goods, that is, things that every rational man is presumed to want. These goods normally have a use whatever a person's rational plan of life. For simplicity, assume that the chief primary goods at the disposition of society are rights and liberties, powers and opportunities, income and wealth. These are the social primary goods. Other primary goods such as health and vigor, intelligence and imagination, are natural goods; although their possession is influenced by the basic structure, they are not so directly under its control. Imagine, then, a hypothetical initial arrangement in which all the social primary goods are equally distributed: everyone has similar rights and duties, and income and wealth are evenly shared. This state of affairs provides a benchmark for judging improvements. If certain inequalities of wealth and organizational powers would make everyone better off than in this hypothetical starting situation, then they accord with the general conception.

Now it is possible, at least theoretically, that by giving up some of their fundamental liberties men are sufficiently compensated by the resulting social and economic gains. The general conception of justice imposes no restrictions on what sort of inequalities are permissible; it only requires that everyone's position be improved. We need not suppose anything so drastic as consenting to a condition of slavery. Imagine instead that men forego certain political rights when the economic returns are significant and their capacity to influence the course of policy by the exercise of these rights would be marginal in any case. It is this kind of exchange which the two principles as stated rule out; being arranged in serial order they do not permit exchanges between basic liberties and economic and social gains. The serial ordering of principles expresses an underlying preference among primary social goods. When this preference is rational so likewise is the choice of these principles in this order.

In developing justice as fairness, I shall, for the most part, leave aside the general conception of justice and examine instead the special case of the two principles in serial order. The advantage of this procedure is that from the first the matter of priorities is recognized and an effort made to find principles to deal with it. One is led to attend throughout to the conditions under which the acknowledgment of the absolute weight of liberty with respect to social and economic advantages, as defined by the lexical order of the two principles, would be reasonable. Offhand, this ranking appears extreme and too special a case to be of much interest; but there is more justification for it than would appear at first sight. Or at any rate, so I shall maintain. Furthermore, the distinction between fundamental rights and liberties and economic and social benefits marks a difference among primary social goods that one should try to exploit. It suggests an important division in the social system. Of course, the distinctions drawn and the ordering proposed are bound to be at best only approximations. There are surely circumstances in which they fail. But it is essential to depict clearly the main lines of a reasonable conception of justice; and under many conditions anyway, the two principles in serial order may serve well enough. When necessary we can fall back on the more general conception.

The fact that the two principles apply to institutions has certain consequences. Several points illustrate this. First of all, the rights and liberties referred to by these principles are those which are defined by the public rules of the basic structure. Whether men are free is determined by the rights and duties established by the major institutions of society. Liberty is a certain pattern of social forms. The first principle simply requires that certain sorts of rules, those defining basic liberties, apply to everyone equally and that they allow the most extensive liberty compatible with a like liberty for all. The only reason for circumscribing the rights defining liberty and making men's freedom less extensive than it might otherwise be is that these equal rights as institutionally defined would interfere with one another.

Another thing to bear in mind is that when principles mention persons, or require that everyone gain from an inequality, the reference is to representative persons holding the various social positions, or offices, or whatever, established by the basic structure. Thus in applying the second principle I assume that it is possible to assign an expectation of well-being to representative individuals holding these positions. This expectation indicates their life prospects as viewed from their social station. In general, the expectations of representative persons depend upon the distribution of rights and duties throughout the basic structure. When this changes, expectations change. I assume, then, that expectations are connected: by raising the prospects of the representative man in one position we presumably increase or decrease the prospects of representative men in other positions. Since it applies to institutional forms, the second principle (or rather the first part of it) refers to the expectations of representative individuals. As I shall discuss below, neither principle applies to distributions of particular goods to particular individuals who may be identified by their proper names. The situation where someone is considering how to allocate certain commodities to needy persons who are known to him is not within the scope of the principles. They are meant to regulate basic institutional arrangements. We must not assume that there is much similarity from the standpoint of justice between an administrative allotment of goods to specific persons and the appropriate design of society. Our common-sense intuitions for the former may be a poor guide to the latter.

Now the second principle insists that each person benefit from permissible inequalities in the basic structure. This means that it must be reasonable for each relevant representative man defined by this structure, when he views it as a going concern, to prefer his prospects with the inequality to his prospects without it. One is not allowed to justify differences in income or organizational powers on the ground that the disadvantages of those in one position are outweighed by the greater advantages of those in another. Much less can infringements of liberty be counterbalanced in this way. Applied to the basic structure, the principle of utility would have us maximize the sum of expectations of representative men (weighted by the number of persons they represent, on the classical view); and this would permit us to compensate for the losses of some by the gains of others. Instead, the two principles require that everyone benefit from economic and social inequalities. It is obvious, however, that there are indefinitely many ways in which all may be advantaged when the initial arrangement of equality is taken as a benchmark. How then are we to choose among these possibilities? The principles must be specified so that they yield a determinate conclusion. I now turn to this problem.

Notes

1. As the text suggests, I shall regard Locke's *Second Treatise of Government*, Rousseau's *The Social Contract*, and Kant's ethical works beginning with *The Foundations of the Metaphysics of Morals* as definitive of the contract tradition. For all of its greatness, Hobbes's *Leviathan* raises special problems. A general historical survey is provided by J W Gough, *The Social Contract*, 2nd ed (Oxford: The Clarendon Press, 1957), and Otto Gierke, *Natural Law and the Theory of Society*, trans, with an introduction by Ernest Barker (Cambridge: The University Press, 1934). A presentation of the contract view as primarily an ethical theory is to be found in G R Grice, *The Grounds of Moral Judgment* (Cambridge: The University Press, 1967). See also §19, note 30.
2. Kant is clear that the original agreement is hypothetical. See *The Metaphysics of Morals*, pt I (*Rechtslehre*), especially §§ 47, 52; and pt II of the essay 'Concerning the Common Saying: This May Be True in Theory but It Does Not Apply in Practice', in *Kant's Political Writings*, ed Hans Reiss and trans by H B Nisbet (Cambridge: The University Press, 1970), 73–87. See Georges Vlachos, *La Pensée politique de Kant* (Paris: Presses Universitaires de France, 1962), 326–35; and J G Murphy, *Kant: The Philosophy of Right* (London: Macmillan, 1970), 109–12, 133–36, for a further discussion.
3. For the formulation of this intuitive idea I am indebted to Allan Gibbard.

Carole Pateman*, 'The Sexual Contract'

Telling stories of all kinds is the major way that human beings have endeavoured to make sense of themselves and their social world. The most famous and influential political story of modern times is found in the writings of the social contract theorists. The story, or conjectural history, tells how a new civil society and a new form of political right is created through an original contract. An explanation for the binding authority of the state and civil law, and for the legitimacy of modern civil government is to be found by treating our society as if it had originated in a contract. The attraction of the idea of an original contract and of contract theory in a more general sense, a theory that claims that free social relations take a contractual form, is probably greater now than at any time since the seventeenth and eighteenth centuries when the classic writers told their tales. But today, invariably, only half the story is told. We hear an enormous amount about the *social* contract; a deep silence is maintained about the *sexual* contract.

The original contract is a sexual-social pact, but the story of the sexual contract has been repressed. Standard accounts of social contract theory do not discuss the whole story and contemporary contract theorists give no indication that half the agreement is missing. The story of the sexual contract is also about the genesis of political right, and explains why exercise of the right is legitimate – but this story is about political right as *patriarchal right* or sex-right, the power that men exercise over women. The missing half of the story tells how a specifically modern form of patriarchy is established. The new civil society created through the original contract is a patriarchal social order.

Social contract theory is conventionally presented as a story about freedom. One interpretation of the original contract is that the inhabitants of the state of nature exchange the insecurities of natural freedom for equal, civil freedom which is protected by the state. In civil society freedom is universal; all adults enjoy the same civil standing and can exercise their freedom by, as it were, replicating the original contract when, for example, they enter into the employment contract or the marriage contract. Another interpretation, which takes into account conjectural histories of the state of nature in the classic texts, is that freedom is won by sons who cast off their natural subjection to their fathers and replace paternal rule by civil government. Political right as paternal right is inconsistent with modern civil society. In this version of the story, civil society is created through the original contract after paternal rule – or patriarchy – is overthrown. The new civil order, therefore, appears to be anti-patriarchal or post-patriarchal. Civil society is created through contract so that contract and patriarchy appear to be irrevocably opposed.

These familiar readings of the classic stories fail to mention that a good deal more than freedom is at stake. Men's domination over women, and the right of men to enjoy equal sexual access to women, is at issue in the making of the original pact. The social contract is a story of freedom; the sexual contract is a story of subjection. The original contract constitutes both freedom and domination. Men's freedom and women's subjection are created through the original contract – and the character of civil freedom cannot be understood without the missing half of the story that reveals how men's patriarchal right over women is established through contract. Civil freedom is not universal. Civil freedom is a masculine attribute and depends upon patriarchal right. The sons overturn paternal rule not merely to gain their liberty but to secure women for themselves. Their success in this endeavour is chronicled in the story of the sexual contract. The original pact is a sexual as well as a social contract: it is sexual in the sense

---

* Carole Pateman, *The Sexual Contract*. Stanford, CA: Stanford University Press; Oxford: Polity Press, 1988, pp. 1–4, 219–221. Copyright by Stanford and Polity Press.

of patriarchal – that is, the contract establishes men's political right over women – and also sexual in the sense of establishing orderly access by men to women's bodies. The original contract creates what I shall call, following Adrienne Rich, 'the law of male sex-right'.[1] Contract is far from being opposed to patriarchy; contract is the means through which modern patriarchy is constituted.

One reason why political theorists so rarely notice that half the story of the original contract is missing, or that civil society is patriarchal, is that 'patriarchy' is usually interpreted patriarchally as paternal rule (the literal meaning of the term). So, for example, in the standard reading of the theoretical battle in the seventeenth century between the patriarchalists and social contract theorists, patriarchy is assumed to refer only to paternal right. Sir Robert Filmer claimed that political power was paternal power and that the procreative power of the father was the origin of political right. Locke and his fellow contract theorists insisted that paternal and political power were not the same and that contract was the genesis of political right. The contract theorists were victorious on this point; the standard interpretation is on firm ground – as far as it goes. Once more, a crucial portion of the story is missing. The true origin of political right is overlooked in this interpretation; no stories are told about its genesis (I attempt to remedy the omission in chapter 4). Political right originates in sex-right or conjugal right. Paternal right is only one, and not the original, dimension of patriarchal power. A man's power as a father comes after he has exercised the patriarchal right of a man (a husband) over a woman (wife). The contract theorists had no wish to challenge the original patriarchal right in their onslaught on paternal right. Instead, they incorporated conjugal right into their theories and, in so doing, transformed the law of male sex-right into its modern contractual form. Patriarchy ceased to be paternal long ago. Modern civil society is not structured by kinship and the power of fathers; in the modern world, women are subordinated to men *as men*, or to men as a fraternity. The original contract takes place after the political defeat of the father and creates modern *fraternal patriarchy*.

Another reason for the omission of the story of the sexual contract is that conventional approaches to the classic texts, whether those of mainstream political theorists or their socialist critics, give a misleading picture of a distinctive feature of the civil society created through the original pact. Patriarchal civil society is divided into two spheres, but attention is directed to one sphere only. The story of the social contract is treated as an account of the creation of the public sphere of civil freedom. The other, private, sphere is not seen as politically relevant. Marriage and the marriage contract are, therefore, also deemed politically irrelevant. To ignore the marriage contract is to ignore half the original contract. In the classic texts, as I shall show in some detail, the sexual contract is displaced onto the marriage contract. The displacement creates a difficulty in retrieving and recounting the lost story. All too easily, the impression can be given that the sexual contract and the social contract are two separate, albeit related, contracts, and that the sexual contract concerns the private sphere. Patriarchy then appears to have no relevance to the public world. On the contrary, patriarchal right extends throughout civil society. The employment contract and (what I shall call) the prostitution contract, both of which are entered into in the public, capitalist market, uphold men's right as firmly as the marriage contract. The two spheres of civil society are at once separate and inseparable. The public realm cannot be fully understood in the absence of the private sphere, and, similarly, the meaning of the original contract is misinterpreted without both, mutually dependent, halves of the story. Civil freedom depends on patriarchal right. . . .

An old anarchist slogan states that 'no man is good enough to be another man's master'. The sentiment is admirable, but the slogan is silent on one crucial issue. In modern civil society all men are deemed good enough to be women's masters; civil freedom depends on patriarchal right. The failure to see patriarchal right as central to the political problem of freedom, mastery and subordination is so deep-seated that even the anarchists, so acutely aware of subjection among men, have had few quarrels with their fellow socialists about sexual domination. From the beginning of the modern era, when Mary Astell asked why, if all men were born free, all women were born slaves, feminists have persistently challenged masculine right; but, despite all the social changes and legal and political reforms over the past three hundred years, the question of women's subordination is still not seen as a matter of major importance, either in the academic study of politics or in political practice. Controversy about freedom revolves round the law of the state and the law of capitalist production: silence is maintained about the law of male sex-right.

The original contract is merely a story, a political fiction, but the invention of the story was also a momentous intervention into the political world; the spell exerted by stories of political origins has to be broken if the fiction is to be rendered ineffective. . . .

Talk of founding has been in vogue in recent years among political theorists, especially in the United States, but how should the real historical 'foundings' of two of the countries with which I am concerned be interpreted? When the First Fleet arrived in Australia in 1788, the men unloaded the ships and built shelters, then, five days later, the female convicts were allowed ashore and into the men's hands. By 1809, the colony was being described as 'little better than an extensive brothel'. As more women convicts were transported, 'the inhabitants of the colony each [selected] one at his pleasure, not only as servants but as avowed objects of intercourse'.[2] Exactly which conjectural history of origins could appropriately be told about these events? The bicentennial of the founding is being celebrated in 1988, but the indigenous people of Australia, like their counterparts in the United States in 1976, see nothing to celebrate. Examples of acts that resemble contractual beginnings can be found in the first white settlements in America, but the 'founding' of white America and Australia took protracted campaigns of conquest and forcible seizure of vast areas of land from indigenous inhabitants.

In order to bring out as sharply as possible something of what is at stake in alternative readings of the original contract, I have exaggerated and described the sexual contract as half the story. The story of political genesis needs to be told again from yet another perspective. The men who (are said to) make the original contract are *white* men, and their fraternal pact has three aspects; the social contract, the sexual contract and the slave contract that legitimizes the rule of white over black.

Notes

1. A Rich, 'Compulsory Heterosexuality and Lesbian Existence', *Signs* 5, no. 4 (1980): 645.
2. In a letter from a settler to Colonel Macquarie in London; cited in A Summers, *Damned Whores and God's Police: The Colonization of Women in Australia* (Harmondsworth: Penguin Books, 1975), 269.

Carole Pateman[*], 'Consent'

The relationship of consent in everyday life to the (postulated) consent of citizens to the liberal democratic state remains unexplored. Consent theorists fail to consider those areas of social life where consent is of practical importance to individuals, but the problems involved form

[*] Carole Pateman, "Women and Consent," in *Political Theory*, Vol. 8, No. 2, May 1980, pp. 149–168. © 1980 Sage Publications, Inc. (selections).

part of the general difficulties and evasions of consent theory. Women are thus easily ignored, because consent in everyday life particularly concerns them. The most intimate relations of women with men are held to be governed by consent; women consent to marriage, and sexual intercourse without a woman's consent constitutes the criminal offense of rape. To begin to examine the unwritten history of women and consent brings the suppressed problems of consent theory to the surface. Women exemplify the individuals who consent theorists have declared are incapable of consenting. Yet, simultaneously, women have been presented as always consenting, and their explicit nonconsent has been treated as irrelevant or has been reinterpreted as 'consent'.

It might be objected that today women have been granted equal citizenship with men in the liberal democracies, so any major difficulties about their consent must lie in the past. To show why this appearance of equality between men and women is misleading, it is necessary to return to the origins of modern consent theory. Consent theorists in the seventeenth and eighteenth centuries were clear why consent was so important both in the state and in the relationship between the sexes. The starting point of early social contract and consent theory was a specific conception of individuals as 'naturally' free and equal, or as born free and equal to each other. The idea that individuals are 'naturally' free and equal raises a fundamental, and revolutionary, question about authority relationships of all kinds; how and why a free and equal individual can ever legitimately be governed by anyone else. Unlike philosophical anarchists, liberal and democratic theorists argue that this question can be satisfactorily answered. It is possible to find a justification for the exercise of authority, but there is only *one* acceptable justification: If their freedom and equality is to be preserved, free and equal individuals must voluntarily commit themselves – for example, by consenting – to enter into such a relationship. Consent theory is thus a specific example of a broader voluntarist theory of society which argues that relationships of authority and obligation must be grounded in the voluntary acts or commitments of individuals.

From the beginning, consent theorists have attempted to avoid the revolutionary implications of voluntarism. They have adopted two main strategies to neutralize the impact of their arguments: First, they have turned to hypothetical voluntarism;[1] second, they have excluded certain individuals and social relationships from the scope of consent. The most familiar example of hypothetical voluntarism is Locke's notorious 'tacit consent'. Not only did Locke argue from a hypothetical social contract, but his 'consent' is merely an inference from, or reinterpretation of, the existence of specific social practices and institutions. Most contemporary discussions of consent are little more than modernized versions of Locke's claim that the consent of future generations (to the social contract made by their forefathers) can always be said to be given if individuals are going peacefully about their daily lives, even though there are 'no Expressions of it at all'.[2] The reinterpretation of certain actions as 'consent' appears at its extreme in Hobbes's theory. His willingness to take individualism to its logical conclusion allowed him to argue that all authority relationships are based on consent, even between parent and infant. The parents' domination over a child derives not from procreation but from 'Consent, either expressed, or by other sufficient arguments declared'. For Hobbes, overwhelming power is sufficient argument, so that in the state of nature the infant's 'consent' to its mother's rule can be assumed.[3] Hobbes's concept of 'consent' merely reinterprets the fact of power and submission; it makes no difference whether submission is voluntary or obtained through threats, even the threat of death. Because Hobbes argues that fear and liberty are compatible, 'consent' has the same meaning whether it arises from submission in fear of a conqueror's sword, or in fear of exposure by a parent, or whether it is a consequence of the (hypothetical) social contract.

Hypothetical voluntarism avoids the 'standard embarrassment' of arguing from actual consent, and the embarrassment is more securely circumvented if only some of the inhabitants of the state of nature or civil society are included in the category of 'free and equal individuals'. Voluntarism presupposes that individuals are rational, that they have, or are able to develop, the moral and intellectual capacities necessary to enable free commitment to be given. 'Free and equal individuals', to use Lockean terminology, own the property in their persons and their attributes, including their capacity to give consent. The individual is the 'guardian of his own consent'.[4] However, the latter formulation should be read literally; the consent is *his* consent. Neither the classic contract theorists nor their successors incorporated women into their arguments on the same footing as men. Contract and consent theory developed partly as an attack on patriarchal theory, but it is necessary to emphasize the limited character of the attack on patriarchal claims that political authority had a 'natural' basis in a father's procreative powers and that sons were 'naturally' in subjection to their fathers. Contract theorists did not extend their criticism to the relationship between men and women, or more specifically, husbands and wives (who are also fathers and mothers).

The state of nature is usually pictured as inhabited by patriarchal families.[5] It was also widely argued that fathers of families entered the social contract, wives being 'concluded by their Husbands'.[6] . . . However, this means that women are excluded from the status of 'individual' that is basic to consent theory; if a wife's subjection to her husband has a 'natural' foundation, she *cannot* also be seen as a 'naturally' free and equal individual. Only if women are seen as 'free and equal individuals' is their consent relevant at all. . . .

Ironically, Rousseau, the only contract theorist who pursued the radical implications of the doctrine, is the most explicit about the reasons why women must be excluded from its scope. Rousseau accepted the patriarchal assertion that women were 'naturally' subordinate to men. He gives a full account of the contrasting 'natural' characters of the sexes, a contrast which, he argues, must be given expression in the sexual double standard.[7] Rousseau provides a clear statement of the claim that women are incapable of consent, but, at the same time, he also denies this and reinterprets explicit nonconsent as its opposite. Rousseau attacked the hypothetical voluntarism of Hobbes's and Locke's versions of the contract argument as a fraud and tantamount to a contract of slavery, but he advocated precisely such a contract as the basis of the relationship between the sexes. In Rousseau's participatory, voluntarist political order, women must remain excluded because of their 'natural' moral characters and their deleterious influence upon the morals and civic virtue of men. In time-honored tradition, Rousseau divides women into the good and the dissolute, or whores. Women can remain good only if they stay within the shelter of domestic life. . . .

Women, Rousseau declares, 'must be trained to bear the yoke from the first . . . and to submit themselves to the will of others',[8] that is, the will of men. The influence of women, even good women, always corrupts men, because women are 'naturally' incapable of attaining the status of free and equal individuals, or citizens, and incapable of developing the capacities required to give consent.

Yet, at the same time, in sexual relationships, the 'consent' of women is all-important. Moreover, their consent can always be assumed to be given – even though apparently it is being refused. According to Rousseau, men are the 'natural' sexual aggressors; women are, 'destined to resist'. Rousseau asks 'what would become of the human species if the order of attack and defense were changed'?[9] Modesty and chasteness are the preeminent female virtues, but because women are also creatures of passion, they must use their natural skills of duplicity and dissemblance to maintain their modesty. In particular, *they must always say 'no' even when they desire to say 'yes'*. And here Rousseau reveals the heart of the problem of women and consent. Apparent refusal of consent can *never*, in a woman, be taken at face value:

> Why do you consult their words when it is not their mouths that speak? . . . The lips always say 'No', and rightly so; but the tone is not always the same, and that cannot lie. . . . Must her modesty condemn her to misery? Does she not require a means of indicating her inclinations without open expression?[10]

A man must learn to interpret a woman's 'consent' when, as in Locke's civil society, there are no obvious expressions of it at all.

> To win this silent consent is to make use of all the violence permitted in love. To read it in the eyes, to see it in the ways in spite of the mouth's denial. . . . If he then completes his happiness, he is not brutal, he is decent. He does not insult chastity; he respects it; he serves it. He leaves it the honor of still defending what it would have perhaps abandoned.[11]

Legal writers in the period of classic contract theory left no doubt about the status of wives and their 'consent'. A wife, as Blackstone wrote in his famous *Commentaries on the Laws of England*, was a legal nonperson; 'by marriage, the husband and wife are one person in law; . . . the very being or legal existence of the woman is suspended. . . .'[12] In what is 'still the most quoted authority on the British law of rape',[13] Hale's *History of the Pleas of the Crown*, it is stated that

> the husband cannot be guilty of a rape committed by himself upon his lawful wife, for by their mutual matrimonial consent and contract the wife hath given up herself in this kind unto her husband, which she cannot retract.[14]

It is hardly surprising that feminists in the mid-nineteenth century so frequently compared wives to the slaves of the West Indies and the American South, for legally and socially a wife was seen as the property of her husband; she could be legally imprisoned in the matrimonial house and could be beaten. John Stuart Mill was moved to comment that although he was

> far from pretending that wives are in general no better treated than slaves . . . no slave is a slave to the same lengths, and in so full a sense of the word as a wife is. . . . [A husband] can claim from her and enforce the lowest degradation of a human being, that of being made the instrument of an animal function contrary to her inclinations.[15]

A century later, a separate legal personality has been granted to women, but their formal legal status is contradicted by social beliefs and practices.

In certain areas of the law where 'consent' is central, notably in the law concerning rape, social reluctance to recognize women as 'free and equal individuals' denies in practice what the law proclaims in principle. Rape is central to the problem of women and consent in everyday life. Rape is widespread, both in and out of marriage, but although women of all ages and classes are attacked, the majority of rapes are not reported.[16] . . .

The legal failure to distinguish between 'acts of sexual assault and consenting sexual relations among adults',[17] or between enforced submission and consent, is grounded in a complex of beliefs about the 'natural' characters of the sexes. Eminent lawyers as well as the public are convinced that the 'naturally' sexually aggressive male must disregard a woman's refusal as merely a token gesture that hides her true desires.[18] Rape victims are divided into 'good' and 'bad' women, and even where violence has unquestionably been used, 'consent' can be held to have been given if the victim can be said to be of 'doubtful reputation' or have 'poor' sexual morals.[19] It is also very difficult for a woman to convince a court that she did not consent when standard works on evidence reinforce the view that women, especially 'unchaste' women, are 'naturally' deceitful and prone to make false statements, including false accusations of rape.[20] Hale's words have been regularly cited in courtrooms for three centuries; 'rape ... is an accusation easily to be made and hard to be proved, and harder to be defended by the party accused, the never so innocent'.[21] Yet a high proportion of rapes that actually are reported are rejected by the police as 'unfounded'.[22] Even allowing for problems of evidence, it is hard to account for these practices except as a direct outcome of an extraordinary perception of women's 'natural' characters. The same perception underlies the conventional requirement that the rape victim's evidence must be corroborated; it is 'only rape complainants, along with children, accomplices and witnesses in treason trials who are [treated as] notoriously unreliable witnesses'.[23] ...

Consent is central to liberal democracy, because it is essential to maintain individual freedom and equality; but it is a problem for liberal democracy, because individual freedom and equality is also a precondition for the practice of consent. The identification of enforced submission with consent in rape is a stark example of the wider failure in liberal democratic theory and practice to distinguish free commitment and agreement by equals from domination, subordination, and inequality. Writers on consent link 'consent', 'freedom', and 'equality', but the realities of power and domination in our sexual and political lives are ignored. Contemporary consent theory presents our institutions as if they were actually as consent demands, as if they were actually constituted through the free agreement of equal persons. The reduction of 'consent' to a mere 'constituent' of liberal democratic ideology leaves consent theorists unable to ask many vital questions. This includes the question whether the character of our socio-political institutions is such that consent ought to be given to (all or some of) them, by men or women. Most liberal theorists would wish to argue that there is one relationship, at least, to which consent ought not to be given. A person ought never to consent to be a slave, because this totally negates the individual's freedom and equality and hence, in a self-contradiction, denies that the individual is capable of consent.[24] However, if this argument is accepted, then should not consent theorists look searchingly at existing institutions, as J. S. Mill examined marriage in his own day, to ensure that there is no denial, or tendency to deny, the very status of individuals that is claimed to be upheld? The problem with this suggestion is that it requires that three centuries of argument about consent be overthrown and that theorists formulate a *critical* theory of voluntarism including both men and women. ...

Consent must always be given *to* something; in the relationship between the sexes, it is always women who are held to consent to men. The 'naturally' superior, active, and sexually aggressive male makes an initiative, or offers a contract, to which a 'naturally' subordinate, passive woman 'consents'. An egalitarian sexual relationship cannot rest on this basis; it cannot be grounded in 'consent'. Perhaps the most telling aspect of the problem of women and consent is that we lack a language through which to help constitute a form of personal life in which two equals freely agree to create a lasting association together.

Notes

1. I have explored this concept at length and discussed its importance for classical contract theorists and their successors in *The Problem of Political Obligation* (Chichester: John Wiley, 1979).
2. J Locke, *Two Treatises of Government*, ed P Laslett (Cambridge: Cambridge University Press, 1967), II, § 119.

3. T Hobbes, *Leviathan*, ed C B Macpherson (Harmondsworth: Penguin Books, 1968), 253–54.
4. R Flathman, *Political Obligation* (New York: Atheneum, 1972), 230.
5. Hobbes is a notable exception to this generalisation. He was consistent enough in his individualism to argue for the freedom and equality of all individuals in the natural state, irrespective of sex. There is no assumption that a female will always 'consent' to (submit to) the authority (protection) of a male. On this point, and for a more detailed account of the arguments of Hobbes and Locke on the relation of husbands and wives in the state of nature and civil society, see T Brennan and C Pateman, ' "Mere Auxiliaries to the Commonwealth": Women and the Origins of Liberalism', *Political Studies* 27, no. 2 (1979): 183–200.
6. The words are those of Locke's friend Tyrrell; cited in G J Schochet, *Patriarchalism in Political Thought* (Oxford: Blackwell, 1975), 202.
7. For an excellent discussion of the sexual double standard – which is 'the reflection of the view that men have property in women' – see K Thomas, 'The Double Standard', *Journal of History of Ideas* 20 (1959): 195–216.
8. J-J Rousseau, *Emile*, trans B Foxley (London: Dent, 1911), 332.
9. Rousseau, *Politics and the Arts*, trans A Bloom (Ithaca, NY: Cornell University Press, 1968), 84.
10. Rousseau, *Emile*, 348.
11. Rousseau, *Politics and the Arts*, 85.
12. Sir W Blackstone, *Commentaries on the Laws of England* (London: Sweet, Maxwell, 1844), 442.
13. B Toner, *The Facts of Rape* (London: Arrow Books, 1977), 95.
14. Sir M Hale, *The History of the Pleas of the Crown* (London: Emlyn, 1778), I, 629.
15. J S Mill, 'The Subjection of Women', in *Essays on Sex Equality*, ed A S Rossi (Chicago: University of Chicago Press, 1970), 159–60.
16. Both rape and unreported rape have only recently begun to receive attention. Reasonable estimates suggest that no more than a third of (extra matrimonial) rapes are reported, and rates of reported rape appear to have increased in the Anglo-Saxon countries in the last twenty years: See figures in E Shorter, 'On Writing the History of Rape', *Signs* 3, no. 2 (1977): 480. P R Wilson, *The Other Side of Rape* (Brisbane: University of Queensland Press, 1978) investigates unreported rapes. The realities of rape are hidden by deeply entrenched cultural myths and stereotypes. One of the most common is that rape is an act perpetrated by a stranger on a woman who probably 'precipitated' the attack. In fact, no woman is immune, whether she is seventy or older, a very small girl, or heavily pregnant, whatever her appearance, and whether or not she is within the shelter of her home. About half of all reported rapes are committed by men known to their victim, including relatives – see summaries of evidence in B Smart and C Smart, 'Accounting for Rape: Reality and Myth in Press Reporting', in *Women. Sexuality and Social Control*, ed B Smart and C Smart (London: Routledge, 1978); L R Harris, 'Towards a Consent Standard in the Law of Rape', *University of Chicago Law Review* 43 (1975): 613–45; C Le Grand, 'Rape and Rape Laws: Sexism in Society and Law', *California Law Review* 61 (1973): 919–41; S Brownmiller, *Against Our Will: Men. Women and Rape* (Harmondsworth: Penguin Books, 1976). Women are also raped by the police who are to apprehend rapists; in Paris, for example, in 1979, three Guardiens de la Paix were convicted of raping a thirteen-year-old girl, and two police patrolmen were convicted of raping a German tourist in their car 'because they were bored'. (Report in *Guardian Weekly*, October 21, 1979.)

17. L Bienen, 'Mistakes', *Philosophy and Public Affairs* 7, no. 3 (1978): 245.
18. See B Toner, *The Facts of Rape* (London: Arrow Books, 1977), 104.
19. See cases cited by P C Wood, 'The Victim in a Forcible Rape Case: A Feminist View', *The American Criminal Law Review* 11 (1973): 344–45. Advocates of legal reform have drawn attention to the common use of evidence about the complainant's prior sexual history, mode of dress, general reputation, and so on in rape cases. Harris, 1975, 617, notes that because the defense of consent admits essential facts, defense lawyers almost invariably attempt to show that the woman is the 'type' who must have consented.
20. See Bienen, 237, and L R Harris, 'Towards a Consent Standard in the Law on Rape', *University of Chicago Law* Review 43 (1975): 626.
21. Hale, 1778, 635.
22. In Victoria in 1974 to 1975 in four police districts, only 50 percent of rape complaints were accepted as 'founded'; evidence in *Royal Commission on Human Relationships* (Canberra: Australian Government Publishing Service, 1977), Vol 5, Pt 7, 178.
23. Toner, 1977, 112.
24. Some further comments on this aspect of the problem of consent with particular reference to promising to obey, can be found in C Pateman, 1979, 19–20; 169–71.

Charles W Mills*, 'The Racial Contract and Ideal Theory'
Race and the Social Contract

Let me begin with some general points about the social contract. The concept is, of course, to be taken not literally but rather as an illuminating metaphor or thought experiment. We are asked to imagine the socio-political order (society, the state) as being self-consciously brought into existence through a 'contract' among human beings in a pre-social, pre-political stage of humanity (the 'state of nature'). The enduring appeal of the metaphor, despite its patent absurdity as a literal representation of the formation of socio-political systems, inheres in its capturing of two key insights. The first (against theological views of divine creation or secular conceptions of an organicist kind) is that society and the polity are artificial human constructs. The second (against ancient and medieval views of natural social hierarchy) is that human beings are naturally equal and that this equality in the state of nature should somehow translate into egalitarian socio-political institutions.[1]

For the Lockean and Kantian contracts that (in conjunction and in competition) define the mainstream of the liberal tradition – but not for the Hobbesian contract – *moral* equality is foundational.[2] The social ontology is classically individualist, and it demands the creation of a polity that respects the equal personhood of individuals and (whether in stronger or weaker versions) their property rights. Basic moral entitlements for the citizenry are then juridically codified and enforced by an impartial state. Economic transactions are, correspondingly, ideally supposed to be non-exploitative, though there will, of course, be controversy about how this concept should be cashed out. So fairness in a broad sense is the overarching contract norm, as befits an apparatus ostensibly founded on principles antithetical to a non-individual-respecting, welfare-aggregating utilitarianism. The moral equality of people in the state of nature demands an equality of treatment (juridical, political, and economic) in the liberal polity they create. The state is not alien or antagonistic to us but the protector of our rights, whether as the constitutionalist Lockean sovereign or the Kantian *Rechtsstaat*. The good polity is the just polity, and the just polity is founded on safeguarding our interests as individuals.

* Charles W Mills, *Black Rights, White Wrongs: The Critique of Racial Criticism*. Oxford: Oxford University Press, 2017, pp. 29–32, 139–141. By Permission of Oxford University Press, USA.

But what if – not merely episodically and randomly, but systematically and structurally – the personhood of some persons was historically disregarded, and their rights disrespected? What if entitlements and justice were, correspondingly, so conceived of that the unequal treatment of these persons, or sub-persons, was *not* seen as unfair, not flagged as an internal inconsistency, but accommodated by suitable discursive shifts and conceptual framings? And what if, after long political struggles, there developed at last a seeming equality that later turned out to be more nominal than substantive, so that justice and equal protection were still effectively denied even while being triumphantly proclaimed? It would mean that we would need to recognize the inadequacy of speaking in the abstract of liberalism and contractarianism. We would need to acknowledge that race had underpinned the liberal framework from the outset, refracting the sense of crucial terms, embedding a particular model of rights-bearers, dictating a certain historical narrative, and providing an overall theoretical orientation for normative discussions. We would need to confront the fact that to understand the actual logic of these normative debates, both what is said and what is not said, we would have to understand not just the ideal, abstract social contract but also its incarnation in the United States (and arguably elsewhere) as a non-ideal racial contract.

Consider the major divisions in the political philosophy of the last few decades. In *Liberalism and the Limits of Justice*, Michael Sandel makes the point that Rawls's A *Theory of Justice* is important because – apart from carrying the Kantianism versus utilitarianism dispute to a higher theoretical level – it was central to not one but two of the major political debates of the 1970s and 1980s, left/social-democratic liberalism versus right/laissezfaire liberalism (John Rawls versus Robert Nozick) and liberalism or contractarianism versus communitarianism (Rawls versus Michael Walzer, Alasdair MacIntyre, Charles Taylor, and Sandel himself).[3] A third major debate, initiated by Rawls's essays of the 1980s and culminating in *Political Liberalism*, could be said to be the debate of the 1990s and 2000s on 'comprehensive' versus 'political' liberalism.[4] In their domination of the conceptual and theoretical landscape, these overarching frameworks tend to set the political agenda, establishing a hegemonic framing of key assumptions and jointly exhaustive alternatives. One locates oneself as a theorist by choosing one or the other of these primary alternatives and then taking up the corresponding socio-political and normative picture, adopting the defining terms, and making the argumentative moves characteristically associated with it. So though other theoretical and political alternatives are not logically excluded, they tend to be marginalized.

But there is another debate – one that has been going on for hundreds of years, if not always in the academy – which is, in a sense, orthogonal to all three of the foregoing and is arguably more pressing than any of them: the conflict between racial liberalism (generally known just as liberalism) and deracialized liberalism. Racial liberalism, or white liberalism, is the actual liberalism that has been historically dominant since modernity: a liberal theory whose terms originally restricted full personhood to whites (or, more accurately, white men) and relegated nonwhites to an inferior category, so that its schedule of rights and prescriptions for justice were all color-coded. Ascriptive hierarchy is abolished for white men, but not white women and people of color.[5] So racism is not an anomaly in an unqualified liberal universalism but generally symbiotically related to a qualified and particularistic liberalism.[6] Though there have always been white liberals who have been anti-racist and anti-imperialist, whose records should not be ignored,[7] they have been in the minority. Indeed the most striking manifestation of this symbiotic rather than conflictual relation is that the two philosophers earlier demarcated as central to the liberal tradition, Locke and Kant, both limited property rights, self-ownership, and personhood racially. Locke invested in African slavery, justified Native American expropriation, and helped to write the Carolina constitution of 1669, which gave masters absolute power over their slaves.[8] Kant, the most important ethicist of the modern period and the famous theorist of personhood and respect, turns out to be one of the founders of modern scientific racism, and thus a pioneering theorist of sub-personhood and disrespect.[9] So the inferior treatment of people of color is not at all incongruent with racialized liberal norms, since by these norms nonwhites are less than full persons.

If this analysis is correct, such inequality, and its historic ramifications, is arguably more fundamental than all the other issues mentioned above, since in principle at least all parties to the many-sided political debate are supposed to be committed to the non-racial moral equality of all. Thus the rethinking, purging, and deracializing of racial liberalism should be a priority for us – and in fact the struggles of people of color for racial equality over the past few hundred years can to a significant extent be most illuminatingly seen as just such a project. As Michael Dawson writes in his comprehensive study of African American political ideologies:

> The great majority of black theorists challenge liberalism as it has been practiced within the United States, not some abstract ideal version of the ideology. . . . [T]here is no necessary contradiction between the liberal tradition in *theory* and black liberalism. The contradiction exists between black liberalism and how liberalism has come to be understood in practice within the American context.[10]

Yet the need for such a reconstruction has been neither acknowledged nor acted on. Rawls and Nozick may be in conflict over left-wing versus right-wing liberalism, but both offer us idealized views of the polity that ignore the racial subordination rationalized by racial liberalism. Rawls and Sandel may be in conflict over contractarian liberalism versus neo-Hegelian communitarianism, but neither confronts how the whiteness of the actual American contract and its conception of the right and of the actual American community and its conception of the good affects their views of justice and the self. Late Rawls maybe in conflict with early Rawls about political versus comprehensive liberalism, but neither addresses the question of the ways in which both versions have been shaped by race, whether through an 'overlapping consensus' (among whites) or a 'reflective equilibrium' (of whites). From the perspective of people of color, these intramural and intra-white debates all fail to deal with the simple overwhelming reality on which left and right, contractarian and communitarian, comprehensive or political liberal, should theoretically all be able to agree: that the centrality of racial exclusion and racial injustice demands a reconceptualization of the orthodox view of the polity and calls for radical rectification.

Rawls on Race/Race in Rawls

Let us now turn to the work of John Rawls, which has been mentioned repeatedly and critically throughout the book but has not yet been engaged with in detail. As pointed out earlier, Rawls's *A Theory of Justice* is widely credited with having revived post–World War II Anglo-American political philosophy, and, with his other four books, is routinely judged to constitute the most important body of work in that field.[11] Indeed, with the collapse of Second World and Third World socialist ideologico-political alternatives, liberalism in one form or another has become globally hegemonic, so that for many commentators, the qualifiers 'postwar' and 'Anglo-American' should just be dropped. Thus the blurb on the jacket of *The Cambridge Companion to Rawls* simply asserts without qualification: 'John

Rawls is the most significant and influential political and moral philosopher of the 20th century'.[12]

Yet for those interested in issues of racial justice, philosophers of color in particular, Rawls's work and the secondary literature it has generated has long been deeply frustrating, producing a weird feeling of incongruity and dissonance.[13] Here is a huge body of work focused on questions of social justice – seemingly the natural place to look for guidance on normative issues related to race – which has nothing to say about racial injustice, the distinctive injustice of the modern world.[14]

What explains this systematic omission? Any elementary sociology of belief would tell us that the demography of the profession (overwhelmingly white) will itself be an obvious major causal factor, group membership in the privileged race tendentially producing certain distinctive interests (uninterests), priorities (marginalities), and concerns (indifferences). But apart from this major extra-ideational factor, I suggest, as indicated in previous chapters, that there is a key internal conceptual factor as-well: Rawls's methodological decision to focus in *A Theory of Justice* on 'ideal theory' – the reconstruction of what a perfectly just society would look like. If this might have seemed reasonable enough when first propounded – after all, what's wrong with striving for the asymptotic realization of perfect justice? – it is, I propose, because of a crucial ambiguity: 'ideally just' as meaning a society without *any* previous history of injustice and 'ideally just' as meaning a society with an unjust history that has now been *completely corrected for*. Rawls really means the former, not the latter. But the difference between the two will obviously make a significant difference to the recommendations respectively appropriate in the two sets of cases. *Preemptive* precautions to prevent injustices entering the 'basic structure' of a society are not the same as *rectificatory* measures aimed at correcting them once they have already entered. Prevention generally differs from cure. Insofar as Rawls's focus is on the former, his prophylactic recommendations will be of limited if any use when it comes to remediation. Thus by a simple conceptual stipulation, the theoretical problems raised of how to adjudicate the redressing of past injustices are immediately shunted aside. In particular, the manifestly *non*-ideal record of our country on race can now be ignored, since such matters fall into an area of dikailogical territory not covered by the mandate of the program. As Thomas Nagel observes in two of the few sentences referring to race (and elliptically and non-specifically at that) in the *Cambridge Companion*:

> Affirmative action . . . is probably best understood in Rawlsian terms as an attempt at corrective justice – an attempt to rectify the residual consequences of a particularly gross violation in the past of the first principle of equal rights and liberties. Affirmative action therefore does not form a part of what Rawls would call 'strict compliance theory' or ideal theory, which is what the two principles of justice are supposed to describe.[15]

In contrast, my 1997 book, *The Racial Contract*, was explicitly and self-describedly a work in non-ideal theory.[16] I sought to show there that – insofar as the contractarian tradition has descriptive pretensions ('contract' as a way of thinking about the creation of society) – the modern 'contract' is better thought of as an exclusionary agreement among whites to create racial polities rather than as a modeling of the origin of colorless, egalitarian, and inclusive socio-political systems. Since Rawls's updating of the contract is purely normative and hypothetical, however, a thought-experiment for generating judgments about justice rather than a historical account, it might seem that my challenge, even if successful, is irrelevant, doubly missing the mark. The contract for Rawls is not meant to be descriptive in the first place, and in the second place, as just emphasized, his normative project is confined to the realm of ideal theory. But my claim would be that this twofold displacement in fact constitutes a double *evasion* and that the ghost of the ostensibly repudiated *factual* dimension of contractarianism continues to haunt the *normative* account, as manifested precisely in this silence on racial justice.[17] A mystified and idealized story of the creation of the modern world, which denies the centrality of racial subordination to its genesis, makes the achievement of corrective racial justice a less pressing matter, if it is seen as necessary at all, for contemporary white ethicists and political philosophers.

In this chapter, I will both document what (little) Rawls does say about race ('Rawls on Race'), and attempt, from a critical philosophy of race perspective ('Race in Rawls'), to bring out what I see as the larger significance of these silences. For me, in other words, they are not contingent but are structurally related to the architecture of what I characterized at the start of the book as 'racial liberalism'. Even now, in a putatively post-racist epoch, a conceptual apparatus inherited from a period of de jure white racial domination continues in numerous ways – in conjunction with white racial privilege – to shape and orient (occident?) the work of white liberals. . . .

Notes

1. See Jean Hampton, 'The Contractarian Explanation of the State', in *Midwest Studies in Philosophy: The Philosophy of the Human Sciences*, eds Peter A French, Theodore E Uehling Jr, and Howard K Wettstein (Notre Dame: University of Notre Dame Press, 1990); Jean Hampton, 'Feminist Contractarianism', in *A Mind of One's Own: Feminist Essays on Reason and Objectivity*, rev 2nd ed, eds Louise M Antony and Charlotte E Witt (Boulder, CO: Westview Press, 2001; orig ed 1993); Jean Hampton, 'Contract and Consent', in *A Companion to Contemporary Political Philosophy*, rev 2nd ed, 2 vols, vol 2, eds Robert E Goodin, Philip Pettit, and Thomas Pogge (Malden, MA: Blackwell, 2007; orig ed [1 vol] 1993).
2. The non-liberal-democratic Hobbesian model is predicated on the approximate physical and mental (rather than moral) equality of self-seeking humans in conflict with one another (the amoral state of nature as a state of war). So Hobbes's solution of a constitutionally unconstrained state – the absolutist sovereign – is obviously uncongenial to those seeking to use the contract model to critique absolutism.
3. Michael J Sandel, *Liberalism and the Limits of Justice*, 2nd ed (New York: Cambridge University Press, 1998; orig ed 1982), 184–85.
4. John Rawls, *Collected Papers*, ed Samuel Freeman (Cambridge, MA: Harvard University Press, 1999); John Rawls, *Political Liberalism*, exp ed (New York: Columbia University Press, 1996; orig ed 1993).
5. Carole Pateman, *The Sexual Contract* (Stanford, CA: Stanford University Press, 1988); Mills, *Racial Contract*.
6. Uday Singh Mehta, *Liberalism and Empire: A Study in Nineteenth-Century British Liberal Thought* (Chicago: University of Chicago Press, 1999); Louis Sala-Molins, *Dark Side of the Light: Slavery and the French Enlightenment*, trans John Conteh-Morgan (Minneapolis: University of Minnesota Press, 2006).

7. Jennifer Pitts, *A Turn to Empire: The Rise of Imperial Liberalism in Britain and France* (Princeton, NJ: Princeton University Press, 2005).
8. James Tully, *An Approach to Political Philosophy: Locke in Contexts* (New York: Cambridge University Press, 1993); Barbara Arneil, *John Locke and America: The Defence of English Colonialism* (New York: Oxford University Press, 1996); David Armitage, 'John Locke, Carolina, and the *Two Treatises of Government*', *Political Theory* 32, no. 5 (October 2004): 602–27; Robert Bernasconi and Anika Maaza Mann, 'The Contradictions of Racism: Locke, Slavery, and the *Two Treatises*', in *Race and Racism in Modern Philosophy*, ed Andrew Valls (Ithaca, NY: Cornell University Press, 2005).
9. Emmanuel Chukwudi Eze, 'The Color of Reason: The Idea of "Race" in Kant's Anthropology', in *Postcolonial African Philosophy: A Reader* (Cambridge, MA: Blackwell, 1997); Robert Bernasconi, 'Who Invented the Concept of Race? Kant's Role in the Enlightenment Construction of Race', in *Race* (Malden, MA; Blackwell, 2001); Robert Bernasconi, 'Kant as an Unfamiliar Source of Racism', in *Philosophers on Race: Critical Essays*, eds Julie K Ward and Tommy L Lott (Malden, MA: Blackwell, 2002); Charles W Mills, 'Kant's *Untermenschen*', in Valls, *Race and Racism*, reprinted as ch 5 of this book.
10. Michael C Dawson, *Black Visions: The Roots of Contemporary African-American Political Ideologies* (Chicago: University of Chicago Press, 2001), 13.
11. John Rawls, *A Theory of Justice*, rev ed (Cambridge, MA: Harvard University Press, 1999; orig ed 1971); John Rawls, *Political Liberalism* (New York: Columbia University Press, 1993); John Rawls, *Political Liberalism*, exp ed (New York: Columbia University Press, 1996); John Rawls, *Collected Papers*, ed Samuel Freeman (Cambridge, MA: Harvard University Press, 1999); John Rawls, *The Law of Peoples, with 'The Idea of Public Reason Revisited'* (Cambridge, MA: Harvard University Press, 1999); John Rawls, *Justice as Fairness: A Restatement*, ed Erin Kelly (Cambridge, MA: Harvard University Press, 2001).
12. Samuel Freeman, ed, *The Cambridge Companion to Rawls* (New York: Cambridge University Press, 2003).
13. See, for example, the contributions to the 'Equal Citizenship: Race and Ethnicity' section of the *Fordham Law Review* 72, no. 5 (April 2004) symposium; 'Rawls and the Law', and, more recently, Christopher J Lebron, *The Color of Our Shame: Race and Justice in Our Time* (New York: Oxford University Press, 2013).
14. I mean by this not that other oppressions and injustices do not exist or are unimportant, but, rather, that both gender and class, for example, predate the modern world as social structures and social identities. Race by contrast – at least in the conventional scholarly judgement (but see Benjamin Isaac, *The Invention of Racism in Classical Antiquity* [Princeton, NJ: Princeton University Press, 2004]) – is distinctively modern, provides the rationale for the European conquest of the world, and insofar as it has facilitated slavery and genocide at a time when human moral equality was supposed to have been broadly established, it is distinctively horrific in the blatancy of the degree of its oppression.
15. Thomas Nagel, 'Rawls and Liberalism', in Freeman, *Cambridge Companion*, 84n3.
16. Charles W Mills, *The Racial Contract* (Ithaca, NY: Cornell University Press, 1997).
17. Charles W Mills, '"Ideal Theory" as Ideology', *Hypatia: A Journal of Feminist Philosophy* 20, no. 3 (August 2005): 165–84, reprinted as ch 5 in this book; Carole Pateman and Charles W Mills, *Contract and Domination* (Malden, MA: Polity Press, 2007).

CASE STUDY

J M Dieterle[*], 'Food Deserts and Lockean Property'

The expression 'food desert' was first used during a 1990s study in Glasgow by the Low Income Project Team of the Nutrition Task Force of Great Britain.[1] The team described food deserts as 'areas of relative exclusion where people experience physical and economic barriers to accessing healthy food'.[2] Distance is the primary physical barrier: access to healthy food is limited because the nearest grocer is too far away to be easily accessible. Food deserts have been identified in many developed countries, including the United Kingdom,[3] Australia,[4] Canada,[5] and New Zealand.[6] However, the most extensive research on and mapping of food deserts has occurred in the United States.[7]

The US Department of Agriculture (USDA) classifies an urban area as a food desert if at least 20 percent of the population lives below the poverty level and there is no mainstream grocery store selling fresh and nutritious food within one mile. Rural areas are classified as food deserts if the nearest mainstream grocer is more than ten miles away.[8] But it is important to note that the measurable distance does not tell the whole story. As Hillary J Shaw notes in *The Consuming Geographies of Food*, one's physical distance from a grocer, if one must walk, is mediated by multiple factors.[9] Walking to the nearest grocer might involve climbing a steep hill or crossing one or more busy roads. There may be no sidewalk or pedestrian path along the most direct route. Heavy grocery bags can impact one's ability to walk long distances to purchase food, especially if one is disabled. The route to the grocer may be through an area that is unsafe at certain times of the day. In rural areas, public transportation may not be available or, if available, may not be reliable. Those who do not have a car or cannot drive may be unable to reach a grocer that stocks healthy food options, even if there is such a grocer within the ten-mile radius. The USDA classifications thus may underestimate the number of people who do not have ready access to healthy, affordable food. Nonetheless, using USDA criteria, 23.5 million US residents live in food deserts.[10]

The demographics of food deserts are telling. Most food deserts in the United States are found in areas that are predominantly nonwhite.[11] In fact, according to the USDA, in all census tracts other than those that are urban and very dense, 'the higher the percentage of minority population, the more likely the area is to be a food desert'.[12] This is true of both urban and rural areas. The proportion of minorities in urban food deserts is 53 percent higher than in urban nonfood deserts. In rural areas, the minority population is 65 percent higher in food desert tracts than in nonfood desert tracts.[13] Poverty levels and unemployment rates are higher in food desert tracts, while median family incomes are substantially lower.[14] However, a 2013 study determined that neighborhoods in the United States that are predominantly African American suffer from the most limited access to venues that sell fresh, healthy food, *regardless of income*. When comparing census tracts of equal poverty levels, black neighborhoods had the fewest supermarkets and white neighborhoods had the most. The authors of the study conclude that poverty level and race are independent indicators of supermarket availability, and that poor African American neighborhoods face a 'double jeopardy'.[15]

The World Health Organization lists three facets of food security: (1) food availability (that a sufficient quantity of healthy, nutritious food is available on a consistent basis); (2) food access (that one has sufficient resources to access healthy, nutritious food); and (3) food use (that one has the knowledge of basic nutrition and sanitation to properly feed oneself).[16] Here, I wish to focus on facet (1): food availability. When there are physical barriers to accessing healthy food, food is essentially

---

[*] J M Dieterle, "Food Deserts and Lockean Property," in J. M. Dieterle ed., *Just Food: Philosophy, Justice and Food*. Lanham, MD: Rowman & Littlefield, 2015, pp. 39–54. © 2015 Rowman & Littlefield.

unavailable. Food insecurity is the direct result. Importantly, unhealthy food *is* often readily available in areas classified as food deserts. Fast food restaurants and 'fringe' food establishments (gas stations, liquor stores, party stores, dollar stores, convenience stores, etc.) are common in food deserts.[17] Such establishments typically carry only a small selection of processed food products. These food products tend to be unhealthy: they are almost always high in salt, fat and sugar and have limited nutritional value.[18] Thus, the 'food' available in food deserts is not sufficient for food security.

My goal in this chapter is to argue that food deserts are a serious matter of justice. This may seem uncontroversial. And, in fact, on most philosophical accounts of justice, it is. On a Rawlsian theory of justice, for example, a sketch of the argument would go something like this: one cannot participate as a free and equal citizen when one is food insecure.[19] Access to nutritious food is a precondition for the attainment of all primary goods, and food distribution should be subject to the difference principle. The distribution of food ought to benefit everyone, and any inequality in its distribution ought to be to the benefit of the least well off. But, clearly, the distribution of food does *not* benefit everyone. Food insecurity is a direct result of food deserts. Further, food deserts harm the least well off disproportionately. More than half of the 23.5 million US residents living in food deserts are in a low-income category.[20] Likewise, food deserts identified in the UK, EU, Australia, Canada and New Zealand are in low-income areas.[21] Clearly, then, the current distribution of food does *not* benefit the least well off, but, instead, makes life more difficult for the least well off. So the argument for injustice of food deserts is fairly straightforward from the Rawlsian perspective.

The argument is also fairly clear-cut from a utilitarian theory of justice. The net balance of social utility that results from the current distribution of food is negative. Not only are the inhabitants of food deserts harmed by the current distribution, but, given the health outcomes associated with food deserts and food insecurity, the consequences for public health are quite dire.[22] Direct costs of food deserts are borne by the individuals who reside in such communities, given that the quality of available food has a profound and negative impact on their health. Indirect costs are borne by the health care industry (who must treat diseases that result from poor diets), by employers (through lost productivity), and by taxpayers and governmental agencies (who in some cases shoulder the financial burden of the health effects of food deserts).[23] So the argument for the injustice of food deserts is also fairly straightforward from the utilitarian perspective.

The interesting question is how a libertarian theory of justice would assess food deserts. One might think that a libertarian would find food deserts unfortunate, but ultimately not a matter of justice. After all, they are the direct outcome of private property rights and capitalistic free markets. Grocery stores went where the money was: to the suburbs.[24] However, I argue that a plausible interpretation of the Lockean theory of property entails the injustice of food deserts. Thus, one who holds a theory of justice that depends on or substantially includes a Lockean theory of property has reason to support limitations on property rights to address the problem of food access. I begin with Locke himself and discuss why he should be committed to the injustice of food deserts. I then turn to Robert Nozick's historical theory of justice and argue that even he should admit that food deserts warrant property rights limitations.

I. Locke

In a Lockean state of nature, the earth and its resources are owned in common by all individuals. Further, individuals have natural rights to preservation and to preserve themselves. Gopal Sreenivasan distinguishes between these two rights as follows:

> These two natural rights may be distinguished by considering the particular duty each right imposes on others when possessed by a rights-bearer. In the former case, others have a duty to

refrain from directly endangering the life of the rights-bearer, in the latter case, others have a duty to refrain from impeding the rights-bearer from actively preserving herself.[25]

Since we have a right to preserve ourselves, we may take from the commons what we need to exercise that right. Suppose, for example, there is a clump of blackberry bushes in my vicinity. I may pick and eat blackberries from those bushes to nourish myself. Further, if I pick more than I can eat, I may keep the surplus as my own. Locke's theory allows us to appropriate, as our own property, any surplus that arises from our labor.

Property acquisition is not unlimited, though. Indeed, Lockean property acquisition is subject to three important limitations. (1) The spoilage limitation: one cannot appropriate more than one can use before it spoils.[26] If I pick more blackberries than I can consume before they rot, I am not entitled to keep the entire surplus as my own. (2) The sufficiency condition (often called the 'enough and as good' proviso): one must leave 'enough and as good' for others.[27] On the (implausible) assumption that blackberries are the only means of fulfilling one's dietary needs in the traversable area, I am not entitled to take all of them from the commons. To appropriate the entire surplus as my own would be to leave others in danger of starvation and thus actively impede them from preserving themselves. Since the blackberries are owned in common by all, I must be sure to leave enough for others to eat. (3) The charity limitation: individuals who are incapable of laboring to produce their own means of sustenance are entitled to subsistence levels of charity from others, provided those others have a surplus.[28] So the charity limitation limits individual acquisition when others are in need and incapable of laboring to support themselves.

Land appropriation is legitimated in much the same way as appropriation of perishable items growing on land owned in common. If I cultivate and improve a plot of land through my labor, then I am entitled to call that land my own, provided I have respected the Lockean limitations on appropriation.

The important Lockean limitation, for my purposes, is (2): the sufficiency condition. In *The Limits of Lockean Rights in Property*, Gopal Sreenivasan argues that the sufficiency condition is Locke's answer to 'the consent problem'. Locke's goal in Chapter V of *The Second Treatise of Government* is to legitimate individual appropriation of land and resources. Given the assumption that the earth and its resources are originally owned in common, individual appropriation seems to be a kind of theft. If one could obtain the consent of the co-owners, of course, appropriation would be legitimate. But it is practically impossible to secure the consent of each and every co-owner when the earth and its resources are commonly owned by all. However, if enough and as good remains once one has appropriated that of which one can make use, then no one is harmed by the appropriation and no one's right to self-preservation is transgressed. As such, consent can be foregone.

The sufficiency condition safeguards individuals' rights to preserve themselves and thus entails that a legitimate appropriation may not jeopardize said individuals' access to those resources necessary to produce their sustenance.[29] Importantly, an appropriation *would* cause harm, and thus *would* violate the sufficiency condition if said appropriation were to impede a fellow rights-bearer from exercising her right to preserve herself. The sufficiency condition ensures that a property appropriation is illegitimate if and when such harm, occurs. In a time and place where arable land is abundant, violations of the sufficiency condition rarely, if ever, occur. There's plenty of land to go around, so no one is impaired in exercising her right to preserve herself. However, land abundance is likely to end with the advent of civil society and the introduction of money. Since money is imperishable, one can amass large amounts of property without the threat of spoilage. Once individuals are free to accumulate such imperishable property, resource scarcity is a likely result. In turn, resource scarcity brings with it the potential to impair others' access to the materials needed to produce their sustenance and thus impede their exercise of the right to self-preservation. But, importantly, given the sufficiency condition, access to the means of preservation is protected. Individual acquisitions that would endanger others' access to said means continue to be illegitimate.

It is worth noting that the claim that the sufficiency condition continues to limit individual appropriation in civil society is not universally accepted by Locke scholars. On the alternate reading of Locke, *both* the spoilage limitation and the sufficiency condition are discharged with the introduction of money and the advent of civil society.[30] However, if the function of the sufficiency condition is to safeguard the right to preserve oneself, then there is every reason to believe that Locke intended it to remain in place.[31] For Locke, the right to preserve oneself is a natural right which cannot be superseded by civil society. The landless cannot be denied access to the means of preservation, even when land itself is scarce. The sufficiency condition protects this access. Note, though, that there is more than one way for the sufficiency condition to be met. Locke does not require that enough and as good *of the same kind* remain to legitimate an appropriation. As long as others have access to the means of preservation, the sufficiency condition is satisfied. Hence, if landowners employ as many people as the land could have sustained had it not been appropriated, then employed but landless individuals presumably are able to earn wages and exchange those wages for sustenance. Their right to preserve themselves is thus theoretically not violated.[32]

In practice, however, things are not so clear. We live in a post-agrarian society. As such, most of us exercise our right to preserve ourselves by laboring for someone else. We labor for wages and exchange our wages for sustenance. However, those living in food deserts are *unable* to exchange their wages for sustenance. Since there is no readily accessible venue for purchasing affordable, nutritious food, food deserts leave individuals without the means to procure the basic necessities of a productive life. As such, residents of food deserts cannot secure the material preconditions of the right to preserve themselves. Enough and as good is *not* available to them: because of private property rights and capitalistic free markets, they are food insecure. Note that this is so *even if* they labor for wages that would be sufficient to purchase their own sustenance if nutritious, healthy food were available.

Of course, there is a difference between *bare subsistence levels* of food and food *adequate to preserve a productive, healthy life.* My argument is that food deserts violate the sufficiency condition because their residents are denied access to the basic necessities of a productive life. But one might contend that the sufficiency condition does not require that level of food security; that Lockean property theory entitles the residents only to bare subsistence levels of food. On this alternative interpretation, one could argue that food deserts are, in fact, consistent with the sufficiency condition, since a subsistence level of food *is* available in food deserts. After all, one *can* survive (at least provisionally) on processed, unhealthy food. However, this alternative interpretation takes a very narrow reading of the right to preserve oneself. My contention is that it is too narrow.

Recall that the right to preserve oneself gives others correlative duties; others may not impede the right-bearer from actively preserving herself. Speaking of these correlative duties, Locke says:

> Every one as he is bound to preserve himself, and not to quit his station wilfully; so by the like reason when his own Preservation comes not in competition, ought he, as much as he can, to preserve the rest of Mankind, and may not unless it be to do Justice on an Offender, take away, or impair the life, or what tends to the Preservation of the Life, Liberty, Health, Limb, or Goods of another.[33]

As Locke notes, our health is essential to the preservation of our life. One may be able to provisionally survive on processed, unhealthy food, but one could not preserve one's life over the long term. So we should read the right to preserve ourselves more inclusively, as including the right to actively preserve our *health.* Thus, if we cannot access the means to procure the basic necessities of a productive life – those things which will keep us healthy and productive – we are thereby impeded in exercising our right to preserve ourselves. As such, when property acquisitions or transfers thwart an individual's exercise of her right to preserve her *health*, they equally thwart her exercise of the right to preserve her life, and the sufficiency condition is violated.[34] A bare subsistence level of unhealthy food is not *enough*, nor is it *as good* as nutritious, healthy food.

Those who are food insecure because they lack access to healthy food are substantially harmed by property acquisitions and transfers that limit food access. Recall that fast food restaurants and 'fringe' food establishments (gas stations, liquor stores, party stores, dollar stores, convenience stores, etc.) are common in areas classified as food deserts. The food for sale in such establishments is typically highly processed and high in fat, sugar and salt. When there are physical barriers to accessing healthy food, but unhealthy food is readily available, negative health outcomes are the likely result. And, in fact, that is exactly what we find. Residents of food deserts have higher rates of diabetes, cancer, obesity and heart disease than residents of other areas. Note that these results are independent of other contributing factors such as income, race and education.[35] A study by the Mari Gallagher Research and Consulting Group found that the death rate from diabetes for those areas of Chicago that are the most out of balance is more than double that of other communities in the surrounding area.[36] The same study found that obesity rates increase the further one gets from a grocery store.[37] And, of course, obesity is a contributing factor in many chronic diseases: heart disease, stroke, diabetes, high blood pressure, some forms of cancer and others.

Food insecurity has devastating effects on children. Studies have shown that food insecure children are twice as likely as food secure children to have fair or poor health. Hospitalization rates in food insecure children are roughly one-third greater than those for children living in food security.[38] Food insecure children have more frequent stomachaches, headaches and colds than children in food secure households.[39] Anxiety scores are more than double those of food secure children.[40] Food insecurity is also linked to developmental problems. Academic impairment is evident in both reading and math scores for children who were food insecure in kindergarten.[41] Food insecure children are more likely than food secure children to have repeated a grade.[42] Iron-deficiency anemia, often associated with food insecurity, impacts children's development of basic motor and social skills.[43] Alaimo, Olson and Frongillo found that children who had suffered from and were treated for iron-deficiency anemia as infants still suffered from impaired memory and social functioning more than ten years later.[44] Food insecure teenagers have difficulty getting along with other children and are more likely to be suspended from school.[45] Food insecure adolescents (fifteen to sixteen years old) are more likely to have depressive disorders and suicide symptoms.[46] And so on.

It seems clear that enough and as good is not available to those who live in food deserts. 'Food' is available, but not the kind of food that will allow one to maintain a healthy, productive life. The Lockean sufficiency condition is a limit on property rights. Since the natural right to preserve oneself is violated if individuals are denied access to the materials needed for their preservation, and food deserts deny people access to such basic materials, property acquisitions and transfers that result in food deserts are in violation of the sufficiency condition. As such, they are unjust. Even though food deserts are the result of private property rights and capitalistic markets, a libertarian in the Lockean tradition has good reason to support state intervention and limitations on property rights to correct the injustice.[47]

Of course, there are assumptions behind Locke's argument that contemporary libertarians might not endorse, such as natural law and the original common ownership of the earth and its resources. I thus now turn to a contemporary libertarian; to see how the argument would play out without these assumptions.

II. Nozick

In Nozick's original state, the earth and its resources are *unowned* – not owned in common as in Locke's state of nature. Recall that the sufficiency condition is necessary for Locke as a mechanism for legitimating appropriation without the consent of the co-owners. But since nothing is owned in Nozick's original state, the consent problem does not arise. Nevertheless, Nozick recognizes that property acquisition should be limited by a theory of justice. His account of justice includes three principles: (1) a principle delineating the process for justly acquiring unowned things (the principle of justice in acquisition); (2) a principle that governs the transfer of property from one person to another (the principle of justice in transfer); and (3) a principle that spells out the process for rectifying past injustices (the principle of rectification). The principle of justice in acquisition includes a version of the sufficiency condition. Nozick requires that 'the situation of others is not worsened'[48] by an appropriation, in the sense that the others are no longer 'able to use freely (without appropriation) what [they] previously could'.[49] He says:

> I assume that any adequate theory of justice in acquisition will contain a proviso similar to the weaker of the ones we have attributed to Locke. A process normally giving rise to a permanent bequeathable property right in a previously unowned thing will not do so if the position of others no longer at liberty to use that thing is thereby worsened.[50]

The sufficiency condition also constrains later actions. Nozick continues:

> Each owner's title to his holding includes the historical shadow of the Lockean proviso on appropriation. This excludes his transferring it into an agglomeration that does violate the Lockean proviso and excludes his using it in a way, in coordination with others or independently of them, so as to violate the proviso by making the situation of others worse than their baseline situation. Once it is known that someone's ownership runs afoul of the Lockean proviso, there are stringent limits on what he may do with (what it is difficult to any longer unreservedly call) 'his property'.[51]

The principle of justice in transfer is thus also subject to the sufficiency condition. One cannot transfer property to another if said transfer makes it the case that others are worse off. Of course, the key question is: worse off than what? Nozick takes the baseline to be a system with *no private property whatsoever*, and he argues that unregulated free markets in a liberal property regime will ensure that the sufficiency condition is met.[52]

Nozick's example of an unjust use of property has to do with water. He notes that an individual may not appropriate or purchase all of the access rights to drinkable water in a given location and then charge exorbitant prices for it.[53] Nor, presumably, could the individual decide to lease all of her access rights to a business that bottles and sells water. Such actions would be in violation of the sufficiency condition since the inhabitants of the area would not have access to one of the things necessary to sustain their lives. They would thus be much worse off than they would be in a no-property situation. As a result, the property rights of the individual owner would be limited.[54]

The sufficiency condition limits an individual's property rights when others are made worse off than their baseline situation. The constraints that limit property rights in such situations also limit property rights when *multiple* owners are involved. Suppose that many individuals independently acquire rights of access to drinkable water in a particular area and none wish to provide water to the local community. (Perhaps all of them wish to profit from leasing their rights to businesses that bottle water and then sell it at exorbitant prices.) Suppose further that all water access points are exhausted by the multiple acquisitions and, as a result, there is no way for local residents to obtain drinkable water without infringing an owner's property rights. In such a situation, the residents are left without access to potable water; they are in the same situation as they would be if one individual owned all of the water rights and denied them access. Said inhabitants are much worse off than they would be in a no-property situation – enough and as good is not available to them – and the sufficiency condition is violated. Here, too, the property rights of the owners would be limited by Nozick's version of the sufficiency condition.

Nozick argues that such situations will rarely – if ever – occur in a system with private property and unregulated free markets:

> I believe that the free operation of a market system will not actually run afoul of the Lockean proviso. . . . If this is correct, the proviso will not play a very important role in the activities of protective agencies and will not provide a significant opportunity for future state action.[55]

Nozick's argument for the claim that a free market system in a liberal property regime will ensure that the sufficiency condition is met relies on the productive capacity of private property. He argues that we are *all* better off than we would be in a no-property situation. The system of private property increases the social product by putting means of production in the hands of those who can use them most efficiently (profitably); experimentation is encouraged, because with separate persons controlling resources, there is no one person or small group whom someone with a new idea must convince to try it out; private property enables people to decide on the pattern and types of risks they wish to bear, leading to specialized types of risk bearing; private property protects future persons by leading some to hold back resources from current consumption for future markets; it provides alternate sources of employment for unpopular persons who don't have to convince any one person or small group to hire them, and so on.[56]

For the sake of argument, I will assume that Nozick is right about the overall benefits of a system of private property. However, note that the benefits do not necessarily accrue to everyone. Those who are without land or money reap few rewards from a system that restricts their access to resources that were originally unowned. The intent of the sufficiency condition, I take it, is to protect *individuals* from being harmed by others' appropriations and transfers of property.[57] That is, the intent is not to ensure that society as a whole is no worse off than it would be without a system of private property, nor even that the majority is no worse off, but, instead, its intent is to make sure *no individual* is made worse off by an appropriation or transfer than she would be in a no-property system. By this standard, it is not clear how a system of unregulated markets is supposed to guarantee that the sufficiency condition is met.

Given that residents of food deserts lack access to the very means of preservation, we seem to have a case where Nozick's sufficiency condition is, in fact, violated. At least prima facie, residents seem to be much worse off than they would be in a system without private property.[58] In fact, the property transfers that have resulted in food deserts are directly analogous to the property transfers that result in individuals being left without access to water in Nozick's own example. Inhabitants of food deserts are food insecure because they lack access to nutritious, affordable food – something necessary for a healthy, productive life. Furthermore, that this is so is *a direct result of* free markets and private property. Grocers have moved to more affluent locations, leaving residents without access to nutritious, healthy food. Of course, Nozick's sufficiency condition is not intended as an end-state principle.[59] He says, 'It focuses on a particular way that appropriative actions affect others, and not on the structure of the situation that results'.[60] But food deserts emerged as a direct result of appropriative actions and transfers of property. Grocers moved to the suburbs, convenience stores and liquor stores took the place of neighborhood markets, and so on. Access to the means of preservation has been limited directly by transfers of property. As such, the sufficiency condition should be in effect. It should limit transfers of property when said transfers leave individuals without access to nutritious, affordable food.

Enough and as good is *not* available to residents of food deserts. Hence, food deserts are in violation of Nozick's version of the sufficiency condition. They are thus unjust, even in a Nozickian minimal state, and the principle of rectification should be invoked to correct the injustice.

III. Conclusion

I have argued that food deserts are a serious matter of justice. My primary thesis is that even someone committed to libertarian principles and a Lockean theory of property has reason to support limitations on property rights to address the problem of food access in food deserts. Note, though, that there is much more to be said about the injustices surrounding food deserts. Improving physical access will not, alone, eliminate food insecurity in food-rich nations.[61] As Hillary J Shaw notes in *The Consuming Geographies of Food*, the problem is multilayered. Even were the problem of physical access solved, a financial layer would remain. Access means little if people cannot afford to purchase fresh, healthy food. Further, there is a third layer, which is more complicated and perhaps less visible: in some cases, food preferences are the problem. People who have access to and the means to purchase fresh, healthy food may very well choose not to eat it.[62] Finally, note that food deserts are an issue of food distribution, but, as so many political theorists have stressed, distribution alone is never the whole story.[63] We need to address the causes of food deserts (poverty, oppression) before we can really solve the problem.

Nonetheless, improving physical access to healthy food is an important first step. Currently, there are grassroots efforts to improve the quality of food in food deserts. Such efforts include urban farming, community gardens, expanded farmers' markets in urban environments, and food trucks in underprivileged areas.[64] But much more is called for to fully address the problem of physical access to fresh, healthy food. We need federal, state and local mobilization to effect change. For example, zoning ordinances can be implemented to limit property rights when exercise of them would result in food deserts and state finances can be utilized to develop food retail in areas where there is little to no access to fresh food.

Pennsylvania's Fresh Food Financing Initiative (FFFI) is one example of a governmental effort to address the food desert problem. The FFFI is a grants and loan program that was set up to encourage development of fresh food retail in underserved areas. Pennsylvania contributed $30 million in state funds to the initiative. So far, eighty-eight projects have been funded and food access has improved for roughly 400,000 residents of Pennsylvania because of FFFI.[65] Due in part to the success in Pennsylvania, the federal government launched the Healthy Food Funding Imitative (HFFI), a partnership between the US Departments of Treasury, Agriculture and Health that aims to improve food access in underserved areas. Like the FFFI, the HFFI provides grants and loans to develop fresh food retail in areas that are now classified as food deserts.[66] Yet, still, this is not enough. Food access remains problematic for millions of people in the United States and other food-rich developed countries.

I conclude with a quote from George A. Kaplan, Thomas Francis Collegiate Professor of Public Health at the University of Michigan. Commenting on a report by the Mari Gallagher Research and Consulting Group on food access in Chicago, he says:

> I find the use of the term 'food desert' particularly interesting. A desert is, of course, a place distinguished by the absence of vegetation, rain, etc., which is the sense in which the word is used in this report. Food deserts are defined as 'areas with no or distant grocery stores'. But the word 'desert' is also a verb – 'to leave someone without help or in a difficult situation and not come back'. This seems to me to capture an important dimension of food deserts not conveyed by the noun. The verb 'desert' focuses on action and agency, emphasizing that the lack of access to good food in some areas is not a natural, accidental phenomenon but is instead the result of decisions made at multiple levels by multiple actors. By focusing on this latter meaning, we can find room for changes to be effected, for different decisions to be made in the future, for movement toward actions that can improve access to healthy food for those who have been deserted. In doing so, we can help in at least one way to improve uneven opportunities, and perhaps provide better health as well.[67]

Notes

1. See Neil Wrigley, '"Food Deserts in British Cities": Policy Context and Research Priorities', *Urban Studies* 39 (2002): 2030 and Hillary J Shaw, *The Consuming Geographies of Food* (New York: Routledge, 2014), 105.
2. Vmt Reisig and A Hobbiss, 'Food Deserts and How to Tackle Them: A Study of One City's Approach', *Health Education Journal* 59 (2000): 138.
3. See Shaw, *Consuming Geographies*, 111–15 for a discussion of food desert research in the UK. Shaw notes that there is no standard metric for classifying an area as a food desert in the UK. Distance from a grocer ranges from one-fourth mile to one mile in the literature. See also Wrigley, '"Food Deserts in British Cities"' for a discussion of the controversy over whether there actually are food deserts in the UK.
4. See Kylie Ball, Anna Timperio and David Crawford, 'Neighborhood Socio-Economic Inequalities in Food Access and Affordability', *Health & Place* 15 (2009): 578–85, for a discussion of food deserts in Melbourne, Australia.
5. See Kristian Larsen and Jason Gilliland, 'Mapping the Evolution of "Food Deserts" in a Canadian City: Supermarket Accessibility in London, Ontario, 1961–2005', *International Journal of Health Geographics* 7 (2008): 16.
6. See J Pearce, T Blakely, K Witten and P Bartie, 'Neighborhood Deprivation and Access to Fast-Food Retailing: A National Study', *American Journal of Preventative Medicine* 32 (2007): 375–82 for discussion of New Zealand food deserts.
7. Although several local studies have been carried out in the UK and other developed nations, as yet, the United States is the only place where systematic mapping has taken place. Furthermore, 'A recent systematic review of 48 studies from 1966 through 2007 … shows equivocal findings about the existence of food deserts in many European countries – but clear evidence of disparities in food access in the United states by income and race'. Paula Tarnapol Whitacre, Peggy Tsai and Janet Mulligan, 'The Public Health Effects of Food Deserts: Workshop Summary' (Washington, DC: National Academy of Sciences, 2009), 30. The review cited is Julie Beaulac, Elizabeth Kristjansson and Steven Cummins, 'A Systematic Review of Food Deserts, 1966–2007', *Preventing Chronic Disease* 6 (2009): A105.
8. USDA, 'Food Deserts', accessed June 3, 2013, http://apps.ams.usda.gov/food-deserts/foodDeserts.aspx.
9. See Shaw, *Consuming Geographies*, 110–11.
10. USDA, 'Food Deserts'.
11. See Paula Dutko, Michele Ver Ploeg and Tracey Farrigan, 'Characteristics and Influential Factors of Food Deserts', USDA Economic Research Report 140 (2012): 11–13; Lisa M Powell, Sandy Slater, Donka Mirtcheva, Yanjun Bao and Frank J Chaloupka, 'Food Store Availability and Neighborhood Characteristics in the United States', *Preventative Medicine* 44 (2007): 189–95; and K Morland, S Wing, A Diez Roux and C Poole, 'Neighborhood Characteristics Associated with the Location of Food Stores and Food Service Places', *American Journal of Preventative Medicine* 22 (2002): 23–29.
12. Dutko, ver Ploeg and Farrigan, 'Characteristics', iii.
13. Dutko, ver Ploeg and Farrigan, 'Characteristics', 11.
14. Dutko, ver Ploeg and Farrigan, 'Characteristics', 13. This holds in both urban and rural areas.
15. Kelly M Bower, Roland J Thorpe Jr, Charles Rohde and Darrell J Gaskin, 'The Intersection of Neighborhood Racial Segregation, Poverty, and Urbanicity and Its Impact on Food Store Availability in the United States', *Preventative Medicine* 58 (2014): 33–39.
16. World Health Organization (WHO), 'Food Security', accessed July 15, 2014, http://www.who.int/trade/glossary/story028/en/. The FAO adds a fourth: stability (that access to food is stable over time and not subject to shocks, economic or otherwise). The WHO criteria fold stability into facet (1) by

including 'on a consistent basis'. See FAO, 'Food Security: Policy Brief' (Rome: Food and Agricultural Organization of the United Nations, 2006).
17. The locution 'fringe food locations' originates with the Mari Gallagher Research and Consulting Group. For their research on food deserts, see http://marigallagher.com/.
18. See Mari Gallagher, 'Examining the Impact of Food Deserts on Public Health in Detroit', Mari Gallagher Research Group, 2007.
19. A complete assessment of food deserts from the Rawlsian perspective would require a full defense of this claim. The idea is that when one lives in food insecurity, one's energy and resources must be devoted to self-preservation. Under such conditions, it would be difficult to assert one's rights, participate in civil society, enjoy freedom of movement, have free choice among occupations, and more. In short, one could not pursue one's conception of the good life if one is living in food insecurity.
20. USDA, 'Food Deserts'.
21. See Shaw, *Consuming Geographies*; Ball, Timperio and Crawford, 'Neighborhood Socioeconomic Inequalities'; Larsen and Gilliland, 'Mapping the Evolution'; and Pearce, Blakely, Witten and Bartie, 'Neighborhood Deprivation'.
22. See below for a discussion of the health outcomes related to food deserts.
23. Mari Gallagher, 'Examining the Impact of Food Deserts on Public Health in Chicago', Mari Gallagher Research and Consulting Group, 2006, 10.
24. The evolution of food deserts is actually slightly more complicated than this. Causes include changes in housing, transportation and banking policies and changes internal to the grocery industry. See Allison Karpyn and Sarah Treuhaft, 'The Grocery Gap: Finding Healthy Food in America', in *A Place at the Table*, ed Peter Pringle (New York: Public Affairs, 2013), for discussion. Even so, they are the direct result of private property rights and capitalistic markets.
25. Gopal Sreenivasan, *The Limits of Lockean Rights in Property* (New York: Oxford University Press, 1995), 23–24.
26. 'But how far has he given it us? To enjoy, As much as any one can make use of to any advantage of life before it spoils . . .' John Locke, *Two Treatises of Government*, introduction and notes by Peter Laslett (New York: Cambridge University Press, 1963), 2nd Treatise, V, 31, 9.
27. 'Nor was this *appropriation* of any parcel of *Land*, by improving it, any prejudice to any other Man, since there was still enough, and as good left . . .' Locke, 2nd Treatise, V, 33, 1.
28. 'As *Justice* gives every Man a Title to the product of his honest Industry, and the fair Acquisitions of his Ancestors descended to him; so *Charity* gives every Man a Title to so much out of another's Plenty, as will keep him from extreme want, where he has no means to subsist otherwise . . .' Locke, 1st Treatise, IV, 43, 35.
29. Sreenivasan, *Limits*, 5.
30. Those who think the sufficiency condition remains in force after the advent of civil society include Robert Nozick, James Tully, A John Simmons and Gopal Sreenivasan. Those who think it does not include C B Macpherson and Jeremy Waldron. Waldron argues that the sufficiency condition is a sufficient (not necessary) condition on appropriation, even in the state of nature. See Robert Nozick, *Anarchy, State, and Utopia* (New York: Basic Books, 1974); James Tully, *A Discourse on Property: John Locke and His Adversaries* (Cambridge: Cambridge University Press, 1980); A John Simmons, *The Lockean Theory of Rights* (Princeton: Princeton University Press, 1992); Sreenivasan, *Limits*; C B Macpherson, *The Political Theory of Possessive Individualism: Hobbes to Locke* (Oxford: Clarendon Press, 1962); and Jeremy Waldron, *The Right to Private Property* (Oxford: Clarendon Press, 1988).
31. Furthermore, note that although Locke explicitly suspends the spoilage limitation when money is introduced, he does not so suspend the sufficiency condition. See Locke, *Two Treatises*, 2nd Treatise, V, 47–50.

32. It is worth noting that Sreenivasan argues that Locke doesn't take the sufficiency condition seriously enough, that, in fact, it entails that appropriation is legitimate up to only the largest universalizable share. But the injustice of food deserts will follow regardless of whether we follow Sreenivasan this far. So here I ignore his contention and concentrate on the more limited Lockean view. After all, if the injustice follows on the limited view, it is more compelling. See Sreenivasan, *Limits*.
33. Locke, *Two Treatises*, 2nd Treatise, II, 6.
34. I assume here the sufficiency condition governs property transfers as well as original acquisition. In this, I follow Nozick and Sreenivasan. See Nozick, *Anarchy, State and Utopia*, and Sreenivasan, *Limits*.
35. See Mari Gallagher, 'Food Desert and Food Balance Community Fact Sheet', Mari Gallagher Research and Consulting Group, 2010, accessed June 1, 2013, http://www.fooddesert.net/wp-content/themes/cleanr/images/FoodDesertFactSheet-revised.pdf.
36. Gallagher, *Chicago*, 7. Note that the Mari Gallagher Research and Consulting Group uses a different measure than does the USDA. Instead of measuring distance from a grocer, they use a metric that determines 'food balance'. The Food Balance Score of a particular area is determined by the distance to the nearest grocer (or other venue where one can purchase fresh, healthy food) divided by the distance to the closest fringe food location. The idea behind the Food Balance Score is that it indicates the level of difficulty in choosing a healthy food venue over a fringe food location.
37. Gallagher, *Chicago*, 9.
38. John T Cook, Deborah A Frank, Carol Berkowitz, Maureen M Black, Patrick H Casey, Diana B Cutts, Alan F Meyers, Nieves Zaldivar, Anne Skalicky, Suzette Levenson, Tim Heeren and Mark Nord, 'Food Insecurity Is Associated with Adverse Health Outcomes among Human Infants and Toddlers', *Journal of Nutrition* 134 (2004): 1432–38. Note that this study controlled for confounding factors, including poverty.
39. Katherine Alaimo, Christine M Olson and Edward A Frongillo Jr, 'Food Insufficiency and American School-Aged Children's Cognitive, Academic, and Psychosocial Development', *Pediatrics* 108 (2001): 44–53. This study controlled for confounding factors.
40. Linida Weinreb, Cheryl Wehler, Jennifer Perloff, Richard Scott, David Hosmer, Linda Sagor and Craig Gundersen, 'Hunger: Its Impact on Children's Health and Mental Health', *Pediatrics* 110 (2002): e41. This study controlled for confounding factors (housing status, mother's distress and stressful life events).
41. Diana F Jyoti, Edward A Frongillo and Sonya J Jones, 'Food Insecurity Affects School Children's Academic Performance, Weight Gain, and Social Skills', *Journal of Nutrition* 135 (2005): 2831–39. Developmental outcomes in this study were measured both with and without controls for confounding factors. The results cited are from the models with controls.
42. Alaimo, Olson and Frongillo, 'Food Insufficiency'. This study controlled for confounding factors.
43. Ruth Rose-Jacobs, Maureen M Black, Patrick H Casey, John T Cook, Diana B Cutts, Mariana Chilton, Timothy Heeren, Suzette M Levenson, Alan F Meyers and Deborah A. Frank, 'Household Food Insecurity: Associations with At-Risk Infant and Toddler Development', *Pediatrics* 121 (2008): 65–72. This study controlled for confounding factors, including poverty.
44. Alaimo, Olson and Frongillo, 'Food Insufficiency'. This study controlled for confounding factors.
45. Alaimo, Olson and Frongillo, 'Food Insufficiency'.
46. Katherine Alaimo, Christine M Olson, and Edward A Frongillo Jr, 'Family Food Insufficiency, but Not Low Family Income, Is Positively Associated with Dysthymia and Suicide Symptoms in Adolescents', *Journal of Nutrition* 132 (2002): 719–25. This study controlled for confounding factors.
47. See below for specific suggestions of limitations that might be a step in the direction of correcting the injustice.
48. Nozick, *Anarchy, State and Utopia*, 175.
49. Nozick, *Anarchy, State and Utopia*, 176.

50. Nozick, *Anarchy, State and Utopia*, 178.
51. Nozick, *Anarchy, State and Utopia*, 180.
52. I address his argument for this claim below.
53. I've changed Nozick's example slightly, as his scenario takes place in a desert. The basic structure of the example is the same.
54. Nozick notes that the owner retains property rights over her water access, but that her rights are *limited* by the sufficiency condition. The rights are overridden to avoid catastrophe. See Nozick, *Anarchy, State and Utopia*, 180–81.
55. Nozick, *Anarchy, State and Utopia*, 182.
56. Nozick, *Anarchy, State and Utopia*, 177.
57. 'The very idea of a proviso is that it protects everyone'. Karl Widerquist, 'Lockean Theories of Property: Justifications for Unilateral Appropriation', *Public Reason* 2 (2010): 14.
58. Of course, we do not – and cannot – know what things would have been like if the Earth's land and resources were unowned. However, it is clear that residents of food deserts are substantially harmed by the current system, in that they lack access to resources necessary for a productive life.
59. Lawrence Becker argues that there is no real difference between end-state theories and historical theories. Since all plausible historical theories will contain provisos limiting acquisitions and transfers, (a) they are just as substantive as end-state theories (the proviso contains the substance); and (b) they will require just as much 'tinkering' to respect the proviso as end-state theories require to preserve the end-state (pattern). See Lawrence C Becker, 'Against the Supposed Difference between Historical and End-State Theories', *Philosophical Studies* 41 (1982): 267–72.
60. Nozick, *Anarchy, State and Utopia*, 181.
61. Despite the fact that the United States is a food-rich nation, one out of every six Americans is food insecure. WHO, 'Food Security'.
62. Shaw, *Consuming Geographies*, 131.
63. See, for example, Iris Marion Young, *Justice and the Politics of Difference* (Princeton: Princeton University Press, 1990); and Elizabeth Anderson, 'What Is the Point of Equality'? *Ethics* 109 (1999): 287–337.
64. Note, however, that most of these efforts concentrate on urban environments. We need programs to alleviate food insecurity in rural food deserts, as well.
65. See The Food Trust, 'What We Do', accessed November 16, 2014, http://the-foodtrust.org/what-we-do/supermarkets.
66. See United States Department of Health and Human Services, 'Community Economic Development Healthy Food Financing Initiative Projects', accessed February 24, 2015, https://www.acf.hhs.gov/hhsgrantsforecast/index.cfm?switch=grant.view&gtt_grants_forecastInfoID=67242, for a description of the initiative.
67. Quoted in Gallagher, *Chicago*, 5.

CASE STUDY

Ronald M Green*, 'Health Care and Justice in Contract Theory Perspective'

No work in the field of social and political philosophy in recent years has been received with as much interest as John Rawls's *A Theory of Justice*.[1] Each passing month new articles in journals of philosophy and political theory appear either applauding or criticizing aspects of Rawls's social-contract view of justice. Whether it is the partisans or critics of Rawls's position who eventually prevail, it is safe to say that in the foreseeable future no responsible discussions of public policy, whether theoretical or applied, can afford to neglect Rawls's book.

In view of this, it is worth asking, What are the implications of Rawls's view for health care policy? Certainly, questions concerning the supply and distribution of health care are central to contemporary discussions of social justice, and it is social justice that is the object of Rawls's inquiry. Despite this, the reader who searches *A Theory of Justice* for a discussion of health care will be puzzled and disappointed; not only does Rawls fail to devote any space to this topic in this lengthy book, but the index itself contains not a single reference to health, sickness, medicine, or medical care. It is true that there are some very brief references to these topics in the text, but these are mere afterthoughts to other discussions.[2]

Why, then, is this major work virtually silent on a matter that many persons believe to be at the forefront of questions of justice in our day? Several explanations might be offered. First, there is the fact that in this book Rawls is primarily interested in developing a theory for the distribution of those basic goods that are created by social cooperation and that are distributed by the social system. He calls these the 'social primary goods', and they include various civil rights and liberties, socially bestowed powers and opportunities, the material goods of wealth and income, and the important social good of self-respect. Rawls distinguishes these from the 'natural primary goods' of intelligence, vigor, imagination, and good health whose distribution, he maintains, is only indirectly affected by the social structure, and he places the natural primary goods outside the scope of his concern (p. 62).

Is this move on his part valid? Not really, one is tempted to say. Critics of Rawls have repeatedly pointed out that for a natural primary good like intelligence, the distinction between what is directly and indirectly mediated by the social structure is artificial. In view of all we know about the effects of family circumstances on learning, for example, it does not seem right to say that intelligence is not in large measure distributed when income shares are decided. If this point has some force with respect to intelligence, it would seem to be even more pertinent where health is concerned. Modern medical technology, with its enormous preventative and therapeutic powers, renders almost archaic the notion that health depends on natural contingencies. Social decisions concerning medical care thus have a vital impact on everyone's health, even where health is construed only in the narrowest sense as freedom from physical disease.[3] Despite Rawls, then, health care ought to be considered a primary social good in his terms, and ought to be directly considered by a theory of justice.

A second reason Rawls may have neglected the issue of health care has to do with his extensive concern in his book with the problem of income distribution. It may be that he believes that the matter of medical care can be made a function of a just distribution of income. Indeed, this view may underlie his definition of health as a natural primary good only indirectly mediated by the social structure (p. 62). Thus, he might believe that once society has been set up so that everyone receives a just share of income, medical care can be arranged for privately out of that share with, perhaps, some special provisions made for those at the bottom of the income ladder. If this is Rawls's final view of the matter, however, it runs against the general tenor of his position. It is very doubtful that the

---

* Ronald M. Green, "Health Care and Justice in Contract Theory Perspective," in R. Veatch and R. Branson, eds., *Ethics and Health Policy*. Cambridge, MA: Ballinger, 1976, pp. 111–126. Rights by Ronald M. Green.

rational agents whose choices define social principles in this theory would neglect to establish separate principles for medical care or would substantially leave its distribution to be determined by one's income share.

A final explanation for Rawls's neglect of health care is less involved than those I have mentioned, and it is the explanation I personally believe to be correct. This is simply that Rawls has not had the space in this book adequately to deal with this issue, and has preferred to pass it by, at least for the time being. *A Theory of Justice* is, after all, a very narrowly defined book. It may seem odd to say this of a volume six hundred pages long, but why should we assume that a topic as important as social justice can be handled in six hundred or even six thousand pages? As it is, the book omits treatment of a number of other vital issues of social justice. We should not be surprised, therefore, that Rawls neglects the issue of health care. It may be that his very silence on this issue reflects a deliberate decision to avoid discussion of an important but complicated problem.

Whatever the reasons for Rawls's unwillingness to engage this issue, it seems clear that a consideration of health care deserves an important place in the kind of theory of justice he advances. In the following discussion, therefore, I want to try to fill in this particular gap in contract theory by suggesting a 'Rawlsian' or social-contract analysis of health care and social justice, accepting the basic lines of his theory and extending them beyond their present bounds.

The main ideas of the kind of social-contract theory worked out by Rawls may have been sketched out by writers in scholarly and popular journals so often by now as to preclude the need for a review of his position. But to help point up those aspects of the theory important for the matter of health care, I think it is useful to summarize the main features of his view. The theory as a whole has two different parts. First, Rawls offers a distinct and fairly novel procedure for arriving at the principles of social justice. Second, he advances several basic principles of justice that he believes a proper application of the procedure would produce.

The theory's choice procedure involves the thought experiment of an imaginary, hypothetical contract situation which Rawls calls 'the original position' (chapter 3). The principles of social justice, according to Rawls, may be thought of as those that would be unanimously chosen in this original position by free, equal, mutually disinterested and rational persons (rational in the simple sense that they can select the best means to any desired end). Rawls further asks us to think of these contract parties as lacking any knowledge of the particularities that distinguish them from one another. They must be thought of as located, as he says, behind a 'veil of ignorance' (pp. 136ff.). This prevents them from knowing their particular natural advantages or disadvantages (their intelligence level, for example, or their physical attributes), their respective places in any existing social order, or even the particular ends and values they actually wish to pursue, what Rawls calls their 'plan of life'. Finally, the veil of ignorance deprives them of the knowledge of those special features which distinguish their society from others, for example its pattern of income distribution or its relative stage of social and economic advance. They are permitted, however, to know true general facts about the human condition and natural and social laws.

The purpose of this elaborate fiction is to insure that strict impartiality rules in the choice of basic moral principles. The idea that moral rules are impartially chosen is not new to Rawls. Impartiality has been sought after by other moral devices such as the utilitarian idea that principles are selected by an impartial 'sympathetic spectator' of the human condition.[4] But there are two reasons why the idea of the original position assists our moral reasoning. First, because it prevents the procedure designed to produce impartiality from completely effacing the important distinction between persons. Though they are stripped of the knowledge of their particularities, members of the original position can still defend their most vital human interests. This accords more with our conception of how moral principles should be produced, Rawls argues, than do some procedures associated with alternative theories, especially utilitarianism, whose 'greatest happiness' principle focuses only on the social order as a whole. Second, the device of the original position assists our thinking by remarkably simplifying the moral choice process. It does this by converting moral choice into the simpler procedure of rational prudence. This means that to determine the principles of social justice, we need not engage in the complicated, opaque, and frequently unfruitful process of weighing one moral intuition against another or one common sense moral rule against other, possibly conflicting, rules. We need only ask, What principles would I as a rational agent in the original position find advantageous to myself? Because of the constraints that this situation imposes on our choice, the results of this prudential deliberation will be acceptable moral principles. Thus, while few of us are skilled in making complicated moral judgments, we are quite good at making individual rational choices, and contract theory seeks to exploit this fact.

From his discussion of the original position, Rawls moves on to the actual choice by contract parties of principles of social justice. These are understood to be enduring principles regulating the major political, social and economic arrangements of a society (pp. 7–11, 54, 64). A theory of justice must concern itself with this basic structure, Rawls argues, and not particular allocations of bundles of goods. This is so because the basic structure itself shapes all of our subsequent decisions and actions. Indeed, unless the priority Rawls gives to principles for the basic structure is kept in mind, his theory can be easily misunderstood. As he makes clear, principles suitable for individual allocations may not be suitable for the long-term functioning of a society's major institutions, and vice versa. Thus, while it is frequently rational to distribute goods on the basis of need (blood plasma on a battlefield), this same principle of distribution may prove inadequate as the sole basis for distributing income in a complex modern economy.

It may be thought that the veil of ignorance rules out the choice of social principles by the contract parties. How, after all, can they select principles advantageous to themselves when they do not know which ends are their own? Rawls responds to this difficulty with the concept of primary goods or values that are of instrumental use to virtually any plan of life. These include the natural and social primary goods mentioned earlier. Thus, the choice of principles of justice comes down to this: from the vantage point of the original position, each contractor selects those principles governing the basic structure that are likely to maximize his own share of the social primary goods, subject to the efforts of others to do the same and the obstacles presented by natural or social circumstances.

As might be suspected, Rawls's final principles are strongly egalitarian. Since the members of the original position are rendered fundamentally similar to one another, and since they are each interested in protecting and furthering their most vital interests, the outcome of the unanimous choice process are principles equally protecting the vital interests of everyone. To put this in a slightly more complicated way, the final principles represent a 'maximin' choice by each contractor. Since each is zealously protective of his most important interests in this situation of uncertainty, he selects only those rules whose potential worst outcome for him in real life is as least damaging as possible (a maximum minimum; hence, 'maximin').

Rawls concedes that a maximin procedure is not always the most rational one for choice under uncertainty. But it tends to become so, he maintains, when certain conditions obtain: when knowledge of the probabilities of various outcomes is limited, when the prospects of gain are not terribly enticing, and when the possibility of losing is intolerable (pp. 153–55). Now in Rawls's view, all of these conditions obtain for the choice in the original position of the basic and enduring principles of social justice. This is especially true, he argues, where the fundamental liberties of citizenship are concerned. These include the liberty to participate in the political process, liberty of speech and conscience, and the various liberties of person such as the freedom from arbitrary arrest and seizure (p. 61). These liberties are so important to many different life plans, Rawls maintains, that even a slight diminution or relative loss of them is a severe threat to the individual. Thus, within the original position, where the chances of winning or losing a greater share are unknown, a maximin choice becomes rational. In this case, a maximum minimum is secured by granting the most extensive equal share of these liberties to everyone.

Rawls's argument with respect to economic distribution is basically the same, but the outcome is less immediately egalitarian. The reason for this is that the contractors are presumed to know true basic facts about economic systems: they know, for example, that human beings naturally differ in their productive abilities and that economic systems can sometimes be made more efficient by employing various incentives (additional material goods or authority) to elicit the exercise of desired talents and abilities. By permitting unequal shares, therefore, the contract parties can insure a more productive society overall. But, of course, these parties are not primarily interested in society 'overall'. A higher level of total or average well-being does not interest them as it does the utilitarian with his 'greatest happiness' principle. What each contractor wants to know is that his prospects in the worst possible representative position (say that of the unskilled worker or someone in the group with less than median income) are as high as possible. Ruled by this logic, the contractors might initially shrink away from permitting inequalities with the consequent loss of efficiency. But they need not do this, Rawls maintains. Instead, they can accept what he calls the 'difference principle' (pp. 75–83, 100–8). This would permit inequalities in income, wealth, or authority only when these clearly work out, in a reasonable period of time, to the advantage of the least-favored representative groups and where the more privileged positions and offices are kept open on a fair basis to all. In other words, efficiency is both desirable and permissible but only when it advantages everyone, in the strictest sense of this term.

Rawls recognizes that inequalities can jeopardize those at the bottom of the income ladder. Though he refuses to define the hypothetical contractors as envious (because envy is an irrational and self-destructive propensity), he concedes that the important social primary good of self-respect can be affected by inequalities in income or authority (p. 546). Since they ordinarily lack many natural talents and abilities, those likely to end up at the bottom of the social order are already shaky in their self-respect: they lack a sense of the worth of their life plans and the confidence needed to fulfill them. Adding income differences to these differences in natural abilities only compounds the problem. But rather than scrap the difference principle and the efficiency it implies, Rawls believes that the contract parties can take various steps to preserve their self-respect. They can insist, for example, that equality of opportunity be implemented by various social measures so as to minimize the effect of class background on one's prospects for achievement. But the most important way contract parties can buttress their self-respect is to insist on the 'lexical' priority over the difference principle of the principle guaranteeing the basic equal liberties of citizenship (pp. 243–50; 541–48). This means that these liberties would have to be insured before inequalities in income were allowed, and it also means that these liberties could not be traded off or made a function of income in any way. Apart from the difference principle, probably no aspect of Rawls's theory has been more controverted than this priority rule.[5] Nevertheless, the force of his view lies in the great importance the basic liberties have for rational agents. This priority is further strengthened by rational agents' unwillingness to permit the more problematically acceptable inequalities allowed by the difference principle to erode the self-respect of the least advantaged group.

Though I have certainly omitted many items needed both to understand fully or criticize Rawls's view, the intuitive sense of his position is clear enough, I hope, to permit its application now to the matter of health care. The immediate task is to follow the deliberations of members of the original position on this subject, or what is the same, to ask which principles I or any rational agent so placed would agree upon where health care is concerned.

Four very general questions would likely confront contract parties as they consider the matter of health care. First, there is the question of how important health services are to rational agents. Should they be considered a primary good (a value all rational agents would want, whatever their other values); and if so, how do they compare with other primary goods like liberty and income? Second, assuming health services to be a scarce good in most societies, how would rational agents want them to be distributed? Should equality prevail, for example, or should some privileged form of access be allowed? Third, there is the question of how extensive the health care services of a society should be, and what priorities a society should establish between health and other socially desirable objectives. This is not the general question of the relative place of health among the primary goods, but the more complicated one of how far a general priority should be carried out. Finally, there is the question of what mechanism, if any, it is rational to select for the implementation of a desired distribution. Should health care be distributed by the free market, by rationing, or by some other procedure? Obviously, these questions and their answers interpenetrate one another. But I shall try roughly to consider them in this same order.

On a very general level the first question permits a ready answer. Access to health care is not only a social primary good, in Rawls's sense of the term, but possibly one of the most important such goods. I have already indicated the central place Rawls believes contract parties would give to the civil liberties. But certainly the same can be said for health care. Even more apparently than governmental interference, disease and ill health interfere with our happiness and undermine our self-confidence and self-respect. Indeed, some who have disputed the priority that Rawls gives to the civil liberties have done so precisely because they believe that other values, especially physical well-being and security, are to be rationally preferred.[6] Fortunately, we do not have to enter this dispute, because conflicts between the civil liberties and health care are not so common as to force a relative evaluation of the two here. But there seems to be little question that in the priorities of rational agents health care stands near to the basic liberties themselves.

The very important place given health care in the prudential deliberations of contract parties has several important implications for the choice of a distributive principle. First, it appears to rule out any utilitarian distribution of this good whether to produce a highest total or highest average level of health care services. We can assume that rational agents in the original position are not primarily interested in aggregates of this sort, but would instead employ cautious maximin reasoning to secure the highest minimal level of health care for themselves and their loved ones.[7] Similarly, their reasoning would rule out any distribution on the basis of desert or merit, for the constraints of the original position rule out agreement on the meritorious qualities a person must possess to be worthy of preferential treatment in a matter as vital as this. As a result, we can expect the parties finally to opt for a principle of equal access to health care: each member of society, whatever his position or background, would be guaranteed an equal right to the most extensive health services the society allows.

This equal right would extend, presumably, only to equal access to health services. It would not signify an equal distribution of health care attention (for example, the same number of hours of medical care each year for everyone). The interests of the contract parties indicate the meaning of 'equality' in its various employments. In this case, since the parties are primarily interested in securing services as they need them, equality extends only to access to the health care system. Within the system care would be distributed on the basis of need or in keeping with whatever other principles impartial rational agents consider appropriate.[8] The social-contract approach thus simplifies a problem that has bothered some writers at this point: how we are to make interpersonal comparisons of individual health care needs.[9] The difficulty is occasioned by the fact that, apart from objective differences in health, some persons experience a greater subjective need for health care than others. Should this be a basis for differing distributions of care? Contract theory bypasses this problem, both because it is not concerned with maximizing some social total of well-being (for which interpersonal comparisons are necessary), and because its focus is not on case to case allocations but on the basic structure of society. As far as this basic structure is concerned, the idea of equal access will suffice. To a large degree we can assume that the problem of differing subjective needs can be handled by professional judgments within the health care system.

An important further implication of contract reasoning at this point is that it would seem to rule out direct income-based distributions of health care. This follows from the value health care has in the plans of rational agents, and from their unwillingness to accept a less-than-equal share for any but the most important reasons. It is true that contract parties may sometimes accept a lesser share of a vital good in order better to secure this good in the future. Thus, during a just defensive war they forego some liberty through conscription in order to preserve their liberties (pp. 303, 380). And they might similarly be prepared to sacrifice some equal access to health care in order to secure such care more firmly in the future. (Permitting physicians to be inoculated first during a plague may be an example.) But they would not permit the tolerated inequalities in a less important good like income to affect their vital equal access to health care. That would allow the tail to wag the dog. Just as they insist on the priority of the basic liberties over the difference principle, in other words, contract parties could be expected to separate access to health care from income considerations. In this respect contract reasoning gives independent rational support to the assertion, common today, that health care is a basic right of all persons regardless of income.

The idea of equal access to health care has more ramifications and complexities than I can touch on here. Other questions come to mind. Should this right be affected, for example, by one's geographical location?[10] Should the health care 'illiteracy' of certain classes and groups be allowed to compromise the exercise of their right of equal access?[11] In each case, I think, the cautious, self-protective reasoning of the contract parties behind the veil of ignorance furnishes a negative answer. Similar reasoning can also guide answers to the many specific questions that a right of equal access must raise.

The question of just how much of a society's productive energy and resources must go into health care poses a particularly difficult set of problems. In general, we have seen, rational agents would consider health care, like liberty, a more important good than income. But this general preference for health care must at some point be qualified, even more so than is the case with liberty. As many writers have noted, provision of the 'best possible' health care is an unreachable goal whose pursuit can absorb all the resources of even the richest society. A right to health care, then, cannot be affirmed like other fundamental rights and liberties. It must eventually be defined in terms of its permissible claim on other resources, particularly those handled by the economic system. Very bluntly, the question is, How much should society spend on health?

It may be, as some have argued, that this question cannot be answered in any general sort of way, and that efforts to do so are 'totalitarian'.[12] Alternatively, it may be contended that this matter is best left to the discretion of legislators within particular societies and should not be handled in terms of general moral principles. But if either of these conclusions is morally acceptable then it would have to be shown that rational agents in the original position would choose either to neglect this issue themselves or leave their future health care prospects up to the whim of majority decision; and neither of these alternatives seems immediately acceptable. The members of the original position as the architects of the basic social system would certainly want to set some upper and lower limits on the availability of health services. They know, of course, that they cannot achieve utter precision in this endeavor, but they have a vital interest in the effort to do so. Furthermore, they are aware that they do not have to be absolutely rigid in their specifications. Since they are permitted to know that societies develop economically over time, they can make their health care principles flexible, as they do in the matter of savings (p. 287). This would allow an adaptation to altered circumstances even as it insured a measure of moral regulation.

Consider, for example, the lower stages of social and economic advance – those typically exhibited in our day by the underdeveloped societies. To neglect the issue of health care's priority at this stage is frequently to allow the health care industry to take a back seat to other social needs, especially economic development. Indeed, some would argue that this is the rational and moral thing to do. Since health care and many other activities require economic support, they ask, why not postpone consumption in this and other goods in order to allow the economy to develop? If many members of several generations suffer ill health, they argue, that will be more than offset by the rapid achievement of economic development and the better health of future generations.

Would contract parties accept this reasoning? It seems not. For one thing, the anti-utilitarian thrust of their thinking extends even to inter-generational issues and prevents, where possible, the sacrifice of any one generation's welfare for the sake of others (p. 286f.). Thus, while investment in health care during the early stages of economic growth may not be allowed to block economic development entirely, neither would such investment be prohibited or given low priority. Each generation, even the first, has an important interest in health. Indeed, there might be good reasons why contract parties would wish at these very early stages of development to give health a very high priority among social investments. We can understand this better if we keep in mind the fact that a savings process must always to some degree disadvantage the earliest generations. They can afford to save the least but must be asked proportionately to save the most, and they receive few immediate rewards for their sacrifices.[13] Health care may be a way of cutting this particular Gordian knot. For one thing, health investment certainly advantages the earliest generations, since even modest improvements in care at these earliest stages produce vast benefits. For another, at these stages health care can have an important effect on productivity by improving the numbers and quality of the labor force.[14] Finally, health care can be a key aspect of programs aimed at reducing the savings-consuming high birth rates of the less-developed societies. As a number of demographers have noted, the persistently high childhood mortality rates of the poorer nations continue to provide a major incentive for numerous offspring. Moreover, these incentives have remained relatively unaffected by mass public health measures. By generally lowering mortality rates, these measures have boosted population growth, but without really giving families any more security that all their children will survive. Despite rising population levels very many couples still aim to have large families. Lowering mortality on a family-to-family basis, therefore, by providing adequate personal health care, can, when supplemented by other measures, help to reduce population growth.[15] As such, health care would be a form of investment likely to receive significant attention from members of the original position.

How much attention? Enough, one might say, to insure that basic preventative and therapeutic services are rapidly brought within the reach of every member of society. Universal basic health care is the desirable goal at this stage. Less desirable, and perhaps actually to be prohibited, are expensive care of the highest quality and costly, esoteric medical research. At this stage such expenditures only distract from the goal of universal basic health care, as well as other health-related goals such as the development of food production and transportation. Among the less-developed societies, it is mainland China that has probably come closest in our day to implementing a program of this sort, even down to the priority placed within the health care system on patient care as against research.[16] This suggests that these priorities are as workable as they are desirable.

How would members of the original position choose to alter these priorities as a society developed economically? For one thing, it would seem rational as development proceeds to go beyond the provision of basic care to more intensive preventative programs, more sophisticated therapies, and more esoteric medical research. Maximin reasoning counsels protecting oneself as much as possible against ill health, whatever its cause. It goes without saying that improvements in quality at these higher stages cannot be made a ground for departures from equality of access. That would represent an inversion of priorities.[17] At these stages, however, the problem of limitless expenditures poses itself anew. Given the sophisticated development of medical technology, there are virtually no limits to what can be spent to preserve individual life and health. To take a bizarre example, where costly research and therapies fail, cryogenic techniques might be used, whatever the cost, to keep the body intact for future revivication. Since each member of the original position seeks to protect his most vital interests, why should he not insist upon such expenditures as soon as the resources become available? And why not do this even if it absorbs all the income that could be devoted, above the level of bare necessities, to making life more satisfying and fruitful? As Arrow points out, a strict maximin solution to this problem could easily lead to the choice of medical procedures so costly as to reduce society to the subsistence level.[18]

Offhand, the logic of contract reasoning does not produce an unequivocal repudiation of such a priority. Indeed, the citizens of many industrialized countries whose economies are marked by abundant consumer goods and luxuries, but often less-than-extensive health services, may have adopted a policy they could not impartially or rationally advocate. Perhaps this is why when some are denied access to scarce dialysis machines, many decry the priorities that would place gadgets for the many over the lives of a few. Still, there are good reasons for not devoting all of the output of an economy above survival to health care. For one thing, economies are complicated mechanisms and developments in one area frequently produce benefits in another. Who would have believed, for example, that a device developed to produce cheaper telephones (the laser) would lead to a superior therapy for glaucoma? Thus, rational agents have good reasons on health care grounds alone to allow the modest development of many of the normal activities of an economy.

Added to this is the common-sense consideration that health is thought to be a state of mental, physical and social well-being and not merely freedom from disease. As such, a healthy existence presumably includes various opportunities for the desired exercise of many human capacities and excellences. In contract terms, we can say that the members of the original position have very good reasons for not settling for a society whose members are free from physical disability but who otherwise live at a level of economic austerity. Thus it is rational for them here to qualify their maximin logic and sacrifice some health care to economic considerations. Just where they would draw the line is hard to say, but a reasonable test may be available. Since contract parties select principles in the original position that they would be prepared to live with in any representative social position, the test of any actual choice made concerning degrees of health care or research is whether those who fall ill would regret the social decisions that rendered the therapy for their condition unavailable. This test is not perhaps totally adequate. It breaks down where the very young are concerned, since they cannot be expected to have availed themselves of the opportunities opened up by the decisions that jeopardize them. But then, this may also mean that we should be cautious about decisions limiting young peoples' access to the most extensive health care services.

If it is true that social decisions limiting health care can sometimes be morally acceptable, this would seem to be the case only in a society whose basic structure otherwise conformed to the principles of social justice. No rational individual, after all, would agree to expose himself to grave health risks without at the same time requiring that the benefits produced by these risks be distributed in ways that he can accept. Though obvious, this awareness has sometimes been lacking in discussions of how scarce life-saving therapies should be allocated.[19] Claims of various contenders have been weighed by several common-sense rules without asking how the larger social context affects the moral acceptability of the final allocation. For example, where 'social contribution' has been made a criterion for receiving scarce therapy, the questions of whether all candidates have had a fair, equal opportunity to make such a contribution, or whether all have really benefited from the contributions of others, have typically been ignored.[20] Here again, contract theory's prior attention to the society's basic structure reveals its moral importance.

The imprecision of any general effort to determine just how much of a society's resources should be devoted to health care leads to the final major question before contract parties: whether particular mechanisms for implementing health care policy might be agreed upon by members of the original position. Specifically, it might be asked whether there are not acceptable mechanisms of social choice that can help reduce reliance on a priori decisions by contract parties and that can allow real members of actual societies to establish their priorities in ways that all can accept. The principle possibility here is use of the free market mechanism, the advantage of the market being that it allows each individual or family to establish priorities between health care and other goods. Among the other advantages of this approach are facilitation of consumer choice in the 'style' of health care delivery,[21] and the possible encouragement of both quality and efficiency in the health care system. In the past, it is true, consumer choice in this area has frequently worked against both quality and efficiency, and it may never be capable of promoting these objectives.[22] But a free market in medical care, in conjunction with such devices as health maintenance organizations financed on a per capita basis, have been thought by some to hold out encouraging prospects in this direction.[23]

The major objection to reliance on the free market is that it seems to reintroduce the income-based distribution of health care already repudiated by the contract parties. But this objection need not be decisive. Through the device of progressive rates on health care (or health insurance and its requisite copayments and deductibles), the goal of equal access can be preserved. Of course, in practice the stipulation and maintenance of just progressive rates may prove impossible, as it has in many other areas, and this would seriously undermine the acceptability of this method. Still, it is at least theoretically possible to proceed in this way.

Assuming truly progressive rates, the free market in health care would function as an instance of 'pure procedural justice' on a parallel with Rawls's hope for the economic system as a whole (pp. 86f., 201). Once properly set up, in other words, the health care industry could operate in a morally acceptable way without the need for constant moral and political regulation. This is desirable in itself, but there are at least two respects (apart from the matter of setting rates) in which this mechanism could only be 'quasi-pure' and would continue to require moral supervision through just political decisions. First, if what I have been saying about the rational importance of health care is correct, then a just society would be expected to have an extensive and well-trained corps of medical practitioners. It is the continuing responsibility of government to see that this is so. At the lower stages of economic development, this would probably require considerable direct governmental involvement in medical training and staffing. At higher stages, where the market mechanism could prevail, it would be the government's job to see that the supply of practitioners is not kept artificially low (or their wages artificially high) by monopolistic practices or by the political intervention of self-interested professional groups.[24] Presumably, in a just society a profession as socially important and as occupationally attractive as medicine would, even without especially high wages, attract competent personnel and be among the most heavily staffed. The government's job is to see that this is the case.

A second reason for assuming the continuing need for political intervention in this area has to do with the importance of collective decision where health is concerned. The matter of savings is an example. Left to themselves, members of any one generation might totally exhaust available resources on consumption, especially in an area as important as health care. Government's responsibility is to prevent this from happening, by establishing a just savings rate and deducting the funds for this prior to the distribution of income. But any savings decisions of this sort require judgments concerning which kinds of expenditures are morally permissible at a given stage, and these judgments must take into account moral principles stipulating permitted degrees of health care. Other instances where collective decision is needed could be cited. The point is that even the best-functioning health care system cannot totally eliminate the need for collective social choice. And whenever choice is made, if it is to be morally acceptable, it must conform to those broad principles established, in the first place, in the original position.

In attempting to sketch the outlines of the kind of health care policy I think would be generated by social-contract theory, I have had two important objectives: First, I have tried partly to fill what I believe to be a major gap in Rawls's contract theory as it presently stands. Second, I have tried to show that the distinguishing aspects of this theory – the device of the original position, the identification of instances where maximin reasoning is appropriate, and the focus on the basic structure – all serve as sound and useful guides to our moral reasoning process. Many of the points I have made have already been emphasized by those using more traditional and intuitive moral approaches. But the aim of contract theory is partly to illuminate the more fundamental rational considerations that underlie our intuitive judgments. In tracing the reasoning of contract parties on this issue, I hope to have at least illustrated the usefulness of this method, and to have identified those basic points in rational deliberation about justice and health care where more focused future discussion and debate is in order.

Notes

1. Cambridge, MA: The Belknap Press of Harvard University Press, 1971. All further references to this book appear in parentheses in the text.
2. None of these brief mentions of health care appear in the index. They include the definition of health as a 'natural primary good' (62); the designation of innoculation procedures and health services as 'public goods' in the special economic sense of that term (268, 270); and the brief, provocative, but unexpanded suggestion that the social minimum of a just society, those payments made to the least-favoured groups, will include 'special payments for sickness' (275).
3. That mental health is a social primary good seems even clearer. For a criticism of Rawls's neglect of mental health see Vinit Haksar, 'Autonomy, Justice and Contractarianism', *British Journal of Political Science* III (1973): 496ff.
4. R M Hare notes this basic similarity between the original position and other procedures and concludes, wrongly I think, that this device makes no contribution to our moral reasoning. See his 'Critical Study: Rawls's Theory of Justice – I', *Philosophical Quarterly* XXIII (1973): 144–55.
5. For a good critical appraisal and qualified defense of this priority rule see Brian Barry, *The Liberal Theory of Justice* (Oxford: Clarendon Press, 1973), chapter 7.
6. See, for example, David Lyons and Michael Teitelman, 'Symposium: *A Theory of Justice* by John Rawls', *Journal of Philosophy* LXIX (1972), 535–57.
7. Assuming this minimal share to be above some low threshold where it acquires worth for rational agents. For a discussion of this threshold problem and maximin reasoning see Barry, chapter 9.
8. I mention need only as the foremost criterion of distribution within the system. Other common-sense rules may have their place. Thus, 'desert' in some special, medically defined sense may properly affect in-system decisions or insurance rates (smokers possibly having to pay more). For a good discussion of this see Gene Outka, 'Social Justice and Equal Access to Health Care', *Journal of Religious Ethics* I (1974), 16f. The problem of allocating scarce therapy poses problems that defy even common-sense analysis, however, and that require the more systematic approach that contract reasoning affords. For an application of contract reasoning to this issue, see James Childress, 'Who Shall Live When Not All Can Live'? *Soundings* LIII (1970), 350ff.
9. See, for example, Kenneth Arrow, 'Some Ordinalist-Utilitarian Notes on Rawls's Theory of Justice', *Journal of Philosophy* LXX (1973): 244.
10. The issue of health care and geographic location is treated at length by David Mechanic, 'Problems in the Future Organization of Medical Practice', *Law and Contemporary Problems* XXXV (1970): 239–45.
11. Low-income groups' failure to use medical services despite the elimination of financial barriers has been noted in Sweden. See Ronald Andersen et al., *Medical Care Use in Sweden and the United States* (Chicago: Center for Health Administration Studies, 1970), 133.

12. This seems to be the view of Paul Ramsey, *The Patient as Person: Exploration in Medical Ethics* (New Haven: Yale University Press, 1970), 266–75.
13. Thus Alexander Herzen's observation that human development displays a kind of chronological unfairness. This is quoted by Isaiah Berlin in his introduction to Franco Venturi, *Roots of Revolution* (New York: Knopf, 1960), xx.
14. The great importance of health care and other forms of 'human investment' in the development process has recently been noted by a number of development economists. For a review of these discussions, see Harvey Leibenstein, 'The Impact of Population Growth on Economic Welfare-Nontraditional Elements', in National Academy of Sciences, *Rapid Population Growth* (Baltimore: Johns Hopkins Press, 1971), 183ff.
15. See, for example, Howard C Taylor and Bernard Berelson, 'Comprehensive Family Planning Services Based on Maternal/Child Health Services: A Feasibility Study for a World Program', *Studies in Family Planning* II (February 1971), 21–54.
16. Ruth and Victor Sidel, 'The Human Services in China', and Frank Riessman, 'Postscript: The Politics of Human Service: China and the United States', *Social Policy* II (1972): 25–34 and 35–39.
17. Here, perhaps, is the basis of a common criticism of the American health system. See, for example, Abraham Ribicoff, 'The Healthiest Nation Myth', and John Knowles, 'Where Doctors Fail', *Saturday Review* LXXX (August 22, 1970): 18–20 and 21–23.
18. Arrow, 'Some Ordinalist-Utilitarian Notes on Rawls's Theory of Justice', 251.
19. Thus, the extensive discussion of this problem by Nicholas Rescher entirely omits to consider this issue. See his 'The Allocation of Exotic Medical Lifesaving Therapy', *Ethics* LXXIX (1969).
20. See for example the account of the deliberations of the Seattle Artificial Kidney Center's selection process in Ramsey, 245ff.
21. Whether the medical system should preserve personal contact with a physician or whether clinically based care is to be preferred is not, I think, a matter of social justice so much as it is a part of one's social ideal. But the preservation of choice here is desirable. For a discussion of this matter see Michael Halberstam, 'Liberal Thought, Radical Theory and Medical Practice', *New England Journal of Medicine* CCLXXXIV (1971): 1180–84.
22. Kenneth Arrow points out that the consumer has the dual characteristic of being ignorant about medicine and loathing to take risks about his health. These characteristics make for poor consumer decision in this area. See his 'Uncertainty and the Welfare Economics of Medical Care', *American Economic Review* LIII (1963): 941. R M Titmuss argues that this problem has been exacerbated by the rapid disappearance of the general practitioner with his traditional role of patient-advocate. See his criticism of free market-medicine in *Monopoly or Choice in Health Services?* Occasional Paper Number 3 of the Institute of Economic Affairs (London, 1964).
23. Clark Havighurst, 'Health Maintenance Organizations and the Market for Health Services', *Law and Contemporary Problems* XXXV (1970): 716–95.
24. For a penetrating critique of the American Medical Association's activities in this area see Reuben Kessel, 'The A.M.A. and the Supply of Physicians', *Law and Contemporary Problems* XXXV (1970): 267–83.

SECTION II

Racial and Gender Justice
The Quest for Civil Rights

That man over there says that women need to be helped into carriages, and lifted over ditches, and to have the best place everywhere. Nobody ever helps me into carriages, or over mud-puddles, or gives me any best place! And ain't I a woman? Look at me! Look at my arm! I have ploughed and planted, and gathered into barns, and no man could head me! And ain't I a woman?
—Sojourner Truth

Only the black woman can say 'when and where I enter, in the quiet, undisputed dignity of my womanhood, without violence and without suing or special patronage, then and there the whole Negro race enters with me'.
—Anna Julia Cooper, *A Voice from the South*

In the first section, the critics of social contract theory pointed to the exclusion of several people from that original contract, calling into question the validity of the consent allegedly given to form society. Both Pateman and Mills suggested that the history of gender and racial subordination required a rethinking of the way we approach political theory in general, and contract theory in particular. As Mills writes, 'The historical reality is that race – white racial privilege and nonwhite racial subordination – has been foundational to the actual "basic structure" of the United states'.[1] And Pateman adds that 'we hear an enormous amount about the *social* contract; a deep silence is maintained about the *sexual* contract. . . . The story of the sexual contract . . . is about political right as *patriarchal right* or sex-right, the power that men exercise over women'.[2] This section focuses on the continuing struggle for inclusion and equality by both groups.

The quotations by Sojourner Truth and Anna Julia Cooper introduce this section and the concept of intersectionality, which is central to the experiences of leaders of antislavery and civil rights movements, such as Maria Stewart, Ida B Wells, W E B Du Bois, and James Baldwin.

The concept of intersectionality was developed by Kimberlé Crenshaw to understand the complex interactions of racism and sexism that erase the specific experiences of routine violence experienced by African American women. As articulated by Crenshaw, intersectionality offers 'a methodology that ultimately will disrupt the tendencies to see race and gender as exclusive or separable'.[3] By describing the simultaneous, multiple and overlapping systems of power that shape our lives and political options, the concept of intersectionality destabilises existing power relations grounded in the living experiences of the marginalised and allows counterhegemonic narratives to come to the surface.

In one of her books, Toni Morrison wrote that 'what was distinctive in the New World was, first of all, its claim to freedom, and second, the presence of the unfree within the heart of the democratic experiment – the critical absence of democracy, its echo, shadow, and silent force in the political and intellectual activity of some not-Americans. The distinguishing features of the not-Americans were their slave status, their social status – and their color'.[4] She pointed to the contradiction, highlighted by several of the authors in this section, between the language of liberty and democracy and the reality of slavery in the New World.

The authors in this section examine the quest for freedom and equality by African Americans before and after the Emancipation Proclamation of 1863. The section opens with a speech delivered in 1832 in Boston by Maria Miller Stewart, a free, young African American woman who is reported to have been the first Black feminist abolitionist in America and the first African American to lecture in defense of women's rights. Speaking six years before Angelina and Sarah Grimke and nearly a decade before Frederick Douglass began his public career in 1841, Stewart anticipated the great abolitionist and civil rights and women's rights speakers that followed her.[5] Her arguments opposed the constraints she faced both as a woman and as a free Black American.

In nineteenth-century America the 'cult of true womanhood' and the 'cult of domesticity' spread as the result of increasing urbanisation, as workers flooded dirty, overcrowded cities. A cultural prescription came to designate the private sphere of the home as the only appropriate domain of women, leaving men control over the public sphere. The 'cult of domesticity', however, applied only to middle-class white women since Black women had to work outside their homes to support their families. In her Franklin Hall address, Stewart addressed and challenged the concept of 'true womanhood' by her very presence in public and by examining the condition of Black women.[6] Twenty years later, in 1852, Frederick Douglass, a former slave who became the greatest abolitionist orator of the antebellum period, was invited by the Ladies Anti-Slavery Society of Rochester to give a Fourth of July speech. In the early 1850s, tensions over slavery were high across the county. The Compromise of 1850 had failed to resolve the controversy over the admission of new slave states to the Union. The Fugitive Slave Act passed by Congress as part of this compromise was bitterly resented by the Northern states. Harriet Beecher Stowe's novel about slavery, *Uncle Tom's Cabin: Or Life among the Lowly*, had been published a few months before and had unexpectedly become a national best-seller. In the speech Douglass denounces the 'shameless hypocrisy' of a nation that celebrates freedom and independence while maintaining a system of slavery, and condemns the injustice of the system of slavery that denies humanity to Black people.

The next two readings address the continued oppression of Blacks even after their legal emancipation in the form of lynching carried out by mobs while law enforcement officers looked the other way. In the year 1892 alone, 161 Black men and women were lynched. That year Frederick Douglass published 'Lynch Law in the South' in the *North American Review*. Although he argued that the men killed in a recent case in Memphis were likely killed because they were 'prosperous', he did not outright deny that all the Black men accused of rape were guilty or that they posed a threat to white Southern women. It took a Southern Black woman to fully discredit such an idea. The twenty-three-year old Ida B Wells, the editor of a small newspaper in Memphis, charged in her paper that white businessmen had instigated three local lynchings against their Black competitors. In retaliation, a group of white men burned the newspaper offices, and she had to flee the South and move to New York City. In New York, and later in Chicago, Ida B Wells focussed on a campaign against lynching that continued for all her life. With her husband, Ferdinand Barnett, she played an active role in the founding of the National Association for the Advancement of Colored People (NAACP). 'A Red Record' was a pamphlet she published in 1895 that provided fourteen pages of statistics related to lynchings between 1892 and 1895 and described them often in graphic detail. 'Lynch Law in America' was a speech Ida B Wells delivered in Chicago in 1900 that documents the unpunished crimes and dehumanising brutality of whites against Blacks. Excerpts of both 'A Red Record' and 'Lynch Law in America' are included here.[7]

Ida B Wells shows that lynching was used by whites to oppress and control Blacks who competed with whites, often under the guise of rape charges. Ironically, she writes that no nation, except for the United States, 'has confessed its inability to protect its women save by hanging, shooting, and burning alleged offenders'.[8] She accuses the United States of a national crime and claims that it is the 'painful duty of the Negro to reproduce a record which shows that a large portion of the American people avow anarchy, condone murder and defy the contempt of civilization'.[9]

Unfortunately, as Carol Anderson writes, there are striking similarities to today: 'The trigger for white rage, inevitably, is black advancement [. . .] it is blackness with ambition, with drive, with purpose, with aspirations, and with demands for full and equal citizenship. It is blackness that refuses to accept subjugation, to give up. A formidable array of policy assaults and legal contortions has consistently punished black resilience, black resolve'.[10] Anderson documents how throughout American history, from the nineteenth century to the twenty-first, white rage has undermined American democracy and maintained a racial divide.

In *The Souls of Black Folk* (1903), Du Bois writes that years have passed since emancipation, but 'the Nation has not yet found peace from its sins; the freedman has not yet found in freedom his promised land' and 'the bright ideals of the past – physical freedom, political power, the training of brains and the training of hands – all these in turn have waxed and waned, until even the last grows dim and overcast'.[11]

Black people, he argued, often faced double standards in their efforts to achieve equality in the wake of enslavement and racial segregation. This double standard led, he argued, to 'twoness', the experience of being 'Black' and 'American', where the two were treated as contradictory, and 'double consciousness', the experience of being seen from the perspective of white supremacy and anti-Black racism, from the perspective of seeing themselves as lowly and inferior.[12] Another aspect of double consciousness involves seeing the contradictions of a system born on the memorable phrase, 'All men are created equal', and the injustice of a social system that limits possibilities for some groups and creates advantages for others. The subsequent criticism of whether 'men' meant 'women too' pushes this point further, as Frederick Douglass, Anna Julia Cooper, and other earlier 19th-century Black critical thinkers contended.

In *Darkwater* Du Bois noticed that double standards affected how history is told, and that the misrepresentation of history as an apology for white supremacy and colonialism led to the degradation of Black people as passive objects of history instead of makers of history. (A similar critic will be formulated in the readings on colonialism in the fifth section.) Du

Bois wrote in 1920 that it was easy for leaders to make people believe that 'every great deed the world ever did was a white man's deed'.[13] And Baldwin seconded that in 1964, observing that white superiority made it so difficult for white men to share power with people of colour that they instead 'set up in themselves a fantastic system of evasions, denials, and justifications', a system that destroys 'their grasp of reality, which is another way of saying their moral sense'.[14]

In *The Fire Next Time*, published in 1963, James Baldwin gives voice to the emerging civil rights movement. It was originally a letter, written by Baldwin to his nephew on the 100th anniversary of the emancipation of Blacks, where he examines the consequences of racial injustice in America and presents a picture of white America as seen through the eyes of a Black man. The title comes from a prophecy recreated from the Bible in a song of a slave:

God gave Noah the rainbow sign,
No more water, the fire next time!

Baldwin writes: 'If we – and I mean the relatively conscious whites and the relatively conscious black, who must, like lovers, insist on, or create, the consciousness of others – do not falter in our duty now, we may be able, handful that we are, to end the racial nightmare, and achieve our country, and change the history of the world'.[15] Otherwise, 'the fire next time'! He contends that Blacks and whites must work to understand and accept one another with love. Towards the end of the letter to his nephew, Baldwin also insists that everyone must understand his or her past and present reality, and that one must commit oneself to act upon that understanding: 'To act is to be committed, and to be committed is to be in danger. The danger, in the minds of white Americans is the loss of their identity: the black man has functioned in the white man's world as a fixed star, as an immovable pillar, and as he moves out of his place, heaven and earth are shaken to their foundations'.[16]

The year of the publication of *The Fire Next Time* (1963) was also the year of the March on Washington for Jobs and Freedom, and that day, August 28, Martin Luther King Jr delivered his famous speech, 'I Have a Dream', to about 250,000 people. Like Baldwin, King observed that one hundred years after emancipation Black people were not free, discrimination was rampant and de facto segregation was still in place. Baldwin had written towards the end of the letter to his nephew, 'This is your home, my friend, do not be driven from it; great men have done great things here, and will again, and we can make America what America must become'.[17] Likewise, King exhorted his people to go back to Mississippi, Alabama, South Carolina, Georgia, Louisiana, to the slums and ghettos in the North, knowing that their situation will change: 'We will not be satisfied until justice rolls down like waters and righteousness like a mighty stream'. And he reminded America of the 'fierce urgency of now'.

The 'fierce urgency of now' was also one of the themes in Ella Baker's speech on January 22, 1964, in Hattiesburg, Mississippi. It was Freedom Day, organised by civil rights groups to urge Black voters to register. And echoing both Du Bois and Baldwin, Baker insists that 'we are just beginning the freedom struggle', and she encourages democratic participation and community engagement at all levels. But freedom was not just the battle for civil rights; it had to include social and economic justice, equal access to job opportunities and basic human needs such as food. She argued that even if 'we were able to vote our full strength', freedom could be not fully achieved 'until we recognize that in this country, in the land of great plenty and great wealth, there are millions of people who go to bed hungry every night'.[18]

In *The Fire Next Time* James Baldwin had written that Blacks and whites needed each other 'if we are really to become a nation – if we are really, that is, to achieve our identity, our maturity, as men and women'.[19] Similarly, Ella Baker argued that freedom was a fundamental aspect of humanity, and racism was a problem for all: 'I am not talking about Negroes, I am talking about people'. And she ended her speech by stating that the movement was fighting for 'a larger freedom that encompasses all mankind. And until that day, we will never turn back'.[20]

More than fifty years after Ella Baker's speech and James Baldwin's reflections in *The Fire Next Time*, it seems that the problem of the twentieth-first century is still 'the problem of the color line'.[21] Police killings of Black men have filled the news; housing segregation and urban poverty still plague communities of colour; as Michelle Alexander writes, 'No task is more urgent for racial justice advocates today than ensuring that America's current racial caste system is its last'.[22] And Eduardo Bonilla-Silva in his book *Racism without Racists* reminds us that we are far from being a post-racial society, and that colour blindness is an ideology that serves to maintain white privilege by negating racial inequality and legitimating the existing social, political and economic arrangements.[23]

A recent study[24] on the sources of racial and ethnic disparities in income using longitudinal data that covered nearly the entire US population from 1989 to 2015 documents that the intergenerational persistence of disparities varied substantially across racial groups, with African Americans having the lowest rates of upward mobility and the highest rates of downward mobility, leading to large income disparities between Blacks and whites that persist across generations. However, such income gap is caused by large differences in wages and employment between white and Black men, while there are no such differences between white and Black women. Another interesting finding in the study that debunks a number of other widely held hypotheses about income inequality is that gaps persisted even when Black and white boys grew up in families with the same income, similar family structures, similar education levels and even similar levels of accumulated wealth. Finally, the Black-white income gap continues even among boys who grow up in the same neighbourhood. Controlling for parental income, Black boys have lower incomes in adulthood than white boys in 99 percent of census tracts. The few areas where Black-white gaps are relatively small tend to be low-poverty neighbourhoods with low levels of racial bias among whites; Black males in such neighbourhoods earn more and are less likely to be incarcerated. However, fewer than 5 percent of Black children grow up in such areas. One of the most popular liberal post-racial ideas that this study disproves is that the fundamental problem is class and not race, and it makes clear that there is something unique about the obstacles Black males face. While Black women also face the negative effects of racism, Black men often experience racial discrimination differently. Black boys are more likely to be disciplined in school. They are pulled over or detained and searched by police officers more often. Black men are stereotyped as being scary, intimidating and violent, and this racist stereotype particularly hurts Black men economically, now that service-sector jobs, requiring interaction with customers, have replaced the manufacturing jobs that employed men with less education.

The study suggests that reducing the Black-white income gap will require measures that target Black boys, such as providing mentors who are not necessarily their parents but who share those children's gender and race, increasing the number of interracial neighbourhoods, and facilitating social interaction across racial groups within a given area.

The essay by Edwidge Danticat, 'Message to My Daughters', concludes this section. She explores the idea that people of the Black diaspora are also refugees and compares a run-down Brooklyn public housing project to a refugee camp, and police abuses she witnessed in her home country of Haiti during the dictatorship to those she saw in her working-class minority neighbourhood in New York. Danticat quotes James Baldwin's words in his letter to his nephew: 'You were born in a society which spelled out with brutal clarity, and in as many ways as possible that you were a worthless human being',[25] and suggests that 'the same letter could have been written to a long roster of dead young men and women . . . Oscar Grant, Aiyana Stanley-Jones, Rekia Boyd, Kimani Gray, Renisha McBride, Trayvon Martin . . . '[26]

Notes

1. Charles W Mills, 'Rawls on Race/Race in Rawls', in *Race, Racism, and Liberalism in the 21st Century*, ed Bill E Lawson, Supplement, *Southern Journal of Philosophy* XLVII (2009): 161–84, 170.
2. Carole Pateman, *The Sexual Contract* (Stanford, CA: Stanford University Press, 1988), 1.
3. Kimberlé Crenshaw, 'Mapping the Margins', *Stanford Law Review* 43 (July 1991): 244.
4. Toni Morrison, *Playing in the Dark* (Cambridge, MA: Harvard University Press, 1990), 48.
5. Laura R Sell, 'Maria W Miller Stewart (1803–1879), First African American Woman to Lecture in Public', in Karlyn Kohrs Campbell, *Women Public Speakers in the United States: A Bio-Critical Sourcebook* (Westport, CT: Greenwood Press, 1993), 339.
6. Like Maria Stewart, Sojourner Truth, in 1851, will also question the meaning of womanhood by asking, 'Ain't I a woman'?
7. On April 26, 2018, the National Memorial for Peace and Justice in Montgomery, Alabama, was dedicated to the victims of American white supremacy, the thousands of Black people who were lynched in a decades-long campaign of racist terror. On eight hundred steel columns there are etched the names of an American county and the people who were lynched there. It is thanks to the records kept by Ida B Wells that we have the names of many of the victims of lynch mobs.
8. Ida B Wells, 'Lynch Law in America' (speech, Chicago, IL, January 1900).
9. Wells, 'Lynch Law in America'.
10. Carol Anderson, *White Rage* (New York and London: Bloomsbury, 2017), 3–4.
11. W E B Du Bois, *The Souls of Black Folk* (Boston and New York: Bedford/St Martin, 1997), 40, 43.
12. Du Bois, *The Souls of Black Folk*, 38–39.
13. W E B Du Bois, *Darkwater: Voices from within the Veil* (Mineola, NY: Dover Publications, 1999), 118.
14. W E B Du Bois, *The Cross of Redemption: Uncollected Writings* (New York: Pantheon Book, 2010), 95.
15. James Baldwin, *The Fire Next Time* (New York: Vintage Books, 1993), 119.
16. Baldwin, *The Fire Next Time*, 9.
17. Baldwin, *The Fire Next Time*, 10.
18. Ella Baker, 'Address at the Hattiesburg Freedom Day Rally' (speech, Hattiesburg, MS, January 21, 1964).
19. Baldwin, *The Fire Next Time*, 111.
20. Baker, 'Address at the Hattiesburg Freedom Day Rally'.
21. Du Bois, *The Souls of Black Folk*, 45.
22. Michelle Alexander, *The New Jim Crow: Mass Incarceration in the Age of Colorblindness* (New York: The New Press, 2012), 19.
23. Eduardo Bonilla-Silva, *Racism without Racists*, 5th ed (Lanham: Rowman & Littlefield, 2018).
24. Raj Chetty, Nathaniel Hendren, Maggie R Jones and Sonya R Porter, 'Race and Economic Opportunity in the United States: An Intergenerational Perspective', March 2018, http://www.equality-of-opportunity.org/assets/documents/ race_paper.pdf.

25. Edwidge Danticat, 'Message to My Daughters'. In *The Fire This Time: A New Generation Speaks about Race*, ed Jesmyn Ward (New York: Scribner, 2016), 212–13.
26. Danticat, 'Message to My Daughters', 213.

Suggested Readings

Alexander, Michelle. *The New Jim Crow*. New York: The New Press, 2012.
Anderson, Carol. *White Rage*. New York and London: Bloomsbury, 2017.
Baldwin, James. *Go Tell It on the Mountain*. New York: Vintage International, 2013.
———. *Notes of a Native Son*. Boston: Beacon Press, 2012.
———. 'The White Man's Guilt'. Collected Essays. Ed Toni Morrison. New York: The Library of America, 1998, 722–27.
Bernasconi, Robert, and Tommy Lott. *The Idea of Race*. Indianapolis: Hackett, 2000.
Carson, Clayborne et al. (eds). *The Eyes on the Prize Civil Rights Reader: Documents, Speeches, and Firsthand Accounts from the Black Freedom Struggle*. New York: Penguin, 1991.
Coates, Ta-Nehisi. *We Were Eight Years in Power: An American Tragedy*. New York: One World Publishing, 2017.
Cooper, Anna J. *A Voice from the South* (1892). Oxford: Oxford University Press, 1988.
Crawford, Vicki L, et al., eds. *Women in the Civil Rights Movement: Trailblazers and Torchbearers, 1941–1965*. Bloomington: Indiana University Press, 1993.
Crenshaw, Kimberlé. 'Mapping the Margins'. *Stanford Law Review* 43 (July 1991): 1241–99.
———. *On Intersectionality. Essential Writings*. New York: The New Press, 2019.
Ellison, Ralph. *Invisible Man*. New York: Vintage International, 1995.
Feimster, Crystal N. *Southern Horrors: Women and the Politics of Rape and Lynching*. Cambridge, MA: Harvard University Press, 2009.
Giddings, Paula J. *Ida: A Sword among Lions: Ida B. Wells and the Campaign Against Lynching*. New York: HarperCollins, 2009.
Gillon, Steven M. *Separate and Unequal: The Kerner Commission and the Unraveling of American Liberalism*. New York: Basic Books, 2018.
Gooding-Williams, Robert. *In the Shadow of Du Bois: Afro-Modern Political Thought in America*. Cambridge, MA: Harvard University Press, 2009.
Hughes, Langston. *The Big Sea*. New York: Hill and Wang, 1996.
King, Martin Luther, Jr. 'I Have a Dream'. Speech at Lincoln Memorial, Washington, DC, 28 August 1963.
———. *A Testament of Hope: The Essential Writings and Speeches*. Edited by James M. Washington. New York: HarperOne, 2003.
———. *Where Do We Go from Here: Chaos or Community?* Boston: Beacon Press, 1968.
———. *Why We Can't Wait*. New York: Harper & Row, 1964.
Morrison, Toni. *Beloved*. New York: Alfred A. Knopf, 2006.
———. *Playing in the Dark*. Cambridge, MA: Harvard University Press, 1992.
Painter, Nell Irvin. *The History of White People*. New York: Norton, 2011.
Ransby, Barbara. *Ella Baker and the Black Freedom Movement: A Radical Democratic Vision*. Chapel Hill: The University of North Carolina Press, 2005.
Richardson, Marilyn (ed). *Maria W. Stewart, America's First Black Woman Political Writer: Essays and Speeches*. Bloomington: Indiana University Press, 1987.
Robinson, Randall. *The Debt: What America Owes to Blacks*. New York: Dutton, 2000.
Truth, Sojourner. *Narrative of Sojourner Truth*. New York: Penguin, 1998.
Wells, Ida B. *The Light of Truth: Writings of an Anti-Lynching Crusader*. Edited by Mia Bay and Henry Louis Gates. New York: Penguin, 2014.

Williams, Patricia J. *The Alchemy of Race and Rights.* Cambridge, MA: Harvard University Press, 1992.

Wytsma, Ken. *The Myth of Equality: Uncovering the Roots of Injustice and Privilege.* Downers Grove, IL: IVP Books, 2017.

Suggested Documentaries and Films

Berry, Channsin D, and Bill Duke, dir. *Dark Girls.* 2012. DVD. Women open up about their experiences being dark, Black women in America. Overwhelmingly these interviews reveal the same thing: to them, Black is not beautiful.

Caouette, Mick, dir. *Mr. Civil Rights: Thurgood Marshall and the NAACP.* South Hill Films/PBS, 2014. DVD. For civil rights attorney Thurgood Marshall, the 1954 *Brown v. Board of Education* Supreme Court decision to desegregate America's public schools completed the final leg of a heroic journey to end legal segregation. Special Feature – A conversation with Supreme Court justices Elena Kagan and John Paul Stevens.

DuVernay, Ava, dir. *Selma.* Pathe, 2014. DVD. A chronicle of Dr Martin Luther King Jr's campaign to secure equal voting rights via an epic march from Selma to Montgomery, Alabama, in 1965.

DuVernay, Ava, dir. *The 13th.* Forward Movement, 2016. DVD. Documentary that provides an in-depth look at the prison system in the United States and reveals the nation's history of racial inequality.

Folayan, Sabaah, dir. *Whose Streets?* Magnolia Pictures, 2017. DVD. A documentary about the Ferguson uprising after the killing of unarmed teenager Michael Brown by the police.

Gates, Henry Louis Jr. *The African Americans: Many Rivers to Cross.* PBS, 2013. DVD. This Emmy Award–winning series explores Black identity and what it means to be an African American in the United States today.

Hampton, Henry. *Eyes on the Prize. PBS, 1987–1990.* DVD. This award-winning series covers all of the major events of the civil rights movement from 1954 to 1985.

Hudlin, Reginald, dir. *Marshall.* Starlight Media, 2017. DVD. 2017 film about a young Thurgood Marshall, the first African American Supreme Court Justice, as he battles through one of his career-defining cases.

Olsson, Goran, dir. *The Black Power Mixtape 1967–1975.* Annika Rogell, 2011. DVD. It tells the story of the Black Power Movement through the eyes of Swedish journalists. Drawn to America in the late 1960s by stories of revolution and urban unrest, the journalists recorded interviews with activists like Stokely Carmichael, Bobby Seale, Angela Davis and Eldridge Cleaver.

Parker, Alan, dir. *Mississippi Burning.* Orion Pictures, 1988. DVD. The film is the story of the murder of three activists in Mississippi during the Freedom Summer of 1964 to register African Americans to vote during the civil rights movements.

Peck, Raoul, dir. *I Am Not Your Negro.* Velvet Films, 2016. DVD. The documentary envisions the book James Baldwin never finished, a narration about race in America, using the writer's original words, as read by actor Samuel L Jackson.

Pollard, Samuel D, dir. *Slavery by Another Name.* PBS, 2012. DVD. The documentary explores how in the years following the Emancipation Proclamation, systematic approaches were taken to reenslave newly freed Blacks in the United States.

Rees, Dee, dir. *Mudbound.* Elevated Films, 2017. DVD. This 2017 film shines light on the daily cruelties in post–World War II Mississippi.

Reiner, Rob, dir. *The Ghosts of Mississippi.* Castle Rock Entertainment, 1996. DVD. The film is based on the true story of the 1994 trial of Byron De La Beckwith, the white supremacist accused of the 1963 assassination of civil rights activist Medgar Evers.

Stanley Jr, Nelson, dir. *Freedom Riders.* Laurens Grant, 2010. DVD. Based on Raymond Arsenault's book *Freedom Riders: 1961 and the Struggle for Racial Justice*, this documentary tells the story of the summer of 1961 when more than four hundred Black and white Americans risked their lives traveling together in the segregated South to protest segregation.

Maria Stewart[*], 'Lecture at Franklin Hall'

Why sit ye here and die? If we say we will go to a foreign land, the famine and the pestilence are there, and there we shall die. If we sit here, we shall die. Come let us plead our cause before the whites: if they save us alive, we shall live – and if they kill us, we shall but die.

Methinks I heard a spiritual interrogation – 'Who shall go forward, and take off the reproach that is cast upon the people of color? Shall it be a woman'? And my heart made this reply – 'If it is thy will, be it even so, Lord Jesus'!

I have heard much respecting the horrors of slavery; but may Heaven forbid that the generality of my color throughout these United States should experience any more of its horrors than to be a servant of servants, or hewers of wood and drawers of water! Tell us no more of southern slavery; for with few exceptions, although I may be very erroneous in my opinion, yet I consider our condition but little better than that. Yet, after all, methinks there are no chains so galling as the chains of ignorance – no fetters so binding as those that bind the soul and exclude it from the vast field of useful and scientific knowledge. O, had I received the advantages of early education, my ideas would, ere now, have expanded far and wide; but, alas! I possess nothing but moral capability – no teachings but the teachings of the Holy Spirit.

I have asked several individuals of my sex, who transact business for themselves, if providing our girls were to give them the most satisfactory references, they would not be willing to grant them an equal opportunity with others? Their reply has been – for their own part, they had no objection; but as it was not the custom, were they to take them into their employ, they would be in danger of losing the public patronage.

And such is the powerful force of prejudice. Let our girls possess what amiable qualities of soul they may; let their characters be fair and spotless as innocence itself; let their natural taste and ingenuity be what they may; it is impossible for scarce an individual of them to rise above the condition of servants. Ah! why is this cruel and unfeeling distinction? Is it merely because God has made our complexion to vary? If it be, O shame to soft, relenting humanity! 'Tell it not in Gath! publish it not in the streets of Askelon'! Yet, after all, methinks were the American free people of color to turn their attention more assiduously to moral worth and

---

[*] Maria Miller Stewart, 'Lecture at Franklin Hall' on 21 September, 1832, Boston, Massachusetts. http://voicesofdemocracy.umd.edu/stewart-lecture-delivered-speech-text/.

intellectual improvement, this would be the result: prejudice would gradually diminish, and the whites would be compelled to say, unloose those fetters!

> Though black their skins as shades of night,
> Their hearts are pure, their souls are white.

Few white persons of either sex, who are calculated for anything else, are willing to spend their lives and bury their talents in performing mean, servile labor. And such is the horrible idea that I entertain respecting a life of servitude, that if I conceived of there being no possibility of my rising above the condition of a servant, I would gladly hail death as a welcome messenger. O, horrible idea, indeed! to possess noble souls aspiring after high and honorable acquirements yet confined by the chains of ignorance and poverty to lives of continual drudgery and toil. Neither do I know of any who have enriched themselves by spending their lives as house-domestics, washing windows, shaking carpets, brushing boots, or tending upon gentlemen's tables. I can but die for expressing my sentiments; and I am as willing to die by the sword as the pestilence; for I am a true born American; your blood flows in my veins, and your spirit fires my breast.

I observed a piece in the *Liberator* a few months since, stating that the colonizationists had published a work respecting us, asserting that we were lazy and idle. I confute them on that point. Take us generally as a people, we are neither lazy nor idle; and considering how little we have to excite or stimulate us, I am almost astonished that there are so many industrious and ambitious ones to be found; although I acknowledge, with extreme sorrow, that there are some who never were and never will be serviceable to society. And have you not a similar class among yourselves?

Again. It was asserted that we were 'a ragged set, crying for liberty'. I reply to it, the whites have so long and so loudly proclaimed the theme of equal rights and privileges, that our souls have caught the flame also, ragged as we are. As far as our merit deserves, we feel a common desire to rise above the condition of servants and drudges. I have learnt, by bitter experience, that continual hard labor deadens the energies of the soul and benumbs the faculties of the mind; the ideas become confined, the mind barren, and, like the scorching sands of Arabia, produces nothing; or, like the uncultivated soil, brings forth thorns and thistles.

Again, continual hard labor irritates our tempers and sours our dispositions; the whole system becomes worn out with toil and fatigue; nature herself becomes almost exhausted, and we care but little whether we live or die. It is true, that the free people of color throughout these United States are neither bought nor sold, nor under the lash of the cruel driver; many obtain a comfortable support; but few, if any, have an opportunity of becoming rich and independent; and the employments we most pursue are as unprofitable to us as the spider's web or the floating bubbles that vanish into air. As servants, we are respected; but let us presume to aspire any higher, our employer regards us no longer. And were it not that the King eternal has declared that Ethiopia shall stretch forth her hands unto God, I should indeed despair.

I do not consider it derogatory, my friends, for persons to live out to service. There are many whose inclination leads them to aspire no higher; and I would highly commend the performance of almost anything for an honest livelihood; but where constitutional strength is wanting, labor of this kind, in its mildest form, is painful. And doubtless many are the prayers that have ascended to Heaven from Africa's daughters for strength to perform their work. Oh, many are the tears that have been shed for the want of that strength! Most of our color have dragged out a miserable existence of servitude from the cradle to the grave. And what literary acquirements can be made, or useful knowledge derived, from either maps, books or charts, by those who continually drudge from Monday morning until Sunday noon? O, ye fairer sisters, whose hands are never soiled, whose nerves and muscles are never strained, go learn by experience! Had we had the opportunity that you have had, to improve our moral and mental faculties, what would have hindered our intellects from being as bright, and our manners from being as dignified as yours? Had it been our lot to have been nursed in the lap of affluence and ease, and to have basked beneath the smiles and sunshine of fortune, should we not have naturally supposed that we were never made to toil? And why are not our forms as delicate, and our constitutions as slender, as yours? Is not the workmanship as curious and complete? Have pity upon us, have pity upon us, O ye who have hearts to feel for other's woes; for the hand of God has touched us. Owing to the disadvantages under which we labor, there are many flowers among us that are

> – born to bloom unseen,
> And waste their fragrance on the desert air.

My beloved brethren, as Christ has died in vain for those who will not accept of offered mercy, so will it be vain for the advocates of freedom to spend their breath in our behalf, unless with united hearts and souls you make some mighty efforts to raise your sons and daughters from the horrible state of servitude and degradation in which they are placed. It is upon you that woman depends; she can do but little besides using her influence; and it is for her sake and yours that I have come forward and made myself a hissing and a reproach among the people; for I am also one of the wretched and miserable daughters of the descendants of fallen Africa. Do you ask, why are you wretched and miserable? I reply, look at many of the most worthy and interesting of us doomed to spend our lives in gentlemen's kitchens. Look at our young men, smart, active and energetic, with souls filled with ambitious fire; if they look forward, alas! what are their prospects? They can be nothing but the humblest laborers, on account of their dark complexions; hence many of them lose their ambition, and become worthless. Look at our middle-aged men, clad in their rusty plaids and coats; in winter, every cent they earn goes to buy their wood and pay their rents; their poor wives also toil beyond their strength, to help support their families. Look at our aged sires, whose heads are whitened with the frosts of seventy winters, with their old wood-saws on their backs. Alas, what keeps us so? Prejudice, ignorance and poverty. But ah! methinks our oppression is soon to come to an end; yea, before the Majesty of heaven, our groans and cries have reached the ears of the Lord of Sabaoth. As the prayers and tears of Christians will avail the finally impenitent nothing; neither will the prayers and tears of the friends of humanity avail us any thing, unless we possess a spirit of virtuous emulation within our breasts. Did the pilgrims, when they first landed on these shores, quietly compose themselves, and say, 'the Britons have all the money and all the power, and we must continue their servants forever'? Did they sluggishly sigh and say, 'our lot is hard, the Indians own the soil, and we cannot cultivate it'? No; they first made powerful efforts to raise themselves, and then God raised up those illustrious patriots, WASHINGTON and LAFAYETTE, to assist and defend them. And, my brethren, have you made a powerful effort? Have you prayed the Legislature for mercy's sake to grant you all the rights and privileges of free citizens, that your daughters may rise to that degree of respectability which true merit deserves, and your sons above the servile situations which most of them fill?

Frederick Douglass[*], 'What to the Slave Is the Fourth of July?'

Fellow Citizens, I am not wanting [lacking] in respect for the fathers of this republic. The signers of the Declaration of Independence were brave men. They were great men, too great enough to give frame to a great age. It does not often happen to a nation to raise, at one time, such a number of truly great men. The point from which I am compelled to view them is not, certainly, the most favorable; and yet I cannot contemplate their great deeds with less than admiration. They were statesmen, patriots and heroes, and for the good they did, and the principles they contended for, I will unite with you to honor their memory. . . .

Fellow-citizens, pardon me, allow me to ask, why am I called upon to speak here today? What have I, or those I represent, to do with your national independence? Are the great principles of political freedom and of natural justice, embodied in that Declaration of Independence, extended to us? and am I, therefore, called upon to bring our humble offering to the national altar, and to confess the benefits and express devout gratitude for the blessings resulting from your independence to us?

Would to God, both for your sakes and ours, that an affirmative answer could be truthfully returned to these questions! Then would my task be light, and my burden easy and delightful. For who is there so cold, that a nation's sympathy could not warm him? Who so obdurate and dead to the claims of gratitude, that would not thankfully acknowledge such priceless benefits? Who so stolid and selfish, that would not give his voice to swell the hallelujahs of a nation's jubilee, when the chains of servitude had been torn from his limbs? I am not that man. In a case like that, the dumb might eloquently speak, and the 'lame man leap as an hart [deer]'.

But such is not the state of the case. I say it with a sad sense of the disparity between us I am not included within the pale of glorious anniversary! Your high independence only reveals the immeasurable distance between us. The blessings in which you, this day, rejoice, are not enjoyed in common. The rich inheritance of justice, liberty, prosperity and independence, bequeathed by your fathers, is shared by you, not by me. The sunlight that brought light and healing to you, has brought stripes and death to me. This Fourth July is yours, not mine. You may rejoice, I must mourn. To drag a man in fetters into the grand illuminated temple of liberty, and call upon him to join you in joyous anthems, were inhuman mockery and sacrilegious irony. Do you mean, citizens, to mock me, by asking me to speak to-day? If so, there is a parallel to your conduct. And let me warn you that it is dangerous to copy the example of a nation whose crimes, towering up to heaven, were thrown down by the breath of the Almighty, burying that nation in irrevocable ruin! I can to-day take up the plaintive lament of a peeled and woe-smitten people!

> By the rivers of Babylon, there we sat down. Yea! we wept when we remembered Zion. We hanged our harps upon the willows in the midst thereof. For there, they that carried us away captive, required of us a song; and they who wasted us required of us mirth, saying, Sing us one of the songs of Zion. How can we sing the Lord's song in a strange land? If I forget thee, O Jerusalem, let my right hand forget her cunning. If I do not remember thee, let my tongue cleave to the roof of my mouth.

Fellow-citizens, above your national, tumultuous joy, I hear the mournful wail of millions! whose chains, heavy and grievous yesterday, are, to-day, rendered more intolerable

---

[*] Frederick Douglass, 'What to the Slave Is the Fourth of July'? *The North Star*, July 5, 1852.

by the jubilee shouts that reach them. If I do forget, if I do not faithfully remember those bleeding children of sorrow this day, 'may my right hand forget her cunning, and may my tongue cleave to the roof of my mouth'! To forget them, to pass lightly over their wrongs, and to chime in with the popular theme, would be treason most scandalous and shocking, and would make me a reproach before God and the world. My subject, then, fellow-citizens, is American slavery. I shall this day and its popular characteristics from the slave's point of view. Standing there identified with the American bondman, making his wrongs mine, I do not hesitate to declare, with all my soul, that the character and conduct of this nation never looked blacker to me than on this 4th of July! Whether we turn to the declarations of the past, or to the professions of the present, the conduct of the nation seems equally hideous and revolting. America is false to the past, false to the present, and solemnly binds herself to be false to the future. Standing with God and the crushed and bleeding slave on this occasion, I will, in the name of humanity which is outraged, in the name of liberty which is fettered, in the name of the constitution and the Bible which are disregarded and trampled upon, dare to call in question and to denounce, with all the emphasis I can command, everything that serves to perpetuate slavery the great sin and shame of America! 'I will not equivocate; I will not excuse'; I will use the severest language I can command; and yet not one word shall escape me that any man, whose judgment is not blinded by prejudice, or who is not at heart a slaveholder, shall not confess to be right and just.

But I fancy I hear some one of my audience say, 'It is just in this circumstance that you and your brother abolitionists fail to make a favorable impression on the public mind. Would you argue more, and denounce less; would you persuade more, and rebuke less; your cause would be much more likely to succeed'. But, I submit, where all is plain there is nothing to be argued. What point in the anti-slavery creed would you have me argue? On what branch of the subject do the people of this country need light? Must I undertake to prove that the slave is a man? That point is conceded already. Nobody doubts it. The slaveholders themselves acknowledge it in the enactment of laws for their government. They acknowledge it when they punish disobedience on the part of the slave. There are seventy-two crimes in the State of Virginia which, if committed by a black man (no matter how ignorant he be), subject him to the punishment of death; while only two of the same crimes will subject a white man to the like punishment. What is this but the acknowledgement that the slave is a moral, intellectual, and responsible being? The manhood of the slave is conceded. It is admitted in the fact that Southern statute books are covered with enactments forbidding, under severe fines and penalties, the teaching of the slave to read or to write. When you can point to any such laws in reference to the beasts of the field, then I may consent to argue the manhood of the slave. When the dogs in your streets, when the fowls of the air, when the cattle on your hills, when the fish of the sea, and the reptiles that crawl, shall be unable to distinguish the slave from a brute, then will I argue with you that the slave is a man!

For the present, it is enough to affirm the equal manhood of the Negro race. Is it not astonishing that, while we are ploughing, planting, and reaping, using all kinds of mechanical tools, erecting houses, constructing bridges, building ships, working in metals of brass, iron, copper, silver and gold; that, while we are reading, writing and ciphering, acting as clerks, merchants and secretaries, having among us lawyers, doctors, ministers, poets, authors, editors, orators and teachers; that, while we are engaged in all manner of enterprises common to other men, digging gold in California, capturing the whale in the Pacific, feeding sheep and cattle on the hill-side, living, moving, acting, thinking, planning, living in families as husbands, wives and children, and, above all, confessing and worshipping the Christian's God, and looking hopefully for life and immortality beyond the grave, we are called upon to prove that we are men!

Would you have me argue that man is entitled to liberty? that he is the rightful owner of his own body? You have already declared it. Must I argue the wrongfulness of slavery? Is that a question for Republicans? Is it to be settled by the rules of logic and argumentation, as a matter beset with great difficulty, involving a doubtful application of the principle of justice, hard to be understood? How should I look to-day, in the presence of Americans, dividing, and subdividing a discourse, to show that men have a natural right to freedom? speaking of it relatively and positively, negatively and affirmatively. To do so, would be to make myself ridiculous, and to offer an insult to your understanding. There is not a man beneath the canopy of heaven that does not know that slavery is wrong for him.

What, am I to argue that it is wrong to make men brutes, to rob them of their liberty, to work them without wages, to keep them ignorant of their relations to their fellow men, to beat them with sticks, to flay their flesh with the lash, to load their limbs with irons, to hunt them with dogs, to sell them at auction, to sunder their families, to knock out their teeth, to burn their flesh, to starve them into obedience and submission to their masters? Must I argue that a system thus marked with blood, and stained with pollution, is wrong? No! I will not. I have better employment for my time and strength than such arguments would imply.

What, then, remains to be argued? Is it that slavery is not divine; that God did not establish it; that our doctors of divinity are mistaken? There is blasphemy in the thought. That which is inhuman, cannot be divine! Who can reason on such a proposition? They that can, may; I cannot. The time for such argument is passed.

At a time like this, scorching irony, not convincing argument, is needed. O! had I the ability, and could reach the nation's ear, I would, today, pour out a fiery stream of biting ridicule, blasting reproach, withering sarcasm, and stern rebuke. For it is not light that is needed, but fire; it is not the gentle shower, but thunder. We need the storm, the whirlwind, and the earthquake. The feeling of the nation must be quickened; the conscience of the nation must be roused; the propriety of the nation must be startled; the hypocrisy of the nation must be exposed; and its crimes against God and man must be proclaimed and denounced.

What, to the American slave, is your 4th of July? I answer; a day that reveals to him, more than all other days in the year, the gross injustice and cruelty to which he is the constant victim. To him, your celebration is a sham; your boasted liberty, an unholy license; your national greatness, swelling vanity; your sounds of rejoicing are empty and heartless; your denunciation of tyrants, brass fronted impudence; your shouts of liberty and equality, hollow mockery; your prayers and hymns, your sermons and thanksgivings, with all your religious parade and solemnity, are, to Him, mere bombast, fraud, deception, impiety, and hypocrisy – a thin veil to cover up crimes which would disgrace a nation of savages. There is not a nation on the earth guilty of practices more shocking and bloody than are the people of the United States, at this very hour.

Go where you may, search where you will, roam through all the monarchies and despotisms of the Old World, travel through South America, search out every abuse, and when you have found the last, lay your facts by the side of the everyday practices of this nation, and you will say with me, that, for revolting barbarity and shameless hypocrisy, America reigns without a rival. . . .

Allow me to say, in conclusion, notwithstanding the dark picture I have this day presented, of the state of the nation, I do not despair of this country. There are forces in operation which must inevitably work [i.e., bring about] the downfall of slavery. 'The arm of the

Lord is not shortened', and the doom of slavery is certain. I, therefore, leave off where I began, with hope. While drawing encouragement from 'the Declaration of Independence', the great principles it contains, and the genius of American Institutions, my spirit is also cheered by the obvious tendencies of the age. Nations do not now stand in the same relation to each other that they did ages ago. No nation can now shut itself up from the surrounding world and trot round in the same old path of its fathers without interference. The time was when such could be done. Long established customs of hurtful character could formerly fence themselves in, and do their evil work with social impunity. Knowledge was then confined and enjoyed by the privileged few, and the multitude walked on in mental darkness. But a change has now come over the affairs of mankind. Walled cities and empires have become unfashionable. The arm of commerce has borne away the gates of the strong city. Intelligence is penetrating the darkest corners of the globe. It makes its pathway over and under the sea, as well as on the earth. Wind, steam, and lightning are its chartered agents. Oceans no longer divide, but link nations together. From Boston to London is now a holiday excursion. Space is comparatively annihilated. Thoughts expressed on one side of the Atlantic are distinctly heard on the other.

The far off and almost fabulous [i.e., fabled] Pacific rolls in grandeur at our feet. The Celestial Empire, the mystery of ages, is being solved. The fiat of the Almighty, 'Let there be Light', has not yet spent its force. No abuse, no outrage whether in taste, sport or avarice, can now hide itself from the all-pervading light. The iron shoe, and crippled foot of China must be seen in contrast with nature. Africa must rise and put on her yet unwoven garment. 'Ethiopia shall stretch out her hand unto God'. In the fervent aspirations of William Lloyd Garrison, I say, and let every heart join in saying it:

> God speed the year of jubilee
> The wide world o'er!
> When from their galling chains set free,
> Th' oppress'd shall vilely bend the knee,
> And wear the yoke of tyranny
> Like brutes no more.
> That year will come, and freedom's reign,
> To man his plundered rights again
> Restore.
> God speed the day when human blood
> Shall cease to flow!
> In every clime be understood,
> The claims of human brotherhood,
> And each return for evil, good,
> Not blow for blow;
> That day will come all feuds to end,
> And change into a faithful friend
> Each foe.
> God speed the hour, the glorious hour,
> When none on earth
> Shall exercise a lordly power,
> Nor in a tyrant's presence cower;
> But to all manhood's stature tower,
> By equal birth!
> That hour will come, to each, to all,

And from his Prison-house, to thrall
Go forth.
Until that year, day, hour, arrive,
With head, and heart, and hand I'll strive,
To break the rod, and rend the gyve [shaclde],
The spoiler of his prey deprive –
So witness Heaven!
And never from my chosen post,
Whate'er the peril or the cost,
Be driven.

Ida B Wells*, 'A Red Record'

Not all nor nearly all of the murders done by white men, during the past thirty years in the South, have come to light, but the statistics as gathered and preserved by white men, and which have not been questioned, show that during these years more than ten thousand Negroes have been killed in cold blood, without the formality of judicial trial and legal execution. . . .

The first excuse given to the civilized world for the murder of unoffending Negroes was the necessity of the white man to repress and stamp out alleged 'race riots'. For years immediately succeeding the war there was an appalling slaughter of colored people, and the wires usually conveyed to northern people and the world the intelligence, first, that an insurrection was being planned by Negroes, which, a few hours later, would prove to have been vigorously resisted by white men, and controlled with a resulting loss of several killed and wounded. It was always a remarkable feature in these insurrections and riots that only Negroes were killed during the rioting, and that all the white men escaped unharmed. . . .

Then came the second excuse, which had its birth during the turbulent times of reconstruction. By an amendment to the Constitution the Negro was given the right of franchise, and, theoretically at least, his ballot became his invaluable emblem of citizenship. In a government 'of the people, for the people, and by the people', the Negro's vote became an important factor in all matters of state and national politics. But this did not last long. The southern white man would not consider that the Negro had any right which a white man was bound to respect, and the idea of a republican form of government in the southern states grew into general contempt. It was maintained that 'This is a white man's government', and regardless of numbers the white man should rule. 'No Negro domination' became the new legend on the sanguinary banner of the sunny South, and under it rode the Ku Klux Klan, the Regulators, and the lawless mobs, which for any cause chose to murder one man or a dozen as suited their purpose best. . . .

The white man's victory soon became complete by fraud, violence, intimidation and murder. The franchise vouchsafed to the Negro grew to be a 'barren ideality', and regardless of numbers, the colored people found themselves voiceless in the councils of those whose duty it was to rule. With no longer the fear of 'Negro Domination' before their eyes, the white man's second excuse became valueless. With the Southern governments all subverted and the Negro actually eliminated from all participation in state and national elections, there could be no longer an excuse for killing Negroes to prevent 'Negro Domination'.

* Ida B Wells, *A Red Record*, 1895. http://instruct.westvalley.edu/kelly/Distance_Learning/Online_Readings/Wells_Barnett.htm/.

Brutality still continued; Negroes were whipped, scourged, exiled, shot and hung whenever and wherever it pleased the white man so to treat them, and as the civilized world with increasing persistency held the white people of the South to account for its outlawry, the murderers invented the third excuse – that Negroes had to be killed to avenge their assaults upon women. There could be framed no possible excuse more harmful to the Negro and more unanswerable if true in its sufficiency for the white man. . . .

A word as to the charge itself. In considering the third reason assigned by the Southern white people for the butchery of blacks, the question must be asked, what the white man means when he charges the black man with rape. Does he mean the crime which the statutes of the civilized states describe as such? Not by any means. With the Southern white man, any mésalliance existing between a white woman and a colored man is a sufficient foundation for the charge of rape. The Southern white man says that it is impossible for a voluntary alliance to exist between a white woman and a colored man, and therefore, the fact of an alliance is a proof of force. In numerous instances where colored men have been lynched on the charge of rape, it was positively known at the time of lynching, and indisputable proven after the victim's death, that the relationship sustained between the man and woman was voluntary and clandestine, and that in no court of law could even the charge of assault have been successfully maintained.

During all the years of slavery, no such charge was ever made, not even during the dark days of the rebellion, when the white man, following the fortunes of war went to do battle for the maintenance of slavery. While the master was away fighting to forge the fetters upon the slave, he left his wife and children with no protectors save the Negroes themselves. And yet during those years of trust and peril, no Negro proved recreant to his trust and no white man returned to a home that had been despoiled.

Likewise, during the period of alleged 'insurrection', and alarming 'race riots', it never occurred to the white man that his wife and children were in danger of assault. Nor in the Reconstruction era, when the hue and cry was against 'Negro Domination' was there ever a thought that the domination would ever contaminate a fireside or strike toward the virtue of womanhood. It must appear strange indeed, to every thoughtful and candid man, that more than a quarter of a century elapsed before the Negro began to show signs of such infamous degeneration.

It is his regret, that, in his own defense, he must disclose to the world the degree of dehumanizing brutality which fixes upon America the blot of a national crime. Whatever faults and failings other nations may have in their dealing with their own subjects or with other people, no other civilized nation stands condemned before the world with a series of crimes so peculiarly national. It becomes a painful duty of the Negro to reproduce a record which shows that a large portion of the American people avow anarchy, condone murder and defy the contempt of civilization.

These pages are written in no spirit of vindictiveness, of all who give the subject consideration must concede that far too serious is the condition of that civilized government in which the spirit of unrestrained outlawry constantly increases in violence and casts its blight over a continually growing area of territory. We plead not for the colored people alone, but for all victims of the terrible injustice which puts men and women to death without form of law. During the year 1894, there were 132 persons executed in the United States by due form of law, while in the same year, 197 persons were put to death by mobs, who gave the victims no opportunity to make a lawful defense. No comment need be made upon a condition of public sentiment responsible for such alarming results. . . .

Ida B Wells*, 'Lynch Law in America'

Our country's national crime is lynching. It is not the creature of an hour, the sudden outburst of uncontrolled fury, or the unspeakable brutality of an insane mob. It represents the cool, calculating deliberation of intelligent people who openly avow that there is an 'unwritten law' that justifies them in putting human beings to death without complaint under oath, without trial by jury, without opportunity to make defense, and without right of appeal. The 'unwritten law' first found excuse with the rough, rugged, and determined man who left the civilized centers of eastern States to seek for quick returns in the gold-fields of the far West. Following in uncertain pursuit of continually eluding fortune, they dared the savagery of the Indians, the hardships of mountain travel, and the constant terror of border State outlaws.

Naturally, they felt slight toleration for traitors in their own ranks. It was enough to fight the enemies from without; woe to the foe within! Far removed from and entirely without protection of the courts of civilized life, these fortune-seekers made laws to meet their varying emergencies. The thief who stole a horse, the bully who 'jumped' a claim, was a common enemy. If caught he was promptly tried, and if found guilty was hanged to the tree under which the court convened.

Those were busy days of busy men. They had no time to give the prisoner a bill of exception or stay of execution. The only way a man had to secure a stay of execution was to behave himself. Judge Lynch was original in methods but exceedingly effective in procedure. He made the charge, impaneled the jurors, and directed the execution. When the court adjourned, the prisoner was dead. Thus lynch law held sway in the far West until civilization spread into the Territories and the orderly processes of law took its place. The emergency no longer existing, lynching gradually disappeared from the West.

But the spirit of mob procedure seemed to have fastened itself upon the lawless classes, and the grim process that at first was invoked to declare justice was made the excuse to wreak vengeance and cover crime. It next appeared in the South, where centuries of Anglo-Saxon civilization had made effective all the safeguards of court procedure. No emergency called for lynch law. It asserted its sway in defiance of law and in favor of anarchy. There it has flourished ever since, marking the thirty years of its existence with the inhuman butchery of more than ten thousand men, women, and children by shooting, drowning, hanging, and burning them alive. Not only this, but so potent is the force of example that the lynching mania has spread throughout the North and middle West. It is now no uncommon thing to read of lynchings north of Mason and Dixon's line, and those most responsible for this fashion gleefully point to these instances and assert that the North is no better than the South.

This is the work of the 'unwritten law' about which so much is said, and in whose behest butchery is made a pastime and national savagery condoned. The first statute of this 'unwritten law' was written in the blood of thousands of brave men who thought that a government that was good enough to create a citizenship was strong enough to protect it. Under the authority of a national law that gave every citizen the right to vote, the newly-made citizens chose to exercise their suffrage. But the reign of the national law was short-lived and illusionary. Hardly had the sentences dried upon the statute-books before one Southern State after another raised the cry against 'negro domination' and proclaimed there was an 'unwritten law' that justified any means to resist it.

---

* Ida B Wells, 'Lynch Law in America', speech in Chicago, IL, January 1900. http://www.sojust.net/speeches/ida_wells_lynch_law.html.

The method then inaugurated was the outrages by the 'red-shirt' bands of Louisiana, South Carolina, and other Southern States, which were succeeded by the Ku-Klux Klans. These advocates of the 'unwritten law' boldly avowed their purpose to intimidate, suppress, and nullify the negro's right to vote. In support of its plans the Ku-Klux Klans, the 'red-shirt' and similar organizations proceeded to beat, exile, and kill negroes until the purpose of their organization was accomplished and the supremacy of the 'unwritten law' was effected. Thus lynchings began in the South, rapidly spreading into the various States until the national law was nullified and the reign of the 'unwritten law' was supreme. Men were taken from their homes by 'red-shirt' bands and stripped, beaten, and exiled; others were assassinated when their political prominence made them obnoxious to their political opponents; while the Ku-Klux barbarism of election days, reveling in the butchery of thousands of colored voters, furnished records in Congressional investigations that are a disgrace to civilization.

The alleged menace of universal suffrage having been avoided by the absolute suppression of the negro vote, the spirit of mob murder should have been satisfied and the butchery of negroes should have ceased. But men, women, and children were the victims of murder by individuals and murder by mobs, just as they had been when killed at the demands of the 'unwritten law' to prevent 'negro domination'. Negroes were killed for disputing over terms of contracts with their employers. If a few barns were burned some colored man was killed to stop it. If a colored man resented the imposition of a white man and the two came to blows, the colored man had to die, either at the hands of the white man then and there or later at the hands of a mob that speedily gathered. If he showed a spirit of courageous manhood he was hanged for his pains, and the killing was justified by the declaration that he was a 'saucy nigger'. Colored women have been murdered because they refused to tell the mobs where relatives could be found for 'lynching bees'. Boys of fourteen years have been lynched by white representatives of American civilization. In fact, for all kinds of offenses – and, for no offenses – from murders to misdemeanors, men and women are put to death without judge or jury; so that, although the political excuse was no longer necessary, the wholesale murder of human beings went on just the same. A new name was given to the killings and a new excuse was invented for so doing.

Again the aid of the 'unwritten law' is invoked, and again it comes to the rescue. During the last ten years a new statute has been added to the 'unwritten law'. This statute proclaims that for certain crimes or alleged crimes no negro shall be allowed a trial; that no white woman shall be compelled to charge an assault under oath or to submit any such charge to the investigation of a court of law. The result is that many men have been put to death whose innocence was afterward established; and today, under this reign of the 'unwritten law'. no colored man, no matter what his reputation, is safe from lynching if a white woman, no matter what her standing or motive, cares to charge him with insult or assault.

It is considered a sufficient excuse and reasonable justification to put a prisoner to death under this 'unwritten law' for the frequently repeated charge that these lynching horrors are necessary to prevent crimes against women. The sentiment of the country has been appealed to, in describing the isolated condition of white families in thickly populated negro districts; and the charge is made that these homes are in as great danger as if they were surrounded by wild beasts. And the world has accepted this theory without let or hindrance. In many cases there has been open expression that the fate meted out to the victim was only what he deserved. In many other instances there has been a silence that says more forcibly than words can, proclaim it that it is right and proper that a human being should be seized by a mob and burned to death upon the unsworn and the uncorroborated charge of his accuser. No matter that our laws presume every man innocent until he is proved guilty; no matter that it leaves a certain class of individuals completely at the mercy of another class; no matter that it encourages those criminally disposed to blacken their faces and commit any crime in the calendar so long as they can throw suspicion on some negro, as is frequently done, and then lead a mob to take his life; no matter that mobs make a farce of the law and a mockery of justice; no matter that hundreds of boys are being hardened in crime and schooled in vice by the repetition of such scenes before their eyes – if a white woman declares herself insulted or assaulted, some life must pay the penalty, with all the horrors of the Spanish Inquisition and all the barbarism of the Middle Ages. The world looks on and says it is well.

Not only are two hundred men and women put to death annually, on the average, in this country by mobs, but these lives are taken with the greatest publicity. In many instances the leading citizens aid and abet by their presence when they do not participate, and the leading journals inflame the public mind to the lynching point with scare-head articles and offers of rewards. Whenever a burning is advertised to take place, the railroads run excursions, photographs are taken, and the same jubilee is indulged in that characterized the public hangings of one hundred years ago. There is, however, this difference: in those old days the multitude that stood by was permitted only to guy or jeer. The nineteenth century lynching mob cuts off ears, toes, and fingers, strips off flesh, and distributes portions of the body as souvenirs among the crowd. If the leaders of the mob are so minded, coal-oil is poured over the body and the victim is then roasted to death. This has been done in Texarkana and Paris, Tex., in Bardswell, Ky., and in Newman, Ga. In Paris the officers of the law delivered the prisoner to the mob. The mayor gave the school children a holiday and the railroads ran excursion trains so that the people might see a human being burned to death. In Texarkana, the year before, men and boys amused themselves by cutting off strips of flesh and thrusting knives into their helpless victim. At Newman, Ga., of the present year, the mob tried every conceivable torture to compel the victim to cry out and confess, before they set fire to the faggots that burned him. But their trouble was all in vain – he never uttered a cry, and they could not make him confess.

This condition of affairs were brutal enough and horrible enough if it were true that lynchings occurred only because of the commission of crimes against women – as is constantly declared by ministers, editors, lawyers, teachers, statesmen, and even by women themselves. It has been to the interest of those who did the lynching to blacken the good name of the helpless and defenseless victims of their hate. For this reason they publish at every possible opportunity this excuse for lynching, hoping thereby not only to palliate their own crime but at the same time to prove the negro a moral monster and unworthy of the respect and sympathy of the civilized world. But this alleged reason adds to the deliberate injustice of the mob's work. Instead of lynchings being caused by assaults upon women, the statistics show that not one-third of the victims of lynchings are even charged with such crimes. The *Chicago Tribune*, which publishes annually lynching statistics, is authority for the following:

In 1892, when lynching reached high-water mark, there were 241 persons lynched. The entire number is divided among the following States:

Alabama.................... 22
Arkansas.................... 25
California.................. 3
Florida...................... 11
Georgia.....................17

Idaho.......................... 8
Illinois........................ 1
Kansas........................ 3
Kentucky..................... 9
Louisiana.................... 29
Maryland..................... 1
Arizona Ter................. 3
Mississippi.................. 16
Montana..................... 4
New York................... 1
North Carolina............ 5
North Dakota.............. 1
Ohio........................... 3
South Carolina............ 5
Tennessee................... 28
Texas.......................... 15
Virginia......................7
West Virginia............. 5
Wyoming.......... 9
Missouri.......... 6
Oklahoma.......... 2

Of this number, 160 were of negro descent. Four of them were lynched in New York, Ohio, and Kansas; the remainder were murdered in the South. Five of this number were females. The charges for which they were lynched cover a wide range. They are as follows:

Rape................................... 46
Murder................................ 58
Rioting................................ 3
Race Prejudice.................... 6
No cause given....................4
Incendiarism....................... 6
Robbery............................... 6
Assault and battery............. 1
Attempted rape...................11
Suspected robbery.............. 4
Larceny...............................1
Self-defense........................ 1
Insulting women................. 2
Desperadoes........................ 6
Fraud................................... 1
Attempted murder.............. 2
No offense stated, boy and girl.......... 2

In the case of the boy and girl above referred to, their father, named Hastings, was accused of the murder of a white man. His fourteen-year-old daughter and sixteen-year-old son were hanged and their bodies filled with bullets; then the father was also lynched. This occurred in November, 1892, at Jonesville, La.

Indeed, the record for the last twenty years shows exactly the same or a smaller proportion who have been charged with this horrible crime. Quite a number of the one-third alleged cases of assault that have been personally investigated by the writer have shown that there was no foundation in fact for the charges; yet the claim is not made that there were no real culprits among them. The negro has been too long associated with the white man not to have copied his vices as well as his virtues. But the negro resents and utterly repudiates the efforts to blacken his good name by asserting that assaults upon women are peculiar to his race. The negro has suffered far more from the commission of this crime against the women of his race by white men than the white race has ever suffered through his crimes. Very scant notice is taken of the matter when this is the condition of affairs. What becomes a crime deserving capital punishment when the tables are turned is a matter of small moment when the negro woman is the accusing party.

But since the world has accepted this false and unjust statement, and the burden of proof has been placed upon the negro to vindicate his race, he is taking steps to do so. The Anti-Lynching Bureau of the National Afro-American Council is arranging to have every lynching investigated and publish the facts to the world, as has been done in the case of Sam Hose, who was burned alive last April at Newman, Ga. The detective's report showed that Hose killed Cranford, his employer, in self-defense, and that, while a mob was organizing to hunt Hose to punish him for killing a white man, not till twenty-four hours after the murder was the charge of rape, embellished with psychological and physical impossibilities, circulated. That gave an impetus to the hunt, and the Atlanta Constitution's reward of $500 keyed the mob to the necessary burning and roasting pitch. Of five hundred newspaper clippings of that horrible affair, nine-tenths of them assumed Hose's guilt – simply because his murderers said so, and because it is the fashion to believe the negro peculiarly addicted to this species of crime. All the negro asks is justice – a fair and impartial trial in the courts of the country. That given, he will abide the result.

But this question affects the entire American nation, and from several points of view: First, on the ground of consistency. Our watchword has been 'the land of the free and the home of the brave'. Brave men do not gather by thousands to torture and murder a single individual, so gagged and bound he cannot make even feeble resistance or defense. Neither do brave men or women stand by and see such things done without compunction of conscience, nor read of them without protest. Our nation has been active and outspoken in its endeavors to right the wrongs of the Armenian Christian, the Russian Jew, the Irish Home Ruler, the native women of India, the Siberian exile, and the Cuban patriot. Surely it should be the nation's duty to correct its own evils!

Second, on the ground of economy. To those who fail to be convinced from any other point of view touching this momentous question, a consideration of the economic phase might not be amiss. It is generally known that mobs in Louisiana, Colorado, Wyoming, and other States have lynched subjects of other countries. When their different governments demanded satisfaction, our country was forced to confess her inability to protect said subjects in the several States because of our State-rights doctrines, or in turn demand punishment of the lynchers. This confession, while humiliating in the extreme, was not satisfactory; and, while the United States cannot protect, she can pay. This she has done, and it is certain will have to do again in the case of the recent lynching of Italians in Louisiana. The United States already has paid in indemnities for lynching nearly a half million dollars, as follows:

Paid China for Rock Springs (Wyo) massacre – $147,748.74
Paid China for outrages on Pacific Coast – $276,619.75

Paid Italy for massacre of Italian prisoners at New Orleans – $24,330.90
Paid Italy for lynchings at Walsenburg, Col – $10,000.00
Paid Great Britain for outrages on James Bain and Frederick Dawson – $2,800.00

Third, for the honor of Anglo-Saxon civilization. No scoffer at our boasted American civilization could say anything more harsh of it than does the American white man himself who says he is unable to protect the honor of his women without resort to such brutal, inhuman, and degrading exhibitions as characterize 'lynching bees'. The cannibals of the South Sea Islands roast human beings alive to satisfy hunger. The red Indian of the Western plains tied his prisoner to the stake, tortured him, and danced in fiendish glee while his victim writhed in the flames. His savage, untutored mind suggested no better way than that of wreaking vengeance upon those who had wronged him. These people knew nothing about Christianity and did not profess to follow its teachings; but such primary laws as they had they lived up to. No nation, savage or civilized, save only the United States of America, has confessed its inability to protect its women save by hanging, shooting, and burning alleged offenders.

Finally, for love of country. No American travels abroad without blushing for shame for his country on this subject. And whatever the excuse that passes current in the United States, it avails nothing abroad. With all the powers of government in control; with all laws made by white men, administered by white judges, jurors, prosecuting attorneys, and sheriffs; with every office of the executive department filled by white men – no excuse can be offered for exchanging the orderly administration of justice for barbarous lynchings and 'unwritten laws'. Our country should be placed speedily above the plane of confessing herself a failure at self-government. This cannot be until Americans of every section, of broadest patriotism and best and wisest citizenship, not only see the defect in our country's armor but take the necessary steps to remedy it. Although lynchings have steadily increased in number and barbarity during the last twenty years, there has been no single effort put forth by the many moral and philanthropic forces of the country to put a stop to this wholesale slaughter. Indeed, the silence and seeming condonation grow more marked as the years go by.

A few months ago the conscience of this country was shocked because, after a two-weeks trial, a French judicial tribunal pronounced Captain Dreyfus guilty. And yet, in our own land and under our own flag, the writer can give day and detail of one thousand men, women, and children who during the last six years were put to death without trial before any tribunal on earth. Humiliating indeed, but altogether unanswerable, was the reply of the French press to our protest: 'Stop your lynchings at home before you send your protests abroad'.

W E B Du Bois*, 'How Does It Feel to Be a Problem'?

Between me and the other world there is ever an unasked question: unasked by some through feelings of delicacy; by others through the difficulty of rightly framing it. All, nevertheless, flutter round it. They approach me in a half-hesitant sort of way, eye me curiously or compassionately, and then, instead of saying directly, How does it feel to be a problem? they say, I know an excellent colored man in my town; or, I fought at Mechanicsville;[1] or, Do not these Southern outrages make your blood boil? At these I smile, or am interested, or reduce the boiling to a simmer, as the occasion may require. To the real question, How does it feel to be a problem? I answer seldom a word.

* W E B Du Bois, *The Souls of Black Folk* (Chicago: A C McClurg & Co, 1903), 1.

And yet, being a problem is a strange experience, – peculiar even for one who has never been anything else, save perhaps in babyhood and in Europe. It is in the early days of rollicking boyhood that the revelation first bursts upon one, all in a day, as it were. I remember well when the shadow swept across me. I was a little thing, away up in the hills of New England, where the dark Housatonic[2] winds between Hoosac and Taghkanic to the sea. In a wee wooden schoolhouse, something put it into the boys' and girls' heads to buy gorgeous visiting-cards – ten cents a package – and exchange. The exchange was merry, till one girl, a tall newcomer, refused my card, – refused it peremptorily, with a glance. Then it dawned upon me with a certain suddenness that I was different from the others; or like, mayhap, in heart and life and longing, but shut out from their world by a vast veil. I had thereafter no desire to tear down that veil, to creep through; I held all beyond it in common contempt, and lived above it in a region of blue sky and great wandering shadows. That sky was bluest when I could beat my mates at examination-time, or beat them at a foot-race, or even beat their stringy heads. Alas, with the years all this fine contempt began to fade; for the worlds I longed for, and all their dazzling opportunities, were theirs, not mine. But they should not keep these prizes, I said; some, all, I would wrest from them. Just how I would do it I could never decide: by reading law, by healing the sick, by telling the wonderful tales that swam in my head, – some way. With other black boys the strife was not so fiercely sunny: their youth shrunk into tasteless sycophancy, or into silent hatred of the pale world about them and mocking distrust of everything white; or wasted itself in a bitter cry, Why did God make me an outcast and a stranger in mine own house? The shades of the prison-house closed round about us all: walls strait and stubborn to the whitest, but relentlessly narrow, tall, and unscalable to sons of night who must plod darkly on in resignation, or beat unavailing palms against the stone, or steadily, half hopelessly, watch the streak of blue above.

After the Egyptian and Indian, the Greek and Roman, the Teuton and Mongolian, the Negro is a sort of seventh son,[3] born with a veil,[4] and gifted with second-sight in this American world, – a world which yields him no true self-consciousness, but only lets him see himself through the revelation of the other world. It is a peculiar sensation, this double-consciousness,[5] this sense of always looking at one's self through the eyes of others, of measuring one's soul by the tape of a world that looks on in amused contempt and pity. One ever feels his two-ness, – an American, a Negro; two souls, two thoughts, two unreconciled strivings; two warring ideals in one dark body, whose dogged strength alone keeps it from being torn asunder.

The history of the American Negro is the history of this strife, – this longing to attain self-conscious manhood, to merge his double self into a better and truer self. In this merging he wishes neither of the older selves to be lost. He would not Africanize America, for America has too much to teach the world and Africa. He would not bleach his Negro soul in a flood of white Americanism, for he knows that Negro blood has a message for the world. He simply wishes to make it possible for a man to be both a Negro and an American, without being cursed and spit upon by his fellows, without having the doors of Opportunity closed roughly in his face.

This, then, is the end of his striving: to be a co-worker in the kingdom of culture, to escape both death and isolation, to husband and use his best powers and his latent genius. These powers of body and mind have in the past been strangely wasted, dispersed, or forgotten. The shadow of a mighty Negro past flits through the tale of Ethiopia the Shadowy and of Egypt the Sphinx. Throughout history, the powers of single black men flash here and there like falling stars, and die sometimes before the world has rightly gauged their brightness. Here in America, in the few days since Emancipation, the black man's turning hither and thither in hesitant and doubtful striving has often made his very strength to lose effectiveness, to seem like absence of power, like weakness. And yet it is not weakness, – it is the contradiction of double aims. The double-aimed struggle of the black artisan – on the one hand to escape white contempt for a nation of mere hewers of wood and drawers of water, and on the other hand to plough and nail and dig for a poverty-stricken horde – could only result in making him a poor craftsman, for he had but half a heart in either cause. By the poverty and ignorance of his people, the Negro minister or doctor was tempted toward quackery and demagogy; and by the criticism of the other world, toward ideals that made him ashamed of his lowly tasks. The would-be black *savant* was confronted by the paradox that the knowledge his people needed was a twice-told tale to his white neighbors, while the knowledge which would teach the white world was Greek to his own flesh and blood. The innate love of harmony and beauty that set the ruder souls of his people a-dancing and a-singing raised but confusion and doubt in the soul of the black artist; for the beauty revealed to him was the soul-beauty of a race which his larger audience despised, and he could not articulate the message of another people. This waste of double aims, this seeking to satisfy two unreconciled ideals, has wrought sad havoc with the courage and faith and deeds of ten thousand thousand people, – has sent them often wooing false gods and invoking false means of salvation, and at times has even seemed about to make them ashamed of themselves.

Away back in the days of bondage they thought to see in one divine event the end of all doubt and disappointment; few men ever worshipped Freedom with half such unquestioning faith as did the American Negro for two centuries. To him, so far as he thought and dreamed, slavery was indeed the sum of all villainies, the cause of all sorrow, the root of all prejudice; Emancipation was the key to a promised land of sweeter beauty than ever stretched before the eyes of wearied Israelites.[6] In song and exhortation swelled one refrain – Liberty; in his tears and curses the God he implored had Freedom in his right hand. At last it came, – suddenly, fearfully, like a dream. With one wild carnival of blood and passion came the message in his own plaintive cadences: –

Shout, O children!
Shout, you're free!
For God has bought your liberty![7]

Years have passed away since then, – ten, twenty, forty; forty years of national life, forty years of renewal and development, and yet the swarthy spectre sits in its accustomed seat at the Nation's feast. In vain do we cry to this our vastest social problem: –

'Take any shape but that, and my firm nerves Shall never tremble'![8]

The Nation has not yet found peace from its sins; the freedman has not yet found in freedom his promised land. Whatever of good may have come in these years of change, the shadow of a deep disappointment rests upon the Negro people, – a disappointment all the more bitter because the unattained ideal was unbounded save by the simple ignorance of a lowly people.

The first decade was merely a prolongation of the vain search for freedom, the boon that seemed ever barely to elude their grasp, – like a tantalizing will-o'-the-wisp, maddening and misleading the headless host. The holocaust of war, the terrors of the Ku-Klux Klan,[9] the lies of carpetbaggers,[10] the disorganization of industry, and the contradictory advice of friends and foes, left the bewildered serf with no new watchword beyond the old cry for freedom. As the time flew, however, he began to grasp a new idea. The ideal of liberty demanded for its attainment powerful means, and these the Fifteenth Amendment gave him.[11] The ballot, which before he had looked upon as a visible sign of freedom, he now regarded as the chief means of gaining and perfecting the liberty with which war had partially endowed him. And why not? Had not votes made war and emancipated millions? Had not votes enfranchised the freedmen? Was anything impossible to a power that had done all this? A million black men started with renewed zeal to vote themselves into the kingdom. So the decade flew away, the revolution of 1876 came,[12] and left the half-free serf weary, wondering, but still inspired. Slowly but steadily, in the following years, a new vision began gradually to replace the dream of political power, – a powerful movement, the rise of another ideal to guide the unguided, another pillar of fire by night after a clouded day. It was the ideal of 'book-learning'; the curiosity, born of compulsory ignorance, to know and test the power of the cabalistic letters of the white man, the longing to know. Here at last seemed to have been discovered the mountain path to Canaan; longer than the highway of Emancipation and law, steep and rugged, but straight, leading to heights high enough to overlook life.

Up the new path the advance guard toiled, slowly, heavily, doggedly; only those who have watched and guided the faltering feet, the misty minds, the dull understandings, of the dark pupils of these schools know how faithfully, how piteously, this people strove to learn. It was weary work. The cold statistician wrote down the inches of progress here and there, noted also where here and there a foot had slipped or someone had fallen. To the tired climbers, the horizon was ever dark, the mists were often cold, the Canaan was always dim and far away. If, however, the vistas disclosed as yet no goal, no resting-place, little but flattery and criticism, the journey at least gave leisure for reflection and self-examination; it changed the child of Emancipation to the youth with dawning self-consciousness, self-realization, self-respect. In those somber forests of his striving his own soul rose before him, and he saw himself, – darkly as through a veil; and yet he saw in himself some faint revelation of his power, of his mission. He began to have a dim feeling that, to attain his place in the world, he must be himself, and not another. For the first time he sought to analyze the burden he bore upon his back, that dead-weight of social degradation partially masked behind a half-named Negro problem. He felt his poverty; without a cent, without a home, without land, tools, or savings, he had entered into competition with rich, landed, skilled neighbors. To be a poor man is hard, but to be a poor race in a land of dollars is the very bottom of hardships. He felt the weight of his ignorance, – not simply of letters, but of life, of business, of the humanities; the accumulated sloth and shirking and awkwardness of decades and centuries shackled his hands and feet. Nor was his burden all poverty and ignorance. The red stain of bastardy, which two centuries of systematic legal defilement of Negro women had stamped upon his race, meant not only the loss of ancient African chastity, but also the hereditary weight of a mass of corruption from white adulterers, threatening almost the obliteration of the Negro home.

A people thus handicapped ought not to be asked to race with the world, but rather allowed to give all its time and thought to its own social problems. But alas! while sociologists gleefully count his bastards and his prostitutes, the very soul of the toiling, sweating black man is darkened by the shadow of a vast despair. Men call the shadow prejudice, and learnedly explain it as the natural defense of culture against barbarism, learning against ignorance, purity against crime, the 'higher' against the 'lower' races. To which the Negro cries Amen! and swears that to so much of this strange prejudice as is founded on just homage to civilization, culture, righteousness, and progress, he humbly bows and meekly does obeisance. But before that nameless prejudice that leaps beyond all this he stands helpless, dismayed, and well-nigh speechless; before that personal disrespect and mockery, the ridicule and systematic humiliation, the distortion of fact and wanton license of fancy, the cynical ignoring of the better and the boisterous welcoming of the worse, the all-pervading desire to inculcate disdain for everything black, from Toussaint[13] to the devil, – before this there rises a sickening despair that would disarm and discourage any nation save that black host to whom 'discouragement' is an unwritten word.

But the facing of so vast a prejudice could not but bring the inevitable self-questioning, self-disparagement, and lowering of ideals which ever accompany repression and breed in an atmosphere of contempt and hate. Whisperings and portents came borne upon the four winds: Lo! we are diseased and dying, cried the dark hosts; we cannot write, our voting is vain; what need of education, since we must always cook and serve? And the Nation echoed and enforced this self-criticism, saying: Be content to be servants, and nothing more; what need of higher culture for half-men? Away with the black man's ballot, by force or fraud, – and behold the suicide of a race! Nevertheless, out of the evil came something of good, – the more careful adjustment of education to real life, the clearer perception of the Negroes' social responsibilities, and the sobering realization of the meaning of progress.

So dawned the time of *Sturm und Drang*: storm and stress to-day rocks our little boat on the mad waters of the world-sea; there is within and without the sound of conflict, the burning of body and rending of soul; inspiration strives with doubt, and faith with vain questionings. The bright ideals of the past, – physical freedom, political power, the training of brains and the training of hands, – all these in turn have waxed and waned, until even the last grows dim and overcast. Are they all wrong, – all false? No, not that, but each alone was over-simple and incomplete, – the dreams of a credulous race-childhood, or the fond imaginings of the other world which does not know and does not want to know our power. To be really true, all these ideals must be melted and welded into one. The training of the schools we need to-day more than ever, – the training of deft hands, quick eyes and ears, and above all the broader, deeper, higher culture of gifted minds and pure hearts. The power of the ballot we need in sheer self-defence, – else what shall save us from a second slavery? Freedom, too, the long-sought, we still seek, – the freedom of life and limb, the freedom to work and think, the freedom to love and aspire. Work, culture, liberty, – all these we need, not singly but together, not successively but together, each growing and aiding each, and all striving toward that vaster ideal that swims before the Negro people, the ideal of human brotherhood, gained through the unifying ideal of Race; the ideal of fostering and developing the traits and talents of the Negro, not in opposition to or contempt for other races, but rather in large conformity to the greater ideals of the American Republic, in order that someday on American soil two world-races may give each to each those characteristics both so sadly lack. We the darker ones come even now not altogether empty-handed: there are to-day no truer exponents of the pure human spirit of the Declaration of Independence than the American Negroes; there is no true American music but the wild sweet melodies of the Negro slave; the American fairy tales and folk-lore are Indian and African; and, all in all, we black men seem the sole oasis of simple faith and reverence in a dusty desert of dollars and smartness. Will America be poorer if she replaces her brutal dyspeptic blundering with light-hearted but determined Negro humility? or her coarse and cruel wit with loving jovial good-humor? or her vulgar music with the soul of the Sorrow Songs?

Merely a concrete test of the underlying principles of the great republic is the Negro Problem, and the spiritual striving of the freedmen's sons is the travail of souls whose burden is almost beyond the measure of their strength, but who bear it in the name of an historic race, in the name of this the land of their fathers' fathers, and in the name of human opportunity.

. . .

The problem of the twentieth century is the problem of the color-line, – the relation of the darker to the lighter races of men in Asia and Africa, in America and the islands of the sea. It was a phase of this problem that caused the Civil War; and however much they who marched South and North in 1861 may have fixed on the technical points of union and local autonomy as a shibboleth, all nevertheless knew, as we know, that the question of Negro slavery was the real cause of the conflict. Curious it was, too, how this deeper question ever forced itself to the surface despite effort and disclaimer. No sooner had Northern armies touched Southern soil than this old question, newly guised, sprang from the earth, – What shall be done with Negroes? Peremptory military commands, this way and that, could not answer the query; the Emancipation Proclamation seemed but to broaden and intensify the difficulties; and the War Amendments made the Negro problems of to-day.

Notes

1. Mechanicsville was a Civil War battle fought on June 26, 1862, just east of Richmond, Virginia.
2. Housatonic is the river that flows through Great Barrington, Massachusetts.
3. The figure of the seventh son carries multiple meanings. Apparently revising Hegel's philosophy of history, Du Bois adds the Negro to Hegel's story of six world-historical peoples. In African American folklore, the seventh son is said to be distinguished in some way, to be able to see ghosts, and to make a good doctor.
4. In African American folklore, a child born with a caul, a veil-like membrane that sometimes covers the head at birth, is said to be lucky, to be able to tell fortunes and to be a 'double-sighted' seer of ghosts. In some West African folk traditions, a child born with a caul is thought to possess a special personality endowed with spiritual potency.
5. Du Bois in this passage echoes the most prominent philosophers and poets writing in the European romantic tradition (such as William Blake, Samuel Taylor Coleridge, Friedrich Schiller and Georg Wilhelm Friedrich Hegel) by promoting the creation of a unified self that synthesises and preserves diverse elements. Though the American Negro was captured in Africa and forced into slavery in America, he knows no nostalgia for an African 'self' that was untainted by the experience of America. Rather, his is a quest for a better, truer, and more encompassing self, the search for a mode of integrity that merges his African and newly acquired American identities yet retains them as distinct.
6. Du Bois envisions blacks in America as the Old Testament Jews (Israelites) who have yet to escape the land of their captivity (Egypt) and enter the promised land (Canaan).
7. From the Negro spiritual 'Shout, O Children'!
8. Shakespeare, *Macbeth*, 3.4.102–3.
9. The Ku Klux Klan is the white fraternal terrorist organisation created in 1866 by Confederate veterans in Pulaski, Tennessee. Its members altered the Greek word for 'circle', *kuklos*, and invented their name. During Reconstruction in the South, the Klan engaged in widespread violence against blacks and their white Republican supporters.
10. Carpetbaggers were northern politicians and businessmen who moved to the South after the Civil War, allegedly to exploit the devastation of the South and the political vacuum left by the defeat of the Confederacy.
11. The Fifteenth Amendment to the US Constitution passed Congress in February 1869 and was ratified by the states in March 1870. It provided that voting rights 'shall not be denied . . . on account of race, color, or previous condition of servitude'.

12. In the disputed presidential election of 1876, Republican Rutherford B Hayes defeated Democrat Samuel Tilden. In three southern states – Louisiana, Florida and South Carolina – the voting returns were disputed, with fraud and intimidation charged by both sides. The election was settled by a congressional committee that declared Hayes the winner in the three contested states as well as by a political compromise (known as the Compromise of 1877).
13. Toussaint was the leader of the Haitian independence movement during the French Revolution.

W E B Du Bois*, 'The Souls of White Folk'

High in the tower, where I sit above the loud complaining of the human sea, I know many souls that toss and whirl and pass, but none there are that intrigue me more than the Souls of White Folk.

Of them I am singularly clairvoyant. I see in and through them. I view them from unusual points of vantage. Not as a foreigner do I come, for I am native, not foreign, bone of their thought and flesh of their language. Mine is not the knowledge of the traveler or the colonial composite of dear memories, words and wonder. Nor yet is my knowledge that which servants have of masters, or mass of class, or capitalist of artisan. Rather I see these souls undressed and from the back and side. I see the working of their entrails. I know their thoughts and they know that I know. This knowledge makes them now embarrassed, now furious! They deny my right to live and be and call me misbirth! My word is to them mere bitterness and my soul, pessimism. And yet as they preach and strut and shout and threaten, crouching as they clutch at rags of facts and fancies to hide their nakedness, they go twisting, flying by my tired eyes and I see them ever stripped, – ugly, human.

The discovery of personal whiteness among the world's peoples is a very modern thing, – a nineteenth and twentieth century matter, indeed. The ancient world would have laughed at such a distinction. The Middle Age regarded skin color with mild curiosity; and even up into the eighteenth century we were hammering our national manikins into one, great, Universal Man, with fine frenzy which ignored color and race even more than birth. Today we have changed all that, and the world in a sudden, emotional conversion has discovered that it is white and by that token, wonderful!

This assumption that of all the hues of God whiteness alone is inherently and obviously better than brownness or tan leads to curious acts; even the sweeter souls of the dominant world as they discourse with me on weather, weal, and woe are continually playing above their actual words an obligation of tune and tone, saying:

> 'My poor, un-white thing! Weep not nor rage. I know, too well, that the curse of God lies heavy on you. Why? That is not for me to say, but be brave! Do your work in your lowly sphere, praying the good Lord that into heaven above, where all is love, you may, one day, be born – white'!

I do not laugh. I am quite straight-faced as I ask soberly:

> 'But what on earth is whiteness that one should so desire it'? Then always, somehow, some way, silently but clearly, I am given to understand that whiteness is the ownership of the earth forever and ever, Amen!

---

* W E B Du Bois, *Darkwater* (New York: Harcourt, Brace and Company, 1920), chapter 2.

Now what is the effect on a man or a nation when it comes passionately to believe such an extraordinary dictum as this? That nations are coming to believe it is manifest daily. Wave on wave, each with increasing virulence, is dashing this new religion of whiteness on the shores of our time. Its first effects are funny: the strut of the Southerner, the arrogance of the Englishman amuck, the whoop of the hoodlum who vicariously leads your mob. Next it appears dampening generous enthusiasm in what we once counted glorious; to free the slave is discovered to be tolerable only in so far as it freed his master! Do we sense somnolent writhings in black Africa or angry groans in India or triumphant banzais in Japan? 'To your tents, O Israel'! These nations are not white!

After the more comic manifestations and the chilling of generous enthusiasm come subtler, darker deeds. Everything considered, the title to the universe claimed by White Folk is faulty. It ought, at least, to look plausible. How easy, then, by emphasis and omission to make children believe that every great soul the world ever saw was a white man's soul; that every great thought the world ever knew was a white man's thought; that every great deed the world ever did was a white man's deed; that every great dream the world ever sang was a white man's dream. In fine, that if from the world were dropped everything that could not fairly be attributed to White Folk, the world would, if anything, be even greater, truer, better than now. And if all this be a lie, is it not a lie in a great cause?

Here it is that the comedy verges to tragedy. The first minor note is struck, all unconsciously, by those worthy souls in whom consciousness of high descent brings burning desire to spread the gift abroad, – the obligation of nobility to the ignoble. Such sense of duty assumes two things: a real possession of the heritage and its frank appreciation by the humble-born. So long, then, as humble black folk, voluble with thanks, receive barrels of old clothes from lordly and generous whites, there is much mental peace and moral satisfaction. But when the black man begins to dispute the white man's title to certain alleged bequests of the Fathers in wage and position, authority and training; and when his attitude toward charity is sullen anger rather than humble jollity; when he insists on his human right to swagger and swear and waste, – then the spell is suddenly broken and the philanthropist is ready to believe that Negroes are impudent, that the South is right, and that Japan wants to fight America.

After this the descent to Hell is easy. On the pale, white faces which the great billows whirl upward to my tower I see again and again, often and still more often, a writing of human hatred, a deep and passionate hatred, vast by the very vagueness of its expressions. Down through the green waters, on the bottom of the world, where men move to and fro, I have seen a man – an educated gentleman – grow livid with anger because a little, silent, black woman was sitting by herself in a Pullman car. He was a white man. I have seen a great, grown man curse a little child, who had wandered into the wrong waiting-room, searching for its mother: 'Here, you damned black – – – ' He was white. In Central Park I have seen the upper lip of a quiet, peaceful man curl back in a tigerish snarl of rage because black folk rode by in a motor car. He was a white man. We have seen, you and I, city after city drunk and furious with ungovernable lust of blood; mad with murder, destroying, killing, and cursing; torturing human victims because somebody accused of crime happened to be of the same color as the mob's innocent victims and because that color was not white! We have seen, – Merciful God! in these wild days and in the name of Civilization, Justice, and Motherhood, – what have we not seen, right here in America, of orgy, cruelty, barbarism, and murder done to men and women of Negro descent.

Up through the foam of green and weltering waters wells this great mass of hatred, in wilder, fiercer violence, until I look down and know that today to the millions of my people no misfortune could happen, – of death and pestilence, failure and defeat – that would not make the hearts of millions of their fellows beat with fierce, vindictive joy! Do you doubt it? Ask your own soul what it would say if the next census were to report that half of black America was dead and the other half dying.

Unfortunate? Unfortunate. But where is the misfortune? Mine? Am I, in my blackness, the sole sufferer? I suffer. And yet, somehow, above the suffering, above the shackled anger that beats the bars, above the hurt that crazes there surges in me a vast pity, – pity for a people imprisoned and enthralled, hampered and made miserable for such a cause, for such a phantasy!

Conceive this nation, of all human peoples, engaged in a crusade to make the 'World Safe for Democracy'! Can you imagine the United States protesting against Turkish atrocities in Armenia, while the Turks are silent about mobs in Chicago and St. Louis; what is Louvain compared with Memphis, Waco, Washington, Dyersburg, and Estill Springs? In short, what is the black man but America's Belgium, and how could America condemn in Germany that which she commits, just as brutally, within her own borders?

A true and worthy ideal frees and uplifts a people; a false ideal imprisons and lowers. Say to men, earnestly and repeatedly: 'Honesty is best, knowledge is power; do unto others as you would be done by'. Say this and act it and the nation must move toward it, if not to it. But say to a people: 'The one virtue is to be white', and the people rush to the inevitable conclusion, 'Kill the "nigger"'!

Is not this the record of present America? Is not this its headlong progress? Are we not coming more and more, day by day, to making the statement 'I am white', the one fundamental tenet of our practical morality? Only when this basic, iron rule is involved is our defense of right nation-wide and prompt. Murder may swagger, theft may rule and prostitution may flourish and the nation gives but spasmodic, intermittent and lukewarm attention. But let the murderer be black or the thief brown or the violator of womanhood have a drop of Negro blood, and the righteousness of the indignation sweeps the world. Nor would this fact make the indignation less justifiable did not we all know that it was blackness that was condemned and not crime.

In the awful cataclysm of World War, where from beating, slandering, and murdering us the white world turned temporarily aside to kill each other, we of the Darker Peoples looked on in mild amaze.

Among some of us, I doubt not, this sudden descent of Europe into hell brought unbounded surprise; to others, over wide area, it brought the *Schadenfreude*[1] of the bitterly hurt; but most of us, I judge, looked on silently and sorrowfully, in sober thought, seeing sadly the prophecy of our own souls.

Here is a civilization that has boasted much. Neither Roman nor Arab, Greek nor Egyptian, Persian nor Mongol ever took himself and his own perfectness with such disconcerting seriousness as the modern white man. We whose shame, humiliation, and deep insult his aggrandizement so often involved were never deceived. We looked at him clearly, with world-old eyes, and saw simply a human thing, weak and pitiable and cruel, even as we are and were.

These super-men and world-mastering demi-gods listened, however, to no low tongues of ours, even when we pointed silently to their feet of clay. Perhaps we, as folk of simpler soul and more primitive type, have been most struck in the welter of recent years by the utter failure of white religion. We have curled our lips in something like contempt as we have witnessed glib apology and weary explanation. Nothing of the sort deceived us. A nation's religion is its life, and as such white Christianity is a miserable failure.

Nor would we be unfair in this criticism: We know that we, too, have failed, as you have, and have rejected many a Buddha, even as you have denied Christ; but we acknowledge our human frailty, while you, claiming super-humanity, scoff endlessly at our shortcomings.

The number of white individuals who are practicing with even reasonable approximation the democracy and unselfishness of Jesus Christ is so small and unimportant as to be fit subject for jest in Sunday supplements and in *Punch*, *Life*, *Le Rire*, and *Fliegende Blätter*. In her foreign mission work the extraordinary self-deception of white religion is epitomized: solemnly the white world sends five million dollars worth of missionary propaganda to Africa each year and in the same twelve months adds twenty-five million dollars worth of the vilest gin manufactured. Peace to the augurs of Rome!

We may, however, grant without argument that religious ideals have always far outrun their very human devotees. Let us, then, turn to more mundane matters of honor and fairness. The world today is trade. The world has turned shopkeeper; history is economic history; living is earning a living. Is it necessary to ask how much of high emprise and honorable conduct has been found here? Something, to be sure. The establishment of world credit systems is built on splendid and realizable faith in fellow-men. But it is, after all, so low and elementary a step that sometimes it looks merely like honor among thieves, for the revelations of highway robbery and low cheating in the business world and in all its great modern centers have raised in the hearts of all true men in our day an exceeding great cry for revolution in our basic methods and conceptions of industry and commerce.

We do not, for a moment, forget the robbery of other times and races when trade was a most uncertain gamble; but was there not a certain honesty and frankness in the evil that argued a saner morality? There are more merchants today, surer deliveries, and wider well-being, but are there not, also, bigger thieves, deeper injustice, and more calloused selfishness in well-being? Be that as it may, – certainly the nicer sense of honor that has risen ever and again in groups of forward-thinking men has been curiously and broadly blunted. Consider our chiefest industry, – fighting. Laboriously the Middle Ages built its rules of fairness – equal armament, equal notice, equal conditions. What do we see today? Machine-guns against assegais; conquest sugared with religion; mutilation and rape masquerading as culture, – all this, with vast applause at the superiority of white over black soldiers!

War is horrible! This the dark world knows to its awful cost. But has it just become horrible, in these last days, when under essentially equal conditions, equal armament, and equal waste of wealth white men are fighting white men, with surgeons and nurses hovering near?

Think of the wars through which we have lived in the last decade: in German Africa, in British Nigeria, in French and Spanish Morocco, in China, in Persia, in the Balkans, in Tripoli, in Mexico, and in a dozen lesser places – were not these horrible, too? Mind you, there were for most of these wars no Red Cross funds.

Behold little Belgium and her pitiable plight, but has the world forgotten Congo? What Belgium now suffers is not half, not even a tenth, of what she has done to black Congo since Stanley's great dream of 1880. Down the dark forests of inmost Africa sailed this modern Sir Galahad, in the name of 'the noble-minded men of several nations', to introduce commerce and civilization. What came of it? 'Rubber and murder, slavery in its worst form', wrote Glave in 1895.

Harris declares that King Leopold's régime meant the death of twelve million natives, 'but what we who were behind the scenes felt most keenly was the fact that the real catastrophe in the Congo was desolation and murder in the larger sense. The invasion of family life, the ruthless destruction of every social barrier, the shattering of every tribal law, the introduction of criminal practices which struck the chiefs of the people dumb with horror – in a word, a veritable avalanche of filth and immorality overwhelmed the Congo tribes'.

Yet the fields of Belgium laughed, the cities were gay, art and science flourished; the groans that helped to nourish this civilization fell on deaf ears because the world round about was doing the same sort of thing elsewhere on its own account.

As we saw the dead dimly through rifts of battle-smoke and heard faintly the cursings and accusations of blood brothers, we darker men said: This is not Europe gone mad; this is not aberration nor insanity; this *is* Europe; this seeming Terrible is the real soul of white culture – back of all culture, – stripped and visible today. This is where the world has arrived, – these dark and awful depths and not the shining and ineffable heights of which it boasted. Here is whither the might and energy of modern humanity has really gone.

But may not the world cry back at us and ask: 'What better thing have you to show? What have you done or would do better than this if you had today the world rule? Paint with all riot of hateful colors the thin skin of European culture, – is it not better than any culture that arose in Africa or Asia'?

It is. Of this there is no doubt and never has been; but why is it better? Is it better because Europeans are better, nobler, greater, and more gifted than other folk? It is not. Europe has never produced and never will in our day bring forth a single human soul who cannot be matched and over-matched in every line of human endeavor by Asia and Africa. Run the gamut, if you will, and let us have the Europeans who in sober truth over-match Nefertari, Mohammed, Rameses and Askia, Confucius, Buddha, and Jesus Christ. If we could scan the calendar of thousands of lesser men, in like comparison, the result would be the same; but we cannot do this because of the deliberately educated ignorance of white schools by which they remember Napoleon and forget Sonni Ali.

The greatness of Europe has lain in the width of the stage on which she has played her part, the strength of the foundations on which she has built and a natural, human ability no whit greater (if as great) than that of other days and races. In other words, the deeper reasons for the triumph of European civilization lie quite outside and beyond Europe, – back in the universal struggles of all mankind.

Why, then, is Europe great? Because of the foundations which the mighty past have furnished her to build upon: the iron trade of ancient, black Africa, the religion and empire-building of yellow Asia, the art and science of the 'dago' Mediterranean shore, east, south, and west, as well as north. And where she has built securely upon this great past and learned from it she has gone forward to greater and more splendid human triumph; but where she has ignored this past and forgotten and sneered at it, she has shown the cloven hoof of poor, crucified humanity, – she has played, like other empires gone, the world fool!

If, then, European triumphs in culture have been greater, so, too, may her failures have been greater. How great a failure and a failure in what does the World War betoken? Was it national jealousy of the sort of the seventeenth century? But Europe has done more to break down national barriers than any preceding culture. Was it fear of the balance of power in Europe? Hardly, save in the half-Asiatic problems of the Balkans. What, then, does Hauptmann mean when he says: 'Our jealous enemies forged an iron ring about our breasts and we knew our breasts had to expand, – that we had to split asunder this ring or else we had to cease breathing. But Germany will not cease to breathe and so it came to pass that the iron ring was forced apart'.

Whither is this expansion? What is that breath of life, thought to be so indispensable to a great European nation? Manifestly it is expansion overseas; it is colonial aggrandizement which explains, and alone adequately explains, the World War. How many of us today fully realize the current theory of colonial expansion, of the relation of Europe which is white, to the world which is black and brown and yellow? Bluntly put, that theory is this: It is the duty of white Europe to divide up the darker world and administer it for Europe's good.

This Europe has largely done. The European world is using black and brown men for all the uses which men know. Slowly but surely white culture is evolving the theory that 'darkies' are born beasts of burden for white folk. It were silly to think otherwise, cries the cultured world, with stronger and shriller accord. The supporting arguments grow and twist themselves in the mouths of merchant, scientist, soldier, traveler, writer, and missionary: Darker peoples are dark in mind as well as in body; of dark, uncertain, and imperfect descent; of frailer, cheaper stuff; they are cowards in the face of mausers and maxims; they have no feelings, aspirations, and loves; they are fools, illogical idiots, – 'half-devil and half-child'.

Such as they are civilization must, naturally, raise them, but soberly and in limited ways. They are not simply dark white men. They are not 'men' in the sense that Europeans are men. To the very limited extent of their shallow capacities lift them to be useful to whites, to raise cotton, gather rubber, fetch ivory, dig diamonds, – and let them be paid what men think they are worth – white men who know them to be well-nigh worthless.

Such degrading of men by men is as old as mankind and the invention of no one race or people. Ever have men striven to conceive of their victims as different from the victors, endlessly different, in soul and blood, strength and cunning, race and lineage. It has been left, however, to Europe and to modern days to discover the eternal world-wide mark of meanness, – color!

Such is the silent revolution that has gripped modern European culture in the later nineteenth and twentieth centuries. Its zenith came in Boxer times: White supremacy was all but world-wide, Africa was dead, India conquered, Japan isolated, and China prostrate, while white America whetted her sword for mongrel Mexico and mulatto South America, lynching her own Negroes the while. Temporary halt in this program was made by little Japan and the white world immediately sensed the peril of such 'yellow' presumption! What sort of a world would this be if yellow men must be treated 'white'? Immediately the eventual overthrow of Japan became a subject of deep thought and intrigue, from St. Petersburg to San Francisco, from the Key of Heaven to the Little Brother of the Poor.

The using of men for the benefit of masters is no new invention of modern Europe. It is quite as old as the world. But Europe proposed to apply it on a scale and with an elaborateness of detail of which no former world ever dreamed. The imperial width of the thing, – the heaven-defying audacity – makes its modern newness.

The scheme of Europe was no sudden invention, but a way out of long-pressing difficulties. It is plain to modern white civilization that the subjection of the white working classes cannot much longer be maintained. Education, political power, and increased knowledge of the technique and meaning of the industrial process are destined to make a more and more equitable distribution of wealth in the near future. The day of the very rich is drawing to a close, so far as individual white nations are concerned. But there is a loophole. There is a chance for exploitation on an immense scale for inordinate profit, not simply to the very rich, but to the middle class and to the laborers. This chance lies in the exploitation of darker peoples. It is here that the golden hand beckons. Here are no labor unions or votes or questioning onlookers or inconvenient consciences. These men may be used down to the very bone, and shot and maimed in 'punitive' expeditions when they revolt. In these dark lands 'industrial development' may repeat in exaggerated form every horror of the industrial history of Europe, from slavery and rape to disease and maiming, with only one test of success, – dividends!

This theory of human culture and its aims has worked itself through warp and woof of our daily thought with a thoroughness that few realize. Everything great, good, efficient, fair, and honorable is 'white'; everything mean, bad, blundering, cheating, and dishonorable is 'yellow'; a bad taste is 'brown'; and the devil is 'black'. The changes of this theme are continually rung in picture and story, in newspaper heading and moving-picture, in sermon and school book, until, of course, the King can do no wrong, – a White Man is always right and a Black Man has no rights which a white man is bound to respect.

There must come the necessary despisings and hatreds of these savage half-men, this unclean *canaille* of the world – these dogs of men. All through the world this gospel is preaching. It has its literature, it has its priests, it has its secret propaganda and above all – it pays!

There's the rub, – it pays. Rubber, ivory, and palm-oil; tea, coffee, and cocoa; bananas, oranges, and other fruit; cotton, gold, and copper – they, and a hundred other things which dark and sweating bodies hand up to the white world from their pits of slime, pay and pay well, but of all that the world gets the black world gets only the pittance that the white world throws it disdainfully.

Small wonder, then, that in the practical world of things-that-be there is jealousy and strife for the possession of the labor of dark millions, for the right to bleed and exploit the colonies of the world where this golden stream may be had, not always for the asking, but surely for the whipping and shooting. It was this competition for the labor of yellow, brown, and black folks that was the cause of the World War. Other causes have been glibly given and other contributing causes there doubtless were, but they were subsidiary and subordinate to this vast quest of the dark world's wealth and toil.

Colonies, we call them, these places where 'niggers' are cheap and the earth is rich; they are those outlands where like a swarm of hungry locusts white masters may settle to be served as kings, wield the lash of slave-drivers, rape girls and wives, grow as rich as Croesus and send homeward a golden stream. They belt the earth, these places, but they cluster in the tropics, with its darkened peoples: in Hong Kong and Anam, in Borneo and Rhodesia, in Sierra Leone and Nigeria, in Panama and Havana – these are the El Dorados toward which the world powers stretch itching palms.

Germany, at last one and united and secure on land, looked across the seas and seeing England with sources of wealth insuring a luxury and power which Germany could not hope to rival by the slower processes of exploiting her own peasants and working-men, especially with these workers half in revolt, immediately built her navy and entered into a desperate competition for possession of colonies of darker peoples. To South America, to China, to Africa, to Asia Minor, she turned like a hound quivering on the leash, impatient, suspicious, irritable, with blood-shot eyes and dripping fangs, ready for the awful word. England and France crouched watchfully over their bones, growling and wary, but gnawing industriously, while the blood of the dark world whetted their greedy appetites. In the background, shut out from the highway to the seven seas, sat Russia and Austria, snarling and snapping at each other and at the last Mediterranean gate to the El Dorado, where the Sick Man enjoyed bad health, and where millions of serfs in the Balkans, Russia, and Asia offered a feast to greed well-nigh as great as Africa.

The fateful day came. It had to come. The cause of war is preparation for war; and of all that Europe has done in a century there is nothing that has equaled in energy, thought, and time her preparation for wholesale murder. The only adequate cause of this preparation was conquest and conquest, not in Europe, but primarily among the darker peoples of Asia and Africa; conquest, not for assimilation and uplift, but for commerce and degradation. For this, and this mainly, did Europe gird herself at frightful cost for war.

The red day dawned when the tinder was lighted in the Balkans and Austro-Hungary seized a bit which brought her a step nearer to the world's highway; she seized one bit and poised herself for another. Then came that curious chorus of challenges, those leaping suspicions, raking all causes for distrust and rivalry and hatred, but saying little of the real and greatest cause.

Each nation felt its deep interests involved. But how? Not, surely, in the death of Ferdinand the Warlike; not, surely, in the old, half-forgotten *revanche* for Alsace-Lorraine; not even in the neutrality of Belgium. No! But in the possession of land overseas, in the right to colonies, the chance to levy endless tribute on the darker world, – on coolies in China, on starving peasants in India, on black savages in Africa, on dying South Sea Islanders, on Indians of the Amazon – all this and nothing more.

Even the broken reed on which we had rested high hopes of eternal peace, – the guild of the laborers – the front of that very important movement for human justice on which we had built most, even this flew like a straw before the breath of king and kaiser. Indeed, the flying had been foreshadowed when in Germany and America 'international' Socialists had all but read yellow and black men out of the kingdom of industrial justice. Subtly had they been bribed, but effectively: Were they not lordly whites and should they not share in the spoils of rape? High wages in the United States and England might be the skillfully manipulated result of slavery in Africa and of peonage in Asia.

With the dog-in-the-manger theory of trade, with the determination to reap inordinate profits and to exploit the weakest to the utmost there came a new imperialism, – the rage for one's own nation to own the earth or, at least, a large enough portion of it to insure as big profits as the next nation. Where sections could not be owned by one dominant nation there came a policy of 'open door', but the 'door' was open to 'white people only'. As to the darkest and weakest of peoples there was but one unanimity in Europe, – that which Herr Dernberg of the German Colonial Office called the agreement with England to maintain white 'prestige' in Africa, – the doctrine of the divine right of white people to steal.

Thus the world market most wildly and desperately sought today is the market where labor is cheapest and most helpless and profit is most abundant. This labor is kept cheap and helpless because the white world despises 'darkies'. If one has the temerity to suggest that these workingmen may walk the way of white workingmen and climb by votes and self-assertion and education to the rank of men, he is howled out of court. They cannot do it and if they could, they shall not, for they are the enemies of the white race and the whites shall rule forever and forever and everywhere. Thus the hatred and despising of human beings from whom Europe wishes to extort her luxuries has led to such jealousy and bickering between European nations that they have fallen afoul of each other and have fought like crazed beasts. Such is the fruit of human hatred.

But what of the darker world that watches? Most men belong to this world. With Negro and Negroid, East Indian, Chinese, and Japanese they form two-thirds of the population of the world. A belief in humanity is a belief in colored men. If the uplift of mankind must be done by men, then the destinies of this world will rest ultimately in the hands of darker nations.

What, then, is this dark world thinking? It is thinking that as wild and awful as this shameful war was, *it is nothing to compare with that fight for freedom which black and brown and yellow men must and will make unless their oppression and humiliation and insult at the hands of the White World cease. The Dark World is going to submit to its present treatment just as long as it must and not one moment longer.*

Let me say this again and emphasize it and leave no room for mistaken meaning: The World War was primarily the jealous and avaricious struggle for the largest share in exploiting darker races. As such it is and must be but the prelude to the armed and indignant protest of these despised and raped peoples. Today Japan is hammering on the door of justice, China is raising her half-manacled hands to knock next, India is writhing for the freedom to knock, Egypt is sullenly muttering, the Negroes of South and West Africa, of the West Indies, and of the United States are just awakening to their shameful slavery. Is, then, this war the end of wars? Can it be the end, so long as sits enthroned, even in the souls of those who cry peace, the despising and robbing of darker peoples? If Europe hugs this delusion, then this is not the end of world war, – it is but the beginning!

We see Europe's greatest sin precisely where we found Africa's and Asia's, – in human hatred, the despising of men; with this difference, however: Europe has the awful lesson of the past before her, has the splendid results of widened areas of tolerance, sympathy, and love among men, and she faces a greater, an infinitely greater, world of men than any preceding civilization ever faced.

It is curious to see America, the United States, looking on herself, first, as a sort of natural peacemaker, then as a moral protagonist in this terrible time. No nation is less fitted for this rôle. For two or more centuries America has marched proudly in the van of human hatred, – making bonfires of human flesh and laughing at them hideously, and making the insulting of millions more than a matter of dislike, – rather a great religion, a world war-cry: Up white, down black; to your tents, O white folk, and world war with black and parti-colored mongrel beasts!

Instead of standing as a great example of the success of democracy and the possibility of human brotherhood America has taken her place as an awful example of its pitfalls and failures, so far as black and brown and yellow peoples are concerned. And this, too, in spite of the fact that there has been no actual failure; the Indian is not dying out, the Japanese and Chinese have not menaced the land, and the experiment of Negro suffrage has resulted in the uplift of twelve million people at a rate probably unparalleled in history. But what of this? America, Land of Democracy, wanted to believe in the failure of democracy so far as darker peoples were concerned. Absolutely without excuse she established a caste system, rushed into preparation for war, and conquered tropical colonies. She stands today shoulder to shoulder with Europe in Europe's worst sin against civilization. She aspires to sit among the great nations who arbitrate the fate of 'lesser breeds without the law' and she is at times heartily ashamed even of the large number of 'new' white people whom her democracy has admitted to place and power. Against this surging forward of Irish and German, of Russian Jew, Slav and 'dago' her social bars have not availed, but against Negroes she can and does take her unflinching and immovable stand, backed by this new public policy of Europe. She trains her immigrants to this despising of 'niggers' from the day of their landing, and they carry and send the news back to the submerged classes in the fatherlands.

All this I see and hear up in my tower, above the thunder of the seven seas. From my narrowed windows I stare into the night that looms beneath the cloud-swept stars. Eastward and westward storms are breaking, – great, ugly whirlwinds of hatred and blood and cruelty. I will not believe them inevitable. I will not believe that all that was must be, that all the shameful drama of the past must be done again today before the sunlight sweeps the silver seas.

If I cry amid this roar of elemental forces, must my cry be in vain, because it is but a cry, – a small and human cry amid Promethean gloom?

Back beyond the world and swept by these wild, white faces of the awful dead, why will this Soul of White Folk, – this modern Prometheus, – hang bound by his own binding, tethered by a fable of the past? I hear his mighty cry reverberating through the world, 'I am white'! Well and good, O Prometheus, divine thief! Is not the world wide enough for two colors, for many little shinings of the sun? Why, then, devour your own vitals if I answer even as proudly, 'I am black'!

Note

1. A feeling of pleasure or satisfaction when something bad happens to someone else.

James Baldwin*, 'Letter to My Nephew'

Dear James:

I have begun this letter five times and torn it up five times. I keep seeing your face, which is also the face of your father and my brother. Like him, you are tough, dark, vulnerable, moody – with a very definite tendency to sound truculent because you want no one to think you are soft. You may be like your grandfather in this, I don't know, but certainly both you and your father resemble him very much physically. Well, he is dead, he never saw you, and he had a terrible life; he was defeated long before he died because at the bottom of his heart, he really believed what white people said about him. This is one of the reasons that he became so holy. I am sure that your father has told you something about all that. Neither you nor your father exhibit any tendency towards holiness: you really *are* of another era, part of what happened when the Negro left the land and came into what the late E. Franklin Frazier called 'the cities of destruction'. You can only be destroyed by believing that you really are what the white world calls a *nigger*. I tell you this because I love you, and please don't you ever forget it.

I have known both of you all your lives, have carried your Daddy in my arms and on my shoulders, kissed and spanked him and watched him learn to walk. I don't know if you've known anybody from that far back; if you've loved anybody that long, first as an infant, then as a child, then as a man, you gain a strange perspective on time and human pain and effort. Other people cannot see what I see whenever I look into your father's face, for behind your father's face as it is today are all those other faces which were his. Let him laugh and I see a cellar your father does not remember and a house he does not remember and I hear in his present laughter his laughter as a child. Let him curse and I remember him falling down the cellar steps, and howling, and I remember, with pain, his tears, which my hand or your grandmother's so easily wiped away. But no one's hand can wipe away those tears he sheds invisibly today, which one hears in his laughter and in his speech and in his songs. I know what the world has done to my brother and how narrowly he has survived it. And I know, which is much worse, and this is the crime of which I accuse my country and my countrymen, and for which neither I nor time nor history will ever forgive them, that they have destroyed and are destroying hundreds of thousands of lives and do not know it and do not

---

* James Baldwin, 'Letter to My Nephew on the One Hundredth Anniversary of the Emancipation', in *The Fire Next Time* (New York: Vintage Books, 1993), 3–10. Permissions by the James Baldwin Estate.

want to know it. One can be, indeed one must strive to become, tough and philosophical concerning destruction and death, for this is what most of mankind has been best at since we have heard of man. (But remember: *most* of mankind is not *all* of mankind.) But it is not permissible that the authors of devastation should also be innocent. It is the innocence which constitutes the crime.

Now, my dear namesake, these innocent and well-meaning people, your countrymen, have caused you to be born under conditions not very far removed from those described for us by Charles Dickens in the London of more than a hundred years ago. (I hear the chorus of the innocents screaming, 'No! This is not true! How *bitter* you are'! – but I am writing this letter to *you*, to try to tell you something about how to handle *them*, for most of them do not yet really know that you exist. I *know* the conditions under which you were born, for I was there. Your countrymen were *not* there, and haven't made it yet. Your grandmother was also there, and no one has ever accused her of being bitter. I suggest that the innocents check with her. She isn't hard to find. Your countrymen don't know that *she* exists, either, though she has been working for them all their lives.)

Well, you were born, here you came, something like fifteen years ago; and though your father and mother and grandmother, looking about the streets through which they were carrying you, staring at the walls into which they brought you, had every reason to be heavy-hearted, yet they were not. For here you were, Big James, named for me – you were a big baby, I was not – here you were: to be loved. To be loved, baby, hard, at once, and forever, to strengthen you against the loveless world. Remember that: I know how black it looks today, for you. It looked bad that day, too, yes, we were trembling. We have not stopped trembling yet, but if we had not loved each other none of us would have survived. And now you must survive because we love you, and for the sake of your children and your children's children.

This innocent country set you down in a ghetto in which, in fact, it intended that you should perish. Let me spell out precisely what I mean by that, for the heart of the matter is here, and the root of my dispute with my country. You were born where you were born and faced the future that you faced because you were black and *for no other reason*. The limits of your ambition were, thus, expected to be set forever. You were born into a society which spelled out with brutal clarity, and in as many ways as possible, that you were a worthless human being. You were not expected to aspire to excellence: you were expected to make peace with mediocrity. Wherever you have turned, James, in your short time on this earth, you have been told where you could go and what you could do (and *how* you could do it) and where you could live and whom you could marry. I know your countrymen do not agree with me about this, and I hear them saying, 'You exaggerate'. They do not know Harlem, and I do. So do you. Take no one's word for anything, including mine – but trust your experience. Know whence you came. If you know whence you came, there is really no limit to where you can go. The details and symbols of your life have been deliberately constructed to make you believe what white people say about you. Please try to remember that what they believe, as well as what they do and cause you to endure, does not testify to your inferiority but to their inhumanity and fear. Please try to be clear, dear James, through the storm which rages about your youthful head today, about the reality which lies behind the words *acceptance* and *integration*. There is no reason for you to try to become like white people and there is no basis whatever for their impertinent assumption that *they* must accept *you*. The really terrible thing, old buddy, is that *you* must accept *them*. And I mean that very seriously. You must accept them and accept them with love. For these innocent people have no other hope. They are, in effect, still trapped in a history which they do not understand; and until they understand it, they cannot be released from it. They have had to believe for many years, and for innumerable reasons, that black men are inferior to white men. Many of them, indeed, know better, but, as you will discover, people find it very difficult to act on what they know. To act is to be committed, and to be committed is to be in danger. In this case, the danger, in the minds of most white Americans, is the loss of their identity. Try to imagine how you would feel if you woke up one morning to find the sun shining and all the stars aflame. You would be frightened because it is out of the order of nature. Any upheaval in the universe is terrifying because it so profoundly attacks one's sense of one's own reality. Well, the black man has functioned in the white man's world as a fixed star, as an immovable pillar: and as he moves out of his place, heaven and earth are shaken to their foundations. You, don't be afraid. I said that it was intended that you should perish in the ghetto, perish by never being allowed to go behind the white man's definitions, by never being allowed to spell your proper name. You have, and many of us have, defeated this intention; and, by a terrible law, a terrible paradox, those innocents who believed that your imprisonment made them safe are losing their grasp of reality. But these men are your brothers – your lost, younger brothers. And if the word *integration* means anything, this is what it means: that we, with love, shall force our brothers to see themselves as they are, to cease fleeing from reality and begin to change it. For this is your home, my friend, do not be driven from it; great men have done great things here, and will again, and we can make America what America must become. It will be hard, James, but you come from sturdy, peasant stock, men who picked cotton and dammed rivers and built railroads, and, in the teeth of the most terrifying odds, achieved an unassailable and monumental dignity. You come from a long line of great poets, some of the greatest poets since Homer. One of them said, *The very time I thought I was lost, My dungeon shook and my chains fell off.*

You know, and I know, that the country is celebrating one hundred years of freedom one hundred years too soon. We cannot be free until they are free. God bless you, James, and Godspeed.

Your uncle,
James

Ella Baker*, 'Address at the Hattiesburg Freedom Day Rally'

This is rather unusual. Aaron Henry said that I had had my fling with all the civil rights organizations. Well, my greatest fling has still to be flung, because as far as I'm concerned I was never working for an organization, I have always tried to work for a cause, and the cause to me is bigger than any organization. Bigger than any group of people, and it is the cause of humanity. The cause is the cause that brings us together, the drive of the human spirit for freedom.

You know, I always like to think that the very God who gave us life, gave us liberty. And if we don't have liberty it is because somebody else has stood between us and that which God has granted us. And so we have come here tonight to renew our struggle, our struggle for that which we are entitled by virtue of being children of the Almighty. The right to be men and women, to grow and to develop to the fullest capacity with which He has endowed us.

---

* Ella Baker, 'Address at the Hattiesburg Freedom Day Rally', 21 January 1964, Hattiesburg, Mississippi. http://voicesofdemocracy.umd.edu/ella-baker-freedom-day-rally-speech-text/.

And as I have listened here tonight, my spirit has rove over a long period of years and I can think of a number of things I would like to say, but if I had anything at all to say tonight is to remind us of something that occurred to me, something that came into focus in a conversation on the night that Medger Evers's body came through Atlanta. A group of people were down at the station among us; we were there for the purpose of identifying with the great tragedy that had occurred in his being shot to death. And after the ceremony, the little ceremony in the station, one of the leading civil right leaders (I won't name any because leadership is one of those things, you know, I won't talk about them too much) but this person said, 'We are in the final stages of the freedom struggle'. And I challenge that.

We are not in the final stages of the freedom struggle. We are really just beginning. We are just beginning the freedom struggle. Let me tell you why. Because even tomorrow if every vestige of racial discrimination were wiped out, if all of us became free enough to go down and to associate with all the people we wanted to associate, we still are not free. We aren't free until within us we have that deep sense of freedom from a lot of things that we don't even mention in these meetings.

And I'm not talking about Negroes, I'm talking about people. People cannot be free until they realize that peace – we can talk about peace – that peace is not the absence of war or struggle, it is the presence of justice. People cannot, pardon me, people cannot be free until there is enough work in the land to give everybody a job. Tomorrow, tomorrow if we were able to vote our full strength and we still voted our full strength, until we recognize that in this country in a land of great and plenty and great wealth there are millions of people who go to bed hungry every night. That tomorrow if we were to call up all the able-bodied men in our country, who could do some work, we wouldn't have work for them to do.

And unless we see this thing in its larger perspective, unless we realize that certainly we must sing, we must have the inspiration of song, the inspiration that comes from songs like this one that was created and demonstrated here tonight, but we also must have the information that comes from lots and lots of study. And so we must come to grips with a lot of problems. We must also know that we are in, in the final analysis, the only group that can make your free is yourself, because we must free ourselves from all of things that keep us back.

And so in conclusion let me quote one of my favorite or improvise one of my favorite thoughts in scripture. And it has to do with the whole struggle I think because it says, 'For now we are nearer than when we first believed'. I forgot the exact quote, but let us 'cast aside the works of darkness and put on the armor of light'.

I love to hear us sing. I've heard a lot of singing in my day. I've been a part of a lot of singing, but I know, and you must know, that singing alone will not do it for us. And we are going to have to have these freedom schools and we are going to have to learn a lot of things in them. We are going to have to be concerned about the kinds of education our children are getting in school, and all of this has to be done along at the same time that we also recognize that our white brothers, the very white brothers in Hattiesburg and in other parts of Mississippi who have kept us in bondage, that they did it because they did not know any better.

They have been fooled, and they have been fooled by those who told them the 'big lie'. The 'big lie' was to the effect that they could do what they wanted in Mississippi with the Negro question. And you know what? The rest of the country for a long time tacitly agreed. That is, they didn't do anything about it.

And so all of us stand guilty at this moment for having waited so long to lend ourselves to a fight for the freedom, not of Negroes, not of the Negroes of Mississippi, but for the freedom of the American spirit, for the freedom of the human spirit for freedom, and this is the reason

I am here tonight, and this is the reason, I think, that these young men who have worked and given their bodies in the movement for freedom. They are here not because they want to see something take place just for the fun of it, they are here because they should know, and I think they do know, that the freedom which they seek is a larger freedom that encompasses all mankind. And until that day, we will never turn back.

CASE STUDY

Eduardo Bonilla-Silva[*], ' "Keeping Them in Their Place": The Social Control of Blacks since the 1960s'

All domination is ultimately maintained through social-control strategies. For example, during slavery, whites used the whip, overseers, night patrols, and other highly repressive practices, along with a number of paternalistic ones, to keep blacks in their place. After slavery was abolished, whites felt threatened by free blacks; hence, very strict written and unwritten rules of racial contact (the Jim Crow laws) were developed to specify 'the place' of blacks in the new environment of 'freedom'. And, as insurance, lynching and other terroristic forms of social control were used to guarantee white supremacy. In contrast, as the Jim Crow practices have subsided, the control of blacks has been chiefly attained through state agencies (police, criminal court system, FBI). Marable describes the new system of control as follows:

> The informal, vigilante-inspired techniques to suppress Blacks were no longer practical. Therefore, beginning with the Great Depression, and especially after 1945, white racists began to rely almost exclusively on the state apparatus to carry out the battle for white supremacy. Blacks charged with crimes would receive longer sentences than whites convicted of similar crimes. The police forces of municipal and metropolitan areas received a *carte blanche* in their daily acts of brutality against Blacks. The Federal and state government carefully monitored Blacks who advocated any kind of social change. Most important, capital punishment was used as a weapon against Blacks charged and convicted of major crimes. The criminal justice system, in short, became a modern instrument to perpetuate white hegemony. Extra-legal lynchings were replaced by 'legal lynchings' and capital punishment.[1]

In the following sections of this chapter, I review the available data to see how well they fit Marable's interpretation of the contemporary system of control.

The State as Enforcer of Racial Order

The United States has the highest per capita incarcerated population in the world.[2] The incarceration rate has risen 600 percent in the past thirty years,[3] and race influences nearly every aspect of incarceration, including arrest rates, conviction rates, the probability of post-incarceration employment, educational opportunities, and marriage outcomes. One in three black males born today can expect to spend some portion of his life behind bars, and Latinos have seen a 43 percent rise in their incarceration rates since 1990.[4] Data on arrest rates show that the contrast between black and white arrest rates since 1950 has been striking. The black arrest rate increased throughout this period, reaching almost one hundred per one thousand by 1978 compared to thirty-five per one thousand for whites.[5] The 1989 data suggest that the arrest rate for blacks has stabilized at around eighty to ninety per one thousand.[6] The implications

---

[*] Eduardo Bonilla-Silva, *Racism without Racists: Color-Blind Racism and the Persistence of Racial Inequality in America*, 5th edition (Lanham, MD: Rowman & Littlefield, 2018), 32–42, 204–5, 232–37. Copyright by Rowman & Littlefield.

for the black community are astounding. Eight to nine percent of all blacks are arrested every year. This means that a substantial number of black families experience the 'services' of the criminal justice system every year, directly (arrested or incarcerated) as well as indirectly (visit to jails, stops by police, etc.).

In terms of how many blacks are incarcerated, we find a pattern similar to their arrest rates. Although blacks have always been overrepresented in the inmate population, as can be seen in the table, this overrepresentation has skyrocketed since 1960. By 1980, the incarceration rate of blacks was six times that of whites.

The statistics for black youth are even more depressing. Black youth aged ten to seventeen, who constitute 15 percent of American youth, account for 25 percent of arrests. Race differences exist at almost every stage of the juvenile justice process: black youth suffer racial profiling by police and higher rates of arrest, detention, and court referral; are charged with more serious offenses; and are more likely to be placed in larger public correctional facilities in contrast to small private group homes, foster homes, and drug and alcohol treatment centers.[7] 'Almost one in four Black men aged twenty to thirty are under the supervision of the criminal justice system any given day'.[8] The rate of incarceration of blacks for criminal offenses is over eight times greater than that of whites, with 1 in 20 black men, in contrast to 1 in 180 white men, in prison.[9] Hence, given these statistics, it is not surprising that today there are more blacks aged twenty to twenty-nine under the supervision of the criminal justice system (incarcerated, on parole, or on probation) than in college.

TABLE 2.1   Percentage of US Residents and Men in Prison or Jail, by Age, Race and Education, 1980, 2000

All US Residents, Men Aged 18–65	1980	2000
All US Residents	0.2%	0.7%
Men Aged 18–65		
All	0.7	2.1
White	0.4	1.0
Hispanic	1.6	3.3
Black	3.0	7.9
Men Aged 20–40		
White	0.6	1.6
Hispanic	2.1	4.6
Black	4.8	11.5
Non-College Men Aged 20–40		
White	0.9	3.2
Hispanic	2.6	5.5
Black	6.0	17.0
High-School-Dropout Men Aged 20–40		
White	2.1	6.7
Hispanic	3.2	6.0
Black	10.7	32.4

Source: Bruce Western, 'The Prison Boom and the Decline of American Citizenship', *Society* 44, no. 5 (2007): 30–36.

This dramatic increase in black incarceration has been attributed to legislative changes in the penal codes and the 'get tough' attitude in law enforcement fueled by white fear of black crime. Furthermore, the fact that blacks are disproportionately convicted and receive longer sentences than whites for similar crimes contributes to their overrepresentation among the penal population. For example, 'according to the Federal Judicial Center, in 1990 the average sentences for blacks on weapons and drug charges were 49 percent longer than those for whites who had committed and been convicted of the same crimes – and that disparity has been rising over time'.[10] Self-report data suggest about 14 percent of U.S. illegal drug users are black; however, blacks constitute 35 percent of those arrested, 55 percent of those convicted, and 74 percent of those incarcerated for drug possession.[11]

Official State Brutality against Blacks

Police departments grew exponentially after the 1960s, particularly in large metropolitan areas with large concentrations of blacks.[12] This growth has been related by various studies to black urban mobilization and rebellion in the 1960s.[13] Another way of measuring the impact of police departments on the life of blacks is surveying how blacks and whites rate police performance. Rosentraub and Harlow, in an article reviewing surveys on the attitudes of blacks and whites toward the police from 1960 through 1981, found that blacks consistently view the police in a much more negative light than do whites despite attempts in the 1970s and 1980s to reduce the friction between black communities and police departments by hiring more black police officers and, in some cases, even hiring black chiefs of police. Blacks are also more inclined to believe that police misconduct occurs frequently and is common in their city and neighborhood.[14]

The level of police force used with blacks has always been excessive. However, since the police have become the more direct enforcer of the social control of blacks since the 1960s, their level of violence against blacks has skyrocketed. For example, in 1975 *46 percent of all the people killed by the police in official action were black.*[15] That situation has not changed much since. Robert Smith reported recently that of the people killed by the police, over half are black; the police usually claim that when they killed blacks it was 'accidental' because they thought that the victim was armed, although in fact the victims were unarmed in 75 percent of the cases; there was an increase in the 1980s in the use of deadly force by the police and the only ameliorating factor was the election of a sensitive mayor in a city; and in the aftermath of the King verdict, 87 percent of civilian victims of police brutality reported in the newspapers of fifteen American major cities were black, and 93 percent of the officers involved were white. Moreover, a record number of black people were killed by law enforcement in 2015, more than the deadliest year of lynching in the United States. But extrajudicial murders of black people in America are not limited to law enforcement, as demonstrated by the Trayvon Martin incident. In February 2012, as Martin walked from the store to his home, he was fatally shot by George Zimmerman, who claimed to be a part of the local neighborhood watch. Zimmerman pursued Martin despite explicit instructions to stand down by a police dispatcher. After a brief altercation, Zimmerman shot Martin in the chest. Due to Florida's 'Stand Your Ground' law, Zimmerman was not initially charged. After a groundswell of national pressure, including marches, protests, and rallies, Zimmerman was eventually charged, tried, and acquitted. This incident shows how the power to punish suspected black 'criminals' may extend even further than formal law enforcement officials. Unfortunately, an ever-lengthening list of names join Martin as this behavior becomes increasingly normalized.[16]

A more mundane form of police brutality in the form of 'stop and frisk' laws in New York City daily terrorize young people of color. Ostensibly aimed at finding weapons and drugs, nearly 90 percent of the stops are black and brown youth. This is despite the fact that, according to antiracist activist Tim Wise,[17] who is white,

White high school students are seven times more likely than blacks to have used cocaine; eight times more likely to have smoked crack; ten times more likely to have used LSD and seven times more likely to have used heroin. . . . What's more, white youth ages 12–17 are more likely to sell drugs: 34 percent more likely, in fact, than their black counterparts. And it is white youth who are twice as likely to binge drink, and nearly twice as likely as blacks to drive drunk. And white males are twice as likely to bring a weapon to school as are black males.

The state-sanctioned abuse of blacks under the cover of enforcing drug laws is clearly not aimed at stopping drug distribution. Rather, it is a manifestation of how supposedly race-neutral laws can be applied at the discretion of officers and departments to control the black population.

Since the late 1990s, a new form of state-sanctioned social control has been written into law in numerous states. Promoted by the right-wing American Legislative Exchange Council, these so-called Stand Your Ground or castle doctrine laws institutionalize racist vigilantism. Twenty states have adopted these laws since 2000, and murder rates in these states, counter to the expectations of advocates for these laws, have increased by 8 percent.[18] And, as one would expect in a racialized society, these laws have not been applied in a racially neutral manner:

> Whites who kill blacks in Stand Your Ground states are far more likely to be found justified in their killings. In non-Stand Your Ground states, whites are 250 percent more likely to be found justified in killing a black person than a white person who kills another white person; in Stand Your Ground states, that number jumps to 354 percent.[19]

Moreover, in response to the 'Black Lives Matter' movement, a number of states have enacted 'Blue Lives Matter' laws, which allow killing law enforcement officers to be classified as hate crimes.[20]

Capital Punishment as a Modern Form of Lynching

The raw statistics on capital punishment seem to indicate racial bias *prima facie*: Of 3,984 people lawfully executed since 1930 (until 1980), 2,113 were black, over half of the total, almost five times the proportion of blacks in the population as a whole.[21] Blacks, who have made up about 13 percent of the population, have accounted for 52 percent of people executed in state or federal jurisdictions since 1930.[22] However, social scientific research on racial sentencing has produced mixed results. A number of authors have found a bias in sentencing,[23] but some have claimed that, as legal factors are taken into account, the bias disappears.[24] Yet recent research has suggested that 'discrimination has not declined or disappeared but simply has become more subtle and difficult to detect'.[25] Despite claims that discrimination has declined in significance, research shows that it may have simply gone underground. Others have pointed out that the discrimination experienced by blacks may occur at earlier stages. For instance, research by Radelet and Pierce suggests that homicides with white victims and black suspects are more likely to be upgraded to a more aggravated description by prosecutors. Hence, additive and linear models will tend to miss the effect of race.[26]

There is a substantial body of research showing that blacks charged of murdering whites are more likely to be sentenced to death than any other victim-offender dyad. Similarly, blacks charged of raping white women also receive the death sentence at a much higher rate. The two tendencies were confirmed by Spohn in a 1994 article using data for Detroit in 1977 and 1978: 'Blacks who sexually assaulted whites faced a greater risk of incarceration than either blacks or whites who sexually assaulted blacks or whites who sexually assaulted whites; similarly, blacks who murdered whites received longer sentences than did offenders in the other two categories'.[27] Data from 1976 to 1981, after the *Furman* statutes were implemented, for the states of Arkansas, Florida, Georgia, Illinois, Mississippi, North Carolina, Oklahoma, and Virginia on people charged with homicide indicate that cases involving white victims are more likely to warrant the death penalty than cases involving black victims. Although the authors find a black suspect–white victim effect in Florida, Georgia, and Illinois, they claim that it disappears when they control for severity of the crime.[28] However, the most respected study on this matter carried out by Professor David C. Baldus to support the claim of Warren McCleskey, a black man convicted of murdering a white police officer in 1978, found that there was a huge disparity in the imposition of the death penalty in Georgia.[29] The study found that in cases involving white victims and black defendants, the death penalty was imposed 22 percent of the time, whereas in the white-black dyad, the death penalty was imposed in only 1 percent of the cases. *Even after controlling for a number of variables, blacks were 4.3 times as likely as whites to receive a death sentence.*[30]

It should not surprise anyone that in a racist society, court decisions on cases involving the death penalty exhibit a race effect. Research on juries suggests that they tend to be older, more affluent, more educated, more conviction-prone, and more white than the average in the community.[31] Moreover, research on the process of selecting jurors for death-penalty cases suggests that the *voir dire* process (questions to select the jury) produces juries that are pro–death penalty.[32] This particular bias has been found to have a racial effect. Gregory D. Russell, in his *The Death Penalty and Racial Bias: Overturning Supreme Court Assumptions*, found indirect data (exhibited via surrogate measures) of racial bias among death-qualified jurors. This finding adds to our understanding of why there is a differential conviction rate for blacks and whites in cases involving the death penalty. As Russell explains,

> The evidence developed did suggest that juries composed of death-qualified jurors are more likely to be white, punitive, and authoritarian. Hence, they are more likely, on this evidence, to exhibit a tendency toward racially biased decisions. Will every juror or jury act in this manner? Of course not. The evidence simply suggests the probability that jurors so composed are more likely than not to be more predisposed to racially biased determinations than other juries, though the appearance of racial bias is quite idiosyncratic.[33]

The racial trends observed by research on the application of the death penalty will not abate any time soon. The 1986 Supreme Court decision *McCleskey v. Kemp*, for example, stipulated that statistical evidence showing racial discrimination was not enough and argued further that evidence of discrimination would be valid only if the plaintiff could prove that a state 'enacted or maintained the death penalty statute *because* of an anticipated racially discriminatory effect'.[34] Given the new contours of the racial order, laws will not be written in ways to overtly discriminate against minorities. In this legal desert created by the Supreme Court, unless Congress enacts a law allowing statistical evidence as proof of discrimination, minorities sentenced to death will have no legal recourse of claiming discrimination. The first attempt to enact such a law (the Racial Justice Act in 1988) failed miserably in Congress. The second attempt during the 1993 discussion of Clinton's crime bill failed also. Meanwhile, the number of incarcerated blacks on death row has reached the 40 percent range.[35]

High Propensity to Arrest Blacks

Blacks complain that police officers mistreat them, disrespect them, assume that they are criminals, violate their rights on a consistent basis, and are more violent when dealing with them. Blacks and other minorities are stopped and frisked by police in 'alarmingly disproportionate numbers'.[36] Why is it that minorities receive 'special treatment' from the police? Studies on police attitudes and on their socialization suggest that police officers live in a 'cops' world' and develop a cop mentality. And that cops' world is a highly racialized one; minorities are viewed as dangerous, prone to crime, violent, and disrespectful.[37]

Various studies have noted that the racist attitudes that police officers exhibit has an impact on their behavior toward minorities. Furthermore, other studies have suggested that police discretion and demographic bias contribute to the over-arrest of blacks. Extra-legal subjective characteristics such as demeanor, appearance, and race have been found to influence the decision of police officers to arrest individuals, as well as other stages in the individual's path through the criminal justice system.[38] In terms of demographic bias, research suggests that because black communities are over-patrolled, the officers patrolling these areas develop a stereotypical view of their residents as more likely to commit criminal acts and are more likely to 'see' criminal behavior than in white communities.[39]

Thus, it is not surprising that blacks are disproportionally arrested compared to whites. It is possible to gauge the level of over-arrest endured by blacks by comparing the proportion of times that they are described by victims as the attackers with their arrest rates. Using this procedure, Farai Chideya contended that

> for virtually every type of crime, African-American criminals are arrested at rates above their commission of the acts. For example, victimization reports indicated that 33 percent of women who were raped said that their attacker was black; however, black rape suspects made up fully 43 percent of those arrested. The disproportionate arrest rate adds to the public perception that rape is a 'black' crime.[40]

Using these numbers, the rate of over-arrest for blacks in cases of rape is 30 percent. As shocking as this seems to be, the rate for cases where the victim is white is even higher. Smith, Visher, and Davidson found that whereas the probability of arrest for cases in which the victim was white and the suspect black was 0.336, for cases of white suspects and black victims the probability dropped to 0.107. Blacks represent 65 percent of those exonerated for rape and half of the exonerations of men convicted of raping white women, even though less than 10 percent of rapes of white women are by black men.[41]

The enormous amount of anecdotal evidence on blacks detained, harassed, or illegally searched for looking 'suspicious' is indicative of the racial consciousness and practices of white police officers. A combination of these disproportionate arrest rates and ongoing police brutality has given rise to the Black Lives Matter movement. After a social media hashtag went viral following the murder of Trayvon Martin in 2012, the movement arguably 'officially' ignited in Ferguson following the killing of Michael Brown in 2014. Since then, the movement has spawned chapters in thirty-one cities, continuing to protest – including interrupting presidential candidates with demands and demanding policy change such as police demilitarization and mandatory body cameras on law enforcement. Unfortunately, the movement has done little to stem the tide of police brutality as 2015 was the deadliest year on record for police killings. The list continues to grow. An article in the *LA Times* chronicles some of the most notable incidents:

Samuel DuBose, 43

Ray Tensing, then a University of Cincinnati police officer, was indicted in July 2015 on a murder charge in the fatal shooting of DuBose, who was unarmed when he was pulled over for a traffic stop. Tensing pulled over DuBose near campus for a missing license plate. His attorney said Tensing feared being dragged under the car as DuBose tried to drive away. The shooting was captured on video by Tensing's body camera and depicts DuBose repeatedly being asked for his driver's license. After DuBose refuses to produce it and gets out of the car, a gunshot is heard.

Freddie Gray, 25

Six Baltimore police officers faced charges ranging from misconduct to second-degree murder in the April 2015 death of Freddie Gray. Gray died when his neck was broken in the back of a police transport van. He had been restrained with handcuffs and leg irons, but not a seat belt. The death set off several days of rioting in Baltimore.

The involuntary manslaughter trial of the first of those charged, Officer William Porter, ended in December in a hung jury. A judge acquitted two other officers in bench trials. The City of Baltimore paid Gray's family $6.4 million as a settlement for civil claims.

Natasha McKenna, 37

McKenna died after being shocked four times with a stun gun while her hands were cuffed and her legs shackled. McKenna, who suffered from mental illness, was in custody in the Fairfax County, Virginia, jail on February 3, 2015, when a deputy used the stun gun on her. She died February 8.

Eric Garner, 43

Garner died July 17, 2014, after a police officer in Staten Island, New York, placed him in an illegal chokehold during an encounter on the sidewalk, where police said Garner was selling illegal cigarettes. A bystander shot video showing Garner's final moments, and it quickly fueled major protests and demands that the officers involved face criminal charges.

The city's medical examiner ruled Garner's death a homicide because of the compression of his neck and chest. Two officers faced an internal investigation in connection with Garner's death: the one who applied the chokehold was put on modified duty, meaning he was stripped of his gun and badge, while a police sergeant was stripped of her gun and badge and charged internally with failure to supervise.

Tamir Rice, 12

Rice was shot and killed in a park in Cleveland on November 22, 2014.

Officers Timothy Loehmann and Frank Garmback responded to a call about a black male sitting on a swing and pointing a gun at people in a city park. The caller expressed doubts about the gun's authenticity and said the male was probably a juvenile, but that information wasn't relayed to the responding officers. Within two seconds of arriving at the scene, Loehmann fired two shots, one hitting Rice in the torso.

Rice's weapon later was found to be a black toy gun. In December 2015, a grand jury declined to indict Loehmann or Garmback.

Rekia Boyd, 22

Boyd was fatally shot by an off-duty Chicago police detective on March 21, 2012, as she stood in an alley with a group of friends. A man in the group exchanged words with the detective, who fired five shots into the alley, hitting Boyd in the back of her head. No weapon was found in the alley[42]. . . .

Post–Civil Rights Social Control and the New Racism

The mechanisms by which blacks experience social control in the contemporary period are not overwhelmingly covert. Yet they share with the previous mechanisms discussed in this chapter their invisibility. The mechanisms to keep blacks in 'their place' are rendered invisible in three ways. First, because the enforcement of the racial order from the 1960s onward has been institutionalized, individual whites can express a detachment from the *racialized* way in which social control agencies operate in America. Second, because these agencies are *legally* charged with defending *order* in society, their actions are deemed neutral and necessary. Thus, it is no surprise that whites consistently support the police in surveys.[43] Finally, the white-dominated media depicts incidents that seem to indicate that racial bias is endemic to the criminal justice system as isolated. For example, cases that presumably expose the racial character of social-control agencies (e.g., the police beating of Rodney King, the police killing of Malice Green in Detroit, the acquittal or lenient sentences received by officers accused of police brutality, etc.) are viewed as 'isolated' incidents and are separated from the larger social context in which they transpire. Ultimately, the emergence of the new racism does not mean that racial violence has disappeared as an enforcer of the racial order. Rather, these incidents are portrayed as nonracial applications of the law. . . .

Obamerica

George Orwell stated a long time ago that 'to see what is in front of one's nose needs constant struggle'.[44] In the 2008 election cycle, Americans did not see what was in front of their noses; they saw what they wanted and longed to see. Whereas blacks and other people of color saw in Obama the impossible dream come true, whites saw the confirmation of their belief that America is indeed a color-blind nation. But facts are, as John Adams said, 'stubborn things',[45] and astute social analysts know that since the late 1970s, racial progress in the United States has stagnated and, in many areas, regressed. Socioeconomic indicators revealed severe racial gaps in income, wealth, housing, and educational and occupational standing in 2008. Now, eight years later, the gaps remain, and, on some indicators, they are wider.

Although all groups experienced slight economic improvements as the recession waned, the racial differences remained stark over Obama's tenure. In 2008, blacks and Latinos were over twice as likely to be unemployed and live in poverty than their white counterparts, while their median incomes were both about 65 percent of whites.[46] In 2016 the unemployment rates for blacks and Latinos were 8.1 percent and 5.6 percent respectively, compared to 4.4 percent for whites.[47] Similarly, in 2015, the median income and poverty rates for blacks and Latinos were $36,898 and 24 percent and $45,148 and 21 percent respectively, while for whites they were $62,850 and 9 percent.[48] It is important to remember that because of factors such as differential labor force participation rate, these numbers may actually underestimate the racial differences. Indeed, a report by the Economic Policy Institute shows that despite moderate increases by both groups, the hourly wage gap between blacks and whites is at its largest since 1979.[49]

Moreover, over half of blacks born into poverty remained in poverty, and of blacks who reach the middle class, over half of their children are downwardly mobile.[50] White households have thirteen times more wealth than black households, the largest gap since 1989, and only 32 and 11 percent of blacks invested in a 401(k) or IRA respectively, relative to 47 and 35 percent of whites.[51] Finally, white families are twice as likely to receive an inheritance than black families, and they receive inheritances that are three times larger than black families.[52]

These statistics are frightening indicators of the worsening economic well-being of blacks, but they do not tell the true extent of the story – as we have seen, the racial wealth disparity can be even more important than income differences.[53] In 2013, white wealth was thirteen times higher than black wealth, the highest it has been since the late 1980s, and in that same year, it was ten times higher than Latino wealth, the highest it has been since the mid-1990s.[54] Much of this huge jump in wealth disparity comes from the racialized effects of the housing market crash. The Center for Responsible Lending reported that by the end of the crash, almost a quarter of black homeowners would lose their homes due to foreclosure.[55] Several major banks (Wells Fargo, Bank of America, and SunTrust) have already agreed to settlements for their targeting of black and Latino customers and communities for subprime mortgages and higher rates,[56] but it is not clear that these practices will be stopped.

The racial inequality that persists today is not the product of 'impersonal market forces'[57] or due to the presumed cultural, moral, ethical, intellectual, or family 'deficiencies' of people of color, as conservative commentators have argued. Racial inequality today is due to the 'continuing significance' of racial discrimination.[58] The scholarly community has documented the persistence of discrimination in the labor and housing markets and has uncovered the coexistence of old-fashioned as well as subtle 'smiling discrimination'.[59] But racial discrimination is not just about jobs and housing: discrimination affects almost every aspect of the lives of people of color. It affects them in hospitals,[60] restaurants,[61] trying to buy cars or hail a cab,[62] driving,[63] flying,[64] or doing almost anything in America. Indeed, 'living while black [or brown]'[65] is quite hard and affects the health (physical and mental) of people of color tremendously, as they seem to always be in 'fight or flight' mode.[66]

Despite the continuing significance of racism in minorities' lives, whites' racial policy attitudes up until at least 2008 had not changed significantly since the 1980s.[67] Instead, most contemporary researchers believe that since the 1970s, whites have developed new ways of justifying the racial status quo distinct from the 'in your face' prejudice of the past. Analysts have labeled whites' post–civil rights racial attitudes as 'modern racism', 'subtle racism', 'aversive racism', 'social dominance', 'competitive racism', or, the term I prefer, 'color-blind racism'. But regardless of the name given to whites' new way of framing race matters, their switch from Jim Crow racism to color-blind racism did not change the basics, as the new version is as good as the old one, if not better, in safeguarding the racial order....

The Revolution Will Not Be Televised: Resistance in Color-Blind Racist America

#BlackLivesMatter. An innocuous, seemingly uncontroversial phrase sits at the center of contemporary black social movement mobilization and embodies what it means to mobilize in a digital age. Black Lives Matter began in 2013. Dismayed by George Zimmerman's acquittal for the 2012 murder of seventeen-year-old Trayvon Martin, three black women activists, Alicia Garza, Patrisse Cullors, and Opal Tometi, took to the social media platform Twitter to express their anger and frustration with the lack of justice that continues to be endemic of the black experience in the United States. The three friends tweeted with the hashtag '#BlackLivesMatter', earning the attention of a variety of artists who took the idea beyond social medial. But Black Lives Matter did not gain the traction to be called a 'movement' until 2014, after the killing of eighteen-year-old Michael Brown in Ferguson, Missouri.[68]

Officer Darren Wilson's extrajudicial murder of Michael Brown, as he reportedly kneeled in the street with his hands in the air, sparked waves of protests in Ferguson. As the tenor of the protests grew increasingly violent when a militarized police force rolled out tanks and riot gear to confront protestors, the original hashtag exploded on Twitter. According to the 'Beyond the Hashtags' report, which analyzed the role of social media in undergirding the movement, the number of tweets using the hashtag peaked at almost 53,000 in August during the initial round of protests in Ferguson. Later, after the local district attorney announced that Darren Wilson would not be indicted in late November 2014, a second round of protests were sparked. These new protests coupled with the non-indictment of Eric Garner's murderer, Officer Daniel Pantaleo, less than two weeks later caused the hashtag to explode. At one point in December, it appeared in over 160,000 individual tweets in *one day*. This increased usage meant that the phrase, indeed the idea 'Black Lives Matter', was growing in popularity and permeating the public consciousness, thus drawing more and more attention to the injustices of Michael Brown and Eric Garner.[69]

Arguably, during this second round of protests in Ferguson, when the black and brown communities' outrage drew even more national attention, #BlackLivesMatter 'officially' transitioned from a social media phenomenon to a social movement. Many respondents interviewed in the 'Beyond the Hashtags' report named the Ferguson protests as the moment when they became aware of the Black Lives Matter movement.[70] Soon after these incidents, the hashtag's creators, Garza, Cullors, and Tometi, formalized this transition by establishing 'Black Lives Matter' as a chapter-based organization, where local chapters must receive approval to earn listing on the webpage. This decentralized chapter-based model has been described as similar to the NAACP (perhaps a more apt description would be the Black Panther Party). At this point, Black Lives Matter had become a 'global phenomenon', comprising not just Black Lives Matter chapters but a broad coalition of organizations falling under the banner 'The Movement for Black Lives'.[71]

In addition to its wide array of goals (such as ending mass incarceration, reparations for slavery, and economic justice), Black Lives Matter should also be commended for its broad inclusiveness of an array of black identities. We must identify this inclusiveness as one of its most notable features. For example, unlike the traditional straight black male dominance of the civil rights and Black Power movements, the Movement for Black Lives boasts a diverse set of leaders. The phrase 'Black Lives Matter' was coined by three black women, all of whom identify as queer, and the three other most prominent figures have been two black women and a gay black man. Moreover, other movement leaders have been overwhelmingly female and they have made a concerted effort to avoid alienating black people on the margins due to gender and sexual identities.

The impact of the movement on public opinion is undeniable. According to a Gallup poll in 2016, twice as many Americans report that they are worried a 'great deal' about race relations than in 2014. That includes increases from 31 percent to 57 percent among black Americans and 14 percent to 27 percent among white Americans.[72] More to the point, a 2015 Pew poll reported that 65 percent of blacks express support for the Black Lives Matter movement and 58 percent believe the movement will 'be effective in helping achieve racial equality' (compared to 40 and 36 percent of whites respectively).[73] Because of the impact of the movement, activists successfully demanded meetings with mainstream politicians, garnering multiple policy meetings with Barack Obama and Bernie Sanders and Hillary Clinton during the 2016 Democratic primary and the subsequent presidential campaign.[74] Even though these meetings have not yielded many results, the movement offers a playbook for response to police brutality, which is its own type of success.

However, the movement's largest impact is increasing the prevalence of police body cameras across the country. But the use of body cameras has netted mixed results. Some studies suggest that the use of body cameras dramatically reduces the number of complaints filed against law enforcement (some claim by up to 93 percent).[75] Other studies suggest that police body cameras are associated with an increase in fatal police shootings.[76] Moreover, their use has been met with a number of other legal and ethical issues. First is the increasing amount of legislation governing who has access to body cam footage. Rather than making the footage freely available in an attempt to offer a sense of true transparency, law enforcement agencies and local governments have placed a number of barriers to acquiring the footage. Sometimes they even require a lawsuit or that law enforcement agencies be afforded the opportunity to redact the footage. Second, there are numerous cases of law enforcement officers claiming that their body cameras malfunctioned or that they forgot to activate them immediately before a violent interaction with a civilian.[77] The lack of footage defeats the purpose of using the body cams at all. Finally, some people have raised privacy concerns about the victims, suspects, and bystanders caught on camera, worried that their identities or other personal information such as addresses may be unnecessarily revealed.[78]

Although Garza, Cullors, and Tometi laid the initial ideological ground-work for the Black Lives Matter movement, the movement has seen the rise of a number of other social movement leaders. Among the most notable are DeRay Mckesson, Brittany Packnett, and Johnetta 'Netta' Elzie, all of whom came to fame by 'live-tweeting' the protests in Ferguson in 2014. Since then, though they remain strongly connected personally, the careers of the three activists have diverged, but in 2015, they collaborated to create 'Campaign Zero', an initiative dedicated to offering specific, research-based policy solutions to reduce police violence.[79] As is the case with many civil rights leaders of the past, some of the activists have become co-opted. Since leaving his job in the Minneapolis school system to become an activist full time in the wake of the Ferguson tragedy, Mckesson has gone on to become firmly integrated into mainstream politics. He launched a campaign for mayor of his hometown of Baltimore in 2016, in which he finished in sixth place in the Democratic primary with about 2.5 percent of the vote. Later that same year, he was appointed interim chief human capital officer of the Baltimore city public school system.[80] Similarly, Packnett has become deeply involved in mainstream politics. After joining a task force assembled by the Missouri governor after the protests in Ferguson, Packnett impressed Barack Obama so much during a meeting that he appointed her to his Task Force on 21st Century Policing. Of her role in the movement she says, 'There are some people who need to be revolutionary, and there are some people who need to be at the table in the White House'.[81] Elzie, on the other hand, has remained much more of an activist, spending most of her time on the road protesting, giving talks at universities, and participating in a variety of other events.[82] The three opposing paths of Mckesson, Packnett, and Elzie demonstrate the assortment of paths available to Black Lives Matter activists and the variety of ways they set out to work toward racial equality. This diversity definitely stands out as one of the strengths of the movement.

Alongside the Black Lives Matter movement, a college campus protest movement emerged. Inspired by the boldness of Black Lives Matter activists, students on about fifty campuses have protested for racial justice on their respective campuses, demanding the removal of racist campus employees, the hiring of more faculty of color, and the implementation of programs and administrators tasked with creating a more inclusive environment, among other things. By all accounts, the students have been successful in forcing university administrations to concede to some of their demands.[83]

The student mobilization began at the University of Missouri in 2015. In early November, a graduate student, Jonathan Butler, began a hunger strike in protest of the campus administration's lackluster response to a number of racist incidents that had transpired on campus in the previous months. Butler demanded that the university president resign. Over the next few days, support for the strike grew exponentially, eventually leading the football team, one of the most prominent in the country, to claim that they would boycott their upcoming game if the president refused to resign. On November 9, the president resigned and the chancellor stepped down from his role to assume a non-administrative research position.[84] The success of the students at the University of Missouri emboldened students across the country, leading to a wave of similar protests.

At Claremont McKenna College in Claremont, California, less than a week after the University of Missouri president resigned, the students forced the dean of students to resign. The students had been pressuring the university for months to increase faculty diversity and funding for multicultural programs, but a comment from the dean of students, coupled with the events in Missouri, pushed the students to a breaking point. The dean of students reportedly emailed a Latina student that she would work harder to include students who 'don't fit our CMC model'. The comments sparked two hunger strikes and a campus protest that led to the dean's resignation.[85]

Even the country's 'elite' higher education institutions have not been exempt from the protests. The same week the president of the University of Missouri resigned, students at Yale University marched in response to ongoing 'racial insensitivity' by the campus administration. The protest had been building for a time, as students battled the university over a variety of issues, including the campus's historical ties to slavery, the lack of faculty diversity, and a professor's insistence that students should be allowed to don offensive Halloween costumes. In response, the university devoted $50 million to an initiative to improve faculty diversity, and the professor who purported to defend 'free expression' soon resigned from the university.[86]

Although these incidents happened in a very narrow period in 2015, student protests have continued well into 2016. The student protests have grown to demand things outside of explicit racial concerns. Students at Duke University occupied an administrative building demanding, among other things, that the university raise its minimum wage to $15 per hour,[87] while students at the Ohio State University occupied an administrative building for a day in an effort to force the university to divest all of its assets from Israeli companies.[88]

We should note that in each case, the students were responding not just to one precipitating event but a pattern of exclusion, tension, and damaging campus policies. The protests are not simple knee-jerk reactions to certain individual events. Instead, they represent the vitality of the current moment and how it has pushed students' desperation and bravery to the fore. Moreover, their demands reflect a deep understanding of the workings of race and racism. Rather than limit their demands to resolving a single conflict, many of the student movements seek to change the entirety of campus racial culture. The protests have already created a climate on college campuses unlike any other time since the 1960s. According to a study by UCLA's Higher Education Research Institute, the percentage of incoming college students in 2015 who expressed that they expect to participate in a protest during their time on campus increased to 8.5 percent, up from just 5.6 percent in 2014. Among black students, the proportion was even higher – at 16 percent in 2015, about a 50 percent increase from 2014. The survey has been conducted every year since 1966 and the percentages of students reporting they expect to participate in a protest is higher than it has been since the question first appeared in 1967.[89] This may represent a collective raise in the social consciousness of college students and suggests that the campus protests are far from over.

As I finish this chapter, a day after Donald J. Trump's inauguration as our forty-fifth president, massive marches and protests across the United States, and all over the world, took place.[90] Although it is hard to predict what these mobilizations will produce, they denote that people of color and progressives in general are alive and well and ready to fight. This, again, is reminiscent of the 1980s and how Reaganism led to massive protests and heightened political work.[91]

Conclusion

This chapter demonstrates the fickle, perhaps ineffective, nature of electoral politics relative to the efficacy of social movement mobilization. Barack Obama, the great black hope for many progressives in the United States, failed to deliver on his grand promise of 'change'. With eight years of compromise, condescension, and center-right politics, he, ultimately, left black Americans worse off than we were before he took office. As he leaves office, he is replaced by President Donald Trump, whose virulent racial rhetoric has led to a spike in overt racism that has accompanied record numbers in police brutality against black Americans. But, as history has shown us, wherever there is oppression there is resistance, and the Black Lives Matter movement seems as if it will continue to be a lasting part of our social fabric and push back against the forces that threaten the lives of oppressed people. The movement has not only 'fought the good fight', it has inspired a wave of young activists to attempt to change the racial climates on their college campuses all across the country. The victories of both Black Lives Matter activists and college campus movements are encouraging. They show, to quote the movie *Independence Day*, that 'we will not go quietly into the night'.

Notes

1. Manning Marable, *How Capitalism Underdeveloped Black America: Problems in Race, Political Economy, and Society* (Cambridge, MA: Southend Press, 2000).
2. Adam Liptak, 'U.S. Imprisons One in 100 Adults, Report Finds', *New York Times*, 29 February, 2008.
3. Devah Pager, 'The Mark of a Criminal Record', *American Journal of Sociology* 108 (2003): 937–75.
4. Marc Mauer and Ryan S King, 'Uneven Justice: State Rates of Incarceration by Race and Ethnicity', The Sentencing Project, June 2007.
5. Gerald D Jaynes and Robin M Williams, *A Common Destiny: Blacks and American Society* (Washington, DC: National Academy Press, 1989).
6. Alfred N Garwood, *Black Americans: A Statistical Sourcebook* (Boulder, CO: Numbers and Concepts, 1991).
7. Donna M Bishop, 'The Role of Race and Ethnicity in Juvenile Justice Processing', in *Our Children, Their Children: Confronting Racial and Ethnic Differences in American Juvenile Justice*, edited by Darnell F Hawking and Kimberly Kempf-Leonard (Chicago and London: University of Chicago Press, 2005).

8. Derrick Bell, *Faces at the Bottom of the Well* (New York: Basic Books, 1992).
9. Renford Reese, *Prison Race* (Durham, NC: Carolina Academic Press, 2006).
10. Farai Chideya, *Don't Believe the Hype: Fighting Cultural Misinformation about African-Americans* (New York: Penguin Books, 1995).
11. Reese, *Prison Race*.
12. Pamela I Jackson, *Minority Group Threat, Crime, and Policing* (New York; Westport, CT; and London: Praeger, 1989).
13. Allen E Liska, Joseph J Lawrence and Michael Benson, 'Perspectives on the Legal Order: The Capacity for Social Control', *American Journal of Sociology* 87 (1981): 413–26.
14. Mark S Rosentraub and Karen Harlow, 'Police Policies and the Black Community: Attitude toward the Police', in *Contemporary Public Policy Perspectives and Black Americans*, edited by Mitchell F Rice and Woodrow Jones Jr, 107–21 (Westport, CT, and London: Greenwood Press, 1984); Ronald Weitzer and Steven Tuch, 'Race and Perception of Police Misconduct', *Social Problems* 51 (2004): 305–25.
15. Lawrence W Sherman, 'Execution without Trial: Police Homicide and the Constitution', *Vanderbilt Law Review* 33 (1980): 71–100.
16. Julia Dahl, 'Trayvon Martin Shooting: A Timeline of Events', CBS, July 12, 2013, retrieved from http://www.cbsnews.com/news/trayvon-martin-shooting-a-timeline-of-events/ (accessed 23 January, 2017).
17. Tim Wise, 'School Shootings and White Denial', 2001, retrieved from www.tim wise.org/2001/03/school-shootings-and-white-denial (accessed 29 March, 2013).
18. Cheng Cheng and Mark Hoekstra, *Does Strengthening Self-Defense Law Deter Crime or Escalate Violence? Evidence from Castle Doctrine* (Cambridge, MA: National Bureau of Economic Research, 2012).
19. Sarah Childress, 'Is There Racial Bias in "Stand Your Ground" Laws'? *Frontline*, July 31, 2012, retrieved from www.pbs.org/wgbh/pages/frontline/criminal-justice/is-there-racial-bias-in-stand-your-ground-laws (accessed 29 March, 2013).
20. Will Bredderman, ' "Blue Lives Matter" Bill Would Grant Cops Hate Crime Protection from Protesters in New York', *Observer*, 3 August, 2016, retrieved from http://observer.com/2016/08/blue-lives-matter-bill-would-grant-cops-hate-crime-protection-from-protesters/ (accessed 23 January, 2017).
21. Samuel R Gross and Robert Mauro, *Death and Discrimination: Racial Disparities in Capital Sentencing* (Boston: Northeastern University Press, 1989).
22. David V Baker, 'The Racist Application of Capital Punishment to African Americans', in *Racial Issues in Criminal Justice: The Case of African Americans*, edited by Marvin D Free Jr. (Westport, CT: Praeger, 2003); Reese, *Prison Race*.
23. Stephen Demuth and Darrell Steffensmeier, 'Ethnicity Effects on Sentence Outcomes in Large Urban Courts: Comparisons among White, Black, and Hispanic Defendants', *Social Science Quarterly* 85 (2004): 994–1011.
24. Charles R Pruitt and James Q Wilson, 'A Longitudinal Study of the Effect of Race in Sentencing', *Law and Society Review* 7 (1983): 613–35.
25. Cassia Spohn, 'Crime and the Social Control of Blacks: Offender/Victim Race and the Sentencing of Violent Offenders', in *Inequality, Crime, and Social Control*, edited by George S Bridges and Martha A Myers, 249–68 (Boulder, CO; San Francisco; and Oxford: Westview Press, 1994).
26. Spohn, 'Crime and the Social Control of Blacks'; Michael L Radelet and Glenn L Pierce, 'The Role of Victim's Race and Geography on Death Sentencing', in *From Lynch Mobs to the Killing State*, edited by Charles J Ogletree Jr and Austin Sarat (New York: New York University Press, 2006).
27. Spohn, Crime and the Social Control of Blacks'.
28. Gross and Mauro, *Death and Discrimination*.

29. David C Baldus, Charles A Pulaski Jr, and George Woodworth, 'Comparative Review of Death Sentences: An Empirical Study of the Georgia Experience', *Journal of Criminal Law & Criminology* 74 (1983): 661–753.
30. Derrick Bell, *Faces at the Bottom of the Well*.
31. Nijole Benokratis, 'Racial Exclusion in Juries', *Journal of Applied Behavioral Science* 18 (1982): 29–47.
32. Craig Haney, 'On the Selection of Capital Juries: The Biasing of the Death-Qualification Process', *Law and Human Behavior* 8 (1984): 121–32.
33. Gregory D Russell, *The Death Penalty and Racial Bias: Overturning Supreme Court Assumptions* (Westport, CT, and London: Greenwood Press, 1994).
34. Gross and Mauro, *Death and Discrimination*.
35. Lee P Brown, 'Crime in the Black Community'.
36. Bell, *Faces at the Bottom of the Well*.
37. John L Cooper, *The Police and the Ghetto* (Port Washington, NY, and London: Kennikat Press, 1980).
38. Alan J Lizote, 'Extra-Legal Factors in Chicago's Criminal Courts: Testing the Conflict Model of Criminal Justice', *Social Problems* 25 (1978): 564–80.
39. Donna M Bishop, 'The Role of Race and Ethnicity in Juvenile Justice Processing', in *Our Children, Their Children: Confronting Racial and Ethnic Differences in American Juvenile Justice*, edited by Darnell F Hawking and Kimberly Kempf-Leonard (Chicago and London: University of Chicago Press, 2005).
40. Chideya, *Don't Believe the Hype*.
41. Douglas Smith, Christy A Visher, and Laura Davidson, 'Equity and Discretionary Justice: The Influence of Race on Police Arrest Decisions', *Journal of Criminal Law and Criminology* 75 (1984): 234–49; Reese, *Prison Race*.
42. Daniel Funke and Tina Susman, 'From Ferguson to Baton Rouge: Deaths of Black Men and Women at the Hands of Police', *Los Angeles Times*, 12 July, 2016, retrieved from http://www.latimes.com/nation/la-na-police-deaths-20160707-snap-htmlstory.html (accessed 23 January, 2017).
43. David J Garrow, *The FBI and Martin Luther King* (New York: Penguin Books, 1983).
44. George Orwell, 'In Front of Your Nose', in *The Collected Essays, Journalism, and Letters of George Orwell*, vol 4, edited by S Orwell and I Angus (New York: Harcourt, Brace, and World, 1946).
45. The exact quote from the second president of the United States is 'facts are stubborn things; and whatever may be our wishes, our inclinations, or the dictates of our passion, they cannot alter the state of facts and evidence'. The quote can be found in the website of law professor Douglas Linder, Famous American Trials, 'Boston Massacre Trials, 1770', at www.law.umkc.edu/faculty/projects/ftrials/bostonmassacre/bostonmassacre.html.
46. *Department of Numbers*, retrieved from http://www.deptofnumbers.com/unemployment/demographics/ (accessed 22 January, 2017); Bernadette D Proctor, Jessica L Semega and Melissa A Kollar, 'Income and Poverty in the United States: 2015', *Current Population Reports*, September 2016, retrieved from https://www.census.gov/content/dam/Census/library/publications/2016/demo/p60-256.pdf (accessed 22 January, 2017).
47. Department of Numbers.
48. Proctor, Semega and Kollar, 'Income and Poverty in the United States: 2015'.
49. Valerie Wilson and William M Rogers III, 'Black-White Wage Gaps Expand with Rising Wage Inequality', 20 September, 2016, retrieved from http://www.epi.org/publication/black-white-wage-gaps-expand-with-rising-wage-inequality/ (accessed 22 January, 2017).
50. Edward Rodriguez and Richard V Reeves, 'Five Bleak Facts on Black Opportunity', 15 January, 2015, retrieved from https://www.brookings.edu/blog/social-mobilitymemos/2015/01/15/five-bleak-facts-on-black-opportunity/ (accessed 22 January, 2017).

51. Rakesh Kochhar and Richard Fry, 'Wealth Inequality Has Widened along Racial, Ethnic Lines since End of Great Recession', 12 December, 2014, retrieved from http://www.pewresearch.org/fact-tank/2014/12/12/racial-wealth-gaps-great-recession/ (accessed 22 January, 2017); National Urban League, '2016 State of Black America: Locked Out: Education, Jobs & Justice', 2016, retrieved from http://nul.iamempowered.com/sites/nul.iamempowered.com/files/black-white-index-051316.pdf (accessed 22 January, 2017).
52. Jeffrey P Thompson and Gustavo A Suarez, 'Exploring the Racial Wealth Gap Using the Survey of Consumer Finances', 2015, retrieved from https://www.federalreserve.gov/econresdata/feds/2015/files/2015076pap.pdf (accessed 22 January, 2017).
53. Melvin Oliver and Thomas Shapiro, *Black Wealth, White Wealth* (New York: Routledge, 1995).
54. This calculation uses the Survey of Consumer Finances. A separate calculation using the Survey of Income and Program Participation shows that the wealth gap as high as 20:1 and 18:1 for whites relative to blacks and Latinos, respectively in 2009. Either way, the point remains the same: the wealth gap between whites and these two groups is large and rising.
55. Center for Responsible Lending, 'Lost Ground, 2011: Disparities in Mortgage Lending and Foreclosures', 17 November, 2011, retrieved from www.responsiblelending.org/mortgage-lending/policy-legislation/regulators/facing-the-foreclosure-crisis.html (accessed 31 March, 2013).
56. Charlie Savage, 'Wells Fargo Will Settle Mortgage Bias Charges', *New York Times*, 12 July, 2012, retrieved from www.nytimes.com/2012/07/13/business/wells-fargo-to-settle-mortgage-discrimination-charges.html (accessed 31 March, 2013).
57. William Julius Wilson, *The Declining Significance of Race: Blacks and Changing American Institutions* (Chicago: University of Chicago Press, 1978); *The Truly Disadvantaged* (Chicago: University of Chicago Press, 1987).
58. Joe R Feagin, 'The Continuing Significance of Race: Antiblack Discrimination in Public Places', *American Sociological Review* 56, no 1 (1991): 101–16.
59. Roy Brooks, *Integration or Separation? A Strategy for Racial Equality* (Cambridge, MA: Harvard University Press, 1996). For a great review of the contemporary landscape of discrimination, see Devah Pager and Hannah Sheppard, 'The Sociology of Discrimination: Racial Discrimination in Employment, Housing, Credit, and Consumer Markets', *Annual Review of Sociology* 34 (2008): 181–209.
60. Janice Blanchard and Nicole Lurie, 'R-e-s-p-e-c-t: Patient Reports of Disrespect in the Health Care Setting and Its Impact on Care', *Journal of Family Practice* 53 (2004): 721–31; Louis A Penner, John H Dovidio, Donald Edmondson, Rhonda K Dailey, Tsveti Markova, Terrance L Albrecht and Samuel L Gaertner, 'The Experience of Discrimination and Black-White Health Disparities in Medical Care', *Journal of Black Psychology* 35 (2009): 180–203.
61. Sarah E Rusche and Zachary W Brewster, '"Because They Tip for Shit"! The Social Psychology of Everyday Racism in Restaurants', *Sociology Compass* 2, no 6 (2008): 2008–29.
62. Ian Ayres, *Pervasive Prejudice?* (Chicago: University of Chicago Press, 2002); Serge Kovaleski and Sewell Chan, 'D.C. Cabs Still Bypass Minorities, Study Finds: City Crackdown Called Sporadic, Inadequate', *Washington Post*, 7 October, 2003, retrieved from www.highbeam.com/doc/1P2-313833.html (accessed 31 March, 2013).
63. Albert Meehan and Michael Ponder, 'Race and Place: The Ecology of Racial Profiling African American Motorists', *Justice Quarterly* 19 (2002): 399–430.
64. Cathy Harris, *Flying While Black: A Whistleblower's Story* (Los Angeles: Milligan, 2001).
65. In the 1960s, sociologist Paul M Siegel wrote a very influential paper titled 'On the Cost of Being a Negro' (*Sociological Inquiry* 35, no 1 [1965]: 41–57) documenting the multiple and deleterious impact of racism on blacks. This idea was updated in the 1990s with the notion of 'living while black', 'driving while black', and so on. In a recent paper, Shaun Gabbidon and Steven A Peterson updated

the evidence: 'Living While Black: A State-Level Analysis of the Influence of Select Social Stressors on the Quality of Life among Black Americans', *Journal of Black Studies* 37, no 1 (2008): 83–102. I added 'brown' to the text in the quote, as many scholars have performed similar analyses for Latinos and Asians and have documented that racism affects them adversely, too.
66. Professor William A Smith has worked tirelessly to demonstrate that racism produces the syndrome he calls 'racial battle fatigue'. The constant thinking, preparing, expecting, and being concerned about the potential for racial discrimination creates an almost-constant state of 'fight or flight' in people of colour, with deleterious health consequences. See William A Smith, Walter Allen and Lynnette Danley, ' "Assume the Position . . . You Fit the Description": Psychosocial Experiences and Racial Battle Fatigue among African American Male College Students', *American Behavioral Scientist* 51, no 4 (2007): 551–78.
67. Steven Tuch and Michael Hughes, 'Whites' Racial Policy Attitudes in the Twenty-First Century: The Continuing Significance of Racial Resentment', *The ANNALS of the American Academy of Political and Social Science* 634 (2011): 134.
68. 'A HerStory of the #BlackLivesMatter Movement', Black Lives Matter, retrieved from http://blacklivesmatter.com/herstory/ (accessed on 23 January, 2017).
69. Deen Freelon, Charlton D Mcilwain and Meredith Clark, 'Beyond the Hashtags: #Ferguson, #BlackLivesMatter, and the Online Struggle for Offline Justice', February 2016, retrieved from http://cmsimpact.org/wp-content/uploads/2016/03/beyond_the_hashtags_2016.pdf (accessed 23 January, 2017).
70. Deen Freelon, Charlton D Mcilwain and Meredith Clark, 'Beyond the Hashtags: #Ferguson, #BlackLivesMatter, and the Online Struggle for Offline Justice'.
71. Freelon, Mcilwain, and Clark, 'Beyond the Hashtags'; 'Platform', The Movement for Black Lives, retrieved from https://policy.m4bl.org/platform/ (accessed 23 January, 2017).
72. Jim Norman, 'U.S. Worries about Race Relations Reach a New High', Gallup, April 11, 2016, retrieved from http://www.gallup.com/poll/190574/worries-race-relations-reach-new-high.aspx (accessed 23 January, 2017).
73. Juliana Menasce Horowitz and Gretchin Livingston, 'How Americans View the Black Lives Matter Movement', Pew Research Center, 8 July, 2016, retrieved from http://www.pewresearch.org/fact-tank/2016/07/08/how-americans-view-the-black-lives-matter-movement/ (accessed 23 January, 2017).
74. Chuck Ross, 'Bernie Sanders to Meet with Black Lives Matter Activist DeRay Mckesson', *Daily Caller*, 15 September, 2015, retrieved from http://dailycaller.com/2015/09/15/bernie-sanders-to-meet-with-black-lives-matter-activist-deray-mckesson/ (accessed 23 January, 2017); Abby Phillip, 'Clinton to Meet with Black Lives Matter Activists in Cleveland', *Washington Post*, 21 October, 2016, retrieved from https://www.washingtonpost.com/news/post-politics/wp/2016/10/21/clinton-to-meet-with-black-lives-matter-activists-in-cleveland/?utm_term=.07b0c131eb1c (accessed 23 January, 2017).
75. Danny Shaw, 'Police Body Cameras "Cut Complaints against Officers" ', BBC News, 29 September, 2016, retrieved from http://www.bbc.com/news/uk-37502136 (accessed 23 January, 2017).
76. Jacob Gershman, 'Study Links Police Bodycams to Increase in Shooting Deaths', *Wall Street Journal*, 12 August, 2016, retrieved from http://blogs.wsj.com/law/2016/08/12/study-links-police-bodycams-to-increase-in-shooting-deaths/ (accessed 23 January, 2017).
77. Robinson Meyer, 'Body Cameras Are Betraying Their Promise', *The Atlantic*, 30 September, 2016, retrieved from http://www.theatlantic.com/technology/archive/2016/09/body-cameras-are-just-making-police-departments-more-powerful/502421/ (accessed 23 January, 2017).
78. Eileen Sullivan, 'Police-Body Cameras May Solve 1 Problem but Create Others for Victims and Innocent Bystanders', *US News*, 11 September, 2015, retrieved from http://www.usnews.com/news/politics/articles/2015/09/11/police-body-cameras-may-solve-one-problem-but-create-others (accessed 23 January, 2017).

79. 'Planning Team', Campaign Zero, retrieved from https://www.joincampaignzero.org/about/ (accessed 23 January, 2017).
80. Erica L Green and Luke Broadwater, 'Civil Rights Activist DeRay Mckesson to Join New City Schools Cabinet', *Baltimore Sun*, 28 June, 2016, retrieved from http://www.baltimoresun.com/news/maryland/baltimore-city/bs-md-ci-deray-mckesson-appointment-20160628-story.html (accessed 23 January, 2017).
81. Wesley Lowery, *They Can't Kill Us All: Ferguson, Baltimore, and a New Era in America's Racial Justice Movement* (New York: Little, Brown and Company, 2016), 226.
82. Aaron Randle, 'Now You See Me: A Look at the World of Activist Johnetta Elzie', *Complex*, 8 March, 2016, retrieved from http://www.complex.com/life/2016/03/johnetta-elzie-profile (accessed 23 January, 2017).
83. Jack Dickey, 'The Revolution on America's Campuses', *Time*, 31 May, 2016, retrieved from http://time.com/4347099/college-campus-protests/ (accessed 23 January, 2017).
84. Victor Luckerson, 'Missouri Shows That College Presidents Can't Be Corporate', *Time*, 11 November, 2015, retrieved from http://time.com/4109421/missouri-shows-that-college-presidents-cant-be-corporate/ (accessed 23 January, 2017); Susan Svrluga, 'U. Missouri President, Chancellor Resign over Handling of Racial Incidents', *Washington Post*, 9 November, 2015, retrieved from https://www.washingtonpost.com/news/grade-point/wp/2015/11/09/missouris-student-government-calls-for-university-presidents-removal/?hpid=hp_hp-top-table-main_missresignation-1124am%3Ahomepage%2Fstory&utm_term=.98ce822783e6 (accessed 23 January, 2017).
85. Teresa Watanabe and Carla Rivera, 'Amid Racial Bias Protests, Claremont McKenna Dean Resigns', *Los Angeles Times*, 13 November, 2015, retrieved from http://www.latimes.com/local/lanow/la-me-ln-claremont-marches-20151112-story.html (accessed 23 January, 2017).
86. Justin Worland, 'Why a Free Speech Fight Is Causing Protests at Yale', *Time*, 10 November, 2015, retrieved from http://time.com/4106265/yale-students-protest/ (accessed 23 January, 2017); Anemona Hartocollis, 'Yale Lecturer Resigns after Email on Halloween Costumes', *New York Times*, 7 December, 2015, retrieved from https://www.nytimes.com/2015/12/08/us/yale-lecturer-resigns-after-email-on-halloween-costumes.html (accessed 23 January, 2017).
87. Amrith Ramkumar and Gautam Hathi, 'Allen Building Sit-In Students Exit Building after Week-Long Protest', *Chronicle*, 8 April, 2016, retrieved from http://www.dukechronicle.com/article/2016/04/allen-building-sit-in-students-exit-building-after-week-long-protest (accessed 23 January, 2017).
88. Josh Logue, 'A Broader Protest Agenda', *Inside Higher Ed*, 19 April, 2016, retrieved from https://www.insidehighered.com/news/2016/04/19/student-protests-year-broaden-beyond-issues-race (accessed 23 January, 2017).
89. Kevin Eagan, Ellen Bara Stolzenberg, Abigail K Bates, Melissa C Aragon, Maria Ramirez Suchard and Cecilia Rios-Aguilar, 'The American Freshman: National Norms Fall 2015', Cooperative Institutional Research Program, 2016, retrieved from https://www.heri.ucla.edu/monographs/TheAmericanFreshman2015.pdf (accessed 23 January, 2017).
90. David Johnson and Chris Wilson, 'See Just How Big Over 200 Women's Marches Were All across the Country', *Time*, 23 January, 2016, retrieved from http://time.com/4643692/womens-march-size-country/ (accessed in 27 January, 2017).
91. Marable, *How Capitalism Underdeveloped Black America*.

CASE STUDY

Edwidge Danticat[*], 'Message to My Daughters'

Soon after the one-year anniversary of the fatal shooting of Michael Brown by the Ferguson police officer Darren Wilson, I was in Haiti, at the southernmost end of the country's border with the Dominican Republic, where hundreds of Haitian refugees had either been deported or driven out of the Dominican Republic by intimidation or threats. Many of these men and women had very little warning that they were going to be picked up or chased away and most of them had fled with nothing but the clothes on their backs.

It was a bright sunny day, but the air was thick with dust. As some friends and I walked through the makeshift resettlement camps on the Haitian side of the border, in a place called Pak Kado, it felt as though we, along with the residents of the camps, were floating through clouds. Around us were lean-tos made of cardboard boxes and sheets. Dust-covered children walked around looking dazed even while playing with pebbles that stood in for marbles, or while flying plastic bags as kites. Elderly people stood on the edge of food and clothes distribution lines, some too weak to wade into the crowd. Later the elderly, along with pregnant women and the disabled, would be given special consideration by the priest and nuns who were giving out the only food available to the camp dwellers, but the food would always run out before they could get to everyone.

A few days after leaving Haiti and returning to the United States, I read a Michael Brown anniversary opinion piece in *The Washington Post* written by Raha Jorjani, an immigration attorney and law professor. In her essay, Jorjani argues that African Americans living in the United States could easily qualify as refugees. Citing many recent cases of police brutality and killings of unarmed black men, women, and children, she wrote:

> Suppose a client walked into my office and told me that police officers in his country had choked a man to death over a petty crime. Suppose he said police fatally shot another man in the back as he ran away. That they arrested a woman during a traffic stop and placed her in jail, where she died three days later. That a 12-year-old boy in his country was shot and killed by the police as he played in the park.
>
> Suppose he told me that all of those victims were from the same ethnic community – a community whose members fear being harmed, tortured or killed by police or prison guards. And that this is true in cities and towns across his nation. At that point, as an immigration lawyer, I'd tell him he had a strong claim for asylum protection under U.S. law.

This is not the first time that the idea of African Americans as internal or external refugees has been floated or applied. The six-million-plus African Americans who migrated from the rural south to urban centers in the northern United States for more than half a century during the Great Migration were often referred to as refugees, as were those people internally displaced by Hurricane Katrina.

Having now visited many refugee and displacement camps, the label 'refugee' at first seemed an extreme designation to assign to citizens of one of the richest countries in the world, especially if it is assigned on a singular basis to those who are black. Still, compared to the relative wealth of the rest of the society, a particularly run-down Brooklyn public housing project where a childhood friend used to live had all the earmarks of a refugee camp. It occupied one of the least desirable parts of town and

---

[*] Edwidge Danticat, 'Message to My Daughters', in *The Fire This Time: A New Generation Speaks about Race*, ed. Jesmyn Ward (New York: Scribner, 2016), 205–16. Permissions by Edwidge Danticat.

provided only the most basic necessities. A nearby dilapidated school, where I attended junior high, could have easily been on the edge of that refugee settlement, where the primary daily task was to keep the children occupied, rather than engaged and learning. Aside from a few overly devoted teachers, we were often on our own. We, immigrant blacks and African Americans alike, were treated by those who housed us, and were in charge of schooling us, as though we were members of a group in transit. The message we always heard from those who were meant to protect us: that we should either die or go somewhere else. This is the experience of a refugee.

I have seen state abuses up close, both in Haiti, where I was born under a ruthless dictatorship, and in New York, where I migrated to a working-class and predominantly African, African American, and Caribbean neighborhood in Brooklyn at the age of twelve. In the Haiti of the 1970s and early '80s, the violence was overtly political. Government detractors were dragged out of their homes, imprisoned, beaten, or killed. Sometimes their bodies were left out in the streets, in the hot sun, for extended periods, to intimidate neighbors.

In New York, the violence seemed a bit more subtle, though no less pervasive. When I started riding the city bus to high school, I observed that a muffled radio message from an annoyed bus driver – about someone talking too loud or not having the right fare – was all it took to make the police rush in, drag a young man off the bus, and beat him into submission on the sidewalk. There were no cell phone cameras back then to record such abuse, and most of us were too terrified to demand a badge number.

Besides, many of us had fled our countries as exiles, migrants, and refugees just to escape this kind of military or police aggression; we knew how deadly a confrontation with an armed and uniformed authoritarian figure could be. Still, every now and then a fellow traveler would summon his or her courage and, dodging the swaying baton, or screaming from a distance, would yell some variation of 'Stop it! This is a child! A child'!

Of course, not all of the police's victims were children. Abner Louima, a family friend, was thirty years old when he was mistaken for someone who had punched a police officer outside a Brooklyn nightclub, on August 9, 1997, sixteen years to the day before Michael Brown was killed. Abner was arrested, beaten with fists, as well as with police radios, flashlights, and nightsticks, and then sexually assaulted with the wooden handle of a toilet plunger or a broom inside a precinct bathroom. After Abner, there was Amadou Diallo, a Guinean immigrant, who was hit by nineteen of the forty-one bullets aimed at him as he retrieved his wallet from his pocket. Then there was Patrick Dorismond, the U.S.-born child of Haitian immigrants, who died trying to convince undercover cops that he was not a drug dealer.

These are only a few among the cases from my era that made the news. There was also sixty-six-year-old Eleanor Bumpurs, who, thirteen years before Abner's assault, was killed by police with a twelve-gauge shotgun inside her own apartment. I have no doubt there were many others. We marched for all of them in the Louima/Diallo/Dorismond decade. We carried signs and chanted 'No Justice! No Peace'! and 'Whose Streets? Our Streets'! even while fearing the latter would never be true. The streets belonged to the people with the uniforms and the guns. The streets were never ours. Our sons and brothers, fathers and uncles, our mothers and sisters, daughters and nieces, our neighbors were, and still are, prey.

My father, a Brooklyn cab driver, used to half joke that police did not beat him up because, at sixty-five years old, he was too skinny and too old, and not worth the effort. Every now and then, when he was randomly stopped by a police officer and deigned to ask why, rather than a beating, he would be given a handful of unwarranted traffic citations that would wipe out a few weeks' hard-earned wages. Today, one might generously refer to such acts as micro-aggressions. That is, until they turn major and deadly, until other unarmed black bodies, with nowhere to go for refuge, find themselves in the path of yet another police officer's or armed vigilante's gun.

When it was announced that Darren Wilson would not be indicted for the killing of Michael Brown, I kept thinking of Abner Louima, whose assault took place when Michael Brown was just eighteen months old. Abner and I have known each other for years. Both our families have attended the same Creole-speaking church for decades, so I called him to hear his thoughts about Michael Brown's killer going free. If anyone could understand all those broken hearts, all the rage, all the desperation, the yearning for justice, what it is to be a member of a seemingly marooned and persecuted group, I thought, he would.

Abner Louima, unlike Michael Brown, had survived. He went on with his life, moved from New York City to south Florida, started businesses. He has a daughter and two sons. One son was eighteen years old when we spoke, the same age Michael Brown was when he died.

How does he feel, I asked him, each time he hears that yet another black person was killed or nearly killed by police?

'It reminds me that our lives mean nothing', he replied.

We are in America because our lives meant nothing to those in power in the countries where we came from. Yet we come here to realize that our lives also mean nothing here. Some of us try to distance ourselves from this reality, thinking that because we are another type of 'other' – immigrants, migrants, refugees – this is not our problem, nor one we can solve. But ultimately we realize the precarious nature of citizenship here: that we too are prey, and that those who have been in this country for generations – walking, living, loving in the same skin we're in – they too can suddenly become refugees.

Parents are often too nervous to broach difficult subjects with their children. Love. Sex. Death. Race. But some parents are forced to have these conversations early. Too early. A broken heart might lead to questions we'd rather not answer, as might an inappropriate gesture, the death of a loved one, or the murder of a stranger.

Each time a black person is killed in a manner that's clearly racially motivated, either by a police officer or a vigilante civilian, I ask myself if the time has come for me to talk to my daughters about Abner Louima and the long list of dead that have come since. My daughters have met Abner, but I have never told them about his past, even though his past is a future they might have to face.

Why don't I tell them? My decision is about more than avoiding a difficult conversation. The truth is, I do not want my daughters to grow up as I did, terrified of the country and the world they live in. But is it irresponsible of me to not alert them to the potentially life-altering, or even life-ending horrors they might face as young black women?

The night President Barack Obama was first elected (would he too qualify for refugee status?), my oldest daughter was three and I was in the last weeks of my pregnancy with my second. When President Obama was inaugurated for the first time, I was cradling both my little girls in my arms.

To think, I remember telling my husband, our daughters will never know a world in which the president of their country has not been black. Indeed, as we watched President Obama's inaugural speech, my oldest daughter was shocked that no woman had ever been president of the United States. That day, the world ahead for my girls seemed full of greater possibility – if not endless possibilities, then at least greater than those for generations past. Many more doors suddenly seemed open to my girls, and the 'joyous daybreak' evoked by Martin Luther King, Jr., in his 'I Have a Dream' speech, a kind of jubilee, seemed to have emerged. However, it quickly became clear that this one man was not going to take all of us with him into the postracial promised land. Or that he even had full access to it. Constant talk of 'wanting him to fail' was racially tinged, as were the 'birther' investigations, and the bigoted commentaries and jokes by both elected officials and ordinary folk. One of the most consistent attacks against the president, was that, like my husband and myself, he was born elsewhere and was not *really* American.

Like Barack Obama's father, many of us had brought our black bodies to America from somewhere else. Some of us, like the president, were the children of such people. We are people who need to have two different talks with our black offspring: one about why we're here and the other about why it's not always a promised land for people who look like us.

In his own version of 'The Talk', James Baldwin wrote to his nephew James in 'My Dungeon Shook', 'You were born in a society which spelled out with brutal clarity, and in as many ways as possible that you were a worthless human being'.

That same letter could have been written to a long roster of dead young men and women, whose dungeons shook, but whose chains did not completely fall off. Among these very young people are Oscar Grant, Aiyana Stanley-Jones, Rekia Boyd, Kimani Gray, Renisha McBride, Trayvon Martin, Michael Bell, Tamir Rice, Michael Brown, Sandra Bland, and counting. It's sad to imagine what these young people's letters from their loved ones may have said. Had their favorite uncle notified them that they could qualify for refugee status within their own country? Did their mother or father, grandmother or grandfather warn them to not walk in white neighborhoods, to, impossibly, avoid police officers, to never play in a public park, to stay away from neighborhood watchmen, to never go to a neighbor's house, even if to seek help from danger?

I am still, in my own mind, drafting a 'My Dungeon Shook' letter to my daughters. It often begins like this. Dear Mira and Leila, I've put off writing this letter to you for as long as I can, but I don't think I can put it off any longer. Please know that there will be times when some people might be hostile or even violent to you for reasons that have nothing to do with your beauty, your humor, or your grace, but only your race and the color of your skin. Please don't let this restrict your freedom, break your spirit, or kill your joy. And if possible do everything you can to change the world so that your generation of brown and black men, women, and children will be the last who experience all this. And please do live your best lives and achieve your full potential. Love deeply. Be joyful. In Jubilee, Mom.

To my draft of this letter, I often add snippets of Baldwin.

'I tell you this because I love you and please don't you ever forget it', Baldwin reminded his James. 'Know whence you came. If you know whence you came, there is no limit to where you can go'.

'The world is before you', I want to tell my daughters, 'and you need not take it or leave it as it was when you came in'.

I want to look happily forward. I want to be optimistic. I want to have a dream. I want to live in jubilee. I want my daughters to feel that they have the power to at least try to change things, even in a world that resists change with more strength than they have. I want to tell them they can overcome everything, if they are courageous, resilient, and brave. Paradoxically, I also want to tell them their crowns have already been bought and paid for and that all they have to do is put them on their heads. But the world keeps tripping me up. My certainty keeps flailing.

So I took them to the border, the one between Haiti and the Dominican Republic, where hundreds of refugees were living, or rather existing. There they saw and helped comfort men, women, and children who look like them, but are stateless, babies with not even a bedsheet between them and a dirt floor, young people who may not be killed by bullets but by the much slower assault of disease.

'These are all our causes', I tried to both tell and show them, brown and black bodies living with 'certain uncertainty', to use Frantz Fanon's words, black bodies fleeing oppression, persecution, and poverty, wherever they are.

'You think your pain and your heartbreak are unprecedented in the history of the world, but then you read', James Baldwin wrote. Or you see. Or you weep. Or you pray. Or you speak. Or you write. Or you fight so that one day everyone will be able to walk the earth as though they, to use Baldwin's words, have 'a right to be here'. May that day come, Mira and Leila, when you can finally claim those crowns of yours and put them on your heads. When that day of jubilee finally arrives, all of us will be there with you, walking, heads held high, crowns a-glitter, because we do have a right to be here.

SECTION III

Economic Justice and Social Welfare

The problem of racism, the problem of economic exploitation, and the problem of war are all tied together. These are the triple evils that are interrelated.
—Martin Luther King Jr

We can have democracy in this country, or we can have great wealth concentrated in the hands of a few, but we cannot have both.
—Louis D Brandeis

The quotations by Martin Luther King Jr and Justice Brandeis highlight the connections between democracy, economic justice and racial justice.

Economic justice requires equal rights to participate in decision making by those who are jointly engaged in economic activity. It also requires distributive justice, a just distribution of goods and means to obtain those goods. Economic justice and distributive justice, however, are different. Rawls's theory is a theory of distributive justice, but it is not a theory of economic justice. It starts with separate individuals, not with individuals as members of society, and their market-maximising behaviour, while the concept of economic justice assumes that ethical principles and social norms prevail over impersonal market mechanisms. Marx, in fact, thought that the concept of distributive justice or equitable distribution should not be the focus of the socialist movement as it dealt with the distribution and exchange of goods rather than with the relations of production under capitalism. Marx claimed that such relations are based on the exploitation of the workers by the capitalists: in fact, one of the defining features of capitalism is that labour is a commodity that can be bought and sold on the market. Since the value of a commodity is determined by the labour-power that is necessary for its production, writes Marx, the value of labour-power (a commodity) is what is required for its existence, such as food, shelter and clothing. It follows that the wage paid by the capitalist is the price of labour-power and covers the cost of the worker's survival, and yet the worker's labour-time is available to the capitalist for a longer period for the production of goods, thus creating added value or profit for the capitalist. Wages, therefore, do not reflect the value that workers create, but are merely the price of the commodity 'labour-power', the market price of labour. As a result, Marx predicted that the working class would suffer impoverishment relative to the growing wealth around it.

Marx's thoughts on the exploitative nature of the relationship between capitalist employers and their employees as well as his views of the increasing economic gap between the poor and the rich ring true today. Today, as Eduardo Bonilla-Silva indicates in his book *Racism without Racists*, Marx's proletariat is mainly composed of dark-skinned people, and primarily African Americans. He shows that the gaps in income and wealth between whites and Blacks are the result of continuing discrimination and structural inequality, housing policies as well as employment segregation. The primarily Black proletariat, or those without property, continues to seek employment from those with property. Economic power and control continue to give the white capitalist class decisive influence over government and politics and control over the supply of labour to ensure that it is sold by employees on terms favourable to the employers. Marx's theories on the exploitative nature of the capitalist employment relationship – which uses up human and natural resources for short-term gain – apply today also in the form of climate and energy issues, as we will see in the section on environmental injustice and the unequal impact of environmental hazards on the poor and people of color. We now have a world capitalist system, with a global rich and global poor, as Marx predicted. There is exploitation across all societies, and the proliferation of sweatshops and export processing zones are all very much in keeping with Marx's account.

Income inequality has risen dramatically since the 1970s and has been highlighted by the financial crisis of 2008, with an increasing concentration of income at the top, stagnation at the middle, and precariousness at the bottom. This has been accompanied by decreased social mobility and opportunity and increased poverty. Increased concentration of income has also led to the concentration of political power and thus a movement towards plutocracy.

In the fall of 2011, the Occupy movement forced into public attention the growing inequality in the United States. The popularity of Thomas Piketty's *Capital in the 21st Century* and his analysis of long-term trends in inequality and the growing prominence of this issue in electoral politics demonstrate that the Occupy discourse about 'the ninety-nine percent' versus 'the one percent' has spread and evolved. In fact, Labour Studies scholar Penny Lewis shows that news-media mentions of 'income inequality' in December 2013 had increased to even higher levels (50 percent more) than at the height of the Occupy movement in 2012.[1]

The Occupy movement originated as Occupy Wall Street in New York City on September 17, 2011. It was organised via Twitter and the Internet by Adbusters, an organisation critical of the corporate control of the media, to coincide with the date of the signing of the US Constitution. The occupation of Wall Street was meant as a protest of the various events that occurred after the 2008 economic collapse: the 2010 Supreme Court ruling in Citizen United that corporations are entitled to have free speech to influence elections, the bailout that did not trickle down as promised, and the growth of income inequality. Adbusters perceived that the original intent of the Framers of the Constitution had been undermined by corporate America. The event was intended to motivate and empower angry Americans to take action, but no one expected the spread and duration of the protest. It revived a form of participatory democracy and collective action that offered hope and an outlet for people to work together in cooperation for the common good, for a democracy for the people. And it initiated a conversation that we all need to be having.

The essay by Heyman and Heyman at the end of this section offers a narrative history of Occupy El Paso, the intersections of race, class and ethnicity, and the particular challenges it faced due to its location at the US-Mexico border. It also shows that the struggle for social and economic justice has not gone away: wherever there is oppression there is resistance of some kind.

Race, gender and class matter also in the way people relate to food and the food system. The food system workers who do low-paying and back-breaking jobs are disproportionately people of colour and migrants (and more women than men have lower-paying jobs in the food system). Farm workers on industrial farms are subjected to abuse by bosses, back-breaking work, harsh conditions, and lack of legal protection, as described in the article by Estabrook on southern Florida's tomato pickers. They work long hours with little compensation for often brutally hard, monotonous work that is akin to slavery and reminds us of Marx's description of the proletarian workers in the factories during the Industrial Revolution.

The continuing relevance of Marx's critique of capitalism and workers' conditions is also documented in Eric Schlosser's book, *Fast Food Nation*, which describes the dangerous jobs in slaughterhouses. Schlosser accuses companies like ConAgra of pursuing profits at the expense of safety for workers and consumers, and factory executives and plant managers allow deplorable and unsafe working conditions in the meatpacking industry because they want to maximise profit and minimise government 'intrusion' into their safety practices. As a consequence of the 'need for speed' in the meatpacking industry, worker injuries are common, and workers have very little sick leave, so many continue to work while hurt, or take drugs, like methamphetamine, to keep working as fast as possible on the line.

In his utopian novel, *Looking Backward* (1888), Bellamy also addresses several themes that are present in Marx. The novel was published at a time when there was widespread fear of working-class strikes and violence and criticism of the accumulation of money by a privileged minority. Bellamy presents a portrait of a utopian society based on centralised planning and cooperative equality, where poverty has been eliminated and each contributes to the common good. Bellamy condemns 19th-century competitive society as degrading and wasteful and compares it to the new society where everyone receives an equal share of the wealth because everyone works at their fullest potential and contributes what they can; people vie for status and honour rather than wealth. The message is that everyone shares equally as income equality is based on our common humanity. As Rawls argues in *A Theory of Justice*, there is no moral reason to distribute wealth according to people's natural endowments since they do not deserve their genetic assets; those who are more productive due to their greater natural abilities have no moral claim to receive more rewards.

In the selection 'Democracy and Charity', Jane Addams, like Bellamy, stresses the difference between charity and equity and focuses on the effects of inequality in a democracy when people try to help those more disadvantaged. Charity, as Addams describes it throughout the chapter, holds the beneficiaries to a standard that the charity visitor herself could not meet; its purpose in view of democracy is also questionable since charity, if perceived as morally good on the basis of someone well-off making a contribution to the poor, is an insufficient way to address suffering because it is one-sided and complacent. It is important that we acknowledge the relationship between social class and cultural expression and thus recognise that democracy calls for humans to perform charitable acts in a different manner than the charity businesses operate. Addams teaches us that since democracy places a high value on diversified experience and requires citizens to pay close attention to context and human action, people should not hold others to standards that they themselves could not reach if placed in similar contexts.

Note

1. Penny Lewis, 'Inequality After Occupy', *Washington Spectator*, 18 March 2014, https://portside.org/2014-03-18/inequality-after-occupy.

Suggested Readings

Ababneh, Sara. 'Troubling the Political: Women in the Jordanian Day-Waged Labor Movement', *International Journal of Middle East Studies* 48 (2016): 87–112.

Avineri, Shlomo. *The Social and Political Thought of Karl Marx.* Cambridge: Cambridge University Press, 1968.

Ball, Terence, and James Farr, eds. *After Marx.* Cambridge: Cambridge University Press, 1984.

Barndt, Deborah. *Tangled Routes: Women, Work, and Globalization on the Tomato Trail.* Rowman & Littlefield Publishers, 2007.

Carver, Terrell, ed. *The Cambridge Companion to Marx.* Cambridge: Cambridge University Press, 1991.

Coalition of Immokalee Workers. 'Anti-Slavery Program'. CIW. ciw-online.org/slavery.

Cohen, G A. *Why Not Socialism?* Princeton, NJ: Princeton University Press, 2011.

Deaton, Angus. *The Great Escape: Health, Wealth, and the Origins of Inequality.* Princeton, NJ: Princeton University Press, 2013.

Desmond, Matthew. *Evicted: Poverty and Profit in the American City.* New York: Crown Books, 2016.

Holmes, Seth. *Fresh Fruit, Broken Bodies: Migrant Farm Workers in the United States.* Berkeley, CA: University of California Press, 2013.

Jayaraman, Saru. *Behind the Kitchen Door.* New York: Cornell University Press, 2013.

King, Martin Luther Jr. *Where Do We Go from Here: Chaos or Community?* Boston, MA: Beacon Press, 1997.

Piketty, Thomas. *Capital in the Twenty-First Century.* Cambridge, MA: Belknap Press, 2017.

Reich, Robert. *The Common Good.* New York: Knopf, 2018.

Sarvasy, Wendy. 'Engendering Democracy by Socializing it: Jane Addams's Contribution to Feminist Political Theorizing'. In *Feminist Interpretations of Jane Addams*, ed Maurice Hamington. College Park, PA: Pennsylvania State University Press, 2010.

Stiglitz, Joseph E. *The Price of Inequality: How Today's Divided Society Endangers Our Future.* New York: W W Norton, 2013.

Suggested Documentaries and Films

Bahrani, Ramin, dir. *99 Houses.* Hyde Park Entertainment, 2014. DVD. A 2015 movie that provides a deep analysis of the meaning of home, the desperation attached to real estate and foreclosures, the pride of ownership and the stability of belonging.

Biberman, Herbert, dir. *Salt of the Earth.* Aamir Khan Productions, 1954. DVD. A drama about mining bosses pitting Mexican Americans against their Anglo counterparts.

Bratt, Peter, dir. *Dolores.* Carlos Santana Production. 2017. DVD. A portrait of Chicana activist Dolores Huerta, who, along Cesar Chavez, tirelessly led the fight for racial and labour justice for farm workers in California to form the UFW.

Chandor, J C, dir. *Margin Call.* Before the Door Pictures, 2011. DVD. A 2011 drama that follows the key people at an investment bank, over a twenty-four-hour period, during the early stages of the 2008 financial crisis.

Ferguson, Charles, dir. *Inside Job.* Sony Pictures Classic, 2010. DVD. A 2010 documentary that takes a closer look at what brought about the 2008 financial meltdown.

Gibney, Alex, dir. *Park Avenue: Money, Power, and the American Dream.* PBS, 2012. DVD. A 2012 documentary that looks at the extreme income concentration and downward mobility.

Hanson, Curtis, dir. *Too Big to Fail.* Deuce Three Productions, 2011. DVD. A 2011 film that chronicles the financial meltdown of 2008.

Kornbluth, Jacob, dir. *Inequality for All.* Sebastian Dungan, 2013. DVD. In his Wealth and Poverty class at UC Berkeley, former Labor Secretary Robert Reich discusses the grave economic and social consequences that may result if the gulf between rich and poor continues to widen.

Linklater, Richard, dir. *Fast Food Nation.* Recorded Picture Company, 2006. DVD. Based on the book by Eric Schlosser, the film examines the health risks involved in the fast food industry as well as its environmental and social consequences.

Loach, Ken, dir. *Bread and Roses.* British Screen, 2000. DVD. Based on the 'Justice for Janitors' campaign of the Service Employees International Union, the film portrays the struggle of poorly paid janitorial workers in Los Angeles and their fight for better working conditions and the right to unionise.

McKay, Adam, dir. *The Big Short.* Regency Enterprises, 2015. DVD. A drama about a handful of wealthy traders who made a killing by betting on the housing collapse.

Moore, Michael, dir. *Capitalism: A Love Story.* Dog Eat Dog Films, 2009. DVD. Michael Moore's exploration of corporate greed and the catastrophic effect on American lives.

Moore, Michael, dir. *Where to Invade Next.* Dog Eat Dog Films, 2015. DVD. A 2015 documentary where Michael Moore, to learn what the USA can learn from other nations, playfully 'invades' them to see what they have to offer.

Singer, Marc, dir. *Dark Days.* Marc Singer, 2000. DVD. A 2000 documentary on the homeless population who live permanently in the underground tunnels of New York City.

Warchus, Matthew, dir. *Pride.* BBC Films, 2014. DVD. A 2014 British film inspired by a true story. It's the summer of 1984, Margaret Thatcher is in power and the National Union of Mineworkers is on strike, prompting a London-based group of gay and lesbian activists to raise money to support the strikers' families.

Karl Marx*, 'The Power of Money'

Money is the *pimp* between man's need and the object, between his life and his means of life. But that which mediates *my* life for me, also *mediates* the existence of other people *for me*. For me it is the *other* person.

> What, man! confound it, hands and feet
> And head and backside, all are yours!
> And what we take while life is sweet,
> Is that to be declared not ours?
> Six stallions, say, I can afford,
> Is not their strength my property?
> I tear along, a sporting lord,
> As if their legs belonged to me.
>
> (Mephistopheles, in *Faust*)[1]

> Shakespeare in *Timon of Athens*:
> Gold? Yellow, glittering, precious gold? No, Gods,
> I am no idle votarist! . . . Thus much of this will make black white, foul fair,
> Wrong right, base noble, old young, coward valiant.
> . . . Why, this
> Will lug your priests and servants from your sides,

---

* Karl Marx, "The Power of Money," from *Economic and Philosophical Manuscripts of 1844*, in Robert C. Tucker, ed., *The Marx-Engels Reader*, 2nd ed, pp. 102–105. Copyright 1978, 1972 by W.W. Norton & Company. Used by permission of W.W. Norton & Company, Inc.

Pluck stout men's pillows from below their heads:
This yellow *slave*
Will knit and break religions, bless the accursed;
Make the hoar leprosy adored, place thieves
And give them title, knee and approbation
With senators on the bench: This is it
That makes the wappen'd widow wed again;
She, whom the spital-house and ulcerous sores
Would cast the gorge at, this embalms and spices
To the April day again. . . . Damned earth,
Thou common whore of mankind, that putt'st odds
Among the rout of nations.[2]

And also later:

O thou sweet king-killer, and dear divorce
Twixt natural son and sire! thou bright defiler
Of Hymen's purest bed! thou valiant Mars!
Thou ever young, fresh, loved and delicate wooer,
Whose blush doth thaw the consecrated snow
That lies on Dian's lap! Thou *visible God*!
That solder'st *close impossibilities,*
And mak'st them kiss! That speak'st with every tongue,
To every purpose! O thou touch of hearts!
Think thy slave man rebels, and by thy virtue
Set them into confounding odds, that beasts
May have the world in empire![3]

Shakespeare excellently depicts the real nature of *money*. To understand him, let us begin, first of all, by expounding the passage from Goethe.

That which is for me through the medium of *money* – that for which I can pay (i.e., which money can buy) – that am *I*, the possessor of the money. The extent of the power of money is the extent of my power. Money's properties are my properties and essential powers – the properties and powers of its possessor. Thus, what I *am* and *am capable* of is by no means determined by my individuality. I am ugly, but I can buy for myself the most *beautiful* of women. Therefore I am not *ugly*, for the effect of *ugliness* – its deterrent power – is nullified by money. I, in my character as an individual, am *lame*, but money furnishes me with twenty-four feet. Therefore I am not lame. I am bad, dishonest, unscrupulous, stupid; but money is honoured, and therefore so is its possessor. Money is the supreme good, therefore its possessor is good. Money, besides, saves me the trouble of being dishonest: I am therefore presumed honest. I am *stupid*, but money is the *real mind* of all things and how then should its possessor be stupid? Besides, he can buy talented people for himself, and is he who has power over the talented not more talented than the talented? Do not I, who thanks to money am capable of *all* that the human heart longs for, possess all human capacities? Does not my money therefore transform all my incapacities into their contrary?

If *money* is the bond binding me to *human* life, binding society to me, binding me and nature and man, is not money the bond of all *bonds*? Can it not dissolve and bind all ties? Is it not, therefore, the universal *agent of divorce*? It is the true *agent of divorce* as well as the true *binding agent* – the [universal][4] *galvano-chemical* power of Society.

Shakespeare stresses especially two properties of money:

(1) It is the visible divinity – the transformation of all human and natural properties into their contraries, the universal confounding and overturning of things: it makes brothers of impossibilities.
(2) It is the common whore, the common pimp of people and nations.

The overturning and confounding of all human and natural qualities, the fraternization of impossibilities – the *divine* power of money – lies in its *character* as men's estranged, alienating and self-disposing *species-nature*. Money is the alienated *ability of mankind*.

That which I am unable to do as a *man*, and of which therefore all my individual essential powers are incapable, I am able to do by means of *money*. Money thus turns each of these powers into something which in itself it is not – turns it, that is, into its *contrary*.

If I long for a particular dish or want to take the mail-coach because I am not strong enough to go by foot, money fetches me the dish and the mail-coach: that is, it converts my wishes from something in the realm of imagination, translates them from their meditated, imagined or willed existence into their *sensuous, actual* existence – from imagination to life, from imagined being into real being. In effecting this mediation, money is the *truly creative* power.

No doubt *demand* also exists for him who has no money, but his demand is a mere thing of the imagination without effect or existence for me, for a third party, for the others, and which therefore remains for me *unreal* and *objectless*. The difference between effective demand based on money and ineffective demand based on my need, my passion, my wish, etc., is the difference between *being* and *thinking*, between the imagined which *exists* merely within me and the imagined as it is for me outside me as a *real object*.

If I have no money for travel, I have no *need* – that is, no real and self-realizing need – to travel. If I have the *vocation* for study but no money for it, I have *no* vocation for study – that is, no *effective*, no *true* vocation. On the other hand, if I have really *no* vocation for study but have the will *and* the money for it, I have an *effective* vocation for it. Being the external, common *medium* and *faculty* for turning an *image* into *reality* and *reality* into a mere *image* (a faculty not springing from man as man or from human society as society), *money* transforms the *real essential powers of man and nature* into what are merely abstract conceits and therefore *imperfections* – into tormenting chimeras – just as it transforms *real imperfections and chimeras* – essential powers which are really impotent, which exist only in the imagination of the individual – into *real powers* and *faculties*.

In the light of this characteristic alone, money is thus the general overturning of *individualities* which turns them into their contrary and adds contradictory attributes to their attributes.

Money, then, appears as this *overturning* power both against the individual and against the bonds of society, etc., which claim to be *essences* in themselves. It transforms fidelity into infidelity, love into hate, hate into love, virtue into vice, vice into virtue, servant into master, master into servant, idiocy into intelligence and intelligence into idiocy.

Since money, as the existing and active concept of value, confounds and exchanges all things, it is the general *confounding* and *compounding* of all things – the world upside-down – the confounding and compounding of all natural and human qualities.

He who can buy bravery is brave, though a coward. As money is not exchanged for any one specific quality, for any one specific thing, or for any particular human essential power, but for the entire objective world of man and nature, from the standpoint of its possessor it therefore serves to exchange every property for every other, even contradictory, property and object: it is the fraternization of impossibilities. It makes contradictions embrace.

Assume *man* to be *man* and his relationship to the world to be a human one: then you can exchange love only for love, trust for trust, etc. If you want to enjoy art, you must be an artistically-cultivated person; if you want to exercise influence over other people, you must be a person with a stimulating and encouraging effect on other people. Every one of your relations to man and to nature must be a *specific expression*, corresponding to the object of your will, of your *real individual* life. If you love without evoking love in return – that is, if your loving as loving does not produce reciprocal love; if through a *living expression* of yourself as a loving person you do not make yourself a *loved person*, then your love is impotent – a misfortune.

Notes

1. Goethe, *Faust* (Part I (New York: Penguin, 1949), 91. Study, III), translated by Philip Wayne.
2. Shakespeare, *Timon of Athens*, Act 4, Scene 3. Marx quotes the Schlegel-Tieck German translation. (Marx's emphasis.)
3. Shakespeare, *Timon of Athens*, Act 4, Scene 3.
4. An end of the page is torn out of the manuscript.

Karl Marx and Friedrich Engels*, 'Communism'

Communism deprives no man of the power to appropriate the products of society; all that it does is to deprive him of the power to subjugate the labour of others by means of such appropriation.

It has been objected that upon the abolition of private property all work will cease, and universal laziness will overtake us.

According to this, bourgeois society ought long ago to have gone to the dogs through sheer idleness; for those of its members who work, acquire nothing, and those who acquire anything, do not work. The whole of this objection is but another expression of the tautology: that there can no longer be any wage-labour when there is no longer any capital. . . .

The charges against Communism made from a religious, a philosophical, and, generally, from an ideological standpoint, are not deserving of serious examination.

Does it require deep intuition to comprehend that man's ideas, views and conceptions, in one word, man's consciousness, changes with every change in the conditions of his material existence, in his social relations and in his social life?

What else does the history of ideas prove, than that intellectual production changes its character in proportion as material production is changed? The ruling ideas of each age have ever been the ideas of its ruling class.

When people speak of ideas that revolutionise society, they do but express the fact, that within the old society, the elements of a new one have been created, and that the dissolution of the old ideas keeps even pace with the dissolution of the old conditions of existence.

When the ancient world was in its last throes, the ancient religions were overcome by Christianity. When Christian ideas succumbed in the 18th century to rationalist ideas, feudal society fought its death battle with the then revolutionary bourgeoisie. The ideas of religious

---

* Karl Marx and Friedrich Engels, "Communism," from *The Communist Manifesto*, in Robert C. Tucker, ed., *The Marx-Engels Reader*, 2nd ed, pp. 486, 489-491. Copyright 1978, 1972 by W.W. Norton & Company. Used by permission of W.W. Norton & Company, Inc.

liberty and freedom of conscience merely gave expression to the sway of free competition within the domain of knowledge.

'Undoubtedly', it will be said, 'religious, moral, philosophical and juridical ideas have been modified in the course of historical development. But religion, morality, philosophy, political science, and law, constantly survived this change'.

'There are, besides, eternal truths, such as Freedom, Justice, etc., that are common to all states of society. But Communism abolishes eternal truths, it abolishes all religion, and all morality, instead of constituting them on a new basis; it therefore acts in contradiction to all past historical experience'.

What does this accusation reduce itself to? The history of all past society has consisted in the development of class antagonisms, antagonisms that assumed different forms at different epochs.

But whatever form they may have taken, one fact is common to all past ages, *viz.*, the exploitation of one part of society by the other. No wonder, then, that the social consciousness of past ages, despite all the multiplicity and variety it displays, moves within certain common forms, or general ideas, which cannot completely vanish except with the total disappearance of class antagonisms.

The Communist revolution is the most radical rupture with traditional property relations; no wonder that its development involves the most radical rupture with traditional ideas. . . .

In place of the old bourgeois society, with its classes and class antagonisms, we shall have an association, in which the free development of each is the condition for the free development of all.

Karl Marx*, 'Capitalism and Exploitation'

Commodities

The Two Factors of a Commodity: Use-Value and Value (the Substance of Value and the Magnitude of Value)

The wealth of those societies in which the capitalist mode of production prevails, presents itself as 'an immense accumulation of commodities', its unit being a single commodity. Our investigation must therefore begin with the analysis of a commodity.

A commodity is, in the first place, an object outside us, a thing that by its properties satisfies human wants of some sort or another. The nature of such wants, whether, for instance, they spring from the stomach or from fancy, makes no difference. Neither are we here concerned to know how the object satisfies these wants, whether directly as means of subsistence, or indirectly as means of production.

Every useful thing, as iron, paper, etc., may be looked at from the two points of view of quality and quantity. It is an assemblage of many properties, and may therefore be of use in various ways. To discover the various uses of things is the work of history. So also is the establishment of socially-recognised standards of measure for the quantities of these useful objects. The diversity of these measures has its origin partly in the diverse nature of the objects to be measured, partly in convention.

The utility of a thing makes it a use-value. But this utility is not a thing of air. Being limited by the physical properties of the commodity, it has no existence apart from that commodity. A commodity, such as iron, corn, or a diamond, is therefore, so far as it is a material

---

* Karl Marx, "Commodities" and "Wages," in David McLlellan with Introduction and Notes (Oxford World's Classics, 1995–2008), *Karl Marx: Capital: An Abridged Edition*, pp. 13–17, 309–314. By Permission of Oxford University Press.

thing, a use-value, something useful. This property of a commodity is independent of the amount of labour required to appropriate its useful qualities. When treating of use-value, we always assume to be dealing with definite quantities, such as dozens of watches, yards of linen, or tons of iron. The use-values of commodities furnish the material for a special study, that of the commercial knowledge of commodities. Use-values become a reality only by use or consumption: they also constitute the substance of all wealth, whatever may be the social form of that wealth. In the form of society we are about to consider, they are, in addition, the material depositories of exchange-value.

Exchange-value, at first sight, presents itself as a quantitative relation, as the proportion in which values in use of one sort are exchanged for those of another sort, a relation constantly changing with time and place. Hence exchange-value appears to be something accidental and purely relative, and consequently an intrinsic value, i.e., an exchange-value that is inseparably connected with, inherent in commodities, seems a contradiction in terms. Let us consider the matter a little more closely.

A given commodity, e.g., a quarter of wheat is exchanged for x blacking, y silk, or z gold, etc. – in short, for other commodities in the most different proportions. Instead of one exchange-value, the wheat has, therefore, a great many. But since x blacking, y silk, or z gold, etc., each represents the exchange-value of one quarter of wheat, x blacking, y silk, z gold, etc., must, as exchange-values, be replaceable by each other, or equal to each other. Therefore, first: the valid exchange-values of a given commodity express something equal; secondly, exchange-value, generally, is only the mode of expression, the phenomenal form, of something contained in it, yet distinguishable from it.

Let us take two commodities, e.g., corn and iron. The proportions in which they are exchangeable, whatever those proportions may be, can always be represented by an equation in which a given quantity of corn is equated to some quantity of iron: e.g., 1 quarter corn = x cwt. iron. What does this equation tell us? It tells us that in two different things – in 1 quarter of corn and x cwt. of iron, there exists in equal quantities something common to both. The two things must therefore be equal to a third, which in itself is neither the one nor the other. Each of them, so far as it is exchange-value, must therefore be reducible to this third.

A simple geometrical illustration will make this clear. In order to calculate and compare the areas of rectilinear figures, we decompose them into triangles. But the area of the triangle itself is expressed by something totally different from its visible figure, namely, by half the product of the base multiplied by the altitude. In the same way the exchange-values of commodities must be capable of being expressed in terms of something common to them all, of which thing they represent a greater or less quantity.

This common 'something' cannot be either a geometrical, a chemical, or any other natural property of commodities. Such properties claim our attention only in so far as they affect the utility of those commodities, make them use-values. But the exchange of commodities is evidently an act characterised by a total abstraction from use-value. Then one use-value is just as good as another, provided only it be present in sufficient quantity. Or, as old Barbon says, 'one sort of wares are as good as another, if the values be equal. There is no difference or distinction in things of equal value. . . . An hundred pounds' worth of lead or iron, is of as great value as one hundred pounds' worth of silver or gold'. As use-values, commodities are, above all, of different qualities, but as exchange-values they are merely different quantities, and consequently do not contain an atom of use-value.

If then we leave out of consideration the use-value of commodities, they have only one common property left, that of being products of labour. But even the product of labour itself has undergone a change in our hands. If we make abstraction from its use-value, we make abstraction at the same time from the material elements and shapes that make the product a use-value; we see in it no longer a table, a house, yarn, or any other useful thing. Its existence as a material thing is put out of sight. Neither can it any longer be regarded as the product of the labour of the joiner, the mason, the spinner, or of any other definite kind of productive labour. Along with the useful qualities of the products themselves, we put out of sight both the useful character of the various kinds of labour embodied in them, and the concrete forms of that labour; there is nothing left but what is common to them all; all are reduced to one and the same sort of labour, human labour in the abstract.

Let us now consider the residue of each of these products; it consists of the same unsubstantial reality in each, a mere congelation of homogeneous human labour, of labour-power expended without regard to the mode of its expenditure. All that these things now tell us is, that human labour-power has been expended in their production, that human labour is embodied in them. When looked at as crystals of this social substance, common to them all, they are – Values.

We have seen that when commodities are exchanged, their exchange-value manifests itself as something totally independent of their use-value. But if we abstract from their use-value, there remains their Value as defined above. Therefore, the common substance that manifests itself in the exchange-value of commodities, whenever they are exchanged, is their value. The progress of our investigation will show that exchange-value is the only form in which the value of commodities can manifest itself or be expressed. For the present, however, we have to consider the nature of value independently of this, its form.

A use-value, or useful article, therefore, has value only because human labour in the abstract has been embodied or materialised in it. How, then, is the magnitude of this value to be measured? Plainly, by the quantity of the value-creating substance, the labour, contained in the article. The quantity of labour, however, is measured by its duration, and labour-time in its turn finds its standard in weeks, days, and hours.

Some people might think that if the value of a commodity is determined by the quantity of labour spent on it, the more idle and unskilful the labourer, the more valuable would his commodity be, because more time would be required in its production. The labour, however, that forms the substance of value, is homogeneous human labour, expenditure of one uniform labour-power. The total labour-power of society, which is embodied in the sum total of the values of all commodities produced by that society, counts here as one homogeneous mass of human labour-power, composed though it be of innumerable individual units. Each of these units is the same as any other, so far as it has the character of the average labour-power of society, and takes effect as such; that is, so far as it requires for producing a commodity, no more time than is needed on an average, no more than is socially necessary. The labour-time socially necessary is that required to produce an article under the normal conditions of production, and with the average degree of skill and intensity prevalent at the time. The introduction of power-looms into England probably reduced by one-half the labour required to weave a given quantity of yarn into cloth. The hand-loom weavers, as a matter of fact, continued to require the same time as before; but for all that, the product of one hour of their labour represented after the change only half an hour's social labour, and consequently fell to one-half its former value.

We see then that that which determines the magnitude of the value of any article is the amount of labour socially necessary, or the labour-time socially necessary for its production. Each individual commodity, in this connexion, is to be considered as an average sample of its class. Commodities, therefore, in which equal quantities of labour are embodied, or which can be produced in the same time, have the same value. The value of one commodity is to the value of any other, as the labour-time necessary for the production of the one is to that necessary for the production of the other. As values, all commodities are only definite masses of congealed labour-time.

The value of a commodity would therefore remain constant, if the labour-time required for its production also remained constant. But the latter changes with every variation in the productiveness of labour. This productiveness is determined by various circumstances, amongst others, by the average amount of skill of the workmen, the state of science, and the degree of its practical application, the social organisation of production, the extent and capabilities of the means of production, and by physical conditions. For example, the same amount of labour in favourable seasons is embodied in 8 bushels of corn, and in unfavourable, only in four. The same labour extracts from rich mines more metal than from poor mines. Diamonds are of very rare occurrence on the earth's surface, and hence their discovery costs, on an average, a great deal of labour-time. Consequently much labour is represented in a small compass. Jacob doubts whether gold has ever been paid for at its full value. This applies still more to diamonds. According to Eschwege, the total produce of the Brazilian diamond mines for the eighty years, ending in 1823, had not realised the price of one-and-a-half years' average produce of the sugar and coffee plantations of the same country, although the diamonds cost much more labour, and therefore represented more value. With richer mines, the same quantity of labour would embody itself in more diamonds, and their value would fall. If we could succeed at a small expenditure of labour, in converting carbon into diamonds, their value might fall below that of bricks. In general, the greater the productiveness of labour, the less is the labour-time required for the production of an article, the less is the amount of labour crystallised in that article, and the less is its value; and vice versa, the less the productiveness of labour, the greater is the labour-time required for the production of an article, and the greater is its value. The value of a commodity, therefore, varies directly as the quantity, and inversely as the productiveness, of the labour incorporated in it.

A thing can be a use-value, without having value. This is the case whenever its utility to man is not due to labour. Such are air, virgin soil, natural meadows, etc. A thing can be useful, and the product of human labour, without being a commodity. Whoever directly satisfies his wants with the produce of his own labour, creates, indeed, use-values, but not commodities. In order to produce the latter, he must not only produce use-values, but use-values for others, social use-values. Lastly nothing can have value, without being an object of utility. If the thing is useless, so is the labour contained in it; the labour does not count as labour, and therefore creates no value.

Wages

The Transformation of the Value (and Respectively the Price) of Labour-Power into Wages On the surface of bourgeois society the wage of the labourer appears as the price of labour, a certain quantity of money that is paid for a certain quantity of labour. Thus people speak of the value of labour and call its expression in money its necessary or natural price. On the other hand they speak of the market-prices of labour, i.e., prices oscillating above or below its natural price.

But what is the value of a commodity? The objective form of the social labour expended in its production. And how do we measure the quantity of this value? By the quantity of the labour contained in it. How then is the value, e.g., of a 12 hours' working-day to be determined? By the 12 working-hours contained in a working-day of 12 hours, which is an absurd tautology.

In order to be sold as a commodity in the market, labour must at all events exist before it is sold. But could the labourer give it an independent objective existence, he would sell a commodity and not labour.

Apart from these contradictions, a direct exchange of money, i.e., of realised labour, with living labour would either do away with the law of value which only begins to develop itself freely on the basis of capitalist production, or do away with capitalist production itself, which rests directly on wage-labour. The working-day of 12 hours embodies itself, e.g., in a money-value of 6s. Either equivalents are exchanged, and then the labourer receives 6s. for 12 hours' labour; the price of his labour would be equal to the price of his product. In this case he produces no surplus-value for the buyer of his labour, the 6s. are not transformed into capital, the basis of capitalist production vanishes. But it is on this very basis that he sells his labour and that his labour is wage-labour. Or else he receives for 12 hours' labour less than 6s., i.e., less than 12 hours' labour. Twelve hours' labour are exchanged against 10, 6, etc., hours' labour. This equalisation of unequal quantities not merely does away with the determination of value. Such a self-destructive contradiction cannot be in any way even enunciated or formulated as a law.

It is of no avail to deduce the exchange of more labour against less, from their difference of form, the one being realised, the other living. This is the more absurd as the value of a commodity is determined not by the quantity of labour actually realised in it, but by the quantity of living labour necessary for its production. A commodity represents, say 6 working-hours. If an invention is made by which it can be produced in 3 hours, the value, even of the commodity already produced, falls by half. It represents now 3 hours of social labour instead of the 6 formerly necessary. It is the quantity of labour required for its production, not the realised form of that labour, by which the amount of the value of a commodity is determined.

That which comes directly face to face with the possessor of money on the market, is in fact not labour, but the labourer. What the latter sells is his labour-power. As soon as his labour actually begins, it has already ceased to belong to him; it can therefore no longer be sold by him. Labour is the substance, and the immanent measure of value, but *has itself no value*.

In the expression 'value of labour', the idea of value is not only completely obliterated, but actually reversed. It is an expression as imaginary as the value of the earth. These imaginary expressions, arise, however, from the relations of production themselves. They are categories for the phenomenal forms of essential relations. That in their appearance things often represent themselves in inverted form is pretty well known in every science except Political Economy.

Classical Political Economy borrowed from every-day life the category 'price of labour' without further criticism, and then simply asked the question, how is this price determined? It soon recognised that the change in the relations of demand and supply explained in regard to the price of labour, as of all other commodities, nothing except its changes, i.e., the oscillations of the market-price above or below a certain mean. If demand and supply balance, the oscillation of prices ceases, all other conditions remaining the same. But then demand and supply also cease to explain anything. The price of labour, at the moment when demand and supply are in equilibrium, is its natural price, determined independently of the relation of demand and supply. And how this price is determined, is just the question. Or a larger period of oscillations in the market-price is taken, e.g., a year, and they are found to cancel one the other, leaving a mean average quantity, a relatively constant magnitude. This had naturally to be determined otherwise than by its own compensating variations. This price which always finally predominates over the accidental market-prices of labour and regulates them, this 'necessary price' (physiocrats) or 'natural price' of labour (Adam Smith) can, as with all other commodities, be nothing else than its value expressed in money. In this way Political Economy expected to penetrate athwart the accidental prices of labour, to the value of labour. As with other commodities, this value was determined by the cost of production. But what is the cost of production – of the labourer, i.e., the cost of producing or reproducing the labourer himself? This question unconsciously substituted itself in Political Economy for the original one; for the search after the cost of production of labour as such turned in a circle and never left the spot. What economists therefore call value of labour, is in fact the value of labour-power, as it exists in the personality of the labourer, which is as different from its function, labour, as a machine is from the work it performs. Occupied with the difference between the market-price of labour and its so-called value, with the relation of this value to the rate of profit, and to the values of the commodities produced by means of labour, etc., they never discovered that the course of the analysis had led not only from the market-prices of labour to its presumed value, but had led to the resolution of this value of labour itself into the value of labour-power. Classical economy never arrived at a consciousness of the results of its own analysis; it accepted uncritically the categories 'value of labour', 'natural price of labour', etc., as final and as adequate expressions for the value-relation under consideration and was thus led . . . into inextricable confusion and contradiction, while it offered to the vulgar economists a secure basis of operations for their shallowness, which on principle worships appearances only.

Let us next see how value (and price) of labour-power, present themselves in this transformed condition as wages.

We know that the daily value of labour-power is calculated upon a certain length of the labourer's life, to which, again, corresponds a certain length of working-day. Assume the habitual working-day as 12 hours, the daily value of labour-power as 3s., the expression in money of a value that embodies 6 hours of labour. If the labourer receives 3s., then he receives the value of his labour-power functioning through 12 hours. If, now, this value of a day's labour-power is expressed as the value of a day's labour itself, we have the formula: Twelve hours' labour has a value of 3s. The value of labour-power thus determines the value of labour, or, expressed in money, its necessary price. If, on the other hand, the price of labour-power differs from its value, in like manner the price of labour differs from its so-called value.

As the value of labour is only an irrational expression for the value of labour-power, it follows, of course, that the value of labour must always be less than the value it produces, for the capitalist always makes labour-power work longer than is necessary for the reproduction of its own value. In the above example, the value of the labour-power that functions through 12 hours is 3s., a value for the reproduction of which 6 hours are required. The value which the labour-power produces is, on the other hand, 6s., because it, in fact, functions during 12 hours, and the value it produces depends, not on its own value, but on the length of time it is in action. Thus, we have a result absurd at first sight – that labour which creates a value of 6s. possesses a value of 3s.

We see, further: The value of 3s. by which a part only of the working-day – i.e., 6 hours' labour – is paid for, appears as the value or price of the whole working-day of 12 hours, which thus includes 6 hours unpaid for. The wage-form thus extinguishes every trace of the division of the working-day into necessary labour and surplus-labour, into paid and unpaid labour. All labour appears as paid labour. In the corvée, the labour of the worker for himself, and his compulsory labour for his lord, differ in space and time in the clearest possible way. In slave-labour, even that part of the working-day in which the slave is only replacing the value of his own means of existence, in which, therefore, in fact, he works for himself alone, appears as labour for his master. All the slave's labour appears as unpaid labour. In wage-labour, on the contrary, even surplus-labour, or unpaid labour, appears as paid. There the property-relation conceals the labour of the slave for himself; here the money-relation conceals the unrequited labour of the wage-labourer.

Hence, we may understand the decisive importance of the transformation of value and price of labour-power into the form of wages, or into the value and price of labour itself. This phenomenal form, which makes the actual relation invisible, and, indeed, shows the direct opposite of that relation, forms the basis of all the juridical notions of both labourer and capitalist, of all the mystifications of the capitalistic mode of production, of all its illusions as to liberty, of all the apologetic shifts of the vulgar economists.

If history took a long time to get at the bottom of the mystery of wages, nothing, on the other hand, is easier to understand than the necessity, the *raison d'être*, of this phenomenon.

The exchange between capital and labour at first presents itself to the mind in the same guise as the buying and selling of all other commodities. The buyer gives a certain sum of money, the seller an article of a nature different from money. The jurist's consciousness recognises in this, at most, a material difference, expressed in the juridically equivalent formulæ: 'Do ut des, do ut facias, facio ut des, facio ut facias'.[1]

Further. Exchange-value and use-value, being intrinsically incommensurable magnitudes, the expressions 'value of labour', 'price of labour', do not seem more irrational than the expressions 'value of cotton', 'price of cotton'. Moreover, the labourer is paid after he has given his labour. In its function of means of payment, money realises subsequently the value or price of the article supplied – i.e., in this particular case, the value or price of the labour supplied. Finally, the use-value supplied by the labourer to the capitalist is not, in fact, his labour-power, but its function, some definite useful labour, the work of tailoring, shoemaking, spinning, etc. That this same labour is, on the other hand, the universal value-creating element, and thus possesses a property by which it differs from all other commodities, is beyond the cognisance of the ordinary mind.

Let us put ourselves in the place of the labourer who receives for 12 hours' labour, say the value produced by 6 hours' labour, say 3s. For him, in fact, his 12 hours' labour is the means of buying the 3s. The value of his labour-power may vary, with the value of his usual means of subsistence, from 3 to 4 shillings, or from 3 to 2 shillings; or, if the value of his labour-power remains constant, its price may, in consequence of changing relations of demand and supply, rise to 4s. or fall to 2s. He always gives 12 hours of labour. Every change in the amount of the equivalent that he receives appears to him, therefore, necessarily as a change in the value or price of his 12 hours' work. This circumstance misled Adam Smith, who treated the working-day as a constant quantity, to the assertion that the value of labour is constant, although the value of the means of subsistence may vary, and the same working-day, therefore, may represent itself in more or less money for the labourer.

Let us consider, on the other hand, the capitalist. He wishes to receive as much labour as possible for as little money as possible. Practically, therefore, the only thing that interests him is the difference between the price of labour-power and the value which its function creates. But, then, he tries to buy all commodities as cheaply as possible, and always accounts for his profit by simple cheating, by buying under, and selling over the value. Hence, he never comes to see that, if such a thing as the value of labour really existed, and he really paid this value, no capital would exist, his money would not be turned into capital.

Moreover, the actual movement of wages presents phenomena which seem to prove that not the value of labour-power is paid, but the value of its function, of labour itself. We may reduce these phenomena to two great classes: (1) Change of wages with the changing length of the working-day. One might as well conclude that not the value of a machine is paid, but that of its working, because it costs more to hire a machine for a week than for a day. (2) The individual difference in the wages of different labourers who do the same kind of work. We find this individual difference, but are not deceived by it, in the system of slavery, where, frankly and openly, without any circumlocution, labour-power itself is sold. Only, in the slave system, the advantage of a labour-power above the average, and the disadvantage of a labour-power below the average, affects the slave-owner; in the wage-labour system it affects the labourer himself, because his labour-power is, in the one case, sold by himself, in the other, by a third person.

For the rest, in respect to the phenomenal form, 'value and price of labour', or 'wages', as contrasted with the essential relation manifested therein, viz., the value and price of labour-power, the same difference holds that holds in respect to all phenomena and their hidden substratum. The former appear directly and spontaneously as current modes of thought; the latter must first be discovered by science. Classical Political Economy nearly touches the true relation of things, without, however, consciously formulating it. This it cannot so long as it sticks in its bourgeois skin.

Note

1. *Facio ut des* is a Latin term which means 'I do so that you give'. This is a species of contract in the civil law which arises when a person agrees to perform anything for a price, either exclusively mentioned or left to the determination of the law to set a value to it. Here, a person agrees to do something for reward. The consideration in such a contract is also termed as *facio ut des*. For example, when a servant hires himself to his master for certain wages or an agreed sum of money.

Edward Bellamy[*], 'Looking Backward'

'How, then, do you regulate wages'? I once more asked.

Dr. Leete did not reply till after several moments of meditative silence. 'I know, of course', he finally said, 'enough of the old order of things to understand just what you mean by that question; and yet the present order is so utterly different at this point that I am a little at loss how to answer you best. You ask me how we regulate wages: I can only reply that there is no idea in the modern social economy which at all corresponds with what was meant by wages in your day'.

'I suppose you mean that you have no money to pay wages in', said I. 'But the credit given the worker at the Government storehouse answers to his wages with us. How is the amount of the credit given respectively to the workers in different lines determined? By what title does the individual claim his particular share? What is the basis of allotment'?

'His title', replied Dr. Leete, 'is his humanity. The basis of his claim is the fact that he is a man'.

---

[*] Edward Bellamy, *Looking Backward : 2000–1887*. Toronto: William Bryce, 1890, pp. 62–66, 89–91.

'The fact that he is a man'! I repeated, incredulously. 'Do you possibly mean that all have the same share'?

'Most assuredly'.

The readers of this book never having practically known any other arrangement, or perhaps very carefully considered the historical accounts of former epochs in which a very different system prevailed, cannot be expected to appreciate the stupor of amazement into which Dr. Leete's simple statement plunged me.

'You see', he said, smiling, 'that it is not merely that we have no money to pay wages in, but, as I said, we have nothing at all answering to your idea of wages'.

By this time I had pulled myself together sufficiently to voice some of the criticisms which, man of the nineteenth century as I was, came uppermost in my mind, upon this to me astounding arrangement. 'Some men do twice the work of others'! I exclaimed. 'Are the clever workmen content with a plan that ranks them with the indifferent'?

'We leave no possible ground for any complaint of injustice', replied Dr. Leete, 'by requiring precisely the same measure of service from all'.

'How can you do that, I should like to know, when no two men's powers are the same'?

'Nothing could be simpler', was Dr. Leete's reply. 'We require of each that he shall make the same effort; that is, we demand of him the best service it is in his power to give'.

'And supposing all do the best they can', I answered, 'the amount of the product resulting is twice greater from one man than from another'.

'Very true', replied Dr. Leete; but the amount of the resulting product has nothing whatever to do with the question, which is one of desert. Desert is a moral question, and the amount of the product a material quantity. It would be an extraordinary sort of logic which should try to determine a moral question by a material standard. The amount of the effort alone is pertinent to the question of desert. All men who do their best do the same. A man's endowments, however god-like, merely fix the measure of his duty. The man of great endowments who does not do all he might, though he may do more than a man of small endowments who does his best, is deemed a less deserving worker than the latter, and dies a debtor to his fellows. The Creator sets men's tasks for them by the faculties he give them; we simply exact their fulfilment'.

'No doubt that is very fine philosophy', I said; 'nevertheless it seems hard that the man who produces twice as much as another, even if both do their best, should only have the same share'.

'Does it indeed seem so to you'? responded Dr. Leete. 'Now, do you know that seems very curious to me? The way it strikes people nowadays is, that a man who can produce twice as much as another with the same effort, instead of being rewarded for doing so, ought to be punished if he does not do so. In the nineteenth century, when a horse pulled a heavier load than a goat, I suppose you rewarded him. Now, we should have whipped him soundly if he had not, on the ground that, being much stronger, he ought to. It is singular how ethical standards change'. The doctor said this with such a twinkle in his eye that I was obliged to laugh.

'I suppose', I said, 'that the real reason that we rewarded men for their endowments, while we considered those of horses and goats merely as fixing the service to be severally required of them, was that the animals, not being reasoning beings, naturally did the best they could, whereas men could only be induced to do so by rewarding them according to the amount of their product. That brings me to ask why, unless human nature has mightily changed in a hundred years, you are not under the same necessity'?

'We are', replied Dr. Leete. 'I don't think there has been any change in human nature in that respect since your day. It is still so constituted that special incentives in the form of prizes, and advantages to be gained, are requisite to call out the best endeavours of the average man in any direction'.

'But what inducement', I asked, 'can a man have to put forth his best endeavours when, however much or little he accomplishes, his income remains the same? High characters may be moved by devotion to the common welfare under such a system, but does not the average man tend to rest back on his oar, reasoning that it is of no use to make a special effort, since the effort will not increase his income, nor its withholding diminish it'?

'Does it then really seem to you', answered my companion, 'that human nature is insensible to any motives save fear of want and love of luxury, that you should expect security and equality of livelihood to leave them without possible incentives to effort? Your contemporaries did not really think so, though they might fancy they did. When it was a question of the grandest class of efforts, the most absolute self-devotion, they depended on quite other incentives. Not higher wages but honour and the hope of men's gratitude, patriotism and the inspiration of duty, were the motives which they set before their soldiers when it was a question of dying for the nation, and never was there an age of the world when these motives did not call out what is best and noblest in men. And not only this, but when you come to analyse the love of money which was the general impulse to effort in your day, you find that the dread of want and desire of luxury were but two of several motives which the pursuit of money represented; the others, and with many the more influential, being desire of power, of social position and reputation for ability and success. So you see that though we have abolished poverty and the fear of it, and inordinate luxury with the hope of it, we have not touched the greater part of the motives which underlay the love of money in former times, or any of those which prompted the supremer sorts of effort. The coarser motives, which no longer move us, have been replaced by higher motives wholly unknown to the mere wage earners of your age. Now that industry of whatever sort is no longer self-service, but service of the nation, patriotism, passion for humanity, impel the worker as in your day they did the soldier. The army of industry is an army, not alone by virtue of its perfect organization, but by reason also of the ardour of self-devotion which animates its members.

'But as you used to supplement the motives of patriotism with the love of glory, in order to stimulate the value of your soldiers, so do we. Based as our industrial system is on the principle of requiring the same unit of effort from every man, that is the best he can do, you will see that the means by which we spur the workers to do their best must be a very essential part of our scheme. With us, diligence in the national service is the sole and certain way to public repute, social distinction, and official power. The value of a man's services in society fixes his rank in it. Compared with the effect of our social arrangements in impelling men to be zealous in business, we deem the object-lessons of biting poverty and wanton luxury on which you depended a device as weak and uncertain as it was barbaric'.

'I should be extremely interested', I said, 'to learn something of what these social arrangements are'.

'The scheme in its details', replied the doctor, 'is of course very elaborate, for it underlies the entire organization of our industrial army; but a few words will give you a general idea of it'.

At this moment our talk was charmingly interrupted by the emergence upon the aerial platform where we sat of Edith Leete. She was dressed for the street, and had come to speak to her father about some commission she was to do for him.

'By the way, Edith', he exclaimed, as she was about to leave us to ourselves, 'I wonder if Mr. West would not be interested in visiting the store with you? I have been telling him something about our system of distribution, and perhaps he might like to see it in practical operation'. . . .

'I should not fail to mention', resumed the Doctor, 'that for those too deficient in mental or bodily strength to be fairly graded with the main body of workers, we have a separate grade, unconnected with the others – a sort of invalid corps, the members of which are provided with a light class of tasks fitted to their strength. All our sick in mind or body, all our deaf and dumb, and lame and blind and crippled, and even our insane, belong to this invalid corps, and bear its insignia. The strongest often do nearly a man's work, the feeblest, of course, nothing; but none who can do anything are willing quite to give up. In their lucid intervals even our insane are eager to do what they can'.

'That is a pretty idea of the invalid corps', I said, 'even a barbarian from the nineteenth century can appreciate that. It is a very graceful way of disguising charity, and must be very grateful to the feelings of its recipients'.

'Charity'! repeated Dr. Leete. 'Did you suppose that we consider the incapable class we are talking of objects of charity'?

'Why, naturally', I said, 'inasmuch as they are incapable of self-support'.

But here the doctor took me up quickly.

'Who is capable of self-support'? he demanded. 'There is no such thing in civilised society as self-support. In a state of society so barbarous as not even to know family co-operation, each individual may possibly support himself, though even then for a part of his life only; but from the moment that men begin to live together, and constitute even the rudest sort of society, self-support becomes impossible. As men grow more civilized, and the subdivision of occupations and services is carried out, a complex mutual dependence becomes the universal rule. Every man, however solitary may seem his occupation, is a member of a vast industrial partnership, as large as the nation, as large as humanity. The necessity of mutual dependence should imply the duty and guarantee of mutual support; and that it did not in your day, constituted the essential cruelty and unreason of your system'.

'That may all be so', I replied, 'but it does not touch the case of those who are unable to contribute anything to the product of industry'.

'Surely, I told you this morning, at least I thought I did', replied Doctor Leete, 'that the right of a man to maintenance at the nation's table depends on the fact that he is a man, and not on the amount of health and strength he may have, so long as he does his best'.

'You said so', I answered, 'but I supposed the rule applied only to the workers of different ability. Does it also hold of those who can do nothing at all'?

'Are they not also men'?

'I am to understand, then, that the lame, the blind, the sick and the impotent, are as well off as the most efficient, and have the same income'?

'Certainly', was the reply.

'The idea of charity on such a scale', I answered, 'would have made our most enthusiastic philanthropists gasp'.

'If you had a sick brother at home', replied Dr. Leete, 'unable to work, would you feed him on less dainty food, and lodge and clothe him more poorly, than yourself? More likely far, you would give him the preference; nor would you think of calling it charity. Would not the word, in that connection, fill you with indignation'?

'Of course', I replied; 'but the cases are not parallel. There is a sense, no doubt, in which all men are brothers; but this general sort of brotherhood is not to be compared, except for rhetorical purposes, to the brotherhood of blood, either as to its sentiment or its obligations'.

'There speaks the nineteenth century'! exclaimed Dr. Leete. 'Ah, Mr. West, there is no doubt as to the length of time that you slept. If I were to give you, in one sentence, a key to what may seem the mysteries of our civilization as compared with that of your age, I should say that it is the fact that the solidarity of the race and the brotherhood of man, which to you were but fine phrases, are to our thinking and feeling, ties as real and as vital as physical fraternity.

'But even setting that consideration aside, I do not see why it so surprises you that those who cannot work are conceded the full right to live on the produce of those who can. Even in your day, the duty of military service for the protection of the nation, to which our industrial service corresponds, while obligatory on those able to discharge it, did not operate to deprive of the privileges of citizenship those who were unable. They stayed at home, and were protected by those who fought, and nobody questioned their right to be, or thought less of them. So, now, the requirement of industrial service from those able to render it does not operate to deprive of the privileges of citizenship, which now implies the citizen's maintenance, him who cannot work. The worker is not a citizen because he works, but works because he is a citizen. As you recognized the duty of the strong to fight for the weak, we, now that fighting is gone by, recognize his duty to work for him.

'A solution which leaves an unaccounted for residuum is no solution at all; and our solution of the problem of human society would have been none at all had it left the lame, the sick, and the blind outside with the beasts, to fare as they might. Better far have left the strong and well unprovided for than these burdened ones, toward whom every heart must yearn, and for whom ease of mind and body should be provided, if for no others. Therefore it is, as I told you this morning, that the title of every man, woman, and child to the means of existence rests on no basis less plain, broad, and simple than the fact that they are fellows of one race – members of one human family. The only coin current is the image of God, and that is good for all we have.

Jane Addams[*], 'Democracy and Charity'

The cure for the ills of Democracy is more Democracy. . . .

Our conceptions of morality, as all our other ideas, pass through a course of development; the difficulty comes in adjusting our conduct, which has become hardened into customs and habits, to these changing moral conceptions. When this adjustment is not made, we suffer from the strain and indecision of believing one hypothesis and acting upon another.

Probably there is no relation in life which our democracy is changing more rapidly than the charitable relation – that relation which obtains between benefactor and beneficiary; at the same time there is no point of contact in our modern experience which reveals so clearly the lack of that equality which democracy implies. We have reached the moment when democracy has made such inroads upon this relationship, that the complacency of the old-fashioned charitable man is gone forever; while, at the same time, the very need and existence of charity, denies us the consolation and freedom which democracy will at last give. . . .

Formerly when it was believed that poverty was synonymous with vice and laziness, and that the prosperous man was the righteous man charity was administered harshly with a good conscience; for the charitable agent really blamed the individual for his poverty, and the very

---

[*] Jane Addams, *Democracy and Social Ethics* (1902) (Champaign: University of Illinois Press, 2001), 13–70 (selections).

fact of his own superior prosperity gave him a certain consciousness of superior morality. We have learned since that time to measure by other standards, and have ceased to accord to the money-earning capacity exclusive respect; while it is still rewarded out of all proportion to any other, its possession is by no means assumed to imply the possession of the highest moral qualities. We have learned to judge men by their social virtues as well as by their business capacity, by their devotion to intellectual and disinterested aims, and by their public spirit, and we naturally resent being obliged to judge poor people so solely upon the industrial side. Our democratic instinct instantly takes alarm. It is largely in this modern tendency to judge all men by one democratic standard, while the old charitable attitude commonly allowed the use of two standards, that much of the difficulty adheres. We know that unceasing bodily toil becomes wearing and brutalizing, and our position is totally untenable if we judge large numbers of our fellows solely upon their success in maintaining it.

The daintily clad charitable visitor who steps into the little house made untidy by the vigorous efforts of her hostess, the washerwoman, is no longer sure of her superiority to the latter; she recognizes that her hostess after all represents social value and industrial use, as over against her own parasitic cleanliness and a social standing attained only through status.

The only families who apply for aid to the charitable agencies are those who have come to grief on the industrial side; it may be through sickness, through loss of work, or for other guiltless and inevitable reasons; but the fact remains that they are industrially ailing, and must be bolstered and helped into industrial health. The charity visitor, let us assume, is a young college woman, well-bred and open-minded; when she visits the family assigned to her, she is often embarrassed to find herself obliged to lay all the stress of her teaching and advice upon the industrial virtues, and to treat the members of the family almost exclusively as factors in the industrial system. She insists that they must work and be self-supporting, that the most dangerous of all situations is idleness, that seeking one's own pleasure, while ignoring claims and responsibilities, is the most ignoble of actions. The members of her assigned family may have other charms and virtues – they may possibly be kind and considerate of each other, generous to their friends, but it is her business to stick to the industrial side. As she daily holds up these standards, it often occurs to the mind of the sensitive visitor, whose conscience has been made tender by much talk of brotherhood and equality, that she has no right to say these things; that her untrained hands are no more fitted to cope with actual conditions than those of her broken-down family.

The grandmother of the charity visitor could have done the industrial preaching very well, because she did have the industrial virtues and housewifely training. In a generation our experiences have changed, and our views with them; but we still keep on in the old methods, which could be applied when our consciences were in line with them, but which are daily becoming more difficult as we divide up into people who work with their hands and those who do not. The charity visitor belonging to the latter class is perplexed by recognitions and suggestions which the situation forces upon her. Our democracy has taught us to apply our moral teaching all around, and the moralist is rapidly becoming so sensitive that when his life does not exemplify his ethical convictions, he finds it difficult to preach.

Added to this is a consciousness, in the mind of the visitor, of a genuine misunderstanding of her motives by the recipients of her charity, and by their neighbors. Let us take a neighborhood of poor people, and test their ethical standards by those of the charity visitor, who comes with the best desire in the world to help them out of their distress. A most striking incongruity, at once apparent, is the difference between the emotional kindness with which relief is given by one poor neighbor to another poor neighbor, and the guarded care with which relief is given by a charity visitor to a charity recipient. The neighborhood mind is at once confronted not only by the difference of method, but by an absolute clashing of two ethical standards.

A very little familiarity with the poor districts of any city is sufficient to show how primitive and genuine are the neighborly relations. There is the greatest willingness to lend or borrow anything, and all the residents of the given tenement know the most intimate family affairs of all the others.

The fact that the economic condition of all alike is on a most precarious level makes the ready outflow of sympathy and material assistance the most natural thing in the world. There are numberless instances of self-sacrifice quite unknown in the circles where greater economic advantages make that kind of intimate knowledge of one's neighbors impossible. An Irish family in which the man has lost his place, and the woman is struggling to eke out the scanty savings by day's work, will take in the widow and her five children who have been turned into the street, without a moment's reflection upon the physical discomforts involved. The most maligned landlady who lives in the house with her tenants is usually ready to lend a scuttle full of coal to one of them who may be out of work, or to share her supper. A woman for whom the writer had long tried in vain to find work failed to appear at the appointed time when employment was secured at last. Upon investigation it transpired that a neighbor further down the street was taken ill, that the children ran for the family friend, who went of course, saying simply when reasons for her non-appearance were demanded, 'It broke me heart to leave the place, but what could I do'? A woman whose husband was sent up to the city prison for the maximum term, just three months, before the birth of her child found herself penniless at the end of that time, having gradually sold her supply of household furniture. She took refuge with a friend whom she supposed to be living in three rooms in another part of town. When she arrived, however, she discovered that her friend's husband had been out of work so long that they had been reduced to living in one room. The friend, however, took her in, and the friend's husband was obliged to sleep upon a bench in the park every night for a week, which he did uncomplainingly if not cheerfully. Fortunately it was summer, 'and it only rained one night'. . . .

The evolutionists tell us that the instinct to pity, the impulse to aid his fellows, served man at a very early period, as a rude rule of right and wrong. There is no doubt that this rude rule still holds among many people with whom charitable agencies are brought into contact, and that their ideas of right and wrong are quite honestly out-raged by the methods of these agencies. When they see the delay and caution with which relief is given, it does not appear to them a conscientious scruple, but as the cold and calculating action of a selfish man. It is not the aid that they are accustomed to receive from their neighbors, and they do not understand why the impulse which drives people to 'be good to the poor' should be so severely supervised. They feel, remotely, that the charity visitor is moved by motives that are alien and unreal. . . .

The poor man who has fallen into distress, when he first asks aid, instinctively expects tenderness, consideration, and forgiveness. If it is the first time, it has taken him long to make up his mind to take the step. He comes somewhat bruised and battered, and instead of being met with warmth of heart and sympathy, he is at once chilled by an investigation and an intimation that he ought to work. He does not recognize the disciplinary aspect of the situation. . . .

The neighborhood understands the selfish rich people who stay in their own part of town, where all their associates have shoes and other things. Such people don't bother themselves about the poor; they are like the rich landlords of the neighborhood experience. But this lady visitor, who pretends to be good to the poor, and certainly does talk as though she were kind-hearted, what does she come for, if she does not intend to give them things which are so plainly needed?

The visitor says, sometimes, that in holding her poor family so hard to a standard of thrift she is really breaking down a rule of higher living which they formerly possessed; that saving, which seems quite commendable in a comfortable part of town, appears almost criminal in a poorer quarter where the next-door neighbor needs food, even if the children of the family do not.

She feels the sordidness of constantly being obliged to urge the industrial view of life. The benevolent individual of fifty years ago honestly believed that industry and self-denial in youth would result in comfortable possessions for old age. It was, indeed, the method he had practised in his own youth, and by which he had probably obtained whatever fortune he possessed. He therefore reproved the poor family for indulging their children, urged them to work long hours, and was utterly untouched by many scruples which afflict the contemporary charity visitor. She says sometimes, 'Why must I talk always of getting work and saving money, the things I know nothing about? If it were anything else I had to urge, I could do it; anything like Latin prose, which I had worried through myself, it would not be so hard'. But she finds it difficult to connect the experiences of her youth with the experiences of the visited family.

Because of this diversity in experience, the visitor is continually surprised to find that the safest platitude may be challenged. She refers quite naturally to the 'horrors of the saloon', and discovers that the head of her visited family does not connect them with 'horrors' at all. He remembers all the kindnesses he has received there, the free lunch and treating which goes on, even when a man is out of work and not able to pay up; the loan of five dollars he got there when the charity visitor was miles away and he was threatened with eviction. He may listen politely to her reference to 'horrors', but considers it only 'temperance talk'. . . .

The subject of clothes indeed perplexes the visitor constantly, and the result of her reflections may be summed up somewhat in this wise: The girl who has a definite social standing, who has been to a fashionable school or to a college, whose family live in a house seen and known by all her friends and associates, may afford to be very simple, or even shabby as to her clothes, if she likes. But the working girl, whose family lives in a tenement, or moves from one small apartment to another, who has little social standing and has to make her own place, knows full well how much habit and style of dress has to do with her position. Her income goes into her clothing, out of all proportion to the amount which she spends upon other things. But, if social advancement is her aim, it is the most sensible thing she can do. She is judged largely by her clothes. Her house furnishing, with its pitiful little decorations, her scanty supply of books, are never seen by the people whose social opinions she most values. Her clothes are her background, and from them she is largely judged. It is due to this fact that girls' clubs succeed best in the business part of town, where 'working girls' and 'young ladies' meet upon an equal footing, and where the clothes superficially look very much alike. Bright and ambitious girls will come to these down-town clubs to eat lunch and rest at noon, to study all sorts of subjects and listen to lectures, when they might hesitate a long time before joining a club identified with their own neighborhood, where they would be judged not solely on their own merits and the unconscious social standing afforded by good clothes, but by other surroundings which are not nearly up to these. For the same reason, girls' clubs are infinitely more difficult to organize in little towns and villages, where every one knows every one else, just how the front parlor is furnished, and the amount of mortgage there is upon the house. These facts get in the way of a clear and unbiassed judgment; they impede the democratic relationship and add to the self-consciousness of all concerned. . . . In some very successful down-town clubs the home address is not given at all, and only the 'business address' is required. Have we worked out our democracy further in regard to clothes than anything else?

The charity visitor has been rightly brought up to consider it vulgar to spend much money upon clothes, to care so much for 'appearances'. She realizes dimly that the care for personal decoration over that for one's home or habitat is in some way primitive and undeveloped; but she is silenced by its obvious need. She also catches a glimpse of the fact that the disproportionate expenditure of the poor in the matter of clothes is largely due to the exclusiveness of the rich who hide from them the interior of their houses, and their more subtle pleasures, while of necessity exhibiting their street clothes and their street manners. Every one who goes shopping at the same time may see the clothes of the richest women in town, but only those invited to her receptions see the Corot on her walls or the bindings in her library. The poor naturally try to bridge the difference by reproducing the street clothes which they have seen. They are striving to conform to a common standard which their democratic training presupposes belongs to all of us. The charity visitor may regret that the Italian peasant woman has laid aside her picturesque kerchief and substituted a cheap street hat. But it is easy to recognize the first attempt toward democratic expression.

The charity visitor finds herself still more perplexed when she comes to consider such problems as those of early marriage and child labor; for she cannot deal with them according to economic theories, or according to the conventions which have regulated her own life. She finds both of these fairly upset by her intimate knowledge of the situation, and her sympathy for those into whose lives she has gained a curious insight. She discovers how incorrigibly bourgeois her standards have been, and it takes but a little time to reach the conclusion that she cannot insist so strenuously upon the conventions of her own class, which fail to fit the bigger, more emotional, and freer lives of working people. The charity visitor holds well-grounded views upon the imprudence of early marriages, quite naturally because she comes from a family and circle of professional and business people. A professional man is scarcely equipped and started in his profession before he is thirty. A business man, if he is on the road to success, is much nearer prosperity at thirty-five than twenty-five, and it is therefore wise for these men not to marry in the twenties; but this does not apply to the workingman. In many trades he is laid upon the shelf at thirty-five, and in nearly all trades he receives the largest wages in his life between twenty and thirty. If the young workingman has all his wages to himself, he will probably establish habits of personal comfort, which he cannot keep up when he has to divide with a family – habits which he can, perhaps, never overcome.

The sense of prudence, the necessity for saving, can never come to a primitive, emotional man with the force of a conviction; but the necessity of providing for his children is a powerful incentive. He naturally regards his children as his savings-bank; he expects them to care for him when he gets old, and in some trades old age comes very early. A Jewish tailor was quite lately sent to the Cook County poorhouse, paralyzed beyond recovery at the age of thirty-five. Had his little boy of nine been but a few years older, he might have been spared this sorrow of public charity. He was, in fact, better able to well support a family when he was twenty than when he was thirty-five, for his wages had steadily grown less as the years went on. Another tailor whom I know, who is also a Socialist, always speaks of saving as a bourgeois virtue, one quite impossible to the genuine working-man. He supports a family consisting of himself, a wife and three children, and his two parents on eight dollars a week. He insists it

[handwritten note: "pressure on children to take care of them when they get old"]

[handwritten note: "Don't give/break down self-respect, we are constantly told. We distrust the human impulses."]

w[...] this amount upon food and shelter, and he
e[...] tendency to put children to work over-
[...] al development and usefulness, and with the
[...] have fed her for fourteen, years, now she can
[...] sual reply when a hardworking father is expostulated
[...] daughter out of school and put her into a factory.

[...] for the charity visitor, who is strongly urging her 'family' toward self-supp[...] at least connive, that the children be put to work early, although she has not [...] that the parents have. It is so easy, after one has been taking the industrial view for a long time, to forget the larger and more social claim; to urge that the boy go to work and support his parents, who are receiving charitable aid. She does not realize what a cruel advantage the person who distributes charity has, when she gives advice. . . .

She has failed to see that the boy who attempts to prematurely support his widowed mother may lower wages, add an illiterate member to the community, and arrest the development of a capable workingman. As she has failed to see that the rules which obtain in regard to the age of marriage in her own family may not apply to the workingman, so also she fails to understand that the present conditions of employment surrounding a factory child are totally unlike those which obtained during the energetic youth of her father. . . .

The struggle for existence, which is so much harsher among people near the edge of pauperism, sometimes leaves ugly marks on character, and the charity visitor finds these indirect results most mystifying. Parents who work hard and anticipate an old age when they can no longer earn, take care that their children shall expect to divide their wages with them from the very first. Such a parent, when successful, impresses the immature nervous system of the child thus tyrannically establishing habits of obedience, so that the nerves and will may not depart from this control when the child is older. The charity visitor, whose family relation is lifted quite out of this, does not in the least understand the industrial foundation for this family tyranny. . . .

The first impulse of our charity visitor is to be somewhat severe with her shiftless family for spending money on pleasures and indulging their children out of all proportion to their means. The [...] which receives beans and coal from the county, and pays for a bicycle on the i[...] ot unknown to any of us. But as the growth of juvenile crime become[...] danger of giving no legitimate and organized pleasure t[...] er that primitive man had games long before he ca[...]

[...] ugh to care for the unworthy among the poor [...] own kin, is certainly a perplexing question. To [...] pon our democratic relations to them which few

[...] ing, ill-regulated kind-heartedness, and we take
he [...] ern parent tells the visitor below how admirably
[...] ng upstairs and laying the foundation for future
nerv[...] it, or rather, the undeveloped stage of our philanthr[...] our tendency to lay constant stress on negative action. [...] f-respect', we are constantly told. We distrust the human [...] as the teachings of our own experience, and in their stead substitute dogmatic ru[...] conduct. We forget that the accumulation of knowledge and the holding

of convictions must finally result in the application of that knowledge and those convictions to life itself; that the necessity for activity and a pull upon the sympathies is so severe, that all the knowledge in the possession of the visitor is constantly applied, and she has a reasonable chance for an ultimate intellectual comprehension. Indeed, part of the perplexity in the administration of charity comes from the fact that the type of person drawn to it is the one who insists that her convictions shall not be unrelated to action. Her moral concepts constantly tend to float away from her, unless they have a basis in the concrete relation of life. She is confronted with the task of reducing her scruples to action, and of converging many wills, so as to unite the strength of all of them into one accomplishment, the value of which no one can foresee.

On the other hand, the young woman who has succeeded in expressing her social compunction through charitable effort finds that the wider social activity, and the contact with the larger experience, not only increases her sense of social obligation but at the same time recasts her social ideals. She is chagrined to discover that in the actual task of reducing her social scruples to action, her humble beneficiaries are far in advance of her, not in charity or singleness of purpose, but in self-sacrificing action. She reaches the old-time virtue of humility by a social process, not in the old way, as the man who sits by the side of the road and puts dust upon his head, calling himself a contrite sinner, but she gets the dust upon her head because she has stumbled and fallen in the road through her efforts to push forward the mass, to march with her fellows. She has socialized her virtues not only through a social aim but by a social process.

The Hebrew prophet made three requirements from those who would join the great forward-moving procession led by Jehovah. 'To love mercy' and at the same time 'to do justly' is the difficult task; to fulfil the first requirement alone is to fall into the error of indiscriminate giving with all its disastrous results; to fulfil the second solely is to obtain the stern policy of withholding, and it results in such a dreary lack of sympathy and understanding that the establishment of justice is impossible. It may be that the combination of the two can never be attained save as we fulfil still the third requirement – 'to walk humbly with God', which may mean to walk for many dreary miles beside the lowliest of His creatures, not even in that peace of mind which the company of the humble is popularly supposed to afford, but rather with the pangs and throes to which the poor human understanding is subjected whenever it attempts to comprehend the meaning of life.

Eduardo Bonilla-Silva[*], 'Racial Economic Inequality'
The Continuing Racial Economic Inequality

The economic life of African Americans has always been influenced by structured racial inequality. A substantial body of literature on white-black employment differences has documented the influence of labor market discrimination, wage differentials, occupational segmentation, as well as income and wealth inequalities, in explaining racially differential

---

[*] Eduardo Bonilla-Silva, *Racism Without Racists: Color-Blind Racism and the Persistence of Racial Inequality in America*, 5th ed., Lanham, MD: Rowman & Littlefield, 2018, pp. 44–49. Copyright by Rowman & Littlefield.

economic outcomes.¹ Despite the well-documented disparities between blacks and whites, many social scientists have focused their attention on the growth of the black middle class.² Some of them have projected the 'success' of this segment to the entire community, creating an image of general economic progress. To be sure, African Americans have experienced significant progress in several areas of their economic life over the past three decades (the economic standing of black women vis-à-vis white women, the opening of jobs that were reserved for whites, the development of a significant middle class, etc.). Yet their overall situation relative to whites has not advanced that much.³ The following sections of this chapter highlight the economic status of blacks and the mechanisms that structure economic inequality at the economic level in the post–civil rights period.

Income and Wage Differentials

Studies analyzing differences in median income between blacks and whites have revealed some convergence; much of it has been attributed to the rising levels of educational attainment of African Americans, in particular among younger cohorts, as well as affirmative action policies.⁴ However, the empirical evidence regarding racial convergence in income is somewhat mixed. Several social scientists have found that the incomes of African Americans began rapid convergence with whites from World War II, but during the recession of the early 1970s, African Americans' income levels began to stagnate and the racial convergence ceased. By the 1990s a substantial black-white earnings gap had reemerged as the black-white family income ratio reached 0.56, a ratio hardly larger than the 0.55 of 1960. In 2014, the median black family income had only marginally improved to 59 percent of white median family income. Interestingly, the decline in blacks' income vis-à-vis whites has been attributed to the decline in enforcement of antidiscrimination laws and affirmative action policies by the federal government. Thus, while blacks made marked advancement from World War II to the early 1970s, their income relative to whites has progressed little over the last several decades.

Furthermore, analysts who focus on income convergence tend to mask serious trends affecting the African American population – like unemployment and underemployment and the decrease in the rate of labor-force participation – by making their comparisons based on full-time workers. Darity and Myers astutely observe that the exclusion of African Americans with zero incomes (i.e., the unemployed and the jobless) in social scientists' assessment of income differences between African Americans and whites masks the persistent racial fault line in economic life.⁵ The gap in unemployment between African Americans and whites increased during the 1970s and the 1980s – the same period in which African Americans' incomes ceased converging with whites.⁶ Even though the racial gap in employment decreased during the economic prosperity of the 1990s, the employment-to-population ratio for black men was 86 percent that of white men and black men were employed seven hours less per week than whites by 1999. By 2014, after the 'Great Recession', black unemployment was 2.3 times higher than white unemployment, almost identical to its recent peak in the 1980s. Moreover, in 2015, black unemployment was higher among all degree levels, suggesting employment differences are not simply the result of educational difference. And in some geographical areas, the differences are vast; for example, in Chicago, only 47 percent of black twenty- to twenty-four-year-olds are employed, compared to 73 percent of white people.⁷

he different earning potential of blacks and
                                            out 60 percent as much as white males;
                                            ent of white females in 1990, saw their
                                            me in 2013. This vast difference is attrib-
ut   rates of return for their education and their
labo   n in the South, all directly related to the racial
dyna   e in earnings disappear when the comparison is
black   ? The answer is no. Farley and Allen carried out
such   ap for black men to be 14 percent. Although this
gap,   eing black, was better than the 19 percent gap of
the 19   percent in 1985 does not give much hope. Thus,
prior to a hasty conclusion that structured racial inequality has declined significantly based on
the fact that the income of full-time male black and white workers has approached 73 percent
in 1986 compared to 43 percent in 1940, we must examine other aspects of their economic
life, such as blacks' occupational distribution, in order to provide a more accurate picture of
their economic standing. More recently, Day and Newburger show that blacks earn less than
whites at every educational level and, similarly, Grodsky and Pager find that even as blacks
move up the occupational hierarchy, their income falls further behind their white peers.[9]

Occupational Mobility and Segmentation

One of the primary reasons why blacks' economic standing is much worse than whites is
because of occupational race-typing. Although recent occupational data show that African
Americans have made substantial progress in obtaining employment in occupational categories from which they previously were, for all practical purposes, excluded, they are still overrepresented among unskilled workers and underrepresented in higher-paying white-collar
jobs. In 1960, whereas 60.4 percent of white men worked in blue-collar jobs, a whopping
76.7 percent of blacks did so.[10] The 2000 U.S. Census shows whites are still more likely than
blacks to be employed in managerial and professional occupations: 35.43 percent of white
males and 40.64 percent of white females compared to 21.65 percent of black males and
31 percent of black females. Blacks, in contrast, are disproportionately employed in service
occupations: 20.23 percent of black males and 26.39 percent of black females compared to
10.85 percent of white males and 17.03 percent of white females. Within service occupations,
black males are most likely to be employed in building and grounds cleaning and maintenance; black females, in health, personal, and food care. Black males are also disproportionately represented in production, transportation, and material moving (26.17 percent of blacks
compared to 17.26 percent of whites). White males are more likely to hold construction jobs
(17.26 percent of whites compared to 12.63 percent of blacks).

Two other factors point to the segmentation experienced by blacks in America. First,
despite the apparent decline in underrepresentation of African Americans in managerial and
professional occupations, those employed in these occupations have lower earnings than
their white counterparts. Second, while the significance of race as a determinant of occupational mobility for African American men may have declined during the period of 1962
through 1973, other research suggests that their occupational mobility is less frequent than
whites and more restricted in terms of destination.[11] Oliver and Shapiro note that 'nearly
two out of five blacks from lower blue-collar backgrounds remain stuck in unskilled and,
for the most part, poorly paid jobs'. Some mainstream researchers have attributed the racial

differences in earnings to the existing educational gap between blacks and whites. However, Cotton found that racial differences among those employed in the managerial and professional occupations could not be explained by educational differences.[12] This is not surprising since research has consistently shown that black men earn less than white men in almost all occupations.[13]

Furthermore, as Collins points out, the relative opening of professional and managerial positions to blacks should not be mistaken for a decline in racial discrimination. While African Americans have succeeded in nontraditional occupations, their occupational mobility still exhibits a distinct racial pattern. Several studies have indicated that, for the most part, Jim Crow–type exclusion discrimination has been replaced with a new web of racial practices that limits their mobility and affects their everyday performance. One of the most pervasive of these practices is pigeonholing blacks in some positions, a practice reminiscent of typecasting blacks for 'nigger jobs' during Jim Crow. For instance, Collins finds that many African American executives fill affirmative action, community relations, minority affairs, or public relations positions that were created during the 1960s and 1970s to respond to civil rights demands, positions than do not provide much mobility.[14]

Racial Practices in the Labor Market

Since the early 1960s social scientists have acknowledged that racial practices in the labor market are important causal factors in explaining the differential employment outcomes of blacks and whites. Yet, until recently, studies on labor-market discrimination assessed discrimination as the unexplained residual in black and white earnings after controlling for a number of variables. Although this measure is useful, it tends to underestimate the extent of discrimination by eliminating differences (e.g., in education and occupational status) that are themselves the product of discriminatory racial practices.[15]

Since the 1990s, analysts have relied on a research strategy to *directly* assess the impact of discrimination. The technique used to examine labor-market discrimination is called an 'employment audit', borrowed from the housing audit strategy, and consists of sending subjects matched in most characteristics except their race to find jobs. By adopting this approach, analysts have been able to estimate the *extent* as well as the *form* of discriminatory racial practices minorities endure in the labor market. Probably the most famous of these studies was one carried out by the Urban Institute in 1991. It was conducted on randomly selected employers in San Diego, Chicago, and Washington, D.C., and found that on average, white testers were significantly favored over black testers. In 20 percent of the audits, blacks were denied job opportunities, and in 31 percent of the audits Latinos were denied job opportunities. In Milwaukee, Wisconsin, Pager divided applicant testers with comparable resumes into four groups: whites without criminal record, whites with criminal record, blacks without criminal record, and blacks with criminal record. White applicants with a criminal record (17 percent) were more likely to be called back for an interview than black applicants without a criminal record (14 percent).[16]

Research indicates that blacks are discriminated against at all levels of the job process. In the search process, they are left behind because most employers rely on informal social networks to advertise their jobs. And since blacks are not part of those networks, they are left out in the cold. Not only does this hinder blacks in their efforts to gain middle-class jobs, but also, as Royster shows in her book *Race and the Invisible Hand*, networks of gatekeepers maintain white privilege in trade careers as well. Specifically, she shows how white students in a trade school who have similar credentials to their black counterparts (in fact, black students in the study are slightly *better*) are given preference by employers who clearly wish to hire their 'own kind'.[17]

Furthermore, recent examination of welfare leavers since the 1996 welfare reform laws indicate that white privilege operates even at low-level service jobs. Employers were less likely to hire black than white welfare leavers and paid the black welfare leavers they did hire less. At the job entry level, in addition to the practices mentioned above, blacks are screened out by tests and the requirement of a high school diploma. These two practices were developed in the late 1950s and 1960s as substitutes for outright exclusion from jobs and were mentioned in the 1964 Civil Rights Act as practices that could have exclusionary results. They are discriminatory because the diploma and the tests are *not* essential to the job performance.

In terms of job promotion, blacks face a glass ceiling because they are pigeonholed in dead-end jobs. Research also suggests that blacks' exclusion from informal social networks restricts their opportunities to demonstrate criteria for promotion, such as loyalty, sound judgment, and leadership potential. Black professionals are also constrained regarding what emotions they can express even when confronted with outright racism in the workplace.[18] Moreover, Baldi and McBrier found that increased minority presence results in a negative effect on blacks. They suggest a group-threat process may be at work where white managers attempt to protect white workers in the face of increased minority presence.[19]

Wealth

The available data on wealth indicate that the disparities in this important area are greater than in any other economic area, and they are increasing. Blacks owned only 3 percent of U.S. assets in 2001, even though they constituted 13 percent of the U.S. population. In 2013, the median net worth of whites, $141,900, was about thirteen times that of blacks, which was only $11,000. This represents the largest gap in black-white wealth since the late 1980s. Although all segments of the population lost a significant portion of wealth in the wake of the Great Recession, white wealth loss plateaued in 2010, while black wealth continued to plummet even faster than during the recession.[20]

A major reason for this disparity in wealth is inheritance and financial gifts from kin. The average financial legacy for white families in 2001 was ten times that of the average black family. Gittleman and Wolff examined factors affecting wealth accumulation from 1984 to 1994 and found no evidence of differences in saving behaviors after controlling for income. Had blacks had comparable inheritance, income, and portfolios during this period, they would have significantly narrowed the racial wealth gap. The researchers conclude, however, that it will be 'extraordinarily difficult for blacks to make up significant ground relative to whites with respect to wealth' because of their much lower rates of inheritance, lower incomes, and the fact that much of their economic assets lie in home equity.[21]

Home equity is less among blacks than whites for several reasons. First, the long history of segregation and redlining ensures that black housing is concentrated in 'less desirable' areas to the white mind. Further, housing stock in black areas appreciates much more slowly than similar housing in white locales, and in areas where the black population is growing, housing prices often fall. Whites are also likely to rate neighborhoods with high black populations as undesirable, promoting segregation.[22]

Notes

1. Mark S Rosentraub and Karen Harlow, 'Police Policies and the Black Community: Attitude toward the Police', in *Contemporary Public Policy Perspectives and Black Americans*, edited by Mitchell F Rice and Woodrow Jones Jr, 107–21. Westport, CT and London: Greenwood Press, 1984.
2. Thomas Sowell, *Civil Rights: Rhetoric or Reality?* (New York: Morrow, 1984); William J Wilson, *The Declining Significance of Race* (Chicago: Chicago University Press, 1978).
3. William A Darity, Jr, Jeremiah Cotton and Herbert Hill. 'Race and Inequality in the Managerial Age'. In *African Americans: Essential Perspectives*, edited by Woernie L Reed, 33–80 (Westport, CT: Auburn House, 1993).
4. Reynolds Farley and Walter R Allen, *The Color Line and the Quality of Life in America* (New York: Russell Sage Foundation, 1987).
5. William A Darity, Jr, and Samuel L Myers, 'Changes in the Black-White Income Inequality, 1968–1978: A Decade of Progress'? *Review of Black Political Economy* 10 (1980): 365–92.
6. Jeremiah Cotton, 'Opening the Gap: The Decline in Black Economic Indicators in the 1980s', *Social Science Quarterly* 70 (1989): 803–19.
7. Alexia Elejalde-Ruiz, 'Chicago's Racial Employment Gaps among Worst in Nation', Chicago *Tribune*, May 25, 2016; Lui Meizhu, Barbara J Robles, Betsy Leondar-Wright, Rose M Brewer and Rebecca Adamson, *The Color of Wealth: The Story behind the U.S. Racial Wealth Divide* (New York: The New York Press, 2006); Valerie Wilson, 'Black Unemployment Is Significantly Higher Than White Unemployment Regardless of Educational Attainment', Economic Policy Institute, December 17, 2015; Valerie Wilson, 'State Unemployment Rates by Race and Ethnicity in the End of 2015 Show a Plodding Recovery', Economic Policy Institute, February 11, 2016.
8. Farley and Allen, *The Color Line and the Quality of Life in America*.
9. Jennifer Cheeseman Day and Eric Newburger, *The Big Payoff: Educational Attainment and Synthetic Estimates of Work-Life Earnings* (Washington, DC: US Census Bureau, 2002).
10. Reynolds Farley, *Blacks and Whites: Narrowing the Gap?* (Cambridge, MA: Harvard University Press, 1984); William O'Hare, Kevin Pollard, Tanya Mann and Mary Kent, 'African Americans in the 1990s', *Population Bulletin* 46, no 1 (1991).
11. Marshall Pomer, 'Labor Market Structure, Intragenerational Mobility, and Discrimination: Black Male Advancement Out of Low-Paying Occupations, 1962–1973', *American Sociological Review* 51 (1986): 650–59, Jeffrey Waddoups, 'Racial Differences in Intersegment Mobility', *Review of Black Political Economy* 20, no 2 (1991): 23–43.
12. Cotton, 'Opening the Gap'.
13. Phillip Moss and Chris Tilly, *Stories Employers Tell: Race, Skill, and Hiring in America* (New York: Russell Sage Foundation, 2001).
14. Ellis Cose, *The Rage of a Privileged Class* (New York: HarperCollins Publishers, 1993).
15. Thomas D Boston, *Race, Class, and Conservatism* (Boston: Unwin Hyman, 1988).
16. Devah Pager, 'The Mark of a Criminal Record'. *American Journal of Sociology* 108 (2003): 937–75.
17. Deirdre A Royster, *Race and the Invisible Hand: How White Networks Exclude Black Men from Blue-Collar Jobs* (Berkeley: University of California Press, 2003).

18. Adia-Harvey Wingfield, 'Are Some Emotions Marked "Whites Only"? Racialized Feeling Rules in Professional Workplaces', *Social Problems* 57, no 2 (2010): 251–68.
19. Stephane Baldi and Debra Branch McBrier, 'Do the Determinants of Promotion Differ for Blacks and Whites'? *Work and Occupations* 24 (1997): 478–97.
20. Meizhu et al., *The Color of Wealth*; Rakesh Kochhar and Richard Fry, 'Wealth Inequality Has Widened Along Racial, Ethnic Lines Since End of Great Recession', Pew Research Center, December 12, 2004.
21. Meizhu et al., *The Color of Wealth*; Maury Gittleman and Edward N Wolff, 'Racial Differences in Patterns of Wealth Accumulation', *Journal of Human Resources* 39 (2004): 193–227.
22. Maria Krysan, Mick P Couper, Reynolds Farley and Tyrone A Forman, 'Does Race Matter in Neighborhood Preferences? Results from a Video Experiment', *American Journal of Sociology* 115, no 2 (2009): 527–59; Chenoa Flippen, 'Unequal Returns to Housing Investments? A Study of Real Housing Appreciation among Black, White, and Hispanic Households', *Social Forces* 82, no 4 (2004): 1523–51.

CASE STUDY

Barry Estabrook[*], 'Politics of the Plate: The Price of Tomatoes'

If you have eaten a tomato this winter, chances are very good that it was picked by a person who lives in virtual slavery.

Driving from Naples, Florida, the nation's second-wealthiest metropolitan area, to Immokalee takes less than an hour on a straight road. You pass houses that sell for an average of $1.4 million, shopping malls anchored by Tiffany's and Saks Fifth Avenue, manicured golf courses. Eventually, gated communities with names like Monaco Beach Club and Imperial Golf Estates give way to modest ranches, and the highway shrivels from six lanes to two. Through the scruffy palmettos, you glimpse flat, sandy tomato fields shimmering in the broiling sun. Rounding a long curve, you enter Immokalee. The heart of town is a nine-block grid of dusty, potholed streets lined by boarded-up bars and bodegas, peeling shacks, and sagging, mildew-streaked house trailers. Mongrel dogs snooze in the shade, scrawny chickens peck in yards. Just off the main drag, vultures squabble over roadkill. Immokalee's population is 70 percent Latino. Per capita income is only $8,500 a year. One third of the families in this city of nearly 25,000 live below the poverty line. Over one third of the children drop out before graduating from high school.

Immokalee is the tomato capital of the United States. Between December and May, as much as 90 percent of the fresh domestic tomatoes we eat come from south Florida, and Immokalee is home to one of the area's largest communities of farmworkers. According to Douglas Molloy, the chief assistant U.S. attorney based in Fort Myers, Immokalee has another claim to fame: It is "ground zero for modern slavery."

---

[*] Barry Estabrook, "Politics of the Plate: The Price of Tomatoes," in Gourmet, March 2009. http//www.gourmet.com/magazine/2000s/2009/03/politics-of-the-plate-the-price-of-tomatoes.htlm

The beige stucco house at 209 South Seventh Street is remarkable only because it is in better repair than most Immokalee dwellings. For two and a half years, beginning in April 2005, Mariano Lucas Domingo, along with several other men, was held as a slave at that address. At first, the deal must have seemed reasonable. Lucas, a Guatemalan in his thirties, had slipped across the border to make money to send home for the care of an ailing parent. He expected to earn about $200 a week in the fields. Cesar Navarrete, then a 23-year-old illegal immigrant from Mexico, agreed to provide room and board at his family's home on South Seventh Street and extend credit to cover the periods when there were no tomatoes to pick.

Lucas's "room" turned out to be the back of a box truck in the junk-strewn yard, shared with two or three other workers. It lacked running water and a toilet, so occupants urinated and defecated in a corner. For that, Navarrete docked Lucas's pay by $20 a week. According to court papers, he also charged Lucas for two meager meals a day: eggs, beans, rice, tortillas, and, occasionally, some sort of meat. Cold showers from a garden hose in the backyard were $5 each. Everything had a price. Lucas was soon $300 in debt. After a month of ten-hour workdays, he figured he should have paid that debt off.

But when Lucas – slightly built and standing less than five and a half feet tall – inquired about the balance, Navarrete threatened to beat him should he ever try to leave. Instead of providing an accounting, Navarrete took Lucas's paychecks, cashed them, and randomly doled out pocket money, $20 some weeks, other weeks $50. Over the years, Navarrete and members of his extended family deprived Lucas of $55,000.

Taking a day off was not an option. If Lucas became ill or was too exhausted to work, he was kicked in the head, beaten, and locked in the back of the truck. Other members of Navarrete's dozen-man crew were slashed with knives, tied to posts, and shackled in chains. On November 18, 2007, Lucas was again locked inside the truck. As dawn broke, he noticed a faint light shining through a hole in the roof. Jumping up, he secured a hand hold and punched himself through. He was free.

What happened at Navarrete's home would have been horrific enough if it were an isolated case. Unfortunately, involuntary servitude – slavery – is alive and well in Florida. Since 1997, law-enforcement officials have freed more than 1,000 men and women in seven different cases. And those are only the instances that resulted in convictions. Frightened, undocumented, mistrustful of the police, and speaking little or no English, most slaves refuse to testify, which means their captors cannot be tried. "Unlike victims of other crimes, slaves don't report themselves," said Molloy, who was one of the prosecutors on the Navarrete case. "They hide from us in plain sight."

And for what? Supermarket produce sections overflow with bins of perfect red-orange tomatoes even during the coldest months – never mind that they are all but tasteless. Large packers, which ship nearly $500 million worth of tomatoes annually to major restaurants and grocery retailers nationwide, own or lease the land upon which the workers toil. But the harvesting is often done by independent contractors called crew bosses, who bear responsibility for hiring and overseeing pickers. Said Reggie Brown, executive vice president of the Florida Tomato Growers Exchange, "We abhor slavery and do everything we can to prevent it. We want to make sure that we always foster a work environment free from hazard, intimidation, harassment, and violence." Growers, he said, cooperated with law-enforcement officers in the Navarette case.

But when asked if it is reasonable to assume that an American who has eaten a fresh tomato from a grocery store or food-service company during the winter has eaten fruit picked by the hand of a slave, Molloy said, "It is not an assumption. It is a fact."

Gerardo Reyes, a former picker who is now an employee of the Coalition of Immokalee Workers (CIW), a 4,000-member organization that provides the only voice for the field hands, agrees. Far from being an anomaly, Reyes told me, slavery is a symptom of a vast system of labor abuses. Involuntary servitude represents just one rung on a grim ladder of exploitation. Reyes said that the victims of this system come to Florida for one reason—to send money to their families back home. "But when they get here, it's all they can do to keep themselves alive with rent, transportation, food. Poverty and misery are the perfect recipe for slavery."

Tomato harvesting involves rummaging through staked vines until you have filled a bushel basket to the brim with hard, green fruits. You hoist the basket over your shoulder, trot across the field, and heave it overhead to a worker in an open trailer the size of the bed of a gravel truck. For every 32-pound basket you pick, you receive a token typically worth about 45 cents – almost the same rate you would have gotten 30 years ago. Working at breakneck speed, you might be able to pick a ton of tomatoes on a good day, netting about $50. But a lot can go wrong. If it rains, you can't pick. If the dew is heavy, you sit and wait until it evaporates. If trucks aren't available to transport the harvest, you're out of luck. You receive neither overtime nor benefits. If you are injured (a common occurrence, given the pace of the job), you have to pay for your own medical care.

Leaning against the railing of an unpainted wooden stoop in front of a putty-colored trailer, a tired Juan Dominguez told an all-too-familiar story. He had left for the fields that morning at six o'clock and returned at three. But he worked for only two of those nine hours because the seedlings he was to plant had been delivered late. His total earnings: $13.76.

I asked him for a look inside his home. He shrugged and gestured for me to come in. In one ten-foot-square space there were five mattresses, three directly on the floor, two suspended above on sheets of flimsy plywood. The room was littered with T-shirts, jeans, running shoes, cheap suitcases. The kitchen consisted of a table, four plastic chairs, an apartment-size stove, a sink with a dripping faucet, and a rusty refrigerator whose door wouldn't close. Bare lightbulbs hung from fixtures, and a couple of fans put up a noisy, futile effort against the stale heat and humidity. In a region where temperatures regularly climb into the nineties, there were no air conditioners. One tiny, dank bathroom served ten men. The rent was $2,000 a month—as much as you would pay for a clean little condo near Naples.

Most tomato workers, however, have no choice but to live like Dominguez. Lacking vehicles, they must reside within walking distance of the football-field-size parking lot in front of La Fiesta, a combination grocery store, taqueria, and check-cashing office. During the predawn hours, the lot hosts a daily hiring fair. I arrived a little before 5 a.m. The parking lot was filled with more than a dozen former school buses. Outside each bus stood a silent scrum of 40 or 50 would-be pickers. The driver, or crew boss, selected one worker at a time, choosing young, fit-looking men first. Once full, the bus pulled away.

Later that day, I encountered some of the men and women who had not been picked when I put in a shift at the Guadalupe Center of Immokalee's soup kitchen. Tricia Yeggy, the director of the kitchen, explained that it runs on two simple rules: People can eat as much as they want, and no one is turned away hungry. This means serving between 250 and 300 people a day, 44 per sitting, beginning at eleven o'clock. Cheerful retirees volunteer as servers, and the "guests" are unabashedly appreciative. The day's selection – turkey and rice soup with squash, corn, and a vigorous sprinkle of cumin – was both hearty and tasty. You could almost forget the irony: Workers who pick the food we eat can't afford to feed themselves.

The CIW has been working to ease the migrants' plight since 1993, when a few field hands began meeting sporadically in a church hall. Lucas Benitez, one of the coalition's main spokespeople, came to the group in its early years. Back then, the challenge was taking small steps, often for individual workers. To make the point, Benitez unfolded a crumpled shirt covered in dried blood. "This is Edgar's shirt," he said.

One day in 1996, a 16-year-old Guatemalan boy named Edgar briefly stopped working in the field for a drink of water. His crew boss bludgeoned him. Edgar fled and arrived at the coalition's door, bleeding. In response to the CIW's call for action, over 500 workers assembled and marched to the boss's house. The next morning, no one would get on his bus. "That was the last report of a worker being beaten by his boss in the field," said Benitez. The shirt is kept as a reminder that by banding together, progress is possible.

Even though the CIW has been responsible for bringing police attention to a half dozen slavery prosecutions, Benitez feels that slavery will persist until overall conditions for field workers improve. The group has made progress on that front by securing better pay. Between the early 1980s and the mid-1990s, the rate for a basket of tomatoes remained 40 cents meaning that workers' real wages dropped as inflation rose. Work stoppages, demonstrations, and a hunger strike helped raise it to 45 cents on average, but the packers complained that competition for customers prevented them from paying more. One grower refused to enter a dialogue with CIW hunger strikers because, in his words, "a tractor doesn't tell the farmer how to run the farm." The CIW decided to try an end run around the growers by going directly to the biggest customers and asking them to pay one cent more per pound directly to the workers. Small change to supermarket chains and fast-food corporations, but it would add about twenty dollars to the fifty a picker makes on a good day, the difference between barely scraping by and earning a livable wage.

The Campaign for Fair Food, as it is called, first took aim at Yum! Brands, owner of Taco Bell, Pizza Hut, KFC, Long John Silver's, and A&W. After four years of pressure, Yum! agreed to the one-cent raise in 2005 and, importantly, pledged to make sure that no worker who picked its tomatoes was being exploited. McDonald's came aboard in 2007, and in 2008 Burger King, Whole Foods Market, and Subway followed, with more expected to join up this year. But the program faces a major obstacle. Claiming that the farmers are not party to the arrangement, the Florida Tomato Growers Exchange, an agricultural cooperative that represents some 90 percent of the state's producers, has refused to be a conduit for the raise, citing legal concerns.

When the Navarrete case came to light, there were no howls of outrage from growers. Or from Florida government circles. When Cesar Navarrete, who pleaded guilty, was sentenced to 12 years in prison this past December, Terence McElroy of the Florida Department of Agriculture and Consumer Services offered his perspective on the crime: "Any legitimate grower certainly does not engage in that activity. But you're talking about maybe a case a year."

Charlie Frost, the Collier County Sheriff's Office detective who investigated and arrested Navarrete, disagrees. With one case wrapped up, he and prosecutor Molloy turned to several other active slavery cases. Sitting in his Naples office and pointing his index finger east, toward the fields of Immokalee, he said, "It's happening out there right now."

Lucas, who received a temporary visa for his testimony, is now back in the fields, still chasing the dream of making a little money to send back home.

BUYING SLAVE-FREE FRUITS

In the warm months, the best solution is to follow that old mantra: buy seasonal, local, and small-scale. But what about in winter? So far, Whole Foods is the only grocery chain that has signed on to the Coalition of Immokalee Workers (CIW) Campaign for Fair Food, which means that it has promised not to deal with growers who tolerate serious worker abuses and, when buying tomatoes, to pay a price that supports a living wage. When shopping elsewhere, you can take advantage of the fact that fruits and vegetables must be labeled with their country of origin. Most of the fresh tomatoes in supermarkets during winter months come from Florida, where labor conditions are dismal for field workers, or from Mexico, where they are worse, according to a CIW spokesman. One option during these months is to buy locally produced hydroponic greenhouse tomatoes, including cluster tomatoes still attached to the vine. Greenhouse tomatoes are also imported from Mexico, however, so check signage or consult the little stickers often seen on the fruits themselves to determine their source. You can also visit the CIW's information-packed website (ciw-online.org) if you are interested in becoming part of the coalition's efforts.

CASE STUDY

Eric Schlosser[*], 'The Most Dangerous Job'

'The Worst'

Some of the most dangerous jobs in meatpacking today are performed by the late-night cleaning crews. A large proportion of these workers are illegal immigrants. They are considered 'independent contractors', employed not by the meatpacking firms but by sanitation companies. They earn hourly wages that are about one-third lower than those of regular production employees. And their work is so hard and so horrendous that words seem inadequate to describe it. The men and women who now clean the nation's slaughterhouses may arguably have the worst job in the United States. 'It takes a really dedicated person', a former member of a cleaning crew told me, 'or a really desperate person to get the job done'.

When a sanitation crew arrives at a meatpacking plant, usually around midnight, it faces a mess of monumental proportions. Three to four thousand cattle, each weighing about a thousand pounds, have been slaughtered there that day. The place has to be clean by sunrise. Some of the workers wear water-resistant clothing; most don't. Their principal cleaning tool is a high-pressure hose that shoots a mixture of water and chlorine heated to about 180 degrees. As the water is sprayed, the plant fills with a thick, heavy fog. Visibility drops to as little as five feet. The conveyer belts and machinery are running. Workers stand on the belts, spraying them, riding them like moving sidewalks, as high as fifteen feet off the ground. Workers climb ladders with hoses and spray the catwalks. They get under tables and conveyer belts, climbing right into the bloody muck, cleaning out grease, fat, manure, left-over scraps of meat.

Glasses and safety goggles fog up. The inside of the plant heats up; temperatures soon exceed 100 degrees. 'It's hot, and it's foggy, and you can't see anything', a former sanitation worker said. The crew members can't see or hear each other when the machinery's running. They routinely spray each other with burning hot, chemical-laden water. They are sickened by the fumes. Jesus, a soft-spoken employee of DCS Sanitation Management, Inc., the company that IBP uses in many of its plants, told

---

[*] Eric Schlosser, "The Worst" and "Kenny," in Eric Schlosser, *Fast Food Nation*, pp. 176–178, 186–190. Copyright 2001 by Eric Schlosser. Reprinted by permission of Houghton Mifflin Harcourt Publishing Company. All rights reserved.

me that every night on the job he gets terrible headaches. 'You feel it in your head', he said. 'You feel it in your stomach, like you want to throw up'. A friend of his vomits whenever they clean the rendering area. Other workers tease the young man as he retches. Jesus says the stench in rendering is so powerful that it won't wash off; no matter how much soap you use after a shift, the smell comes home with you, seeps from your pores.

One night while Jesus was cleaning, a coworker forgot to turn off a machine, lost two fingers, and went into shock. An ambulance came and took him away, as everyone else continued to clean. He was back at work the following week. 'If one hand is no good', the supervisor told him, 'use the other'. Another sanitation worker lost an arm in a machine. Now he folds towels in the locker room. The scariest job, according to Jesus, is cleaning the vents on the roof of the slaughterhouse. The vents become clogged with grease and dried blood. In the winter, when everything gets icy and the winds pick up, Jesus worries that a sudden gust will blow him off the roof into the darkness.

Although official statistics are not kept, the death rate among slaughterhouse sanitation crews is extraordinarily high. They are the ultimate in disposable workers: illegal, illiterate, impoverished, untrained. The nation's worst job can end in just about the worst way. Sometimes these workers are literally ground up and reduced to nothing.

A brief description of some cleaning-crew accidents over the past decade says more about the work and the danger than any set of statistics. At the Monfort plant in Grand Island, Nebraska, Richard Skala was beheaded by a dehiding machine. Carlos Vincente – an employee of T and G Service Company, a twenty-eight-year-old Guatemalan who'd been in the United States for only a week – was pulled into the cogs of a conveyer belt at an Excel plant in Fort Morgan, Colorado, and torn apart. Lorenzo Marin, Sr., an employee of DCS Sanitation, fell from the top of a skinning machine while cleaning it with a high-pressure hose, struck his head on the concrete floor of an IBP plant in Columbus Junction, Iowa, and died. Another employee of DCS Sanitation, Salvador Hernandez-Gonzalez, had his head crushed by a pork-loin processing machine at an IBP plant in Madison, Nebraska. The same machine had fatally crushed the head of another worker, Ben Barone, a few years earlier. At a National Beef plant in Liberal, Kansas, Homer Stull climbed into a blood-collection tank to clean it, a filthy tank thirty feet high. Stull was overcome by hydrogen sulfide fumes. Two coworkers climbed into the tank and tried to rescue him. All three men died. Eight years earlier, Henry Wolf had been overcome by hydrogen sulfide fumes while cleaning the very same tank; Gary Sanders had tried to rescue him; both men died; and the Occupational Safety and Health Administration (OSHA) later fined National Beef for its negligence. The fine was $480 for each man's death.

Kenny

During my trips to meatpacking towns in the High Plains I met dozens of workers who'd been injured. Each of their stories was different, yet somehow familiar, linked by common elements – the same struggle to receive proper medical care, the same fear of speaking out, the same underlying corporate indifference. We are human beings, more than one person told me, but they treat us like animals. The workers I met wanted their stories to be told. They wanted people to know about what is happening right now. A young woman who'd injured her back and her right hand at the Greeley plant said to me, 'I want to get on top of a rooftop and scream my lungs out so that somebody will hear'. The voices and faces of these workers are indelibly with me, as is the sight of their hands, the light brown skin criss-crossed with white scars. Although I cannot tell all of their stories, a few need to be mentioned. Like all lives, they can be used as examples or serve as representative types. But ultimately they are unique, individual, impossible to define or replace – the opposite of how this system has treated them.

Raoul was born in Zapoteca, Mexico, and did construction work in Anaheim before moving to Colorado. He speaks no English. After hearing a Monfort ad on a Spanish-language radio station, he applied for a job at the Greeley plant. One day Raoul reached into a processing machine to remove a piece of meat. The machine accidentally went on. Raoul's arm got stuck, and it took workers twenty minutes to get it out. The machine had to be taken apart. An ambulance brought Raoul to the hospital, where a deep gash in his shoulder was sewn shut. A tendon had been severed. After getting stitches and a strong prescription painkiller, he was driven back to the slaughterhouse and put back on the production line. Bandaged, groggy, and in pain, one arm tied in a sling, Raoul spent the rest of the day wiping blood off cardboard boxes with his good hand.

Renaldo was another Monfort worker who spoke no English, an older man with graying hair. He developed carpal tunnel syndrome while cutting meat. The injury got so bad that sharp pain shot from his hand all the way up to his shoulder. At night it hurt so much he could not fall asleep in bed. Instead he would fall asleep sitting in a chair beside the bed where his wife lay. For three years he slept in that chair every night.

Kenny Dobbins was a Monfort employee for almost sixteen years. He was born in Keokuk, Iowa, had a tough childhood and an abusive stepfather, left home at the age of thirteen, went in and out of various schools, never learned to read, did various odd jobs, and wound up at the Monfort slaughterhouse in Grand Island, Nebraska. He started working there in 1979, right after the company bought it from Swift. He was twenty-three. He worked in the shipping department at first, hauling boxes that weighed as much as 120 pounds. Kenny could handle it, though. He was a big man, muscular and six-foot-five, and nothing in his life had ever been easy.

One day Kenny heard someone yell, 'Watch out'! then turned around and saw a ninety-pound box falling from an upper level of the shipping department. Kenny caught the box with one arm, but the momentum threw him against a conveyer belt, and the metal teeth on the rim of the belt pierced his lower back. The company doctor bandaged Kenny's back and said the pain was just a pulled muscle. Kenny never filed for workers' comp, stayed home for a few days, then returned to work. He had a wife and three children to support. For the next few months, he was in terrible pain. 'It hurt so fucking bad you wouldn't believe it', he told me. He saw another doctor, got a second opinion. The new doctor said Kenny had a pair of severely herniated disks. Kenny had back surgery, spent a month in the hospital, got sent to a pain clinic when the operation didn't work. His marriage broke up amid the stress and financial difficulty. Fourteen months after the injury, Kenny returned to the slaughterhouse. 'GIVE UP AFTER BACK SURGERY? NOT KEN DOBBINS'!! a Monfort newsletter proclaimed. 'Ken has learned how to handle the rigors of working in a packing plant and is trying to help others do the same. Thanks, Ken, and keep up the good work'.

Kenny felt a strong loyalty to Monfort. He could not read, possessed few skills other than his strength, and the company had still given him a job. When Monfort decided to reopen its Greeley plant with a nonunion workforce, Kenny volunteered to go there and help. He did not think highly of labor unions. His supervisors told him that unions had been responsible for shutting down meatpacking plants all over the country. When the UFCW tried to organize the Greeley slaughterhouse, Kenny became an active and outspoken member of an anti-union group.

At the Grand Island facility, Kenny had been restricted to light duty after his injury. But his supervisor in Greeley said that old restrictions didn't apply in this new job. Soon Kenny was doing tough, physical labor once again, wielding a knife and grabbing forty- to fifty-pound pieces of beef off a table. When the pain became unbearable, he was transferred to ground beef, then to rendering. According to a former manager at the Greeley plant, Monfort was trying to get rid of Kenny, trying to make his work so unpleasant that he'd quit. Kenny didn't realize it. 'He still believes in his heart that people are honest and good', the former manager said about Kenny. 'And he's wrong'.

As part of the job in rendering, Kenny sometimes had to climb into gigantic blood tanks and gut bins, reach to the bottom of them with his long arms, and unclog the drains. One day he was unexpectedly called to work over the weekend. There had been a problem with *Salmonella* contamination. The plant needed to be disinfected, and some of the maintenance workers had refused to do it. In his street clothes, Kenny began cleaning the place, climbing into tanks and spraying a liquid chlorine mix. Chlorine is a hazardous chemical that can be inhaled or absorbed through the skin, causing a litany of health problems. Workers who spray it need to wear protective gloves, safety goggles, a self-contained respirator, and full coveralls. Kenny's supervisor gave him a paper dust mask to wear, but it quickly dissolved. After eight hours of working with the chlorine in unventilated areas, Kenny went home and fell ill. He was rushed to the hospital and placed in an oxygen tent. His lungs had been burned by the chemicals. His body was covered in blisters. Kenny spent a month in the hospital.

Kenny eventually recovered from the overexposure to chlorine, but it left his chest feeling raw, made him susceptible to colds and sensitive to chemical aromas. He went back to work at the Greeley plant. He had remarried, didn't know what other kind of work to do, still felt loyal to the company. He was assigned to an early morning shift. He had to drive an old truck from one part of the slaughterhouse complex to another. The truck was filled with leftover scraps of meat. The headlights and the wipers didn't work. The windshield was filthy and cracked. One cold, dark morning in the middle of winter, Kenny became disoriented while driving. He stopped the truck, opened the door, got out to see where he was – and was struck by a train. It knocked his glasses off, threw him up in the air, and knocked both of his work boots off. The train was moving slowly, or he would've been killed. Kenny somehow made it back to the plant, barefoot and bleeding from deep gashes in his back and his face. He spent two weeks at the hospital, then went back to work.

One day, Kenny was in rendering and saw a worker about to stick his head into a pre-breaker machine, a device that uses hundreds of small hammers to pulverize gristle and bone into a fine powder. The worker had just turned the machine off, but Kenny knew the hammers inside were still spinning. It takes fifteen minutes for the machine to shut down completely. Kenny yelled, 'Stop'! but the worker didn't hear him. And so Kenny ran across the room, grabbed the man by the seat of his pants, and pulled him away from the machine an instant before it would have pulverized him. To honor this act of bravery, Monfort gave Kenny an award for 'Outstanding Achievement in CONCERN FOR FELLOW WORKERS'. The award was a paper certificate, signed by his supervisor and the plant safety manager.

Kenny later broke his leg stepping into a hole in the slaughterhouse's concrete floor. On another occasion he shattered an ankle, an injury that required surgery and the insertion of five steel pins. Now Kenny had to wear a metal brace on one leg in order to walk, an elaborate, spring-loaded brace that cost $2,000. Standing for long periods caused him great pain. He was given a job recycling old knives at the plant. Despite his many injuries, the job required him to climb up and down three flights of narrow stairs carrying garbage bags filled with knives. In December of 1995 Kenny felt a sharp pain in his chest while lifting some boxes. He thought it was a heart attack. His union steward took him to see the nurse, who said it was just a pulled muscle and sent Kenny home. He was indeed having a massive heart attack. A friend rushed Kenny to a nearby hospital. A stent was inserted in his heart, and the doctors told Kenny that he was lucky to be alive.

Not long afterward, Monfort fired Kenny Dobbins. Despite the fact that Kenny had been with the company for almost sixteen years, despite the fact that he was first in seniority at the Greeley plant, that he'd cleaned blood tanks with his bare hands, fought the union, done whatever the company had asked him to do, suffered injuries that would've killed weaker men, nobody from Monfort called him with the news. Nobody even bothered to write him. Kenny learned that he'd been fired when his payments to the company health insurance plan kept being returned by the post office. He called Monfort repeatedly to find out what was going on, and a sympathetic clerk in the claims office finally told Kenny that the checks were being returned because he was no longer a Monfort employee. When I asked company spokesmen to comment on the accuracy of Kenny's story, they would neither confirm nor deny any of the details.

Today Kenny is in poor health. His heart is permanently damaged. His immune system seems shot. His back hurts, his ankle hurts, and every so often he coughs up blood. He is unable to work at any job. His wife, Clara – who's half-Latina and half-Cheyenne, and looks like a younger sister of Cher's – was working as a nursing home attendant when Kenny had the heart attack. Amid the stress of his illness, she developed a serious kidney ailment. She is unemployed and recuperating from a kidney transplant.

As I sat in the living room of their Greeley home, its walls decorated with paintings of wolves, Denver Broncos memorabilia, and an American flag, Kenny and Clara told me about their financial condition. After almost sixteen years on the job, Kenny did not get any pension from Monfort. The company challenged his workers' comp claim and finally agreed – three years after the initial filing – to pay him a settlement of $35,000. Fifteen percent of that money went to Kenny's lawyer, and the rest is long gone. Some months Kenny has to hock things to get money for Clara's medicine. They have two teenage children and live on Social Security payments. Kenny's health insurance, which costs more than $600 a month, is about to run out. His anger at Monfort, his feelings of betrayal, are of truly biblical proportions.

'They used me to the point where I had no body parts left to give', Kenny said, struggling to maintain his composure. 'Then they just tossed me into the trash can'. Once strong and powerfully built, he now walks with difficulty, tires easily, and feels useless, as though his life were over. He is forty-five years old.

CASE STUDY

Josiah Heyman and Merlyn Heyman[*], 'Occupy in a Border City: El Paso, Texas, U.S.A.'

1. Introduction

El Paso, Texas, located on the U.S. border with Mexico, is a socially and culturally distinctive place, and a site where the Occupy movement's concerns about economic and political justice hold heightened relevance.

Occupy El Paso creatively synthesized global Occupy discourse with border regional concerns. It appealed to bilingual and bicultural youth, with roots in immigration from Mexico, who have worked

---

[*] Josiah Heyman and Merlyn Heyman, 'Occupy in a Border City: El Paso, Texas, U.S.A.,' in Todd A Comer, ed., *What Comes after Occupy? The Regional Politics of Resistance* (Cambridge: Cambridge Scholars Publishing, 2015). Permission by Josiah and Merlyn Heyman.

in the military and flexible service production, while episodically participating in higher education. Though the burst of enthusiasm for Occupy was short-lived, it may foretell the future politics and aspirations of a 'new working class', as Kathleen Arnold perceptively terms it.

K. R. Arnold proposes that changes in global capitalism have weakened the partial, relatively privileged working class of recent U.S. history, and instead a new working class has emerged.[1] Members of this class are concentrated in the service sector, and subject to flexible production regimes. People of many origins come together in this new working class, immigrant and non-immigrant, white and people of color, women and men, and gay and straight. The new working class life experience, according to Arnold, includes, often, coerced work in prison, free labor, paid labor, and sporadic movement among government benefits and paid work; to this list, we add movement in and out of the military and higher education. While older workers are also subject to these processes, they particularly characterize the life experience of young adults. The new working class is emerging, Arnold suggests, in the context of a political struggle between democracy and state 'prerogative power'[2] in the setting of global capitalism. We find that this helpfully frames the Occupy experience in El Paso.

The chapter begins by introducing the reader to El Paso and the U.S.-Mexico border. Occupy El Paso faced simultaneously local and transnational fields of power, inequality, and injustice in the borderlands.

The problematic term 'occupy' is discussed – it is a problematic term given that indigenous and Latino El Paso forms part of 'Occupied America'.[3] It then unfolds a narrative history of Occupy El Paso as a basis for examining key themes and lessons in the remainder of the chapter.

Speaking to the 'new working class' framework, it characterizes Occupy El Paso participants, acknowledging their diversity but noting the predominant role of Latin@ and multiracial youth characteristic of this border city.

A challenge in the border setting was that many compelling issues of social justice (immigrant rights, violence in Mexico, farmworker and other labor rights, etc.) were already being confronted by social movement organizations; Occupy El Paso provided solidarity to these organizations, but this fact reduced its own development. Meanwhile, issues specific to the new working class tended to go unrecognized by local Occupiers in favor of dramatized leftist concerns. The chapter also considers the challenges Occupy El Paso faced in transcending the international border – this despite the personal history and political commitments of many members which were bound up with Mexico – and asks what lessons can be learned from this.

While parts of the chapter dwell on Occupy El Paso's own borders, it also recounts its rebellious energy, though in a tragic cause. For a period, Occupy El Paso was at the forefront of a struggle over crony capitalism focused on real estate in the city, an engagement that grew organically from the closure of its encampment. Consistent with Arnold's perspective, the spatial repression of Occupy El Paso was a step along the path of the elite's subversion of democracy in the city. This history deftly characterizes Occupy El Paso: its ample and integrative, but also diffuse embrace of numerous values and issues, its short life cycle based on a burst of enthusiasm, its horizontal ethos and limited organizational capacity for sustaining struggle over time, the rapid coming and going of participants, its naiveté and squabbling, and so forth. While sometimes frustrating, these features emerged from Occupy El Paso's vital quality: its distinctive youthfulness. The chapter thus closes by emphasizing new possibilities in the Occupy experience for the young people of the 'new working class'.

2. The Local Setting

El Paso, Texas, is on the U.S.-Mexico border, with close connections to Mexico, especially its neighbor Ciudad Juárez, Chihuahua. El Paso was once part of the Mexican 'Paso del Norte' region, with Mexican and Native American settlements along its desert riverbanks. After 1848, it was torn away from Mexico by warfare and an imposed treaty. The resulting international border has been a mechanism of state power and thus a cause of social division, but also a basis for interaction and thus a source of mutual commitment. The U.S. side of the border contains a massive police force, including a border wall, over 20,000 Border Patrol officers, nearly as many Port of Entry inspectors, and so forth. Migrants rely on human smugglers to evade these perilous but ultimately ineffective barriers, but many hundreds die annually in the process. The Mexican side has witnessed horrific violence (in some years, Ciudad Juárez has had more deaths than Baghdad), driven by the international trade in guns, drugs, and money. Side by side with this bloodshed, Juárez is the epitome of contemporary global capitalism, with youthful workers in its *maquiladora* export assembly plants earning approximately $60 a week churning out computers, televisions, washing machines, and other goods for prosperous consumers in the United States and elsewhere. The border is thus an important site and symbol of inequality and human suffering. Yet it is more than this; divided yet also combined, it is a vibrant human community.

Personal relations and sentiments often cross the political border. There is extensive cross-border movement, including everyday visiting and migration (both documented and undocumented). Many people are transnationals, having residences in both countries, or living in one country and regularly visiting the other one. Identification with 'the border' and possessing a sense of connection across it is typical, though bounded nationalism is also common in both countries. Given its history and proximity to Mexico, it is unsurprising that El Paso is 83 percent 'Hispanic', as of the 2010 census, almost all of Mexican origin. Spanish-English bilingualism and Mexican–North American biculturalism are the most common linguistic and cultural repertoires in El Paso. However, monolingualism and monoculturalism in either direction are also widespread, which poses interactional and communicative barriers. Historically, El Paso was an explicitly racist city (Anglo-Americans dominating African-Americans and Chican@s[4]); this era largely has passed at the interpersonal level, so that on the surface, race relations are egalitarian, but structural racial inequality remains strong (e.g., differential distribution of education and occupations). Mexican identity continues to be stigmatized as foreign and associated with poverty and backwardness. These subtle but pervasive biases occur among Chican@s as well as non-Mexican origin people.

El Paso is, in important ways, iconic of Occupy's concerns about inequality and economic justice. The city is distinctly poor, characteristic of all U.S. border cities except San Diego. El Paso's median household income is $38,259; U.S. median household income is $52,762 according to the U.S. census.[5] Two of the ten poorest zip codes in the United States with over 5,000 tax returns are in El Paso, including the single poorest one.[6] Distinctive socio-economically marginalized communities are found in the inner city (old Mexican-origin *barrios*) and outlying unplanned settlements (so-called *colonias*, to some extent resembling Mexican squatter settlements on the U.S. side, but built on remote, undeveloped plots leased from landlords). A vast poor to middle income, if often economically insecure, population is spread across the city in a geographically unmarked fashion. Regional capitalist development historically centered on cheap labor (farm work and men's pants manufacture). Today, El Paso's economy centers on the state, with an enclave of good government jobs (e.g., Drug Enforcement Agency, Border Patrol, border and Latin America surveillance, etc.) surrounded by a vast sea of low-wage services, informal enterprises, and widespread underemployment. El Paso is a military base city; Fort Bliss is one of the largest installations in the country in terms of the number of service members, and a center for the return of troops from Iraq and Afghanistan deployments, as well as the surveillance of Latin America.

Politically, El Paso is a left-liberal city, with a marked concern for economic justice. There is ambivalence about social-cultural issues but change is occurring rapidly; for example, El Paso has strongly favored drug legalization, a response to Paseño[7] empathy with the violence in Mexico, as evidenced by the 2012 election of Beto O'Rourke to Congress substantially on the basis of his drug policy reform position.[8] While social justice organizations are discussed later in the chapter, El Paso's population as a whole tends to be little engaged in politics of any kind.

Occupy El Paso obviously did not encompass all these dimensions of El Paso and the border region. But it was an organic growth from many of these roots, especially as experienced by young people. It was not artificial or alienated from its place. The composition of its members, its values and concerns, and its forms of action and challenges, all emerged from U.S. border life, galvanized by the wider examples of the world Occupy and *Indignado* movements.

3. Occupy El Paso

Occupy El Paso's history resembled many U.S. Occupies. Anarchist computer activists, influenced by the example of Occupy Wall Street in New York City, started planning meetings in late September. The first Occupy demonstration was held on October 15, 2011, and the Occupation of the central downtown open space, San Jacinto Plaza, began on October 17. A University of Texas at El Paso (UTEP) Chicana grad student served as liaison with City Hall. Because of a lack of lead time, the City Manager issued her a permit for 24 hour a day camping at the plaza, which was to be ratified or denied by City Council on October 25. Thirty to forty Occupiers attended the City Council meeting and 21 spoke in support. Included in this group was a homeless man, originally from Rhode Island, who spoke about the development of a sense of community, where he, as a non-local non-Hispanic, had been accepted, was given tasks to perform, fed, and had his consciousness raised regarding the class structure of the United States. (He subsequently returned home, rejoined family, found work, and occasionally kept in touch via e-mail.) The Resolution passed, giving Occupy permission to camp in San Jacinto Plaza through November 13, 2011. Perhaps, prophetically, at this meeting the city council also approved a resolution to support a retail stimulus program for the area surrounding the plaza.

The actual encampment consisted mostly of young people, although a few older ones also camped. Significant numbers of people visited the encampment at various times during the day and in the evening to attend the 7:00 p.m. General Assemblies. Among the participants were young parents, and two four-year-olds became mainstays of the group and were soon able to lead the chants. Almost immediately, the Occupiers were joined by about 20 homeless people, none of whom were natives of El Paso. They were male and female, and at least two were veterans, one of Iraq and one of Viet Nam. The homeless who chose to participate in general assemblies and chores were full members of Occupy El Paso.[9] A significant contingent from El Paso Adapt, a disability rights organization, were part of Occupy El Paso. Many were wheelchair users and several slept in the park. Most campers were male. Females were more likely to visit during the days and evenings, and sleep at home, though a few did camp. Although we do not know of any gendered threats, concern about safety did cause a gender bias in the encampment. However, influential people were gender balanced; the occupier who obtained the permit was a woman, while the person who coordinated most general assemblies was a man (both were young).

There were two main clusters of tents divided by a functional area with food, a medic tent, sign and banner storage, and so forth. For a while, a large teepee was located in one side of the plaza, installed by a neo-Aztec *Kalpulli* group. A library had a large variety of contributed books.

After the first few, unorganized days of occupation, the local branch of the national Food Not Bombs established a kitchen with regular meal times and shared work expectations for participants. They did a wonderful job of feeding people. People had to participate in chores if they were going to eat. Some were not interested and left. It became clear that even this small 'society' of 50–70 people living together in a park needed norms to live together peaceably. The 'RULES/REGLAS' of Occupy El Paso were worked out and posted in both English and Spanish. Committees were established to deal with food preparation, sanitation/clean-up, and 'security'. The Viet Nam vet was the camp medic.

When Occupy El Paso began it experienced the comfortable temperatures of the desert Southwest. The encampment had an almost festive atmosphere. Much attention was given to artistic and clever expression, through posters and banners, of the political views of participants. Musicians were also among the Occupiers. Spontaneous protests marched through downtown, often led by drummers and other musicians, with members carrying signs and chanting, past banks and other businesses, sometimes down to the Segundo Barrio (the old inner city barrio, between downtown and the Mexican border). One Sunday afternoon the group marched uphill to St. Patrick's Cathedral, where upset and concerned parishioners were reassured by the warm and fraternal greeting of the Mexican parish priest.

Two important social justice organizations, the Border Network for Human Rights (BNHR) and the Sin Fronteras Farmworkers Center, made special visits to the plaza. BNHR provided a lavish tamale feast. The Farmworkers, together with Kalpulli dancers, marched to the plaza to demonstrate solidarity, and Occupiers in turn made two visits to the Sin Fronteras building, almost at the border, deep in the Segundo Barrio. Occupy El Paso put on a massive Thanksgiving feast for the farmworkers, and shared food together at the center, with sometimes hesitant but often lively conversations in Spanish; and likewise Occupy cooked and served a bountiful Christmas *tamalada* (tamale meal) to the farmworkers, with a vigorous discussion of food justice and labor and a teach-in on indigenous issues.

Occupy El Paso considered at one of the early General Assemblies the issue of using the term 'Occupy' because of its political implications for indigenous peoples. Some wanted to use 'De-Occupy' instead. Some of the leading figures in Occupy El Paso were also leaders of MEChA, Movimiento Estudiantil Chican@ de Aztlán, at UTEP. In criticizing the term 'occupy', they referred to Rodolfo Acuña's influential interpretation of Chican@ history, *Occupied America*.[10] Native Americans and Chican@s were, after all, in this land long before the Anglos showed up – a popular local saying is 'we didn't cross the border, the border crossed us'. Chican@s in El Paso are well aware of this fact, as well as of the Native American component in their heritage. While the term 'occupy' continued in use, its flaws were widely acknowledged.

People physically occupied San Jacinto Plaza, from October 17 until November 13, when the permit expired. The City Manager had implicitly promised to allow Occupy to relocate to another city park two blocks away, but she reneged on this understanding, and the city avoided issuing a new permit for overnight camping. The encampment was thoroughly cleaned out, and almost all tents removed. Most participants departed for other places – El Paso, other cities, and a few homeless encampments in the area. There were two nights of symbolic civil disobedience in which people occupied a few tents overnight – the first night resulting in seven tickets, and the second night resulting in seven arrests. All arrestees were bailed out by a large group of supporters, who held a candlelight vigil by the county jail. Physical protest and occupation ended, however, after the second night. The halt was not caused just by repression. It occurred in the context of sagging personal energy and organizational capacity, including the reluctance of individuals to be arrested and limited ability of the group to raise bail.

Occupy El Paso continued meeting regularly (three days a week at the plaza, and, during some cold weeks, at Mujer Obrera, a labor and social justice center). In January 2012, the group undertook a series of strategic meetings, resulting in a set of initiatives (e.g., weekend afternoon assemblies/outreach opportunities at parks in various residential areas of the city, three of which were carried out). Instead of re-energizing and focusing Occupy El Paso, the visioning process occurred during a period of gradually declining participation. Lack of a core encampment certainly contributed. Many youthful participants moved on, though some continued or reappeared after pauses.

A non-comprehensive list of events organized by Occupy El Paso after the end of the encampment include: the festive meals with the farmworkers discussed above; a group of creative young people who did a 'mic check' at Walmart on Black Friday; a demonstration (with Occupy Las Cruces, New Mexico, and the Brown Berets) calling attention to the harms caused by the North American Free

Trade Agreement (NAFTA) on January 1, 2012, its 18th anniversary. There was also a 'mic check' challenging the chief Mexican negotiator of NAFTA, Herminio Blanco, at his speaking appearance at the UTEP. Two days (February 29–March 1, 2012) of Occupy Colleges events were held at UTEP, drawing attention to the political economy of college costs, and some tabling was done at El Paso Community College. When the weather warmed up, a 'return to Occupy' festival was held at the plaza, with art, music, signs, and personal statements of what Occupy meant to people. A large May Day rally was held at the plaza, with the participation of immigrant rights, farmworker, labor union, and peace organizations. A particularly interesting event brought elderly (still active) leftist Catholic priests and nuns to transmit their wealth of experiences and insights about non-violent civil disobedience to younger activists.

During this time, Occupy El Paso also supported with turnout and participation a number of local labor and social movement events, including worksite picketing by SEIU hospital workers; a kick-off rally by the National Nurses Union, a Robin Hood (financial transaction) tax rally by National Nurses United; several picketing events against wage thieves organized by the Labor Justice Committee of El Paso; the Cesar Chavez day march and memorial of the Sin Fronteras Farmworkers Center; and the group consultations and regional conference of the Human Rights at Home campaign, sponsored in El Paso by the Border Network for Human Rights.

After May Day 2012, Occupy El Paso became entirely dormant with weekly General Assemblies finally halting. The remaining echo is the Occupy El Paso Facebook page, which remains energetic, but without complementary real-world activities; it largely consists of forwarded items from around the global internet, and occasionally social justice events and issues in El Paso. While Facebook helped the group communicate during its active, face-to-face period, over the long run it distracted from the Occupy project, or at least mystified its rapid decline, as users substituted forwarding items and commenting (or arguing) on postings for deeper participation.[11]

4. Occupy El Paso and the Struggle for Space

Occupy El Paso was integral to the struggle over space, real estate capital, and insider political dealings in the city. This struggle had begun before Occupy El Paso, with organizing and protests over the extension of the downtown redevelopment plan southward to two bridges to Mexico, impacting the Segundo Barrio, a poor residential and small scale retail neighborhood. For a time, the plans were stalled. Informed by the antecedent social movement, several members of Occupy became concerned about maintaining open public spaces and spending public monies on projects to serve the underserved people in this poor city. The City's sudden about face on permitting the Occupy encampment, discussed above, reinforced these concerns.

The blocks facing the Plaza include small shops/restaurants, two large office buildings, the Chase Bank Building, and the Bank of America building. The only complaints concerning Occupy El Paso came from the Mills Building management on the west side of the Plaza. This historic building was restored and owned by one of the richest men in El Paso, the billionaire owner of Western Refining, who invested heavily in downtown real estate. At the time of Occupy, he had proposed taking over part of the Plaza for an outdoor café across from his building, thus using one of the few public spaces downtown to benefit his prosperous customers. It is possible that he complained directly to the City Manager and Council members, and this was part of the reason why Occupy El Paso's permit was not renewed or adequate space provided nearby.

Occupiers began to track initiatives by private capital and the City to reshape the downtown area. Members attended City Council meetings from Fall 2011 through Summer 2012. The City Manager announced that there would be large quality of life bond issues on the ballot in November 2012. During spring 2012, City Council discussed and decided the items to be included were parks, bicycle paths, public pools, community centers, and a downtown arena for sports and large concerts – this last item was to cost $180 million. With several comparable venues in the city, who needed and/or wanted the downtown arena? Clearly, well-connected owners of downtown real estate. Occupy El Paso became the nexus of discussions around the city concerning these questions of public investments.

There had been talk of trying to bring an affiliated minor league baseball team to El Paso. (El Paso currently has the Diablos, an independent league team, which plays in Cohen Stadium in the Northeast section of the city. The team was recently bought by the Tigua Indian tribe. The northeast, near the military base, is considered to be déclassé.)

The City Manager announced that the baseball stadium would not be funded via the bond issues. However, a key occupier heard a city council member boast that something 'important' was happening with the new baseball team (without public disclosure), and people would have to 'move fast'. This deal had been worked on in secret starting in 2010 by large capitalists, the City Manager, and the Council Members 'owned' by the capitalists. These capitalists owned many buildings in downtown whose value they hoped would be enhanced with a baseball stadium, as well as the unneeded, unwanted arena.

On Thursday afternoons, the agenda for the next Tuesday City Council meeting is announced. On Thursday, June 21, the agenda included funding for a $50 million baseball stadium to be paid for by the citizens of El Paso, and visitors through an increase in the hotel tax. The baseball stadium was intended for a Triple AAA team purchased by the billionaire owner of Western Refining/downtown real estate investor, together with the near-billionaire son of a large-scale military housing developer. The next Tuesday, June 26, with negligible time for democratic discussion and involvement, this plan was rammed through and passed by the City Council. Occupy El Paso got out the word, and other critics also stepped forward, but the framework was crafted to neuter effective public participation.

The details as they emerged were more enraging, corrupt, and wasteful than could have been imagined. The baseball stadium 'had' to go where the then city hall was located. City offices were to be scattered among several downtown buildings that would be purchased and renovated at taxpayer expense, improving the market for downtown commercial real estate. One of the buildings was the *El Paso Times* building (the main English language newspaper). What chance existed for unbiased reporting? An intensive, nasty purchased advertising campaign, funded by developers with monetary interests in these projects, filled the televisions and mailboxes of El Paso. They characterized opponents to the stadium (including key occupiers) as not wanting a better future for the children of El Paso. Over $400,000 was spent on this propaganda effort, and it worked. The voters supported the bond issues and the raising of the hotel tax (both items phrased on the ballot in manipulative ways). A genuinely democratic process might well have resulted in a new baseball stadium, but manipulation of council agendas and votes, and orchestrated 'public opinion' leading into tricky referendums, are indisputably fake 'democracy'.

It was like watching a train wreck; Occupy El Paso members and other activists knew what was at stake, who had the power, and how they intended to capture the public's money to be spent for private benefit, but concerned citizens were unable to prevent it. Activists, including occupiers, petitioned and protested around city hall (which became a symbol of the struggle), but to no effect. Occupy had had a role in transmitting attention and knowledge across 2011–2012, but the decline in enthusiasm and participation by summer and fall 2012, especially among youth, meant that it had little capacity for protest or organizing at the time of key decisions. For example, no one participated in a proposed 'circle of hands' around city hall.

On April 14, 2013, city hall was imploded. The baseball stadium is under construction. The $50 million cost is now up to $68 million and counting. What will attendance at baseball games be? How will average families afford tickets? We don't expect the team to be here very long. El Paso will be paying for the stadium long after the team has left town. Public monies were captured for private interests, so two middle-aged 'boys' have a place to play team owner. . . .

5. Lessons from Occupy El Paso

5.1 The Participants Occupy El Paso's members came from varied backgrounds, but broadly, its social composition emerged organically from the U.S. border region. The largest group of participants was twenty-something (and a few teen) Chican@s and a smaller number of Anglo-Americans.[12] Many Chican@ youth, but not all, grew up as transnationals, visiting family in Mexico. Anglo-American youth generally grew up in El Paso in close association with the Chican@ youth just described. This was the first engagement in political activism for most young adults. Experienced peace and justice activists, both Chican@ and Anglo-American, supplemented the youthful core. During the main, fall 2011 period, older activists generally deferred to youthful leaders. After the beginning of 2012, experienced activists took more of the initiative and influence, but this indicated the declining participation in and energy of Occupy El Paso more than a 'capture' of the group by such persons. Indeed, the measures taken under their influence sought to bring back the engagement and voices of all participants, but the central problem was the decline in presence and commitment of the youthful enthusiasts from the original encampment. This disengagement will be discussed below; here, the goal is to characterize the people of Occupy El Paso.

Many Occupiers, of course, could provide interesting examples. The two central 'leaders' mentioned previously – Occupy is a horizontal movement, but unquestionably there were key influential figures – were a Chicana female graduate student and mother of a preschooler, and a male Chicano first year college student from a poor, working class background.

An exemplary active participant was a young woman, born in Mexico and raised in both countries, who attended college (where she had been a drug legalization activist) and was working as a home health care aide (previously as a call center operative). Another was a U.S.-born and raised child of Mexican immigrants who had gained modest (lower middle class) success; he found this tiny instance of the 'American dream' confining, and traveled across the United States, visiting Occupy sites, seeking a more artistic and social-value based way of life, while periodically working as a laborer, house painter, and sous-chef. The experienced activist who was most influential during the encampment was a long-time participant in alternative trade, peace, and social justice. He was from an academic family, whose parents were Anglo-American and Mexican, affiliated with the Catholic left. Finally, a good example of a personally quiet but committed participant was a young Iraq war veteran, gay, of Mexican origin, who attended the local university.

The presence of higher education in several of these examples should not be misinterpreted as indicating an elitist separation of Occupy from the wider El Paso community. UTEP is an urban commuter university with over 60% of its students being first in their family to attend college, and El Paso Community College is comparable. Flexible work, child-raising, taking classes, and time with laboring and immigrant family members, form a commonly shared experience of young adulthood in the new working class.

A sensitive indicator in El Paso of social-cultural composition is the choice of language, Spanish or English, in public events and interactions.

Over 60% of Paseños are fluent bilinguals, although this number is likely lower for young adults. On each side of this bilingual center are large linguistic minorities: English and Spanish monolinguals with no or limited capacity in the other language. Almost all of the general assemblies were conducted in English, consistent with public speech choices typical of young Chican@s. Key occupiers all spoke English fluently, and varied considerably in their Spanish fluency. Bilingual Occupiers conscientiously provided simultaneous interpretation to the small number of limited English-proficient attendees.

There was a robust ethos of accessibility. Dialogues and speeches fluidly shifted to Spanish when circumstances called for it, such as plaza visits by farmworkers from the Centro Sin Fronteras, most of whom were limited English-proficient. Personal conversations varied widely among English, Spanish, and Spanish-English code-switching, locally termed Spanglish. Chants (formalized political speech) used both Spanish and English. Occupy El Paso, though grounded in the main tendencies of U.S.-side border youth, resisted the linguistic and cultural 'borders' between the United States and Mexico.

5.2 The Values Occupy El Paso was distinctly place conscious. This can be seen in many of the activities recounted above. It also is illustrated by the *Declaration of El Paso/Declaración de El Paso*,[13] which merges language from Occupy Wall Street with border-specific calls to change. The document initially endorses the Declaration of the Occupation of New York City, and provides its text. The issues and values of the world Occupy and *Indignado* movements, including the critique of social inequality, corporate power, and corruption of politics by big money, resonated in a poor city where redistribution of resources for the public good remains a vital agenda. Then, the Occupy El Paso declaration turns to border-specific issues, in a strong and original text.

The list of critical observations about the status quo and demands for change cannot be reviewed in its entirety. Here we summarize some distinctive ones. The document begins by noting that Occupy Wall Street's general concerns disproportionately affect communities of color like El Paso. It repeatedly focuses on migration, indicting the global political-economic system that creates millions of economic refugees, who are then criminalized and denied the right to cross borders, and it attacks border militarization and enforcement escalation. It speaks of 'a class of working people whose rights are consistently violated due to the fact that they have no documentation' and calls for 'an immigration policy . . . [that responds] to the human needs of all people', and it expresses solidarity with domestic workers and farmworkers, many of them migrants, who are pervasive in El Paso.

The declaration addresses issues felt acutely by border youth, including the alienating style of education (e.g., limited bilingual education), the prison-industrial complex and imprisonment of people of color, and the 'poverty draft' into the military. It takes note of wars of economic domination: '[to] use violence to ensure economic prosperity of the rich in the United States at the expense of human lives and livelihoods in the U.S. and abroad'. This language is interesting in light of the involvement of young veterans in the group. Equitable and dignified treatment for LGBQT individuals was likewise meaningful to group members. Notably, given the composition of the encampment, the declaration voices strong support for people with disabilities and the homeless.

Occupy El Paso took particular note of issues affecting Mexico, which are relatively well known in the U.S. borderlands but much less so in the U.S. interior. The declaration addressed the human cost in both countries of 'free trade' and removal of controls over corporations and capital. It made reference to the *maquiladoras* just across the border, and their pay rates and working conditions that fail to support human development. Finally, it spoke to one of the most pressing issues of the time, extreme violence in Mexico, calling for changes in drug policy (to weaken criminal organizations), weapons and munitions policy (in which the U.S. is the main supplier of tools of death), U.S. police and military aid to Mexico's violent and repressive state, and the asylum policy for persecuted Mexicans arriving at the border. In summary, Occupy El Paso declared that 'We stand for open borders, food sovereignty and the end of exploitative free trade agreements that have left us all in economic crisis'.

5.3 Relationships to Existing Social Justice Organizations This commitment to place informed Occupy El Paso's mutually supportive relations with established social justice organizations, many of them distinctive to El Paso and border issues. They included the Border Network for Human Rights, a large base-community organization centered on human rights for immigrants; Annunciation House, a 'no questions asked' migrant residence and advocacy organization; the Sin Fronteras farmworker organizing and assistance center; the Labor Justice Committee, a worker-based organization focused on combating wage theft; and La Mujer Obrera, an alternative economic enterprise based among garment factory workers whose jobs were exported from El Paso to Mexico and Central America following NAFTA. Other allied organizations included the National Nurses Organizing Committee and the Service Employees International Union, which were organizing the hospital sector in El Paso during the Occupy period, and other labor organizations. There were also threads of connection to environmental justice movements, the Catholic left (particularly strong in El Paso), and local peace organizations.

The organizations just named, all with physical offices and dedicated staffs, have greater capacity for action than Occupy El Paso. As narrated earlier, they often organized activities for which Occupy El Paso provided volunteer assistance and attendance. This increased participant enthusiasm in Occupy El Paso, and helped to educate many neophyte activists. Occupy El Paso likewise received attendees and material support at its events. However, the presence of established local issue networks, activities, and organizations may have reduced opportunities for Occupy El Paso to develop its own focus, sense of identity, member commitment, and so forth....

5.4 Crossing Borders? The Occupy movement, together with the antecedent *Indignado* movement, envisioned values and struggles as crossing conventional national borders. Occupy El Paso, located on just such a border, showed both strengths and limitations in these terms. Some Occupy El Paso members had transnational life experiences, such as growing up in both Ciudad Juárez and El Paso. The group was aware of issues in Mexico and issues that spanned the two countries, as indicated by the NAFTA anniversary protest at the foot of an international bridge. Importantly, Occupy El Paso was interwoven with the El Paso movement (and through this, movements in Mexico) that responded to the extreme violence in Ciudad Juárez. In 2009, a large conference organized by city elites and university professors questioned U.S. drug policy, in connection to violence in Mexico; student leadership emerged during this event. In fall 2010, an alliance of students and faculty, including several Occupiers, created a touching and impressive binational memorial and protest at the border fence. Simultaneously with the start of Occupy El Paso, in October 2011, and with shared participants, a student-based conference at UTEP focused on activism skills in conjunction with U.S. policy issues (e.g., guns and munitions) linked to violence in Mexico. Occupy El Paso formed part of the audience for a U.S. press conference condemning the arrest of activists in Juárez, and subsequently a human rights protest at the Mexican consulate. There were also network connections from Occupy to two visits of the Mexican human rights and anti-violence leader Javier Sicilia to El Paso, although in these instances and those of the previous sentence, the organizers came from established social justice networks....

6. Conclusion: Limitations and Possibilities

Occupy El Paso suffered from characteristic problems of horizontal social movements in individualistic societies (that is, lacking traditions of collective cooperation and identity): interpersonal conflict, inconsistent commitment and follow-through, naïveté about the depth and complexity of goals and activities, and so forth. The youth of most key members and the (correct) reluctance of experienced activists to dominate the assemblies exacerbated these issues. However, the crucial limitation was also the initial strength of Occupy El Paso: that it emerged from a powerful impulse, a wave of enthusiasm and urge to express dissent. The timing of Occupy El Paso within the struggles over real estate capital, democracy, and downtown development illustrates the role of enthusiasm. Initial phases of that struggle antedated Occupy El Paso. Communications via the internet, unrelated to this El Paso timeline, then stimulated the encampment. Yet due to that moment of enthusiasm, in November 2011 Occupy El Paso became central to the struggle over space, involving the end of its permit and civil disobedience to the enforcement of the no overnight camping ordinance. Without a unifying encampment, participation in regular meetings declined, and youthful members drifted away. But Occupy El Paso continued to have an important role in the struggle, as members went to City Council meetings, monitored statements and actions, and kept the struggle for democracy and social-spatial justice alive in the spring and early summer of 2012. By the time of the key city council votes in summer 2012, and subsequent petitions and street protests in fall 2012, new critics of city policy emerged, and Occupy El Paso, its enthusiasm spent, faded from the struggle.

Occupy El Paso played an admirable role in this struggle, but one bounded in time by the accident of its moment of enthusiasm. It had energy and size in fall 2011, but the heart of the struggle was the midsummer of 2012, when it lacked capacity to act as a group (though individuals did contribute). It emerged from a moment of world-wide communication, but was incompletely synchronized to a concrete local struggle for which the activities and values of Occupy were well suited. Enthusiasm, then, must form part of a wider combination of elements to be brought together for a long run struggle for justice. Understanding how to achieve that is an important agenda.

Enthusiasm for values and actions, diffused across new media, and focused on performative and symbolic expression, may seem to be characteristics of youth. They come with limitations already identified.

Yet it is unhelpful to focus criticism on youthfulness. For example, the decline in involvement was not simply fickleness or faddishness. It reflected the life-ways of young, mostly working class people. They often departed from the group to take up jobs when they needed money. The jobs often involved complicated schedules. Others faded from the group as they focused on completing college work, or coped with child raising and family care. Transportation to meetings in the city center was a problem – many occupiers did not have functional cars or gas money. After the end of the encampment that had concentrated the group, this became an especially erosive force. Finally, many young Occupiers lived geographically fractured lives, with separated families in El Paso and other distant cities, and departure from the group sometimes occurred because of family imperatives.

The initial wave of enthusiasm and expression of ideas and values was, above all, a start. The young adults of Occupy El Paso went through a learning experience. They talked constantly about issues and values of justice and democracy. They encountered important social justice organizations. They participated in numerous public events. They struggled to organize a voluntary community. The more experienced and committed activists, who perhaps had more lasting power and were not as driven by enthusiasm, did not need these lessons; but the lessons themselves are crucial.

The youthful core of Occupy El Paso fits well Arnold's proposal of a new working class. In this region constituted primarily by the children and grandchildren of Mexican immigrants, members of this class provide flexible labor in the new global service economy, epitomized by bilingual call centers. They undergo discipline of corporations and states, in military service, workplaces, and the criminal justice system. They experience controlled and reduced democracy in the public sphere, including the diversion of public funds and spaces to private hands in their home city.

Future struggles for social justice depend on this new generation, not aging punks (such as the authors) and others of our ilk. In El Paso, as worldwide, the Occupy movement changed discourses, bringing public attention to inequality, economic justice, corporate power, the value of public goods, and big money corrupting politics and governance. El Paso was already receptive to these messages, and Occupy reinforced these perspectives. The young people active in Occupy El Paso learned lessons in political values and practical organizing. If the new working class responds to the Occupy burst of enthusiasm, if the new working class finds voice and expression, this is a very good thing. We should be proud.

Notes

1. K R Arnold, *America's New Working Class: Race, Gender, and Ethnicity in a Biopolitical Age* (University Park, PA: Pennsylvania State University Press, 2008), 3–11.
2. Arnold, *America's New Working Class*, 3.
3. Rodolfo Acuña, *Occupied America: A History of Chicanos*, 7th ed. (Boston: Longman, 2011).
4. We use Chican@ for the El Paso Mexican-origin population to be consistent with the public speech preference of Occupy (it is rarely used in the community, however). The @ symbol covers both female (a) and male (o) noun endings in Spanish. Anglo-American, or Anglo for short, roughly glosses as 'white' in borderlands usage. Other terms resemble current US usage.
5. American Fact Finder. Washington, DC: US Census Bureau, 2012. http://factfinder2.census.gov/faces/nav/jsf/pages/community_facts.xhtml (accessed 3 June 2014). Database searches: El Paso County median household income and US median household income.
6. Mongabay.com. *100 Lowest Income Zip Codes in the United States.* http://wealth.mongabay.com/tables/100_lowest_income-5000.html (accessed 3 June 2014).
7. Paseños is the Spanish language term for people from El Paso, which is common in local usage.
8. B O'Rourke, and S M Byrd, *Dealing Death and Drugs: The Big Business of Dope in the U.S. and Mexico, an Argument to End the Prohibition of Marijuana* (El Paso: Cinco Puntos Press, 2011).
9. For more on Occupy El Paso and the homeless, see C Smith, E Castañeda and J Heyman, 'The Homeless and Occupy El Paso: Creating Community among the 99%', *Social Movement Studies* 11, nos 3–4 (2012): 356–66.
10. R Acuña, *Occupied America: A History of Chicanos*, 7th ed. (Boston: Longman, 2011).
11. The public Occupy El Paso Facebook page is at http://www.facebook.com/OccupyElPaso (accessed 4 June 2014). There was also a standard web page with Occupy El Paso documents and message boards, rarely used after the fall of 2011, and taken down in September of 2012. It was at http://occupyelpaso.org/ (copy in files of the authors).
12. No publicly known member of the local Native American community, Ysleta del Sur, participated, but neo-indigenous people with roots in the Chican@ community did. No African Americans (a small population locally) participated extensively.
13. Occupy El Paso, *Declaration of El Paso/La Declaración de El Paso*, 2011. http://www.facebook.com/notes/occupy-el-paso/occupy-el-paso-declaration/292757994095006 (accessed 4 June 2013).

SECTION IV

Environmental Justice
Confronting Racism and Imperialism

One of the key components in environmental justice is getting people to the table to speak for themselves . . . they need to be in the room where policy is being made.
—Robert Bullard

It really boils down to this: that all life is interrelated. We are all caught in an inescapable network of mutuality, tied into a single garment of destiny. Whatever affects one destiny, affects all indirectly.
—Martin Luther King Jr

The concept of environmental justice shows how race, class and gender mediate people's lives and affect the burden of environmental degradation they experience. The concepts of racial and gender justice addressed in section 2 and of economic justice in section 3 intersect in this section, since people of colour and low-income people are more likely to live in urban neighbourhoods dominated by toxic industries and rural areas polluted by pesticides. Environmental justice is also closely related to reproductive justice, as described in this section in the article on the Native American women's struggles for their environmental, cultural and reproductive rights.

Gender roles also shape the access to and management of resources. For example, in many countries of the Global South women are primarily responsible for tending the land and providing sustenance for their families, but they are often denied control and rights over resources. Agrarian reforms have often distributed land to male heads of households, thus adversely impacting women's land use rights. In Kenya, for example, women's environmental interests focussed on access to land and other resources for livelihood security.[1]

The threats caused by global climate change are also not neutral, and poor people in developing countries experience the worst consequences, partly due to their lower adaptive capacities. Women in rural areas in developing countries are highly dependent on local resources for their livelihood because of their responsibilities to secure food and water for their families. Due to their limited access to decision making and economic assets, poor women in developing countries are the most affected by climate change.

In his essay, Peter Wenz argues that environmental justice is about how some of us consume key environmental resources at the expense of others, sometimes in distant places, and about how the power to effect change and influence environmental decision making is unequally distributed. The disproportionate impacts on poor people violate principles of distributive justice and thus are not morally justifiable. Based on the generally accepted principle of 'commensurate burdens and benefits' that states that those who derive benefits should sustain commensurate burdens, and on the principle of equal consideration demonstrated in Rawls's thought experiment, Wenz shows that different views of distributive justice such as libertarianism, utilitarianism and cost-benefit analysis, as well as a free-market approach, are all inadequate to determine the just distribution of toxic waste. He suggests an approach that would assign points to different types of locally undesirable land uses (LULUs) and require that all communities earn LULU points, and, based on the Principle of Commensurate Benefits and Burdens, wealthy communities would be required to earn more LULU points than poorer ones.

In the essay that opens this section, Robert Bullard writes that environmental racism is evident in practices that expose racial minorities in the United States and people of colour around the world to disproportionate shares of environmental hazards such as toxic chemicals in factories, toxic herbicides and pesticides in agriculture, radiation from uranium mining, lead from paint on older buildings, and toxic wastes illegally dumped. In its early formulation in the United States in the early 1980s, environmental justice activism and research focused on the relationship between race and poverty and the spatial distribution of toxic waste and industrial sites producing pollution impacts, including accusations of environmental racism and the deliberate targeting of poor Black communities in locating polluting sites. Today the concept of environmental justice has expanded to include transport issues, food justice, deforestation, lead poisoning, and biopiracy. The forms of social difference that are featured in recent environmental justice research include questions of age, gender, disability, the environmental rights of indigenous people, and the responsibilities to future generations.

The initial environmental justice spark in the United States sprang from the protests in a poor, rural and overwhelmingly Black county in North Carolina, Warren County.[2] In 1982 Warren County was designated as the site of a hazardous waste landfill. The landfill would receive PCB-contaminated soil from illegal dumping of toxic waste along roadways. In response to the state's decision, the NAACP and others staged a massive protest. In six weeks of marches and protests more than five hundred people were arrested as they attempted to prevent the passage of trucks to the site. While the protest failed to prevent the siting of the disposal facility, it became a cause célèbre, defining the start of the environmental justice movement in the United States and the assertion that environmentally significant decisions could have racist intent. The story of ordinary people driven to desperate measures to protect their communities from a toxic assault drew national media attention and inspired other people who had lived through similar injustice. The Warren County protests also marked the first instance of an environmental protest by people of colour that garnered widespread national attention.

As James Cone discusses, to civil rights activists the actions of the North Carolina state government in forcing a toxic landfill onto a small African American community were an extension of the racism they had encountered for decades in housing, education and employment. This time it was environmental racism. Many early leaders in the environmental justice movement in fact came out of the civil rights movement and brought to it the same tactics they had used in civil rights struggles—marches, petitions, rallies, coalition building, litigation and nonviolent direct action.[3]

Many authors in this section address the limits of mainstream environmentalism and argue that it has not addressed the fact that 'social inequality and imbalances of social power are at the heart of environmental degradation, resource depletion, pollution, and even overpopulation'.[4] James Cone suggests that white environmentalists must engage with people of colour and learn about their communities and struggles in order to oppose environmental racism. The environmental crisis, according to these authors, cannot be solved without social justice. As the environmentalist Paul Hawken writes,

> The environmental movement is critical to our survival. Our house is literally burning, and it is only logical that environmentalists expect the social justice movement to get on the environmental bus. But it is the other way around; the only way we are going to put out the fire is to get on the social justice bus and heal our wounds, because, in the end, there is only one bus.[5]

To differentiate their perspective from that of the mainstream environmental movement that they see as out of touch with the social and economic realities of the poor and people of colour, the American Indian and Hispanic women leaders in the environmental justice movement in the study by Prindeville in New Mexico describe themselves as 'third world' or 'indigenous' environmentalists whose focus is on the survival of their communities.[6]

Another important aspect of the environmental justice movement is their demand for political recognition through democratic participatory politics. Both the Latino communities described by Figueroa[7] and the American Indian and Hispanic women interviewed by Prindeville[8] address the importance of cultural recognition and political empowerment that are linked to democratic participation. Both groups describe how their people's history of environmental and cultural conquest shapes their movement where environmental justice includes concerns of social justice, preservation of traditions, language, culture, and identity.

Finally, the article on the Indigenous Peoples of North America connects environmental justice with reproductive justice. Reproductive justice proposes a paradigm shift beyond demanding reproductive rights to a broader reproductive health agenda. It is an intersectional theory emerging from the experiences of women of colour whose multiple communities face a complex set of reproductive oppressions. It is based on the understanding that the impacts of race, class, gender and sexual identity oppressions are not additive but integrative, thus producing the paradigm of intersectionality. The concept of environmental reproductive justice ensures that a community's reproductive abilities are not impaired by environmental contamination. In the case of the Mohawk Nation at Akwesasne the contamination of the fish by PCBs and other toxins dumped in the St Lawrence River by industries such as General Motors resulted in hormonal changes in girls, thyroid disease in menopausal women, and the contamination of breast milk. The Mother's Milk Project, started by a midwife who argued for the development of health studies, is an example of community organising by Native American women to protect the life and culture of their tribe and fight against environmental pollution.[9] In fact, the contamination of their environment is closely tied to the community's ability to reproduce, whether physically, through the birth of healthy children, or culturally, through the passing on of traditional practices.

Notes

1. Dianne Rocheleau and David Edmunds, 'Women, Men and Trees: Gender, Power and Property in Forest and Agrarian Landscapes', *World Development* 25, no. 8: 1351–71.
2. James H Cone, 'Whose Earth Is It Anyway'? in James H Cone, *Risks of Faith: The Emergence of a Black Theology of Liberation, 1968–1998* (Boston: Beacon Press, 1999), 139.
3. Cone, 'Whose Earth Is It Anyway'? 139–40.

4. Robert Bullard, 'Anatomy of Environmental Racism and the Environmental Justice Movement', in *Confronting Environmental Racism*, ed Robert Bullard (Brooklyn: South End Press, 1993), 23.
5. Paul Hawken, *Blessed Unrest: How the Largest Social Movement in History Is Restoring Grace, Justice, and Beauty to the World* (New York and London: Penguin Books, 2007), 190.
6. Diane-Michelle Prindeville, 'For the People: American Indian and Hispanic Women in New Mexico's Environmental Justice Movement', in *Our Backyard: A Quest for Environmental Justice*, eds Gerald Robert Visgilio and Diane M. Whitelaw (Lanham: Rowman & Littlefield, 2003), 150.
7. Robert Melchior Figueroa, 'Other Faces: Latinos and Environmental Justice', in *Faces of Environmental Racism: Confronting Issues of Global Justice*, eds L. Westra and P. Wenz (Lanham: Rowman & Littlefield, 1995), 167–84.
8. Prindeville, 'For the People', 139–57.
9. Jael Silliman, Marlene Gerber Fried, Loretta Ross, and Elena Gutierrez, 'The Mother's Milk Project', in *Undivided Rights: Women of Color Organize for Reproductive Justice*, ed Jael Silliman, Marlene Gerber Fried, Loretta Ross, and Elena Gutierrez (Brooklyn: South End Press, 2004), 123–41.

Suggested Readings

Agyeman, Julian. *Sustainable Communities and the Challenge of Environmental Justice.* New York: New York University Press, 2005.

Alkon, Alison Hope, and Julian Agyeman, eds. *Cultivating Food Justice: Race, Class, and Sustainability.* Cambridge, MA: MIT Press, 2011.

Bullard, Robert, ed. *Confronting Environmental Racism: Voices from the Grassroots.* Cambridge, MA: South End Press, 1999.

Dobson, Andrew, ed. *Fairness and Futurity: Essays on Environmental Sustainability and Social Justice.* New York: Oxford University Press, 1999.

Hawken, Paul. *Blessed Unrest: How the Largest Social Movement in History Is Restoring Grace, Justice, and Beauty to the World.* New York and London: Penguin Books, 2007.

Kelly, Petra. *Thinking Green! Essays on Environmentalism, Feminism, and Nonviolence.* Berkeley, CA: Parallax Press, 1994.

Krauss, Celene. 'Challenging Power: Toxic Waste Protests and the Politicization of White, Working-Class Women'. In *Community Activism and Feminist Politics*, ed Nancy Naples. New York: Routledge, 1998, 129–50.

Pellow, David Naguib. *Garbage Wars: The Struggle for Environmental Justice in Chicago.* Cambridge, MA: MIT Press, 2004.

Pellow, David Naguib. 'Toward a Critical Environmental Justice Studies: Black Lives Matter as an Environmental Justice Challenge'. *Du Bois Review: Social Science Research on Race* 13, no 2 (October 2016): 221–36.

Ross, Loretta, Elena Gutierrez, Marlene Gerber, and Jael Silliman. *Undivided Rights: Women of Color Organize for Reproductive Justice.* Cambridge, MA: South End Press, 2004.

Schlosberg, David. *Defining Environmental Justice: Theories, Movements, and Nature.* Oxford, UK: Oxford University Press, 2007.

Shiva, Vandana. *Stolen Harvest: The Hijacking of the Global Food Supply.* Cambridge, MA: South End Press, 2000.

_____. *Earth Democracy: Justice, Sustainability, and Peace.* Cambridge, MA: South End Press, 2005.

Shrader-Frechette, Kristin. *Environmental Justice: Creating Equity, Reclaiming Democracy.* Oxford, UK: Oxford University Press, 2002.

Stein, Rachel, ed. *New Perspectives on Environmental Justice: Gender, Sexuality, and Activism.* New Brunswick, NJ: Rutgers University Press, 2004.

Suggested Films and Documentaries

Fox, Josh, dir. *Gasland.* New Video, 2010. DVD. Filmmaker Josh Fox goes on a cross-country journey that uncovers a trail of secrets, lies and contamination. One of many contamination stories that Fox discovers is residents of a Pennsylvania town who reports that they are able to light their drinking water on fire.

Geller, Phylis, dir. *Coal Country.* Evening Star Production, 2008. DVD. The film tells of the dramatic struggle around the use of coal, which provides over half of electricity in America. The filmmakers of *Coal Country* seek to understand the meaning behind promises of 'cheap energy' and 'clean coal' and if they are achievable and at what costs.

Hart Reed, Shannon, dir. *Sisters on the Planet.* Oxfam, 2011. DVD. 'The Sisters on the Planet Initiative', created by Oxfam, brings together women leaders to raise awareness about climate change and to help vulnerable communities adapt to the crisis. The film tells the story of four women – Martina-Uganda, Muriel-Brazil, Sharon-Mississippi, and Sahena-Bangladesh – and their different struggles brought on by climate change in their respective communities.

Kenner, Robert, dir. *Food, Inc.* Dogwood Pictures, 2008. DVD. The documentary unveils America's food industry showing how the nation's supply is now controlled by a handful of corporations that often put profit ahead of consumer health, the livelihood of the American farmer, the safety of workers, and the environment.

Salina, Irena, dir. *Flow: For the Love of Water.* Oscilloscope Laboratories, 2008. DVD. An award-winning documentary investigation into 'The World Water Crisis', which experts have labeled the most important political and environmental issue of the 21st century.

Soechtig, Stephanie, and Jason Lindsey, dir. *Tapped.* Atlas Films, 2009. DVD. It gives a behind-the-scenes look into the unregulated and unseen world of the water industry that aims to privatise the one resource that should not become a commodity: water.

Robert D Bullard[*], 'Anatomy of Environmental Racism and the Environmental Justice Movement'

Communities are not all created equal. In the United States, for example, some communities are routinely poisoned while the government looks the other way. Environmental regulations have not uniformly benefited all segments of society. People of color (African Americans, Latinos, Asians, Pacific Islanders, and Native Americans) are disproportionately harmed by industrial toxins on their jobs and in their neighborhoods. These groups must contend with dirty air and drinking water – the byproducts of municipal landfills, incinerators, polluting industries, and hazardous waste treatment, storage, and disposal facilities.

* Robert Bullard, 'Anatomy of Environmental Racism and the Environmental Justice Movement', in *Confronting Environmental Racism*, ed Robert Bullard (Boston: South End Press, 1993), 15–22. Permissions by Robert Bullard.

Why do some communities get 'dumped on' while others escape? Why are environmental regulations vigorously enforced in some communities and not in others? Why are some workers protected from environmental threats to their health while others (such as migrant farmworkers) are still being poisoned? How can environmental justice be incorporated into the campaign for environmental protection? What institutional changes would enable the United States to become a just and sustainable society? What community organizing strategies are effective against environmental racism? These are some of the many questions addressed in this book.

This chapter sketches out the basic environmental problems communities of color face, discusses how the mainstream environmental movement does not provide an adequate organizational base, analysis, vision, or strategy to address these problems, and, finally, provides a glimpse of several representative struggles within the grassroots environmental justice movement. For these purposes, the pervasive reality of racism is placed at the very center of the analysis.

Internal Colonialism and White Racism

The history of the United States has long been grounded in white racism. The nation was founded on the principles of 'free land' (stolen from Native Americans and Mexicans), 'free labor' (cruelly extracted from African slaves), and 'free men' (white men with property). From the outset, institutional racism shaped the economic, political, and ecological landscape, and buttressed the exploitation of both land and people. Indeed, it has allowed communities of color to exist as internal colonies characterized by dependent (and unequal) relationships with the dominant white society or 'Mother Country'. In their 1967 book, *Black Power*, Carmichael and Hamilton were among the first to explore the 'internal' colonial model as a way to explain the racial inequality, political exploitation, and social isolation of African Americans. As Carmichael and Hamilton write:

> The economic relationship of America's black communities [to white society] . . . reflects their colonial status. The political power exercised over those communities goes hand in glove with the economic deprivation experienced by the black citizens.
> Historically, colonies have existed for the sole purpose of enriching, in one form or another, the 'colonizer'; the consequence is to maintain the economic dependency of the 'colonized'. (1967, 16–17)

Generally, people of color in the United States – like their counterparts in formerly colonized lands of Africa, Asia, and Latin America – have not had the same opportunities as whites. The social forces that have organized oppressed colonies internationally still operate in the 'heart of the colonizer's mother country' (Blauner 1972, 26). For Blauner, people of color are subjected to five principal colonizing processes: they enter the 'host' society and economy involuntarily; their native culture is destroyed; white-dominated bureaucracies impose restrictions from which whites are exempt; the dominant group uses institutionalized racism to justify its actions; and a dual or 'split labor market' emerges based on ethnicity and race. Such domination is also buttressed by state institutions. Social scientists Omi and Winant (1986, 76–78) go so far as to insist that 'every state institution is a racial institution'. Clearly, whites receive benefits from racism, while people of color bear most of the cost.

Environmental Racism

Racism plays a key factor in environmental planning and decision-making. Indeed, environmental racism is reinforced by government, legal, economic, political, and military institutions. It is a fact of life in the United States that the mainstream environmental movement is only beginning to wake up to. Yet, without a doubt, racism influences the likelihood of exposure to environmental and health risks and the accessibility to health care. Racism provides whites of all class levels with an 'edge' in gaining access to a healthy physical environment. This has been documented again and again.

Whether by conscious design or institutional neglect, communities of color in urban ghettos, in rural 'poverty pockets', or on economically impoverished Native-American reservations face some of the worst environmental devastation in the nation. Clearly, racial discrimination was not legislated out of existence in the 1960s. While some significant progress was made during this decade, people of color continue to struggle for equal treatment in many areas, including environmental justice. Agencies at all levels of government, including the federal EPA, have done a poor job protecting people of color from the ravages of pollution and industrial encroachment. It has thus been an up-hill battle convincing white judges, juries, government officials, and policymakers that racism exists in environmental protection, enforcement, and policy formulation.

The most polluted urban communities are those with crumbling infrastructure, ongoing economic disinvestment, deteriorating housing, inadequate schools, chronic unemployment, a high poverty rate, and an overloaded health-care system. Riot-torn South Central Los Angeles typifies this urban neglect. It is not surprising that the 'dirtiest' zip code in California belongs to the mostly African-American and Latino neighborhood in that part of the city (Kay 1991). In the Los Angeles basin, over 71 percent of the African Americans and 50 percent of the Latinos live in areas with the most polluted air, while only 34 percent of the white population does (Mann 1991). This pattern exists nationally as well. As researchers Wernette and Nieves note:

> In 1990, 437 of the 3,109 counties and independent cities failed to meet at least one of the EPA ambient air quality standards . . . 57 percent of whites, 65 percent of African Americans, and 80 percent of Hispanics live in 437 counties with substandard air quality. Out of the whole population, a total of 33 percent of whites, 50 percent of African Americans, and 60 percent of Hispanics live in the 136 counties in which two or more air pollutants exceed standards. The percentage living in the 29 counties designated as nonattainment areas for three or more pollutants are 12 percent of whites, 20 percent of African Americans, and 31 percent of Hispanics. (1992, 16–17)

Income alone does not account for these above-average percentages. Housing segregation and development patterns play a key role in determining where people live. Moreover, urban development and the 'spatial configuration' of communities flow from the forces and relationships of industrial production which, in turn, are influenced and subsidized by government policy (Gottdiener 1988). There is widespread agreement that vestiges of race-based decision-making still influence housing, education, employment, and criminal justice. The same is true for municipal services such as garbage pickup and disposal, neighborhood sanitation, fire and police protection, and library services. Institutional racism influences decisions on local land use, enforcement of environmental regulations, industrial facility siting, management of economic vulnerability, and the paths of freeways and highways.

People skeptical of the assertion that poor people and people of color are targeted for waste-disposal sites should consider the report the Cerrell Associates provided the California Waste Management Board. In their 1984 report, *Political Difficulties Facing Waste-to-Energy Conversion Plant Siting*, they offered a detailed profile of those neighborhoods most likely to organize effective resistance against incinerators. The policy conclusion based on this analysis is clear. As the report states:

> All socioeconomic groupings tend to resent the nearby siting of major facilities, but middle and upper socioeconomic strata possess better resources to effectuate their opposition. Middle and higher socioeconomic strata neighbor-hoods should not fall within the one-mile and five-mile radius of the proposed site. (43)

Where then will incinerators or other polluting facilities be sited? For Cerrell Associates, the answer is low-income, disempowered neighborhoods with a high concentration of nonvoters. The ideal site, according their report, has nothing to do with environmental soundness but everything to do with lack of social power. Communities of color in California are far more likely to fit this profile than are their white counterparts.

Those still skeptical of the existence of environmental racism should also consider the fact that zoning boards and planning commissions are typically stacked with white developers. Generally, the decisions of these bodies reflect the special interests of the individuals who sit on these boards. People of color have been systematically excluded from these decision-making boards, commissions, and governmental agencies (or allowed only token representation). Grassroots leaders are now demanding a shared role in all the decisions that shape their communities. They are challenging the intended or unintended racist assumptions underlying environmental and industrial policies.

Toxic Colonialism Abroad

To understand the global ecological crisis, it is important to understand that the poisoning of African Americans in South Central Los Angeles and of Mexicans in border *maquiladoras* have their roots in the same system of economic exploitation, racial oppression, and devaluation of human life. The quest for solutions to environmental problems and for ways to achieve sustainable development in the United States has considerable implications for the global environmental movement.

Today, more than 1,900 *maquiladoras*, assembly plants operated by American, Japanese, and other foreign countries, are located along the 2,000-mile U.S.-Mexico border (Center for Investigative Reporting 1990; Sanchez 1990). These plants use cheap Mexican labor to assemble products from imported components and raw materials, and then ship them back to the United States (Witt 1991). Nearly half a million Mexicans work in the *maquiladoras*. They earn an average of $3.75 a day. While these plants bring jobs, albeit low-paying ones, they exacerbate local pollution by overcrowding the border towns, straining sewage and water systems, and reducing air quality. All this compromises the health of workers and nearby community residents. The Mexican environmental regulatory agency is understaffed and ill-equipped to adequately enforce the country's laws.

The practice of targeting poor communities of color in the Third World for waste disposal and the introduction of risky technologies from industrialized countries are forms of 'toxic colonialism', what some activists have dubbed the 'subjugation of people to an ecologically-destructive economic order by entities over which the people have no control'

(Greenpeace 1992, 3). The industrialized world's controversial Third World dumping policy was made public by the release of an internal, December 12, 1991, memorandum authored by Lawrence Summers, chief economist of the World Bank. It shocked the world and touched off a global scandal. Here are the highlights:

> 'Dirty' Industries: Just between you and me, shouldn't the World Bank be encouraging MORE migration of the dirty industries to the LDCs [Less Developed Countries]? I can think of three reasons:
>
> 1) The measurement of the costs of health impairing pollution depends on the foregone earnings from increased morbidity and mortality. From this point of view a given amount of health impairing pollution should be done in the country with the lowest cost, which will be the country with the lowest wages. I think the economic logic behind dumping a load of toxic waste in the lowest wage country is impeccable and we should face up to that.
>
> 2) The costs of pollution are likely to be non-linear as the initial increments of pollution probably have very low cost. I've always thought that under-polluted areas in Africa are vastly UNDER-polluted; their air quality is probably vastly inefficiently low compared to Los Angeles or Mexico City. Only the lamentable facts that so much pollution is generated by non-tradable industries (transport, electrical generation) and that the unit transport costs of solid waste are so high prevent world welfare-enhancing trade in air pollution and waste.
>
> 3) The demand for a clean environment for aesthetic and health reasons is likely to have very high-income elasticity. The concern over an agent that causes a one in a million change in the odds of prostate cancer is obviously going to be much higher in a country where people survive to get prostate cancer than in a country where under 5 [year-old] mortality is 200 per thousand. Also, much of the concern over industrial atmosphere discharge is about visibility impairing particulates. These discharges may have very little direct health impact. Clearly trade in goods that embody aesthetic pollution concerns could be welfare enhancing. While production is mobile the consumption of pretty air is a non-tradable.
>
> The problem with the arguments against all of these proposals for more pollution in LDCs (intrinsic rights to certain goods, moral reasons, social concerns, lack of adequate markets, etc.) could be turned around and used more or less effectively against every Bank proposal. . . .

Beyond the Race vs. Class Trap

Whether at home or abroad, the question of who *pays* and who *benefits* from current industrial and development policies is central to any analysis of environmental racism. In the United States, race interacts with class to create special environmental and health vulnerabilities. People of color, however, face elevated toxic exposure levels even when social class variables (income, education, and occupational status) are held constant (Bryant and Mohai 1992). Race has been found to be an independent factor, not reducible to class, in predicting the distribution of 1) air pollution in our society (Gianessi, Peskin, and Wolff 1979; Wernette and Nieves 1992); 2) contaminated fish consumption (West, Fly, and Marans 1990); 3) the location of municipal landfills and incinerators (Bullard 1983, 1987, 1990, 1991); 4) the location of abandoned toxic waste dumps (United Church of Christ Commission for Racial Justice 1987); and 5) lead poisoning in children (Agency for Toxic Substances and Disease Registry 1988).

Lead poisoning is a classic case in which race, not just class, determines exposure. It affects between three and four million children in the United States – most of whom are African Americans and Latinos living in urban areas. Among children five years old and younger, the percentage of African Americans who have excessive levels of lead in their blood far exceeds the percentage of whites at all income levels (Agency for Toxic Substances and Disease Registry 1988, 1–12).

The federal Agency for Toxic Substances and Disease Registry found that for families earning less than $6,000 annually an estimated 68 percent of African-American children had lead poisoning, compared with 36 percent for white children. For families with incomes exceeding $15,000, more than 38 percent of African-American children have been poisoned, compared with 12 percent of white children. African-American children are two to three times more likely than their white counterparts to suffer from lead poisoning independent of class factors.

One reason for this is that African Americans and whites do not have the same opportunities to 'vote with their feet' by leaving unhealthy physical environments. The ability of an individual to escape a health-threatening environment is usually correlated with income. However, racial barriers make it even harder for millions of African Americans, Latinos, Asians, Pacific Islanders, and Native Americans to relocate. Housing discrimination, redlining, and other market forces make it difficult for millions of households to buy their way out of polluted environments. For example, an affluent African-American family (with an income of $50,000 or more) is as segregated as an African-American family with an annual income of $5,000 (Jaynes and Williams 1989). Thus, lead poisoning of African-American children is not just a 'poverty thing'.

White racism helped create our current separate and unequal communities. It defines the boundaries of the urban ghetto, *barrio*, and reservation, and influences the provision of environmental protection and other public services. Apartheid-type housing and development policies reduce neighborhood options, limit mobility, diminish job opportunities, and decrease environmental choices for millions of Americans. It is unlikely that this nation will ever achieve lasting solutions to its environmental problems unless it also addresses the system of racial injustice that helps sustain the existence of powerless communities forced to bear disproportionate environmental costs.

The Limits of Mainstream Environmentalism

Historically, the mainstream environmental movement in the United States has developed agendas that focus on such goals as wilderness and wildlife preservation, wise resource management, pollution abatement, and population control. It has been primarily supported by middle- and upper-middle-class whites. Although concern for the environment cuts across class and racial lines, ecology activists have traditionally been individuals with above-average education, greater access to economic resources, and a greater sense of personal power (Buttel and Flinn 1978; Morrison 1986; Bullard, 1990; Bullard and Wright 1987; Bachrach and Zautra 1985).

Not surprisingly, mainstream groups were slow in broadening their base to include poor and working-class whites, let alone African Americans and other people of color. Moreover, they were ill-equipped to deal with the environmental, economic, and social concerns of these communities. During the 1960s and 1970s, while the 'Big Ten' environmental groups focused on wilderness preservation and conservation through litigation, political lobbying, and technical evaluation, activists of color were engaged in mass direct action mobilizations for basic civil rights in the areas of employment, housing, education, and health care. Thus, two parallel and sometimes conflicting movements emerged, and it has taken nearly two decades for any significant convergence to occur between these two efforts. In fact, conflicts still remain over how the two groups should balance economic development, social justice, and environmental protection.

In their desperate attempt to improve the economic conditions of their constituents, many African-American civil rights and political leaders have directed their energies toward bringing jobs to their communities. In many instances, this has been achieved at great risk to the health of workers and the surrounding communities. The promise of jobs (even low-paying and hazardous ones) and of a broadened tax base has enticed several economically impoverished, politically powerless communities of color both in the United States and around the world (Center for Investigative Reporting and Bill Moyers 1990; Bullard 1990; Bryant and Mohai 1992). Environmental job blackmail is a fact of life. You can get a job, but only if you are willing to do work that will harm you, your families, and your neighbors.

Workers of color are especially vulnerable to job blackmail because of the greater threat of unemployment they face compared to whites and because of their concentration in low-paying, unskilled, nonunionized occupations. For example, they make up a large share of the nonunion contract workers in the oil, chemical, and nuclear industries. Similarly, over 95 percent of migrant farmworkers in the United States are Latino, African-American, Afro-Caribbean, or Asian, and African Americans are overrepresented in high-risk, blue-collar, and service occupations for which a large pool of replacement labor exists. Thus, they are twice as likely to be unemployed as their white counterparts. Fear of unemployment acts as a potent incentive for many African-American workers to accept and keep jobs they know are health threatening. Workers will tell you that 'unemployment and poverty are also hazardous to one's health'. An inherent conflict exists between the interests of capital and that of labor. Employers have the power to move jobs (and industrial hazards) from the Northeast and Midwest to the South and Sunbelt, or they may move the jobs offshore to Third World countries where labor is even cheaper and where there are even fewer health and safety regulations. Yet, unless an environmental movement emerges that is capable of addressing these economic concerns, people of color and poor white workers are likely to end up siding with corporate managers in key conflicts concerning the environment.

Indeed, many labor unions already moderate their demands for improved work-safety and pollution control whenever the economy is depressed. They are afraid of layoffs, plant closings, and the relocation of industries. These fears and anxieties of labor are usually built on the false but understandable assumption that environmental regulations inevitably lead to job loss (Brown 1980, 1987).

The crux of the problem is that the mainstream environmental movement has not sufficiently addressed the fact that social inequality and imbalances of social power are at the heart of environmental degradation, resource depletion, pollution, and even overpopulation. The environmental crisis can simply not be solved effectively without social justice. . . .

References

Agency for Toxic Substances and Disease Registry. *The Nature and Extent of Lead Poisoning in Children in the United States: A Reprint to Congress.* Atlanta: US Department of Health and Human Services, 1988.

Bachrach, Kenneth M, and Alex J Zautra. 'Coping with Community Stress: The Threat of a Hazardous Waste Landfill'. *Journal of Health and Social Behavior* 26 (June 1985): 127–41.

Blauner, Robert. *Racial Oppression in America.* New York: Harper and Row, 1972.
Brown, Michael H. *Laying Waste: The Poisoning of America by Toxic Chemicals.* New York: Pantheon Books, 1980.
———. *The Toxic Cloud: The Poisoning of America's Air.* New York: Harper and Row, 1987.
Bryant, Bunyan, and Paul Mohai. *Race and the Incidence of Environmental Hazards.* Boulder, CO: Westview Press, 1992.
Bullard, Roberts D. 'Solid Waste Sites and the Black Houston Community'. *Sociological Inquiry* 53 (Spring 1983): 273–88.
———. *Invisible Houston: The Black Experience in Boom and Bust.* College Station, TX: Texas A & M University Press, 1987.
———. *Dumping in Dixie: Race, Class, and Environmental Quality.* Boulder, CO: Westview Press, 1990.
———. 'Environmental Justice for All'. *EnviroAction,* Environmental News Digest for the National Wildlife Federation (November 1991).
Bullard, Robert D, and Beverly H Wright. 'Blacks and the Environment'. *Humboldt Journal of Social Relations* 14 (1987): 165–84.
Buttel, Frederick, and William L Flinn. 'Social Class and Mass Environmental Beliefs: A Reconsideration'. *Environment and Behavior* 10 (September 1978): 433–50.
Carmichael, S, and C V Hamilton. *Black Power.* New York: Vintage, 1967.
Center for Investigative Reporting and Bill Moyers. *Global Dumping Grounds: The International Trade in Hazardous Waste.* Washington, DC: Seven Locks Press, 1990.
Cerrell Associates, Inc. *Political Difficulties Facing Waste-to-Energy Conversion Plant Siting.* California Waste Management Board, Technical Information Series. Prepared by Cerrell Associates, Inc, for the California Waste Management Board. Los Angeles, CA: Cerrell Associates, Inc, 1984.
Gianessi, Leonard, H M Peskin, and E Wolff. 'The Distributional Effects of Uniform Air Pollution Policy in the U.S.' *Quarterly Journal of Economics* (May 1979): 281–301.
Gottdiener, Mark. *The Social Production of Space.* Austin, TX: University of Texas Press, 1988.
Greenpeace. 'The "Logic" Behind Hazardous Waste Export'. *Greenpeace Waste Trade Update* (First Quarter, 1992): 1–2.
Jaynes, Gerald D, and Robin M Williams, Jr. *A Common Destiny: Blacks and American Society.* Washington, DC: National Academy Press, 1989.
Kay, Jane. 'Fighting Toxic Racism: L.A.'s Minority Neighborhood Is the "Dirtiest" in the State'. *San Francisco Examiner,* 7 April 1991: A1.
Mann, Eric. *L.A.'s Lethal Air: New Perspectives for Policy, Organizing, and Action.* Los Angeles: Labor/Community Strategy Center, 1991.
Morrison, Denton E. 'How and Why Environmental Consciousness Has Trickled Down'. In *Distributional Conflict in Environmental Resource Policy,* edited by Allan Schnaiberg, Nicholas Watts and Klaus Zimmermann, 187–220. New York: St Martin's Press, 1986.
Omi, Michael, and Howard Winant. *Racial Formation in the United States: From the 1960's to the 1980's.* New York: Routledge, Kegan and Paul, 1986.
Sanchez, Roberto. 'Health and Environmental Risks of the Maquiladora in Mexicali'. *Natural Resources Journal* 30 (Winter 1990): 163–86.
United Church of Christ Commission for Racial Justice. *Toxic Wastes and Race in the United States. A National Report of the Racial and Socio-Economic Characteristics of Communities with Hazardous Waste Sites.* New York: United Church of Christ, 1987.
Wernette, D R, and L A Nieves. 'Breathing Polluted Air'. *EPA Journal* 18 (March/April 1992): 16–17.

West, Pat C., F Fly, and R Marans. 'Minority Anglers and Toxic Fish Consumption: Evidence from a State-Wide Survey of Michigan'. In *Proceedings of the Michigan Conference on Race and the Incidence of Environmental Hazards*, edited by B Bryant and P Mohai, 108–22. Ann Arbor, MI: University of Michigan School of Natural Resources, 1989.

Witt, Matthew. "An Injury to One is Un Agravio a Todos: The need for a Mexico-U.S. Health Card Safety Movement." *New Solutions, a Journal of Environmental and Occupational Health Policy* 1 (March 1991): 28–33.

James Cone[*], 'Whose Earth Is It Anyway'?

> *The earth is the Lord's and all that is in it,*
> *The world, and those who live in it.*
> —Psalm 24:1 (NRSV)

> *We say the earth is our mother –*
> *we cannot own her; she owns us.*[1]
> —Pacific peoples

The logic that led to slavery and segregation in the Americas, colonization and Apartheid in Africa, and the rule of white supremacy throughout the world is the same one that leads to the exploitation of animals and the ravaging of nature. It is a mechanistic and instrumental logic that defines everything and everybody in terms of their contribution to the development and defense of white world supremacy. People who fight against white racism but fail to connect it to the degradation of the earth are anti-ecological – whether they know it or not. People who struggle against environmental degradation but do not incorporate in it a disciplined and sustained fight against white supremacy are racists whether they acknowledge it or not. The fight for justice cannot be segregated but must be integrated with the fight for life in all its forms.

Until recently, the ecological crisis has not been a major theme in the liberation movements in the African American community. 'Blacks don't care about the environment' is a typical comment by white ecologists. Racial and economic justice has been at best only a marginal concern in the mainstream environmental movement. 'White people care more about the endangered whale and the spotted owl than they do about the survival of young blacks in our nation's cities' is a well-founded belief in the African American community. Justice fighters for blacks and the defenders of the earth have tended to ignore each other in their public discourse and practice. Their separation from each other is unfortunate because they are fighting the same enemy – human beings' domination of each other and nature.

The leaders in the mainstream environmental movement are mostly middle- and upper-class whites who are unprepared culturally and intellectually to dialogue with angry blacks. The leaders in the African American community are leery of talking about anything with

---

[*] James H Cone, 'Whose Earth Is It Anyway'? in James H Cone, *Risks of Faith: The Emergence of a Black Theology of Liberation, 1968–1998* (Boston, MA: Beacon Press, 1999), 138–45. Permissions by James H Cone.

whites that will distract from the menacing reality of racism. What both groups fail to realize is how much they need each other in the struggle for 'justice, peace and the integrity of creation'.[2]

In this essay, I want to challenge the black freedom movement to take a critical look at itself through the lens of the ecological movement and also challenge the ecological movement to critique itself through a radical and ongoing engagement of racism in American history and culture. Hopefully, we can break the silence and promote genuine solidarity between the two groups and thereby enhance the quality of life for the whole inhabited earth – humankind and otherkind.

Expanding the Race Critique

No threat has been more deadly and persistent for black and Indigenous peoples than the rule of white supremacy in the modern world. For over five hundred years through the wedding of science and technology, white people have been exploiting nature and killing people of color in every nook and cranny of the planet in the name of God and democracy. According to the English historian Basil Davidson, the Atlantic slave trade 'cost Africa fifty million souls'.[3] Author Eduardo Galeano claims that 150 years of Spanish and Portuguese colonization in Central and South America reduced the Indigenous population from 90 million to 3.5 million.[4] During the twenty-three-year reign of terror of King Leopold II of Belgium in the Congo (1885–1908), scholarly estimates suggest that approximately 10 million Congolese met unnatural deaths – 'fully half the territory's population'.[5] The tentacles of white supremacy have stretched around the globe. No people of color have been able to escape its cultural, political and economic domination.

Blacks in the U.S. have been the most visible and articulate opponents of white racism. From Frederick Douglas and Sojourner Truth to Martin Luther King, Jr., Malcolm X, and Fannie Lou Hamer, African Americans have waged a persistent fight against white racism in all its overt and covert manifestations. White racism denied the humanity of black people, with even theologians debating whether blacks had souls. Some said blacks were subhuman 'beasts'.[6] Other more progressive theologians, like Union Seminary's Reinhold Niebuhr, hoped that the inferiority of the Negro was not 'biological' but was due instead to 'cultural backwardness', which could gradually with education be overcome.[7]

Enslaved for 244 years, lynched and segregated another 100, blacks, with militant words and action, fought back in every way they could – defending their humanity against all who had the nerve to question it. Malcolm X, perhaps the most fierce and uncompromising public defender of black humanity, expressed the raw feelings of most blacks: 'We declare our right on this earth . . . to be a human being, to be respected as a human being, to be given the rights of a human being in this society, on this earth, in this day, which we intend to bring into existence by any means necessary'.[8]

Whites bristled when they heard Malcolm talk like that. They not only knew Malcolm meant what he said but feared that most blacks agreed with him – though they seldom said so publicly. Whites also knew that if they were black, they too would say a resounding 'amen'! to Malcolm's blunt truth. 'If you want to know what I'll do', Malcolm told whites, 'figure out what you'll do'.[9]

White theologians thanked God for being 'truly longsuffering', 'slow to anger and plenteous in mercy' (Ps. 103:8), as Reinhold Niebuhr put it, quoting the Hebrew Scriptures. Niebuhr knew that white people did not have a leg to stand on before the bar of God's justice regarding their treatment of people of color. 'If', Niebuhr wrote, 'the white man were to expiate his sins committed against the darker races, few would have the right to live'.[10]

Black liberation theology is a product of a fighting spirituality derived from nearly four hundred years of black resistance. As one who encountered racism first as a child in Bearden, Arkansas, no day in my life has passed in which I did not have to deal with the open and hidden violence of white supremacy. Whether in the society or the churches, at Adrian College or Union Seminary, racism was always there – often smiling and sometimes angry. Since writing my first essay on racism in the white church and its theology thirty years ago, I decided that I would never be silent about white supremacy and would oppose it with my whole being.

While white racism must be opposed at all cost, our opposition will not be effective unless we expand our vision. Racism is profoundly interrelated with other evils, including the degradation of the earth. It is important for black people, therefore, to make the connection between the struggle against racism and other struggles for life. A few black leaders recognized this need and joined the nineteenth century abolitionist movement with the Suffragist movement and the 1960s civil rights movement with the second wave of the women's movement. Similar links were made with the justice struggles of other U.S. minorities, gay rights struggles, and poor peoples' fight for freedom around the world. Martin Luther King, Jr.'s idea of the 'beloved community' is a potent symbol for people struggling to build one world community where life in all its forms is respected. 'All life is interrelated', King said. 'Whatever affects one directly affects all indirectly. . . . There is an interrelated structure of reality'.

Connecting racism with the degradation of the earth is a much-needed work in the African American community, especially in black liberation theology and the black churches. Womanist theologians have already begun this important intellectual work. Delores Williams explores a 'parallel between defilement of black women's bodies' and the exploitation of nature. Emilie Townes views 'toxic waste landfills in African American communities' as 'contemporary versions of lynching a whole people'. Karen Baker-Fletcher, using prose and poetry, appropriates the biblical and literary metaphors of dust and spirit to speak about the embodiment of God in creation. 'Our task', she writes, 'is to grow large hearts, large minds, reconnecting with earth, Spirit, and one another. Black religion must grow ever deeper in the heart'.[11]

The leadership of African American churches turned its much-needed attention toward ecological issues in the early 1990s. The catalyst, as usual in the African American community, was a group of black churchwomen in Warren County, North Carolina, who in 1982 lay their bodies down on a road before dump trucks carrying soil contaminated with highly toxic PCBs (polychlorinated biphenyl) to block their progress. In two weeks, more than four hundred protesters were arrested, 'the first time anyone in the United States had been jailed trying to halt a toxic waste landfill'.[12] Although local residents were not successful in stopping the landfill construction, that incident sparked the attention of civil rights and black church leaders and initiated the national environmental justice movement. In 1987 the United Church of Christ Commission of Racial Justice issued its groundbreaking 'Report on Race and Toxic Wastes in the United States'. This study found that 'among a variety of indicators race was the best predictor of the location of hazardous waste facilities in the U.S.'[13] Forty percent of the nation's commercial hazardous waste landfill capacity was in three predominantly African American and Hispanic communities. The largest landfill in the nation is found in Sumter County, Alabama, where nearly 70 percent of its seventeen thousand residents are black and 96 percent are poor.

In October 1991 the First National People of Color Environmental Leadership Summit was convened in Washington, D.C. More than 650 grassroots and national leaders from fifty states, the District of Columbia, Mexico, Puerto Rico, and the Marshall Islands participated. They represented more than three hundred environmental groups of color. They all agreed that 'If this nation is to achieve environmental justice, the environment in urban ghettoes, barrios, reservations, and rural poverty pockets must be given the same protection as that provided to the suburbs'.[14]

The knowledge that people of color are disproportionately affected by environmental pollution angered the black church community and fired up its leadership to take a more active role in fighting against 'environmental racism', a phrase that was coined by Benjamin Chavis who was then the Director of the UCC Commission on Racial Justice.[15] Bunyan Bryant, a professor in the School of Natural Resources and Environment at the University of Michigan and a participant in the environmental justice movement, defines environmental racism as 'an extension of racism':

> It refers to those institutional rules, regulations, and policies or government or corporate decisions that deliberately target certain communities for least desirable land uses, resulting in the disproportionate exposure of toxic and hazardous waste on communities based upon certain prescribed biological characteristics. Environmental racism is the unequal protection against toxic and hazardous waste exposure and the systematic exclusion of people of color from environmental decisions affecting their communities.[16]

The more blacks found out about the racist policies of the government and corporations the more determined they became in their opposition to environmental injustice. In December 1993, under the sponsorship of the National Council of Churches, leaders of mainline black churches held a historic two-day summit meeting on the environment in Washington, D.C. They linked environmental issues with civil rights and economic justice. They did not talk much about the ozone layer, global warming, the endangered whale, or the spotted owl. They focused primarily on the urgent concerns of their communities: toxic and hazardous wastes, lead poisoning, landfills and incinerators. 'We have been living next to the train tracks, trash dumps, coal plants and insect-infested swamps for many decades', Bishop Frederick C. James of the A.M.E. Church said. 'We in the Black community have been disproportionately affected by toxic dumping, disproportionately affected by lead paint at home, disproportionately affected by dangerous chemicals in the workplace'. Black clergy also linked local problems with global issues. 'If toxic waste is not safe enough to be dumped in the United States, it is not safe enough to be dumped in Ghana, Liberia, Somalia nor anywhere else in the world', proclaimed Charles G. Adams, pastor of Hartford Memorial Baptist Church in Detroit. 'If hazardous materials are not fit to be disposed in the suburbs, they are certainly not fit to be disposed of in the cities'.[17]

Like black church leaders, African American politicians also are connecting social justice issues with ecology. According to the League of Conservation Voters, the Congressional Black Caucus has 'the best environmental record of any voting bloc in Congress'.[18] 'Working for clean air, clean water, and a clean planet', declared Rep. John Lewis of Georgia, 'is just as important, if not more important, than anything I have ever worked on, including civil rights'.[19]

Black and other poor people in all racial groups receive much less than their fair share of everything good in the world and a disproportionate amount of the bad. Middle class and elite white environmentalists have been very effective in implementing the slogan 'Not in My Backyard' (NIMBY). As a result, corporations and the government merely turned to the backyards of the poor to deposit their toxic waste. The poor live in the least desirable areas of our cities and rural communities. They work in the most polluted and physically dangerous workplaces. Decent health care hardly exists. With fewer resources to cope with the dire consequences of pollution, the poor bear an unequal burden for technological development while the rich reap most of the benefits. This makes racism and poverty ecological issues. If blacks and other hard-hit communities do not raise these ethical and political problems, they will continue to die a slow and silent death on the planet.

Ecology touches every sphere of human existence. It is not just an elitist or a white middle class issue. A clean safe environment is a human and civil rights issue that impacts the lives of poor blacks and other marginal groups. We therefore must not let the fear of distracting from racism blind us to the urgency of the ecological crisis. What good is it to eliminate racism if we are not around to enjoy a racist free environment?

The survival of the earth, therefore, is a moral issue for everybody. If we do not save the earth from destructive human behavior, no one will survive. That fact alone ought to be enough to inspire people of all colors to join hands in the fight for a just and sustainable planet.

Expanding the Ecological Critique. We are indebted to ecologists in all fields and areas of human endeavor for sounding the alarm about the earth's distress. They have been so effective in raising ecological awareness that few people deny that our planet is in deep trouble. For the first time in history, humankind has the knowledge and power to destroy all life – either with a nuclear bang or a gradual poisoning of the land, air, and sea.

Scientists have warned us of the dire consequences of what human beings are doing to the environment. Theologians and ethicists have raised the moral and religious issues. Grassroots activists in many communities are organizing to stop the killing of nature and its creatures. Politicians are paying attention to people's concern for a clean, safe environment. 'It is not so much a question of whether the lion will one day lie down with the lamb', writes Alice Walker, 'but whether human beings will ever be able to lie down with any creature or being at all'.[20]

What is absent from much of the talk about the environment in First World countries is a truly radical critique of the culture most responsible for the ecological crisis. This is especially true among white ethicists and theologians in the U.S. In most of the essays and books I have read, there is hardly a hint that perhaps whites could learn something of how we got into this ecological mess from those who have been the victims of white world supremacy. White ethicists and theologians sometimes refer to the disproportionate impact of hazardous waste on blacks and other people of color in the U.S. and Third World and even cite an author or two, here and there throughout the development of their discourse on ecology. They often include a token black or Indian in anthologies on ecotheology, ecojustice, and ecofeminism. It is 'politically correct' to demonstrate a knowledge of and concern for people of color in progressive theological circles. But people of color are not treated *seriously*, that is, as if they have something *essential* to contribute to the conversation. Environmental justice concerns of poor people of color hardly ever merit serious attention, not to mention organized resistance. How can we create a genuinely mutual ecological dialogue between whites and people of color if one party acts as if they have all the power and knowledge?

Since [the first] Earth Day in 1970, the environmental movement has grown into a formidable force in American society and ecological reflections on the earth have become a dominant voice in religion, influencing all disciplines. It is important to ask, however, whose problems define the priorities of the environmental movement? Whose suffering claims its attention? 'Do environmentalists care about poor people'?[21] Environmentalists usually respond something like Rafe Pomerance puts it: 'A substantial element of our agenda has related to improving the environment for everybody'.[22] Others tell a different story. Former Assistant Secretary of Interior James Joseph says that 'environmentalists tend to focus on those issues that provide recreative outlets instead of issues that focus on equity'. Black activist Cliff Boxley speaks even more bluntly, labeling the priorities of environmentalists as 'green bigotry'. 'Conservationists are more interested in saving the habitats of birds than in the construction of low-income housing'.[23]

Do we have any reason to believe that the culture most responsible for the ecological crisis will also provide the moral and intellectual resources for the earth's liberation? White ethicists and theologians apparently think so, since so much of their discourse about theology and the earth is just talk among themselves. But I have a deep suspicion about the theological and ethical values of white culture and religion. For five hundred years whites have acted as if they owned the world's resources and have forced people of color to accept their scientific and ethical values. People of color have studied dominant theologies and ethics because our physical and spiritual survival partly depended on it. Now that humanity has reached the possibility of extinction, one would think that a critical assessment of how we got to where we are would be the next step for sensitive and caring theologians of the earth. While there is some radical questioning along these lines, it has not been persistent or challenging enough to compel whites to look outside of their dominating culture for ethical and cultural resources for the earth's salvation. One can still earn a doctorate degree in ethics and theology at American seminaries, even at Union Seminary in New York, and not seriously engage racism in this society and the world. If we save the planet and have a society of inequality, we wouldn't have saved much.

According to Audre Lorde, 'the master's tools will never dismantle the master's house'.[24] They are too narrow and thus assume that people of color have nothing to say about race, gender, sexuality, and the earth – all of which are interconnected. We need theologians and ethicists who are interested in mutual dialogue, honest conversation about justice for the earth and all of its inhabitants. We need whites who are eager to know something about the communities of people of color – our values, hopes, and dreams. Whites know so little about our churches and communities that it is often too frustrating to even talk to them about anything that matters. Dialogue requires respect and knowledge of the other – their history, culture and religion. No one racial or national group has all the answers but all groups have something to contribute to the earth's healing.

Many ecologists speak often of the need for humility and mutual dialogue. They tell us that we are all interrelated and interdependent, including human and otherkind. The earth is not a machine. It is an organism in which all things are a part of each other. 'Every entity in the universe', writes Catherine Keller, 'can be described as a process of interconnection with every other being'.[25] If white ecologists really believe that, why do most still live in segregated communities? Why are their essays and books about the endangered earth so monological – that is, a conversation of a dominant group talking to itself? Why is there so much talk of love, humility, interrelatedness, and interdependence, and yet so little of these values reflected in white people's dealings with people of color?

Blacks and other minorities are often asked why they are not involved in the mainstream ecological movement. To white theologians and ethicists I ask, why are you not involved in the dialogue on race? I am not referring primarily to President Clinton's failed initiative, but to the initiative started by the Civil Rights and Black Power movements and black liberation theology more than forty years ago. How do we account for the conspicuous white silence on racism, not only in the society and world but especially in theology, ethics, and ecology? I have yet to read a white theologian or ethicist who has incorporated a sustained, radical critique of white supremacy in their theological discourse similar to their engagement of Anti-Semitism, class contradictions, and patriarchy.

To be sure, a few concerned white theologians have written about their opposition to white racism but not because race critique was essential to their theological identity. It is usually just a gesture of support for people of color when solidarity across differences is in vogue. As soon as it is no longer socially and intellectually acceptable to talk about race, white theologians revert back to their silence. But as Elie Wiesel said in his Nobel Peace Prize Acceptance Speech, 'we must always take sides. Neutrality helps the oppressor, never the victim. Silence encourages the tormentor, never the tormented'.[26] Only when white theologians realize that a fight against racism is a fight for their humanity will we be able to create a coalition of blacks, whites and other people of color in the struggle to save the earth.

Today ecology is in vogue and many people are talking about our endangered planet. I want to urge us to deepen our conversation by linking the earth's crisis with the crisis in the human family. If it is important to save the habitats of birds and other species, then it is at least equally important to save black lives in the ghettoes and prisons of America. As Gandhi said, 'the earth is sufficient for everyone's need but not for everyone's greed'.[27]

Notes

1. Cited in Samuel Rayan, 'The Earth Is the Lord's', in *Ecotheology: Voices from South and North*, ed David G Hallman (Geneva: WCC Publications, 1994), 142.
2. See *Justice, Peace and the Integrity of Creation*, papers and Bible studies, ed James W van Hoeven for the World Alliance of Reformed Churches Assembly, Seoul, Korea, August 1989; and Preman Niles, *Resisting the Threats to Life: Covenanting for Justice, Peace and the Integrity of Creation* (Geneva: WCC Publications, 1989).
3. Basil Davidson, *The African Slave Trade: Precolonial History 1450–1850* (Boston: Little, Brown, 1961), 80.
4. Eduardo Galeano, *Open Veins of Latin America: Five Centuries of the Pillage of a Continent* (London: Monthly Review Press, 1973), 50.
5. See Adam Hochschild, 'Hearts of Darkness: Adventures in the Slave Trade', *San Francisco Examiner Magazine*, 16 August, 1998, 13. This essay is an excerpt from his book, *King Leopold's Ghosts: A Story of Greed, Terror and Heroism in Colonial Africa* (New York: Houghton Mifflin, 1998). Louis Turner suggests that five to eight million were killed in the Congo. See his *Multinational Companies and the Third World* (New York: Hill and Wang, 1973), 27.
6. See Chas Carroll, *The Negro a Beast* (St. Louis: American Book and Bible House, 1900).
7. See Reinhold Niebuhr, 'Justice to the American Negro from State, Community and Church' in his *Pious and Secular America* (New York: Charles Scribner's Sons, 1958), 81.
8. Malcolm X, *By Any Means Necessary* (New York: Pathfinder Press, 1970), 56.
9. *Malcolm X Speaks*, ed George Breitman (New York: Grove Press, 1965), 197–98.
10. Reinhold Niebuhr, 'The Assurance of Grace' in *The Essential Reinhold Niebuhr: Selected Essays and Addresses*, edited and introduced by Robert M Brown (New Haven: Yale University Press, 1986), 65.

11. See Delores Williams, 'A Womanist Perspective on Sin' in *A Troubling in My Soul: Womanist Perspectives on Evil and Suffering*, ed Emilie M Townes (Maryknoll, NY: Orbis, 1993), 145–47; and her 'Sin, Nature, and Black Women's Bodies', in *Ecofeminism and the Sacred*, ed Carol J Adams (New York: Continuum, 1993), 24–29; Emilie Townes, *In a Blaze of Glory: Womanist Spirituality as Social Witness* (Nashville: Abingdon, 1995), 55; and Karen Baker-Fletcher, *Sisters of Dust, Sisters of Spirit: Womanist Wordings on God and Creation* (Minneapolis: Fortress, 1998), 93.
12. Robert Bullard, *Dumping in Dixie: Race, Class, and Environmental Quality* (Boulder, CO: Westview Press, 1990), 31.
13. Cited in Bunyan Bryant and Paul Mohai, eds, *Race and the Incidence of Environmental Hazards: A Time for Discourse* (Boulder, CO: Westview Press, 1992), 2. See also 'African American Denominational Leaders Pledge Their Support to the Struggle against Environmental Racism', *The A.M.E. Christian Recorder*, May 18, 1998, 8, 11.
14. Cited in Robert D Bullard, ed, *Unequal Protection: Environmental Justice and Communities of Color* (San Francisco: Sierra Club Books, 1994), 20.
15. Benjamin Chavis is now known as Benjamin Chavis Muhammad and is currently serving as the National Minister in Louis Farrakhan's Nation of Islam.
16. Bunyan Bryant, 'Introduction' in his edited work, *Environmental Justice: Issues, Policies, and Solutions* (Washington, DC: Island Press, 1995), 5. Benjamin Chavis defined environmental racism as 'racial discrimination in environmental policymaking. It is racial discrimination in the enforcement of regulations and laws. It is racial discrimination in the deliberate targeting of communities of color for toxic waste disposal and the siting of polluting industries. It is racial discrimination in the official sanctioning of the life-threatening presence of poisons and pollutants in communities of color. And, it is racial discrimination in the history of excluding people of color from the mainstream environmental groups, decisionmaking boards, commissions, and regulatory bodies' ('Foreword' in Robert Bullard, ed, *Confronting Environmental Racism: Voices from the Grassroots* [Boston: South End Press, 1993], 3.)
17. *National Black Church Environmental and Economic Justice Summit*, Washington, DC, 1 and 2 December, 1993, The National Council of Churches of Christ in the USA, Prophetic Justice Unit. This is a booklet with all the speeches of the meeting, including the one by Vice President Gore.
18. See Ronald A Taylor, 'Do Environmentalists Care about Poor People'? *U.S. News and World Report*, 2 April, 1984, 51.
19. John Lewis's quotation is cited in Deeohn and David Hahn-Baker, 'Environmentalists and Environmental Justice Policy' in Bunyan Bryant, ed, *Environmental Justice*, 68.
20. Alice Walker, *Living by the Word: Selected Writings 1973–1987* (San Diego: Harcourt Brace Jovanovich, 1988), 173.
21. See Ronald A Taylor, 'Do Environmentalists Care about Poor People'?
22. Taylor, 'Do Environmentalists Care about Poor People'? 51.
23. Taylor, 'Do Environmentalists Care about Poor People'?
24. Audre Lorde, *Sister Outsider* (Trumansburg, NY: Crossing Press, 1984), 110.
25. Catherine Keller, *From a Broken Web: Separation, Sexism, Self* (Boston: Beacon Press, 1986), 5.
26. See Elie Wiesel, 'Nobel Peace Prize Acceptance Speech', December 10, 1986.
27. Cited in Leonado Boff, *Cry of the Earth, Cry of the Poor* (Maryknoll, NY: Orbis, 1997), 2.

Peter S Wenz*, 'Just Garbage'

Environmental racism is evident in practices that expose racial minorities in the United States, and people of color around the world, to disproportionate shares of environmental hazards.[1] These include toxic chemicals in factories, toxic herbicides and pesticides in agriculture, radiation from uranium mining, lead from paint on older buildings, toxic wastes illegally dumped, and toxic wastes legally stored. In this chapter, which concentrates on issues of toxic waste, both illegally dumped and legally stored, I will examine the justness of current practices as well as the arguments commonly given in their defense. I will then propose an alternative practice that is consistent with prevailing principles of justice.

A Defense of Current Practices

Defenders often claim that because economic, not racial, considerations account for disproportionate impacts on nonwhites, current practices are neither racist nor morally objectionable. Their reasoning recalls the Doctrine of Double Effect. According to that doctrine, an effect whose production is usually blameworthy becomes blameless when it is incidental to, although predictably conjoined with, the production of another effect whose production is morally justified. The classic case concerns a pregnant woman with uterine cancer. A common, acceptable treatment for uterine cancer is hysterectomy. This will predictably end the pregnancy, as would an abortion. However, Roman Catholic scholars who usually consider abortion blameworthy consider it blameless in this context because it is merely incidental to hysterectomy, which is morally justified to treat uterine cancer. The hysterectomy would be performed in the absence of pregnancy, so the abortion effect is produced neither as an end-in-itself, nor as a means to reach the desired end, which is the cure of cancer.

Defenders of practices that disproportionately disadvantage nonwhites seem to claim, in keeping with the Doctrine of Double Effect, that racial effects are blameless because they are sought neither as ends-in-themselves nor as means to reach a desired goal. They are merely predictable side effects of economic and political practices that disproportionately expose poor people to toxic substances. The argument is that burial of toxic wastes, and other locally undesirable land uses (LULUs), lower property values. People who can afford to move elsewhere do so. They are replaced by buyers (or renters) who are predominantly poor and cannot afford housing in more desirable areas. Law professor Vicki Been puts it this way: 'As long as the market allows the existing distribution of wealth to allocate goods and services, it would be surprising indeed if, over the long run, LULUs did not impose a disproportionate burden upon the poor'. People of color are disproportionately burdened due primarily to poverty, not racism. This defense against charges of racism is important in the American context because racial discrimination is illegal in the United States in circumstances where economic discrimination is permitted.[2] Thus, legal remedies to disproportionate exposure of nonwhites to toxic wastes are available if racism is the cause, but not if people of color are exposed merely because they are poor.

There is strong evidence against claims of racial neutrality. Professor Been acknowledges that even if there is no racism in the process of siting LULUs, racism plays at least some part

---

* Peter S Wenz, 'Just Garbage', in *Faces of Environmental Racism: Confronting Issues of Global Justice*, eds L Westra and P Wenz (Lanham, MD: Rowman & Littlefield, 1995), 57–71. Copyright by Rowman & Littlefield.

in the disproportionate exposure of African Americans to them. She cites evidence that 'racial discrimination in the sale and rental of housing relegates people of color (especially African Americans) to the least desirable neighborhoods, regardless of their income level'.[3]

Without acknowledging for a moment, then, that racism plays no part in the disproportionate exposure of nonwhites to toxic waste, I will ignore this issue to display a weakness in the argument that justice is served when economic discrimination alone is influential. I claim that even if the only discrimination is economic, justice requires redress and significant alteration of current practices. Recourse to the Doctrine of Double Effect presupposes that the primary effect, with which a second effect is incidentally conjoined, is morally justifiable. In the classic case, abortion is justified only because hysterectomy is justified as treatment for uterine cancer. I argue that disproportionate impacts on poor people violate principles of distributive justice, and so are not morally justifiable in the first place. Thus, current practices disproportionately exposing nonwhites to toxic substances are not justifiable even if incidental to the exposure of poor people.

Alternate practices that comply with acceptable principles of distributive justice are suggested below. They would largely solve problems of environmental racism (disproportionate impacts on nonwhites) while ameliorating the injustice of disproportionately exposing poor people to toxic hazards. They would also discourage production of toxic substances, thereby reducing humanity's negative impact on the environment.

The Principle of Commensurate Burdens and Benefit

We usually assume that, other things being equal, those who derive benefits should sustain commensurate burdens. We typically associate the burden of work with the benefit of receiving money, and the burdens of monetary payment and tort liability with the benefits of ownership.

There are many exceptions. For example, people can inherit money without working, and be given ownership without purchase. Another exception, which dissociates the benefit of ownership from the burden of tort liability, is the use of tax money to protect the public from hazards associated with private property, as in Superfund legislation. Again, the benefit of money is dissociated from the burden of work when governments support people who are unemployed.

The fact that these exceptions require justification, however, indicates an abiding assumption that people who derive benefits should shoulder commensurate burdens. The ability to inherit without work is justified as a benefit owed to those who wish to bequeath their wealth (which someone in the line of inheritance is assumed to have shouldered burdens to acquire). The same reasoning applies to gifts.

Using tax money (public money) to protect the public from dangerous private property is justified as encouraging private industry and commerce, which are supposed to increase public wealth. The system also protects victims in case private owners become bankrupt as, for example, in Times Beach, Missouri, where the government bought homes made worthless due to dioxin pollution. The company responsible for the pollution was bankrupt.

Tax money is used to help people who are out of work to help them find a job, improve their credentials, or feed their children. This promotes economic growth and equal opportunity. These exceptions prove the rule by the fact that justification for any deviation from the commensuration of benefits and burdens is considered necessary.

Further indication of an abiding belief that benefits and burdens should be commensurate is grumbling that, for example, many professional athletes and corporate executives are overpaid. Although the athletes and executives shoulder the burden of work, the complaint is that their benefits are disproportionate to their burdens. People on welfare are sometimes criticized for receiving even modest amounts of taxpayer money without shouldering the burdens of work, hence recurrent calls for 'welfare reform'. Even though these calls are often justified as means to reducing government budget deficits, the moral issue is more basic than the economic. Welfare expenditures are minor compared to other programs, and alternatives that require poor people to work are often more expensive than welfare as we know it.

The principle of commensuration between benefits and burdens is not the only moral principle governing distributive justice, and may not be the most important, but it is basic. Practices can be justified by showing them to conform, all things considered, to this principle. Thus, there is no move to 'reform' the receipt of moderate pay for ordinary work, because it exemplifies the principle. On the other hand, practices that do not conform are liable to attack and require alternate justification, as we have seen in the cases of inheritance, gifts, Superfund legislation, and welfare.

Applying the principle of commensuration between burdens and benefits to the issue at hand yields the following: In the absence of countervailing considerations, the burdens of ill health associated with toxic hazards should be related to benefits derived from processes and products that create these hazards.

Toxic Hazards and Consumerism

In order to assess, in light of the principle of commensuration between benefits and burdens, the justice of current distributions of toxic hazards, the benefits of their generation must be considered. Toxic wastes result from many manufacturing processes, including those for a host of common items and materials, such as paint, solvents, plastics, and most petrochemical-based materials. These materials surround us in the paint on our houses, in our refrigerator containers, in our clothing, in our plumbing, in our garbage pails, and elsewhere.

Toxins are released into the environment in greater quantities now than ever before because we now have a consumer-oriented society where the acquisition, use, and disposal of individually owned items is greatly desired. We associate the numerical dollar value of the items at our disposal with our 'standard of living', and assume that a higher standard is conducive to, if not identical with, a better life. So toxic wastes needing disposal are produced as by-products of the general pursuit of what our society defines as valuable, that is, the consumption of material goods.

Our economy requires increasing consumer demand to keep people working (to produce what is demanded). This is why there is concern each Christmas season, for example, that shoppers may not buy enough. If demand is insufficient, people may be put out of work. Demand must increase, not merely hold steady, because commercial competition improves labor efficiency in manufacture (and now in the service sector as well), so fewer workers can produce desired items. More items must be desired to forestall labor efficiency-induced unemployment, which is grave in a society where people depend primarily on wages to secure life's necessities.

Demand is kept high largely by convincing people that their lives require improvement, which consumer purchases will effect. When improvements are seen as needed, not merely desired, people purchase more readily. So our culture encourages economic expansion by blurring the distinction between wants and needs.

One way the distinction is blurred is through promotion of worry. If one feels insecure without the desired item or service, and so worries about life without it, then its provision is easily seen as a need. Commercials, and other shapers of social expectations, keep people worried by adjusting downward toward the trivial what people are expected to worry about. People worry about the provision of food, clothing, and housing without much inducement. When these basic needs are satisfied, however, attention shifts to indoor plumbing, for example, then to stylish indoor plumbing. The process continues with needs for a second or third bathroom, a kitchen disposal, and a refrigerator attached to the plumbing so that ice is made automatically in the freezer, and cold water can be obtained without even opening the refrigerator door. The same kind of progression results in cars with CD players, cellular phones, and automatic readouts of average fuel consumption per mile.

Abraham Maslow was not accurately describing people in our society when he claimed that after physiological, safety, love, and (self-) esteem needs are met, people work toward self-actualization, becoming increasingly their own unique selves by fully developing their talents. Maslow's Hierarchy of Needs describes people in our society less than Wenz's Lowerarchy of Worry. When one source of worry is put to rest by an appropriate purchase, some matter less inherently or obviously worrisome takes its place as the focus of concern. Such worry-substitution must be amenable to indefinite repetition in order to motivate purchases needed to keep the economy growing without inherent limit. If commercial society is supported by consumer demand, it is worry all the way down. Toxic wastes are produced in this context.

People tend to worry about ill health and early death without much inducement. These concerns are heightened in a society dependent upon the production of worry, so expenditure on health care consumes an increasing percentage of the gross domestic product. As knowledge of health impairment due to toxic substances increases, people are decreasingly tolerant of risks associated with their proximity. Thus, the same mindset of worry that elicits production that generates toxic wastes, exacerbates reaction to their proximity. The result is a desire for their placement elsewhere, hence the NIMBY syndrome – Not in My Back Yard. On this account, NIMBYism is not aberrantly selfish behavior, but integral to the cultural value system required for great volumes of toxic waste to be generated in the first place.

Combined with the principle of Commensurate Burdens and Benefits, that value system indicates who should suffer the burden of proximity to toxic wastes. Other things being equal, those who benefit most from the production of waste should shoulder the greatest share of burdens associated with its disposal. In our society, consumption of goods is valued highly and constitutes the principal benefit associated with the generation of toxic wastes. Such consumption is generally correlated with income and wealth. So other things being equal, justice requires that people's proximity to toxic wastes be related positively to their income and wealth. This is exactly opposite to the predominant tendency in our society, where poor people are more proximate to toxic wastes dumped illegally and stored legally.

Rejected Theories of Justice

Proponents of some theories of distributive justice may claim that current practices are justified. In this section I will explore such claims.

A widely held view of justice is that all people deserve to have their interests given equal weight. John Rawls's popular thought experiment in which people choose principles of justice while ignorant of their personal identities dramatizes the importance of equal consideration of interests. Even selfish people behind the 'veil of ignorance' in Rawls's 'original position' would choose to accord equal consideration to everyone's interests because, they reason, they may themselves be the victims of any inequality. Equal consideration is a basic moral premise lacking serious challenge in our culture, so it is presupposed in what follows. Disagreement centers on application of the principle.

Libertarianism

Libertarians claim that each individual has an equal right to be free of interference from other people. All burdens imposed by other people are unjustified unless part of, or consequent upon, agreement by the party being burdened. So no individual who has not consented should be burdened by burial of toxic wastes (or the emission of air pollutants, or the use of agricultural pesticides, etc.) that may increase risks of disease, disablement, or death. Discussing the effects of air pollution, libertarian Murray Rothbard writes, 'The remedy is simply to enjoin anyone from injecting pollutants into the air, and thereby invading the rights of persons and property. Period'.[4] Libertarians John Hospers and Tibor R. Machan seem to endorse Rothbard's position.[5]

The problem is that implementation of this theory is impractical and unjust in the context of our civilization. Industrial life as we know it inevitably includes production of pollutants and toxic substances that threaten human life and health. It is impractical to secure the agreement of every individual to the placement, whether on land, in the air, or in water, of every chemical that may adversely affect the life or health of the individuals in question. After being duly informed of the hazard, someone potentially affected is bound to object, making the placement illegitimate by libertarian criteria.

In effect, libertarians give veto power to each individual over the continuation of industrial society. This seems a poor way to accord equal consideration to everyone's interests because the interest in physical safety of any one individual is allowed to override all other interests of all other individuals in the continuation of modern life. Whether or not such life is worth pursuing, it seems unjust to put the decision for everyone in the hands of any one person.

Utilitarianism

Utilitarians consider the interests of all individuals equally, and advocate pursuing courses of action that promise to produce results containing the greatest (net) sum of good. However, irrespective of how 'good' is defined, problems with utilitarian accounts of justice are many and notorious.

Utilitarianism suffers in part because its direct interest is exclusively in the sum total of good, and in the future. Since the sum of good is all that counts in utilitarianism, there is no guarantee that the good of some will not be sacrificed for the greater good of others. Famous people could receive (justifiably according to utilitarians) particularly harsh sentences for criminal activity to effect general deterrence. Even when fame results from honest pursuits, a famous felon's sentence is likely to attract more attention than sentences in other cases of similar criminal activity. Because potential criminals are more likely to respond to sentences in such cases, harsh punishment is justified for utilitarian reasons on grounds that are unrelated to the crime.

Utilitarianism suffers in cases like this not only from its exclusive attention to the sum total of good, but also from its exclusive preoccupation with future consequences, which makes the relevance of past conduct indirect. This affects not only retribution, but also reciprocity and gratitude, which utilitarians endorse only to produce the greatest sum of future benefits. The direct relevance of past agreements and benefits, which common sense assumes, disappears in utilitarianism. So does direct application of the principle of Commensurate Burdens and Benefits.

The merits of the utilitarian rejection of common sense morality need not be assessed, however, because utilitarianism seems impossible to put into practice. Utilitarian support for any particular conclusion is undermined by the inability of anyone actually to perform the kinds of calculations that utilitarians profess to use. Whether the good is identified with happiness or preference-satisfaction, the two leading contenders at the moment, utilitarians announce the conclusions of their calculations without ever being able to show the calculation itself.

When I was in school, math teachers suspected that students who could never show their work were copying answers from other students. I suspect similarly that utilitarians, whose 'calculations' often support conclusions that others reach by recourse to principles of gratitude, retributive justice, commensuration between burdens and benefits, and so forth, reach conclusions on grounds of intuitions influenced predominantly by these very principles.

Utilitarians may claim that, contrary to superficial appearances, these principles are themselves supported by utilitarian calculations. But, again, no one has produced a relevant calculation. Some principles seem *prima facie* opposed to utilitarianism, such as the one prescribing special solicitude of parents for their own children. It would seem that in cold climates more good would be produced if people bought winter coats for needy children, instead of special dress coats and ski attire for their own children. But utilitarians defend the principle of special parental concern. They declare this principle consistent with utilitarianism by appeal to entirely untested, unsubstantiated assumptions about counterfactuals. It is a kind of 'Just So' story that explains how good is maximized by adherence to current standards. There is no calculation at all.

Another indication that utilitarians cannot perform the calculations they profess to rely upon concerns principles whose worth is in genuine dispute. Utilitarians offer no calculations that help to settle the matter. For example, many people wonder today whether or not patriotism is a worthy moral principle. Detailed utilitarian calculations play no part in the discussion.

These are some of the reasons why utilitarianism provides no help to those deciding whether or not disproportionate exposure of poor people to toxic wastes is just.

Free Market Approach

Toxic wastes, a burden, could be placed where residents accept them in return for monetary payment, a benefit. Since market transactions often satisfactorily commensurate burdens and benefits, this approach may seem to honor the principle of commensuration between burdens and benefits.

Unlike many market transactions, however, whole communities, acting as corporate bodies, would have to contract with those seeking to bury wastes. Otherwise, any single individual in the community could veto the transaction, resulting in the impasse attending libertarian approaches.[6] Communities could receive money to improve such public facilities as schools, parks, and hospitals, in addition to obtaining tax revenues and jobs that result ordinarily from business expansion.

The major problem with this free market approach is that it fails to accord equal consideration to everyone's interests. Where basic or vital goods and services are at issue, we usually think equal consideration of interests requires ameliorating inequalities of distribution that markets tend to produce. For example, one reason, although not the only reason, for public education is to provide every child with the basic intellectual tools necessary for success in our society. A purely free market approach, by contrast, would result in excellent education for children of wealthy parents and little or no education for children of the nation's poorest residents. Opportunities for children of poor parents would be so inferior that we would say the children's interests had not been given equal consideration.

The reasoning is similar where vital goods are concerned. The United States has the Medicaid program for poor people to supplement market transactions in health care precisely because equal consideration of interests requires that everyone be given access to health care. The 1994 health care debate in the United States was, ostensibly, about how to achieve universal coverage, not about whether or not justice required such coverage. With the exception of South Africa, every other industrialized country already has universal coverage for health care. Where vital needs are concerned, markets are supplemented or avoided in order to give equal consideration to everyone's interests.

Another example concerns military service in time of war. The United States employed conscription during the Civil War, both world wars, the Korean War, and the war in Vietnam. When the national interest requires placing many people in mortal danger, it is considered just that exposure be largely unrelated to income and market transactions.

The United States does not currently provide genuine equality in education or health care, nor did universal conscription (of males) put all men at equal risk in time of war. In all three areas, advantage accrues to those with greater income and wealth. (During the Civil War, paying for a substitute was legal in many cases.) Imperfection in practice, however, should not obscure general agreement in theory that justice requires equal consideration of interests, and that such equal consideration requires rejecting purely free market approaches where basic or vital needs are concerned.

Toxic substances affect basic and vital interests. Lead, arsenic, and cadmium in the vicinity of children's homes can result in mental retardation of the children.[7] Navaho teens exposed to radiation from uranium mine tailings have seventeen times the national average of reproductive organ cancer.[8] Environmental Protection Agency (EPA) officials estimate that toxic air pollution in areas of South Chicago increase cancer risks one hundred to one thousand times.[9] Pollution from Otis Air Force base in Massachusetts is associated with alarming increases in cancer rates.[10] Non-Hodgkin's Lymphoma is related to living near stone, clay, and glass industry facilities, and leukemia is related to living near chemical and petroleum plants.[11] In general, cancer rates are higher in the United States near industries that use toxic substances and discard them nearby.[12]

In sum, the placement of toxic wastes affects basic and vital interests just as do education, health care, and wartime military service. Exemption from market decisions is required to avoid unjust impositions on the poor, and to respect people's interests equally. A child dying of cancer receives little benefit from the community's new swimming pool.

Cost-Benefit Analysis (CBA)

CBA is an economist's version of utilitarianism, where the sum to be maximized is society's wealth, as measured in monetary units, instead of happiness or preference satisfaction. Society's wealth is computed by noting (and estimating where necessary) what people are willing to pay for goods and services. The more people are willing to pay for what exists in society, the better off society is, according to CBA.

CBA will characteristically require placement of toxic wastes near poor people. Such placement usually lowers land values (what people are willing to pay for property). Land that is already cheap, where poor people live, will not lose as much value as land that is currently expensive, where wealthier people live, so a smaller loss of social wealth attends placement of toxic wastes near poor people. This is just the opposite of what the Principle of Commensurate Burdens and Benefits requires.

The use of CBA also violates equal consideration of interests, operating much like free market approaches. Where a vital concern is at issue, equal consideration of interests requires that people be considered irrespective of income. The placement of toxic wastes affects vital interests. Yet CBA would have poor people exposed disproportionately to such wastes.[13]

In sum, libertarianism, utilitarianism, free market distribution, and cost-benefit analysis are inadequate principles and methodologies to guide the just distribution of toxic wastes.

LULU Points

An approach that avoids these difficulties assigns points to different types of locally undesirable land uses (LULUs) and requires that all communities earn LULU points.[14] In keeping with the Principle of Commensurate Benefits and Burdens, wealthy communities would be required to earn more LULU points than poorer ones. Communities would be identified by currently existing political divisions, such as villages, towns, city wards, cities, and counties.

Toxic waste dumps are only one kind of LULU. Others include prisons, half-way houses, municipal waste sites, low-income housing, and power plants, whether nuclear or coal fired. A large deposit of extremely toxic waste, for example, may be assigned twenty points when properly buried but fifty points when illegally dumped. A much smaller deposit of properly buried toxic waste may be assigned only ten points, as may a coal-fired power plant. A nuclear power plant may be assigned twenty-five points, while municipal waste sites are only five points, and one hundred units of low-income housing are eight points.

These numbers are only speculations. Points would be assigned by considering probable effects of different LULUs on basic needs, and responses to questionnaires investigating people's levels of discomfort with LULUs of various sorts. Once numbers are assigned, the total number of LULU points to be distributed in a given time period could be calculated by considering planned development and needs for prisons, power plants, low-income housing, and so on. One could also calculate points for a community's already existing LULUs. Communities could then be required to host LULUs in proportion to their income or wealth, with new allocation of LULUs (and associated points) correcting for currently existing deviations from the rule of proportionality.

Wherever significant differences of wealth or income exist between two areas, these areas should be considered part of different communities if there is any political division between them. Thus, a county with rich and poor areas would not be considered a single community for purposes of locating LULUs. Instead, villages or towns may be so considered. A city with rich and poor areas may similarly be reduced to its wards. The purpose of segregating areas of different income or wealth from one another is to permit the imposition of greater LULU burdens on wealthier communities. When wealthy and poor areas are considered as one larger community, there is the danger that the community will earn its LULU points by placing hazardous waste near its poorer members. This possibility is reduced when only relatively wealthy people live in a smaller community that must earn LULU points.

Practical Implications

Political strategy is beyond the scope of this chapter, so I will refrain from commenting on problems and prospects for securing passage and implementation of the foregoing proposal. I maintain that the proposal is just. In a society where injustice is common, it is no surprise that proposals for rectification meet stiff resistance.

Were the LULU points proposal implemented, environmental racism would be reduced enormously. To the extent that poor people exposed to environmental hazards are members of racial minorities, relieving the poor of disproportionate exposure would also relieve people of color.

This is not to say that environmental racism would be ended completely. Implementation of the proposal requires judgment in particular cases. Until racism is itself ended, such judgment will predictably be exercised at times to the disadvantage of minority populations. However, because most people of color currently burdened by environmental racism are relatively poor, implementing the proposal would remove 80 to 90 percent of the effects of environmental racism. While efforts to end racism at all levels should continue, reducing the burdens of racism is generally advantageous to people of color. Such reductions are especially worthy when integral to policies that improve distributive justice generally.

Besides improving distributive justice and reducing the burdens of environmental racism, implementing the LULU points proposal would benefit life on earth generally by reducing the generation of toxic hazards. When people of wealth, who exercise control of manufacturing processes, marketing campaigns, and media coverage, are themselves threatened disproportionately by toxic hazards, the culture will evolve quickly to find their production largely unnecessary. It will be discovered, for example, that many plastic items can be made of wood, just as it was discovered in the late 1980s that the production of many ozone-destroying chemicals is unnecessary. Similarly, necessity being the mother of invention, it was discovered during World War II that many women could work in factories. When certain interests are threatened, the impossible does not even take longer.

The above approach to environmental injustice should, of course, be applied internationally and intranationally within all countries. The same considerations of justice condemn universally, all other things being equal, exposing poor people to vital dangers whose generation predominantly benefits the rich. This implies that rich countries should not ship their toxic wastes to poor countries. Since many poorer countries, such as those in Africa, are inhabited primarily by nonwhites, prohibiting shipments of toxic wastes to them would reduce significantly worldwide environmental racism. A prohibition on such shipments would also discourage production of dangerous wastes, as it would require people in rich countries to live with whatever dangers they create. If the principle of LULU points were applied in all countries, including poor ones, elites in those countries would lose interest in earning foreign currency credits through importation of waste, as they would be disproportionately exposed to imported toxins.

In sum, we could reduce environmental injustice considerably through a general program of distributive justice concerning environmental hazards. Pollution would not thereby be eliminated, since to live is to pollute. But such a program would motivate significant reduction in the generation of toxic wastes, and help the poor, especially people of color, as well as the environment.

Notes

1. Vicki Been, 'Market Forces, Not Racist Practices, May Affect the Siting of Locally Undesirable Land Uses', in *At Issue: Environmental Justice*, ed by Jonathan Petrikin (San Diego, CA: Greenhaven Press, 1995), 41.
2. See *San Antonio Independent School District v. Rodriguez*, 411 R.S. 1 (1973) and *Village of Arlington Heights v. Metropolitan Housing Development Corporation*, 429 U.S. 252 (1977).
3. Been, 'Market Forces, Not Racist Practices', 41.
4. Murray Rothbard, 'The Great Ecology Issue', *The Individualist* 21, no 2 (February 1970): 5.
5. See Peter S Wenz, *Environmental Justice* (Albany, NY: State University of New York Press, 1988), 65–67 and associated endnotes.
6. Christopher Boerner and Thomas Lambert, 'Environmental Justice Can Be Achieved through Negotiated Compensation', in *At Issue: Environmental Justice*.
7. F Diaz-Barriga et al., 'Arsenic and Cadmium Exposure in Children Living Near to Both Zinc and Copper Smelters', summarized in *Archives of Environmental Health* 46, no 2 (March/April 1991): 119.
8. Dick Russell, 'Environmental Racism', *Amicus Journal* (Spring 1989): 22–32, 24.
9. Marianne Lavelle, 'The Minorities Equation', *National Law Journal* 21 (September 1992): 3.
10. Christopher Hallowell, 'Water Crisis on the Cape', *Audubon* (July/August 1991): 65–74, especially 66 and 70.
11. Athena Linos et al., 'Leukemia and Non-Hodgkin's Lymphoma and Residential Proximity to Industrial Plants', *Archives of Environmental Health* 46, no 2 (March/April 1991): 70–74.
12. L W Pickle et al., *Atlas of Cancer Mortality among Whites: 1950–1980*, HHS publication # (NIH) 87-2900 (Washington, DC: US Department of Health and Human Services, Government Printing Office: 1987).
13. Wenz, *Environmental Justice*, 216–18.
14. The idea of LULU points comes to me from Frank J Popper, 'LULUs and Their Blockage', in *Confronting Regional Challenges: Approaches to LULUs, Growth, and Other Vexing Governance Problems*, ed by Joseph DiMento and Le Roy Graymer (Los Angeles, CA: Lincoln Institute of Land Policy, 1991), 13–27, especially 24.

CASE STUDY

Diane-Michele Prindeville[*], 'For the People: American Indian and Hispanic Women in New Mexico's Environmental Justice Movement'

The Environmental Justice Movement in New Mexico

The environmental justice movement is active in New Mexico in local, state, and tribal politics. The state's history, political culture, large racial/ethnic minority population, political economy, and location have all contributed to the founding and growth of environmental justice groups throughout New Mexico. The legacy of colonization, first by Spain and then by the United States, has left an indelible

---

[*] Diane-Michele Prindeville, 'For the People: American Indian and Hispanic Women in New Mexico's Environmental Justice Movement', in *Our Backyard: A Quest for Environmental Justice*, eds Visgilio and Whitelaw (Lanham, MD: Rowman & Littlefield, 2003), 139–57. Copyright by Rowman & Littlefield.

mark on New Mexico's culture, economy, and politics. Unresolved conflicts involving Indian sovereignty, Spanish land grants, the U.S. government, and private developers continue to fuel debates over rights to land and water.[1] Tensions persist between the economic draw of tourism on the one hand and the commercialization of indigenous peoples and their cultures on the other. What's more, New Mexico's economic dependence on both the federal government and the defense industry has left a legacy of environmental destruction. Specifically, hazardous and nuclear wastes, produced through the mining of uranium and the manufacture and testing of nuclear weapons in the state, have led to countless deaths due to radiation exposure and have resulted in significant environmental contamination of soil and groundwater.[2] In addition, the Waste Isolation Pilot Project (WIPP), a national storage site for medium- and low-level radioactive wastes, has been constructed in New Mexico, despite considerable protest. The combination of these factors and their social, economic, and political impact serve to make the environmental justice movement's agenda especially relevant to New Mexicans. Consequently, grassroots organizations have formed throughout the state in both urban centers and rural areas, on and off Indian lands.

These grassroots groups have grown, building coalitions with other organizations and forming what has become known as the environmental justice movement. In New Mexico, American Indian and Hispanic women have been particularly active in this movement and make up a significant portion of the leadership. In the early 1990s, for example, members of the Navajo Nation and the Mescalero Apache tribe successfully defeated proposals to place hazardous waste storage facilities on their tribal lands. In both cases, the grassroots campaigns were spearheaded by women. Also during this period, under the leadership of its first female governor, Isleta Pueblo adopted its own nationally recognized environmental standards in order to combat pollution generated by the city of Albuquerque. Similarly, neighborhood groups in Albuquerque's South Valley, a predominantly Hispanic area, pressured the city to investigate the source of groundwater contamination that resulted in a number of wells being capped. When the pollution was found to emanate from the nearby weapons research laboratory located at Kirtland Air Force Base, community leaders, with the help of a local environmental justice organization, managed to negotiate the cleanup of several toxic sites.

Like similar groups around the country, New Mexico's environmental justice organizations identify concerns arising from environmental and economic conditions, such as community development, neighborhood safety, pollution, the availability of low-income housing and public transportation, employment opportunities, and workplace hazards.[3] Local groups have campaigned to influence public policies involving the siting of undesirable land uses,[4] groundwater contamination,[5] industrial air emissions and effluent discharges,[6] airport noise, soil erosion and toxicity,[7] and waste reduction and incineration.[8] Additionally, these organizations are involved in issues surrounding neighborhood and cultural preservation,[9] Indian sovereignty,[10] indigenous people's rights,[11] and civil rights abuses. These grassroots organizations form coalitions with other groups in a variety of activities to protect sacred Indian lands,[12] to protest anti-immigration or English-only laws, to boycott union-busting companies, or to advocate for community health and safety.[13] Besides responding to problems, these organizations work proactively to highlight citizen concerns and to develop solutions.[14]

In general, New Mexico's grassroots environmental groups (1) endorse policies that favor the disenfranchised, (2) focus on equality and distributional impacts, (3) advocate direct action, and (4) solicit the support of local civic and religious groups.[15] While they vary with regard to membership, objectives, and strategies, environmental justice groups in New Mexico share broad goals and policy agendas with similar organizations around the country.[16] In fact, numerous New Mexico groups maintain ties with organizations that also seek environmental, economic, and social justice for indigenous peoples across the United States and in other countries. For instance, the Southwest Network for

Environmental and Economic Justice (SNEEJ) was established in 1990 as a regional multi-issue coalition by the South West Organizing Project, a vocal social justice group based in Albuquerque. The following 'Statement of Solidarity' was presented by SNEEJ leaders at the People of Color Regional Activist Dialogue held in Albuquerque the same year. It outlines both the group's mission and the precepts underlying the environmental justice movement.

> We are a multi-cultural, multi-national, grassroots network whose focus is to address the fact that communities of color, as well as economically oppressed communities, suffer disproportionately from toxic contamination. We are deliberately targeted through genocide of indigenous people, the threatening of future generations, racism, sexism, and a lack of economic and social justice. (SNEEJ, April 8, 1990)

For the most part, New Mexico's numerous grassroots environmental organizations are neither as radical as Earth First! nor as tied to the establishment as the Sierra Club.[17] Instead, they tend to reflect local racial and class diversity, offering opportunities for political involvement to people of color and the poor, which these other associations do not.[18] Individuals become involved and remain active because of the relevance of the problems being addressed: jobs, health, family, and neighborhood safety.

Women's Political Activism and the Environmental Justice Movement

Historically, social movements have been a primary vehicle for women's political participation.[19] As one scholar notes, 'In the procedural or pluralistic democracy of the United States, organizations and organized interest groups represent the major vehicle for input into decision making regarding policy and resource allocations at all levels of government'.[20] Successful citizen organizations enable individuals to effect change through collective action. In doing so, they cause a shift from the impersonal, unilateral decision making of politicians, businesses, and technicians to mediated resolutions arrived at through negotiation with community leaders. This form of grassroots involvement is particularly accessible to women who are already a part of community networks that provide resources, support, and communication links with other residents. These networks are familiar and informal. They build on existing relationships established among women through their neighborhoods, children's schools, places of worship, clubs and civic organizations, and places of work.[21] Furthermore, community organizing activities employ many of the skills that women develop through their roles as homemakers and mothers. Women's involvement in community-based groups also provides occasions for social interaction, status and recognition, an increased sense of personal and political efficacy, confidence building, and greater personal satisfaction.[22]

Through their participation in local grassroots associations, women create a legitimate voice to represent their interests in the governing bureaucracy, what one scholar calls 'activist mothering'.[23] When such organizations are managed and led by women, they often cultivate local women's leadership, provide greater opportunities for women's involvement, and enable participants to develop skills transferable to other forums. As an avenue for political participation, grassroots organizing has proven to be especially accessible to women, often leading to greater opportunities for leadership.[24] While women are not proportionally represented in highly visible leadership positions within the environmental justice movement, it is estimated that 90 percent of those who actively participate are women.[25] In fact, a great many environmental justice groups in the United States and abroad are founded and run by women of color.[26] These activists, who tend to work through structurally and ideologically democratic organizations to improve conditions in their communities,[27] are often mothers fighting problems that threaten the health and well-being of their families and neighborhoods.[28] Their motivation, however, is not solely a product of their biological or gendered sociocultural roles of 'mother' and 'nurturer'. Rather, their motives for involvement in such grassroots politics, and in electoral politics, are far more complex. As G. Di Chiro notes,

> The question of community survival in the face of cultural imperialist attacks by the dominant, white male, industrial complex figures conspicuously in many women of color's involvements in environmental justice works. Women in many communities and cultures have customarily been seen to be the repositories of or given the responsibilities for maintaining local, cultural traditions and histories.[29]

Both American Indian and Hispanic women activists have traditionally engaged in struggles to remedy social and economic concerns; this work continues through their leadership in contemporary environmental justice organizations. Whether they are native women fighting the federal government over deployment of nuclear weapons on tribal lands or Mexican American mothers organizing against the placement of yet more undesirable land uses in their *barrio*, they share common approaches to leadership and their activism is often similarly motivated. The focus of this chapter is the role of American Indian and Hispanic women in New Mexico's environmental justice movement and their contributions to the political, social, and economic well-being of their communities.

Research Methodology

Sample Selection Using nonrandom purposive sampling, a total of fifty women active in New Mexico politics were selected for participation in this study. I obtained their names using a reputational 'snowball' technique in which each woman interviewed was asked the names of other women involved in environmental politics in the state. The bulk of the participants (forty-five) were leaders known for their involvement in environmental policymaking or for their roles as advocates for communities of color. The remaining five leaders favored environmental and social justice policies, but their primary political involvement was with other issues. The reliability and validity of my sampling strategy was reinforced when the same women were repeatedly identified as policy leaders by different study participants in numerous organizational settings. Generalization to the larger population of women leaders across the United States is not intended, nor would it be appropriate, using this methodology.

Both indigenous and Hispanic women were interviewed for this project, including volunteers and paid staff of grassroots organizations (activists) as well as appointed and elected officials at various levels of government (public officials).

Table 4.1 provides a breakdown of the racial/ethnic identity of the leaders interviewed as well as the positions they held. While the indigenous leaders were evenly split between activists and officials, among Hispanics there were two more grassroots activists than public officials. Overall, though, the study participants were fairly evenly distributed among staff (thirteen) and volunteers (thirteen) of grassroots organizations and appointed (twelve) and elected (twelve) public officials.

American Indian women and women of Hispanic origin eighteen years and older make up roughly 313,500 persons or about 17 percent of New Mexico's population.[30] While the precise number of people who hold leadership positions in communities throughout the state is unknown, we can safely assume that women are a minority within this elite group.

TABLE 4.1. Racial/Ethnic Identity of Leaders and Position Held

	Grassroots Activists		Public Officials		
Race/Ethnicity	Staff	Volunteer	Appointed	Elected	Total
Indigenous[1]	6	7	7	6	26
Hispanic[2]	7	6	5	6	24
Total	13	13	12	12	50
Percent	26	26	24	24	100

1. This group consists of twenty-five American Indian women and one Native Hawaiian.
2. This group of Hispanas includes two women who self-identify as 'Mestizas', acknowledging both their Native American and Spanish heritage.

Subsequently, the small universe from which to draw a sample resulted in my interviewing many, if not most, of the indigenous and Hispanic women leaders in New Mexico politics. Due to their relatively small number, high level of political activity, and aggressive coalition building, and because they constitute a political elite, the women interviewed for this study were in many cases acquainted with each other. To protect their identity, and so that no quote is directly attributable to any individual, pseudonyms have been used throughout.

The twenty-six grassroots activists included employees and volunteers who were, or had been, policymakers, such as directors or board members in nonprofit, community-based organizations working for environmental and social justice. Their organizations varied in scope as well as focus. Those with a local scope served a particular neighborhood or an entire city. Some groups worked throughout the state of New Mexico, while others were limited to serving the members of particular Indian tribes. Some of the organizations had a larger geographic scope that included several states within the Southwestern region of the country. A few of the organizations represented groups throughout the nation, while others reached across national boundaries to serve even broader constituencies.

Several of the public officials had gained valuable political experience as former community activists. The public officials included elected and appointed officials who had campaigned on issues related to environmental quality or who had served on formal legislative committees or in federal, state, tribal, or local agencies addressing environmental and social justice concerns. The public officials were a very diverse group comprising elected or appointed leaders at the local, county, state, tribal, and national levels of government. While most of the officials held positions in the legislative or executive branches, two women worked in the judicial branch. All twenty-four public officials personally advocated environmental or social justice policies.

Data Collection and Analysis Using an interview guide composed of open-ended questions to collect my data, I met with the leaders at various locations throughout New Mexico between April 1994 and June 1996 (with the exception of three interviews conducted in November 1991 as part of a pilot project). Interviews were tape recorded with the permission of the participant and handwritten notes were taken simultaneously. A transcribed record of each interview was later made from my field notes and audiotapes. The interviews lasted between approximately forty-five minutes and two hours, with an average length of one hour.

Two interview guides were prepared, one for the activists and one for the public officials, with only minimal variations to account for the leaders' different circumstances. While the interview guides followed a similar set of questions, participants spoke in their own words and were encouraged to pursue related issues expounding on areas they thought relevant. Both the format of the guide and the interview process stressed participants' definitions of concepts and issues, encouraged them to structure their own accounts of a problem or policy concern, allowed for detailed descriptions by the participants, and facilitated their communicating their particular ideas of what is relevant.[31] The flexible interview format gave participants special, nonstandardized treatment consistent with the research goal of developing as rich and as accurate a profile as possible of each of the leaders.[32] The use of loosely structured interviews, administered in person and employing open-ended questions, emphasizes the life experience of project participants. This technique allows respondents to tell their own stories, to offer their own subjective meanings, and to link these meanings to their understandings of the social world.[33] The flexibility afforded by this method allows for continual refinement of the interview schedule, clarification of questions and responses (because the researcher continually moves back and forth between data collection and analysis), inclusion of field observations in the analysis, and the exploration of previously unexamined concepts.[34] The result is rich data that reveal the complexities of human experience and emotion providing context, authenticity, specificity, and vivid description.

Discussion of the Findings

By obtaining mass support and adopting active leadership roles, indigenous and Hispanic women in New Mexico's environmental justice movement influence public policy and shape the politics of the state. The political activism of the indigenous and Hispanic women leaders I interviewed spans grassroots and electoral politics. While the New Mexico leaders' motives may incorporate traditional maternal and domestic concerns, the reasons for their political involvement are not limited to their gendered identities as women, wives, or mothers. Instead, their involvement in politics originates from many sources, including their early political socialization, their particular experiences of politicization, their affinity with and commitment to their racial/ethnic communities, their identification with and desire to improve the condition of women as a group, and their political ideologies.

Paths to Leadership

Although there is some overlap, the paths to leadership taken by the fifty women interviewed can be traced to three general sources. First, women mobilized as youths participated in social justice causes while in high school or college. Their exposure to varied political ideologies and their involvement in social movements and party organizations provided them with contacts and valuable experience. In many cases, this experience helped the young women to determine their future career goals and life choices, cementing their commitment to political activism. Second, while fulfilling their roles as mothers and homemakers, several women developed valuable planning and organizational skills, which aided their ascent to leadership. Women active in their children's education found occasions to influence school policy and programs. In numerous cases, their experiences led to their serving on local or state school boards and these positions led to yet other opportunities for political involvement. Third, women free to volunteer their time initiated or joined efforts to protect, maintain, or enhance the quality of life in their communities. As spokespersons for their neighborhood associations, for example, women gained exposure and experience in dealing with bureaucracies, local officials, and the media. As they gained prominence, these women were invited to serve on city boards and commissions. Similarly, women who volunteered their time to work for a political party or service organization gained experience, useful insights into political processes, administrative skills, and contacts. In some cases, women benefited from mentorship, specific leadership training and development opportunities, and financial or other support when running their own campaigns for public office.

Leaders' Motives for Political Involvement

While these New Mexico leaders were a diverse group with regard to their demographic characteristics and trajectories into politics, they also shared particular goals and reported comparable experiences of political socialization. With few exceptions, these women were not catapulted into politics by some life-altering catalytic event. On the contrary, they were socialized into public life early on by family members and others who helped to prepare them for assuming positions of influence in their communities. Most significantly, these women expressed similar motives for assuming leadership: the desire to fulfill their civic obligation by improving the quality of life for residents of their racial/ethnic communities. In fact, racial and ethnic identity figured prominently in the leaders' motives for political action as they sought to preserve water and soil quality, to revive centuries-old artistic or agropastoral traditions, to repatriate native lands or artifacts, to prevent the commercialization of indigenous cultures, and to politically empower their peoples. Several women were motivated to participate in politics by the goal of preserving traditional New Mexico culture and practices for future generations, despite the tremendous development pressures facing their economically depressed communities.

Characteristic of the environmental justice movement, numerous leaders identified relationships between people of color, their land and labor, and environmental health issues. For example, one leader mobilized against the company that had mined her tribe's land for years, leaving the water and soil severely contaminated. She believed that the industry's mining of uranium on the reservation was directly responsible for the unusually high rate of cancer in the community. A cancer survivor herself, Donna had begun to make connections between patterns she saw in the siting of hazardous facilities and native lands.

> Everywhere you look there are all kinds of Native American Indians . . . dying of cancer. . . . My question is why? Why are these companies trying to store this stuff on our reservations? . . . Are they trying to kill us all? What are they trying to do? . . . We see the scars the company left behind. Why should we let these companies come in and demolish everything . . . in sight? They promise a lot of stuff, but right now I don't think I'd believe any of them anymore. I'm scared about the future for my grandkids. What will there be left for them? (Donna)

A Hispanic leader became politically active after falling seriously ill and being fired from her job at a high-tech manufacturing plant in Albuquerque. Monica's experience motivated her to found an organization with the express purpose of seeking redress in the form of resources and medical services for other women poisoned by their jobs in the computer chip industry. For Monica, inequalities based on gender, race/ethnicity, and class became visible as a result of her own experience; the vast majority of the assembly workers in the industry and, therefore, those most affected by dangerous working conditions, were working-class women of color like herself.

For women of color, the political activities associated with environmental justice are predicated on the critical linkage between race and the environment. Leaders such as Juana saw toxic contamination of their communities as systematic genocide, believing that government and industry target communities of color for environmentally undesirable land uses that will result in the annihilation of their people. Indeed, environmental racism is a recurring theme in many of the narratives of indigenous women activists; as one scholar writes, 'it is a genocidal analysis, rooted in the Native American cultural identification, the experience of colonialism, and the imminent endangerment of their culture'.[35]

Leaders' Environmental Ideologies

To better understand their conceptualizations of 'environmentalism', I examined the basis of the New Mexico leaders' environmental beliefs. In general, these fell within one of four categories: preservation, sustainable use or conservation, environmental justice, and spiritual beliefs. As the leaders' environmental ethics were often richly described and conceptually complex, their beliefs were seldom contained within just one category. Therefore, most of the leaders expressed environmental beliefs that straddled, for example, preservation, sustainable use, and environmental justice. Rather than signaling their lack of commitment to one point of view, the findings reveal the multifaceted nature of the leaders' environmental ideologies, their appreciation for the complexities involved in seeking solutions to difficult environmental problems, and their understanding of the tremendous cultural variation of perspectives of the environment.

Like mainstream environmentalism, 'preservation' stressed the value of maintaining wilderness areas and biodiversity – not only for the enjoyment and use of future generations, but also because nature has value in and of itself. As one leader stated, an environmentalist is,

> [S]omeone who takes an active role in preserving many things, including culture, nature, people. [Someone] who looks at the world like we all fit together for a reason. If we lose the Mexican wolf or a plant species then we'll lose indigenous people. There is an interconnectedness. (Lucia)

'Sustainable use' referred to the conservation of land and natural resources and implied a preference for environmentally sustainable forms of economic development. In contrast to preservation, conservation largely placed human needs above those of nonhuman life. To illustrate, one leader was particularly critical of the national environmental movement's lack of concern for issues affecting the lives of poor people and people of color:

> [Mainstream environmentalists] are economically and biologically illiterate; they do not understand local conditions. They take off on their fantasies about a pristine type environment and what it should look like and try to apply that to every piece of land. . . . 'Trickle down' environmentalism is 'If we litigate and if we legislate, it will trickle down and it will create a healthy environment'. And just like trickle down economics, it does not get rid of poverty. (Marta)

Support for the principles of environmental justice meant that the leaders' environmental beliefs incorporated issues relative to social and economic justice and included racial and gender equity goals, in addition to improving environmental quality. For example, environmental justice implies sharing both the costs and benefits of environmental policies so that no one racial/ethnic or socioeconomic group assumes disproportionate rewards or burdens (such as the cost of hosting a toxic waste facility). As one activist explained,

> The grassroots environmental justice movement's focus is on survival. Economic needs must be addressed. The environmental movement is more leisure and recreation-oriented; they deal with different issues. For example, we need trees for firewood, land for grazing. We see [the environment] as one whole thing. The environment reflects on our spiritual development – protecting the earth for our survival. (Terri)

'Spiritual beliefs', relative to the environment, were grounded in the notion that both the natural environment and all nonhuman life within it are sacred and, therefore, are valued for their own sake. Life was seen as an interconnected web in which maintaining a harmonious balance is essential to its integrity. One woman explained that,

> [Environment] has a different meaning for most Indian people. We can't separate it from our everyday being. You grow up learning and being a part of the environment, not a separate entity. I find it real sad that people separate the words 'Indian' and 'environmentalist'. To me it's one and the same. Like being a civil rights activist and an Indian, they're synonymous. (Carmen)

TABLE 4.2. Leaders' Environmental Ideologies

Activists Officials' Ideology	Indig.	Hisp.	Indig.	Hisp.	Total	Percent
Environmentalist	4	5	4	8	21	42
Non-Environmentalist	1	0	0	1	2	4
Third World Environmentalist	8	8	9	2	27	54

As indicated in table 4.2, leaders identified themselves as either 'environmentalists' or 'third world environmentalists'. Fewer than half (21, or 42 percent) actually called themselves environmentalists. Most (27, or 54 percent) preferred to identify as 'third world' environmentalists, promoting an environmentalism that incorporates participatory decision making and locally determined priorities that reflect the concerns and values of indigenous and third world peoples.

The 'environmentalists' demonstrated mainstream environmental values, such as preservation of wilderness areas and maintaining biodiversity, and saw the appropriate role of humans as that of stewards of the earth. These leaders sometimes worked in cooperation with or supported the work of national environmental organizations, approaching policy change from the same ideological perspective: that of classical liberalism. This meant that these self-identified environmentalists believed in the capacity of (and employed) the existing political and economic systems to promote environmental quality within their communities. As one leader stated, 'I believe we need to take care of the environment for ourselves and our children. We've seen the benefits of regulations and major legislation such as the Clean Air and Clean Water Acts' (Gina).

However, several of the New Mexico leaders objected to the white middleclass bias they believed was inherent in mainstream environmentalism.

> I never said I was an environmentalist, but I believe in the environment. . . . I believe in preserving, in respecting the use of resources. Respect for the environment is essential. If you take care of the earth and you take care of the heavens – important things in life – that will always be there to sustain your life. (Erica)

Despite some of these leaders' involvement in or association with environmental groups, for the most part people of color do not join such organizations for recreational or aesthetic purposes.[36] This is not to suggest that they are not interested in the environment; on the contrary, they may be very concerned with maintaining the health and safety of their communities. Ironically, because racial/ethnic minorities are more likely to experience undesirable or even hazardous living conditions (due to pollutants emanating from nearby industries or waste dumps, for example), they are unlikely to associate their struggle with that of environmentalists. Consequently, twenty-nine of the fifty New Mexico leaders did not consider themselves 'environmentalists', even though they espoused values that included respect for nature and preservation of the earth's resources.

The majority of the leaders described themselves as 'new', 'third world', or 'indigenous' environmentalists. As one woman explained,

> An indigenous environmentalist is one who believes in the spiritual value of nature. One who sees nature not only in a patch of forest, but also in the middle of downtown. An indigenous environmentalist does not see anything 'wild' about nature. (Linda)

The 'third world' environmentalists differentiated their perspective from that of the mainstream environmental movement, claiming that the latter is out of touch with the economic and social realities of the poor, the working class, and people of color. Di Chiro, who interviewed women of color in the environmental movement, similarly found that they were reluctant to call themselves environmentalists 'due to the dominance of the mainly white, middleclass, and uncritically "preservationist" political culture from which much of the mainstream environmental discourse has developed'.[37] The principal differences between the New Mexico leaders I interviewed and those in the mainstream environmental movement were their approaches, philosophies, and constituencies. Proponents of the environmental justice movement were concerned with the economic and political empowerment of third world communities. 'Environment' was defined broadly to include 'where we live, work, and play'.

Indeed, the problems that third world environmentalists face are far more immediate and personally threatening than the traditional environmental concern for preservation of wilderness areas and nonhuman species, which they regard as being of less consequence than the survival of their people and their communities.[38] The New Mexico leaders who identified with the environmental justice movement frequently advocated incorporating the cultural beliefs of third world peoples relative to sustainable use (conservation) into contemporary environmentalism. Marta's comments, in particular, illustrate this view.

> When you have settlers that have come onto the land and have survived more than a century, if they came to settle as farmers and ranchers, they will have developed a relationship to the resources in that ecology that they have had to respect [in order to] survive in very harsh climates, which we have. The science that gets learned over several generations, in terms of how people relate to the land and its resources to keep it healthy, is a science that is today being thrown out the window by environmentalists and the government. So keeping the culture strong is an environmental mission. (Marta)

Belief in the value of indigenous people's knowledge and experience of the earth is central to the environmental justice movement. Winona LaDuke, an indigenous environmentalist, ties environmental protection to cultural preservation and economic autonomy for her tribe.[39] The perspectives of the environmental justice movement shared by the third world environmentalists included a strong belief in the rights of citizens to participate in making environmental decisions; a general distrust of government based upon direct experiences with public officials and agencies; a basic belief that human health – rather than aesthetics, wilderness preservation, or other issues – is their primary concern; a skepticism about science and industry; and a prevalent belief that economic growth is not necessarily good and does not benefit everyone equally. Several New Mexico leaders also shared the opinion that 'our land is being ripped off with the help of the top ten mainstream environmental organizations that have colluded with industry, the military, and government, and agribusiness' (Juana). These leaders' involvement in environmental issues was often highly personal, because threats to the environment were interpreted as threats to their families and communities.

Leaders' Environmental Policy Initiatives

In the course of their political activism, the New Mexico leaders participated in the formulation and implementation of fifty-one separate environmental policy initiatives. These initiatives incorporated such issues as water quality and water rights, conservation of indigenous or Hispanic peoples' traditional lands and land uses, long-range land-use planning, preservation of soil quality, waste management, and production and use of renewable energy sources. Specifically, grassroots activists pressed for policies to provide information and technical assistance to communities of color for the purpose of developing environmental programs; facilitate the negotiation of agreements between communities and industry or government agencies for pollution abatement and site cleanup; encourage increased citizen participation in environmental policymaking; create programs for the prevention of soil and groundwater contamination; and provide reparation to victims of toxic poisoning. Public policies advocated by officials included similar components, such as the development of regulations and implementation of programs to enhance air and water quality; the cleanup of toxic sites; ensuring tribal control of mineral rights on Indian lands; and the formulation of land-use plans to guide urban development. As one leader stated,

> For several years, I've sponsored a beverage container recycling act – the 'bottle bill'. I carry legislation that relates to sewer and water hookups for low-income people so that we can get them into systems that will give them safer water. I like issues that relate to landfills, reduce and reuse of materials, safety for our water table. Mostly anything that protects our water and air, our infrastructure. (Sonia)

As is characteristic of the environmental justice movement, the leaders' policy agendas included human rights and public service initiatives, which were often tied to more 'traditional' environmental concerns, such as sustainable development. For example, promoting sustainable economic development, preserving traditional agricultural practices, and improving the Rio Grande's water quality were equally important goals for one leader who stated that her organization's mission was 'to restore the water to drinkable quality and to keep the communities active and alive along the Rio Grande' (Miranda). Several of the leaders believed that communities of color are specifically targeted for placement of polluting industries and facilities. To support their claims, they cited specific examples of cancer clusters, the contamination of well sites, incidences of health and safety violations by both government and industry, and other such problems. Their efforts to publicize these concerns resulted in the production of video documentaries aired by local public television stations, the publication of numerous studies and position papers by various organizations, public hearings held around the state, and feature stories in the news media.

The process of formulating public policy requires that (democratic) governments provide the means by which citizens, both as individuals and as representatives of groups, are enabled to participate actively. The New Mexico leaders recognized that community members must be included as principal actors in the policymaking process to identify local needs and to permit consultation prior to policy design, during program implementation, and throughout evaluation procedures. Empowering community members to effectively participate in public decision making was a policy priority for both activists and officials. The New Mexico leaders promoted consensus building, shared decision making, and community participation in goal setting and public policy formulation. Each leader exhibited egalitarian views and supported participatory forms of democracy. Some strove for political and economic transformation of their racial/ethnic community by increasing public awareness and access to information through forums, workshops, and public hearings. Others sought to empower community members through leadership training and education. In several cases, grassroots activists recruited their membership to promote gender equality and ethnic/racial diversity and to ensure representation of poor and low-income citizens in their organizations' leadership. In general, the New Mexico leaders sought to increase political participation by enabling community members to help themselves, by providing advocacy, by facilitating coalition building, and by sharing information.

My findings suggest that the fifty New Mexico leaders are devoted political actors who value democratic participation and work to improve social, environmental, and economic conditions in their communities. Their participation is animated by the overarching goal of achieving economic equity and social justice for their communities. The politics of these leaders are heavily influenced by their racial/

ethnic and gender identity as they seek to represent the interests of their communities, to advance the position of women in society, and to empower individual citizens to participate actively in public life. Both their racial/ethnic identity and environmental ideology inform and shape their public policy agendas and their roles in New Mexico's environmental politics.

Conclusion

The New Mexico leaders' environmental ideologies and public policy initiatives reflected, to varying degrees, the history and situation of their racial/ethnic group in the United States, the leaders' motives for political involvement, identification with their racial/ethnic group, and personal experience of politics. In general, they rejected the mainstream Euro-American environmental movement in favor of alternative ideologies that incorporated the cultural values, beliefs, and life situations of people of color into their political agendas. Together, the motives, political goals, and ideology of the New Mexico leaders shaped their public policy agendas.

While their agendas included a broad array of concerns, they generally focused on three shared objectives: (1) to safeguard the rights of community members and empower them to participate in public decision-making processes, (2) to secure services and resources to improve social and economic conditions for racial/ethnic minorities and for women, and (3) to promote the conservation of natural resources and the use of sustainable development practices. Although the scope of their work extended from solving neighborhood-level problems to forming networks with organizations internationally, their common focus was achieving environmental justice for their racial/ethnic communities. This entailed providing for the health and safety of community members, empowering politically marginalized individuals and groups, and establishing programs to meet their social and economic needs. While the public officials advocated more policies aimed at community development and the grassroots activists pursued greater numbers of environmental policies, the New Mexico leaders overwhelmingly supported policies to empower community members.

Significantly, whether they were activists or officials, indigenous or Hispanic, the leaders' policy initiatives reflected the goals of the environmental justice movement, incorporating such notions as gender equity; social, economic, and environmental justice; and increased participation in public decision making. These research findings are significant for at least a couple of reasons. First, they demonstrate greater support for 'mainstream' environmentalism by American Indian and Hispanic women than might be expected based on existing literature. Second, they reveal the ingenuity of the New Mexico leaders in adapting elements of mainstream social movements to the needs of their own particular racial/ethnic communities. Furthermore, the alternative forms of environmentalism espoused by the leaders reveal their underlying concerns with preserving their culture, achieving racial and gender equity, increasing political participation, and maintaining or improving environmental quality. These findings are also important because they identify common themes and confirm the results of a handful of studies that examine the political goals and public policy agendas of American Indian and Hispanic women.[40] In combination, these studies reveal that indigenous and Hispanic women leaders enter politics for the people – in order to improve the quality of life in their racial/ethnic communities by empowering community members and increasing participation in public decision-making processes.

Notes

1. See especially S Rodriguez, 'Land, Water, and Ethnic Identity in Taos', in *Land, Water, and Culture: New Perspectives on Hispanic Land Grants*, ed C L Briggs and J R Van Ness, 313–403 (Albuquerque: University of New Mexico Press, 1987).

2. M Guerrero, 'Albuquerque Revisits Radioactive Dumping', *Voces Unidas* 4, no 2 (1994): 5; M L Jones, 'Missiles over Dineh', *Voces Unidas* 4, no 1 (1994): 11; and C Seidman, 'That Their Children May Inherit the Earth', *Sage Magazine* (October 1994): 10–12.
3. D Salazar and L A Moulds, 'Toward an Integrated Politics of Social Justice and Environment: African American Leaders in Seattle' (paper presented at the annual meeting of the Western Political Science Association, Portland, Oregon, March 1995); B Marquez, 'The Politics of Environmental Justice in Mexican American Neighborhoods' (paper presented at the annual meeting of the Western Political Science Association, Albuquerque, New Mexico, March 1994); and L Head, 'Take Back New Mexico'! *Voces Unidas* 3, no 2 (1993): 1 (2).
4. J Fleck, 'Nuclear Waste Plan Rejected', *Albuquerque Journal*, 2 February, 1995; Partners in the Environment, 'New Mexico: The Land of Enchantment'? *EAGLE* 1, no 6 (1993): 5 (2).
5. R Contreras and R Shaw, 'Isleta Pueblo's First Woman Governor', *Voces Unidas* 3, no 2 (1993): 10 (2), and T Anaya and B F Chavis Jr, 'People of Color Unite to Combat Environmental Racism', *Albuquerque Journal*, 25 October, 1991.
6. T Enslin, 'Keep Radioactive Waste Water Out of Sewers', *Albuquerque Journal*, 1 November, 1991; F Moreno, producer, *Environment, Race and Class: The Poisoning of Communities of Color* (Albuquerque, NM: Community Cable Channel 27), aired 31 August, 1991.
7. V Taliman, 'Uranium Miners Made Profits, Left Town, and Stuck Natives with Open Pits and Contamination Worries', *Voces Unidas* 1, no 3 (1991): 6.
8. Inter-Hemispheric Education Resource Center, 'Concerned Citizens of Sunland Park', *BorderLines* 2, no 1 (1994): 4–5, and R Fernandez, 'Los Lunas Stops Waste Incinerator', *Voces Unidas* 3, no 3 (1993): 12.
9. L Naranjo, 'Martineztown Defeats Courthouse'! *Voces Unidas* 4, no 2 (1994): 4.
10. Jones, 'Missiles over Dineh'; A Gedicks, *The New Resource Wars: Native and Environmental Struggles against Multinational Corporations* (Boston: South End, 1993); and SouthWest Organizing Project, 'Carletta Tilousi: Fighting for Her People', *Voces Unidas* 1, no 4 (1991): 13.
11. L Pulido, 'Sustainable Development at Ganados del Valle', in *Confronting Environmental Racism: Voices from the Grassroots*, ed R D Bullard (Boston: South End, 1993), 123–39, and D Peña, 'The "Brown" and the "Green": Chicanos and Environmental Politics in the Upper Rio Grande', *Capitalism Nature Socialism: A Journal of Socialist Ecology* 3, no 1 (1992): 79–103.
12. R M Laws, 'Spiritual Conflict Underlies Nuclear Waste Controversy', *Albuquerque Journal*, 8 March, 1995, and L Taylor et al., 'The Importance of Cross-Cultural Communication between Environmentalists and Land-Based People', *Workbook* 13, no 3 (1988): 90–93.
13. Seidman, 'Inherit the Earth'; and R Contreras, 'Toxic Survivors Seek Protection', *Voces Unidas* 3, no 2 (1993): 7.
14. F Romero, 'Grupitos: Citizen Involvement at the Kitchen Table', *Nuestro Pueblo* 7, no 2 (Summer 1997); SouthWest Organizing Project, 'Five Years Later: SWOP's Letter to the "Group of Ten" Revisited', *Voces Unidas* 5, no 3 (1995), special insert: 1–4; and SouthWest Organizing Project, 'The Selling of New Mexico', *Voces Unidas* 4, no 2 (1994a), special insert.
15. D M Prindeville and J G Bretting, 'Indigenous Women Activists and Political Participation: The Case of Environmental Justice', *Women & Politics* 19, no 1 (1998): 39–58; C Mack-Canty, 'Women Political Activists: Taking the State Back Out' (paper presented at the annual meeting of the Western Political Science Association, Tucson, Arizona, March 1997); and SouthWest Organizing Project, 'Grassroots Democracy in Action: An Interview with Richard Moore', *Voces Unidas* 4, no 3 (1994b): 9 (3).
16. See Salazar and Moulds, 'Toward an Integrated Politics'; D. Alston, *'Taking Back Our Lives': A Report to the Panos Institute on Environment, Community Development and Race in the United States* (Washington, DC: Panos Institute, 1990), and M Guerrero and L Head, 'Informed Collective Action – A Powerful Weapon', in *Taking Back Our Lives*, ed Alston, 24 (4).

17. Marquez, 'Politics of Environmental Justice'.
18. Prindeville and Bretting, 'Indigenous Women Activists'; S Cable and C Cable, *Environmental Problems, Grassroots Solutions: The Politics of Grassroots Environmental Conflict* (New York: St Martin's, 1995), and D Taylor, 'Environmentalism and the Politics of Inclusion', in *Confronting Environmental Racism*, ed Bullard, 53–61.
19. N E McGlen and K O'Connor, *Women, Politics, and American Society* (Englewood Cliffs, NJ: Prentice Hall, 1995), and J M Bystydzienski, 'Introduction', in *Women Transforming Politics: Worldwide Strategies for Empowerment*, ed J M Bystydzienski, 1–8 (Indianapolis: Indiana University Press, 1992).
20. T Aragón de Valdez, 'Organizing as a Political Tool for the Chicana', *Frontiers* 5, no 2 (1980): 7.
21. L A Tilly and P Gurin, 'Women, Politics and Change', in *Women, Politics and Change*, ed L A Tilly and P Gurin, 3–34 (New York: Russell Sage Foundation, 1990), and S Morgen and A Bookman, 'Rethinking Women and Politics: An Introductory Essay', in *Women and the Politics of Empowerment*, ed A Bookman and S Morgen, 3–29 (Philadelphia: Temple University Press, 1988).
22. C Hardy-Fanta, *Latina Politics, Latino Politics: Gender, Culture, and Political Participation in Boston* (Philadelphia: Temple University Press, 1993); S Cable, 'Women's Social Movement Involvement: The Role of Structural Availability in Recruitment and Participation Processes', *Sociological Quarterly* 33, no 1 (1992): 35–50; and L Albrecht and R M Brewer, 'Bridges of Power: Women's Multicultural Alliances for Social Change', in *Bridges of Power: Women's Multicultural Alliances*, ed L Albrecht and R M Brewer, 2–22 (Philadelphia: New Society, 1990).
23. N A Naples, 'Women's Community Activism: Exploring the Dynamics of Politicization and Diversity', in *Community Activism and Feminist Politics: Organizing across Race, Class, and Gender*, ed N A Naples, 327–49 (New York: Routledge, 1998), and N A Naples, 'Activist Mothering: Cross-Generational Continuity in the Community Work of Women from Low-Income Urban Neighborhoods', *Gender and Society* 6, no 3 (1992): 441–63. Also see A Orleck, 'Tradition Unbound: Radical Mothers in International Perspective', in *The Politics of Motherhood: Activist Voices from Left to Right*, ed A Jetter, A Orleck, and D Taylor, 3–11 (Hanover, NH: University Press of New England, 1997).
24. McGlen and O'Connor, *Women, Politics*; S Thomas, *How Women Legislate* (New York: Oxford University Press, 1994); and Hardy-Fanta, *Latina Politics*.
25. G Di Chiro, 'Defining Environmental Justice: Women's Voices and Grassroots Politics', *Socialist Review* 22, no 4 (1992): 109.
26. Di Chiro, 'Defining Environmental Justice', 109. Also see R Paehlke and P Vaillancourt Rosneau, 'Environment/Equity: Tensions in North American Politics', *Policy Studies Journal* 21, no 4 (1993): 672–86.
27. Mack-Canty, 'Women Political Activists'; Taylor, 'Environmentalism'; and Cable, 'Women's Social Movement Involvement'.
28. T Kaplan, *Crazy for Democracy: Women in Grassroots Movements* (New York: Routledge, 1997), and Seidman, 'Inherit the Earth'.
29. Di Chiro, 'Defining Environmental Justice', 115.
30. US Census Bureau, *Census 2000. Summary File 2*, Matrices PCT3 and PCT4. 'Census of Population – Geographic Area, New Mexico Race, or Ethnic Groups'. http://factfinder.census.gov/servlet/QTTable?ds_name=DEC_2000_SF2_U&geo_id=04000US35&qr_name=DEC_2000_SF2_U_QTP1 (6 May, 2002).
31. J Lofland and L Lofland, *Analyzing Social Settings: A Guide to Qualitative Observation and Analysis*, 3rd ed (Belmont, CA: Wadsworth, 1995).
32. M S Feldman, *Strategies for Interpreting Qualitative Data* (London: Sage, 1995), and G McCracken, *The Long Interview* (Newbury Park, CA: Sage, 1988).
33. Feldman, *Strategies*; Lofland and Lofland, *Analyzing Social Settings*; and M B Miles and A M Huberman, *Qualitative Data Analysis*, 2nd ed (London: Sage, 1994).

34. J A Holstein and J F Gubrium, *The Active Interview* (Beverly Hills, CA: Sage, 1995); Lofland and Lofland, *Analyzing Social Settings*; and A Strauss and J Corbin, *Basics of Qualitative Research: Grounded Theory Procedures and Techniques* (London: Sage, 1990).
35. C Krauss, 'Women and Toxic Waste Protests: Race, Class and Gender as Resources of Resistance', *Qualitative Sociology* 16, no 3 (1993): 257. Also see W Churchill and W LaDuke, 'The Earth Is Our Mother: Struggles for American Indian Land and Liberation in the Contemporary United States', in *The State of Native America: Genocide, Colonization, and Resistance*, ed M A Jaimes, 139–88 (Boston: South End, 1992), and M A Jaimes, 'American Indian Women: At the Center of Indigenous Resistance in North America', in *The State of Native America*, ed Jaimes, 311–44.
36. Taylor, 'Environmentalism', and Alston, 'Taking Back Our Lives'.
37. Di Chiro, 'Defining Environmental Justice', 94.
38. Marquez, 'Politics of Environmental Justice'.
39. Orleck, 'Tradition Unbound'.
40. See for example, M Pardo, 'Doing It for the Kids: Mexican American Activists, Border Feminists'? in *Feminist Organizations: Harvest of the Women's Movement*, ed M M Ferree and P Y Martin, 356–71 (Philadelphia: Temple University Press, 1995); K B Chiste, 'Aboriginal Women and Self-Government: Challenging Leviathan', *American Indian Culture and Research Journal* 18, no 3 (1994): 19–43; P Cruz Takash, 'Breaking Barriers to Representation: Chicana/Latina Elected Officials in California', *Urban Anthropology* 22, nos 3–4 (1993): 325–60; and M McCoy, 'Gender or Ethnicity: What Makes a Difference? A Study of Women Tribal Leaders', *Women & Politics* 12, no 3 (1992): 57–68.

CASE STUDY

Robert Melchior Figueroa[*], 'Other Faces: Latinos and Environmental Justice'

One of the classic cases of environmental racism involves the Latino community of Kettleman City, California, where ChemWaste Management, the largest disposal corporation in the United States, wanted to build a second toxic waste facility. Members of that Latino community won their struggle. But this case is not an isolated event. Numerous cases of environmental injustice have involved persons of Hispanic descent fighting for social and environmental justice, including:

- The Chicano community of San Luis, Colorado, continues its ongoing struggle to preserve its sustainable living, maintain its cultural landscape, and challenge auspicious land claims against a history of destructive mining and timber operations.
- Historically, Cesar Chavez and the United Farm Workers represent one of the critical U.S. labor movements that raised job-related environmental burdens.
- Transcending the stereotype of a single-issue political movement, the grassroots organization Mothers of East Los Angeles touts a strong local membership with an impressive multi-issue agenda that includes victorious struggles against a variety of environmental burdens. . . .

These are some of the cases explored in this chapter that will provide insights by studying the role Latinos play in the environmental justice movement.[1] From this account will also emerge a deeper

[*] Robert Melchior Figueroa, 'Other Faces: Latinos and Environmental Justice', in *Faces of Environmental Racism: Confronting Issues of Global Justice*, eds L Westra and P Wenz (Lanham, MD: Rowman & Littlefield, 1995), 167–75, 177–80, 182–84. Copyright by Rowman & Littlefield.

understanding of how issues of environmental justice and environmental racism transcend the black-and-white view of racial and environmental injustice.

Latino Contributions to the Environmental Justice Movement

Despite the cultural variety in Latino ancestry, the cultures are connected by shared qualities. The historical origins of these cultures have roots to indigenous peoples whose worlds and resources were conquered by the civilizations of the Iberian Peninsula: the Spanish and/or Portuguese. In the same way that we consider indigenous environmental struggles as cases involving environmental justice, so too were these Latino cultures born among environmental injustices that result from the simultaneity of environmental and cultural conquest. Resource extraction, agricultural domination, and the destruction of sustainable practices are symptoms of conquest, displacement, cultural domination, and assimilation. Thus, environmental justice, as a form of social justice, implicitly connects concerns of culture, social justice, and the environment, and is historically based in Latino cultures. The cultural identity of the Latino includes a historical and present environmental identity. That is to say, a Latino's identity includes environmental values and practices that are interpreted, sustained, and refined through cultural identification, beliefs, and behaviors. This environmental identity is historically reflected, because cultural struggles have always involved the preservation of lifestyles and traditions that fundamentally include environmental relationships, values, and practices.

Likewise, in the present, Latino communities work to save their environmental identities when they mobilize against environmental injustices that tear at the cultural fabric. One common cultural association among Latino groups is their deep connection with the Spanish language. While many self-identifying Latinos are not fluent in Spanish, Latino identity involves the celebrated use of Spanish language in many ways, with the spoken language being the most prevalent. Given that environmental identity emerges as a facet of cultural identity, one consideration for environmental justice in Latino communities is the recognition and respect for the use of Spanish. The use and control of language has always been a candidate for sustaining hegemony, which is partly why Latino communities are particularly affected by the important role language plays for environmental justice and environmental racism.

El Pueblo para el Aire y Agua Limpio

An oft-cited Latino case that has played a critical role in the environmental justice literature is the victory of *El Pueblo para el Aire y Agua Limpio* (People for Clean Air and Water) over ChemWaste Management (CWM) in Kettleman City, California. *El Pueblo* struggled to halt a second CWM facility in its community, this time a hazardous waste incinerator to go with the existing toxic landfill. Kettleman City is a small community of farm workers, more than 60 percent of whom speak only Spanish. Citizens felt that democratic rights and political participation were easily violated because the political process was not carried out in the language of the community's citizen majority. In the verdict of *El Pueblo para el Aire y Agua Limpio v. Kings County*, CWM lost because the company provided only English versions of its reports, project details, and other critical information, failing to recognize the Spanish majority. CWM also failed to report the cumulative effects of the two facilities and the agricultural impacts.

The *El Pueblo* case provides a model for environmental justice mobilization for several reasons. First, it identifies the kind of actions commonly used to undermine the political participation of Latinos, especially Spanish-speaking citizens. The oversight of the cultural language of a community designates a facet of racism. To say that these citizens ought to be speaking and knowing English denies the convenience with which CWM was able to produce reports that did not satisfactorily inform those most directly affected by the environmental burden.

Second, this case exemplifies the marriage of civil rights with environmental concerns, this time through environmental policy. *El Pueblo* won its case through civil rights protection that is housed in environmental legislation, not civil rights legislation per se. California environmental law requires a meaningful democratic process, including the satisfaction of information rights and public hearings. Thus, *El Pueblo* and Kettleman City further represents the extent to which culture, civil rights, and environmental concerns are intertwined.

An Early Grassroots Heritage

One earmark of environmental justice activities is the grassroots activism that communities must launch against mainstream political machines, corporations, and environmental institutions. The fact that the parties that will experience the highest level of impacts are not fully included in the democratic process, though they are distributed environmental burdens, points to the heart of violations against political recognition and distributive justice. Whenever government and nongovernmental environmental organizations become involved with environmental justice conflicts, they must adapt to the local grassroots groups or they will be perceived and treated as part of the problem the community is struggling against – in this case, the paternalism and institutional oppression of mainstream political organizations. Latino grassroots groups must respond to these forms of paternalism and disenfranchisement in a culturally specific way, often involving the importance of language and labor sectors. The kinds of grassroots responses that are available, as well as the responses required for achieving justice, reflect the political characteristics of the community's environmental identity. The residents and members of these grassroots organizations identify communally and culturally, not simply as interest-maximizing individuals with common goals, but as individuals who are similarly situated by virtue of their experiences in this particular geographical and social setting.

Cesar Chavez and the United Farm Workers

Agribusiness in the United States has grown through the decades along with industry and other business sections. And for the most part, the majority of laborers in agribusiness have been members of ethnic and racial minorities. The only exception to this rule was during the Great Depression, when the dustbowl forced poor white farmers westward, and agribusiness took advantage of their desperate need for work. Otherwise, the most exploited agricultural workers have run the gamut of historical ethnic minorities, from African Americans as slaves and then sharecroppers, to Native Americans. Next came Chinese immigrants during the late 1800s, until Japanese workers arrived, and then Filipino workers. The exploitation of Mexican workers began during World War II and continued through the postwar period of the 1940s. Latinos now dominate the agricultural labor force and suffer much of the historical racism that agribusiness has always maintained. Today, field-workers, predominately Latino, harvest 85 percent of this country's fruits and vegetables.[2]

The struggle of agricultural workers is nothing less than an environmental justice struggle, and the predominance of people of color makes this struggle one of environmental racism. Agribusiness and government agencies have historically refused to set equitable boundaries for farmworkers' rights, their health, or their safety. Most industries had to face the obligation of social justice for workers, especially organized workers, as early as 1938, when the Fair Labor Relations Act went into effect. This law, which granted workers the right to join unions and engage in collective bargaining, was explicitly denied to agricultural laborers. Likewise, the Fair Labor Standards Act of 1938 excluded farm labor from minimum wage standards and permitted farm labor a comparatively lower working age than other labor markets.[3] Even the heralded Occupational Safety and Health Act (OSHA) of 1970 did not extend workers' safety and environmental protection to farmworkers. The issues surrounding farmworkers involved racism, little or no legal protection, unregulated minimal wages, deportation threats, abject poverty, poor health care, violence, and a disparately distributed environmental burden in the form of numerous pesticides that are harmful to human health. Cesar Chavez and the United Farm Workers (UFW) revealed the struggles that coupled cultural recognition with labor issues and social justice with environmental conditions.

The organizing by Chavez and UFW took social justice into the realm of Rachel Carson's tremendous book, *Silent Spring* (Boston: Houghton Mifflin, 1994). Her work exposed the health and environmental hazards of DDT, and in doing so, took on the government, the military, and a whole community of scientists. By the late 1960s, Carson's insights changed policies and lead to the eventual outlawing of DDT use in the United States. However, there were some oversights regarding the extent to which social justice was relevant to chemical contamination, in particular, the immediate impact on agricultural workers who were in direct contact with the chemicals. Of course, most of these workers were poor and members of ethnic minorities – and in California, that would mean Latinos.

One may rightly debate the beginnings of the contemporary environmental movement; however, it is certain that *Silent Spring* represents a founding place in schools of environmentalism. It was within only a few years of Carson's publication that Chavez and UFW successfully mobilized in 1965 against the injustices of California table-grape growers. These strikes and the subsequent national boycotts lead to collective bargaining agreements between UFW and growers. In each of these mobilizations, Chavez fought for the protection of farmworkers and the 'prohibition on the use of DDT, Aldrin, Dieldrin, and parathon on union ranches'.[4] Despite the popularity of the classic environmental work that Carson brought to the public, it was ten years before the UFW's national boycott campaign forced the EPA to prohibit the use of DDT on farms with manual labor. With steady pressure, many other pesticides became prohibited. However, the detrimental impacts will be felt for generations and the use of dangerous pesticides continues, as does the inability of many Latinos to address the problem.

It took Chavez, the UFW, and other leaders – such as Baldemar Velasquez in Ohio, now president of the Farm Labor Organizing Committee – to address both deleterious environmental effects *and* civil injustices surrounding the use of dangerous chemicals. The grassroots organizing of Latino leaders reveals a legacy that is often overlooked by critics of the environmental justice movement. Often, grassroots groups fighting for environmental justice have been seen as dealing with a single issue. The image of NIMBYists (Not in My Back Yard) and antitoxins campaigns are taken to be weak forms of grassroots action – perhaps successful for a single battle but ineffective against the web of issues that surrounds the cases. Including Chavez and his fellow leaders as a part of the environmental justice movement refutes the single-issue criticism. The national boycott campaign encompassed issues of environmental protection, public health, corporate influence of government policy, labor struggles, civil rights, and racism. Instead of the single issue life span, Chavez leaves a Latino legacy of a multi-issue grassroots organization.

Grassroots Voices and Social Location

The grassroots emphasis in the environmental justice movement is born with the early rally cry 'We Speak for Ourselves', emphasizing the movement's explicit purpose to empower communities through their own voices – the local voices of the grass roots.[5] Becoming full participants throughout the decision-making process allows collectivities to be heard and their input to be considered. It also offers collectivities a chance to reassess the attitudes and values that perpetuate cultural stigma. Analysis from the politics of recognition includes the notion of cultural collectivities as they relate to communities of discourse: the social locations and contexts from which people's concerns and identities receive social legitimization. These issues of voice are particularly emphasized by the ethical and political problems in the arena of environmental policy. One critical concern is that the 'deeper' environmental issues have been defined almost strictly in terms of so-called natural environments, neglecting urban and rural human environments that are threatened. Another concern is that membership in mainstream environmental groups has tended to be almost completely white and predominantly affluent. The canvassing practices and the choice environments receiving attention have both intentionally and habitually left out the voices of those with differing environmental concerns, so much so that until the late twentieth century such alternative interests were merely dim shadows of environmental concern. Were environmentalists speaking for all environments or simply the environments of their own selection, or the selection of their funded organization? The environmental justice movement represents one response to establishing an environmental voice for people of color and the poor amidst the din of exclusionary habits.

From the politics of recognition arise several relevant issues pertaining to the relationship between the environmental justice movement and cultural representation through the ability to 'speak for ourselves'. Linda Martin Alcoff provides an insightful analysis that maps directly onto the concerns of political recognition in environmental justice. Alcoff notes two critical claims in the problem of speaking for others:

> First, there has been a growing awareness that where an individual speaks from affects both the meaning and truth of what she says and thus she cannot assume an ability to transcend her location. In other words, a speaker's location (which I take here to refer to her *social* location or social identity) has an epistemically significant impact on that speaker's claims and can serve either to authorize or de-authorize her speech. . . . The second claim holds that not only is location epistemically salient but certain privileged locations are discursively dangerous. In particular, the practice of privileged persons speaking for or on behalf of less privileged persons has actually resulted (in many cases) in increasing or reinforcing the oppression of the group spoken for.[6]

In the environmental justice context these issues express the direct concerns of grassroots activism. Both the inability to completely transcend one's social location and the epistemic significance for political empowerment are reasons why an active, local voice is crucial. Very few distributive approaches can directly address the idea of social location because distributive theories tend to ignore the significance of the connections between culture and epistemology as they relate to the politics of place. Perhaps distributive accounts of working class communities or industrial communities could be considered to give some significance to social location, because the expression of economic interests is more easily heard over the cultural expression. Yet, with purely distributive accounts there still lacks a cultural context from which we can work to achieve political empowerment and institutional restructuring. The crucial points raised by Alcoff are that speaking for others denies the fact that others are socially located in a way that allows them to make important political differences for effectively serving the interests of others. This social location is expressed in cultural terms that are destined to be overheard without participation and political recognition.

Madres de Este de Los Angeles

The impact of including the voices from other social locations is illustrated through the Latina grass roots of *Madres de Este de Los Angeles*, or Mothers of East Los Angeles (MELA). According to Gabriel Gutierrez, MELA was formed in May 1985 to protest the proposed siting of a prison.[7] Borrowing from the *madre* movements in South America, Father John Morreta coined *Madres de Este de Los Angeles* from an adaptation of *Madres de la Plaza de Mayo*, the Argentine mothers who rallied for the return of their children, kidnapped and possibly killed by the Argentine military.[8] Community men and husbands remain on the sidelines of the organization. MELA's members – and there are hundreds of them – do not pay dues, and the organization has no hierarchical leadership roles. Juana Beatriz Gutierrez, mother of nine, homemaker, and previously an active member for the

Neighborhood Watch Program, is the most likely candidate to be credited with MELA's founding. Others at the founding meeting and members with untiring political stamina, such as Erlinda Robles, certainly deserve mention as the organization's inspirational momentum.

After blocking a state prison proposal in a Latino community, MELA then put a stop to plans for an oil pipeline that would run through East Los Angeles, with some parts of it above ground and adjacent to an elementary school. MELA also has worked with other grassroots groups, including local chapters of environmental organizations such as Greenpeace and the National Resources Defense Council. Each mobilization also included coalitions with ad hoc neighborhood groups fighting similar struggles throughout California. MELA has sustained close connections with California state Assemblywoman Gloria Molina and U.S. Rep. Lucille Roybal-Allard to mobilize communities against environmental burdens and to achieve a political voice. MELA extended this voicing process through major information and hearing campaigns that included accessing undisclosed information and lobbying for direct action by the California state government.

MELA represents the values that participatory justice can carry over distributive justice. MELA, community residents of Vernon in East Los Angeles, and other activist groups refused to settle with compensatory measures used to ensure the siting of a hazardous waste incinerator project. MELA exemplifies the fact that citizen autonomy and the actualization of participatory rights often determine a community's ability to respond to the distribution of environmental burdens. Consistent with the social locations of MELA's members, recent actions have voiced a demand for social transformation in other venues. Among these are the creation of a Chicano/Chicana Studies Department at the University of California, Los Angeles, and on other campuses; initiating community-based scholarship programs; antigang actions; and urban environmental projects. . . .

San Luis, Colorado

In the San Luis Valley of southern Colorado, farmers and townspeople have wrestled to maintain traditional ways of life that inexorably connect the culture to the land, the heritage to the environment. The original peoples of the land were among the high-plains Native American nations, including the Apache and clans of the Southern Mountain Utes. Other cultural origins include a series of migrations by Chicanos into the San Luis Valley by grantee-permission given by the Sangre de Cristo Land Grant in 1843. The grantees invited Chicano migration into the San Luis Valley, and in 1851 La Plaza de San Luis Culebra became the area's first settlement, making what is now San Luis the oldest town in Colorado.[9]

Farmers in San Luis have maintained one of the only two commons left in the United States, the other being Boston Commons. The commons system and the traditional land and resource uses involved a long history of community interdependence. La Sierra, the mountain watershed of the valley, is the nexus of the community's environmental identity. The philosophy of the commons and the farmers' agro-history evolved from a cultural synthesis into the Chicano land heritage. For instance, the land parcels display the riparian long-lot farming that was imported with the Mexican/Spanish migration into the Southwest and formerly inherited from early Roman practices. As Devon Pena and Joseph Gallegos record:

> The settlers received private riparian long-lots in the bottomlands of the seven major creeks in the Culebra microbasin; but the majority of the land, including the vast foothill woodlands and mountain forests and parks, was set aside as an *ejido*, a commons.[10]

With the riparian long-lot parcels, farmers use gravity irrigation systems called *acequias*, the use of which dates back to Muslim history in Spain during the Crusades. The system constitutes a 'mother ditch', or *acequia madre*, that runs a course into numerous localized *acequias*, which sustain the agro-ecology of the riparian long-lot parcels. The traditional resource use of *acequias* and the commons-based land management produce a sustainable, biologically diverse agriculture while reflecting the multicultural influences of the Latino heritage with preserved Native American, Spanish, Roman, and North African impressions. Thus, the people of San Luis created a cultural landscape that represents their Latino history. Attempts to acquire, privatize, and/or control the area's resources would have an immediate impact on the production and maintenance of the cultural land-scape.

As early as the 1890s, after a series of surreptitious land purchases, the people of the Culebra microbasin began feeling the serious threat of land speculation and private enclosure of the commons. Every move to enclose the commons, as well as actions to privatize the water use, would be challenged by Chicanos by maintaining land-use traditions that involved constant management of the *acequias*. The traditional use of the land prevented possible land-abandonment litigation.

Although land speculators, resource developers, and mining companies took notice of the San Luis Valley in the 1850s and sporadic threats arose in the 1890s, it was not until the 1960s that enclosure of the commons became a direct and immediate threat. A North Carolina lumberman, Jack Taylor, bought the 'Mountain Tract'. The tract long known as La Sierra became the infamous Taylor Ranch, the site of a toxic mining operation and, more recently, a major logging operation that has caused tremendous amounts of soil erosion, virtually destroying the watershed.[11]

Two decades of antimining actions and constant land and water rights disputes set the backdrop for an ultimate cultural insult: the over-story removal in the forest of Taylor Ranch.[12] During the late 1990s, an important environmental alliance struggled against the logging activities on Taylor Ranch. Local farmers, ranchers, businesses, and residents formed a coalition with environmentalists from the region led by Ancient Forest Rescue (AFR). San Luis has become a point of political, personal, and environmental interest, attracting diverse groups that have come to respect the importance of the cultural landscape as part of the community's environmental identity. However, this coalition did not begin without the specter of discriminatory environmentalism. At first, AFR had to be made aware of the historical and the cultural contexts. AFR was initially perceived as a group of young white activists who were myopically focused on the ancient forests and operations on Taylor Ranch and uninterested in the long-term struggles of the people and unaware of the sustainable land practices that depend on La Sierra. Would AFR be a transient voice that would pass through the town without respect for the cultural impacts of its actions?

Fortunately, some AFR members had developed a repertoire of cultural diversity training, the need for which had been established in earlier coalitions with Native American groups. In order to be received as intended, environmentalists had to take the time to listen to the people of San Luis and to learn the cultural importance underlying political actions against Taylor Ranch. Eventually, San Luis evolved into one of the clearest cases of an environmental justice coalition between outside environmentalists and local residents and activists. The Chicano community came to realize that white environmentalists could share in its cultural pride and plight. The merging of these two groups led to a transformation in environmental identities. For more than two years, AFR members lived and worked with San Luis farmers, ranchers, and townspeople. The environmentalists found the cultural dimension in their cause, and the local residents found an ally willing to coexist with the community to develop resistance strategies. The environmentalists joined the long heritage of the people there and their struggle to avoid cultural and political invasion.

The case represents two important reflections on environmental racism. First, San Luis details a unique history of environmental alliance in a deeply traditional Chicano community. Where discriminatory environmentalism affects most communities of color, the San Luis case proves that white environmentalists can coexist, collaborate, and coordinate political action with communities of color. Second, the extent to which the cultural identity is affected by environmental practices reveals a display of racism in the disrespect for the rich environmental identity. The logging operations cut clear through the lifeblood of the community. One can only legitimate the destruction of the ancient forest of La Sierra if one is capable of ignoring the community's cultural landscape and history. One can only privately own La Sierra if one ignores the prior claim of a commons. And one can conscientiously destroy the land and forest of La Sierra only if one wishes to destroy the endangered Chicano culture of San Luis....

Closing Thoughts

To be sure, Latinos share struggles against environmental racism. In urban and rural contexts, Latino struggles reflect many plights of African Americans. In traditional land-use struggles and cultural survival, Latinos echo the struggles of Native Americans. And in their struggles for environmental equity, Latinos represent many of the ways that economically depressed communities must work to achieve environmental fairness. The issues and cases of this discussion also reflect some of the ways that Latinos widen environmental justice arenas by carving a space for people of color into mainstream environmental concerns about logging, grazing, and old growth forest protection. Thus, we find Latinos playing important roles in antitoxins campaigning; in traditional land rights disputes; in indigenous struggles; in grassroots organizing; in sustainable development; and in reestablishing culturally specific environmental practices while generating critical environmental alliances.

What is missing from this analysis? The many cases of Latino struggles throughout the Midwest, the South, and the East Coast, *and* a thorough discussion of the environmental colonialism, in the *maquiladoras* along the U.S.-Mexican border and in the communities of Puerto Rico. The absence of detailed discussions about these critical examples of Latino struggles associated with the United States must be admittedly recognized as a gaping hole in the study provided here. These other cases cannot be left out of a comprehensive assessment of Latinos and environmental justice, but this is one of many points of my analysis – that Latinos present an impressive and critically important breadth to the environmental justice movement.

Each of the Latino cases that I have discussed sketches valuable lessons for understanding environmental justice. The cases teach us about the vital relationship between respect for environmental identity and achieving environmental justice. While distributive equity must certainly be met for the amelioration of environmental racism, these cases also indicate the existence of injustices against culturally molded environmental identities. Thus, environmental racism must be addressed from both the dimensions of distributive justice and the politics of recognition. Without concentrating our attention on cultural recognition and direct participation, environmental discrimination and discriminatory environmentalism are not successfully ameliorated. This is true for Latinos and any community struggling and striving for environmental justice.

On a final note, these Latino cases reveal lessons about the transformative nature of the environmental justice movement. We learn that environmental identities, from communities of color and from mainstream environmentalism, *do* have a transformative power to meet the rethinking environmental justice demands of political, cultural, and environmental assumptions.

Notes

1. Growing up, I was taught to refer to my Puerto Rican identity as *Hispanic*. Filling out applications and census forms only contributed to this practice. The use of this term to designate the peoples of Latin American descent remains prevalent. However, the use of the term *Latino* has been introduced to explicitly distinguish people of Latin American descent from people of Spain. It may correctly be said that all Latinos are of Latin American descent, but not all Hispanics are, since *Hispanics* is also capable of including people of Spain. For this distinction, I chose to refer to peoples in the United States who

are of Latin American descent as *Latinos*. I do this fully cognizant and respectful of the fact that many people of Latin American descent refer to themselves as Hispanics and by other related terms.
2. For details on the ethnic history and racist legacy of the agricultural business, see Marion Moses, 'Farmworkers and Pesticides', in *Confronting Environmental Racism: Voices from the Grassroots*, ed R D Bullard (Boston: South End Press, 1993), 160–78. For discussion on the migration of Latino agricultural workers throughout the South and their continued fight for union protection, see Sandy Smith-Nonini, 'The Union Is the Only Way', *Southern Exposure* 28, no 2 (Summer 1999): 46–47, 51–52.
3. Moses, 'Farmworkers and Pesticides', 171–72.
4. Moses, 'Farmworkers and Pesticides', 176.
5. Early into the environmental justice movement, the phrase 'We Speak for Ourselves' signified the crisis of exclusion and lack of recognition in the decision-making process and the participatory remedy to these injustices. See Dana Alston, ed, *We Speak for Ourselves: Social Justice, Race, and Environment* (Washington, DC: The Panos Institute, 1990).
6. Linda Martin Alcoff, 'The Problem of Speaking for Others', in *Who Can Speak?: Authority and Critical Identity*, ed J Roof and R Wiegman (Urbana: University of Illinois Press, 1995), 98–99.
7. Gabriel Gutierrez, 'Mothers of East Los Angeles Strike Back', in *Unequal Protection: Environmental Justice and Communities of Color*, ed R D Bullard (San Francisco: Sierra Club Books, 1994), 220–33.
8. Gutierrez, 'Mothers of East Los Angeles Strike Back', 223–24.
9. Devon Pena and Joseph Gallegos, 'Nature and Chicanos in Southern Colorado', in *Confronting Environmental Racism: Voices from the Grassroots*, ed R D Bullard (Boston: South End Press, 1992), 141–60.
10. Pena and Gallegos, 'Nature and Chicanos in Southern Colorado', 147.
11. These details on the history, agro-ethnography, and environmental struggles of San Luis are extrapolated from Pena and Gallegos, 'Nature and Chicanos in Southern Colorado'.
12. Information on the logging practices and environmental justice struggles is drawn from two primary sources: the film *Sin Aqua No Hay Vida* (Boulder, CO: Wet Mountain Productions, 1998) and several years of research conversations with Jay Bowman, one of the film's producers. Other sources of information often came directly from participants in antilogging actions, particularly students from my environmental justice courses at the University of Colorado at Boulder.

CASE STUDY

Elizabeth Hoover, Katsi Cook, Ron Plain, Kathy Sanchez, Vi Waghiyi, Pamela Miller, Renee Dufault, Caitlin Sislin and David O Carpenter[*], 'Indigenous Peoples of North America: Environmental Exposures and Reproductive Justice'

American Indian (AI) and Alaska Native (AN) peoples compose 1.7% of the population of the United States (Census Briefs 2012), and First Nations, Metis, and Inuit peoples compose 3.8% of the population of Canada (Statistics Canada 2006). Although these groups differ markedly in some aspects of culture and lifestyle, they unfortunately suffer from many common problems. Rates of poverty,

[*] Elizabeth Hoover et al., 'Indigenous People of North America: Environmental Exposure and Reproductive Justice', in *Environmental Health Perspectives* 120, no 12 (December 2012): 1645–49. https://ehp.niehs.nih.gov/1205422/.

unemployment, substance abuse, and violence are high, and overall life expectancy for indigenous people is less than that among whites. Mortality rates for AN populations are 60% higher than those of the U.S. white population (Day and Lanier 2003), and mortality rates in AI populations are about twice that of the general U.S. population (Kunitz 2008). AI/AN adults (16.1%) were more likely than black adults (12.6%), Hispanic adults (11.8%), Asian adults (8.4%), or white adults (7.1%) to have ever been told they had diabetes. These rates vary by region, from 5.5% among AN adults to 33.5% among AI adults in southern Arizona (Centers for Disease Control and Prevention 2011). Similarly, rates of diabetes among indigenous populations in Canada are 3–5 times higher than the general population (Sharp 2009). In addition, AI/AN have the lowest cancer survival rates among any racial group in the United States (U.S. Commission on Civil Rights 2004).

Many health conditions in indigenous communities are attributed to poverty, lifestyle, genetics, and an inadequate health care delivery system, but in many cases they are also compounded by exposure to environmental contaminants. These exposures affect not only current community residents, and those born into these exposed communities, but also generations to come. Exposure to environmental contaminants can increase these health risks for both the mother and her unborn children. Exposure of the unborn to environmental chemicals such as methylmercury, pesticides, and polychlorinated biphenyls (PCBs) not only increases the risk of developing several diseases later in life (Grandjean 2008) but also results in impairment of intellectual function for life (Carpenter 2006). In this commentary we will explore the linkages between environmental and reproductive health and justice issues in Native North American communities.

Environmental and Reproductive Health and Justice

The U.S. Environmental Protection Agency (EPA 2012) defines environmental justice as:

> the fair treatment and meaningful involvement of all people regardless of race, color, national origin, or income with respect to the development, implementation, and enforcement of environmental laws, regulations, and policies.

In tribal communities in the United States, environmental mitigation is significantly behind that of nontribal communities (U.S. EPA 2004). The situation is equally concerning for indigenous communities in Canada, where legislation that deals directly with the inequalities created by environmental injustice is for the most part nonexistent (Dhillon and Young 2010). As Mascarenhas (2007) observed,

> whether by conscious design or institutional neglect, Native American communities face some of the worst environmental devastation in the nation.

Sites ranging from industry to mining to military bases, as well as the release of pesticides and other agricultural by-products, negatively affect not only the surrounding environment, but the health, culture, and reproductive capabilities of the communities they border. Because of subsistence lifestyles, spiritual practices, and other cultural behaviors, tribes have multiple exposures from resource use that could result in disproportionate environmental impacts (U.S. EPA 2004).

Reproductive justice is:

> the right to have children, not have children, and parent the children we have in safe and healthy environments – [and] is based on the human right to make personal decisions about one's life, and the obligation of government and society to ensure that the conditions are suitable for implementing one's decisions. (SisterSong 2012).

As such, reproductive justice, a term that has not yet appeared in the environmental health literature, embeds reproductive rights in an intersectional framework that includes social justice and human rights (Luna 2010). Reproductive justice stresses both individual and group rights because the ability of a woman to determine her reproductive destiny is in many cases directly tied to conditions in her community (Shen 2006). The concept of environmental reproductive justice involves ensuring that a community's reproductive capabilities are not inhibited by environmental contamination.

In the case studies we highlight below, struggles for environmental and reproductive justice have often converged as communities have become concerned about the impact of environmental contamination on their ability to reproduce and create culturally competent tribal citizens. These issues were explored in July 2011 in an Environmental Reproductive Health Symposium and Retreat organized by the First Environment Collaborative in Hot Springs, South Dakota, near the homeland of the Lakota Sioux.

The focus of this meeting was to explore the common issues of exposure to environmental contaminants and the health consequences of this exposure. The intent was to facilitate and nurture partnerships among the indigenous community organizations, researchers, scientists, and health care providers. The recommendations that came from the symposium include the need for additional community-based research that will support efforts to achieve environmental reproductive justice, and the need to support policy regulations that will better protect indigenous communities from both local and more widespread sources of environmental contamination. Below we present the environmental and reproductive health issues faced by each of the indigenous communities who were represented at this symposium, and discuss the need to develop the concept of environmental reproductive justice.

Aamjiwnaang

Perhaps the most strikingly contaminated community is that of the Aamjiwnaang near Sarnia, Ontario, Canada, a 12-km^2 reserve that is home to about 850 Anishnaabe First Nations people. The reserve is surrounded by 62 major industrial facilities located within 25 km, including oil refineries, chemical manufacturers (40% of Canada's chemical industry), and manufacturers of plastics, polymers, and agricultural products. The area is known as 'Chemical Valley'. Levels of air pollutants, including volatile organic compounds, are high (Atari and Luginaah 2009). In 1996, hospital admissions for women in Chemical Valley were 3.11 times the expected rates for women and 2.83 times those for men than would be expected based on other rates for Ontario. These admissions were especially pronounced for cardiovascular and respiratory ailments, and were hypothesized to be pollution related (Fung et al. 2007). About 40% of Aamjiwnaang residents require use of an inhaler, and 17% of adults and 22% of children are reported to have asthma (MacDonald and Rang 2007). The ratio of male births declined over the period 1984–1992 from > 0.5 to about 0.3, a change that may at least partly reflect effects of chemical exposures (Mackenzie et al. 2005.) Releases of chemicals have also interfered with the community's cultural life, affecting hunting, fishing, medicine gathering, and ceremonial activities (MacDonald and Rang 2007).

St. Lawrence Island (SLI)

The SLI Yupik live in two villages of about 800 people each. SLI, the largest island in the Bering Sea, lies just 240 km south of the Arctic Circle and is distant from industrial contamination sources. However, the Arctic acts as a 'cold trap' and is a hemispheric sink for persistent organic pollutants (POPs) that are transported through a process known as global distillation via atmospheric transport from warmer regions (Wania 2003). In addition, there are two abandoned military sites on the island that contain fuels, pesticides, PCBs, metals, and solvents.

POPs bioaccumulate and biomagnify in the lipid-rich Arctic food webs, some to dangerous levels. The rendered oils of bow-head whale, seals, and walrus contain PCB concentrations of 193–421 ppb (Welfinger-Smith et al. 2011). For reference, the U.S. EPA risk-based consumption limit for PCBs in fish to avoid excess risk of cancer is 1.5 ppb (Welfinger-Smith et al. 2011). Rendered oils, blubber, and other fatty tissues from marine mammals are critical components of the traditional diet that provide important nutritional and cultural benefits. Blood serum of the Yupik people contains PCB levels 4–12 times higher than that of the general U.S. population. The predominant source is global transport; however, the former military site at Northeast Cape contributes to the PCB exposure (Carpenter et al. 2005). Although traditional foods are the primary source of exposure to POPs, harvest and consumption of these foods is a defining attribute of the SLI Yupik way of life – a necessary part of maintaining cultural identity. Although a systematic health study has not been done in this community, the residents believe they suffer from excess rates of cancer, thyroid disease, diabetes, and cardiovascular and other chronic diseases (Carpenter et al. 2005; Henifin 2007). This was most forcefully stated in a film interview of Annie Alowe, a SLI woman dying of breast cancer who believed it was caused by the chemical contamination (Miller and Riordan 1999).

Tewa Pueblo

In addition to deposition of petrochemical and military waste, mining tends to heavily impact native communities. Uranium mining and mine tailings are major problems in both South Dakota and New Mexico. There was extensive uranium mining in the Southwest in the past, often on Indian land, and the mounds of mine tailings leached uranium into drinking and groundwater (Landa and Gray 1995). Uranium is both radioactive and has direct metal toxicity, which results in increased risk of cancer, birth defects, and kidney disease (Craft et al. 2004). In addition to mining effluents, the Tewa community in northern New Mexico is also exposed to toxic and radioactive wastes coming from releases from the Los Alamos National Laboratory, spread by air and surface and groundwater. Although a systematic health study has not been conducted in these populations, some environmental testing has been commissioned by local nonprofit organizations, which found PCB levels 25,000 times the standard for human health and 1,000 times over the standard for wildlife habitat in Los Alamos Canyon (Amigos Bravos and Concerned Citizens for Nuclear Safety 2006). Amigos Bravos won a settlement in May 2011 against the U.S. EPA and Los Alamos over discharge permits that will require clean up of a number of sites, increase monitoring, and install pollution control measures (van Buren 2011). However, these measures do little to determine the impact this contamination has had on the health and culture of the region's residents.

Oglala Lakota, Pine Ridge

Although starkly beautiful in landscape and home to myriad artists and storytellers, the Pine Ridge Indian Reservation in South Dakota, home to 25,000 Oglala Lakota people, is notoriously poverty stricken. Forty-nine percent of the residents live below the federal poverty level, and the infant mortality rate is five times higher than the national average (Ruffin 2011). Native Americans in the Northern Plains region have a cancer mortality rate approximately 40% higher than that of the overall population (Rogers and Petereit 2005). Although these health disparities are often attributed to the intense poverty in this region, since the late 1970s community organizations like Women of All Red Nations (WARN) have suspected links between Lakota health issues and the region's history of uranium mining. WARN has cited the high rates of miscarriage and reproductive cancers among Lakota women as evidence of the adverse effects of uranium contamination (Unger 2004). The Pine Ridge reservation lies southeast of the Black Hills, which was the site of extensive uranium mining and milling during the 1940s–1970s. A series of studies traced gross alpha-radiation in groundwater and surface water sources in the Pine Ridge town of Red Shirt to the Edgemont uranium mill site (Jones 2011). Dozens of other abandoned mining and milling sites surround traditional Lakota territory, and the residents are currently fighting the expansion of uranium mining in the region in order to protect future generations.

Akwesasne

The community that has perhaps been best studied is the Mohawk Nation at Akwesasne (located at the juncture of New York, Ontario, and Quebec), whose members traditionally derived most of their protein from fish from the St. Lawrence River and its tributaries. Three aluminum foundries were established upstream of Akwesasne, and all used PCBs as hydraulic fluids that leaked and contaminated the rivers, the fish, and consequently the people (Hwang et al. 1996). After analysis of fish by state and federal officials, tribal leaders advised the members to cease eating local fish in 1986. Although this has resulted in a decline in the levels of PCBs in breast milk and serum, PCB levels are still elevated compared with the general U.S. population (Fitzgerald et al. 1998). In addition, significantly higher levels of PCBs were found in Mohawk adolescents who were breastfed as infants (Gallo et al. 2011). Higher serum PCB concentrations were also associated with decrements in cognitive (Haase et al. 2009; Newman et al. 2009) and thyroid function (Schell et al. 2008) and elevated risk of diabetes (Codru et al. 2007), cardiovascular disease, and hypertension (Goncharov et al. 2008). Mohawk girls were more likely to have reached puberty at 12 years of age if they had higher serum PCBs (Denham et al. 2005), which could be due to the estrogenic effects of PCBs. Serum levels of PCBs in Mohawk men were associated with lower serum testosterone levels (Goncharov et al. 2009). Thus many aspects of Mohawk health may be adversely impacted by their exposure to PCBs.

Environmental Justice, Indigenous People, and the Law

Indigenous communities are disproportionately exposed to environmental contaminants based on where they live and the cultural activities that put them in close contact with their environment. However, federal and state laws often make it easier for extractive and polluting enterprises to access tribal lands. Federal legislation and jurisprudence applicable to tribal lands are distinct from rules that apply to nontribal lands, and are typically inconsistent and inequitable. From Chief Justice John Marshall's 1831 arbitrary definition of tribes as 'domestic dependent nations' (*Cherokee Nation v. State of Georgia* 1831), to a 1985 Supreme Court decision that the Western Shoshone people lost title to their land because of 'gradual encroachment' by the federal government (*U.S. v. Dann 1985*) (a concept that appears nowhere in the law before or since), federal courts and bureaucracies have long wielded language to constrain and derogate tribal peoples according to the political will of the day.

Because of these structural inequities, tribal jurisdictions are attractive to corporations seeking a lesser degree of environmental regulation, oversight, and enforcement than are imposed by state governments. Moreover, due to current social and structural inequalities, indigenous communities seeking environmental justice often experience barriers to their participation in prescribed environmental decision-making processes (Cole and Foster 2001).

Litigation under federal environmental laws and federal Indian law is fraught with challenges. Federal Indian law, a body of judge-made law arising mostly from litigation primarily before the United States Supreme Court, overwhelmingly denies environmental and cultural rights to Native American people. In addition, federal environmental legislation rarely recognizes environmental justice as a cause for action. Even when activists achieve victories in the courts, legislation and administrative agency rule makings can often undo years of environmental justice litigation. For these reasons, it is essential to develop policies that would better protect AI/AN communities from pollution, rather than leaving the matter to courts.

Native Communities and Research

Because indigenous communities often do not have the legal, political, or economic means to resist the placement of polluting industries, indigenous people may suffer excess illness as a consequence of involuntary environmental exposures. However, because of historic antagonism to and distrust of non-native governments and academics, often these communities have not been studied to determine the extent of illness. In the past, some researchers entered indigenous communities with pre-developed projects, did not ask for community input, pressured residents into taking part in the studies, treated Natives as subjects and not colleagues, sensationalized problems in the community in their publications, used blood samples for unauthorized projects (Schnarch 2004), and did not give results to the community (Schell and Tarbell 1998).

These experiences have led some native communities to avoid engaging in research and others to make themselves available only to research projects that will include them as equal partners. The Akwesasne Mohawk developed an effective partnership with researchers, which resulted in > 50 published papers. Mohawk authors Arquette et al. (2002) highlighted the importance of continued collaborative research because of the need for better site- and Nation-specific data. This will provide tribal decision makers with specific information about contaminant levels in various local media and biota. These types of studies can also collect information about traditional cultural practices and natural resource use – information that can then be used to support the protection of natural resources and support the transfer of traditional knowledge and cultural practices to future generations.

To conduct such research, scientists and community members must develop equal and cooperative partnerships (Harding et al. 2012). Utilizing the community's kinship network is important in garnering support for a study, recruiting study participants, and disseminating information. Especially important for the success of future environmental and reproductive health studies is increasing the number of indigenous midwives, physicians, and researchers who understand the potential health impacts of exposure to environmental contaminants.

Environmental Reproductive Justice

Concerns about the community's ability to reproduce, whether physically through the birth of healthy children or culturally through the passing on of traditional practices, has sparked interest in the need for environmental health research. As stated above, in Aamjiwnaang there was the noticeable decrease in male birth ratio (Mackenzie et al. 2005), which residents attribute to their proximity to petrochemical plants. At Akwesasne, a midwife pushed for health studies because of concerns of local mothers about the number of miscarriages in the community and the possibility of contaminated breast milk. Studies found that Mohawk women who ate local fish had higher levels of contaminants in their breast milk than a control group (Fitzgerald et al. 1998). Breastfeeding rates for AI/AN populations are well below the national average (Spieler 2010), an issue that health care providers are seeking to rectify. Indigenous mothers need to be confident that their breast milk is safe for their infants if these statistics are to be improved.

The reproductive capabilities of Mohawk women in Akwesasne are also affected by contamination; for example, PCB exposure has been associated with reducing the age of menarche in Mohawk girls (Denham et al. 2005). The Tewa Pueblo are concerned about the potential of birth defects connected to radiation exposure, and the women of Pine Ridge have attributed their high rates of mis-carriage and reproductive organ cancers to contamination from uranium mines (Unger 2004). SLI Yupik people attribute their perceived high rate of cancer and other diseases to contamination from military sources and long-range transport (Carpenter et al. 2005; Henifin 2007; Miller and Riordan 1999).

In addition to concerns about the physical reproduction of community members, indigenous people are concerned about how environmental contamination impacts the reproduction of cultural knowledge. In Aamjiwnaang, oral traditions once passed down from grandfathers during fishing or grandmothers during berry picking and medicine gathering are being lost as those activities are no longer practiced because of concerns about these foods being contaminated. Rocks once used for sweat lodges are no longer being collected from local streams because the streams have become contaminated.

The cedar used for making tea, smudging, and washing babies contains vanadium at concentrations as high as 6 mg/kg (ALS Laboratory Group Analytical Report, unpublished data), reflecting local releases to air of > 611 tons of vanadium between 2001 and 2010 (Environment Canada 2012). At Akwesasne, community members report a loss of language and culture around subsistence activities like fishing, which have been largely abandoned because of fears of exposure to contaminants. The generational reproduction of culturally informed interpersonal relationships has been affected as much as physical reproduction. We want to expand the definition of reproductive justice to include the capacity to raise children in culturally appropriate ways. For many indigenous communities, to reproduce culturally informed citizens requires a clean environment.

Conclusion

Modern environmental law in North America is predicated on federal-state partnerships that did not initially account for pollution and environmental degradation of Native America (Grijalva 2011). Current regulatory gaps make it difficult to prevent and rectify environmental contamination that impacts AI/AN communities. This contamination threatens not only the health of indigenous communities, it also infringes on their reproductive rights, including the ability to impart cultural land-based knowledge to their children. Thus there is a great need for the concept of environmental reproductive justice in environmental health research. Continued research, involving collaborative partnerships among researchers, health care providers, and community members, is needed to determine the impact of environmental contamination on community members' health and to develop necessary remediation, preventative measures, and protective policy interventions.

References

Amigos Bravos, Concerned Citizens for Nuclear Safety. 2006. Historic and Current Discharges from Los Alamos National Laboratory: Analysis and Recommendations. Final Report. Available: http://www.amigosbravos.org/docs/pdf/06LANLDischargeReport.pdf (accessed 10 October 2011).

Arquette, M, M Cole, K Cook, B LaFrance, M Peters, J Ransom, et al. 2002. 'Holistic Risk-Based Environmental Decision Making: A Native Perspective'. *Environ Health Perspect* 110 (suppl 2): 259–64.

Atari, D O, and I N Luginaah. 2009. 'Assessing the Distribution of Volatile Organic Compounds Using Land Use Regression in Sarnia, "Chemical Valley", Ontario, Canada'. *Environ Health* 8:16. doi:10.1186/1476-069X-8-16 (Online 16 April 2009).

Carpenter, D O. 2006. 'Environmental Contaminants and Learning and Memory. *Internat Cong Series* 1287:183–89.

Carpenter, D O, A P DeCaprio, D O'Hehir, F Akhtar, G Johnson, R J Scrudato, et al. 2005. 'Polychlorinated Biphenyls in Serum of the Siberian Yupik People from St. Lawrence Island, Alaska'. *Int J Circumpolar Health* 64:322–35.

Census Briefs. 2012. 'The American Indian and Alaska Native Population: 2010'. Available: http://www.census.gov/prod/cen2010/briefs/c2010br-10.pdf (accessed 27 February 2012).

Centers for Disease Control and Prevention. 2011. National Diabetes Fact Sheet. Available: http://www.cdc.gov/diabetes/pubs/estimates11.htm#4 (accessed 1 June 2012).

Cherokee Nation v. State of Georgia. 1831. 30 U.S. (5 Pet.) 1. U.S. Supreme Court, Washington, DC, 5 March 1831.

Codru, N, M J Schymura, S Negoita, Akwesasne Task Force on Environment, R Rej, and D O Carpenter. 2007. 'Diabetes in Relation to Serum Levels of Polychlorinated Biphenyls and Chlorinated Pesticides in Adult Native Americans'. *Environ HealthPerspect* 115:1442–47.

Cole, L W, and S R Foster. 2001. 'From the Ground Up: Environmental Racism and the Rise of the Environmental Justice Movement'. New York: New York University Press.

Craft, E, A Ábu-Qare, M Flaherty, M Garofolo, H Rincavage, and M Abou-Donia. 2004. 'Depleted and Natural Uranium: Chemistry and Toxicological Effects'. *J Toxicol Environ Health B Crit Rev* 7:297–317.

Day, G E, and A P Lanier. 2003. 'Alaska Native Mortality, 1979–1998'. *Public Health Rep* 118:518–30.

Denham, M, L M Schell, G Deane, M V Gallo, J Ravenscroft, and A P DeCaprio, et al. 2005. 'Relationship of Lead, Mercury, Mirex, Dichlorodiphenyldichloroethylene, Hexachlorobenzene, and Polychlorinated Biphenyls to Timing of Menarche among Akwesasne Mohawk Girls'. *Pediatrics* 115:e127–e134.

Dhillon, C, and M G Young. 2010. 'Environmental Racism and First Nations: A Call for Socially Just Public Policy Development'. *Cdn J Hum Soc Sci* 1:23–37.

Environment Canada. 2012. National Pollutant Release Inventory, Tracking Pollution in Canada. Available: http://www.ec.gc.ca/inrp-npri/ (accessed 26 July 2012).

Fitzgerald, E F, S A Hwang, B Bush, K Cook, and P Worswick. 1998. 'Fish Consumption and Breast Milk PCB Concentrations among Mohawk Women at Akwesasne'. *Am J Epidemiol* 148:164–72.

Fung, K, I Luginaah, and K Gorey. 2007. 'Impact of Air Pollution on Hospital Admissions in Southwestern Ontario, Canada: Generating Hypotheses in Sentinel High-Exposure Places'. *Environ Health*; doi:10.1186/1476-069X-6-18 (Online 5 July 2007).

Gallo, M V, L M Schell, A P DeCaprio and A Jacobs. 2011. 'Levels of Persistent Organic Pollutant and Their Predictors among Young Adults'. *Chemosphere* 83:1374–82.

Goncharov, A, R F Haase, A Santiago-Rivera, G Morse, Akwesasne Task Force on the Environment, R J McCaffrey, et al. 2008. 'High Serum PCBs Are Elevation of Serum Lipids and Cardiovascular Disease in a Native American Population'. *Environ Res* 106:226–39.

Goncharov, A, R Rej, S Negoita, M Schymura, A Santiago-Rivera, G Morse, et al. 2009. 'Lower Serum Testosterone Associated with Elevated Polychlorinated Biphenyl Concentrations in Native American Men'. *Environ Health Perspect* 117:1454–60.

Grandjean, P. 2008. 'Late Insights into Early Origins of Disease'. *Basic Clin Pharmacol Toxicol* 102:94–99.

Grijalva, J M. 2011. 'Self-Determining Environmental Justice for Native America'. *Environmental Justice* 4:187–92.

Haase, R, R J McCaffrey, A L Santiago-Rivera, G S Morse and A Tarbel. 2009. 'Evidence of an Age-Related Threshold Effect of Polychlorinated Biphenyls (PCBs) on Neuropsychological Functioning in a Native American Population'. *Environ Res* 109:73–85.

Harding, A, B Harper, D Stone, C O'Neill, P Berger, S Harris and J Donatuto. 2012. 'Conducting Research with Tribal Communities: Sovereignty, Ethics, and Data-Sharing Issues'. *Environ Health Perspect* 120:6–10.

Henifin, K A. 2007. *Toxic Politics at 64N, 171W: Addressing Military Contaminants on St Lawrence Island, Alaska* (PhD Dissertation). Corvallis, OR: Oregon State University.

Hwang, S A, E F Fitzgerald, and B Bush. 1996. 'Exposure to PCBs from Hazardous Waste among Mohawk Women and Infants at Akwesasne'. *J Franklin Inst* 333A:17–23.

Jones, L. 2011. 'Uranium Activities' Impacts on Lakota Territory'. *Indigenous Policy J*. XII. Available: http://02b7adb.netsolhost.com/ipjournal/post/2011/10/21/Uranium-Activities%E2%80%99-Impacts-on-Lakota-Territory.aspx (accessed 27 February 2012).

Kunitz, S J. 2008. 'Changing Patterns of Mortality among American Indians'. *Am J Public Health* 98:404–12.

Landa, E R, and J R Gray. 1995. 'US Geological Survey Research on the Environmental Fate of Uranium Mining and Milling Wastes'. *Environ Geol* 26:19–31.

Luna, Z T. 2010. 'Marching toward Reproductive Justice: Coalitional (Re)framing of the March for Women's Lives'. *Sociol Inq* 80:554–78.

MacDonald, E, and S Rang. 2007. 'Exposing Canada's Chemical Valley: An Investigation of Cumulative Air Pollution Emissions in the Sarnia, Ontario Area. An Ecojustice Report'. Available: http://www.ecojustice.ca/publications/reports/reportexposing-canadas-chemical-valley/attachment (accessed 10 October 2011).

Mackenzie, C A, A Lockridge, and M Keith. 2005. 'Declining Sex Ratio in a First Nation Community'. *Environ Health Perspect* 113:1295–98.

Mascarenhas, M. 2007. 'Where the Waters Divide: First Nations, Tainted Water and Environmental Justice in Canada'. *Local Environ* 12:565–77.

Miller, P K, and J Riordan. 1999. 'I Will Fight Until I Melt [Video]'. Available: http://www.akaction.org/Multimedia/Video/ANNIE_ALOWA_15_6.MOV (accessed 9 October 2012).

Newman, J, M V Gallo, L M Schell, A P DeCaprio, M Denham, G D Deane, et al. 2009. 'Analysis of PCB Congeners Related to Cognitive Functioning in Adolescents'. *Neurotoxicology* 30:686–96.

Rogers, D, and D Petereit. 2005. 'Cancer Disparities Research Partnerships in Lakota Country: Clinical Trials, Patient Services, and Community Education for the Oglala, Rosebud, and Cheyenne River Sioux Tribes'. *Am J Public Health* 95:2129–32.

Ruffin, J. 2011. 'A Renewed Commitment to Environmental Justice in Health Disparities Research'. *Am J Public Health* 101 (suppl 1):S12–S14.

Schell, L M, M V Gallo, M Denham, J Ravenscroft, A P DeCaprio, and D O Carpente. 2008. 'Relationship of Thyroid Hormone Levels to Levels of Polychlorinated Biphenyls, Lead, p,p'-DDE, and Other Toxicants in Akwesasne Mohawk Youth'. *Environ Health Perspect* 116:806–13.

Schell, L M, and A Tarbell. 1998. 'A Partnership Study of PCBs and the Health of Mohawk Youth: Lessons from Our Past and Guidelines for Our Future'. *Environ Health Perspect* 106 (suppl 3):833–40.

Schnarch, B. 2004. 'Ownership, Control, Access, and Possession (OCAP) or Self Determination Research: A Critical Analysis of Contemporary First Nations Research and Some Options for First Nations Communities'. *J Aboriginal Health* 1:80–95.

Sharp, D. 2009. 'Environmental Toxins, a Potential Risk Factor for Diabetes among Canadian Aboriginals'. *Int J Circumpolar Health* 68:316–26.

Shen, E. 2006. 'Reproductive Justice: Towards a Comprehensive Movement'. *Collective Voices* 1:1–3.

SisterSong. 2012. 'Why Is Reproductive Justice Important for Women of Color'? Available: http://www.sistersong.net/index.php?option=com_content&view=article&id=141&Ite mid=81 (accessed 27 February 2012).

Spieler, L. 2010. 'American Indians and Alaska Natives: Breastfeeding Disparities and Resources'. *Breastfeed Med* 5:219–20.

Statistics Canada. 2006. Aboriginal Identity (8), Sex (3) and Age Groups (12) for the Population of Canada, Provinces, Territories, Census Metropolitan Areas and Census Agglomerations, 2006 Census – 20% Sample Data. Available: http://www12.statcan.ca/census-recensement/2006/dp-pd/tbt/Rp-eng.cfm?LANG=E&APATH=3&DETAIL=0&DIM=0&FL=A&FREE=0&GC=0&GID=837928&GK=0&GRP=1&PID=89122&PRID=0&PTYPE=88971,97154&S=0&SHOWALL=0&SUB=0&Temporal=2006&THEME=73&VID=0&VNAMEE=&VNAMEF= (accessed 27 February 2012).

Unger, N. 2004. 'Women, Sexuality and Environmental Justice in American History'. In *New Perspectives on Environmental Justice*, ed R Stein. New Brunswick, NJ: Rutgers University Press, 45–62.

US Commission on Civil Rights. 2004. Native American Health Care Disparities Briefing. Available: http:// www.law.umaryland.edu/marshall/usccr/documents/nativeamerianhealthcaredis.pdf (accessed 1 June 2012).

US EPA (US Environmental Protection Agency). 2004. Tribal Superfund Program Needs Clear Direction and Actions to Improve Effectiveness. Report no. 2004-P-00035. Available: http://www.epa.gov/oig/reports/2004/20040930-2004-P00035.pdf (accessed 30 July 2011).

US EPA (US Environmental Protection Agency). 2012. Environmental Justice Program and Civil Rights. Available: http://www.epa.gov/region1/ej/ (accessed 5 November 2012).

U.S. v. Dann. 1985. 470 U.S. 39. U.S. Supreme Court, Washington, DC, 20 February 1985.

van Buren, M. 2011. 'LANL and Taos Nonprofit Reach Pollution Settlement'. *The Taos News*. Thursday, 5 May 2011. Available: http://www.taosnews.com/news/article_228a8261-66e85269-bac2-38a95c0d993c.html (accessed 10 October 2011).

Wania, F. 2003. 'Assessing the Potential of Persistent Organic Chemicals for Long-Range Transport and Accumulation in Polar Regions'. *Environ Sci Technol* 37:1344–51.

Welfinger-Smith, G, J L Minholz, S Byrne, V Waghiyi, J Gologergen, J Kava, et al. 2011. 'Organochlorine and Metal Contaminants in Traditional Foods from St. Lawrence Island, Alaska'. *J Toxicol Environ Health A* 74:1–20.

SECTION V

Global Justice
Confronting Colonialism and Imperialism

Until the lions have their own historians, the history of the hunt will always glorify the hunter.
—Chinua Achebe

Memory is never a quiet act of introspection or retrospection. It is a painful re-membering, a putting together of the dismembered past to make sense of the trauma of the present.
—Homi Bhabha

The last reading in the previous section addressed Native American women's struggle for the survival of their people, their identity and culture, still suffering from the long-term devastating effects of European colonisation of North America. In fact, colonialism impacted the environment, health, culture and identity of the colonised in every area of the world where Europeans settled. The intersectionality of race, gender and class becomes clear once more in the international context and in the divisions between the Global South and the Global North.

The political end of European colonialism as a result of two world wars and the rise of movements for independence and self-determination did not end cultural imperialism and its effects. The imperial culture was appropriated in projects of countercolonial resistance, thus giving rise to post-colonial literary work as the interaction between colonial and indigenous cultures. As a result, post-colonial theory came into being as a mixture of imperial language and local experience. One may say that the post-colonial condition starts with the onset rather than the end of colonial occupation since the psychological resistance to colonialism begins with its onset, and post-colonial theory is a theoretical resistance to the amnesia of the colonial aftermath and the repression of painful memories of colonial subordination, as expressed in the above quotation by Bhabha. Colonisation, as Said argued, is a 'fate with lasting, indeed grotesquely unfair results'.[1]

Some would date the start of Postcolonial Studies as a discipline in the Western academy from the publication of Edward Said's *Orientalism* in 1978, a critique of Western knowledge and scholarship about the East as generated from false assumptions and marked by a 'subtle and persistent Eurocentric prejudice against Arabo-Islamic peoples and their cultures'.[2] Said argued that a long tradition of romanticised images of Asia and the Middle East in Western culture has served as an implicit justification for European and American colonial and imperial ambitions. These images portray 'Eastern' societies as fundamentally similar to one another, and fundamentally dissimilar to 'Western' societies. This establishes 'the East' as antithetical to 'the West', and the 'Orient' is constructed as a negative inversion of Western culture. As Said puts it, 'Orientalism was ultimately a political vision of reality whose structure promoted the difference between the familiar (Europe, West, "us") and the strange (the Orient, the East, "them")'.[3]

Said showed that the myth of the Oriental was possible because of European political dominance of the Middle East and Asia. Influenced by the French philosopher Michel Foucault, Said argued that Orientalism is a full-fledged discourse, not just a simple idea, and that all knowledge is produced in situations of unequal relations of power. A person who dominates another is the only one in the position to write a book about it, to establish it, to define it. Creating an image of the Orient and a body of knowledge about the Orient and subjecting it to systematic study became the prototype for taking control of the Orient. By taking control of the scholarship, the West also took political and economic control.

It follows, therefore, as Mignolo argues, that philosophy and scholarship must be decolonised. Decolonisation works from the double bind of the 'colonial difference': as Bernasconi writes, 'Western philosophy traps African philosophy in a double bind: either African philosophy is so similar to Western philosophy that it makes no distinctive contribution and effectively disappears; or it is so different that its credentials to be genuine philosophy will always be in doubt'.[4] Decolonisation becomes an undoing of the colonial difference and a redoing, 'another thinking', which includes a critique of Occidentalism from the perspective of the colonial history of North Africa.

Europe, as a body of scholarship that defines how academics view the world, must be returned to its rightful place as one world region amongst many, without the privilege that it has continued to hold in academic circles, where the theory of development presented a linear history where modernity, capitalism and civilisation appear 'first in Europe and then elsewhere'.[5] As Said writes, 'Without examining Orientalism as a discourse one cannot possibly understand the enormously systematic discipline by which European culture was able to manage – and even produce – the Orient politically, sociologically, militarily, ideologically, scientifically, and imaginatively during the post-Enlightenment period'.[6] Similarly, 'Provincializing Europe', suggests Dipesh Chakrabarty, implies that Western social science and the universal ideas of the Enlightenment need to be recognised in their limitations in explaining the historical experiences of political modernity in South Asia.

Aimé Césaire, in *Discourse on Colonialism*, describes the brutal impact of European capitalism and colonialism on both the coloniser and colonised, exposing the contradictions and hypocrisy implicit in Western notions of 'progress' and 'civilisation' upon encountering the 'savage', 'uncultured', or 'primitive'. Like Fanon and Gandhi after him, Césaire calls for the decolonisation of the African mind, the liberation of the colonised people from their imposed sense of inferiority. 'The problem of colonialism includes not only the interrelations of objective historical conditions but also the human attitudes toward these conditions', remarked Fanon.[7] For Fanon, as well as for Gandhi, national and cultural liberation were central to the project of independence, and both addressed the 'inferiority complex' of the colonised that culminates, for Fanon, in the native's desire to be White. Fanon attempted to articulate the cultural and psychological effects of colonialism as they were experienced by those subjected to them. 'How does it feel to be a problem'? as Du Bois put it.[8] What was it like to find oneself transformed into a colonial subject? How does it feel to have your culture devalued and appropriated, your language debased into a vernacular, detached from all forms of power which are accessible and enacted only in a foreign tongue? How does it feel today to be a 'post-colonial subject'? What, in short, has been the human experience of colonialism and decolonisation? What are the psychological effects for both coloniser and colonised? This juxtaposition of the objective with the subjective, of seeing yourself as a subject who is also an object, amounts to what Du Bois described as 'double consciousness'.

Fanon, however, like other critics of colonialism, does not include gender in his discussion of the coloniser and the colonised. As Oyèrónkẹ́ Oyěwùmí reminds us in her book, *The Invention of Women: Making an African Sense of Western Gender Discourses*, the histories of both coloniser and colonised have been written from the male point of view and have marginalised women and their experiences. She demonstrates how the colonial experience threw women 'to the very bottom of a history that was not theirs'.[9] The precolonial seniority system was replaced by a patriarchal system in which women were inferior and subordinate to men, a system that unfortunately survived the demise of colonialism.

How should we respond to the cultural injustices of colonialism? How should we respond to continuing cultural injustice? As previous readings have shown and Oyèrónkẹ́ Oyěwùmí has discussed in her study of Nigeria, injustices that started in a somewhat distant past are still continuing and the effects of colonialism are still present. In his essay, Rajeev Bhargava underlines the importance of coming to terms with the past in a search for ethnocentric biases and truth telling. Every story was told from the standpoint of the coloniser, and the colonised were included only as mere objects, never as subjects. A major conceptual reorientation is needed, a 'provincializing' of Europe, as Chakrabarty suggests. 'It means looking from the other side of the photograph, experiencing how differently things look when you live in Baghdad rather than in Boston and understanding why'.[10] This may involve a financial commitment to research and education and the hiring of people with knowledge and understanding about non-Western cultures. However, indigenous traditions and original cultural forms may not be recovered, and alternative modernities may be reconstructed from the interactions of different cultures on an egalitarian basis. Following Gandhi's example, Bhargava suggests that we must unmask false universals and recognise that we are 'different, unfamiliar, and strange'.[11] Only this way we can find 'a morally acceptable place for each other in our respective cultures'.[12]

The section concludes with two case studies. The first addresses the Japanese colonisation of Korea and the case of the 'Comfort Women' and suggests alternative approaches to reparations from the Japanese state and people to the Korean women. The second case study turns to Cuba and the influence of José Martí's thought on the post-colonial critique of the economic, political and cultural conditions of post-coloniality and the strategies needed to eliminate the effects of colonialism in the Global South.

Notes

1. Edward Said, *Orientalism* (London and New York: Penguin, 1978), 207.
2. Keith Windschuttle, 'Edward Said's *Orientalism* Revisited', *The New Criterion*, January 17, 1999.
3. Said, *Orientalism*, 43.
4. Walter D Mignolo, 'Philosophy and the Colonial Difference', in *Latin American Philosophy: Currents, Issues, Debates*, ed Eduardo Mendieta (Bloomington: Indiana University Press, 2003), 82.
5. Dipesh Chakrabarty, *Provincializing Europe: Postcolonial Thought and Historical Difference* (Princeton, NJ: Princeton University Press, 2000), 8.
6. Said, *Orientalism*, 3.
7. Frantz Fanon, *Black Skin, White Masks* (New York: Grove Press, Inc., 2008), 84.
8. W E B Du Bois, *The Souls of Black Folk* (Boston and New York: Bedford/St Martin, 1997), 37.

9. Oyèrónkẹ́ Oyěwùmí, *The Invention of Women: Making an African Sense of Western Gender Discourses* (Minneapolis: University of Minnesota Press, 1997), 153.
10. Dipesh Chakrabarty, *Provincializing Europe: Postcolonial Thought and Historical Difference* (Princeton, NJ: Princeton University Press, 2000), 243.
11. Rajeev Bhargava, 'Reparations for Cultural Injustice', in *Reparations*, eds Jon Miller and Rahul Kumar (Oxford: Oxford University Press, 2007), 247.
12. Bhargava, 'Reparations for Cultural Injustice', 248.

Suggested Readings

Achebe, Chinua. *Arrow of God*. New York: Doubleday, 1969.
_____. *The Education of a British Protected Child*. New York: Knopf, 2009.
Amin, Samir. *L'eurocentrisme: Critique d'une ideologie*. Paris: Anthropos, 1988.
Appiah, Kwame Anthony. 'There Is No Such Thing as Western Civilization'. *The Guardian*, November 9, 2016.
Bhabha, Homi. *The Location of Culture*. London and New York: Routledge, 1994.
Desai, Gaurav, and Supriya Nair, eds. *Postcolonialisms: An Anthology of Cultural Theory and Criticism*. New Brunswick: Rutgers University Press, 2005.
Desai, Kiran. *The Inheritance of Loss*. New York: Atlantic Monthly Press, 2006.
Etemad, Bouda. *Possessing the World: Taking the Measurements of Colonization from the Eighteenth to the Twentieth Century*. Trans Andrene Everson. New York and Oxford: Berghahn Books, 2007.
Gandhi, Leela. *Postcolonial Theory: Sydney, Australia: A Critical Introduction*. Sydney, Australia: Allen & Unwin, 1998.
Gandhi, Mohandas. *Hind Swaraj and Other Writings*. Cambridge: Cambridge University Press, 1997.
Kincaid, Jamaica. *Annie John*. New York: New American Library, 1986.
_____. *Lucy*. New York: Plume, 1991.
Loomba, Ania. *Colonialism/Postcolonialism*. London and New York: Routledge, 2005.
Lu, Catherine. 'Colonialism as Structural Injustice: Historical Responsibility and Contemporary Redress'. *Journal of Political Philosophy* 19 (2011): 261–81.
Lugones, Maria. 'Toward a Decolonial Feminism'. *Hypatia* 25, no. 4 (Fall 2010): 742–59.
McLeod, John, ed. *The Routledge Companion to Postcolonial Studies*. London and New York: Routledge, 2007.
Myhre, Knut Christian. 'The Bookseller of Kabul'. *Anthropology Today* 20, no. 3 (June 2004): 19–22.
Roy, Arundhati. *Walking with the Comrades*. New York: Penguin: 2011.
Soyinka, Wole. *Death and the King's Horseman*. New York: Norton, 2003.
Spivak, Gayatri Chakravorty. 'Can the Subaltern Speak'? In *The Post-Colonial Studies Reader*, eds Bill Ashcroft, Gareth Griffith, and Helen Tiffin. London and New York: Routledge, 1995, 24–28.
Tan, Kok-Chor. 'Colonialism, Reparations and Global Justice'. In *Reparations*, eds Jon Miller and Rahul Kumar. Oxford and New York: Oxford University Press, 2007.
Ypi, Lea. 'What's Wrong with Colonialism'? *Philosophy and Public Affairs* 41, no. 2 (2013): 158–91.

Suggested Documentaries and Films

Asante, Amma, dir. *A United Kingdom.* BBC Films, 2016. DVD. The story of King Seretse Khama of Botswana and how his loving but controversial marriage to a British white woman, Ruth Williams, put his kingdom into political and diplomatic turmoil.

Chadwick, Justin, dir. *Mandela: Long Walk to Freedom.* Pathe, 2013. DVD. A chronicle of Nelson Mandela's life journey from his childhood in a rural village through to his inauguration as the first democratically elected president of South Africa.

George, Terry, dir. *Hotel Rwanda.* United Artists, 2004. DVD. It recounts the efforts of hotelier Paul Rusesabagina to save his family and others during the Rwandan Civil War, a conflict beginning in 1990 between the Hutu-led government and the Rwandan Patriotic Front (RPF), which largely consisted of Tutsi refugees whose families had fled to Uganda after the 1959 Hutu revolt against colonial rule. The film is a harrowing portrayal of a country losing itself in chaos as the international community looked away.

Noyce, Phillip, dir. *Rabbit-Proof Fence.* Rumbalara Films, 2002. DVD. A 2002 film showing the policies by the Australian government to remove Aboriginal children of mixed race by force from their families and raise them in training schools that would prepare them for lives as factory workers or domestic servants. The children affected are known today in Australia as the Stolen Generation.

Peck, Raoul, dir. *Lumumba.* Jacques Bidou, 2000. DVD. The true story of controversial leader of independent Congo, Patrice Lumumba.

Pontecorvo, Ponte, dir. *The Battle of Algiers.* Rizzoli, Rialto Pictures, 1966. DVD. Filmed in a semi-documentary format, this film deals with the battle of Algiers (1956–1957), part of the broader fight for Algerian independence (1954–1962) from French colonial rule.

Rouch, Jean, dir. *Moi, un Noir.* Les Films de la Pléiade, 1958. DVD. *I, a Negro* depicts young Nigerian immigrants who left their country to find work in the Ivory Coast, in the Treichville quarter of Abidjan, the capital.

Rouch, Jean, dir. *The Human Pyramid.* Les Films de la Pléiade, 1961. DVD. Rouch meets with white colonial French high school students and their black African classmates (all non-actors) and persuades them to improvise a drama about integrating the mutually wary groups.

Walter D Mignolo[*], 'Philosophy and the Colonial Difference'

In the fifties, the distinguished ethno-historian and expert on ancient Mexico Miguel León-Portilla published his classic book, *La filosofía Nahuatl* (Nahuatl philosophy).[1] He did not have to wait long for criticism, and one of the major attacks concerned his 'imprudent' use of the term 'philosophy' to designate something that the Aztecs or Nahuatl-speaking people could have been engaged in. But the criticisms were ambiguous. The 'lack' of philosophical discourse among the Aztecs could have meant that they were 'barbarians', uncivilized, or undeveloped. On the

---

[*] Walter D Mignolo, 'Philosophy and the Colonial Difference', in *Latin American Philosophy: Currents, Issues, Debates*, ed Eduardo Mendieta (Bloomington: Indiana University Press, 2003), 80–86. Copyright by *Philosophy Today*.

other hand, it could have meant just that they were 'different'. In this case, Nahuatl-speaking people may not have had 'philosophy', but the 'difference' should not be considered a lack but an assertion that they had or did something else. Europeans, in turn, did not have whatever that 'something' else could have been. In another study, León-Portilla reflected on the social role of the *tlamatini*. He did not translate this social role as 'philosopher' but described it as 'those who have the power of the word'.[2] León-Portilla, like others, had difficulties in defining what philosophy is so that he could then show that the Aztec or Nahuatl-speaking people indeed had it. He managed, however, to give an acceptable picture of what philosophy was for the Greeks and then matched it with the remains of Aztec documentation from the early sixteenth century, before Cortes's arrival in Mexico-Tenochtitlan.

León-Portilla overlooked the fact that philosophy, in Greece, went together with the emergence of what is today considered the Western alphabet and Western literacy. Indeed, if I had to define what philosophy is (following the Greek legacy), I would begin by saying that it is something that is linked to writing and to alphabetic writing. I would add that it was alphabetic writing, linked to the concept of philosophy, that allowed Western men of letters, from the sixteenth century on, to establish the difference between philosophy and other forms of knowledge. There is a caveat in this argument, however: the Arabic language and the Arabic early contact with and translation of philosophical texts from Greek to Arabic. I will not pursue this point, since I am concentrating on Latin America, but it is indeed an issue to keep in mind for an understanding of the emergence of the colonial difference.

Beyond overlooking the complicity of alphabetic writing in the Western self-description of philosophy, León-Portilla accepted without further question (and here he is not alone) that philosophy is a Greek invention and the natural point of reference for deciding whether something is or is not philosophy. We could certainly extend this argument to other practices. But let us stay with philosophy. So, the argument goes, philosophy did not exist before the Greeks invented it. Therefore, communities or civilizations before the Greeks, or even having simultaneous histories after the Greeks, invented philosophy but, with not much contact between them, did not have philosophy – such as the Aztecs in the early sixteenth century, for example, or the Chinese, before the Greeks and during the Greek golden age of philosophical thinking. There is something odd in this historiographical picture, particularly because it is the result of an argument that positions philosophy as a good thing to have, a crucial achievement of which other cultures have been or are deprived.

You may be wondering at this point, what does all of this have to do with Latin American philosophy? A great deal, indeed, since I am talking around the colonial difference, and the colonial difference came into being during the so-called conquest of America, which is, in a different macro-narrative, the emergence of the Atlantic commercial circuit and of the modern/colonial world. But to explain this, I have to stay a little longer with the famous Greeks. Why, indeed, did León-Portilla title his book *La filosofía Nahuatl*, and why did people react to this title by asking whether Nahuatl-speaking people did or did not have philosophy? Why is Greek philosophy the reference point? And if Greek philosophy is not the reference point, then, what are we talking about? Perhaps we should change the perspective from which we think about this issue. Instead of assuming that there is something like philosophy, that the Greeks invented it, and that, thereafter, the rest of the planet had to deal with it, we should first ask, What was the 'thing' that the Greeks called philosophy? Second, we should ask why, once the Greeks invented it, philosophy was appropriated by the West (since the Arabs were 'first' to translate and pursue it) and then converted into a point of reference to establish borders between philosophy and its difference. Well, I am arguing that 'philosophy and its difference' became an issue in the sixteenth century and that the issue was the making of the colonial difference.

Now, I do not know whether before the sixteenth century the problem encountered by León-Portilla was a common one. It may have been. Certainly, communities had their self-description and many ways of distinguishing themselves from other communities. But never before the sixteenth century had the differentiation acquired the dimension that it had in the modern/colonial world, a world that was made, shaped, and controlled by European powers, from the Spanish to the British empires and through Dutch, French and German colonialism. The European Renaissance (in southern Europe) and then the European Enlightenment (in northern Europe) did two things simultaneously. First, the self-image of the West began to be built by constructing the macro-narrative of Western civilization; second, the colonial difference began to be built with the philosophical debate around the humanity of the Amerindians. Certainly, Vitoria, Sepulveda, and las Casas did not ask themselves whether the Amerindians had philosophy. They assumed that they did not. And in this respect, León-Portilla made a brave and important move by assuming that there was a Nahuatl philosophy. But the problem lies elsewhere.

I am arguing that the problem León-Portilla had is the problem of the colonial difference. His contribution was bringing it to the foreground, even though, at that time (1959), the philosophical debate around decolonization was just at its inception. Frantz Fanon's *The Wretched of the Earth* was published in 1961. We will discuss why the debate around decolonization is important below. First, though, let's remember that León-Portilla's dilemma was not a problem for sixteenth-century Spanish philosophers or, even less, for eighteenth-century French philosophers, as we know because of the 'debates on the New World' and Hegel's follow-up in his lessons on the philosophy of history. León-Portilla is Mexican, while Sepúlveda et al. were Spaniards, and the eighteenth-century philosophers, including Hegel, were either French, German, or British. This is not a problem of nationality, but of local histories – and of local histories from where you 'feel' and 'think', whether philosophically or not. León-Portilla may have felt the colonial difference when he decided to write *Nahuatl Philosophy*.

But what is this colonial difference? Robert Bernasconi is a specialist in Continental philosophy, and well versed in Heidegger, Levinas, and Derrida. Reflecting on the challenges that African philosophy currently poses to Continental philosophy, Bernasconi states, 'Western philosophy traps African philosophy in a double bind: either African philosophy is so similar to Western philosophy that it makes no distinctive contribution and effectively disappears; or it is so different that its credentials to be genuine philosophy will always be in doubt'.[3] Now, I am quoting Bernasconi not as an authority, to stamp with his quotation what I have been arguing so far, but as an ethnographic informant. Furthermore, I think that the elegance and force of his argument allow precisely for that. Otherwise, his argument would have been made at the pure level of the enunciated without putting at risk the very act of enunciation. That is, Bernasconi would have maintained the philosophical authority of someone who reports the difference without putting himself or herself at risk in the act of reporting. I am quoting Bernasconi because of the double bind in which Western philosophy has placed African philosophy. That double bind is the colonial difference, and the structure of power that maintains it is the coloniality of power. León-Portilla did not articulate the issue in that way. He argued for the existence of Nahuatl philosophy because Nahuatl philosophy has been negated since the very inception of conquest and colonization. What did his critics do? They questioned the pertinence of attributing philosophy to the Nahuatls. Which means that the quarrel was prompted by the colonial difference, the double bind between an excessive similarity and an excessive difference. Where do we go from here? Decolonization of philosophy and, more generally, of cultures of scholarship still seems to be a viable project. I quote Bernasconi again, this time on decolonization. What is new here is that as an expert in Continental philosophy he has heard the claim that philosophers, social scientists, and humanists in the Third World have been making for at least thirty years:

> The existential dimension of African philosophy's challenge to Western philosophy in general and Continental philosophy in particular is located in the need to decolonize the mind. This task is at least as important for the colonizer as it is for the colonized. For Africans, decolonizing the mind takes place not only in facing the experience of colonialism, but also in recognizing the precolonial, which establishes the destructive importance of so-called ethnophilosophy and sage philosophy, as well as nationalist-ideological philosophy.[4]

Decolonization, in the project of Moroccan philosopher Abdelkebir Khatibi, is the hidden side of the moon, the darker side of modernization. In its nineteenth-century version, modernization was linked to the civilizing mission; after World War II, it was linked to developmental ideology; and in the nineties it was linked to globalization and the market ideology, yet its hidden side was, and still is, colonization. While imperialism and globalization place the accent on the hegemonic forces of regulation and control, colonization (or, better, coloniality of power) places the accent on the receiving end of imperial and global designs. That is why decolonization as a project is most likely to come from the receiving end of global designs than from the local histories where global designs are drawn and implemented. For Khatibi, if decolonization is the darker side of modernization, it is also the irreducible complement of deconstruction. Khatibi conceived decolonization as a double critique, of Western and Islamic fundamentalism – a step that is beyond deconstruction, since deconstruction remains a critique of Western logocentrism by Western logocentrism itself.[5] In this sense, deconstruction runs parallel to postmodern critiques of modernity. Decolonization, as double critique, instead presupposes the colonial difference. It works precisely from the colonial difference, from the double bind between assimilation (say, Arabic philosophy is so similar to Western philosophy that it makes no contribution) and marginalization (it is so different that its credentials will be always in doubt). Decolonization, for Khatibi, is simultaneously an undoing and a redoing: an undoing (double critique) of the colonial difference and a redoing in terms of what I have elsewhere called 'border thinking',[6] as the ground of future epistemologies and political projects. Khatibi calls it *'une pensée autre'*, 'another thinking', emerging from a double critique but, also, as a critique of Occidentalism from the perspective of the colonial history of North Africa, from the Spanish in the sixteenth century to the French in the nineteenth.

In Latin America, decolonization of scholarship arose in the middle to late sixties, with the impact of Frantz Fanon and of political decolonization in Asia and Africa. Philosophy of liberation was the philosophical version of what later became identified as decolonization. . . .

If we think back to León-Portilla's book, we may see that it opened up a can of worms that, unfortunately, went unnoticed in Latin American philosophical circles, even in the late sixties, when the question of whether there was a Latin American philosophy occupied the minds of philosophers. There was a parallel, at that time, between sub-Saharan African and Latin American philosophers who were becoming aware of the colonial difference. For to ask 'Is there an African or a Latin American philosophy'? is to respond to the demands of the colonial difference. León-Portilla did it in this way, as an ethno-cultural historian and not as a philosopher. He did not ask whether the Nahuatl had philosophy. He assumed that they did, but in doing so, he had to make an enormous effort to put the Nahuatls next to the Greeks and then defend his move to his ferocious critics – that is, to the 'malaise' produced by the colonial difference.

Now, the cards are on the table. Philosophy is a regional and historical practice, initiated in Greece and taken up by and in the making of Europe, from the Renaissance to the Enlightenment. Coupled with religious and economic expansion, philosophy became the yardstick by which other ways of thinking are measured. Perspectives have been changing, and now 'philosophy' is located on the edge of the colonial difference. It is recognized because Western expansion has touched every corner of the planet, and displaced because what is good for one local history is not necessarily good for other local histories. To think from the colonial difference means, today, assuming philosophy as a regional practice and simultaneously thinking against and beyond its normative and disciplinary regulations.[7] After all, it was to a certain way of 'thinking' that the Greeks called philosophy. In that sense, philosophy may have been invented by the Greeks, but thinking goes well beyond the Greeks – and beyond philosophy itself. The future demands thinking beyond the Greeks and Eurocentrism. Raúl Fornet-Betancourt, a Cuban philosopher residing in Germany, proposed 'intercultural philosophy' to solve some of the puzzles presented by the colonial difference.[8] It is certainly a way of dealing with thinking beyond Eurocentrism. However, one of the issues that should be confronted is the translation of 'cultural differences' into colonial differences and vice versa. The double translation will show that the very concept of 'culture' is a colonial construction and that, indeed, 'cultural difference' is the effect and the work of coloniality of power. Or, if you wish, 'cultural difference' is basically a semantic question, while 'colonial difference' underlines power relations, the coloniality of power, in the very making of cultural differences. The colonial difference is the underlying logic, and power relations holding together cultural differences have been articulated by the coloniality of power, from early Christian global designs to the current global coloniality driven by the metaphysics of the market. Intellectual decolonization, and in the case at hand the decolonization of philosophy, could help to undo the colonial difference and imagine possible futures beyond the alternative offered by global coloniality and the current reproduction (mass finances, mass mediation, mass migration) of the colonial difference.

Notes

1. Miguel León-Portilla, *La filosofía Nahuatl* (Mexico City: Universidad Autonoma de Mexico, 1956).
2. Miguel León-Portilla, *Major Trends in Mexican Philosophy*, translated by A Robert Caponigri (Notre Dame: University of Notre Dame Press, 1966). For philosophy in the Andes, see also Walter D Mignolo, 'Decir es fuera de lugar sujetos dicentes, roles sociales y formas de inscripción', *Revista de crítica literaria latinoamericana* 41 (1995): 9–32.
3. Robert Bernasconi, 'African Philosophy's Challenge to Continental Philosophy', in *Postcolonial African Philosophy: A Critical Reader* (Oxford: Blackwell, 1997), 188.
4. Bernasconi, 'African Philosophy's Challenge to Continental Philosophy', 191.
5. Abdelkebir Khatibi, 'Double Critique: I. Décolonisation de la sociologie'. In Abdelkebir Khatibi, *Maghreb Pluriel*, ed Emmanuel Chukwudi Eze (Paris: Denoël, 1983), 43–63.
6. Walter D Mignolo, *Local Histories/Global Designs. Coloniality, Subaltern Knowledge and Border Thinking* (Princeton, NJ: Princeton University Press, 2000).

7. Augusto Salazar Bondy, *Existe una filosofía en Nuestra America?* (Mexico City: Siglo XXI, 1996 [1968]).
8. See Chukwudi Eze, *Postcolonial African Philosophy*; Enrique Dussel, *The Underside of Modernity: Apel, Ricoeur, Rorty, Taylor and the Philosophy of Liberation*, trans and ed by Eduardo Mendieta (Atlantic Highlands, NJ: Humanities Press International, 1996); Enrique Dussel, *Postmodernidad y Transmodernidad. Dialogos con la filosofía de Gianni Vattimo* (México: Universidad Iberoamericana, 1999).
9. Raúl Fornet-Betancourt, *Filosofía Intercultural* (Mexico City: Universidad Pontifica de Mexico, 1994).

Dipesh Chakrabarty[*], 'The Idea of Provincializing Europe'

Provincializing Europe is not a book about the region of the world we call 'Europe'. That Europe, one could say, has already been provincialized by history itself. Historians have long acknowledged that the so-called European age in modern history began to yield place to other regional and global configurations toward the middle of the twentieth century.[1] European history is no longer seen as embodying anything like a 'universal human history'.[2] No major Western thinker, for instance, has publicly shared Francis Fukuyama's 'vulgarized Hegelian historicism' that saw in the fall of the Berlin wall a common end for the history of all human beings.[3] The contrast with the past seems sharp when one remembers the cautious but warm note of approval with which Kant once detected in the French Revolution a 'moral disposition in the human race' or Hegel saw the imprimatur of the 'world spirit' in the momentousness of that event.[4]

I am by training a historian of modern South Asia, which forms my archive and is my site of analysis. The Europe I seek to provincialize or decenter is an imaginary figure that remains deeply embedded in *clichéd and shorthand forms* in some everyday habits of thought that invariably subtend attempts in the social sciences to address questions of political modernity in South Asia.[5] The phenomenon of 'political modernity' – namely, the rule by modern institutions of the state, bureaucracy, and capitalist enterprise – is impossible to *think* of anywhere in the world without invoking certain categories and concepts, the genealogies of which go deep into the intellectual and even theological traditions of Europe.[6] Concepts such as citizenship, the state, civil society, public sphere, human rights, equality before the law, the individual, distinctions between public and private, the idea of the subject, democracy, popular sovereignty, social justice, scientific rationality, and so on all bear the burden of European thought and history. One simply cannot think of political modernity without these and other related concepts that found a climactic form in the course of the European Enlightenment and the nineteenth century.

These concepts entail an unavoidable – and in a sense indispensable – universal and secular vision of the human. The European colonizer of the nineteenth century both preached this Enlightenment humanism at the colonized and at the same time denied it in practice. But

---

[*] Dipesh Chakrabarty, *Provincializing Europe: Postcolonial Thought and Historical Difference* (Princeton: Princeton University Press, 2000), 3–6. Copyright by Princeton University Press.

the vision has been powerful in its effects. It has historically provided a strong foundation on which to erect – both in Europe and outside – critiques of socially unjust practices. Marxist and liberal thought are legatees of this intellectual heritage. This heritage is now global. The modern Bengali educated middle classes – to which I belong and fragments of whose history I recount later in the book – have been characterized by Tapan Raychaudhuri as the 'the first Asian social group of any size whose mental world was transformed through its interactions with the West'.[7] A long series of illustrious members of this social group – from Raja Rammohun Roy, sometimes called 'the father of modern India', to Manabendranath Roy, who argued with Lenin in the Comintern – warmly embraced the themes of rationalism, science, equality, and human rights that the European Enlightenment promulgated.[8] Modern social critiques of caste, oppressions of women, the lack of rights for laboring and subaltern classes in India, and so on – and, in fact, the very critique of colonialism itself – are unthinkable except as a legacy, partially, of how Enlightenment Europe was appropriated in the subcontinent. The Indian constitution tellingly begins by repeating certain universal Enlightenment themes celebrated, say, in the American constitution. And it is salutary to remember that the writings of the most trenchant critic of the institution of 'untouchability' in British India refer us back to some originally European ideas about liberty and human equality.[9]

I too write from within this inheritance. Postcolonial scholarship is committed, almost by definition, to engaging the universals – such as the abstract figure of the human or that of Reason – that were forged in eighteenth-century Europe and that underlie the human sciences. This engagement marks, for instance, the writing of the Tunisian philosopher and historian Hichem Djait, who accuses imperialist Europe of 'deny[ing] its own vision of man'.[10] Fanon's struggle to hold on to the Enlightenment idea of the human – even when he knew that European imperialism had reduced that idea to the figure of the settler-colonial white man – is now itself a part of the global heritage of all postcolonial thinkers.[11] The struggle ensues because there is no easy way of dispensing with these universals in the condition of political modernity. Without them there would be no social science that addresses issues of modern social justice.

This engagement with European thought is also called forth by the fact that today the so-called European intellectual tradition is the only one alive in the social science departments of most, if not all, modern universities. I use the word 'alive' in a particular sense. It is only within some very particular traditions of thinking that we treat fundamental thinkers who are long dead and gone not only as people belonging to their own times but also as though they were our own contemporaries. In the social sciences, these are invariably thinkers one encounters within the tradition that has come to call itself 'European' or 'Western'. I am aware that an entity called 'the European intellectual tradition' stretching back to the ancient Greeks is a fabrication of relatively recent European history. Martin Bernal, Samir Amin, and others have justly criticized the claim of European thinkers that such an unbroken tradition ever existed or that it could even properly be called 'European'.[12] The point, however, is that, fabrication or not, this is the genealogy of thought in which social scientists find themselves inserted. Faced with the task of analyzing developments or social practices in modern India, few if any Indian social scientists or social scientists of India would argue seriously with, say, the thirteenth-century logician Gangesa or with the grammarian and linguistic philosopher Bartrihari (fifth to sixth centuries), or with the tenth- or eleventh-century aesthetician Abhinavagupta. Sad though it is, one result of European colonial rule in South Asia is that the intellectual traditions once unbroken and alive in Sanskrit or Persian or Arabic are now only matters of historical research for most – perhaps all – modern social scientists in the region.[13] They treat these traditions as truly dead, as history. Although categories that were once subject to detailed theoretical contemplation and inquiry now exist as practical concepts, bereft of any theoretical lineage, embedded in quotidian practices in South Asia, contemporary social scientists of South Asia seldom have the training that would enable them to make these concepts into resources for critical thought for the present. And yet past European thinkers and their categories are never quite dead for us in the same way. South Asian(ist) social scientists would argue passionately with a Marx or a Weber without feeling any need to historicize them or to place them in their European intellectual contexts. Sometimes – though this is rather rare – they would even argue with the ancient or medieval or early-modern predecessors of these European theorists.

Yet the very history of politicization of the population, or the coming of political modernity, in countries outside of the Western capitalist democracies of the world produces a deep irony in the history of the political. This history challenges us to rethink two conceptual gifts of nineteenth-century Europe, concepts integral to the idea of modernity. One is historicism – the idea that to understand anything it has to be seen both as a unity and in its historical development – and the other is the very idea of the political. What historically enables a project such as that of 'provincializing Europe' is the experience of political modernity in a country like India. European thought has a contradictory relationship to such an instance of political modernity. It is both indispensable and inadequate in helping us to think through the various life practices that constitute the political and the historical in India. Exploring – on both theoretical and factual registers – this simultaneous indispensability and inadequacy of social science thought is the task this book has set itself....

Notes

1. See, for instance, Oscar Halecki, *The Limits and Divisions of European History* (Notre Dame, IN: University of Notre Dame Press, 1962), chapter 2 and passim.
2. Janet Abu-Lughod, *Before European Hegemony: The World System A.D. 1250–1350* (New York and Oxford: Oxford University Press, 1989); Eric Wolf, *Europe and the People without History* (Berkeley and Los Angeles: University of California Press, 1982); K N Chaudhuri, *Asia before Europe: Economy and Civilisation of the Indian Ocean from the Rise of Islam to 1750* (Cambridge: Cambridge University Press, 1990). Among more recent titles, see J M Blaut, *The Colonizer's Model of the World: Geographical Diffusionism and Eurocentric History* (New York, London: Guilford Press, 1993); Martin W Lewis and Karen E Wigen, *The Myth of Continents: A Critique of Metageography* (Berkeley and Los Angeles: University of California Press, 1997). See also Sanjay Subrahmanyam, 'Connected Histories: Notes towards a Reconfiguration of Early Modern Eurasia', *Modern Asian Studies* 31, no 3 (1997): 735–62.
3. Michael Roth, 'The Nostalgic Nest at the End of History', in his *The Ironist's Cage: Memory, Trauma and the Construction of History* (New York: Columbia University Press, 1995), 163–74.
4. Immanuel Kant, 'An Old Question Raised Again: Is the Human Race Constantly Progressing?' in his *The Conflict of Faculties*, translated by Mary J Gregor (Lincoln and London: University of Nebraska Press, 1992), 153. Jean Hyppolite, *Genesis and Structure of Hegel's 'Phenomenology of Spirit'*, translated by Samuel Cherniak and John Heckman (Evanston: Northwestern University Press, 1974), 426. See also Charles Taylor, *Hegel* (Cambridge: Cambridge University Press, 1978), 416–21.

5. It is important to keep in mind that it is not my purpose here to discuss the long history and genealogy of the fundamental categories of European social and political thought. Two such possible genealogies, for example, of the 'public sphere' and the 'civil society' are Jürgen Habermas, *The Structural Transformation of the Public Sphere: An Inquiry into a Category of Bourgeois Society*, translated by Thomas Burger and Frederick Lawrence (Cambridge: MIT Press, 1989), and Dominique Colas, *Civil Society and Fanaticism: Conjoined Histories*, translated by Amy Jacobs (Stanford: Stanford University Press, 1997). But these genealogies are completely 'internalist' accounts of European intellectual history. For a postcolonial history of European (French) thought, see Alice Bullard, *Constellations of Civilization and Savagery: New Caledonia and France 1770–1900* (forthcoming).
6. I distinguish here between thought and practice. To be a member of the parliamentary body in India does not require one to know the history of anything called 'the parliament' in any depth. Yet a textbook explaining to the children of India what the role of 'the parliament' is would find it impossible to address this task without some engagement with European history.
7. Tapan Raychaudhuri, *Europe Reconsidered: Perceptions of the West in Nineteenth Century Bengal* (Delhi: Oxford University Press, 1988), ix.
8. On Rammohun Roy, see V C Joshi, ed, *Raja Rammohun Roy and the Process of Modernization in India* (Delhi: Nehru Memorial Museum and Library, 1973); on M N Roy, see Sanjay Seth, *Marxist Theory and Nationalist Politics: The Case of Colonial India* (Delhi: Sage Publications, 1995).
9. See the last chapter of this book.
10. Hichem Djait, *Europe and Islam: Cultures and Modernity*, translated by Peter Heinegg (Berkeley and Los Angeles: University of California Press, 1985), 101.
11. See the conclusion to Frantz Fanon, *The Wretched of the Earth*, translated by Constance Farrington (New York: Grove Press, 1963).
12. See Martin Bernal, *The Black Athena: The Afroasiatic Roots of Classical Civilization*, vol 1 (London: Vintage, 1991); Samir Amin, *Eurocentrism*, translated by Russell Moore (New York: Zed, 1989), 91–92, on 'the myths of Greek ancestry'. I understand that several of Bernal's claims are being disputed in the scholarship today. But his point about the contributions made by non-Greek persons to so-called Greek thought remains.
13. This is not to deny the fact that Sanskrit learning enjoyed a brief renaissance under British rule in the early part of the nineteenth century. But this revival of Sanskrit should not be confused with the question of survival of an intellectual tradition. Modern research and studies in Sanskrit have on the whole been undertaken within the intellectual frameworks of the European human sciences. Sheldon Pollock's forthcoming book, *The Language of the Gods in the World of Men: Sanskrit and Power to 1500*, directly engages with the problematic intellectual legacies of this practice. See also Pollock's forthcoming essays 'The Death of Sanskrit', in *Comparative Studies in Society and History*, and 'The New Intellectuals of Seventeenth-Century India', in *Indian Economic and Social History Review*. See also John D Kelly, 'What Was Sanskrit for? Metadiscursive Strategies in Ancient India'; Sheldon Pollock, 'The Sanskrit Cosmopolis, 300–1300 C.E.: Transculturation, Vernacularization, and the Question of Ideology'; and Saroja Bhate, 'Position of Sanskrit in Public Education and Scientific Research in Modern India', all in Jan E M Houben, ed, *Ideology and Status of Sanskrit* (Leiden, New York, Cologne: E Brill, 1996), 87–107, 197–247, and 383–400, respectively. The very use of the word *ideology* in the title of this book would appear to support my thesis. Similar points could be made with respect to

scholarship and intellectual traditions available, say, in the eighteenth century in Persian and Arabic. I am, unfortunately, less aware of contemporary research of this problem with respect to these two languages. I also acknowledge the highly respectable line of modern scholars of Indian philosophy who over generations have attempted conversations between European and Indian traditions of thought. Two contemporary exemplars of this tradition would be J N Mohanty and the late B K Matilal. But, sadly, their thinking has yet to have any major impact on social science studies of South Asia.

Aimé Césaire*, 'Discourse on Colonialism'

A civilization that proves incapable of solving the problems it creates is a decadent civilization.

A civilization that chooses to close its eyes to its most crucial problems is a stricken civilization.

A civilization that uses its principles for trickery and deceit is a dying civilization.

The fact is that the so-called European civilization – 'Western' civilization – as it has been shaped by two centuries of bourgeois rule, is incapable of solving the two major problems to which its existence has given rise: the problem of the proletariat and the colonial problem; that Europe is unable to justify itself either before the bar of 'reason' or before the bar of 'conscience'; and that, increasingly, it takes refuge in a hypocrisy which is all the more odious because it is less and less likely to deceive.

Europe is indefensible.

Apparently that is what the American strategists are whispering to each other.

That in itself is not serious.

What is serious is that 'Europe' is morally, spiritually indefensible.

And today the indictment is brought against it not by the European masses alone, but on a world scale, by tens and tens of millions of men who, from the depths of slavery, set themselves up as judges.

The colonialists may kill in Indochina, torture in Madagascar, imprison in Black Africa, crack down in the West Indies. Henceforth the colonized know that they have an advantage over them. They know that their temporary 'masters' are lying.

Therefore that their masters are weak.

And since I have been asked to speak about colonization and civilization, let us go straight to the principal lie which is the source of all the others.

Colonization and civilization?

In dealing with this subject, the commonest curse is to be the dupe in good faith of a collective hypocrisy that cleverly misrepresents problems, the better to legitimize the hateful solutions provided for them.

In other words, the essential thing here is to see clearly, to think clearly – that is, dangerously – and to answer clearly the innocent first question: what, fundamentally, is colonization? To agree on what it is not: neither evangelization, nor a philanthropic enterprise, nor a desire to push back the frontiers of ignorance, disease, and tyranny, nor a project undertaken for the greater glory of God, nor an attempt to extend the rule of law. To admit once for all, without flinching at the consequences, that the decisive actors here are the adventurer and the pirate, the wholesale grocer and the ship owner, the gold digger and the merchant, appetite

* Aimé Césaire, *Discourse on Colonialism* (New York: Monthly Review Press, 1972), 9–12, 20–25. Copyright by Monthly Review Press.

and force, and behind them, the baleful projected shadow of a form of civilization which, at a certain point in its history, finds itself obliged, for internal reasons, to extend to a world scale the competition of its antagonistic economies.

Pursuing my analysis, I find that hypocrisy is of recent date; that neither Cortés discovering Mexico from the top of the great teocalli, nor Pizarro before Cuzco (much less Marco Polo before Cambaluc), claims that he is the harbinger of a superior order; that they kill; that they plunder; that they have helmets, lances, cupidities; that the slavering apologists came later; that the chief culprit in this domain is Christian pedantry, which laid down the dishonest equations *Christianity = civilization, paganism = savagery*, from which there could not but ensue abominable colonialist and racist consequences, whose victims were to be the Indians, the yellow peoples, and the Negroes.

That being settled, I admit that it is a good thing to place different civilizations in contact with each other; that it is an excellent thing to blend different worlds; that whatever its own particular genius may be, a civilization that withdraws into itself atrophies; that for civilizations, exchange is oxygen; that the great good fortune of Europe is to have been a crossroads, and that because it was the locus of all ideas, the receptacle of all philosophies, the meeting place of all sentiments, it was the best center for the redistribution of energy.

But then I ask the following question: Has colonization really *placed civilizations in contact*? Or, if you prefer, of all the ways of *establishing contact*, was it the best?

I answer *no*.

And I say that between *colonization* and *civilization* there is an infinite distance; that out of all the colonial expeditions that have been undertaken, out of all the colonial statutes that have been drawn up, out of all the memoranda that have been despatched by all the ministries, there could not come a single human value. . . .

I see clearly what colonization has destroyed: the wonderful Indian civilizations – and neither Deterding nor Royal Dutch nor Standard Oil will ever console me for the Aztecs and the Incas.

I see clearly the civilizations, condemned to perish at a future date, into which it has introduced a principle of ruin: the South Sea Islands, Nigeria, Nyasaland. I see less clearly the contributions it has made.

Security? Culture? The rule of law? In the meantime, I look around and wherever there are colonizers and colonized face to face, I see force, brutality, cruelty, sadism, conflict, and, in a parody of education, the hasty manufacture of a few thousand subordinate functionaries, 'boys', artisans, office clerks, and interpreters necessary for the smooth operation of business.

I spoke of contact.

Between colonizer and colonized there is room only for forced labor, intimidation, pressure, the police, taxation, theft, rape, compulsory crops, contempt, mistrust, arrogance, self-complacency, swinishness, brainless élites, degraded masses.

No human contact, but relations of domination and submission which turn the colonizing man into a classroom monitor, an army sergeant, a prison guard, a slave driver, and the indigenous man into an instrument of production.

My turn to state an equation: colonization = 'thingification'.

I hear the storm. They talk to me about progress, about 'achievements', diseases cured, improved standards of living.

I am talking about societies drained of their essence, cultures trampled underfoot, institutions undermined, lands confiscated, religions smashed, magnificent artistic creations destroyed, extraordinary *possibilities* wiped out.

They throw facts at my head, statistics, mileages of roads, canals, and railroad tracks.

I am talking about thousands of men sacrificed to the Congo-Océan.¹ I am talking about those who, as I write this, are digging the harbor of Abidjan by hand. I am talking about millions of men torn from their gods, their land, their habits, their life – from life, from the dance, from wisdom.

I am talking about millions of men in whom fear has been cunningly instilled, who have been taught to have an inferiority complex, to tremble, kneel, despair, and behave like flunkeys.

They dazzle me with the tonnage of cotton or cocoa that has been exported, the acreage that has been planted with olive trees or grapevines.

I am talking about natural *economies* that have been disrupted – harmonious and viable *economies* adapted to the indigenous population – about food crops destroyed, malnutrition permanently introduced, agricultural development oriented solely toward the benefit of the metropolitan countries, about the looting of products, the looting of raw materials.

They pride themselves on abuses eliminated.

I too talk about abuses, but what I say is that on the old ones – very real – they have superimposed others – very detestable. They talk to me about local tyrants brought to reason; but I note that in general the old tyrants get on very well with the new ones, and that there has been established between them, to the detriment of the people, a circuit of mutual services and complicity.

They talk to me about civilization, I talk about proletarianization and mystification.

For my part, I make a systematic defense of the non-European civilizations.

Every day that passes, every denial of justice, every beating by the police, every demand of the workers that is drowned in blood, every scandal that is hushed up, every punitive expedition, every police van, every gendarme and every militiaman, brings home to us the value of our old societies.

They were communal societies, never societies of the many for the few.

They were societies that were not only ante-capitalist, as has been said, but also *anti-capitalist*.

They were democratic societies, always.

They were cooperative societies, fraternal societies.

I make a systematic defense of the societies destroyed by imperialism.

They were the fact, they did not pretend to be the idea; despite their faults, they were neither to be hated nor condemned. They were content to be. In them, neither the word *failure* nor the word *avatar* had any meaning. They kept hope intact.

Whereas those are the only words that can, in all honesty, be applied to the European enterprises outside Europe. My only consolation is that periods of colonization pass, that nations sleep only for a time, and that peoples remain.

This being said, it seems that in certain circles they pretend to have discovered in me an 'enemy of Europe' and a prophet of the return to the ante-European past.

For my part, I search in vain for the place where I could have expressed such views; where I ever underestimated the importance of Europe in the history of human thought; where I ever preached a *return* of any kind; where I ever claimed that there could be a *return*.

The truth is that I have said something very different: to wit, that the great historical tragedy of Africa has been not so much that it was too late in making contact with the rest of the world, as the manner in which that contact was brought about; that Europe began to 'propagate' at a time when it had fallen into the hands of the most unscrupulous financiers and captains of industry;

that it was our misfortune to encounter that particular Europe on our path, and that Europe is responsible before the human community for the highest heap of corpses in history.

In another connection, in judging colonization, I have added that Europe has gotten on very well indeed with all the local feudal lords who agreed to serve, woven a villainous complicity with them, rendered their tyranny more effective and more efficient, and that it has actually tended to prolong artificially the survival of local pasts in their most pernicious aspects.

I have said – and this is something very different – that colonialist Europe has grafted modern abuse onto ancient injustice, hateful racism onto old inequality.

That if I am attacked on the grounds of intent, I maintain that colonialist Europe is dishonest in trying to justify its colonizing activity *a posteriori* by the obvious material progress that has been achieved in certain fields under the colonial regime – since *sudden change* is always possible, in history as elsewhere; since no one knows at what stage of material development these same countries would have been if Europe had not intervened; since the technical outfitting of Africa and Asia, their administrative reorganization, in a word, their 'Europeanization', was (as is proved by the example of Japan) in no way tied to the European *occupation*; since the Europeanization of the non-European continents could have been accomplished otherwise than under the heel of Europe; since this movement of Europeanization *was in progress*; since it was even slowed down; since in any case it was distorted by the European takeover.

The proof is that at present it is the indigenous peoples of Africa and Asia who are demanding schools, and colonialist Europe which refuses them; that it is the African who is asking for ports and roads, and colonialist Europe which is niggardly on this score; that it is the colonized man who wants to move forward, and the colonizer who holds things back.

Note
1. A railroad line connecting Brazzaville with the port of Pointe-Noire. (Trans)

Frantz Fanon*, 'The Black Man and Language'

When I meet a German or a Russian speaking bad French I try to indicate through gestures the information he is asking for, but in doing so I am careful not to forget that he has a language of his own, a country, and that perhaps he is a lawyer or an engineer back home. Whatever the case, he is a foreigner with different standards.

There is nothing comparable when it comes to the black man. He has no culture, no civilization, and no 'long historical past'.

Perhaps that is why today's Blacks want desperately to prove to the white world the existence of a black civilization.

Whether he likes it or not, the black man has to wear the livery the white man has fabricated for him. Look at children's comic books: all the Blacks are mouthing the ritual 'Yes, boss'. In films the situation is even more acute. Most of the American films dubbed in French reproduce the grinning stereotype *Y a bon Banania*. In one of these recent films, *Steel Sharks*, there is a black guy on a submarine speaking the most downright classic dialect imaginable. Furthermore, he is a true nigger, walking behind the quartermaster, trembling at the latter's slightest fit of anger, and is killed in the end. I am convinced, however, that in the original

---
* Frantz Fanon, *Black Skin, White Masks* (New York: Grove Press, Inc, 2008), 17–23. Copyright by Grove Press.

version he did not have this way of expressing himself. And even if he did I can't see why in a democratic France, where 60 million citizens are colored, anyone would dub the same idiocies from America. The reason is that the black man has to be portrayed in a certain way, and the same stereotype can be found from the black man in *Sans pitié* – 'Me work hard, me never lie, me never steal' – to the servant in *Duel in the Sun*.

All they ask of the black man is to be a good nigger; the rest will follow on its own. Making him speak pidgin is tying him to an image, snaring him, imprisoning him as the eternal victim of his own essence, of a *visible appearance* for which he is not responsible. And of course, just as the Jew who is lavish with his money is suspect, so the black man who quotes Montesquieu must be watched. Let me make myself clear: 'watched' insofar as he might start something. I do not contend that the black student is suspect to his peers or his professors. But outside university circles there is an army of fools. It is a question not of educating them but of teaching the black man not to be a slave of their archetypes.

Granted, these fools are the product of a psychological-economic structure. But that does not get us anywhere.

When a black man speaks of Marx, the first reaction is the following: 'We educated you and now you are turning against your benefactors. Ungrateful wretches! You'll always be a disappointment'. And then there's that sledgehammer argument from the plantation owners in Africa: our enemy is the elementary-school teacher.

The fact is that the European has a set idea of the black man, and there is nothing more exasperating than to hear: 'How long have you lived in France? You speak such good French'.

It could be argued that this is due to the fact that a lot of black people speak pidgin. But that would be too easy. You're traveling by train and ask:

'Excuse me, could you please tell me where the restaurant car is'?

'Yes, sonny boy, you go corridor, you go straight, go one car, go two car, go three car, you there'.

Let's be serious. Speaking pidgin means imprisoning the black man and perpetuating a conflictual situation where the white man infects the black man with extremely toxic foreign bodies. There is nothing more sensational than a black man speaking correctly, for he is appropriating the white world. I often have conversations with foreign students. They speak French badly. Little Robinson Crusoe, alias Prospero, is in his element. He explains, informs, comments, and helps them with their studies. But with the black man, he is utterly stupefied; the black man has put himself on an equal footing; the game is no longer possible; he's a pure replica of the white man, who has to surrender to the facts.[1]

After everything that has just been said, it is easy to understand why the first reaction of the black man is to say *no* to those who endeavor to define him. It is understandable that the black man's first action is a *reaction*, and since he is assessed with regard to his degree of assimilation, it is understandable too why the returning Antillean speaks only French: because he is striving to underscore the rift that has occurred. He embodies a new type of man whom he imposes on his colleagues and family. His old mother no longer understands when he speaks of her pj's; her ramshackle dump, and her lousy joint. All that embellished with the appropriate accent.

In every country in the world there are social climbers, those who think they've arrived. And opposite them there are those who keep the notion of their origins. The Antillean returning from the *métropole* speaks in Creole if he wants to signify that nothing has changed. It can be sensed on the docks where friends and relatives are waiting for him – waiting for him not only in the literal sense, but in the sense of waiting to catch him out. They need only one minute to make their diagnosis. If he says: 'I am so happy to be back among you.

Good Lord, it's so hot in this place; I'm not sure I can put up with it for long', they have been forewarned – it's a European who's come back.

In a different respect, when a group of Antillean students meet in Paris they have two options:

> Either support the white world – i.e., the real world – and with the help of French be able to address certain issues and aim at a certain degree of universalism in their conclusions.
>
> Or reject Europe, 'Yo',[2] and come together thanks to Creole by settling comfortably in what we'll call the Martinican *Umwelt*. By this we mean – and this goes especially for our Antillean brothers – that when one of our comrades in Paris or another university town attempts to address a problem in all seriousness he is accused of putting on airs, and the best way of disarming him is to brandish the Antilles and shift into Creole. This is one of the reasons why so many friendships fall through after a few months of life in Europe.

Since our argument is the disalienation of Blacks, we would like them to realize that every time there is a break-down in understanding among themselves faced with the white world, there is a lack of judgment.

A Senegalese who learns Creole to pass for an Antillean is a case of alienation.

The Antilleans who make a mockery out of him are lacking in judgment.

As we have seen, we are not mistaken in thinking that a study of the Antillean's language can reveal several characteristics of his world. As we said at the beginning, there are mutual supports between language and the community.

To speak a language is to appropriate its world and culture. The Antillean who wants to be white will succeed, since he will have adopted the cultural tool of language. I can remember just over a year ago in Lyon, following a lecture where I had drawn a parallel between black and European poetry, a French comrade telling me enthusiastically: 'Basically, you're a white man'. The fact I had studied such an interesting question in the white man's language gave me my credentials.

It should be understood that historically the black man wants to speak French, since it is the key to open doors which only fifty years ago still remained closed to him. The Antillean who falls within our description goes out of his way to seek the subtleties and rarities of the language – a way of proving to himself that he is culturally adequate.[3]

It has been said that the Antillean orator has a power of expression which leaves the Europeans gasping. In 1945, during an electoral campaign, Aimé Césaire, who was running for parliament, was speaking at a boys' school in Fort-de-France in front of a packed auditorium. In the middle of his talk a woman fainted. The next day a colleague describing the event commented: 'His French was so dynamite the woman fell to the floor and started ketching malkadi'.[4] The power of language.

A few other facts deserve closer attention – for instance, M. Charles-André Julien introducing Aimé Césaire as a 'black poet with a university *agrégation*' or else quite simply the expression 'a great black poet'.

These ready-made phrases that seem to be commonsense – after all Aimé Césaire is black and a poet – contain a hidden nuance, a persisting crux. I know nothing about Jean Paulhan except that he writes interesting books. I have no idea how old Roger Caillois is; the only evidence I have of him is when his presence streaks across the sky from time to time. And let no one accuse me of affective anaphylaxis. What I mean to say is that there is no reason why Monsieur Breton should say of Césaire: 'Here is a black man who handles the French language unlike any white man today'.[5]

And even if Monsieur Breton were telling the truth, I don't see where the paradox lies; I don't see why there should be any emphasis, because after all Aimé Césaire is Martinican with a university *agrégation*.

Let us return to Michel Leiris:

> If in the Antillean writer there is a desire to break with the literary forms associated with official education, such a desire, striving toward a freer future, would not assume the appearance of folklore. Seeking above all in literature to formulate a message that is their very own and, in the case of some of them at least, to be the spokesmen of a real race with unrecognized potential, they scorn the artifice which for them, whose intellectual education has been almost exclusively French, would represent recourse to a language they could only use as a second language they have learned.[6]

But, Blacks will retort, we should be honored that a white man such as Breton writes such things about us.

Let us move on. . . .

Notes

1. 'I knew some Negroes at the School of Medicine. . . . In short, they were a disappointment. The color of their skin should have given *us* the opportunity of being charitable, generous, and scientifically friendly. They failed in their duty and to satisfy our goodwill. All our tearful tenderness, all our artful concern, was to no avail. We had no Negroes to cajole, we had nothing to hate them for either; on the scales involving small jobs and meager daily deceits, they weighed virtually as much as we did'. Michel Salomon, 'D'un juif à des nègres', *Présence Africaine* 5, 776.
2. A generic term for *other people*, especially *Europeans*.
3. See, for example, the almost unbelievable number of anecdotes stemming from the parliamentary elections of any number of candidates. That rag of a paper by the name of *Le Canard Déchaîné* has constantly buried M B with damning Creolisms. This is in fact the sledgehammer used in the French Antilles: *Can't speak French properly*.
4. Fell into convulsions.
5. Introduction to *Cahier d'un retour au pays natal* (Notebook of a Return to My Native Land).
6. Michel Leiris, 'Martinique, Guadeloupe, Haiti', *Les Temps Modernes*, February 1950, 1346.

Frantz Fanon[*], 'On National Culture'

. . . Today we know that in the first phase of the national struggle colonialism tries to disarm national demands by putting forward economic doctrines. As soon as the first demands are set out, colonialism pretends to consider them, recognizing with ostentatious humility that the territory is suffering from serious underdevelopment which necessitates a great economic and social effort. And, in fact, it so happens that certain spectacular measures (centers of work for the unemployed which are opened here and there, for example) delay the crystallization of national consciousness for a few years. But, sooner or later, colonialism sees that it is not

---

[*] Frantz Fanon, *The Wretched of the Earth* (New York: Grove Press, 2004), 146–49, 168, 173–75. Copyright by Grove Press.

within its powers to put into practice a project of economic and social reforms which will satisfy the aspirations of the colonized people. Even where food supplies are concerned, colonialism gives proof of its inherent incapability. The colonialist state quickly discovers that if it wishes to disarm the nationalist parties on strictly economic questions then it will have to do in the colonies exactly what it has refused to do in its own country. . . .

I am ready to concede that on the plane of factual being the past existence of an Aztec civilization does not change anything very much in the diet of the Mexican peasant of today. I admit that all the proofs of a wonderful Songhai civilization will not change the fact that today the Songhais are underfed and illiterate, thrown between sky and water with empty heads and empty eyes. But it has been remarked several times that this passionate search for a national culture which existed before the colonial era finds its legitimate reason in the anxiety shared by native intellectuals to shrink away from that Western culture in which they all risk being swamped. Because they realize they are in danger of losing their lives and thus becoming lost to their people, these men, hotheaded and with anger in their hearts, relentlessly determine to renew contact once more with the oldest and most pre-colonial springs of life of their people.

Let us go further. Perhaps this passionate research and this anger are kept up or at least directed by the secret hope of discovering beyond the misery of today, beyond self-contempt, resignation, and abjuration, some very beautiful and splendid era whose existence rehabilitates us both in regard to ourselves and in regard to others. I have said that I have decided to go further. Perhaps unconsciously, the native intellectuals, since they could not stand wonderstruck before the history of today's barbarity, decided to back further and to delve deeper down; and, let us make no mistake, it was with the greatest delight that they discovered that there was nothing to be ashamed of in the past, but rather dignity, glory, and solemnity. The claim to a national culture in the past does not only rehabilitate that nation and serve as a justification for the hope of a future national culture. In the sphere of psycho-affective equilibrium it is responsible for an important change in the native. Perhaps we have not sufficiently demonstrated that colonialism is not simply content to impose its rule upon the present and the future of a dominated country. Colonialism is not satisfied merely with holding a people in its grip and emptying the native's brain of all form and content. By a kind of perverted logic, it turns to the past of the oppressed people, and distorts, disfigures and destroys it. This work of devaluing pre-colonial history takes on a dialectical significance today. . . .

In such a situation the claims of the native intellectual are not a luxury but a necessity in any coherent program. The native intellectual who takes up arms to defend his nation's legitimacy and who wants to bring proofs to bear out that legitimacy, who is willing to strip himself naked to study the history of his body, is obliged to dissect the heart of his people . . . .

To fight for national culture means in the first place to fight for the liberation of the nation, that material keystone which makes the building of a culture possible. There is no other fight for culture which can develop apart from the popular struggle. To take an example: all those men and women who are fighting with their bare hands against French colonialism in Algeria are not by any means strangers to the national culture of Algeria. The national Algerian culture is taking on form and content as the battles are being fought out, in prisons, under the guillotine, and in every French outpost which is captured or destroyed. . . .

While at the beginning the native intellectual used to produce his work to be read exclusively by the oppressor, whether with the intention of charming him or of denouncing him through ethnic or subjectivist means, now the native writer progressively takes on the habit of addressing his own people.

It is only from that moment that we can speak of a national literature. Here there is, at the level of literary creation, the taking up and clarification of themes which are typically nationalist. This may be properly called a literature of combat, in the sense that it calls on the whole people to fight for their existence as a nation. It is a literature of combat, because it molds the national consciousness, giving it form and contours and flinging open before it new and boundless horizons; it is a literature of combat because it assumes responsibility, and because it is the will to liberty expressed in terms of time and space.

On another level, the oral tradition – stories, epics, and songs of the people – which formerly were filed away as set pieces are now beginning to change. The storytellers who used to relate inert episodes now bring them alive and introduce into them modifications which are increasingly fundamental. There is a tendency to bring conflicts up to date and to modernize the kinds of struggle which the stories evoke, together with the names of heroes and the types of weapons. The method of allusion is more and more widely used. The formula 'This all happened long ago' is substituted with that of 'What we are going to speak of happened somewhere else, but it might well have happened here today, and it might happen tomorrow'. The example of Algeria is significant in this context. From 1952–53 on, the storytellers, who were before that time stereotyped and tedious to listen to, completely overturned their traditional methods of storytelling and the contents of their tales. Their public, which was formerly scattered, became compact. The epic, with its typified categories, reappeared; it became an authentic form of entertainment which took on once more a cultural value. Colonialism made no mistake when from 1955 on it proceeded to arrest these storytellers systematically.

The contact of the people with the new movement gives rise to a new rhythm of life and to forgotten muscular tensions, and develops the imagination. Every time the storyteller relates a fresh episode to his public, he presides over a real invocation. The existence of a new type of man is revealed to the public. The present is no longer turned in upon itself but spread out for all to see. The storyteller once more gives free rein to his imagination; he makes innovations and he creates a work of art. It even happens that the characters, which are barely ready for such a transformation – highway robbers or more or less antisocial vagabonds – are taken up and remodeled. The emergence of the imagination and of the creative urge in the songs and epic stories of a colonized country is worth following. The storyteller replies to the expectant people by successive approximations, and makes his way, apparently alone but in fact helped on by his public, toward the seeking out of new patterns, that is to say national patterns. Comedy and farce disappear, or lose their attraction. As for dramatization, it is no longer placed on the plane of the troubled intellectual and his tormented conscience. By losing its characteristics of despair and revolt, the drama becomes part of the common lot of the people and forms part of an action in preparation or already in progress. . . .

Edward Said[*], 'Orientalism'

On a visit to Beirut during the terrible civil war of 1975–1976 a French journalist wrote regretfully of the gutted downtown area that 'it had once seemed to belong to . . . the Orient of Chateaubriand and Nerval'.[1] He was right about the place, of course, especially so far as a

---

[*] Edward Said, *Orientalism* (London and New York: Penguin, 1978), 1–14. Used by permission of Pantheon Books, an imprint of the Knopf Doubleday Publishing Group, a subdivision of Penguin Random House LLC. All rights reserved.

European was concerned. The Orient was almost a European invention, and had been since antiquity a place of romance, exotic beings, haunting memories and landscapes, remarkable experiences. Now it was disappearing; in a sense it had happened, its time was over. Perhaps it seemed irrelevant that Orientals themselves had something at stake in the process, that even in the time of Chateaubriand and Nerval Orientals had lived there, and that now it was they who were suffering; the main thing for the European visitor was a European representation of the Orient and its contemporary fate, both of which had a privileged communal significance for the journalist and his French readers.

Americans will not feel quite the same about the Orient, which for them is much more likely to be associated very differently with the Far East (China and Japan, mainly). Unlike the Americans, the French and the British – less so the Germans, Russians, Spanish, Portuguese, Italians, and Swiss – have had a long tradition of what I shall be calling *Orientalism*, a way of coming to terms with the Orient that is based on the Orient's special place in European Western experience. The Orient is not only adjacent to Europe; it is also the place of Europe's greatest and richest and oldest colonies, the source of its civilizations and languages, its cultural contestant, and one of its deepest and most recurring images of the Other. In addition, the Orient has helped to define Europe (or the West) as its contrasting image, idea, personality, experience. Yet none of this Orient is merely imaginative. The Orient is an integral part of European *material* civilization and culture. Orientalism expresses and represents that part culturally and even ideologically as a mode of discourse with supporting institutions, vocabulary, scholarship, imagery, doctrines, even colonial bureaucracies and colonial styles. In contrast, the American understanding of the Orient will seem considerably less dense, although our recent Japanese, Korean, and Indochinese adventures ought now to be creating a more sober, more realistic 'Oriental' awareness. Moreover, the vastly expanded American political and economic role in the Near East (the Middle East) makes great claims on our understanding of that Orient.

It will be clear to the reader (and will become clearer still throughout the many pages that follow) that by Orientalism I mean several things, all of them, in my opinion, interdependent. The most readily accepted designation for Orientalism is an academic one, and indeed the label still serves in a number of academic institutions. Anyone who teaches, writes about, or researches the Orient – and this applies whether the person is an anthropologist, sociologist, historian, or philologist – either in its specific or its general aspects, is an Orientalist, and what he or she does is Orientalism. Compared with *Oriental studies* or *area studies*, it is true that the term *Orientalism* is less preferred by specialists today, both because it is too vague and general and because it connotes the high-handed executive attitude of nineteenth-century and early-twentieth-century European colonialism. Nevertheless books are written and congresses held with 'the Orient' as their main focus, with the Orientalist in his new or old guise as their main authority. The point is that even if it does not survive as it once did, Orientalism lives on academically through its doctrines and theses about the Orient and the Oriental.

Related to this academic tradition, whose fortunes, transmigrations, specializations, and transmissions are in part the subject of this study, is a more general meaning for Orientalism. Orientalism is a style of thought based upon an ontological and epistemological distinction made between 'the Orient' and (most of the time) 'the Occident'. Thus a very large mass of writers, among whom are poets, novelists, philosophers, political theorists, economists, and imperial administrators, have accepted the basic distinction between East and West as the starting point for elaborate theories, epics, novels, social descriptions, and political accounts concerning the Orient, its people, customs, 'mind', destiny, and so on. *This* Orientalism can accommodate Aeschylus, say, and Victor Hugo, Dante and Karl Marx. A little later in this introduction I shall deal with the methodological problems one encounters in so broadly construed a 'field' as this.

The interchange between the academic and the more or less imaginative meanings of Orientalism is a constant one, and since the late eighteenth century there has been a considerable, quite disciplined – perhaps even regulated – traffic between the two. Here I come to the third meaning of Orientalism, which is something more historically and materially defined than either of the other two. Taking the late eighteenth century as a very roughly defined starting point Orientalism can be discussed and analyzed as the corporate institution for dealing with the Orient – dealing with it by making statements about it, authorizing views of it, describing it, by teaching it, settling it, ruling over it: in short, Orientalism as a Western style for dominating, restructuring, and having authority over the Orient. I have found it useful here to employ Michel Foucault's notion of a discourse, as described by him in *The Archaeology of Knowledge* and in *Discipline and Punish*, to identify Orientalism. My contention is that without examining Orientalism as a discourse one cannot possibly understand the enormously systematic discipline by which European culture was able to manage – and even produce – the Orient politically, sociologically, militarily, ideologically, scientifically, and imaginatively during the post-Enlightenment period. Moreover, so authoritative a position did Orientalism have that I believe no one writing, thinking, or acting on the Orient could do so without taking account of the limitations on thought and action imposed by Orientalism. In brief, because of Orientalism the Orient was not (and is not) a free subject of thought or action. This is not to say that Orientalism unilaterally determines what can be said about the Orient, but that it is the whole network of interests inevitably brought to bear on (and therefore always involved in) any occasion when that peculiar entity 'the Orient' is in question. How this happens is what this book tries to demonstrate. It also tries to show that European culture gained in strength and identity by setting itself off against the Orient as a sort of surrogate and even underground self.

Historically and culturally there is a quantitative as well as a qualitative difference between the Franco-British involvement in the Orient and – until the period of American ascendancy after World War II – the involvement of every other European and Atlantic power. To speak of Orientalism therefore is to speak mainly, although not exclusively, of a British and French cultural enterprise, a project whose dimensions take in such disparate realms as the imagination itself, the whole of India and the Levant, the Biblical texts and the Biblical lands, the spice trade, colonial armies and a long tradition of colonial administrators, a formidable scholarly corpus, innumerable Oriental 'experts' and 'hands', an Oriental professorate, a complex array of 'Oriental' ideas (Oriental despotism, Oriental splendor, cruelty, sensuality), many Eastern sects, philosophies, and wisdoms domesticated for local European use – the list can be extended more or less indefinitely. My point is that Orientalism derives from a particular closeness experienced between Britain and France and the Orient, which until the early nineteenth century had really meant only India and the Bible lands. From the beginning of the nineteenth century until the end of World War II France and Britain dominated the Orient and Orientalism; since World War II America has dominated the Orient, and approaches it as France and Britain once did. Out of that closeness, whose dynamic is enormously productive even if it always demonstrates the comparatively greater strength of the Occident (British, French, or American), comes the large body of texts I call Orientalist.

It should be said at once that even with the generous number of books and authors that I examine, there is a much larger number that I simply have had to leave out. My argument, however, depends neither upon an exhaustive catalogue of texts dealing with the Orient nor upon a clearly delimited set of texts, authors, and ideas that together make up the Orientalist canon. I have depended instead upon a different methodological alternative – whose backbone in a sense is the set of historical generalizations I have so far been making in this Introduction – and it is these I want now to discuss in more analytical detail.

II

I have begun with the assumption that the Orient is not an inert fact of nature. It is not merely *there*, just as the Occident itself is not just *there* either. We must take seriously Vico's great observation that men make their own history, that what they can know is what they have made, and extend it to geography: as both geographical and cultural entities – to say nothing of historical entities – such locales, regions, geographical sectors as 'Orient' and 'Occident' are man-made. Therefore as much as the West itself, the Orient is an idea that has a history and a tradition of thought, imagery, and vocabulary that have given it reality and presence in and for the West. The two geographical entities thus support and to an extent reflect each other.

Having said that, one must go on to state a number of reasonable qualifications. In the first place, it would be wrong to conclude that the Orient was *essentially* an idea, or a creation with no corresponding reality. When Disraeli said in his novel *Tancred* that the East was a career, he meant that to be interested in the East was something bright young Westerners would find to be an all-consuming passion; he should not be interpreted as saying that the East was *only* a career for Westerners. There were – and are – cultures and nations whose location is in the East, and their lives, histories, and customs have a brute reality obviously greater than anything that could be said about them in the West. About that fact this study of Orientalism has very little to contribute, except to acknowledge it tacitly. But the phenomenon of Orientalism as I study it here deals principally, not with a correspondence between Orientalism and Orient, but with the internal consistency of Orientalism and its ideas about the Orient (the East as career) despite or beyond any correspondence, or lack thereof, with a 'real' Orient. My point is that Disraeli's statement about the East refers mainly to that created consistency, that regular constellation of ideas as the pre-eminent thing about the Orient, and not to its mere being, as Wallace Stevens's phrase has it.

A second qualification is that ideas, cultures, and histories cannot seriously be understood or studied without their force, or more precisely their configurations of power, also being studied. To believe that the Orient was created – or, as I call it, 'Orientalized' – and to believe that such things happen simply as a necessity of the imagination, is to be disingenuous. The relationship between Occident and Orient is a relationship of power, of domination, of varying degrees of a complex hegemony, and is quite accurately indicated in the title of K. M. Panikkar's classic *Asia and Western Dominance*.[2] The Orient was Orientalized not only because it was discovered to be 'Oriental' in all those ways considered commonplace by an average nineteenth-century European, but also because it *could be* – that is, submitted to being – *made* Oriental. There is very little consent to be found, for example, in the fact that Flaubert's encounter with an Egyptian courtesan produced a widely influential model of the Oriental woman; she never spoke of herself, she never represented her emotions, presence, or history. *He* spoke for and represented her. He was foreign, comparatively wealthy, male, and these were historical facts of domination that allowed him not only to possess Kuchuk Hanem physically but to speak for her and tell his readers in what way she was 'typically Oriental'. My argument is that Flaubert's situation of strength in relation to Kuchuk Hanem was not an isolated instance. It fairly stands for the pattern of relative strength between East and West, and the discourse about the Orient that it enabled.

This brings us to a third qualification. One ought never to assume that the structure of Orientalism is nothing more than a structure of lies or of myths which, were the truth about them to be told, would simply blow away. I myself believe that Orientalism is more particularly valuable as a sign of European-Atlantic power over the Orient than it is as a veridic discourse about the Orient (which is what, in its academic or scholarly form, it claims to be). Nevertheless, what we must respect and try to grasp is the sheer knitted-together strength of Orientalist discourse, its very close ties to the enabling socio-economic and political institutions, and its redoubtable durability. After all, any system of ideas that can remain unchanged as teachable wisdom (in academies, books, congresses, universities, foreign-service institutes) from the period of Ernest Renan in the late 1840s until the present in the United States must be something more formidable than a mere collection of lies. Orientalism, therefore, is not an airy European fantasy about the Orient, but a created body of theory and practice in which, for many generations, there has been a considerable material investment. Continued investment made Orientalism, as a system of knowledge about the Orient, an accepted grid for filtering through the Orient into Western consciousness, just as that same investment multiplied – indeed, made truly productive – the statements proliferating out from Orientalism into the general culture.

Gramsci has made the useful analytic distinction between civil and political society in which the former is made up of voluntary (or at least rational and noncoercive) affiliations like schools, families, and unions, the latter of state institutions (the army, the police, the central bureaucracy) whose role in the polity is direct domination. Culture, of course, is to be found operating within civil society, where the influence of ideas, of institutions, and of other persons works not through domination but by what Gramsci calls consent. In any society not totalitarian, then, certain cultural forms predominate over others, just as certain ideas are more influential than others; the form of this cultural leadership is what Gramsci has identified as *hegemony*, an indispensable concept for any understanding of cultural life in the industrial West. It is hegemony, or rather the result of cultural hegemony at work, that gives Orientalism the durability and the strength I have been speaking about so far. Orientalism is never far from what Denys Hay has called the idea of Europe,[3] a collective notion identifying 'us' Europeans as against all 'those' non-Europeans, and indeed it can be argued that the major component in European culture is precisely what made that culture hegemonic both in and outside Europe: the idea of European identity as a superior one in comparison with all the non-European peoples and cultures. There is in addition the hegemony of European ideas about the Orient, themselves reiterating European superiority over Oriental backwardness, usually overriding the possibility that a more independent, or more skeptical, thinker might have had different views on the matter.

In a quite constant way, Orientalism depends for its strategy on this flexible *positional* superiority, which puts the Westerner in a whole series of possible relationships with the Orient without ever losing him the relative upper hand. And why should it have been otherwise, especially during the period of extraordinary European ascendancy from the late Renaissance to the present? The scientist, the scholar, the missionary, the trader, or the soldier was in, or thought about, the Orient because he *could be there*, or could think about it, with very little resistance on the Orient's part. Under the general heading of knowledge of the Orient, and within the umbrella of Western hegemony over the Orient during the period from the end of the eighteenth century, there emerged a complex Orient suitable for study in the academy, for display in the museum, for reconstruction in the colonial office, for theoretical illustration in anthropological, biological, linguistic, racial, and historical theses about mankind and the universe, for instances of economic and sociological theories of development, revolution, cultural personality, national or religious character. Additionally, the imaginative examination of things Oriental was based more or less exclusively upon a sovereign Western consciousness out of whose unchallenged centrality an Oriental world emerged, first according to general ideas about who or what was an Oriental, then according to a detailed logic governed not simply by empirical reality but by a battery of desires, repressions, investments, and projections. If we can point to great Orientalist works of genuine scholarship like Silvestre de Sacy's *Chrestomathie arabe* or Edward William Lane's *Account of the Manners and Customs of the Modern Egyptians*, we need also to note that Renan's and Gobineau's racial ideas came out of the same impulse, as did a great many Victorian pornographic novels (see the analysis by Steven Marcus of 'The Lustful Turk'[4]).

And yet, one must repeatedly ask oneself whether what matters in Orientalism is the general group of ideas overriding the mass of material – about which who could deny that they were shot through with doctrines of European superiority, various kinds of racism, imperialism, and the like, dogmatic views of 'the Oriental' as a kind of ideal and unchanging abstraction? – or the much more varied work produced by almost uncountable individual writers, whom one would take up as individual instances of authors dealing with the Orient. In a sense the two alternatives, general and particular, are really two perspectives on the same material: in both instances one would have to deal with pioneers in the field like William Jones, with great artists like Nerval or Flaubert. And why would it not be possible to employ both perspectives together, or one after the other? Isn't there an obvious danger of distortion (of precisely the kind that academic Orientalism has always been prone to) if either too general or too specific a level of description is maintained systematically?

My two fears are distortion and inaccuracy, or rather the kind of inaccuracy produced by too dogmatic a generality and too positivistic a localized focus. In trying to deal with these problems I have tried to deal with three main aspects of my own contemporary reality that seem to me to point the way out of the methodological or perspectival difficulties I have been discussing, difficulties that might force one, in the first instance, into writing a coarse polemic on so unacceptably general a level of description as not to be worth the effort, or in the second instance, into writing so detailed and atomistic a series of analyses as to lose all track of the general lines of force informing the field, giving it its special cogency. How then to recognize individuality and to reconcile it with its intelligent, and by no means passive or merely dictatorial, general and hegemonic context?

III

I mentioned three aspects of my contemporary reality: I must explain and briefly discuss them now, so that it can be seen how I was led to a particular course of research and writing.

1. *The distinction between pure and political knowledge.* It is very easy to argue that knowledge about Shakespeare or Wordsworth is not political whereas knowledge about contemporary China or the Soviet Union is. My own formal and professional designation is that of 'humanist', a title which indicates the humanities as my field and therefore the unlikely eventuality that there might be anything political about what I do in that field. Of course, all these labels and terms are quite unnuanced as I use them here, but the general truth of what I am pointing to is, I think, widely held. One reason for saying that a humanist who writes

about Wordsworth, or an editor whose specialty is Keats, is not involved in anything political is that what he does seems to have no direct political effect upon reality in the everyday sense. A scholar whose field is Soviet economics works in a highly charged area where there is much government interest, and what he might produce in the way of studies or proposals will be taken up by policymakers, government officials, institutional economists, intelligence experts. The distinction between 'humanists' and persons whose work has policy implications, or political significance, can be broadened further by saying that the former's ideological color is a matter of incidental importance to politics (although possibly of great moment to his colleagues in the field, who may object to his Stalinism or fascism or too easy liberalism), whereas the ideology of the latter is woven directly into his material – indeed, economics, politics, and sociology in the modern academy are ideological sciences – and therefore taken for granted as being 'political'.

Nevertheless the determining impingement on most knowledge produced in the contemporary West (and here I speak mainly about the United States) is that it be nonpolitical, that is, scholarly, academic, impartial, above partisan or small-minded doctrinal belief. One can have no quarrel with such an ambition in theory, perhaps, but in practice the reality is much more problematic. No one has ever devised a method for detaching the scholar from the circumstances of life, from the fact of his involvement (conscious or unconscious) with a class, a set of beliefs, a social position, or from the mere activity of being a member of a society. These continue to bear on what he does professionally, even though naturally enough his research and its fruits do attempt to reach a level of relative freedom from the inhibitions and the restrictions of brute, everyday reality. For there is such a thing as knowledge that is less, rather than more, partial than the individual (with his entangling and distracting life circumstances) who produces it. Yet this knowledge is not therefore automatically nonpolitical.

Whether discussions of literature or of classical philology are fraught with – or have unmediated – political significance is a very large question that I have tried to treat in some detail elsewhere.[5] What I am interested in doing now is suggesting how the general liberal consensus that 'true' knowledge is fundamentally non-political (and conversely, that overtly political knowledge is not 'true' knowledge) obscures the highly if obscurely organized political circumstances obtaining when knowledge is produced. No one is helped in understanding this today when the adjective 'political' is used as a label to discredit any work for daring to violate the protocol of pretended suprapolitical objectivity. We may say, first, that civil society recognizes a gradation of political importance in the various fields of knowledge. To some extent the political importance given a field comes from the possibility of its direct translation into economic terms; but to a greater extent political importance comes from the closeness of a field to ascertainable sources of power in political society. Thus an economic study of long-term Soviet energy potential and its effect on military capability is likely to be commissioned by the Defense Department, and thereafter to acquire a kind of political status impossible for a study of Tolstoi's early fiction financed in part by a foundation. Yet both works belong in what civil society acknowledges to be a similar field, Russian studies, even though one work may be done by a very conservative economist, the other by a radical literary historian. My point here is that 'Russia' as a general subject matter has political priority over nicer distinctions such as 'economics' and 'literary history', because political society in Gramsci's sense reaches into such realms of civil society as the academy and saturates them with significance of direct concern to it.

I do not want to press all this any further on general theoretical grounds: it seems to me that the value and credibility of my case can be demonstrated by being much more specific, in the way, for example, Noam Chomsky has studied the instrumental connection between the Vietnam War and the notion of objective scholarship as it was applied to cover state-sponsored military research.[6] Now because Britain, France, and recently the United States are imperial powers, their political societies impart to their civil societies a sense of urgency, a direct political infusion as it were, where and whenever matters pertaining to their imperial interests abroad are concerned. I doubt that it is controversial, for example, to say that an Englishman in India or Egypt in the later nineteenth century took an interest in those countries that was never far from their status in his mind as British colonies. To say this may seem quite different from saying that all academic knowledge about India and Egypt is somehow tinged and impressed with, violated by, the gross political fact – and yet *that is what I am saying* in this study of Orientalism. For if it is true that no production of knowledge in the human sciences can ever ignore or disclaim its author's involvement as a human subject in his own circumstances, then it must also be true that for a European or American studying the Orient there can be no disclaiming the main circumstances of *his* actuality: that he comes up against the Orient as a European or American first, as an individual second. And to be a European or an American in such a situation is by no means an inert fact. It meant and means being aware, however dimly, that one belongs to a power with definite interests in the Orient, and more important, that one belongs to a part of the earth with a definite history of involvement in the Orient almost since the time of Homer.

Put in this way, these political actualities are still too undefined and general to be really interesting. Anyone would agree to them without necessarily agreeing also that they mattered very much, for instance, to Flaubert as he wrote *Salammbô*, or to H. A. R. Gibb as he wrote *Modern Trends in Islam.* The trouble is that there is too great a distance between the big dominating fact, as I have described it, and the details of everyday life that govern the minute discipline of a novel or a scholarly text as each is being written. Yet if we eliminate from the start any notion that 'big' facts like imperial domination can be applied mechanically and deterministically to such complex matters as culture and ideas, then we will begin to approach an interesting kind of study. My idea is that European and then American interest in the Orient was political according to some of the obvious historical accounts of it that I have given here, but that it was the culture that created that interest, that acted dynamically along with brute political, economic, and military rationales to make the Orient the varied and complicated place that it obviously was in the field I call Orientalism.

Therefore, Orientalism is not a mere political subject matter or field that is reflected passively by culture, scholarship, or institutions; nor is it a large and diffuse collection of texts about the Orient; nor is it representative and expressive of some nefarious 'Western' imperialist plot to hold down the 'Oriental' world. It is rather a *distribution* of geopolitical awareness into aesthetic, scholarly, economic, sociological, historical, and philological texts; it is an *elaboration* not only of a basic geographical distinction (the world is made up of two unequal halves, Orient and Occident) but also of a whole series of 'interests' which, by such means as scholarly discovery, philological reconstruction, psychological analysis, landscape and sociological description, it not only creates but also maintains; it *is*, rather than expresses, a certain *will* or *intention* to understand, in some cases to control, manipulate, even to incorporate, what is a manifestly different (or alternative and novel) world; it is, above all, a discourse that is by no means in direct, corresponding relationship with political power in the raw, but rather is produced and exists in an uneven exchange with various kinds of power, shaped to a degree by the exchange with power political (as with a colonial or imperial establishment), power intellectual (as with reigning sciences like comparative linguistics or anatomy, or any of the modern policy sciences), power cultural (as with orthodoxies and canons of taste, texts, values), power moral (as with ideas about what 'we' do and what 'they' cannot do or understand as 'we' do). Indeed, my real argument is that Orientalism is – and does not simply represent – a considerable dimension of modern political-intellectual culture, and as such has less to do with the Orient than it does with 'our' world.

Because Orientalism is a cultural and a political fact, then, it does not exist in some archival vacuum; quite the contrary, I think it can be shown that what is thought, said, or even done about the Orient follows (perhaps occurs within) certain distinct and intellectually knowable lines. Here too a considerable degree of nuance and elaboration can be seen working as between the broad superstructural pressures and the details of composition, the facts of textuality. Most humanistic scholars are, I think, perfectly happy with the notion that texts exist in contexts, that there is such a thing as intertextuality, that the pressures of conventions, predecessors, and rhetorical styles limit what Walter Benjamin once called the 'overtaxing of the productive person in the name of . . . the principle of "creativity" ', in which the poet is believed on his own, and out of his pure mind, to have brought forth his work.[7] Yet there is a reluctance to allow that political, institutional, and ideological constraints act in the same manner on the individual author. A humanist will believe it to be an interesting fact to any interpreter of Balzac that he was influenced in the *Comédie humaine* by the conflict between Geoffroy Saint-Hilaire and Cuvier, but the same sort of pressure on Balzac of deeply reactionary monarchism is felt in some vague way to demean his literary 'genius' and therefore to be less worth serious study. Similarly – as Harry Bracken has been tirelessly showing – philosophers will conduct their discussions of Locke, Hume, and empiricism without ever taking into account that there is an explicit connection in these classic writers between their 'philosophic' doctrines and racial theory, justifications of slavery, or arguments for colonial exploitation.[8] These are common enough ways by which contemporary scholarship keeps itself pure.

Perhaps it is true that most attempts to rub culture's nose in the mud of politics have been crudely iconoclastic; perhaps also the social interpretation of literature in my own field has simply not kept up with the enormous technical advances in detailed textual analysis. But there is no getting away from the fact that literary studies in general, and American Marxist theorists in particular, have avoided the effort of seriously bridging the gap between the superstructural and the base levels in textual, historical scholarship; on another occasion I have gone so far as to say that the literary-cultural establishment as a whole has declared the serious study of imperialism and culture off limits.[9] For Orientalism brings one up directly against that question – that is, to realizing that political imperialism governs an entire field of study, imagination, and scholarly institutions – in such a way as to make its avoidance an intellectual and historical impossibility. Yet there will always remain the perennial escape mechanism of saying that a literary scholar and a philosopher, for example, are trained in literature and philosophy respectively, not in politics or ideological analysis. In other words, the specialist argument can work quite effectively to block the larger and, in my opinion, the more intellectually serious perspective.

Here it seems to me there is a simple two-part answer to be given, at least so far as the study of imperialism and culture (or Orientalism) is concerned. In the first place, nearly every nineteenth-century writer (and the same is true enough of writers in earlier periods) was extraordinarily well aware of the fact of empire: this is a subject not very well studied, but it will not take a modern Victorian specialist long to admit that liberal cultural heroes like John Stuart Mill, Arnold, Carlyle, Newman, Macaulay, Ruskin, George Eliot, and even Dickens had definite views on race and imperialism, which are quite easily to be found at work in their writing. So even a specialist must deal with the knowledge that Mill, for example, made it clear in *On Liberty* and *Representative Government* that his views there could not be applied to India (he was an India Office functionary for a good deal of his life, after all) because the Indians were civilizationally, if not racially, inferior. The same kind of paradox is to be found in Marx, as I try to show in this book. In the second place, to believe that politics in the form of imperialism bears upon the production of literature, scholarship, social theory, and history writing is by no means equivalent to saying that culture is therefore a demeaned or denigrated thing. Quite the contrary: my whole point is to say that we can better understand the persistence and the durability of saturating hegemonic systems like culture when we realize that their internal constraints upon writers and thinkers were *productive*, not unilaterally inhibiting. It is this idea that Gramsci, certainly, and Foucault and Raymond Williams in their very different ways have been trying to illustrate. Even one or two pages by Williams on 'the uses of the Empire' in *The Long Revolution* tell us more about nineteenth-century cultural richness than many volumes of hermetic textual analyses.[10]

Therefore I study Orientalism as a dynamic exchange between individual authors and the large political concerns shaped by the three great empires – British, French, American – in whose intellectual and imaginative territory the writing was produced. What interests me most as a scholar is not the gross political verity but the detail, as indeed what interests us in someone like Lane or Flaubert or Renan is not the (to him) indisputable truth that Occidentals are superior to Orientals, but the profoundly worked over and modulated evidence of his detailed work within the very wide space opened up by that truth. One need only remember that Lane's *Manners and Customs of the Modern Egyptians* is a classic of historical and anthropological observation because of its style, its enormously intelligent and brilliant details, not because of its simple reflection of racial superiority, to understand what I am saying here.

The kind of political questions raised by Orientalism, then, are as follows: What other sorts of intellectual, aesthetic, scholarly, and cultural energies went into the making of an imperialist tradition like the Orientalist one? How did philology, lexicography, history, biology, political and economic theory, novel-writing, and lyric poetry come to the service of Orientalism's broadly imperialist view of the world? What changes, modulations, refinements, even revolutions take place within Orientalism? What is the meaning of originality, of continuity, of individuality, in this context? How does Orientalism transmit or reproduce itself from one epoch to another? In fine, how can we treat the cultural, historical phenomenon of Orientalism as a kind of *willed human work* – not of mere unconditioned ratiocination – in all its historical complexity, detail, and worth without at the same time losing sight of the alliance between cultural work, political tendencies, the state, and the specific realities of domination? Governed by such concerns a humanistic study can responsibly address itself to politics *and* culture. But this is not to say that such a study establishes a hard-and-fast rule about the relationship between knowledge and politics. My argument is that each humanistic investigation must formulate the nature of that connection in the specific context of the study, the subject matter, and its historical circumstances. . . .

Notes

1. Thierry Desjardins, *Le Martyre du Liban* (Paris: Pion, 1976), 14.
2. K M Panikkar, *Asia and Western Dominance* (London: George Allen & Unwin, 1959).

3. Denys Hay, *Europe: The Emergence of an Idea*, 2nd ed (Edinburgh: Edinburgh University Press, 1968).
4. Steven Marcus, *The Other Victorians: A Study of Sexuality and Pornography in Mid-Nineteenth Century England* (1966; reprint ed, New York: Bantam Books, 1967), 200–19.
5. See my *Criticism between Culture and System* (Cambridge, MA: Harvard University Press, forthcoming).
6. Principally in his *American Power and the New Mandarins: Historical and Political Essays* (New York: Pantheon Books, 1969) and *For Reasons of State* (New York: Pantheon Books, 1973).
7. Walter Benjamin, *Charles Baudelaire: A Lyric Poet in the Era of High Capitalism*, trans Harry Zohn (London: New Left Books, 1973), 71.
8. Harry Bracken, 'Essence, Accident and Race', *Hermathena* 116 (Winter 1973): 81–96.
9. In an interview published in *Diacritics* 6, no 3 (Fall 1976): 38.
10. Raymond Williams, *The Long Revolution* (London: Chatto & Windus, 1961), 66–67.

Oyèrónkẹ́ Oyěwùmí*, 'Colonizing Bodies and Minds: Gender and Colonialism'

Theorists of colonialization like Frantz Fanon and Albert Memmi tell us that the colonial situation, being a Manichaean world,[1] produces two kinds of people: the colonizer and the colonized (also known as the settler and the native), and what differentiates them is not only skin color but also state of mind.[2] One similarity that is often overlooked is that both colonizers and colonized are presumed male. Colonial rule itself is described as 'a manly or husbandly or lordly prerogative'.[3] As a process, it is often described as the taking away of the manhood of the colonized. While the argument that the colonizers are men is not difficult to sustain, the idea of the colonized being uniformly male is less so. Yet the two following passages from Fanon are typical of the portrayal of the native in the discourses on colonization: 'Sometimes people wonder that the native rather than give his wife a dress, buys instead a transistor radio'.[4] And, 'The look that the native turns on the settler's town is a look of lust, a look of envy; it expresses *his* dreams of possession – all manner of possession: to sit at the settler's table, to sleep in the settler's bed, with *his wife* if possible. The colonized man is an envious man'.[5] But what if the native were female, as indeed many of them were? How is this feeling of envy and desire to replace the colonizer manifested or realized for women? Or, for that matter, does such a feeling exist for women?

The histories of both the colonized and the colonizer have been written from the male point of view – women are peripheral if they appear at all. While studies of colonization written from this angle are not necessarily irrelevant to understanding what happened to native females, we must recognize that colonization impacted males and females in similar and dissimilar ways. Colonial custom and practice stemmed from 'a world view which believes in the absolute superiority of the human over the nonhuman and the subhuman, the *masculine* over the *feminine* . . ., and the modern or progressive over the traditional or the savage'.[6]

---

* Oyèrónkẹ́ Oyěwùmí, *The Invention of Women: Making an African Sense of Western Gender Discourses* (Minneapolis: University of Minnesota Press, 1997), 121–56 (selections). Copyright 1997 by the Regents of University of Minnesota.

Therefore, the colonizer differentiated between male and female bodies and acted accordingly. Men were the primary target of policy, and, as such, they were the natives and so were visible. These facts, from the standpoint of this study, are the justification for considering the colonial impact in gender terms rather than attempting to see which group, male or female, was the most exploited. The colonial process was sex-differentiated insofar as the colonizers were male and used gender identity to determine policy. From the foregoing, it is clear that any discussion of hierarchy in the colonial situation, in addition to employing race as the basis of distinctions, should take into account its strong gender component. The two racially distinct and hierarchical categories of the colonizer and the native should be expanded to four, incorporating the gender factor. However, race and gender categories obviously emanate from the preoccupation in Western culture with the visual and hence physical aspects of human reality. Both categories are a consequence of the bio-logic of Western culture. Thus, in the colonial situation, there was a hierarchy of four, not two, categories. Beginning at the top, these were: men (European), women (European), native (African men), and Other (African women). Native women occupied the residual and unspecified category of the Other.

In more recent times, feminist scholars have sought to rectify the male bias in the discourses on colonization by focusing on women. One major thesis that emerged from this effort is that African women suffered a 'double colonization': one form from European domination and the other from indigenous tradition imposed by African men. Stephanie Urdang's book *Fighting Two Colonialisms* is characteristic of this perspective.[7] While the depth of the colonial experience for African women is expressed succinctly by the idea of doubling, there is no consensus about what is being doubled. From my perspective, it is not colonization that is two, but the forms of oppression that flowed from the process for native females. Hence, it is misleading to postulate two forms of colonization because both manifestations of oppression are rooted in the hierarchical race/gender relations of the colonial situation. African females were colonized by Europeans as Africans and as African women. They were dominated, exploited, and inferiorized as Africans together with African men and then separately inferiorized and marginalized as African women.

It is important to emphasize the combination of race and gender factors because European women did not occupy the same position in the colonial order as African women. A circular issued by the British colonial government in Nigeria shows the glaringly unequal position of these two groups of women in the colonial system. It states that 'African women should be paid at 75% of the rates paid to the European women'.[8] Furthermore, whatever the 'status' of indigenous customs, the relations between African men and women during this period can be neither isolated from the colonial situation nor described as a form of colonization, particularly because African men were subjects themselves.[9] The racial and gender oppressions experienced by African women should not be seen in terms of addition, as if they were piled one on top of the other. In the context of the United States, Elizabeth Spelman's comment on the relationship between racism and sexism is relevant. She writes: 'How one form of oppression is experienced is influenced by and influences how another form is experienced'.[10] Though it is necessary to discuss the impact of colonization on specific categories of people, ultimately its effect on women cannot be separated from its impact on men because gender relations are not zero-sum – men and women in any society are inextricably bound.

This chapter will examine specific colonial policies, practices, and ideologies and ascertain how they impacted males and females in different ways. In this regard, the gender identity of the colonizers is also important. At the level of policy, I shall look at administrative, educational, legal, and religious systems. It will become clear that certain ideologies and values flowed out of these policies and practices, and in an often unstated, but no less profound, way they shaped the behavior of the colonized. Colonization was a multifaceted process involving different kinds of European personnel, including missionaries, traders, and state officials. Hence, I treat the process of Christianization as an integral part of the colonial process. Finally, colonization was, above all, the expansion of the European economic system in that 'beneath the surface of colonial political and administrative policy lay the unfolding process of capital penetration'.[11] The capitalist economic system shaped the particular ways in which colonial domination was effected.

The State of Patriarchy

The imposition of the European state system, with its attendant legal and bureaucratic machinery, is the most enduring legacy of European colonial rule in Africa. The international nation-state system as we know it today is a tribute to the expansion of European traditions of governance and economic organization. One tradition that was exported to Africa during this period was the exclusion of women from the newly created colonial public sphere. In Britain, access to power was gender-based; therefore, politics was largely men's job; and colonization, which is fundamentally a political affair, was no exception. Although both African men and women as conquered peoples were excluded from the higher echelons of colonial state structures, men were represented at the lower levels of government. The system of indirect rule introduced by the British colonial government recognized the male chief's authority at the local level but did not acknowledge the existence of female chiefs. Therefore, women were effectively excluded from all colonial state structures. The process by which women were bypassed by the colonial state in the arena of politics – an arena in which they had participated during the precolonial period – is of particular interest in the following section.

The very process by which females were categorized and reduced to 'women' made them ineligible for leadership roles. The basis for this exclusion was their biology, a process that was a new development in Yorùbá society. The emergence of women as an identifiable category, defined by their anatomy and subordinated to men in all situations, resulted, in part, from the imposition of a patriarchal colonial state. . . .

Likewise, colonization was presented as a 'man-sized' job – the ultimate test of manhood – especially because the European death-rate in West Africa at this time was particularly high. Only the brave-hearted could survive the 'white man's grave', as West Africa was known at the time. According to Callaway, Nigeria was described again and again as a man's country in which women[12] (European women) were 'out of place' in a double sense of physical displacement and the symbolic sense of being in an exclusively male territory. Mrs. Tremlett, a European woman who accompanied her husband to Nigeria during this period, lamented about the position of European women: 'I often found myself reflecting rather bitterly on the insignificant position of a woman in what is practically a man's country. . . . If there is one spot on earth where a woman feels of no importance whatever, it is in Nigeria at the present day'.[13] If the women of the colonizer were so insignificant, then one could only imagine the position of the 'other' women, if their existence was acknowledged at all.

Yet on the eve of colonization there were female chiefs and officials all over Yorùbáland. Ironically, one of the signatories to the treaty that was said to have ceded Ìbàdàn to the British was Làńlàtù, an *iyálóde*, an anafemale chief.[14] The transformation of state power to male-gender power was accomplished at one level by the exclusion of women from state structures. This was in sharp contrast to Yorùbá state organization, in which power was not gender-determined.

The alienation of women from state structures was particularly devastating because the nature of the state itself was undergoing transformation. Unlike the Yorùbá state, the colonial state was autocratic. The African males designated as chiefs by the colonizers had much more power over the people than was vested in them traditionally. In British West Africa in the colonial period, (male) chiefs lost their sovereignty while increasing their powers over the people,[15] although we are to believe that their powers derived from 'tradition' even where the British created their own brand of 'traditional chiefs'. Martin Chanock's astute comment on the powers of chiefs in colonial Africa is particularly applicable to the Yorùbá situation: 'British officials, . . . where they came across a chief, . . . intended to invest *him* retroactively not only with a greater range of authority than he had before but also with authority of a different type. There seemed to be no way of thinking about chiefly authority . . . which did not include judicial power'.[16] Thus male chiefs were invested with more power over the people while female chiefs were stripped of power. Through lack of recognition, their formal positions soon became attenuated.

At another level, the transfer of judicial power from the community to the council of male chiefs proved to be particularly negative for women at a time when the state was extending its tentacles to an increasing number of aspects of life. In pre-British Yorùbá society, adjudication of disputes rested with lineage elders. Therefore, very few matters came under the purview of the ruler and the council of chiefs. But in the colonial administration, the Native Authority System, with its customary courts, dealt with all civil cases including marriage, divorce, and adultery.

It is precisely at the time that the state was becoming omnipotent that women were excluded from its institutions. This omnipotence of the state was a new tradition in Yorùbá society, as it was in many African societies. The omnipotence of the state has deep roots in European politics. Fustel De Coulanges's analysis of the Greek city-states in antiquity attests to this fact:

> There was nothing independent in man; his body belonged to the state, and was devoted to its defence. . . . If the city had need of money, it could order the women to deliver up their jewels. Private life did not escape the omnipotence of the state. The Athenian law, in the name of religion, forbade men to remain single. Sparta punished not only those who remained single, but those who married late. At Athens, the state could prescribe labor, and at Sparta idleness. *It exercised its tyranny in the smallest things*; at Locri the laws forbade men to drink pure wine; at Rome, Miletus and Marseilles, wine was forbidden to women.[17]

Remarkably, Edward Shorter, writing about European societies, echoes De Coulanges's earlier observations: 'Traditional European communities regulated such matters as marital sexuality or the formation of the couple. What may be startling, however, is the extent to which these affairs were removed from informal regulation by public opinion and *subjected to public policy*'.[18] To mention a few examples: there was a 'fornication penalty' against women who were pregnant out of wedlock – no bridal crowns for pregnant brides; and before a man was allowed to join a guild, the guild insisted 'not only that [the] man himself not be illegitimate (or even conceived before marriage), but that his parents be respectably born as well'.[19] Above all, the community had the power to halt marriages.[20] We must not forget that in Europe at this time women were largely excluded from formal public authority; therefore, the public policy referred to by Shorter was male-constituted. No doubt, some of these matters were regulated by African societies, but the regulation was in the hands of the lineage and possibly nonfamilial opinion. Consequently, the probability that any one category of people, such as anafemales, could have been excluded from the decision-making process of the family was much less than in Europe.

It was into this unfortunate tradition of male dominance that Africans were drafted – this was particularly disadvantageous to women because marriage, divorce, and even pregnancy came under the purview of the state. Given the foregoing, it is clear that the impact of colonization was profound and negative for women. Appraisals of the impact of colonization that see certain 'benefits' for African women are mistaken in light of the overarching effect of the colonial state, which effectively defined females as 'women' and hence second-class colonial subjects unfit to determine their own destiny. The postindependence second-class status of African women's citizenship is rooted in the process of inventing them as women. Female access to membership in the group is no longer direct; access to citizenship is now mediated through marriage, through the 'wifization of citizenship'. . . .

Upgrading Males: Sex Discrimination in Colonial Education

The introduction of Christianity and Western education was critical to the stratification of colonial society along both class and gender lines. The initial disadvantage of females in the educational system is arguably the main determinant of women's inferiority and lack of access to resources in the colonial period and indeed in the contemporary period. How did this happen? In the first half-century of British colonization in Yorùbáland, Christianity and Western education were inseparable because they were the monopoly of Christian missionaries. The school was the church, and the church was the school. From the point of view of missionaries, the process of Christianizing and educating the African heathens was to be a process of Europeanization. The goal of the missionaries was to transform African societies, not preserve them.

As envisaged by the missionaries, the African family system was to be targeted for reform and, in turn, to be the vehicle for the 'civilization' of these societies. One missionary in Yorùbáland was to betray this bias when he posed the question: 'Is it proper to apply the sacred name of a home to a compound occupied by two to six or a dozen men each perhaps with a plurality of wives'?[21] 'Spiritual rebirth' and the reconstruction of African societies were intertwined in the minds of the missionaries.

To this end, schools were established to facilitate evangelization. Possibly the most important rationale for the establishment of schools in Yorùbáland during this early period of missionary work is summarized in Baptist missionary T. J. Bowen's book published in 1857:

> Our designs and hopes in regard to Africa, are not simply to bring as many individuals as possible to the knowledge of Christ. We desire to establish the Gospel in the hearts and minds and social life of the people, so that truth and righteousness may remain and flourish among them, without the instrumentality of foreign missionaries. This cannot be done without civilization. To establish the Gospel among any people, they must have Bibles, and therefore must have the art to make them or the money to buy them. They must read the Bible and this implies instruction.[22]

Two important points stand out. First, the European missions needed African missionaries for the purpose of Christianizing their own kind. This is not surprising in that during this period, West Africa was still known as the white man's grave because few Europeans could survive in the environment. Therefore, it was imperative to make use of African personnel if Christianity was to be firmly planted. Second, the ability to read the Bible was seen as critical to the maintenance of individual faith. In light of the foregoing, it is not surprising that males were the target of missionary education. They were seen as potential clerks, catechists, pastors, and missionaries in the service of the church. There was no place for women in these professions except as wives, as helpmates to their husbands, which indeed was the role of the few women missionaries.

In 1842, the very first school was established in Badagri by the Wesleyan mission. By 1845, the Church Missionary Society (CMS) had established a boarding school for boys. Abẹ́òkúta, further inland, was to become the base and education capital of Yorùbáland. By 1851, three thousand Yorùbá emigrants commonly called Sàró,[23] many of them Christians, had settled in this town. One of the most prominent among them was Samuel Ajayi Crowther, who was to become the first African Anglican bishop. Immediately after they arrived in Abẹ́òkúta, Crowther and his wife established two schools, one for boys and one for girls. We are told that Mrs. Crowther's sewing school was very popular, that 'even the *babalawos* [diviner-priests] brought their little girls to Mrs. Crowther for instruction'.[24] Separate-sex practices were established early, as was reflected even in the curriculum of schools that were coeducational. Ajayi summarizes the timetable of the CMS schools in 1848 as follows:

9:00 am	Singing, Rehearsals of Scripture Passages, Reading One Chapter of Scripture, Prayers.
9:15–12 noon	Grammar, Reading, Spelling, Writing, Geography, Tables [except Wednesday, when there was Catechism in place of Grammar].
2:00–4:00 pm	Ciphering [i.e., Arithmetic], Reading, Spelling, Meaning of Words.
4:00 pm	Closing Prayers.[25]

Source: A. Fajana, *Education in Nigeria 1942–1939: An Historical Analysis* (Lagos: Longman, 1978).

He adds: 'This was more or less repeated every day except Friday, which was devoted to rehearsals of Scripture passages, revision and examinations. Girls followed a similar curriculum, but with important changes. In the afternoon session, from Monday to Thursday, they had Sewing and Embroidery'.[26]

Although males were the primary focus of missionary education, it is clear that the education of females was not irrelevant to the missionaries' scheme. In fact, they had a vested interest in producing mothers who would be the foundation of Christian families. They were clearly concerned that the home influence 'could be destroying the good seed sown in school'.[27] The case of the Harrisons and their female wards demonstrates the thinking of missionaries on what this 'home influence' looked like. Mr. and Mrs. Harrison kept the female pupils away from their mothers, who were presumed to be trying 'to keep their daughters down to their old bad ways'.[28] T. H. Popleslour, a missionary and educator, underlined the importance of the family in the education of the child:

> The instruction at school comprehends [*sic*] but a part in education. That in the mouldering [*sic*] of a useful and Christian character the life outside the school must always be taken into consideration in the influences operating for good or ill . . . The parents can play an important part (if they are Christians). How can a heathen who sees no evil in lying, stealing, deception, fornication . . . teach morality? How can they teach their children the fear of God?[29]

For the Christian missions, both girls and boys needed to be educated, but for different places in the new society the colonizers were in the process of fabricating. Thus, priority was given to male education, and provisions were made for some form of higher education for males in some places....

It is clear that, initially, the response of Yorùbá parents to schooling for children was not that favorable. They were reluctant to lose the services of their children, both male and female, on the farms and in the markets. Therefore, the missions had to find incentives to get parents to send their children to school. Thus, in Ìjàyè, both the Baptist and CMS paid pupils to come to school. Even in the coastal areas like Lagos and Badagri, inducements had to be provided. Free gifts from Europe were one such inducement.[30] As time went on, there were complaints from parents that schoolchildren had become lazy and disrespectful to elders. The preference for boarding schools was partially related to the desire of parents to pass the cost of raising their 'unproductive' children to missionaries if schooling was to deprive them of the services of these children. This situation was soon to change as parents realized the value of education in salaried employment and important positions that the educated came to occupy. None of this was available to females. It is no wonder, then, that parents subsequently were not as eager to educate their daughters as their sons. Western schools were very appropriate for educating boys for their future roles, but the training of girls for the adult life mapped out by the European missionaries and colonial officials did not require that kind of education.

By the 1870s, among the Lagos elite – the Sàró particularly – the mothers had found a good reason for educating their daughters. Namely, educated women were sought after for marriage by educated men. Consequently, the creation of female secondary schools by the Methodist, Anglican, and Catholic missions was due to the effort of women's organizations. They used their privileged positions as wives and daughters of prominent men to establish schools for girls.[31] In Victorian Lagos, some of the up-and-coming Yorùbá professional men were beginning to realize what an educated woman could do for their status and career in colonial society. Kristin Mann, in her pioneering study of marriage in colonial Lagos, shows that educated women were in demand for marriage.[32] Not surprisingly, the ideal for such women was to become housewives....

In other words, regardless of qualifications, merit, or seniority, *women were to be subordinated to men in all situations.* Maleness was thus projected as one of the qualifications for employment in the colonial senior civil service. The promotion of anasex as social identity and as a determinant of leadership and responsibility is in stark contrast to the seniority system that was the hallmark of precolonial Yorùbá social organization. Men were to become the 'inheritors' of the colonial state. In many ways, women were dispossessed; their exclusion from education and employment was profound and proved devastating over time. Men had more than a head start, not only in numbers but in what Western education and values came to represent in African societies. The ability to negotiate the 'modern' world, which led to wealth, status, and leadership roles, was increasingly determined by access to Western education and its use for advancement.

Perhaps the most damaging lasting effect of the association of men with education, gainful employment, and leadership may be its psychological effect on both men and women. This is reflected both structurally and ideologically in the school systems. The notion that females are not as mentally capable as males is commonplace among some of the Western-educated in contemporary Nigerian society. It is part of the colonial legacy. For example, Dr. T. Solarin, one of the most prominent educators in Nigeria, has touched on the problem of sex inequality in education. Mayflower, the high school he founded, became coeducational in 1958. Initially, there was a lot of resistance from male students who felt that girls would not perform as well as boys in school because of their mental inferiority.[33] Dr. Solarin was to betray the same kind of thinking. Commenting on the differential achievements of men and women, he pointed out that Europe had produced women like Joan of Arc and Madame Curie, but 'Africa of all continents had sat ever so long and so cruelly on its womanhood'.[34] His sympathy for African women notwithstanding, it is remarkable that, based on the Western standards of achievement that he was invoking, Africa has not produced men of the stature of Madame Curie either. Discounting our history, Dr. Solarin failed to deduce this fact, believing the Western-propagated notion that African women are the most oppressed in the world. This example illustrates the degree to which ideas about racial superiority of Europeans and patriarchy are intertwined in the minds of the colonized – Solarin assumed that in Europe, women were treated as equal to men, in spite of all the evidence to the contrary. One wonders what his reaction would have been to the fact that despite Madame Curie's exceptional achievement of two Nobel prizes, she was not admitted into the French Academy of Sciences because of her sex.[35]

Masculinizing the òrìṣà: Sex Bias in Godly Places

The introduction of Christianity, which is male-dominant, was another factor in the process of establishing male dominance in Yorùbá society. Christian missions in Africa have been rightly described as the hand-maidens of colonization. Like John the Baptist, they prepared the way. They did so in Yorùbáland, just as in other parts of Africa. Christianity arrived in Yorùbáland in the 1840s, decades before most of the area was brought under British rule. The major missionary groups were the Church Missionary Society (CMS) (from Britain), the Wesleyan Methodists, the Southern Baptists (from the United States), and the Catholics. The CMS was the largest and most significant in the early period. The first mission stations were established in Badagri and Abẹ́òkúta, but they soon expanded to towns such as Ìjàyè, Ògbómòṣọ́, Ọ̀yọ́, and Ìbàdàn.

In general, Christian missionaries were well received by the various Yorùbá states. In fact, there was competition among them to secure the presence of missionaries within their borders. Although Yorùbá religion always had room for the adoption of new gods, the reason Yorùbá rulers sought European missionaries was political, not religious. Yorùbá rulers needed the presence and skills of missionaries in order to secure access to trade with the Europeans on the coast and to enhance their position in the power struggle among Yorùbá states during this time period. Abẹ́òkúta, which became the center of missionary activities in Yorùbáland, enjoyed the patronage of Europeans, including their military support. The first Christian community in Yorùbáland was founded in Abẹ́òkúta. Initially, the community was made up mostly of Sàró, but with time they were able to recruit converts from the local population. From the records, it is not very clear what sort of people were drawn to Christianity and what number of males and females converted. Among the Igbó of southeastern Nigeria, social outcasts and slaves, that is, marginalized persons, were the first converts. In Yorùbáland, probably because of the presence of an already Christianized Yorùbá population – the Sàró – the pattern appears to have been different.

Men seem to have been the primary targets for evangelization, a fact borne out in the debate over polygamy. The most serious and most enduring conflict between the church and its Yorùbá converts was the Yorùbá custom of multiple marriage. It became the most explosive factor in the relationship between Yorùbá would-be Christians and the evangelists. For the missionaries, having multiple wives was not only primitive but against God's law: polygamy was adultery, pure and simple.[36] Therefore, the minimum a Yorùbá convert was expected to do before being baptized was to divest himself of all but one of his wives. J. F. A. Ajayi has noted that it is remarkable that the missions were so dogmatic in their opposition to polygamy but were tolerant of slavery. The following quote, attributed to the secretary of the CMS, shows this: 'Christianity will ameliorate the relationship between master and slave; polygamy is an offense against the law of God, and therefore is incapable of amelioration'.[37]

From the perspective of this study, what is equally interesting is how women appear in this debate. One would have thought that since Yorùbá men were the ones who had multiple conjugal partners and thus fell outside the Christian ethos, the woman would have been the natural target for Christianization. Not so. What we find is this recurring question: Should the church baptize the wife of a polygamist?[38] The fact that the question arose at all shows that women were not treated as individual souls for the purpose of salvation. Their individual faith was secondary to the more important question of whose wives they were. Regardless of the fact that salvation was to be constituted by an individual coming to Christ, women were not viewed as individuals – they were seen only as wives. Yorùbá missionary Ajayi Crowther was quick to point out to the church that 'the wife of a polygamist was an involuntary victim of a social institution and should not be denied baptism because of that'.[39] But were women victims of polygamy or victims of the church during this period? My point is that if a polygamist became a Christian, it was only then that the question arose as to which wives were to be discarded and which children were bastards. Women and children were to be penalized for a cultural conflict that was not of their own making. In fact, they were being penalized for being good cultural citizens. The implication of conversion was not lost on the Yorùbá, yet the church failed to address this thorny issue. The admonition of some of the Yorùbá missionaries that polygamy should be tolerated but progressively reformed fell on deaf ears.

By 1891, various conflicts between the Yorùbá Christian community and the missions resulted in secession. In popular discourse, there is the claim that the intolerance of the church for polygamy was one of the main reasons for the break. In 1891, the first African church independent of the missions was founded in Lagos. J. B. Webster, in his pioneering study of independent churches in Yorùbáland, however, asserts that the emergence of indigenous churches in Yorùbáland was a tribute to how committed the Yorùbá had become to Christianity.[40] From my standpoint, this Yorùbá commitment to Christianity was necessarily a commitment to Judeo-Christian patriarchy, and this represented a bad omen for women.

Nevertheless, a new era was dawning in the history of the church in Yorùbáland. In the mission churches, women had been taken for granted; they had been excluded from the clergy and had had no official role whatsoever. But with the founding of the independent churches, women began to assume roles that were more prominent and that were more in tune with the traditional representation of anafemales in Yorùbá religion. As a matter of fact, quite a number of these churches were established by women. The most prominent of them was cofounded by Abíọ́dún Akínsọ̀wọ́n in 1925, but there were many others.[41] Women also played important roles in the day-to-day running of the churches and as prophets. . . .

An upshot of the Christianization of Yorùbá society was the introduction of notions of gender into the religious sphere, including into the indigenous religious system. In traditional Yorùbá religion, anasex-distinctions did not play any part, whether in the world of humans or in that of the gods. Like other African religions, Yorùbá religion had three pillars. First, there was Olódùmarè (God – the Supreme Being). Olódùmarè did not have a gender identity, and it is doubtful that s/he was perceived as a human being before the advent of Christianity and Islam in Yorùbáland. Second, the òrìṣà (gods) were the manifestations of the attributes of the supreme being and were regarded as his/her messengers to humans. They were the most obvious focus of Yorùbá worship. Though there were anamale and anafemale *òrìṣà*, as in other institutions this distinction was inconsequential; therefore, it is best described as a distinction without difference. For example, both Ṣàngó (the god of thunder) and Ọya (the female river god) were known for their wrath. Furthermore, a census of the *òrìṣà* to determine their sex composition is impossible since the total number of *òrìṣà* is unknown and is still expanding. In addition, not all the *òrìṣà* were thought of in gendered terms; some were recognized as male in some localities and female in others. Third, there were the ancestors, both male and female, venerated by members of each lineage and acknowledged yearly in the Egúngún masquerade: a cult of ancestor veneration. In the world of humans, the priesthood of various gods was open to both males and females. In general, the singular predictor of who worshiped which *òrìṣà* was lineage membership and town of origin. From the foregoing, it is clear that Yorùbá religion, just like Yorùbá civic life, did not articulate gender as a category; therefore, the roles of the *òrìṣà*, priests, and ancestors were not gender-dependent. . . .

The implications of replacing female symbols with male ones and transforming gender-neutral gods into male gods in African religions are yet to be analyzed. However, the work of feminist theologians regarding Judeo-Christian patriarchy's effect on women in the West is indicative of what is in store for African women as the patriarchalizing of their religions continue. In regard to Judeo-Christian religions, Carol Christ asserts: 'Religions centered on the worship of a male God create "moods" and "motivations" that keep women in a state of psychological dependence on men and male authority, while at the same time legitimating the *political* and *social* authority of fathers and sons in the institutions of society'.[42] The organization of religion in any given society, including religious symbols and values, reflects the social organization. Therefore, as African women are increasingly marginalized in society, it is not surprising that they are shortchanged in religious systems as well. The ramifications of patriarchalized religions may be greater in Africa than in the West because religion permeates all aspects of African life; the notion of a nonreligious space even today is questionable.

No Woman's Land

Another landmark of European penetration of indigenous societies, whether in Africa or in the Americas, was the commercialization of land. Land became a commodity to be bought and sold. The focus of this section is to analyze the effect of the commodification of land and how females were shortchanged in the transition from collective rights of access to private ownership.

In nineteenth-century Yorùbáland, as in most parts of Africa, land was not a commodity to be individually owned, bought, and sold. The following statement from the memoirs of Anna Hinderer, a European missionary living in Ìbàdàn at the time, shows the Yorùbá conception of property and ownership: 'When Mr. Hinderer, on first settling at Ìbàdàn, asked what price he must pay for some land . . . , the chief said laughing,"Pay! Who pays for the ground? All the ground belongs to God; you cannot pay for it"'.[43] If there was any claim to land, it was lineage-based and communally based.[44] Land was never sold – it was given to newcomers either by the *ọba* or by representatives of lineages. The lineage was the landholding unit, and all members of the family, male and female, had rights of usage. As Samuel Johnson noted, 'No portion of such farms can be alienated from the family without the unanimous consent of all the members thereof . . . '.[45]

This Yorùbá 'no man's land' system of land tenure thus started to undergo transformation in the colonial period, to the detriment of women. Their land rights were affected by a number of developments, best illustrated by the case of Lagos, which was occupied by the British in 1861. Changes there were indicative of what was to take place in other Yorùbá towns following European rule.

Land sales evolved quite early in Lagos because of the presence of European merchants and a Westernized class of Yorùbá – the Sàró. Land grants to European merchants from the *ọba* of Lagos were understood as outright sales. In the case of the Sàró, their Western education and values predisposed them to the buying and selling of land. More directly, the system of crown grants of land was used in which local 'owners of property held their land as a grant from the British Crown'.[46] For example, an ordinance was issued in 1869 that provided for property ownership for any person who 'had been in occupation either by *himself* or his sub-tenant'.[47] This Crown grant system served to propagate further the idea of land for sale. The idea that persons occupying land had a right of ownership must have turned many a family property into private property, usually male-owned. First, the movement from collective ownership of land to private and individual ownership was stacked against women because by colonial definition (as the wording of the ordinance suggests) only men could be individuals. Second, given that marriage residence in Yorùbáland was in general patrilocal, it is not likely that a woman occupied land '*by himself*'. I should be quick to note that the apparent disadvantage in this case stemmed not from the Yorùbá tradition of patrilocality but from the colonial law that occupation of land constituted ownership, thereby abrogating the precolonial rights of access conferred by birth. After all, the idea that a man occupied land by himself and not on behalf of the lineage was a result of the new dispensation and could only be sustained by the European idea of a male household head whose authority was absolute. More significantly, relative to men, many women lacked both cultural capital and currency that had become necessary for accumulation in Victorian Lagos.

> Social historian Kristin Mann is correct when she articulated that in Victorian Lagos, the ability to read and write in English ensured the early educated Christians advantages in a community where the government and private citizens increasingly wrote down, in the language of colonial rulers, important communications and commercial and legal transactions. . . . Illiterate merchants soon found they had to hire literate clerks.[48]

Among the Sàró, the number of educated women was far less than men; and besides, the Victorian values of such women meant that they saw the business of acquiring property and breadwinning as properly within the sphere of men. Nevertheless, Sàró women benefited from their privileged status, and in fact some of them took advantage of their education. The situation in Abẹ́òkúta was almost identical to that of Lagos, as the former was the other locality where the Sàró were concentrated. The sale of land in Abẹ́òkúta became so rapid and generated so many problems that in 1913 the council issued an order limiting sale to indigenes of the town.[49]

The production of cash crops such as cocoa proved to be another factor that increased the value of land. In gender terms, it is also important because it generated new wealth from which women were by and large marginalized. This process can be seen further inland. In Ìbàdàn, Ife, and Ondo, the commercialization of land and its rapid sale were due to the expansion of cocoa cultivation. Though the British did not introduce cocoa into Yorùbáland, they quickly recognized the potential of its exploitation for the benefit of the colonial government. They promoted its spread and subsequently monopolized its marketing. The major impact of cocoa cultivation on women was that they were marginal to the biggest opportunity for gaining wealth that opened up during this period. According to Sara Berry, the pioneers of the cocoa cultivation were Yorùbá men who had been exposed to Christianity.[50] The literature has assumed a link between women's marginality in cocoa production and their lack of association with farming in the precolonial period. However, in chapter 2, I demonstrated that the evidence shows that farming was not a gender-defined occupation in precolonial Yorùbáland. Even if we accept the notion of a gender division of labor, the disadvantage of women still needs to be accounted for considering that even in societies where females were recognized as farmers and took part in the cocoa boom, as among the Ashanti of Ghana, women did not seem to do as well as men during the colonial period; despite the claim that Yorùbá women had been dominant in trade, this did not guarantee their continued dominance in the colonial period. No comparable opportunity for accumulating wealth opened up to women. Therefore, we begin to see a gender gap in access to wealth. This gap was heightened because cocoa production gave men an advantage in trade and provided them with capital. Again, this fact shows that the polarization of trade and farming as distinct occupational types is misleading.

The individuation of land ownership and the scarcity attendant upon commercialization did not augur well for women's rights. Simi Afonja has documented that in Ondo since the colonial period, women's rights have been abrogated, especially in the case of children who want to enforce their rights of access based on their mother's membership in a lineage.[51] Jane Guyer found that in another Yorùbá locality, as a result of the value placed on land used to grow cocoa, patrilineages were unwilling to pass it down through females. They preferred to pass this land through males in the second generation, though they remained willing to pass food-crop land through both male and female members of the lineage.[52]

Perhaps the most serious development resulting from land sale was the ideology explaining the new reality of land sales and abrogation of women's rights as 'our custom' rather than as a 'tradition' that developed in the colonial period. Gavin Kitching, in his discussion of the impact of the European land-tenure system on the Kikuyu of Kenya, points out that it was in the colonial period that Africans started to conceptualize their land-use patterns in terms of Western notions of land purchase, sale, and tenancy.[53] Such developments were also evident in Yorùbáland. Fadipe notes that by the 1930s, there existed an erroneous belief in some Yorùbá localities that 'the sale of land has been a long tradition among them'.[54] In the same way, the marginalization of females from family land has also been presented as a 'long tradition'. Simi Afonja cites a seventy-year-old man in the town of Ife who stated that 'it was unheard of for the commoner women to own landed property and houses in the past'.[55] However, Afonja did not raise the next logical question as to which 'past' he was referring to, particularly because private property in land and houses for any person was unknown in Yorùbáland until the nineteenth century in Lagos and Abẹ́òkúta and much later in the hinterland. . . .

The Wages of Colonization

Central to colonial rule was the question of how to extract wealth from the colonies for the benefit of the occupying European powers. To this end, by the turn of the century, the British colonial administration started to build a railway line that would link various parts of their three colonies that were to become Nigeria. For this study, the railways are important because railway service pioneered wage labor and proved to be the largest employer of labor in colonial Nigeria. Women were largely excluded from the wage-labor force (although there have been relatively large improvements since independence, female representation in the formal sector remains much lower than that of men).

By 1899, over ten thousand men were employed in the construction of the railways. Later, more men were employed to operate the system. Most of the original workers were Yorùbá. According to W. Oyemakinde, unlike other parts of Nigeria and indeed other areas of Africa, there was no labor shortage for the construction of the railways in Yorùbáland because there was already in existence a 'floating population' of men.[56] These were displaced persons who had been enslaved in the wake of the Yorùbá civil wars in the nineteenth century. This population was easily recruited as labor by the colonial government. However, despite the presence of females among this population, and in spite of the fact that some of the initial work on the railways involved head-loading supplies, which was no different from what males and females did in the nineteenth century, women were not employed in any considerable numbers. It is not clear what happened to the 'floating' female population.

More importantly, the introduction of capitalist relations in the form of wage labor was a novelty in the Yorùbá economy and was to have major repercussions, particularly in the definition of work. All through the nineteenth century, in spite of the expansion of trade with Europe, no free-market developed in Yorùbáland as regards labor. In fact, domestic slavery (as distinct from the Atlantic slave trade) expanded during this period due to the increased demand for labor, as trade with Europe in agricultural produce expanded. Oyemakinde notes that in colonial Yorùbáland wage labor became the avenue for former slaves to buy their freedom.[57] The implications of this statement are far-reaching in light of the fact that females did not have access to wages. Does it then mean that female enslavement was prolonged? This is an interesting question that cannot be answered in this study. Historical studies of slavery and the slave trade in Africa remain trapped in Eurocentric concerns and misrepresentations.

Apart from access to cash, which wage labor meant for men, there were other more subtle but equally profound effects. Because men were paid a wage, their labor acquired exchange value while women's labor retained only its use value, thereby devaluing work that became associated with women. Walter Rodney's analysis of work in the colonial situation is elucidating:

> Since men entered the money sector more easily and in greater numbers than women, women's work became greatly inferior to that of men within the new value system of colonialism: men's work was 'modern' and women's work was 'traditional' and 'backward'. Therefore, the deterioration in the status of African women was bound up with the consequent loss of the right to set indigenous standards of what work had merit and what did not.[58]

This gender distinction was to lead to the perception of men as workers and women as nonworkers and therefore appendages of men. Women's work became invisible. Yet in reality the starvation wages that men were paid by the colonial government were insufficient to reproduce the family, and women's labor remained as necessary as ever for the survival of the community. It is well documented that African men, unlike their European counterparts, were paid a single and not a family wage. In fact, by 1903, the initial attraction of wage work on the railways in Nigeria gave way to a labor shortage and trade union organization by disgruntled workers.[59]

In addition, wage labor involved migration away from places of origin to centers of government and commerce that were developing all over the colony at the time. It meant that women moved with their husbands away from kin groups. The case of Madame Bankole, a subject in an ethnographic study of Yorùbá migrant families, is not atypical:

> In 1949 she married . . . another Ijebu man who was a supervisor in the telegraph office and had recently been widowed. He was transferred frequently from place to place, and she went with him, changing her trade each time. From Warri in the western Niger delta she

transported palm oil to Ìbàdàn and re-sold it there to retailers. Then from Jos and Kano she sent rice and beans to a woman to whom she sublet her . . . stall, and received crockery in return that she sold in the North. She also cooked and sold food in the migrant quarters of those towns. From 1949 to 1962 she moved around with him.[60]

What is most striking about Madame Bankole's experience is her resourcefulness and entrepreneurial spirit, responding to the market and her situation. But on a more subtle note, Madame Bankole had become a wife, an appendage whose situation was *determined* by her husband's occupation. Although she retained one of the dominant indigenous occupations of Yorùbáland, the focus of her existence appears to have shifted from trade to marriage as an occupation. The combination of male wage labor and migration produced a new social identity for females as dependents and appendages of men. Regardless of the fact that in precolonial Ọ̀yọ́ the position of an *aya* was junior to that of her conjugal partner, the perception of an *aya* as a dependent and an appendage was a new one. For example, in spite of the fact that Madame Bankole was not dependent in economic terms, there is a perception of her dependency built into the new family situation. The anafemales had moved from being *aya* to *wife*.

A corollary of women's exaggerated identity as wives was that other identities became muted. As couples moved away from kin groups, women's identity as offspring (daughters) and members of the lineage became secondary to their identities as wives. Though Madame Bankole retained a dominant precolonial occupation in Yorùbáland (i.e., trading), the fact that she had to fold up shop whenever her husband's job demanded shows that she and her occupation were secondary. The family itself was slowly being redefined as the man plus his dependents (wife/wives and children) rather than as the 'extended' family, including siblings and parents. The emergence of men as apparent sole breadwinners was to shape the kind of opportunities and resources that were made available by both the colonial and the neocolonial state that followed. For example, the reason why men had more educational opportunities is often ascribed to the notion that they were the 'breadwinners'. The symbolism of bread is particularly apt since both bread and the male as sole breadwinner are colonial infusions into Yorùbá culture. The definition of men as the 'breadwinners' resulted in discrimination against women in the taxation system, which has continued to the present. Women cannot claim any exemptions for children as long as the fathers of such children are still alive. As Fola Ighodalo notes, one of the first female permanent secretaries in the Nigerian civil service said about the tax regulation: 'This particular regulation has completely disregarded the social circumstances of Nigeria where polygamy is a way of life and under which many women have to carry solely the responsibility for the maintenance, education and every care of their children'.[61]

The notion that only men really work shows up in the compilation of national statistics on labor force participation. The percentage of women in the formal sector remains small.[62] This is accounted for by the fact that most women are self-employed and their engagements are not defined as work, despite their participation in the cash economy. It is important to point out that I am not referring here to their contribution of goods and services in the home but employment outside the home as traders and farmworkers, to give two examples. From the standpoint of national statistics-accounting, Madame Bankole was unemployed.

Becoming Women, Being Invisible

We can discern two vital and intertwined processes inherent in European colonization of Africa. The first and more thoroughly documented of these processes was the racializing and the attendant inferiorization of Africans as the colonized, the natives. The second process, which has been the focus of this chapter, was the inferiorization of females. These processes were inseparable, and both were embedded in the colonial situation. The process of inferiorizing the native, which was the essence of colonization, was bound up with the process of enthroning male hegemony. Once the colonized lost their sovereignty, many looked to the colonizer for direction, even in the interpretation of their own history and culture. Many soon abandoned their own history and values and embraced those of the Europeans. One of the Victorian values imposed by the colonizers was the use of body-type to delineate social categories; and this was manifested in the separation of sexes and the presumed inferiority of females. The result was the reconceptualization of the history and customs of the natives to reflect this new race and gender bias of the Europeans. . . .

For African women, the tragedy deepened in that the colonial experience threw them to the very bottom of a history that was not theirs. Thus, the unenviable position of European women became theirs by imposition, even as European women were lifted over Africans because their race was privileged. More specifically, in the Yorùbá case, females became subordinated as soon as they were 'made up' into women – an embodied and homogenized category. Thus by definition they became invisible. The precolonial Yorùbá seniority system was displaced by a European system of hierarchy of the sexes in which the female sex is always inferior and subordinate to the male sex. The ultimate manifestation of this new system was a colonial state that was patriarchal and that has unfortunately survived the demise of 'the empire'. Whatever the values, history, and world-sense of any cultural group in Africa, the colonial government held political control and 'the specifically symbolic power to impose the principles of the construction of reality'.[63] The reality created and enforced was the inferiority of Africans and the inferiority of females until the colonized chart their own reality. . . .

Notes

1. This is a bifurcated world – a world cut in two. Abdul Jan Mohammed elaborates the idea of Manichaeanism in the colonial world as 'a field of diverse yet interchangeable oppositions between White and Black, good and evil, superiority and inferiority, civilization and savagery, intelligence and emotion, rationality and sensuality, self and Other, subject and object' ('The Economy of Manichean Allegory: The Function of Racial Difference in Colonialist Literature', in *Race, Writing, and Difference*, ed Henry Louis Gates Jr [Chicago: University of Chicago Press, 1988], 82).
2. Frantz Fanon, *The Wretched of the Earth* (New York: Grove Weidenfeld, 1963); Albert Memmi, *The Colonizer and the Colonized* (Boston: Beacon Press, 1965).
3. Ashis Nandy, *The Intimate Enemy: Loss and Recovery of Self under Colonialism* (Delhi: Oxford University Press, 1983), 5. Dominance is often expressed in sexual terms; consequently, colonisation is seen as a process of taking away the manhood of the colonised, and national liberation seen as a step towards its restoration.
4. Fanon, *Wretched of the Earth*, 63.
5. Fanon, *Wretched of the Earth*, 39; emphasis added.
6. Nandy, *Intimate Enemy*, x; emphasis added.
7. Stephanie Urdang, *Fighting Two Colonialisms: Women in Guinea-Bissau* (London: Zed Press, 1979); Elizabeth Schmidt, *Peasants, Traders, and Wives: Shona Women in the History of Zimbabwe, 1870–1939* (Portsmouth, NH: Heinemann Educational Books, 1992), makes the claim that Shona women of Zimbabwe were beholden to two patriarchies – indigenous and European.

8. Cited in Nina Mba, *Nigerian Women Mobilized: Women's Political Activity in Southern Nigeria, 1900–1965* (Berkeley: University of California, Institute of International Studies, 1982), 65.
9. It is misleading to assume that the relationship between African men and women was untouched by colonisation. After all, according to Memmi, 'I discovered that few aspects of my life and personality were untouched by the fact of colonization. Not only my own thoughts, my passions and my conduct, but the conduct of others towards me was affected' (*Colonizer*, viii).
10. Elizabeth Spelman, *Inessential Woman: Problems of Exclusion in Feminist Thought* (Boston: Beacon Press, 1988), 123.
11. Bill Freund, *The Making of Contemporary Africa* (Bloomington: Indiana University Press, 1984), 111.
12. Callaway appears to be impervious to the fact that there were gender distinctions among the Africans, despite the fact that part of her motivation for writing was to restore a gendered analysis of colonisation.
13. Quoted in Helen Callaway, *Gender, Culture, Empire: European Women in Colonial Nigeria* (Oxford: MacMillan Press, 1987), 5.
14. Samuel Johnson, *The History of the Yorubas* (New York: Routledge and Kegan Paul, 1921), 656.
15. M Crowder and O Ikime, *West African Chiefs* (Ife: University of Ife Press, 1970), xv.
16. Martin Chanock, 'Making Customary Law: Men, Women and the Courts in Colonial Rhodesia', in *African Women and the Law: Historical Perspectives*, ed M J Hay and Marcia Wright (Boston: African Studies Center, Boston University, 1982), 59; emphasis added.
17. Fustel De Coulanges, *The Ancient City: A Study on the Religion, Laws and Institutions of Greece and Rome* (np, 1983 [1987]), 293–94; emphasis added.
18. Edward Shorter, *The Making of the Modern Family* (New York: Vintage Books, 1983), 50; emphasis added.
19. Shorter, *The Making of the Modern Family*, 51.
20. Shorter, *The Making of the Modern Family*, 52.
21. J F A Ajayi, *Christian Missions in Nigeria 1841–1891* (Evanston, IL: Northwestern University Press, 1965), 15.
22. T J Bowen, *Central Africa* (Charleston: Southern Baptist Publication Society, 1857), 321–22.
23. On the Sàró, see chap 3, n16, above.
24. A Fajana, *Education in Nigeria 1942–1939: An Historical Analysis* (Lagos: Longman, 1978), 25.
25. Ajayi, *Christian Missions*.
26. Ajayi, *Christian Missions*, 139.
27. Fajana, *Education in Nigeria*, 29.
28. Fajana, *Education in Nigeria*, 37.
29. Quoted in Fajana, *Education in Nigeria*, 30.
30. Ajayi, *Christian Missions*, 135.
31. Mba, *Nigerian Women*, 62.
32. Kristin Mann, *Marrying Well: Marriage, Status, and Social Change among the Educated Elite in Colonial Lagos* (Cambridge: Cambridge University Press, 1985).
33. T Solarin, *To Mother with Love: An Experiment in Auto-Biography* (Ìbàdàn: Board Publications, 1987), 223.
34. Solarin, *To Mother with Love*, 226.

35. See Lorna Schiebinger, *The Mind Has No Sex? Women in the Origins of Modern Science* (Cambridge, MA: Harvard University Press, 1989), 10–11.
36. Ajayi, *Christian Missions*, 106.
37. Quoted in Ajayi, *Christian Missions*, 107.
38. Ajayi, *Christian Missions*.
39. Ajayi, *Christian Missions*, 106.
40. J B Webster, *The African Churches among the Yoruba, 1882–1922* (London: Clarendon Press, 1961).
41. See J D Y Peel, *Aladura: A Religious Movement among the Yoruba* (London: Oxford University Press, 1968), 71.
42. Carol Christ, 'Why Women Need the Goddess: Phenomenological, Psychological, and Political Reflections', in *Womanspirit Rising: A Feminist Reader in Religion*, ed C P Christ and J Plaskow (San Francisco: Harper and Row, 1979), 275.
43. Hinderer, *Seventeen Years*, 60. Anna Hinderer, *Seventeen Years in the Yoruba Country: Memorials of Anne Hinderer* (London: Seeley, Jackson and Holliday, 1877), 60.
44. Fadipe, *Sociology of the Yoruba*, 169. N. A. Fadpie, *The Sociology of the Yoruba* (Ìbàdàn: Ìbòdàn University Press, 1970), 169.
45. Johnson, *History of the Yorubas*, 96.
46. Coker, *Family Property*. G. B. A. Coker, *Family Property among the Yoruba* (London: Sweet and Maxwell, 1958).
47. Coker, *Family Property*, 189–90; emphasis added.
48. Mann, *Marrying Well*, 19–20.
49. T O Elias, *Nigerian Land Law and Custom* (London: Routledge and Kegan Paul, 1951), 186.
50. Sara Berry, *Cocoa, Custom and Socio-Economic Change in Rural Western Nigeria* (Oxford: Clarendon Press, 1975), 46–49.
51. Simi Afonja, 'Land Control: A Critical Factor in Yoruba Gender Stratification', in *Women and Class in Africa*, ed C Robertson and I Berger (New York: Africana Publishing, 1986).
52. Cited in Afonja, 'Land Control'.
53. Gavin Kitching, *Class and Economic Change in Kenya: The Making of an African Petit Bourgeoisie* (New Haven, CT: Yale University Press, 1980), 285.
54. Fadipe, *Sociology of the Yoruba*, 171.
55. Simi Afonja, 'Changing Modes of Production and the Sexual Division of Labor among the Yoruba', in *Women's Work, Development and Division of Labor by Gender*, ed H Safa and E Leacock (South Hadley, MA: Bergin and Garvey, 1986), 131.
56. W Oyemakinde, 'Railway Construction and Operation in Nigeria 1895–1911', *Journal of Historical Society of Nigeria* 7, no 2 (1974): 305.
57. Oyemakinde, 'Railway Construction', 305.
58. Walter Rodney, *How Europe Underdeveloped Africa* (Washington, DC: Howard University Press, 1972), 227.
59. Oyemakinde, 'Railway Construction', 312.
60. Dan Aronson, *The City Is Our Farm: Seven Migrant Yoruba Families* (Cambridge, MA: Schenkman Publishing Co, 1978), 128–29.
61. Fola Ighodalo, 'Barriers to the Participation of Nigerian Women in the Modern Labor Force', in *Nigerian Women and Development*, ed O Ogunsheye et al. (Ìbàdàn: Ìbàdàn University Press, 1988), 363.
62. Ighodalo, 'Barriers to the Participation of Nigerian Women', 356.
63. Callaway, *Gender*, 55.

Rajeev Bhargava*, 'Reparations for Cultural Injustice'

Is another response possible between violence and forcible exclusion on the one hand and silence and denial on the other? What possibly could this response be? How should we respond to continuing cultural injustice? What should the sufferer demand from the traducer or from himself? I take it as a given that prosecution is an absurd remedy for cultural injustice. If any morally adequate response is appropriate, then it must take some form of reparation. Why so? And what should be the content of such reparative claims?

Recall the attributes of cultural injustice: (*a*) the displacement and dislocation of indigenous cultures and the loss of their basic cultural forms. (*b*) The generation of damaged selves and schizophrenia in the colonized.[1] (*c*) The imposition on the colonized of the position of a perpetual chaser of the colonizer. Because he is cast as an imitator, he is forever condemned to be behind the colonizer, always pursuing purposes not of his own making. Such a situation leaves no scope for alternating and reciprocal leadership. (*d*) The inferiorization of the culture of the colonized. (*e*) Given to inferiorizing the colonized for long, the colonizer develops grave indifference to the fate of the colonized. He is morally deadened to the vulnerable and the estranged – a massive moral defect. In sum, at the deepest level, colonialism not only gravely damages colonized cultures and selves but also relations between the colonized and the colonizer.[2]

How are damaged cultures and broken relationships to be mended? Should the colonizers financially compensate for the damage and dislocation they caused to the cultures of the colonized? It is hard to calculate the monetary value of cultures and anyway inappropriate to do so. Therefore, like prosecution, this too seems an absurd requirement. What then should be the content of such reparative claims? A significant cause of broken relationship between the colonized and the colonizer is the failure on the part of the colonizer to extend the principle of moral equality to the colonized. How can moral indifference be replaced by an attitude that grants equal moral standing and worth to people of formerly colonized cultures? How can the basic attitude of the colonizer be changed? How can the circulation of crude stereotypes about other cultures be stopped? This is related to other questions. How can asymmetries of cultural power be transformed into relations of cultural equality? How can monologic interactions become dialogic? Two reparative strategies are relevant here, if we have traducer-response in mind. First, an apology for past wrongs. Apologies, as Martha Minow reminds us 'acknowledge the fact of harms, accept some degree of responsibility, avow sincere regret, and promise not to repeat the offence'.[3] Sincere apologies depend on experiencing shame and then making a positive use of this emotion to improve oneself and to reconstruct the world in which one has to live, a relevant traducer-response is to feel shame.

The promise not to repeat the offence is as difficult as, and presupposes, the acknowledgment of harms and the acceptance of responsibility. Because if the promise is to be fulfilled, it must be accompanied by a genuine cognitive resolve to change the ways in which the colonizers have viewed the colonized. This entails a major transformation on the way in which Western knowledge systems have been organized and regulated. It is also linked to the second reparative strategy: truth telling. Thus, stories of empire building, colonialism and imperialism and the cultural and cognitive damage they caused must be constructed. History, social science, humanities, the arts, and the media more generally each have a role to play

---

* Rajeev Bhargava, 'Reparations for Cultural Injustice', in *Reparations*, ed Jon Miller and Rahul Kumar (Oxford: Oxford University Press, 2007), 241–51. By permission of Oxford University Press.

in dismantling these powerful intellectual-cum-cultural colonizing systems and showing the collusion between belief-systems and colonialism. Coming to terms with the past is not only a political but a powerful cultural and intellectual act of truth telling. Such truth telling must be inspired by a persistent and engaging search for ethnocentric biases. New theoretical structures and strategies of perception are required to contest the previous dominant Western ways of saying things. Once upon a time, every single story was told from the standpoint of the colonizer. The colonized were included as a mere object, never as a subject. Changing this requires a major conceptual re-orientation toward the needs of the non-Western world.[4] Let me give an example from my own experience. Indian universities generally tend to be lukewarm to social and political philosophy. This is partly because of a lack of interest among academics in normative issues but also because of certain features of political philosophy itself. Its content may well be universal but its form is certainly parochial, no doubt partly because there are few non-Western scholars who take it up. Much of academic political philosophy takes little inspiration from non-Western societies, makes hardly any references to the problems they face and takes little notice of how cross-cultural issues acquire a distinct inflection in their cultures. Most of the examples discussed in political philosophy have no immediate relation to these societies. Besides, there are few non-Western philosophers who could become a role model for Indian students. No wonder that political scientists in India take virtually no interest in political philosophy. All this makes the task of a political philosopher in India very difficult. These difficulties are compounded by the unavailability of journals all of which are published abroad. It is hardly surprising therefore, that Indian students though enthused by political philosophy, do not display a great deal of self-confidence or competence in doing it. Changing all this means literally turning the world upside down. 'It means looking from the other side of the photograph, experiencing how differently things look when you live in Baghdad rather than in Boston and understanding why. It means realizing that when the West looks at the non-Western world, what it sees is often more a mirror image of itself and its assumptions than what the non-West is really like and how non-Western people actually feel and perceive themselves'.[5] This requires sustained intellectual commitment framed by a larger moral commitment to equal consideration and respect for all including the vulnerable and the stranger and a resolve to build common spaces where different cultures can enter into dialog with one another on equal terms. It also requires building a larger culture that allows ordinary people in colonizing countries to morally disassociate themselves from those practices of their governments and multinational corporations that perpetuate injustice.[6]

This resolve may also carry financial implications. The rectification of intellectual blunders committed in the past may be possible only by the institutionalization of systematic learning about other cultures and civilizations. This may require more than a token gesture of setting up an area studies program or a research institute. It may involve setting aside huge sums of money for research and education, educational scholarships, and the hiring of people with knowledge and understanding about these cultures. It would most certainly require correcting imbalances in the media by instituting more scrupulous policies of selecting the right people for the job and for ensuring adequate and culturally sensitive coverage of events in former colonies.

I have spoken above of traducer-response. Let me turn my attention once again to sufferer-response. What is an appropriate sufferer-response? I believe it too must change its character. Monological resistance may well be justifiable as a temporary act of defiance. But in the long run, sufferer-responses must cease to be restricted only to sufferers and must encompass the traducer. Surely, to rectify continuing cultural injustice, we need not monadic, isolated and disengaged responses but those which, though separate, are mutually engaged. This mutual engagement is mandatory for another important reason. I have hitherto spoken of colonizers and colonized and assumed that all colonizers are traducers and all colonized are sufferers. This is incorrect for two reasons. First, those descendants of colonizers who have unambiguously dissociated themselves from the acts of the colonial state and colonizers should be included, if at all, with the greatest of caution. The mere fact of being a white man or a white woman does not make one a traducer. Second, those among the colonized who had begun to collaborate and had benefited from colonization and those of their descendants who have still failed to morally dissociate themselves from the process of colonization can barely be counted among the sufferers. The mere fact of being, say, an Indian does not make one into an unambiguous victim or sufferer. I do not mean to suggest that colonizers and the colonized elite share equal responsibility for the suffering of the colonized people. However, the colonized elite has some responsibility, if not for their own initial suffering, then at least for the contribution they made toward the suffering of others in the reproduction of cultural injustices. Such people were surely morally tainted. It is no longer possible then, as it once might have been, to identify all perpetrators of injustice as Western and all victims as non-Western. The historical responsibility for the continuing cultural injustice of colonialism is distributed among both the colonizers and at least a part of the colonized elite. From here on, therefore, when I speak of traducers, I exclude some descendants of the colonizers and include some descendants of the colonized. Likewise, when I speak of sufferers, I do not mean to imply that every colonized person was a victim of cultural injustice to the same degree. These points must be kept in mind when we are thinking of appropriate responses to cultural injustices. If what is mentioned above is correct, then within the larger plot of working out a better understanding and reconciliation between colonial traducers and colonized sufferers is the subplot of better mutual understanding and reconciliation between colonized traducers and colonized sufferers. The colonizers have an obligation to the colonized. Among the colonized, the elites too have special obligation toward the colonized sufferers. The collaborative nature of the colonial enterprise at least in its middle phase implies that a proper response to it must also be worked out jointly.[7] An intellectual coming to terms with the past, a proper acknowledgment and telling of the truth about cultural colonialism must be the result of a joint effort of Western and non-Western intelligentsia.

However, this is easier said than done. No matter how complicitous the non-Western elites were or are in the production of cultural injustice, there is no getting away from the fact that huge asymmetries of knowledge and power still remain intact. We must reckon with the fact that Western people including those who have dissociated themselves from colonialism continue to function with little knowledge of the non-Western world. This is not the case with non-Western intellectuals. Indeed, it is impossible for them to function as intellectuals without a great deal of knowledge about Western intellectual traditions. I do not here mean merely that there are inequities of empirical knowledge of each other. I have in mind something deeper. The very assumptions and presuppositions underlying our enquiries into our own world are shot through with categories derived from Western experience. It is self-evident by now that the categories of Western thought are inadequate for our experience and lifeworld. Yet, it is these categories with which we cannot help but begin. We recognize that they should be neither the starting point of our investigations nor its finished product. Yet, this is an ever-present danger of our enquiries. We know for example that contemporary political theory is useful for our societies but we know better still that it is a product of a context that has practically no relation to our own. In short, the deep problem today for the sufferers of cultural injustice is that Western categories have both an undeniable universal potential and that they are fully intermingled with the specificity of Western practices and, worse, possess a deep imprint of Western domination and hegemony. We can neither ignore Western ideas nor fully show how they can be rescued from the pernicious effects of their own imperial imprint.[8] Western thought to non-Western people is both recognizably their own *and* alien.

It appears then that apart from working jointly with their western counterparts, the sufferers of cultural injustice also have to work on their own and work out their own distinctive responses. To begin with, they must know which responses to eschew. First, they should not yield to the temptation of 'postcolonial revenge'.[9] They should not retreat from anything Western merely on the ground that it is Western. They should neither blindly reject nor accept it. Second, they should avoid the pitfalls of a naive and dangerous nativism or an intellectually impoverished cultural nationalism. Third, as already implied above, the elites among the formerly colonized should not behave as if they had no hand whatsoever in their own victimization or in the victimization of their fellow citizens. Indeed, they should more openly acknowledge their active role in the neglect or inferiorization of their own tradition and culture.

What then should they do? First, sufferers of cultural injustice must turn their biculturalism into a strength rather than perpetually view it as a sign of their subjection. As they identify the eurocentrism and parochialism of Western categories, they should also see in this an invitation for the creative renewal of a potentially common tradition – that is one among many and yet shared. This can be done only if it is reinvigorated by non-Western peoples with their own outlook and interests in mind. Western traditions were also frozen by the impact of colonialism or by the sheer intellectual lethargy of its inheritors. It needs 'outsiders' to rejuvenate it. This is already happening with concepts such as secularism and democracy.

However, the renewal of Western traditions by non-Western people is not possible unless they are committed to a focused, collective effort to retrieve their own forgotten and neglected traditions. This entails the examination of texts that have so far been gathering dust in unknown sites. But can these indigenous traditions ever be recovered? Can cultures of the colonized be restored to a state in which they were before colonization? Can they be relocated where they were before their displacement by colonialism? Can basic cultural forms be recovered? It is doubtful if 'original cultural forms' can ever be recovered. There is a sense in which there is no going back to pure indigenous cultures because every rediscovery is at least partly a reinvention. We know that every revival of tradition has turned out to be its reinvention. Restoration may be possible for cultural artifacts that are physically embodied but for artifacts such as conceptual frameworks that are largely disembodied, this is extremely difficult. Yet the slow painstaking process of a part recovery of the voice and history of the colonized can begin by putting together and reinterpreting traces of evidence and meaning present in largely forgotten texts.

Retrieving intellectual traditions is not, of course, just a matter of locating texts and reading them creatively. It also means connecting with those people who escaped the deep impact of colonial modernity and who, therefore, are still steeped in traditions from which elites are themselves cut off. It is this collaborative effort between modern scholars, traditional pundits, organic intellectuals, and people on the ground that will help to rebuild forgotten cultural and intellectual traditions. This would also help articulate concepts embedded in social and cultural practices so that they are available as a resource for creative use. Only thus might the sufferers of colonialism be able to construct alternative modernities that are shaped by the experience of interacting cultures on an egalitarian basis and which respect the autonomy of all participants.

This is not as hopeless a task as might seem at first sight. In a way, it has been happening less self-consciously during much of the colonial encounter. In any encounter between cultures, some lending and borrowing is inevitable. This certainly is the grain of truth in the contact-zone perspective. In the making of the modern Bengali novel, modern and traditional conventions were mixed freely. Bankim drew freely from conventions of classical Sanskrit drama and epic poetry for describing nature, on Vaishnav lyrics for the representation of sexuality and eroticism. On folk comedy for farcical effects, on oral literature like the ballad for direct address to the reader, on Hindu mythology for prophesies and other forms of providential intervention.[10] Anticolonial movements reworked local resources to mobilize for decolonization.[11] Gandhi's movement for swaraj built on local resources in its methods at the same time as it borrowed from Western authors such as Tolstoy and Emerson.

One version of this attempt is already present in Gandhi's response. He took it on himself not only to liberate the non-Western peoples but also the West from the history and psychology of British colonialism.[12] For example, Gandhi believed that he could use the resources of androgyny available both in the east and in the repressed, marginalized Western traditions to challenge the hypermasculine worldview of colonialism. In his view, activism and courage could be liberated from aggressiveness and made compatible with the feminine principle.

Gandhi identified with the marginalized traditions of the West and made them his own. For him, 'India held in trusteeship aspects of the West lost to the West itself'.[13] Borrowing from the West was never for him a problem by itself. Choosing to borrow an object or an idea to suit one's own purposes is very different from being forced or manipulated into having it. Indeed, Gandhi freely acknowledged that the idea of nonviolence had its roots not in the sacred texts of India but in the Sermon on the Mount.[14] Yet, it was important for Gandhi to make sense of the West in Indian terms. This entailed grasping that the modern West offered one possible lifestyle among many, which unfortunately for both the West and India became cancerous, so Gandhi thought, by virtue of its disproportionate spread and power. In the end, however, it was not enough for Gandhi to make sense of the West in Indian terms but also to have a genuine place for it within Indian civilization. This was the very least he also expected from the best proponents of Western civilization.

The general point that emerges from Gandhi's project is this: what we have hitherto believed as universals is only one particular masquerading as such. These are false, abstract universals. If we are to arrive at genuine, concrete, transcultural universals, then we must first accept that we are different, unfamiliar, and strange. There are no easy and neat shortcuts to communication across cultures. Once we accept the difficulty and messiness of translation across cultures as also the initial circle of prejudice that surrounds us, we may be able to find a morally acceptable place for each other in our respective cultures. Then we can also hope for a richer, greater commonness.

Notes

1. As Fanon put it, 'colonialism forces the people it dominates to ask themselves the question constantly: "In reality, who am I"?' Frantz Fanon, quoted in Robert Young, *Postcolonialism: An Historical Introduction* (Oxford and Malden, MA: Blackwell, 2001), 139.
2. Janna Thompson has helpfully made distinction between two theories of reparations which she calls 'reparation as restoration' and 'reparation as reconciliation'. I locate my

own perspective on reparation within the second theory – that is, as part of a broader theory of reconciliation. On my own perspective on reconciliation, see Rajeev Bhargava, 'Restoring Decency to Barbaric Societies', in *Truth vs. Justice*, eds Robert I Rotberg and Dennis Thompson (Princeton, NJ: Princeton University Press, 2000).

3. Martha Minow, *Between Vengeance and Forgiveness* (Boston, MA: Beacon Press, 1998), 112.
4. See Young, *Postcolonialism*.
5. Young, *Postcolonialism*, 2.
6. On moral disassociation, see James P Sterba, 'Understanding Evil: American Slavery, the Holocaust, and the Conquest of the American Indians', *Ethics* (1996):106.
7. This point was important also because reparative claims presuppose that we have properly identified both the claimants who are entitled to reparation as well as those who have the obligation to provide it. On these points, see Janna Thompson, *Taking Responsibility for the Past* (Cambridge: Polity, 2002), ch 3.
8. Some of these issues are also raised by Dipesh Chakrabarty, *Provincializing Europe: Postcolonial Thought and Historical Difference* (Delhi: Oxford University Press, 2000), and Jan Nederveen Pieterse and Bhikhu Parekh, eds, *The Decolonisation of Imagination* (Delhi: Oxford University Press, 1997).
9. I borrow this phrase from Leila Gandhi, *Post-Colonial Theory: An Introduction* (Sydney: Allen and Unwin, 1998), x.
10. See Ranajit Guha, *Dominance without Hegemony: History and Power in Colonial India* (Delhi: Oxford University Press, 1998), 179.
11. On this, see Pieterse and Parekh, *The Decolonisation of Imagination*, 6.
12. See M K Gandhi, *Hind Swaraj* in, e.g., M K Gandhi, *Hind Swaraj and Other Writings*, ed Anthony J Parel (Cambridge: Cambridge University Press, 1997). For an illuminating discussion of these issues, see Ashis Nandy, *The Intimate Enemy: Loss and Recovery of Self Under Colonialism* (New Delhi: Oxford University Press, 1983).
13. Nandy, *The Intimate Enemy*, 74.
14. Nandy, The Intimate Enemy.

CASE STUDY

Kinhide Mushakoji[*], 'The Case of the "Comfort Women": Sexual Slavery by the Japanese Military'

The state-run military sexual slavery case known as the 'Comfort Women' is a case where the state of Japan used its power as colonial ruler and/or as military occupier to institutionalize a military brothel system, 'recruiting' by abduction, deceit, and other constraining means women and girls from its colonies and occupied territories to work in the military brothels established and run by and for the Imperial Armed Forces. In this case, the usually clandestine sector of sexual slavery became a state institution. This institution was based on a blatant violation of the fundamental rights and dignity of the victims. In this situation, the victims, declared by the Universal Declaration on Human Rights to

---

[*] Kinhide Mushakoji, 'Engendering the Japanese "Double Standard" Patriarchal Democracy: The Case of the "Comfort Women" and Military Sexual Slavery', in *Gender, Globalization, and Democratization*, eds Kelly, Bayes, Hawkesworth and Young (Lanham: MD: Rowman & Littlefield, 2001), 211–22. Copyrights by Rowman & Littlefield.

be 'born free and equal in dignity and rights', were discriminated against and exploited by the Japanese military personnel within state-run brothels called 'Comfort Stations'. That the state of Japan explicitly created and sponsored these brothels, modeled on the traditional public brothel system, makes the action especially unacceptable and illustrates in an extreme way the commodification of women by the Japanese state and society.

The Japanese society, more precisely its male members, have to face the fact that traditional, ethical double standards legitimizing the prostitution sector in general and the public brothel system in particular have helped justify this blatant abuse of women's rights. The Japanese state, according to the universal principles accepted by all modern democratic states, must be held responsible for this state-run military sexual slavery, that is, for the 'Comfort Stations' and the 'Comfort Women'. The responsibility of the Japanese state and people has become the object of public debate after half a century. All these years, the existence of the 'Comfort Women' was vaguely known but was occluded from public awareness. The victims were ashamed to disclose their past due to the stigma of prostitution. This is a direct consequence of one side of the double standard discourse that stresses the exclusive role of the patriarchal family institution as having a monopoly on legitimate sexual intercourse, thereby facilitating treating women in prostitution as 'bad women'. Only when the debate in the United Nations about women's rights and violence against women, especially during armed conflict, drew public attention did some of the victims get the courage to speak publicly. Members of various feminist movements also began to demand state compensation from the government of Japan for the victims. The case triggered a public debate in Japan that helped externalize the different value judgments about sexual slavery hidden in the minds of Japanese citizens.

The position of the Japanese government was that international law does not require the state of Japan to pay compensation to the 'Comfort Women'. The government tried to pacify the objections raised by the advocates of the 'Comfort Station' victims in their own countries as well as in Japan by setting up an Asian Women's Fund. Through this fund, the Japanese government supported distributing to the victims atonement money collected from Japanese citizens, while simultaneously denying responsibility for compensating the victims. This support created a strong dissatisfaction among many citizens who had launched a movement to help the victims. The movement leaders decided to crush the fund. In their eyes the fund had been built to justify the government policy of avoiding state compensation and public recognition of state wrongdoing (Yoshiaki 1997: 38–45). This institutionalized violence against women by the state itself was not just a crime committed by it, but also involved the Japanese civil society, since the 'Comfort Stations' were a variant of the public brothel system, the hidden sector of the Japanese society where the males in this highly patriarchal society still practice sexual slavery. Although the form of the brothels and their regulation by the state varied in different regimes and historical conditions, the essence of the system is longstanding. The case of the 'Comfort Women' is not only an act of the state that requires compensation; it is also the consequence of an institutionalized practice of sexual slavery that continues to thrive in contemporary Japan. The practice of sexual slavery is daily becoming a more and more serious ethical and pragmatic issue as the sex industry becomes increasingly globalized and more widespread.

To define in a purely legalistic manner how the Japanese state and civil society must cope with the case of the 'Comfort Women', with state-run military sexual slavery, is insufficient, for the case requires coming to terms with the private sense of discrimination and stigmatization of the victims of the sexual slavery caused by the patriarchal Japanese culture. Unless a new discourse of caring for these victims triggers a transformation of the attitude of the Japanese vis-à-vis the prostitution sector, state compensation will only strengthen the stigmatization of the women in prostitution. The compensation will be made because the 'good women' of the colonies and occupied territories of Japan were forced to become 'bad women', not because their human rights were violated.

In the case of 'prostitution' the two ethical standards enable accepting the institution as a necessary evil and not unjust as such, while simultaneously stigmatizing the women in prostitution as 'bad women'. Under such ethics, occultation occurs. The wrong committed to the victims, 'good women' turned by force into 'bad women', should be redressed, but the institution, brothels called 'Comfort Stations', were not considered bad in themselves, if they had 'normal' 'bad women' (i.e., women in prostitution) working there. The national sense of morality operating within the institutional framework of the existing state order is unable to recognize that its policy of creating the 'Comfort Station' institution is questionable and unethical. Instead, the double standard promotes the view that the victims should be compensated, but the state should not be penalized. According to the above-mentioned traditional discourse on charity, sympathy, and caring, the stigmatized and brutalized women become the objects of sympathy and atonement, but this discourse denies any links with a universal discourse on rights and responsibilities. The opposition between the public legal position and a private sense of sympathy and caring constrained by conventional double standards about prostitution has led the debate into a complex exchange of statements based on different discourses reflecting particular interests and beliefs. This exchange, as well as the facts of the situation, creates an ideal case for analyzing the double standard regarding the hidden sector of prostitution and sex industries not only in feudal imperialist Japan but also in the 'democratized' Japan of the post–World War II period.

Put in its historical context, the 'Comfort Women' case involving state-run military sexual slavery can be described as follows. In the latter half of nineteenth century, modern Japan developed a new domestic order corresponding to the requirements of a modernizing capitalist state with a cohesive and expansionist orientation. The state-regulated brothel sector was a clandestine and yet important unit of this domestic order. Meiji Japan was built as a patriarchal, capitalist, state-controlled society unified by the emperor. This patriarch was the mediator and integrator of the familial/capitalist, developmentalist Japanese society; and the society was one that created a gender division of labor with a production sector dominated by its male population, a reproduction sector where women were forced to play the role of wives and mothers, and a third brothel sector where sex slaves were provided to the male population as a bonus and an encouragement to their productive activities.

The state of Japan throughout its modern history skillfully used the patriarchal male-centered double standard on trafficking and prostitution in order to strengthen its domestic and external power as a modern state. First, the domestic political economic structure of modernizing Japan in the latter half of the nineteenth century maximized its capacity to produce goods indispensable for its industrialization by developing a well-integrated and docile masculine labor force and a parallel traditional patriarchal family structure enabling it to reproduce this docile masculine labor force through equally docile wives/mothers.

This division of labor between factories and families was complemented by the public brothel system that served as a 'safety valve' by permitting extramarital sexual satisfaction for its masculine labor force. When Japan began its external expansion through colonization and military aggressions, the same means was militarized in support of military 'virility(!?)' and safety from venereal diseases as the Imperial Army invaded neighboring countries from the 1930s through the end of World War II in 1945.

The Japanese government created the 'Comfort Stations' as a military brothel system. The victims of this prostitution system, the 'Comfort Women', and the ethical issues involved were concealed from public attention after the defeat of Japan in 1945, while sexual slavery, which had turned into a growing commercialized sex industry, prospered. In the early 1970s Japanese women concerned about the growing sex tourism toward Korea were told by their Korean sisters that a military version of sexual slavery had existed in the form of military sexual slavery before 1945 (Matsui 1997: 53–58). Already in the 1970s, Japan was exploiting the women of East and Southeast Asia in countries it was dominating economically.

The Japanese people were involved in this institutionalized gender violence and continue to be involved in it. The Japanese people, accepted and reproduced throughout their history a male-dominant, patriarchal, ethical double standard discourse that stigmatized as 'bad' the women prostitutes involved in commercial prostitution while considering the existence of brothels and the extramarital satisfaction of male sexual needs a necessary evil for maintaining male morale and the strength of the nation.

In the Edo period, the public brothel system was a place where the masculine members of the society, irrespective of their status and rank, developed an 'egalitarian' brothel culture called the *kuruwa* culture. In the modernizing Japan of the Meiji era, the government, which had adopted Western laws and formal institutions, maintained the public brothel as an institution useful for supporting the modernization and industrialization of Japan. Before the World War II defeat, this exercise in violence against women victimized both Japanese women and women from the countries colonized by Japan. Now that the public brothel system has been abolished, commercial, global sex industries have replaced it, exploiting women from a variety of developing countries. In this historical context of colonialism and neocolonialism, the debate surrounding the 'Comfort Women' and military sexual slavery unmasks an ethical double standard that promotes sexist and racist exploitation of women within Japan's sphere of influence.

The 'Comfort Station' was a wartime, state-imposed version of the modern Japanese public brothel system, different only in its brutal military aspect and its sponsorship by the state itself. Women as a group were the most affected of the victims of militarist Japan, which committed many atrocities and other violations of the human rights of the peoples in the regions occupied or colonized by it. Yet, many observers of Japan, both in its military and economic expansionist phases, ignored the crucial importance of the different forms of violence against women, especially as it was conducted in the prostitution sector of military and commercial sexual slavery, until the 'Comfort Women' issue drew international attention and triggered a debate polarizing the Japanese civil society in the 1990s.

The Discursive Space of the Debate about State Compensation

The debate about state compensation to the victims of the Japanese state-run military sexual slavery called 'Comfort Women' and about the role of the Asian Women's Fund involved different discourses about the legal responsibility of the state and the moral obligations of the society. The 'Comfort Women' debate interests us particularly because the discursive space created by the different discourses used in this debate helps us divulge and determine the complex epistemological construct that defines the prostitution sector. Setting aside the debate about whether state-run military sexual slavery did or did not exist (a debate that resembles the one on the existence of the Holocaust and has no direct implication to our concern on sexual slavery itself), the most important divide in the debate was about the legal and moral responsibility of the state of Japan and of the Japanese people.

This point has been made in an unambiguous manner by the UN Special Rapporteur on Violence Against Women, Its Causes and Consequences, Ms. Radhika Coomaraswamy.

> The Special Rapporteur sees the Fund, as created, as an expression of the Japanese Government's moral concern for the fate of 'comfort women'. However, it is a clear statement denying any legal responsibility for the situation of these women and this is reflected in particular in the desire to raise funds from the private sector. Although the Special Rapporteur welcomes the initiative from [a] moral perspective, it must be understood that it does not vindicate the legal claims of the 'comfort women' under public international law. (Report of the Special Rapporteur 1996: Para. 134)

This statement helps identify and classify the three different positions taken by the Japanese government and by different sectors of the Japanese civil society in the debate over state compensation and the Asian Women's Fund. These positions differ, as we said already, in terms of their interpretation of the legal and moral responsibility of the state of Japan and of its citizens.

The first position is officially proclaimed by the Foreign Ministry of Japan, which denies any legal ground for state compensation vis-à-vis the victims of the state sexual slavery. The Foreign Ministry argued that the state of Japan deals only with other states and cannot enter into legal rapport with victims without negotiating with the states with which Japan has already completed state-to-state compensation (with the exception of North Korea). The government additionally asserts that it can only be bound by international conventions and treaties signed prior to the sexual enslavement of the 'Comfort Women'. Those signed after the fact cannot be applied. Since no state commitments existed at the time of the 'Comfort Stations', to claim compensation now represents a retroactive application of legal obligations. This argument does not negate the universality of human rights as legal norms. It simply does not recognize the universality of human rights qua *idées de droit*. Such recognition would make possible a retroactive application to itself of the idea of crimes against humanity, which would include crimes related to violence against women exercised by states during violent conflicts (Iwamatsu 1998: 93–140). The Japanese state position is a legalistic one that ignores the *idées de droit* underlying the concept of state compensation and instead insists on a narrow legalistic interpretation of the *règles de droit*. It is a typical legal approach of non-Western states that have introduced rules of law with no prior process of democratization having generated the new *idées* for the new *règles*. Such discourse represents the formal side of the double standard discourse on the prostitution sector. This discourse recognizes the legality of prostitution without establishing the rights of the women who are exploited in it. The denial of any responsibility to give compensation to the 'Comfort Women' victims is logically correct so long as one adopts this discourse.

The second position was taken by movements and intellectuals critical of the government policy (including myself) who considered it essential to safeguard the universal application of human rights by having the state of Japan assume full responsibility for past violations of the fundamental rights of the 'Comfort Station' victims (Nihon no Senso Sekinin Shiryo Centre 1999). Those upholding this position believed that state compensation to individual victims was not only a valid practice but also an act of rectification expected from any responsible party, whether a private person or a state. Not to recognize that states could deal directly with private persons, as was practiced in the European Human Rights Regime, was to deny that human rights norms could apply to states in any situation. From the perspective of the second position, military sexual slavery was a crime against humanity that could and should be applied retroactively. Furthermore, because Japan had ratified the 1923 Convention against trafficking, the Japanese state had already recognized prostitution and sexual slavery as illegal when the Imperial Army instituted the 'Comfort Women' enslavement policy. This position, in spite of its call for compensation for blatant abuses of human rights, did not advocate that the state take moral measures of atonement to try to transform the Japanese patriarchal, ethical standard that still promotes sexual slavery. The need for the Japanese state to give compensation to the victims of the military sexual slavery it institutionalized is legally self-evident, especially when one refers to the *idées de droit* on human rights, especially women's rights about violence against them. This discourse, however, leaves undefined the exploitative nature of the prostitution sector and the loss of dignity of the women exploited in it.

Within this second position compensation might have to be given to 'good women' who were forcefully degraded to become 'bad women' in prostitution. However, such compensation would be required by the state only because the state had used its power to coerce women into state institutionalized sexual slavery. The state would not be held responsible in those cases where states tolerate and only regulate such institutions. The second position does not force the issue of the state having to assume the responsibility of omission, that of not protecting women's rights as human rights. Such an omission appears less serious than the responsibility of commission of forced sexual slavery by the state of Japan. In my view, however, such an omission needs to become the concern of the international community. This is especially the case for military-base sexual slavery regulated by the base authorities.

The third position was held by those who supported the government's decision to establish the Asian Women's Fund, which would be paid for by private citizens and organizations but would allow the Japanese government to avoid making state compensation. The Ministry of Foreign Affairs under the instruction of the socialist Prime Minister Murayama invented this face-saving compromise to appease the politicians while keeping intact the position of the government bureaucracy. The Ministry of Foreign Affairs held that no legal grounds existed for state compensation, but that the government could establish a fund to receive donations from the Japanese people to express their desire to apologize to the victims. This formula was a skillful move to avoid assuming state responsibility. The fund payments were a clear replacement for state compensation and would foreclose any further objections to the Japanese government's decision to refuse giving compensation to the victims. Supporters of the second position, however, argued that this use of the fund implied that a state's legal obligations, based on universal rights, could be replaced by legally meaningless acts based on a moral concern. This replacement of a universal *idées de droit* by a personalized sense of 'caring' was unacceptable for the second position.

The government, which never did revise its position, took a decision contradicting itself by establishing the Asian Women's Fund as a concession to the third position with the support of citizens who did not necessarily recognize the legality of the government's refusal to give compensation, but who wanted to express their sense of guilt and sympathy to the victims of the military sexual slavery. Many of them believed that since state compensation was unlikely, the minimum moral obligation of the Japanese people was to express their deep feeling by giving the victims atonement money. A sense of urgency to take some measures to support the victims whose age did not permit further delay supported this action. This was a natural conclusion to be drawn from their discourse emphasizing personal 'caring' of each of the individual victims.

Practically all the supporters of the fund available for contact did not believe in the formal argument that state compensation is a necessary condition that should logically precede any moral measures. Many recognized the need of state compensation but placed greater importance on the need to develop a humane discourse expressing guilt and the will of the Japanese people to compensate the victims at least partially. In contrast to the holders of the second position, a few lawyers and law professors preferred the more humane 'caring' approach of the Asian Women's Fund to the Western universalist legal argument demanding state compensation. Many of the supporters of the Asian Women's Fund preferred to define the case of the 'Comfort Women' as an unfortunate case of gender violence caused by the combination of specific cultural and historical circumstances. Their discourse was, thus, basically a *gemeinschaft*-like private one, stressing charity, sympathy, and caring on the personal level.

We have already stressed the fact that this discourse is quite different from the formal, universal, *gesellschaft*-like discourse of those who demand state compensation. 'Atonement' is a concept belonging to a *gemeinschaft*-like moral discourse, quite different from the concept of 'compensation' based on an *idées de droit* of formal and universal rights calling for state responsibility. The distinction between a legal measure based on the concept of responsibility and a moral measure based on a vague sense of guilt combined with a sentiment of sympathy is not clearly perceived by most of the supporters of the fund.

The advocates of the third position did not negate the universality of human rights norms, but tried to develop a personalized nonconfrontational moral discourse without either denying or confirming the validity of the *idées de droit* proclaimed by the holders of the second position. They neither rejected nor accepted these ideas as the basis of the *règles de droit* regarding state compensation as the holders of the first and second positions did. For the supporters of the fund, it was important, if not sufficient, to take an action of moral atonement, which was undoubtedly akin to the human rights discourse, to the extent that it emphasizes, as does the Universal Declaration of Human Rights, 'the spirit of brotherhood' (and sisterhood?!) (Onuma, Shimomura, and Wada 1998). The position of the supporters of the Asian Women's Fund is in line with the universal *idées de droit* of human rights, but it does not support its formal universal application in the form of *règles de droit*. 'Sisterhood' is in their case personal and informal and overlooks completely the legal responsibility of the state. This third position uses a discourse directly inherited from the premodern *gemeinschaft*-like ethics that attempts, as we saw before, a rectification of the despotic rule of imposed law, through a patriarchal benevolent ethics of 'caring'.

The supporters of the fund avoided contesting the legal arguments of the Japanese Ministry of Foreign Affairs that deny the need for any legal measures that would recognize the responsibility of the state of Japan. Unlike the confrontational proclamation of the legal responsibility by the holders of the second position, those who hold the third position take a noncritical attitude vis-à-vis the government. By avoiding a discussion of the issues of the legal responsibility of the state of Japan, their highly moral discourse resembles so many status-quo–oriented discourses that appeal to the conscience of the power holders rather than making universally valid demands in a confrontational way.

The exclusion of the imperative requirement of state compensation from the third-position discourse has a definitely negative effect on human rights promotion and democratization. It helps the government of Japan in its attempt to divert world public opinion from the question of state compensation to the 'Comfort Station' victims. The state is, nevertheless, the target of verbal attacks by the Japanese right-wing movements who deny any responsibility, legal or moral, for the 'Comfort Women'. The right wing sees the attention given to the case as a ploy promoted by the left wing. The Foreign Ministry meanwhile continues to avoid being identified with this extremist position, thanks to its support for the Asian Women's Fund that it helped create as a means for satisfying the expressed wish of the socialist Prime Minister Murayama.

The sense of guilt and the sympathy toward the victims of one's own group could have existed in any society, premodern and nondemocratic, as part of the moral discourse of any religion that stresses kindness and compassion toward other human beings. The conflict between such moral discourse and a universal recognition of state responsibility in the modern *idées de droit* is the result of an opposition between a traditional discourse and a modern one. The conflict between the second and the third positions, thus, represented the two discourses that are normally compartmentalized in the public and the private life of the Japanese society (and of other non-Western societies), which democratizes in the public domain while maintaining its traditional discourse in private life. This debate, deeply rooted in the modernizing Japanese culture, attracted everybody's interest and diverted the attention of both social movements and of the public media from any confrontation between the first and the second positions. As a consequence, the Japanese government did not have to discuss the legality of its refusal to make compensation to the victims of its military sexual slavery.

The majority of the 'Comfort Women' victims themselves, in spite of their material interest in accepting the 'atonement' money, sided with the second position arguing that the Asian Women's Fund's atonement money was an attempt by the Japanese government to escape its responsibility. This caused a painful division among the victims in the Philippines.

In response to the criticism about replacing state compensation, the Asian Women's Fund developed an extremely meaningful new program called *Songen Jigyo*, or activities regarding the dignity of women. The program funded activities to fight against different forms of violence against women, including trafficking of women and children, and different efforts to transform the patriarchal culture in Japan and in other Asian societies. These activities are based on a recognition that social and cultural traditions accepting prostitution as an institution while stigmatizing the women in prostitution were at the root of the state-run military sexual slavery and continue to be a root cause of privatized commercial sexual slavery.

Recognition of the above contradiction leads to recognizing also that the Enlightenment discourse cannot simultaneously condemn the prostitution sector as an institution of sexual slavery and proclaim that the women in prostitution are exercising a legally acceptable activity. If the women in prostitution have to be destigmatized, then their work will need to be legally acceptable. This means that women in prostitution should be equally respectable as women in the family. Such recognition can only take place if the sex sector is defined as a normal industrial sector, not as a clandestine sector exploiting women as sex slaves.

The case of the 'Comfort Women' military sexual slavery is a typical example of the patriarchal power that distorts gender relations by legitimizing the slavery institution and the masculine exploiter, while failing to accept the legitimacy of prostitution that would endanger the family (the key institution in any patriarchal society). This dilemma can be overcome only by a creative application of the discourse of caring, not in its patriarchal conformist version, but in its creative version proposed by some feminists. One can deconstruct any kind of stigma if one cares genuinely about an individual, since caring addresses the person herself, and the label of 'sex slave' loses its derogative value in front of one's care about the victim as a person.

Only when some feminists raised their voice against the Japanese military sexual slavery did the victims get the courage to tell publicly that they had been 'Comfort Women', a stigmatized status that could not have been announced publicly unless they were assured by the anti–'Comfort Women' movement that they were cared for and had nothing to fear from public opinion. Only when a significant portion of the public realized that the 'Comfort Women' was an unacceptable institution of sexual slavery, and its victims were not to be stigmatized as 'Comfort Women' but rather cared for and 'atoned' as victims, were the 'Comfort Women' able to come forward.

The double standard discourse justifying other kinds of sexual slavery, military or commercial, should be deconstructed in the same way, by an application of a universal *idées de droit* condemning the sexual slavery institution combined with a personalized caring approach to the women in prostitution, whose dignity should be cared for with no distinction between them and women in families.

Activities of the *Songen Jigyo* were based on the realization that the state-run military sexual slavery of the 'Comfort Women' was but an extreme case of the sexual exploitative culture that still supports the operating, globalized sex industry of Japan. To eradicate this problem will require more than a one-time state payment to the victims of 'Comfort Stations'. Critics of the *Songen Jigyo* argued that it is a means of deflecting the criticism the Asian Women's Fund received for trying to give atonement to the 'Comfort Women'.

In spite of this shortcoming, the third position has an advantage over the second because it attempts to treat the victims of the military sexual slavery not as abstract human persons possessing universal rights but also as living and mortal individuals who should be cared for as individuals in their concrete environment, each with specific needs – material and moral. Most participants in debates over the hidden sex sector typically discuss it as an object of abstract discussions while ignoring individual women. The discourse adopted by the holders of this third position, however, efficiently put into question the very labeling of individual women as wives, mothers, or women in prostitution. In other words, this discourse can lead to questioning categories imposed by the patriarchal state and society in order to strengthen its power over the labeled women.

Conclusion

The above description of the three different positions in the 'Comfort Women' debate reveals an important lacuna. The aforementioned statement by Ms. Coomaraswamy makes crystal clear the need for the state and the people of Japan to: (1) recognize the legal responsibility of the state of Japan toward the victims of its military sexual slavery, giving them due apologies and compensation; and (2) make efforts to transform the patriarchal brothel culture of Japan so that no kind of sexual slavery will be able to victimize women and girls, whether from within Japan or from the neighboring countries of Japan. The Japanese people must assume this important moral responsibility. This combination of legal and moral responsibilities is unfortunately not implemented, let alone proposed, by any of the agents involved in the 'Comfort Women' debate. Neither the state nor the Asian Women's Fund nor the movements demanding state compensation propose an integral approach to the 'Comfort Women' issue, coping with both the legal and moral aspects of the problem.

This is a fourth and most preferable position, one that adopts a discourse that can combine a legal and a moral approach to the 'Comfort Women' question as well as cope with all forms of sexual slavery. The only way to deconstruct the double standard discourse is by establishing unambiguously the illegality of the sex sector on the one hand, and on the other hand proclaiming the responsibility of the society to accept the women in prostitution as equal in dignity with women in the family sector, eliminating all grounds for discrimination and stigmatization.

The difficulty in arriving at this position is partially created by the opposition that has developed during the debate between the holders of the second and the third positions. Yet, a more fundamental problem lies in the very nature of the two discourses and their relationship to the double standard discourse on the hidden clandestine sex sector.

The difficulty in joining the second and the third positions discussed above is due to the contradiction between their discourses. Their discursive orientations stress respectively, (1) the priority of universal human rights standards grounded in individual rights and dignity, and (2) the ethical position that 'caring' for an individual victim's welfare is more precious than any legal regulations. As we saw already, one cannot take sides between these two positions if the hidden prostitution sector of the Japanese society is to be democratized. The double standard discourse that continues to justify the existence of this sector combines a public discourse and a private discourse that have to be corrected simultaneously. The application of universal human rights *idées de droit* and *règles de droit* is indispensable to deconstruct the institutional frameworks of the prostitution sector. A personalized caring of the exploited women is also indispensable if one wants to avoid justifying the sex industries while removing all stigma from the women in prostitution. Their rights and dignity do not emanate from the legality of the prostitution sector but from their personal dignity that cannot be violated even on the private, informal level. A measure that applies the *règles de droit* about state compensation toward its victims of human rights violation is a necessary condition for the rectification of this affront. An additional extralegal effort by the Japanese society transforming the masculine stigmatization of the 'bad women' in the prostitution sector needs to be added, and the two together will constitute the sufficient conditions for overcoming the double standard discourse at the base of the sexual slavery, state-run or private, military or commercial institutions.

The case of the 'Comfort Women' debate shows the difficulty of democratizing a situation where two opposite movements, one against the institution and the other caring for the victims, have to be developed simultaneously. The difficulty comes from the fact that the former needs to adopt the discourse of the Western Enlightenment tradition while the latter has to ignore it and develop an endogenous discourse, a democratized version of the traditional caring discourse. One movement needs to engage in the legal fighting for the institutionalization of formal democracy based on universal *idées de droit*. The other needs to stress the insufficiency of a formal introduction of exogenous values in the public life of the state and to insist on the necessity of developing a process of democratizing private community life based on a new endogenous social and cultural discourse.

The combination of the two discourses goes against the law of the excluded middle that helped to create all the modern dichotomies of public/private, universal/particular, legal/moral, and so forth. This dichotomy helped the double standards discourse that compartmentalize two logics: one about the institution, the other about the individual members. The new discourse should deconstruct these dichotomies and combine in an integral whole the legal application of a universal *idées de droit* to the hidden sector while simultaneously applying the moral approach of a particular and personalized, societal caring for its members.

We may conclude in more general terms that the patriarchal power continues to impose on democratizing societies a double standards discourse based on a formal acceptance of exogenous democratic *idées de droit* while ignoring their practical violation in particular concealed clandestine sectors of the society. In these hidden sectors, the critique of the undemocratic nature of specific institutions is diverted toward personal targets, mainly vulnerable and exploited women who receive unjustified stigmatization in place of the institution victimizing them. Engendering democracy, even in existing 'democratic' countries, implies the elimination of the hidden sector of enslavement and discrimination, especially the sex industry sector that enslaves and commodifies women. It is important to take note of the fact that this effort requires a deconstruction of the public/private, modern/traditional, legal/extra-legal dichotomies, even of the sexual slavery/right to prostitution opposition that originates from the double standards patriarchal discourse. All hidden sectors where gender and racial discriminations are practiced by the democratic state and civil society should be divulged and deconstructed. The dichotomous discourses that occlude the true structures of the patriarchal and neocolonial exploitation should also be transformed into a more just and more caring discourse.

References

Iwamatsu, Shigetoshi. 'The Dual Structure of Aggression of the Japanese Ruling Elite'. In *Sensou Sekinin to Kaku Haizetsu* (War-Time Responsibility and the Abolition of the Nuclear Bomb, 93–140). Tokyo: Sanichi Shobo, 1998.

Matsui, Yayori. *Asia Tono Rentai* (Solidarity with Asia). Ajia Josei: Shiryo Center (Asian Women's Documentation Center), 1997: 53–58.

Nihon no Senso Sekinin Shiryo Centre, ed. 'Symposium: Nationalism to ianfu "mondai"'. (Nationalism and the 'Comfort Women' Problem). In *Yujo* (Traditional Women in the Prostitution of Traditional Japan), edited by Aoki Shoten and Nishiyama, Matsunosuke. Tokyo: Fuji Shuppan, 1999.

Onuma, Yasuaki, Michiko Shimomura, and Haruki Wada, eds. *Ianfu Mondai to Asia Josei Kikin* ('Comfort Women' and the Asian Fund). Tokyo: Teshindo, 1998.

'Report of the Special Rapporteur on Violence against Women, Its Causes, and Consequences'. Ms. Radhika Coomaraswamy, in accordance with the Commission of Human Rights resolution 1994–45. Report on the mission to the Democratic People's Republic of Korea, the Republic of Korea and Japan on the issue of military sexual slavery in wartime. United Nations, Economic and Social Council, E/CN 4/1996/Add.1, 4 January 1996. Para. 134.

Yoshiaki, Yoshimi. "'Jugun-Ianfu' Mondai towa." (What is the "Confort Women" Problem). Asia Forum, ed. Moto "Ianfu" no Shogen: 50 Nen no Chinmoku wo Yabutte (Testimony of the Former "Confort Women": Breaking 50 Years of Silence) *Koseisha*, 1997: 38–45.

CASE STUDY

Ofelia Schutte*, 'Resistance to Colonialism: The Latin American Legacy of José Martí'

José Martí's Legacy of 'Nuestra América', or Whose Nation? Whose Culture?

Cuba is one of the most interesting countries in the Western Hemisphere when it comes to the analysis of colonialism and postcoloniality. Unlike most other 'Hispanic-American' nations, which obtained their independence from Spain in the earlier parts of the century, during Martí's lifetime (1853–1895) Cuba was still a colony of Spain. A fervent partisan of Cuba's national independence, Martí lived abroad for most of his adult life, often engaged in projects aimed at liberating his native island from colonialism. Martí lived in New York City during the last period of his short life, from 1880 to 1895 (and prior to departing to fight for Cuba's independence, where he was killed in May 1895 by Spanish troops). It seems that in addition to sharpening his keen political sense and his love for that part of the Americas that he called 'our America' (*nuestra América*) – a term to which I will return in a moment – Martí's sojourn in the United States allowed him to conceptualize colonialism as a recurring political system in modern times. He had a double sense of vision as he envisioned Cuba's liberation from colonial status. On the one hand, there was the evident necessary war to be fought against the colonial power, Spain. But, on the other hand, there was the diplomatic struggle to prevent what Martí foresaw as an emerging economic and political colonialism of the government and business interests of the United States toward the Hispanic Caribbean, Mexico, Central, and South America. In the case of Cuba, this meant fighting for Cuba's independence on two separate fronts: one, against Spain's past and current dominance; the other, against the United States' emerging and projected future dominance.

In the case of the Hispanic American republics, the struggle Martí proposed was to resist U.S. economic and political hegemony on political and diplomatic terms. In fact, it seems to me that Martí probably saw the latter goal as a necessary condition for helping to maintain Cuba's independence in the long term. So, while he gave his life for Cuba's actual independence from Spain, he was also preparing the ground for a united Latin America resisting the expansion of U.S. economic and political power over the entire hemisphere.[1] Martí envisioned a united front emerging from Latin America itself, against a second round of colonialism, this time instigated not by Europe but by the United States in a phase of intensive capitalist expansion – what in 1894 Martí called simply 'the America that is not ours' (OC 6:35).[2] The name of the collective entity Martí wished to safeguard from U.S. interventionism and expansionism is what he called 'nuestra América' (our America) – a term he seems to have used initially during his stay in Guatemala between 1877 and 1879 to designate an anti-colonialist Indo-Hispanic America (OC 7:98; OC 18:131 ff).[3] As the years passed, Martí's notion of 'our America' developed further, referring to the indigenous, black, and mestizo populations along with all the peoples whose cultural and political priorities were to the 'natural' and creative humanity found in America rather than the norms and values imported or received by force from abroad (Martí [1891] OC 6:17; 2002, 290–91). Such peoples could overcome 'the hierarchical constitution of the colonies' ('*la constitución jerárquica de las colonias*') by the 'democratic organization of the Republic' ('*la organización democrática de la República*') (Martí [1891], OC 6:19; 2002, 292). He is referring here to the forms and structures of power, which could either promote or undermine good government.

---

* Ofelia Schutte, 'Resistance to Colonialism: The Latin American Legacy of Jose Martí', in *Colonialism and Its Legacies*, ed Jacob T Levy (with Iris Marion Young) (Lanham, MD: Lexington Books, 2011), 181–204. Copyright by Rowman and Littlefield.

But, at the same time, the new republics were frail when compared to the huge economic power of the United States, which he believed was intent on preventing their full development to suit its own expanding economic interests.

In a famous passage dated from November 1889 at a time when the government of the United States had organized the first hemispheric congress of American states, Martí wrote:

> Spanish America knew how to free itself from the tyranny of Spain; and now, after judging the precedents, causes, and factors of the invitation [to the aforementioned congress], it is urgent to state – because it is the truth – that the hour has come for Spanish America to declare its second independence.[4] (Martí [1889] OC 6:46)

What is the 'second independence' to be from, if not from another type of colonialism?[5] At the time, the goal of Latin American liberalism was the *political* independence of the new national republics. In the language of Latin American nineteenth-century political liberalism, 'independence' or 'national independence' meant freedom from colonial rule. But the liberals' interpretation of independence was insufficiently critical of the economic dependence they were establishing with Western powers. Rising above his contemporaries' views of these matters, Martí defended the continent's ethnic diversity while analyzing an emerging pattern of hemispheric *economic* domination for the primary benefit of the interests of the more powerful party which could severely undermine the presumed national independence of the less powerful. Martí's analysis of the economic dependence to which the Hispanic American countries would be subjected is based jointly on a cultural analysis of what he sees as the driving spirit behind the United States' will to dominance: 'a people that begins to look at freedom, which is the universal and perennial aspiration of the human being, as its own privilege, and to invoke it [freedom] in order to deprive other peoples of it' (Martí, OC 6:53).[6]

Martí's analysis of cultural politics gained immensely from his unique biographical position as a Cuban exile who had both traveled and lived in Spain and several Latin American countries, as well as eventually settling in New York City in the 1880s and early 1890s.[7] Making the most of a large network of contacts and compatriots throughout the Americas, he paid close attention to political and economic events in Latin America and the United States as he put together his plan to found the Cuban Revolutionary Party. Founded in Key West, Florida, in 1892, the CRP aimed at unifying Cubans and earning favorable world opinion in support of the final stage of Cuba's war of independence against Spanish colonial rule.[8]

Martí was able both to foresee and clarify some of the dangers imminent to the South as the United States increasingly exercised its economic powers over existing Hispanic lands at the end of the nineteenth century.[9] Despite his clearly articulated analysis of the U.S. agenda as it convened the existing Latin American governments for a meeting in Washington in 1889–1890, the political resistance he hoped to see from the Latin American governments invited to Washington was not to take place. Nonetheless, parts of the political strategy that he developed over one hundred years ago to resist the North's cultural hegemony are still relevant today. His perspective is challenging. It involves the commitment to both denounce injustice and struggle against it – a choice not everyone is willing to take. The legacies of colonialism are not easily defeated. Postcolonial political criticism needs to have both a vision and a strategy if it is to succeed. When we focus on resistance to colonialism, it seems that a large component of this resistance must be strategy. Martí's article 'Nuestra América' (1891) contains an outline for such a strategy.

'Nuestra América' as a Political Strategy

Given the fact that Martí had already articulated his view that a 'second independence' was needed for the nineteenth-century Hispanic American republics, based on his detection of what I would call a 'colonial intentionality' on the part of the U.S. expansionist political and economic interests to use the Latin American countries primarily to suit their own benefit at the latter's expense, the text 'Nuestra América' can be looked at as a rhetorical strategy to rally the unified sentiment of his Latin American readers against U.S. hegemony in the region. It is in embracing the vision of 'Nuestra América' ('Our America') as different from the America to our North that Martí hoped to rally a movement of resistance to the U.S. economic and political hegemony taking place – or, as in the cases of Cuba and Puerto Rico, imminently positioned to take place – *after* the demise of Spanish colonialism.

Martí begins 'Nuestra América' with a call to a battle of ideas based on the 'weapons of judgment', which he claims are much more valuable than the actual tactics of war. This confirms the view I proposed earlier regarding his desire for a united front that would bear diplomatic weight against U.S. hegemony in the region. Characterizing a village mentality as one that fails to be concerned about the relationship between the local and the global (I am rephrasing him using current terms) and, in that context, failing to see that 'giants in seven-league boots' can step on them, Martí calls for the awakening of any remaining village mentality in America ([1891] 2002, 288).

The obstacles Martí faced for people to rally behind his vision of 'nuestra América' rested not only in ignorance and apathy with regard to the need for political change, but in important structural problems that were a part of Latin American history. Martí's essay addresses both the external menace and the internal outlooks that must be changed to resist it. Among the latter, two of the most important were (1) overcoming the hierarchical and authoritarian mentality inherited from the colonial period and (2) embracing the multiracial composition of the continent which he called '*nuestra América mestiza*' ([1891] OC 6:19).[10] I argue that without invoking the terms 'colonialism' and 'racism' in this essay, Martí was fighting a combination of both.[11] He also constantly battled the Ibero-American upper- and middle-class prejudices against working and humble people, reporting that their gaze was focused on imitating European fashionable trends: 'These sons of carpenters who are ashamed that their father was a carpenter! These men born in America who are ashamed of the mother that raised them because she wears an Indian apron' ([1891] 2002, 289). He does not argue that whoever is born in America, or is of indigenous, black, or mestizo origin, or comes from a certain class, is in a cognitively privileged position to understand his or her political situation. In fact, he is fully aware that the masses, just as with the middle class, can only make progress if their consciousnesses are awakened and take on an anti-colonialist stance.

Martí bases the process of liberation from colonialism on the mediating role played by instituting an anti-colonialist republic and, of course, by the consciousness of all those who create and defend it, even giving up their lives if necessary ([1891] 2002, 293). So far this coincides with liberal political sentiments of the time, which took a stand against the conservative ideologies inherited from the colony and which tried to provide a mediating role for incorporating indigenous and mestizo contributions toward a new national project.[12] But Martí also inserted a strong dose of anti-hierarchical 'Americanism' with naturalist features into his platform. It is his naturalism that provides the conceptual link between affirming a multiethnic America and overcoming the hierarchical mentality of the colonial period. He claimed that in our America one had 'to govern with the soul of the earth and not against or without it' ([1891] 2002, 292).[13] The failure to govern appropriately meant that postcolonial Latin America was tired of having to accommodate between 'the discordant and hostile elements it inherited from its perverse, despotic colonizer' and 'the imported forms and ideas' ([1891] 2002, 292) that, lacking local reality, have delayed 'the logical government' (*el gobierno lógico*) (Martí [1891] OC 6:19).

What does Martí mean by 'the logical government'? From what he says in the essay, he seems to mean a government founded on the specific needs of its people, not on imported, so-called universal formulas derived from European models – or for that matter, from models imported from the

United States. This position is key to the importance his thought carries for postcolonial critics and movements up to our own time. While Martí invokes Enlightenment notions of reason and freedom, and of 'the right of man [human being] to the exercise of his reason' (*'el derecho del hombre al ejercicio de su razón'* [OC 6:19]) in his view the exercise of reason is not necessarily mediated by European values or extraterritorial powers. He refers favorably to 'the natural man' or to the 'real man': 'the natural man . . . knocks down the justice [*justicia*] accumulated in books because it is not administered in accordance with the evident [*patentes*] needs of the country' ([1891] OC 6:18). Further on he invokes an Enlightenment ideal of moderation, appealing to the 'serene harmony of Nature' (OC 6:19–20) and the 'continent of light', where with the help of a new generation engaged in 'critical reading [*lectura crítica*] . . . the real man is being born to America, in these times' ([1891] 2002, 293).

The real or natural man (or human being) of whom Martí speaks is someone for whom the European concept of racial divisions and the socially hierarchical society built on it do not apply. He places the distinction among races as something that can provoke 'futile hatreds' among peoples and instead proclaims that 'the justice of nature' reveals 'the universal identity of man' or, in today's terms, of the human being ([1891] 2002, 295–96). 'The soul', he continues, 'equal and eternal, emanates from bodies that are diverse in form and in color. Anyone who promotes and disseminates opposition and hatred among the races is committing a sin against humanity' ([1891] 2002, 296). On this view he claims that 'there is no racial hatred, because there are no races' ([1891], 2002, 294). By 'race' Martí appears to mean a class of human beings that, on account of their color or related physical characteristics, is thought to be superior or inferior to any other human type. Although the concept post-dates him, Martí appears to think of 'race' as a socially constructed category. Specifically, he thought of it as a category that delimits the humanity of the human being. In other words, for Martí, the notion of 'race' was always already imbedded within the discourse of racism. In historical terms, he was probably correct but he lacked the critical framework by which to speak of 'race' as a socially constructed category. What he did was to claim that in 'nature' there was no such thing (this point will be returned to later when the implications of his views for the Cuban revolution of 1895 are discussed).

The 'natural man' (or human being) of whom Martí speaks refers to people of every color, all of whom he embraced in his alternative concept of 'nuestra América mestiza' ([1891] OC 6:19).[14] He reasoned that racial prejudices were socioculturally constructed and could indeed result in significant injustice toward targeted populations. This is why he warns that there are indeed some acquired characteristics, dispositions, and interests that accumulate over time in various peoples and that, at restless national moments, can trigger in a dominant group what I have called 'colonial intentionalities' toward others whose appearance, color, and customs differ from theirs. Such colonial intentionalities are described by Martí as 'ideas and habits of expansion, acquisition, vanity, and greed . . . that . . ., in a period of internal disorder or precipitation of a people's cumulative character' could rise to the forefront and threaten the weaker countries, which are represented as 'perishable and inferior' by the dominant power ([1891] 2002, 296). Surely he uses diplomatic terms here to point out the potential for U.S. expansionism toward the 'isolated' and relatively 'weak' Latin American republics. He thinks the problem that he has outlined – in our terms, the nascent conditions for neocolonialism – cannot be averted and that, for the sake of the coming centuries' peace, the facts of the impending problem should be brought to light ([1891] 2002, 296).

Just as Martí enunciated a policy of governing according to the needs of specific peoples in the light of reason and avoiding racial prejudice, he held a view of the type of education that the peoples of 'our America' should receive in order to reach maturity in their democratic forms of government. . . . 'The battle is not between civilization and barbarity', he declared, 'but between false erudition and nature' ([1891] 2002, 290). Here we see that Martí recognized the binary by which Western colonizing thought places 'barbarity' on the side of 'nature', raising its own colonizing project to that of a civilizing mission. But he wisely pointed out that this binary is a form of 'false erudition' and a false antagonism between culture and nature. Since due to their exclusive reliance on Western models no Hispanic American university curricula analyzed what is 'unique to the peoples of America', he asks what kind of education will those aspiring to govern their countries receive ([1891] 2002, 291). In a pragmatic but also moral vein, he decried that unless the pursuit of truth included seeking out the truth about your own people – and by this he meant seeking out the subaltern populations that were marginalized from knowledge, culture, and power – it would not be possible to solve the problems that affect the people or the country.

Just as education should place priority on Our American history, the manner of government should derive from the very own 'constitution' of the country (*la constitución propia del país*) ([1891] OC 6:17),[15] even if the aim seems to be conceived by Martí as a universal one: to attain a state in which all those who contribute to it, especially through their work, enjoy freedom and prosperity.... While Martí appealed to Enlightenment concepts of 'reason' and 'liberty', for him, both of these were grounded in the recognition and appreciation of a non-Eurocentric approach to Latin America's sociocultural reality. Over the span of the twentieth century, a significant tradition of Latin American philosophical and political thought has been based on this Martían *nuestra Americanista* ideal, which has functioned as a criterion of freedom from colonialism and neocolonialism in diverse contexts. Perhaps the best known of these is the selective appropriation of Martí's ideas by the Marxist leadership of the Cuban revolution. But many other examples abound, including a strong influence on a sector of twentieth-century Latin American philosophy (Schutte 1993; Cerutti Guldberg 1998) and on the politics of United States, Latino, and Chicano studies since the 1980s (Saldívar 1990; Acosta-Belén 1999)....

'Race' and 'Nature' in Our America

As mentioned above, Martí advocated complete equality of rights among the races. Illustrating this point in his 1893 article, 'My Race', which is devoted to Cuban racial issues, he notes that 'no man has any special rights because he belongs to one race or another: say "man" and all rights have been stated' (2002, 318). Martí's position stands out for its anti-discriminatory quality, particularly with regard to white-on-black racism. But what can members of discriminated races do to obtain or defend their rights if the prevailing historical understanding of 'human' is insufficient to promulgate them? Martí held that, whether used by blacks or whites, it is a form of racism to use race as a marker of superiority or of a 'special character' (2002, 319) that would grant some persons or group of persons 'differential rights' (*derechos diferenciales*) over others on account of their race. But he made one exception – namely, 'the right of the black man to maintain and demonstrate that his color does not deprive him of any of the capacities and rights of the human race' (2002, 319).[16] He called this principle – which could be extended to what we know of today as affirmative action – a '*just* racism' (emphasis added; 2002, 319). Strongly committed to a racial equality platform for all Cubans, Martí believed that the Cuban revolution's victory over colonialism would redress the problems of racism and slavery that the Spanish colonial regime had imposed on the island.[17] With history's hindsight, we must move beyond Martí on this matter since the outcome of historical events has shown that racism, as an effect of colonialism, has not been eradicated from our Latin American cultures. In fact, Martí's death in 1895 kept him from theorizing on this any further as conditions took a turn against the advent of the free, racially egalitarian republic for which he laid down his life.

Clearly, Martí opposed any notion of biological racial identification as a basis for qualifying a person's moral, civic, or political status. He claims that 'blacks, like whites, can be grouped according to their character – timid or brave, self-abnegating or egotistical', and that the principle for uniting in political parties or comparable associations was 'an affinity of character', which was 'more powerful than an affinity of color' (2002, 319–20). He made these statements in conjunction with the claim that in Cuba there would not be a race war – something that the colonial (racist) Spanish propaganda had voiced would be a threat if the island were to achieve national independence. The anti-colonial Cuban forces had forcefully declared the end of slavery while both blacks and whites fought side by side against Spain in the various phases of the Cuban revolution.[18] Martí and other Cuban revolutionary leaders promoted the concept of full racial equality at the foundation of the Cuban nation but, as some argue, at the cost of limiting the public debate about racial differences in Cuba. . . .

Martí did not take time to distinguish the human right of people to be able to affirm their cultural heritages – a practice that can be distinguished philosophically, but perhaps not always politically, from the racist practice of ascribing biological superiority to a particular race. Nonetheless, from the position that he takes in 'Nuestra América', it is clear that he strongly affirms the right of peoples to defend their cultural heritage – so much so that this is the basic premise he defends in 'Nuestra América'. He does distinguish, however, between affirming one's cultural heritage and the practice of cultural imperialism. In fact he attempts to persuade the reader that articulating and communicating a Latin American *nuestra Americanista* perspective is a strong deterrence to the cultural imperialism of the North. From this angle it does not contradict his views to argue that, given the resiliency of white dominance, it is imperative for blacks, mestizo, and indigenous peoples to defend their cultural heritages in the strongest possible terms. This is why his symbol of a multicolored America, contained in the figure of *nuestra América mestiza*, continues to be so powerful. . . .

Martí's Legacy and the Critique of Colonial Discourse

Martí's double legacy – one to Latin America through his concept of *nuestra América* and his stand against hemispheric cultural and economic imperialism; the other, to Cuba, through his concept of a truly independent, self-governed, and racially egalitarian, republic – has traversed the whole of the twentieth century and continues to be relevant today. During this period of over one century conceptual frameworks, literary styles, and political ideologies have come and gone – some for good, while others adapted or readapted in response to changing circumstances. New conceptual frameworks have also emerged such as post-structuralism and postcolonialism. The hemispheric context in which Martí wrote can now no longer be so easily separated from a global context. This means that some of the commonalities and differences between Latin America and other colonized regions in the global South – principally Asia and Africa – also demand our attention. The capitalist globalization of the economy in the last part of the twentieth century and the beginning of the twenty-first have also fueled our hemisphere's South-to-North migration so that we can no longer assert (if it had ever been possible) that 'nuestra América' was limited geographically to the Caribbean and Latin America. Indeed, today 'nuestra América' has also unleashed its presence within and alongside the borders of the continental United States. Post-colonial theory takes into account such matters and is a logical place for Martí's *nuestra Americanista* perspective to find an intellectual place.

The discussion of Cuba's position in the aftermath of Spanish colonialism was complicated by the Spanish-American War of 1898 and the subsequent U.S. hegemony over the island, particularly until the end of Cuba's 'first republic' in 1933. With the 1959 revolution Cuban nationalism gradually fell in the arms of Marxism-Leninism. But, even so, Latin American Marxism was a different kind of creature than the forms Marxism had taken in Europe, the Soviet Union, and Asia.[19] The cultural roots of Cuban Marxist-led nationalism became evident after the dissolution of the Soviet Union, when the nation was forced to adapt to changing political and economic global conditions, but not to the extent that it would comply with the U.S. government's idea of how the country ought to be governed. Martí's view of not importing the structure of government from abroad plus appeals to notions of national sovereignty led Cubans to claim that as an independent republic they had the right to chart their own course and not to capitulate to pressure from the North. The impasse regarding what constitutes colonialism in our own times has not subsided. Critics refer to the Cuban government as a dictatorship, while others contend that, above all, freedom for Cuba means freedom from U.S. imperialism. Regardless of its internal method of government Cuba became a symbol, for many people around the world, of a small island that has continued to defy the world's greatest superpower in the face of considerable economic and political obstacles. Ironically, the United States has contributed significantly to this image by taking unusually harsh measures against its neighbor especially at a time when it trades profusely with communist China and has established diplomatic relations with Vietnam. It makes one wonder whether Cuba's exceptional treatment by the United States is not an instance, among others, of the dreaded new form of economic colonialism that Martí hoped could be averted before it was too late.

Meanwhile, in the United States, recent non-Cuban readings of Martí credit him with opposing colonialism and promoting a diverse, multicultural concept of Our America (with especial relevance to the dialectic of contemporary North/South transnational relations). José Saldívar adapts Martí's ideas to the call for diversifying the canon in American Studies in such a way that the subaltern works of Latinas/os, Native Americans, and American writers of color can find prominent recognition for their cultural productions. In what he called 'the dialectics of our America', Saldívar extrapolated Martí's analysis of U.S. political, economic, and cultural hegemony over Latin America to challenge the marginalization of ethnic literatures and criticism from the field of American Studies in the United States. Influenced by Edward Said's critique of Orientalist discourse as well as Roberto Fernández Retamar's Marxist cultural analyses of Latin American and Caribbean resistance to Western colonialism and U.S. imperialism, Saldívar – from the standpoint of Chicano studies – revalidated Martí's notion of *nuestra América* as a useful perspective for reclaiming the missing voices from Our America in the North American literary canon. He likens Martí's role in promoting the notion of *nuestra América*, which serves to ground the legacy of anti-colonialist Latin American and Caribbean cultural production, to Emerson's essay, 'The American Scholar' (1837), 'which established the grounds for a national, popular American literature' (Saldívar 1990, 66).[20] But for Saldívar, what radicalizes Martí's conception of *nuestra América* even further, enabling its implications and repercussions to link up with the late twentieth-century debates on the role of postcolonial intellectuals in U.S. ethnic and cultural studies, is the materialist reconversion of Martí's notion by the Cuban Marxist postcolonial critic Roberto Fernández Retamar.[21] 'Fernández Retamar has produced perhaps the most powerful model of oppositional critical practice in Our America since Martí', wrote Saldívar in 1990 (Saldívar 1990, 73; Fernández Retamar 1989).

From the encounters of radical and progressive writers gathered at the Casa de las Américas Cuban cultural center, directed by Fernández Retamar, Saldívar deduced (correctly, in my view) that there was much that the literature of the Americas (North and South) had in common, but that to appreciate what they had in common one had to apply a genealogy regarding the regimes of power they were resisting. In this regard, José Martí's 'Nuestra América' – later enhanced by the Calibanesque rebellion against colonialism embraced by Fernández Retamar and many other postcolonial writers and intellectuals – was the definitive text through which subsequent alliances for or against colonialist regimes of power could be interpreted. The outcome of this analysis is to link together powerful works by writers of color in the United States with the Latin American and Caribbean leftist postcolonial writers, understanding that, despite the wide differences in style or languages of composition, what unites them are their alternative visions for 'our America' and their resistance to that 'other America' which is not ours – the America complicit with the work of Western colonialism.

For many U.S. Latinos/as in the United States, the social implications of Martí's notion of 'nuestra América' are even more powerful than their academic repercussions. In this vein, Martí's anti-colonialist vision of two oppositional Americas, broadly construed and reinterpreted in our own times of global capitalist acceleration impelled by the United States and the transnational migration of people from South to North, is both conscious of internal differentiations among Latin America's exploited groups and especially relevant to the construction of a contemporary oppositional pan-Latina/o or trans-Latino hemispheric consciousness. As the Puerto Rican feminist and Latina scholar Edna Acosta-Belén states: '[Martí's] pan-national affirmation of a multicultural and multiracial *nuestra América* also takes on great contemporary significance as we strive to put an end to European and Anglo-American ethnocentrism by decolonizing and deconstructing the cultural mythologies and received knowledge about subaltern groups perpetuated within the dominant Western tradition' (Acosta-Belén 1999, 86). In fact, Martí's idealization of a voluntary *nuestra Americanista* identity over a century ago now seems immensely helpful as a strategy to guide the construction of the new pan-ethnic 'Latina/o' identities imposed on or adopted by immigrants from the Caribbean and Latin America to the United States. One of the advantages of Martí's notion of *nuestra América* noted by Acosta-Belén, in addition to its oppositional anti-colonialist quality, is its transcending of national boundaries, in a way that can ground 'reciprocal interactions and bidirectional exchanges' among the U.S. Latina/o and Latin American/Caribbean populations, rather than treat each as a separate entity lodged within national borders (Acosta-Belén 1999, 82–83).

With regard to international relations, Jeffrey Belnap, coeditor of an important recent anthology on Martí, points to the importance of Martí's formulation of '*nuestra América*' for contemporary geopolitics in a transnational hemisphere. Belnap refers to 'the incisive lucidity of Martí's most influential piece of newspaper prose, "Our America" (1891), an essay that, after a century, still serves as a necessary touchstone for any analysis of inter-American cultural politics' (Belnap 1998, 192).[22] The same judgment is shared by many Latin Americans. For example, the Argentine-Mexican philosopher Horacio Cerutti Guldberg, writing on the one hundredth anniversary of its publication, stated that Martí's essay 'appears to have been written yesterday or, better said, tomorrow' (Cerutti Guldberg 1996, 119). Martí's essay continues to serve critics of colonialism as a guide for the interpretation of hemispheric relations, Latin American culture, and most recently, Latino culture in the United States....

To conclude, I have argued that we must expand our concept of postcolonialism in the United States to make room for Latin American thinkers, many of whom, like Martí, wrote outside the parameters of postmodern critique.[23] He is not alone in this role, but his relevance is sufficiently important to warrant major consideration.[24] Moreover, there is a difference between theorizing about Latin American postcoloniality with a focus on South America and the Caribbean, Mexico, and Central America regions (that have historically been much more vulnerable to U.S. intervention); as Mignolo has posited, our 'loci of enunciation' will yield different perspectives on 'theorizing postcolonial cultural histories' (Mignolo 2000, 180, 182–84). In this vein, the Uruguayan critic Hugo Achúgar reminds us that 'one thing is to be postcolonial in English and another in Spanish, Portuguese, Bayano, Quechua, Aymara, Guarani, Papiamento and equivalents' (Achúgar 1998, 278). As Achúgar states, postcolonial thought in Latin America can be modern, postmodern, or non-Western, and includes, as Martí's vision of Our America did, both migrants and non-migrants. As a Cuban-American, I could not possibly begin to understand colonialism in this hemisphere without reading Martí. His thought reveals aspects of our present-day cultural and political realities whose roots go back to conditions in the making for well over a century. Martí's brilliant and passionate thinking continues to enrich our understanding of the many facets of resistance to colonialism, both historically and even today.

Notes

1. Surely Martí did not imagine that – as the twentieth century demonstrated – Cuba would undergo a political revolution that would attempt to resist U.S. hegemony on its own or with the help of an extra-continental power such as the Soviet Union, without the backing of the majority of Hispanic American republics.

2. In the 1891 article 'Nuestra América', Martí contrasted the Indo-Hispanic, African-descendant, and creole cultures of 'our America' with the Anglo-based cultures of the United States. Roberto Fernández Retamar has called attention to Martí's use elsewhere of the expression 'European America' (Roberto Fernández Retamar, *Caliban and Other Essays*, trans Edward Baker [Minneapolis: University of Minnesota Press, 1989], 21, 24, 27 and passim; Martí, *Obras Completas de José Martí* [hereafter cited as OC] 25+ volumes [Havana: Editorial Nacional de Cuba, 1963–65], 8:442), a term that Retamar takes as a defining contrast to 'nuestra América'. Martí referred to 'la América Europea' (European America) in an 1884 article describing a graduating ceremony at Vassar. The article contains an interesting statement regarding his support for the advanced education of women (mellowed by his simultaneous endorsement of women's 'feminine' traits). See 'Una distribución de diplomas en un colegio de los Estados Unidos' in OC 8:440–45.
3. For a discussion of Martí's political formation during this period, see also Fernández Retamar, 'Prólogo', in José Martí, *Política de nuestra América*, edited by José Aricó (Mexico City: Siglo XXI, 1979), 26–28.
4. 'De la tiranía de España supo salvarse la América española; y ahora, después de ver con ojos judiciales los antecedentes, causas y factores del convite, urge decir, porque es la verdad, que ha llegado para la América española la hora de declarar su segunda independencia' (OC 6:46).
5. In fact, Martí used the term *colonialismo* to describe the nature of the economic manipulation the United States was engaging in before and during the 1889 hemispheric congress. He refers to 'the [economic] battle the United States is preparing to have with the rest of the world' and questions why the United States should wage its [trade] battles against Europe 'over the American republics, and try out *in free peoples its system of colonization*'? (emphasis added; OC 6:57). This article was written in New York on 2 November 1889, and published 20 December 1889, in *La Nación*, Buenos Aires.
6. 'un pueblo que comienza a mirar como privilegio suyo la libertad, que es aspiración universal y perenne del hombre, y a invocarla para privar a los pueblos de ella' (OC 6:53).
7. For a chronology of Martí's life, see *José Martí: Selected Writings*, ed and trans by Esther Allen, Introduction by Roberto González Echevarría (New York: Penguin, [1893] 2002), xxvii–xxxii. For a biographical essay on Martí's life and the historical reception of his work in Cuba and Latin America, see Oscar Martí, 'Martí and the Heroic Image', *José Martí's 'Nuestra América': From National to Hemispheric Cultural Studies*, ed Jeffrey Belnap and Raúl Fernández (Durham, NC: Duke University Press, 1998), 317–38.
8. The two earlier stages of the war had been the Ten Years' War or Big War (1868–1878) and the Little War (1879–1880).
9. The earlier part of the nineteenth century had shown the territorial expansion of the United States over previously Hispanic lands in the northern part of the continent. Florida was purchased from Spain in 1819. Texas, California, Arizona, New Mexico, and parts of Colorado, Nevada, and Utah were part of Mexico in the earlier part of the nineteenth century. Texas was part of Mexico until 1835 and California until 1847. The rest were ceded to the United States by the Treaty of Guadalupe Hidalgo that concluded the Mexican-American War in 1848 (see James Dunkerley, 'Latin America since Independence', in *The Cambridge Companion to Modern Latin American Culture*, edited by John King [New York: Cambridge University Press, 2004], 29). In 1855 the United States offered to buy Cuba from Spain for one hundred million dollars. Spain was not interested (Martí 2002, xxvii).
10. Various translators have used 'our *mestizo* America' to translate this phrase, although for Martí 'our America' is gendered female and is described as having the qualities of a nurturing, freedom-loving mother. I am therefore retaining the term *mestiza* in the feminine. It is a *mestiza* America (not a masculinised 'mestizo' America) that Martí invokes and theorizes as 'ours'. A famous speech of his from December 1889 'Madre América' ('Mother America') invokes the continent that nourishes its children to independence from colonialism in feminine, maternal terms. See 'Mother America', in *Our America by José Martí: Writings on Latin America and the Cuban Struggle for Independence*, ed Philip S Foner (New York: Monthly Review Press, 1977), 69–83.

11. The debate over whether Martí took sufficient steps to fight racism in Cuba will be considered below.
12. For a classic study on nineteenth-century Latin American intellectual liberalism, including its limitations, see Beatriz González Stephan, *La historiografía literaria del liberalismo hispano-americano del siglo XIX* (Havana: Casa de las Américas, 1987).
13. In terms of contemporary global politics, Martí's position in favour of indigenous peoples and peasants, and against the power of foreign corporations over regional and local resources, could be seen as having some interesting affinities with the movement that the Indian environmental activist Vandana Shiva calls 'earth democracy'.
14. The term *mestizaje* has had multiple meanings and uses in the history of Latin America. It is important to take its meaning in context. It is widely known that the term has been used in racist ways to whiten and erase the presence and contributions of African-descendant and indigenous peoples. However, it has also been used to challenge racism. I take it that Martí invoked the expansive, rather than the reductionist, sense of 'mestizaje'.
15. The translation by Esther Allen is possibly misleading here by referring to 'the country's natural constitution' (Martí 2002, 290). Philosophically speaking, what is 'propio' is neither reducible nor equivalent to what is natural, since it can be 'propio' (of one's very own, of its very own) in a cultural or historic sense. I also prefer to read the next sentence ('El gobierno no es más que el equilibrio de los elementos naturales del país' [OC 6:17]) as meaning that government is nothing but the balance of the country's natural elements, which allows for personal judgement and collective action in recognising and/or facilitating such a balance, rather than Allen's 'The government is no more than an equilibrium among the country's natural elements' (Martí 2002, 290). If Martí had meant the latter, he could have used the proposition *entre*, meaning 'among', but he did not.
16. I do not think that Martí's principle of 'just racism' is incompatible with the twentieth-century principles of affirmative action (called 'reverse discrimination' by its opponents in the United States) as long as the measures are understood to be temporary and the measures' objectives are as stated. He apparently did not think such measures would be necessary in post-revolutionary nineteenth-century Cuba because the Republic itself would be founded on non-discriminatory principles, and during the struggle many black leaders had already taken positions of power and responsibility in the revolutionary movement. The Spanish American War, which interrupted the Cuban patriots' struggle for independence from Spain and imposed US control over the island in 1898, cut short the vision for which Martí gave up his life in 1895. With the United States imposing its own (anti-*nuestra Americanista*) conditions for granting Cuban independence, the difficulties of achieving Martí's racial egalitarianism became fully apparent. For a comprehensive study of the racial question in Cuba, see Alejandro de la Fuente, *A Nation for All: Race, Inequality, and Politics in Twentieth-Century Cuba* (Chapel Hill: University of North Carolina Press, 2001).
17. Spain did not abolish slavery in Cuba until 1886, and it did so in the aftermath of the treaty ending the Ten Years' War in 1878 (See Foner, 13–14 and note 14). As a youth Martí witnessed slavery in both the city and the countryside of Cuba. A section of his *Versos sencillos* describes the impact upon witnessing the slave trade and a lynching on a small boy (presumably himself) who 'swore / to wash the crime away with his life'. 'Un niño lo vio: tembló / De pasión por los que gimen: / Y, al pie del muerto, juró / Lavar con su vida el crimen' (2002), 280–81. See also Hebert Pérez, 'Martí, Race, and Cuban Identity', *Monthly Review* 55, no 6 (2003).
18. In 'My Race' Martí claimed that the first Cuban constitution of independence (1869) proclaimed by the rebels freed the slaves, but this goal was not actually achieved within rebels' control until 23 December 1870, when the last provisions against slavery were removed (Foner, 314). De la Fuente dates the themes of abolition and equality among the rebels as becoming prominent in 1871 (Fuente, 26).
19. One of the most prominent founders of Latin American Marxism was José Carlos Mariátegui (1894–1930). For an analysis of his work, see Ofelia Schutte, *Cultural Identity and Social Liberation in Latin American Thought* (Albany: SUNY Press, 1993), 18–71.

20. A similar point was made by Foner in the Preface to his edition of Martí (1977, 9). Foner attributes the observation about Emerson to Gordon Lewis but does not provide a reference for it.
21. Retamar published his influential essay, 'Calibán', for the first time in *Casa de las Américas*, in 1968 (Havana, September–October 1971).
22. Jeffrey Belnap, "Headbands, Hemp Sandals, and Headdresses," *José Martí's "Nuestia América": From National to Hemispheric Studies*, ed. J. Belnap and R. Fernández (Durham, NC: Duke University Press, 1998), 192.
23. Walter Mignolo proposed the category 'postoccidentalism' (in place of 'postmodernism' or 'postcolonialism') to name the tradition of Latin American thought, but despite its conceptual value, the term has not caught on ('Posoccidentalismo: el argumento desde América Latina', in *Teorías sin Disciplina: Latinoamericanismo, poscolonialidad y globalizatión en debate*, edited by S Castro-Gómez and E Mendieta [Mexico City: University of San Francisco and Miguel Angel Porrúa Editores, 1998], 33). Mignolo credits Roberto Fernández Retamar ('Our America and the West', *Social Text* 15, Fall [1976] 1986) for the term *postoccidental*.
24. For additional reading and perspectives beyond Martí, see José Carlos Mariátegui, *Seven Interpretive Essays on Peruvian Reality*, trans Marjory Urquidi (Austin: University of Texas Press, [1928] 1971); Fernández Retamar 1986, 1989; Schutte 1993; Mignolo, *The Darker Side of the Renaissance* (Ann Arbor: University of Michigan Press, 1995); John Beverley et al., *The Postmodernism Debate in Latin America* (Durham, NC: Duke University Press, 1995); Santiago Castro-Gómez and Eduardo Mendieta, eds, *Teorías sin Disciplina: Latinoamericanismo, poscolonialidad y globalización en debate* (Mexico City: University of San Francisco and Miguel Angel Porrúa Editores, 1998); Sara Castro-Klarén, ed, *Latin American Women's Narrative: Practices and Theoretical Perspectives* (Madrid and Frankfurt: Iberoamericana and Vervuert, 2003); Eduardo Mendieta, *Latin American Philosophy: Currents, Issues, Debates* (Bloomington: Indiana University Press, 2003); Mark Thurner and Andrés Guerrero, eds, *After Spanish Rule: Postcolonial Predicaments of the Americas* (Durham, NC: Duke University Press, 2003).

References

Achúgar, Hugo. "Leones, cazadores e historiadores: A propósito de las políticas de la memoria y del conocimiento." In *Teorías sin Disciplina: poscolonialidad y globalización en debate*. Ed. S. Castro-Gómez and E. Mendieta. Mexico City: University of San Francisco and Miguel Angel Porrúa Editores, 1998, 271–285.

Acosta-Belén, Edna. 1999. "Hemispheric Remappings: Revisiting the Concept of Nuestra América." In *Identities on the Move: Transnational Processes in North America and the Caribbean Basin*. Ed. L. R. Goldin. Austin: University of Texas Press, 1999, 81–106.

Cerutti Guldberg, Horacio. *Memoria Comprometida*. Heredia, Costa Rica: Universidad Nacional, 1996.

Martí, José. [1891] 1979. "Nuestra América." In *Política de nuestra América*. Ed. José Aricó, 37–42. Mexico City: Siglo XXI.

Mignolo, Walter D. "Human Understanding and (Latin) American Interests – The Politics and Sensibilities of Geohistorical Locations." In *A Companion to Postcolonial Studies*. Ed. Henry Schwarz and Sangeeta Ray. Malden, MA: Blackwell, 2000, 180–202.

Saldívar, José David. 1990. "The Dialectics of Our America." In *Do the Americas Have a Common Literature?* Ed. Gustavo Pérez Firmat, 62–84.

Schutte, Ofelia. 1993. Cultural Identity and Social Liberation in Latin American Thought. Albany: SUNY Press.

SECTION VI

Transitional and Restorative Justice
Working towards a Just World

Forgiving and being reconciled to our enemies or our loved ones are not about pretending that things are other than they are. It is not about patting one another on the back and turning a blind eye to the wrong. True reconciliation exposes the awfulness, the abuse, the hurt, the truth. It could even sometimes make things worse. It is a risky undertaking but, in the end, it is worthwhile, because in the end only an honest confrontation with reality can bring real healing. Superficial reconciliation can bring only superficial healing.
—Desmond Tutu

Harambee: Let's pull together (Swahili)

How do we address the wrongs committed by colonialism and its lasting effects? Rajeev Bhargava, 'Reparations for Cultural Injustice', in the previous section provides an approach to reparations that suggests a major conceptual reorientation. Scholars of transitional justice also pursue a different kind of justice to be applied in cases of grave human rights violations that were seen as normal and tolerated by the colonial or settler state.

In Book V of the *Nicomachean Ethics*, Aristotle writes that different kinds of justice are needed to address the different ways in which something can be just, as each kind offers normative guidance on how to deal with a specific issue. For example, retributive justice deals with punishment for breaking a rule. Corrective justice is concerned with restoring to the injured parties what they have lost, and distributive justice allocates social goods and burdens.

Jennifer Llewellyn in the excerpt in this section suggests that in addition to the types of justice presented by Aristotle, restorative justice is another kind of justice that is appropriately applied to transitional contexts. Restorative justice is concerned with restoring relationships as the response to wrongdoing; it starts from the belief that the ability of human beings to flourish requires relationships of mutual respect and concern. Proponents of restorative justice seek something better than the alternatives, such as retributive justice, which have been tried with limited success in the past. In the 1970s and 1980s, faith in the criminal justice system was diminished by several years of attempts to rehabilitate offenders and the unsatisfactory results that followed. During the 1980s, politicians perceived a shift in public opinion away from rehabilitation and towards greater punitive measures, so they began enacting tougher sentencing laws with longer jail terms, elimination of parole, mandatory sentences, and juvenile 'waivers' for treatment as adults. Yet despite creating the highest levels of incarceration in US history and one of the highest rates amongst industrialised countries, crimes rates continued to rise, and the system was increasingly seen as ineffective as well as unresponsive to the needs of crime victims and their communities. A victims' rights movement started asking for increased services and compensation for crime victims, and intervention in the criminal justice process. In this period there was also a rise in interest in community-based problem solving and indigenous forms of justice. It was not until the mid-1990s, however, that the 'restorative justice' movement achieved prominence as an alternative to an adversarial model of punitive justice that relied too much on attorneys and judges and in which victims' needs were not met and where they often felt treated as merely pieces of evidence and twice victimised by both the offender and the criminal justice system. As Howard Zehr writes, victims need a sense of empowerment in order to heal as power has been taken away from them, but so do offenders, as often for them crime is a way to assert their power, identity and worth in a world that defines worth as access to power. For offenders, the criminal justice process fosters anger, denial of responsibility and feelings of powerlessness. 'So the system is not working for victims, and neither is it working for offenders'.[1]

Restorative justice conceptualises crime as a problem in the relationship amongst the offender, the victim and the community. Thus, the goal is to restore such relationship in the aftermath of crime. As Gottschall and Armour show in their article in this section, restorative justice principles may offer insight into how to reunite former offenders with their communities. They particularly focus on the effects of the American War on Drugs on poor Black communities and the mass incarceration of Black men, arguing that the penal system and its policies actually 'create more crime, destabilize impoverished communities of color, and forge lasting, toxic consequences for us all'.[2] There is a need to rebuild relations of trust and mutual respect, and the rehabilitative potential of restorative justice through community involvement seems a better alternative to heal a damaged society and to deal with a history of massive injustice and violence.

Restorative justice advocates contend that the new paradigm of restorative justice that places the victim as a central decision maker in a process of personal encounters and joint negotiations is not really new as it represents a return to ancient and tribal practices of indigenous peoples where the goal of resolution was not simply to assign blame for transgressions, but 'to restore wholeness to the individual and the community'.[3] In his essay in this section, Chris Cunneen explores transitional and restorative justice in the context of Indigenous peoples in settler colonial states (Canada, the United States, Australia and New Zealand). Although these countries are not usually seen as 'transitional societies', Cunneen challenges that view and suggests that the effects of settler colonialism on the Indigenous peoples of those countries call for the need to confront and remedy past injustices arising from their colonial histories. In his very interesting and provocative article, he suggests a new way of looking at the link between transitional and restorative justice and their connections to Indigenous concepts of justice. He writes that Indigenous justice as healing may provide an important part of the reparative process for historical injustice and challenge the problem of high levels of criminalisation. Indigenous justice thus bridges the notions of transitional and restorative justice and becomes a decolonising strategy.

The appeal of restorative justice to transitional justice stems from some similarities between the two, as they both emphasise inclusive and non-adversarial frameworks with the goal of preventing the repetition of the past. As Ruth Teitel suggests, they are both conceived as 'a form of dialogue between victims and their perpetrators rather than a punitive blame allocation exercise'.[4]

Transitional justice is a distinct form of justice. The problems addressed by this type of justice are different from those addressed by theories of retributive, corrective and distributive justice. Retributive justice asks what the just treatment of a perpetrator of a crime is, and its answer is proportional punishment. Corrective justice asks what a just response is to the losses suffered by a victim of crime, and its answer is some form of compensation. Distributive justice asks what a just distribution of goods is, and the answers vary according to the goods to be distributed (as we saw in Section One with Rawls's theory of justice). Transitional justice asks what constitutes the just pursuit of societal transformation: how to transform a society that has been subjected to human rights abuses and grave injustices.

The contemporary notion of transitional justice emerged in the late 1980s during the transitions of democracy in Latin America, and in the early 1990s with the collapse of the Soviet Union. In the debate on how to address the crimes of past regimes, it became clear that a model of justice different from the standard retributive type was required. In transitional societies, there are both pragmatic and moral obstacles that preclude the standard application of trial, conviction and punishment to most cases of wrongdoing. There is the risk that adhering to the rule of law by prosecuting previous human right abusers could perpetuate political violence. Numerous human right abuses are committed during repression and conflict, and so the sheer numbers of crimes can overwhelm the criminal justice system. Evidence may be destroyed by government officials prior to a transition, and corruption often undermines the ability of courts to distinguish the guilty from the innocent. Finally, in some cases, such as in South Africa, the possibility of a transition may have been conditioned on the granting of amnesty to those who participated in wrongdoing in the past (see Mallinder's and Llewellyn's articles in this section).

While in established democracies law is used to ensure political stability and to punish those who transgress it, in transitional societies accountability is not the primary goal. In her book *Between Vengeance and Forgiveness*, Martha Minow characterises restorative justice's goal as seeking 'repair of social connections and peace rather than retribution against offenders' and as 'building connections and enhancing communication between perpetrators and those they victimized, and forging ties across the community'.[5] Dealing with past wrongs matters only insofar as the failure to do so would inhibit relational transformations. The establishment of peace is often the key priority within transitional settings, which requires the suspension of ordinary criminal justice mechanisms. This has included the implementation of several of the tools of restorative justice such as a focus on reparations and healing of victims and hearings directed at truth finding that emphasise community involvement.

The truth commission is the tool of transitional justice that is most commonly characterised as restorative in nature, as truth commissions provide a public forum for victims and allow victims and offenders to meet with a view to dialogue and personal healing. In the early days of the South African Truth and Reconciliation Commission (TRC), Archbishop Desmond Tutu declared that while Western justice was mainly retributive, the African understanding was more restorative and intended to redress or restore a balance that had been knocked askew. Although as many critics suggest, meaningful encounters and opportunities for reparations were often lacking from the process in the South African TRC in its attempt to achieve a peaceful and democratic future for the country, such a model of justice in a post-conflict environment may be a more beneficial approach in facilitating the repairing of harm where other mechanisms have failed.

Suggested Readings

Balint, J, Evans, J and McMillan, N. 'Rethinking Transitional Justice, Redressing Indigenous Harm: A New Conceptual Approach', *International Journal of Transitional Justice* 8:94–216.
Borer, T, ed. *Telling the Truths: Truth Telling and Peacebuilding in Post-Conflict Societies*. Notre Dame, IN: University of Notre Dame Press, 2005.
Clamp, Kerry, ed. *Restorative Justice in Transitional Settings*. New York: Routledge, 2016.
Cunneen, C, and Hoyle, C. *Debating Restorative Justice*. Oxford: Hart Publishing, 2010.
Hayner, Priscilla B. *Unspeakable Truths: Confronting State Terror and Atrocity*. New York: Routledge, 2000.
London, Ross. 'A New Paradigm Arises'. In *A Restorative Justice Reader*, 2nd edition. Edited by Gerry Johnstone. London and New York: Routledge, 2013, 5–11.
Minow, Martha. *Between Vengeance and Forgiveness: Facing History after Genocide and Mass Violence*. Boston: Beacon Press, 1999.
Simic, Olivera, ed. *An Introduction to Transitional Justice*. New York: Routledge, 2016.
Thompson, Janna. *Taking Responsibility for the Past: Reparation and Historical Injustice*. Cambridge: Polity Press, 2002.
Tutu, Desmond M. *No Future without Forgiveness*. New York: Doubleday, 1999.
Ukpokolo, Isaac E, ed. *Themes, Issues and Problems in African Philosophy*. New York: Palgrave Macmillan, 2017.
Zehr, Howard. 'Retributive Justice, Restorative Justice'. In *A Restorative Justice Reader*, 2nd edition. Edited by Gerry Johnstone. London and New York: Routledge, 2013, 23–35.

Suggested Films and Documentaries

Hoffman, Deborah, and Frances Reid, dir. *Long Night's Journey into Day*. Johnny Symons, 2001. DVD. A documentary that studies South Africa's Truth and Reconciliation Commission, set up by the post-apartheid democratic government to consider amnesty for perpetrators of crimes committed under apartheid's reign.
International Institute for Restorative Practices Graduate School, pro. *Beyond Zero Tolerance: Restorative Practices in Schools*. 2006. DVD. In this 2006 documentary, students, teachers and administrators speak candidly about restorative justice and the effects it has had on their schools.
Kuhimbisa, Edgar, dir. *Voices of the People: A Community-Led Transitional Justice Process in Uganda*. JLOS Media Production, 2013. DVD. This 2013 documentary provides highlights of community feedback and views on the transitional justice process in Uganda.
York, Steve, dir. *A Force More Powerful*. PBS, 1999. DVD. A PBS documentary on how non-violent power overcame oppression and authoritarian rule.

Notes

1. Howard Zehr, 'Retributive Justice, Restorative Justice', *A Restorative Justice Reader*, 2nd edition, ed Gerry Johnstone (London and New York: Routledge, 2013), 24.
2. Hon. Joan Gottschall and Molly Armour, 'Rethinking the War on Drugs: What Insights Does Restorative Justice Offer'? in *Restorative Justice in Practice: A Holistic Approach*, ed Sheila M Murphy and Michael P Seng (Lake Mary, FL: Vandeplas Publishing, 2015), 98.
3. Ross London, 'A New Paradigm Arises', in *A Restorative Justice Reader*, 2nd edition, ed Gerry Johnstone (London and New York: Routledge, 2013), 6.

4. Ruth Teitel, 'Transitional Historical Justice', in *Justice in Time: Responding to Historical Injustice*, ed Lukas H. Meyer (Baden-Baden: Nomos Verlagsgesellschaft, 2004), 80.
5. Martha Minow, *Between Vengeance and Forgiveness: Facing History after Genocide and Mass Violence* (Boston: Beacon Press, 1998), 92.

Jennifer Llewellyn[*], 'Truth Commissions through a Restorative Lens'

Approaching restorative justice as a theory of justice, and not partial justice or a special kind of justice, offers a different view of truth commissions, and their potential and significance for transitional contexts. First and foremost, this understanding of restorative justice as full justice means that truth commissions, insofar as they are restorative justice institutions, ought to be the first and best choice for transitional contexts even where prosecutions (domestic or international) are possible. Indeed, this view of truth commissions turns the 'justice to the extent possible' defence on its head. If justice is understood as fundamentally restorative – that is, requiring the restoration of relationships as the response to wrongdoing – then full justice could not be achieved through retributive-focused prosecutions. There are, of course, some circumstances in which restorative justice might not be possible. For example, continuing hostilities or violence might be a constructive bar to beginning the work of restoration.[1] In such circumstances when the full justice of restoration is impossible, the partial justice of prosecutions might be an alternative. Indeed, it might pave the way for restorative justice by incapacitating those who continue to cause harm to relationships. This would reverse the relationship between prosecution and truth commissions from that currently assumed so that prosecution would represent 'justice to the extent possible' and thus be the second-best option to truth commissions (Llewellyn 2003).

Justice re-envisioned as restorative supports the use of truth commissions as the mechanisms best able to respond to past abuse and violence with a view to building a just future. It makes clear the role truth commissions might play in doing justice in times of transition. But it also points to the potential for such institutions to be of broader significance beyond transition and recovery. The conception of restorative justice as a theory of justice, apt for so-called normal times just as for transitions, points to another way in which truth commissions might play a fundamental role for transitional contexts. As transitional contexts struggle to imagine and construct a future different from their repressive pasts, truth commissions might serve as an example of what justice means and how just institutions might function in the future. Truth commissions, in their design and operation, offer an experience of how to do justice post-transition. They might thus serve as a training ground, building capacity for citizens to do justice in the future (Llewellyn 2005).

Restorative justice fully understood as a theory of justice suggests that truth commissions ought to be favoured over prosecutions for doing justice in response to gross human rights abuse and violence because they are capable of being restorative. This is not to say that they are necessarily nor automatically so. Indeed, there are many truth commissions that, while making some contribution to restoration (through discerning the truth of what happened or providing a forum for victims to tell their story and feel heard, etc.), are not in their design or orientation fully restorative. A helpful distinction is to be made here between processes that

---

[*] Jennifer Llewellyn, "Truth Commissions and Restorative Justice", in Gerry Johnstone and Daniel W. Van Ness, eds., *Handbook of Restorative Justice*. © 2011 Routledge, pp. 357–358, 361–366, reproduced by permission of Taylor & Francis Books UK.

are restoratively oriented, in the sense that they are less retributive or serve to pave the way for the restoration of relationships, and those that take restoration as their goal or orienting principle. Some models of truth commissions might serve restorative interests, but yet not be fully restorative. It is important to consider what implications a fully restorative approach to truth commissions would have for the design, implementation and operation of these institutions. . . .

Instituting Restorative Justice: Lessons from South Africa

The South African Truth and Reconciliation Commission (TRC) is instructive as an example of how truth commissions might be restorative institutions. The South African TRC represents a significant development in truth commissions as institutional models of restorative justice. The South African commission self-identified as concerned with restorative justice (Truth and Reconciliation Commission 1998: vol 1, ch 5, para 80 [hereafter TRC report]; Tutu 1999: 54–55). In using the South African commission as a basis for considering how truth commissions might be restorative institutions, I do not hold it out as a perfect or ideal example. The South African TRC is nevertheless worthy of careful attention because it represents the most advanced model thus far of a truth commission oriented towards restorative justice. It is instructive to examine the ways in which the South African commission attempted to embody the principles of restorative justice in its response to gross human rights abuse and violence. However, in looking to the commission for what it has to teach about creating institutions for restorative justice, it is important to attend to both its successes and failures in this respect.

A note of caution is warranted before undertaking this examination. In recognizing the weaknesses of the South African commission there is a danger of falling into retrospective critique. It is easy to find fault from a distance and with the luxury of time. This is not my intent. Rather, the model developed by the TRC is so significant an advance in the potential of truth commissions as institutions of justice that it deserves attention to ensure the insights of this experience are preserved for others who will face similar tasks in future. While in retrospect we can and must identify aspects of the commission process that could be improved, at the same time we must acknowledge how remarkable it is that the South African commission achieved the innovations and successes it did. The commission did not have time in advance of its work to contemplate and delineate a theoretical framework to inform its work. The commission came to restorative justice as it sought to explain the convictions of those working within the commission – far from sacrificing justice, as its critics charged, the commission was in fact doing justice. In some sense this makes the South African commission an even more powerful example of the potential of restorative justice in response to gross human rights abuse because its identification with restorative justice was not the result of an experiment aimed at proving the truth of restorative dogma, but rather flowed from the reality and demands of justice in that context.

Finally, it is important to be clear that this consideration of the South African commission should not be taken as a blueprint for restorative justice-based truth commission processes. Restorative justice is fundamentally committed to restoring relationships and doing this requires careful attention to the specific details and the context of those relationships. Restorative processes must thus be designed after consideration of the needs of particular parties and the issues involved. It is not possible or desirable, then, to provide a model of a restorative process absent knowledge or experience of the specific context. To be restorative, such processes must emerge from the context in which they will operate. If they are to comprehend the nature of the harms to relationships and how to address them, restorative justice-based truth commissions should be homegrown – developed through a process that includes all the parties concerned.

The struggle to do justice in transitional contexts has been the subject of a great deal of international attention over the last two decades. In response to contexts lacking the resources, skills and/or the will to ensure justice is done, the international community has come to the rescue with money, expertise and sometimes even ready-made institutions (tribunals or truth commissions). If restorative justice is taken as the goal in transitional contexts, this will have implications for international assistance. Ready-made international models will not achieve the restoration of relationships absent attention to context and without involvement and commitment of the parties concerned. Thus, while outsiders might assist in developing the skills and capacity needed for participation in such processes, they cannot create or run such institutions. The South African model, therefore, ought not to be taken as one simply to replicate. It is significant not for its institutional detail, but as an example of how restorative justice might inform an institutional model designed to deal with gross human rights abuse and violence.

What insights, then, might we draw from the South African TRC as a model of a restorative process? Arguably the most significant innovation of the South African commission was the inclusion of perpetrators in the process through the provision of amnesty. Restorative justice processes aim to bring all those affected by wrongdoing together to make a plan to address the resulting harm with a view to restoring relationships. Inclusion of perpetrators is thus vital to a restorative process. Other restoratively oriented processes aimed primarily at the needs of victims and communities might be possible without the participation of the perpetrator, but would leave a significant aspect of the work of restoration undone. Until the South African TRC, truth commissions were typically preceded or followed by a general amnesty. These previous models thus offered little incentive (and in many cases made no attempt) to involve those responsible for the abuse or violence in the process. While the South African commission was also created in the shadow of an amnesty provision agreed to at the last minute of the political negotiations for the transfer of power (Constitution of the Republic of South Africa No. 200 1993),[2] the South African Parliament chose to build this amnesty grant into the truth commission process. Amnesty was not a blanket provision applying across the board, but rather was granted to individuals who applied for it, offered full disclosure of their acts, demonstrated a political motive and showed proportionality between their motive and the means (Promotion of National Unity and Reconciliation Act No. 34 1995, s 20, as amended by the Promotion of National Unity and Reconciliation Amendment Act No. 87 1995; hereafter TRC Act). Amnesty thus became part of the truth commission process as it was offered in exchange for truth. The significance of this development of including perpetrators was not simply that it allowed greater access to information. It was also significant from the perspective of restorative justice, for bringing perpetrators into the process created an opportunity for accountability and reintegration.

In addition to the participation of perpetrators, another significant aspect of the South African TRC as a restorative justice-based truth commission was its definition, inclusion and treatment of victims. The TRC encompassed relatives and dependants within its definition of victims, thereby recognizing that the harm resulting from wrongdoing extended beyond direct victims to those connected to the victim (TRC Act, s 1 [xix]). The TRC reflected restorative principles in providing opportunities for victims to tell their stories and identify their needs for reparations. The commission was committed to ensuring respect for victims and their experiences in all their dealings (TRC Act, s 11),[3] corresponding to the victim-centred approach of restorative justice (Llewellyn and Howse 1998: 69). The commission did not, however, attend to the needs of victims at the expense of fair and respectful treatment of perpetrators.

The TRC also embodied the principles of restorative justice through the public's involvement in the process. This is consistent with the understanding at the core of restorative justice that communities play a fundamental role in the creation and resolution of conflict and that wrongdoing affects communities. The importance of public participation is most obvious perhaps in transitional contexts recovering from gross human rights abuse and violence. In such contexts, communities face the challenge of rebuilding and healing from the harmful effects of past conflict. Bringing community into the process to play a role in understanding and developing a response to the harmful effects of past abuse and violence restores a sense of community and reinforces the values of a healthy community.

The South African TRC included community as both witnesses of, and participants in, the process. The commission's hearings were public unless cause was shown to hold a closed hearing (TRC Act, s 33).[4] These hearings were also broadcast on public radio and television ensuring access to the widest possible number of citizens. Community members were involved in some of the hearings thereby offering an opportunity for them to bring context to the events and highlight the wide-ranging effects of abuse and violence. Communities were also consulted broadly on the issue of reparations. In addition, the appointed commissioners brought the public into the process. Typically in a restorative justice process it is not ideal or advisable to rely upon the facilitator to bring community perspectives. In the case of the South African TRC, however, members of the commission were not charged with the central role of facilitating the process (though occasionally some members did act in this capacity). Generally, commission staff fulfilled this function. The commissioners were thus freed to represent community views and concerns. Indeed, commissioners were selected from civil society groups through a public process (Truth and Reconciliation Commission 1998, vol 1, ch 1, para 37, hereafter TRC Report).[5]

Finally, the TRC stands as an example of a restorative justice process in its forward-looking orientation. The commission was tasked with making recommendations to ensure a better future. It was not focused purely on affixing blame for past crimes. The goal of the South African TRC was thus a restorative one – to make a plan for the future aimed at restoring relationships to ones of equal respect, concern and dignity. The words of the mandate of the commission reflect this ambition to 'promote unity and reconciliation in a spirit of understanding which transcends the conflicts and divisions of the past' (TRC Act, s 3(1)).

The South African commission is significant for what its developments reveal about the potential of truth commissions to be institutions of restorative justice. It was not, however, without flaws or weaknesses when viewed from the perspective of restorative justice. The design and operation of the South African commission raise some concerns and cautions for those who might follow in its footsteps in attempting to develop a restorative truth commission.

The most significant weakness of the commission, from a restorative point of view, was structural. The commission separated the processes designed to deal with victims and perpetrators. Perpetrators were dealt with through the Amnesty Committee and victims through the Human Rights Violation Committee (TRC Act, ss 17 and 14, respectively). This separation caused a number of problems for the commission as a restorative justice process. It reduced the opportunities for face-to-face encounters between the parties involved (victims, perpetrators and community). These encounters are fundamental to restorative justice as they provide an opportunity for dialogue about the nature of the harms and how to address them. Such encounters were not wholly absent, however. They occurred during victim appearances at amnesty hearings and informally when the commission arranged and facilitated meetings between victims and perpetrators outside the formal amnesty and victims' hearings (TRC report, vol 5, ch 9, para 62 et seq).[6] In addition to the standard victims' hearing held by the Human Rights Violation Committee, there were special hearings into events of particular significance. These special event hearings offer some guidance as to how such encounters might become more central to truth commission processes. All the parties involved in a major event during the conflict were brought together in these hearings. They 'allowed [the Commission] to explore the motives and perspectives of the different role players' (TRC report, vol 5, ch 1, para 33). While these hearings still did not fully conform to the principles of restorative justice in that victims, perpetrators and the community were dealt with at separate times, the hearings did bring all three groups into the same process so that they might hear one another and understand one another's perspectives on the events.[7]

These processes were, however, the exception rather than the norm in the South African process. When they happened they provided an opportunity for communities to address collective experiences and harms. These experiences teach how important it is for restorative processes to create space in which those involved can encounter one another and engage in dialogue aimed at making a plan to restore relationships in the future.

The separation of the amnesty and victim processes was also problematic for the South African TRC as a restorative process because it resulted in the exclusion of perpetrators from the process of repairing harm. Perpetrators were not required under the amnesty provision to make any reparations to their victims or to the community. In fact, no formal option existed within the process whereby perpetrators could voluntarily participate in making reparation to their victims and to the community.[8] Restorative justice requires that the perpetrator take an active role in repairing the harm caused by wrongdoing because it is crucial for reintegration and, ultimately, for the restoration of relationships. An institutional model of restorative justice, then, should ensure all parties are actively engaged in the process of reparation.

The commission suffered another related problem in realizing its potential as a restorative process as a result of its limited power over reparations. Not only were the perpetrators not required or given the opportunity to participate in reparations, the commission itself had only recommending power with respect to reparations (TRC Act, ss 3(1)(c), 3(1)(d), 4(b), 4(f), 4(h)). This meant that, while the commission could grant amnesty to perpetrators, thereby offering them an immediate benefit, it was not similarly empowered to respond to victims' needs. The South African government retained the right to determine reparations, including when and whether they would be granted. In the South African context, this was possibly the greatest threat to the restorative potential of the commission (Llewellyn 2004: 178–79). The government recently acted upon some of the recommendations of the commission and provided a measure of reparation for victims. However, they waited over five years after the commission submitted its reparation recommendations (Terreblanche 2003a). The delay cast serious doubt on their intentions to make good on reparations in any significant way and threatens the foundation laid for restoration laid by the commission (Llewellyn 2004). Without reparations a significant aspect of the work of restoration remains undone. Perhaps even more worrisome is that failure to make good on reparations could cast doubt on the legitimacy and sincerity of the process as a whole, given that victims participated on the basis of a commitment to address their harm. The struggle over reparations in South Africa makes clear the importance of a sufficient commitment to follow through on the outcomes of the restorative process.

Another lesson can be learnt from the South African experience about the relationship between truth commissions and trials. Amnesty in the South African commission was used as a means to bring perpetrators into the process. For their participation and willingness to contribute to restoration (at the very least in the form of truth-telling and public accountability for their actions), perpetrators were granted amnesty so that they might be reintegrated into society. If amnesty is to be meaningful, however, the failure to apply or be granted amnesty must be met with some consequence. From the perspective of restorative justice, the problem here is not simply that of the free-rider, it is also that those who have not chosen to participate in the restorative process may continue to cause harm either directly through their actions or resulting from their lack of accountability. It is thus important that a restorative justice truth commission be backed by mechanisms aimed at ensuring accountability for those who do not participate. Prosecution is typically the mechanism used for such purposes. Failure to pursue prosecutions against those who were refused or failed to apply for amnesty may thus be problematic for the prospects of restorative justice (Llewellyn 2003). South Africa has not as yet pursued a significant number of prosecutions related to crimes committed in the past.[9] Additionally, the failure to enforce the threat of prosecutions in one context might jeopardize the success of restorative-based truth commissions in the future as perpetrators may refuse to participate, instead counting on there being no future consequences. Unfortunately, the failure to pursue further prosecutions following a truth commission process is not always a matter of will on the part of governments. It is often a consequence of scarce resources and the many demands for urgent and basic needs faced by transitional contexts (Llewellyn 2005).[10]

Finally, the experience of the South African commission offers insights into the importance of preparation for the participants – particularly for the victim and perpetrator – so that they can understand the nature of the process and its goals. The South African commission had support personnel available for victims who testified before public hearings but significantly less support was available to the thousands of victims who spoke to statement-takers about their experiences. Less support still was provided to offenders; typically legal counsel was their primary support. Follow-up is equally, if not more, important than preparation to the restoration of relationships. It is important to support victims after the process and to ensure that reparation recommendations are carried out. For the perpetrator, it is important to provide support for reintegration if restoration is to become a reality. The South African commission's follow-up was weak. There were no formal provisions made with respect to reintegration of perpetrators or follow through on reparations. Additionally, whatever limited psychological support existed for victims was one of the first services to be eliminated towards the end of the commission's work.

Conclusion

Restorative justice is being invoked with increased frequency as an approach to dealing with gross human rights abuse and mass violence, yet the full promise and potential of restorative justice to address these circumstances have not been realized. The developments brought by the South African TRC show the possibility of truth commissions to be restorative justice processes. The time is ripe for careful attention to the application of restorative justice principles and practices in response to large-scale, systemic abuse and violence, both in transitional contexts and established democracies. Such attention will be fruitful for these contexts, and for the development and understanding of restorative justice, as it reveals that justice can only be realized if relationships are restored to ones of equal dignity, concern and respect.

References

Katz, M L (1996) 'Apartheid Era Unveiled: South African Commission May Reopen Massacre Case'. *USA Today*, 14 October: 4A.

Leebaw, B. (2001) 'Restorative Justice for Political Transitions: Lessons from the South African Truth and Reconciliation Commission'. *Contemporary Justice Review* 4: 267–89.

Llewellyn, J. (2003) 'Justice to the Extent Possible: The Relationship between the International Criminal Court and Domestic Truth Commissions', in *The Highway to the International Criminal Court: All Roads Lead to Rome*, eds H Dumont and A Boisvert. Montreal: Journée Maximilien-Caron.

Llewellyn, J. (2004) 'Doing Justice in South Africa: Restorative Justice and Reparation', in *To Repair the Irreparable: Reparation and Reconstruction in South Africa*, eds E Doxtader and C Villa-Vicencio. Cape Town: David Philip.

Llewellyn, J. (2005) 'Restorative Justice in Transitions and Beyond: The Justice Potential of Truth Telling Mechanisms for Post-Peace Accord Societies', in *Telling the Truths: Truth Telling and Peacebuilding in Post-Conflict Societies*, ed T Borer. Notre Dame, IN: University of Notre Dame Press.

Llewellyn, J, and R Howse. (1998) *Restorative Justice: A Conceptual Framework*. Ottawa: Law Commission of Canada.

Naidu, E. (2005) 'No General Amnesty for Apartheid Crimes'. *Sunday Independent*, 3 July.

Tepperman, J D (2002) 'Truth and Consequences'. *Foreign Affairs*, 81: 129–45.

Terreblanche, C. (2003a) 'Government Ready to Pay Apartheid Reparations'. *Independent Online*, 16 November.

Terreblanche, C. (2003b) 'New Deal Stops Short of General Amnesty'. *Independent Online*, 18 May.

Truth and Reconciliation Commission. (1998) *Truth and Reconciliation Commission of South Africa Report* (vols 1 and 5). Cape Town: Truth and Reconciliation Commission.

Tutu, D. M. *No Future without Forgiveness*. (New York: Doubleday, 1999).

Notes

1. This does not mean that there can be no violence ongoing. Many transitions from conflict and repression are marked by so-called spoiler violence or isolated acts of violence aimed at disrupting the transition undermining the peace. A general end to hostilities and a commitment by the major parties to move beyond the abuses and violence of the past are necessary in order to create a safe space for the work of a truth commission to begin.
2. It was contained in the 'postamble' to the interim constitution. The interim constitution was drafted by a multiparty negotiating council and set out principles for the transition period and the development of the final constitution. The interim constitution was in force from 1993 to December 1996 when the new constitution was promulgated. The provisions contained in the postamble were incorporated into the final constitution tabled 8 May 1996 under s 22 of Schedule 6 on Transitional Arrangements (Constitution of the Republic of South Africa No 200 1993).

3. The Promotion of National Unity and Reconciliation Act identified seven principles to guide the treatment of victims in all aspects of the commission's work. Victims were to (1) be treated with compassion and respect for their dignity; (2) be treated equally and without discrimination of any kind; (3) encounter expeditious, fair, inexpensive and accessible procedures when making application to the commission; (4) be informed through the press and other media of their rights in seeking redress through the commission; (5) have their inconvenience minimised and when necessary measures taken to protect their safety and that of their family, and to protect their privacy; (6) be able to communicate in their chosen language; and (7) be able to access informal mechanisms for the resolution of disputes, including mediation, arbitration and any procedure provided for by customary law and practice, where appropriate (TRC Act, s 11).
4. The presumption of transparency can also be found elsewhere in the Act (See ss 29 and 30).
5. The commissioners were Archbishop Desmond Tutu (chairperson), Dr Alex Boraine (vice-chairperson), Mary Burton (former Black Sash president), Advocate Chris de Jager (lawyer, former Member of Parliament and human rights commissioner), Rev Bongani Finca (Minster in the Reformed Presbyterian Church), Ms Sisi Kamphephe (lawyer and vice-chairperson of Mediation and Conciliation Centre), Mr Richard Lyster (Director, Legal Resources Centre, Durban), Mr Wynand Malan (lawyer and former Member of Parliament), Ms Hlengiwe Mkhize (Director, Mental Health and Substance Abuse, Department of Health), Mr Dumisa Ntsebeza (lawyer), Dr Wendy Orr (medical doctor), Dr Mapule Ramashala (clinical psychologist), Dr Fazel Randera (medical doctor and deputy chairperson, Human Rights Committee), Dr Yasmin Sooka (lawyer and president, World Conference on Religion and Peace, South Africa Chapter), Ms Glenda Wildschut (chairperson, Trauma Centre for Victims of Violence and Torture), Rev K M Mqojo (Methodist minister) and Advocate Denzil Potgieter (lawyer).
6. The inclusion of amnesty into the overall work of the commission was important from the perspective of restorative justice as it brought perpetrators into the process and kept open the possibility of reintegration and thus restoration of relationships. However, the amnesty process itself was not, for the most part, a restorative one. In fact, the amnesty hearings more closely resembled adversarial court processes than the other hearings of the commission. The structure of this process limited the participation of the victims and community and the opportunities for restorative encounters. This is one of the weaknesses of the commission if viewed as a restorative process.
7. An example of such a hearing was that concerning the 'Trojan Horse' incident which occurred in Athlone, Cape Town, in October 1985. The hearing was held in Athlone in the presence of community members and heard testimony from the community, victims and perpetrators. These hearings are addressed in the TRC report (vol 5, ch 1 paras 33–37).
8. The case of Brian Victor Mitchell, who was granted amnesty with respect to the Trust Feeds Massacre, serves as a well-publicised example of a perpetrator who sought a way to make amends for his actions. There was no official mechanism within the commission to do this so he struggled to find some means of doing it on his own (see Amnesty Application No 2586/96). The commission did, however, informally assist Mitchell in making contact with the community. The commission discusses this example in its report as one in which some important steps towards reconciliation were ultimately made (TRC report 1998: vol 5, ch 9, paras 70–82).
9. The current government even floated the prospect of a general amnesty for acts committed during apartheid, although it has recently announced that no such amnesty

will be granted. However, as part of a new prosecution policy some indemnity may be granted in connection with apartheid-related crimes. Details of the policy have yet to be released, but it would not offer immunity from civil claims (Terreblanche 2003b; Naidu 2005).

10. The experience of South Africa with two early attempts to prosecute apartheid crimes demonstrates how difficult and costly these prosecutions can be. The trials of General Magnus Malan and Eugene de Kock, two of apartheid's most notorious perpetrators, were long, expensive (costing a combined R17 million) and ultimately unsuccessful (Katz 1996; Leebaw 2001: 276; Tepperman 2002: 143–44).

Louise Mallinder*, 'Amnesties in the Pursuit of Reconciliation, Peacebuilding, and Restorative Justice'

Introduction

For centuries, amnesty laws were a habitual element of peacebuilding and reconciliation around the world.[1] Amnesties were used to calm insurrections or to mark the ends of wars between states.[2] Ruling elites often portrayed the introduction of these laws as gestures of mercy and benefaction designed to restore relations between the state and the citizenry, or between the peoples of belligerent countries.[3] During the past 30 years, amnesty laws have remained a key component of peace negotiations around the world. For example, a 2007 survey of peace agreements made between 1980 and 2006 found that while 'provisions for prosecutions and truth commissions are rare in peace agreements . . . the use of amnesty is comparatively common'.[4] However, with the development of the field of transitional justice from the early 1990s, reliance on national amnesty laws to promote peacebuilding and reconciliation has provoked increasing international controversy.[5]

The roots of this controversy lie in the end of the Cold War, which marked the start of a new era in global politics in which legalism and the rule of law became increasingly important in international relations.[6] These changes were manifest in a growing privileging of legal discourse within political transitions,[7] and a rapid expansion of international criminal law and institutions, including the creation of the ad hoc tribunals, the hybrid courts, and the International Criminal Court (ICC).[8] These developments had multiple and contrasting impacts on amnesty laws. For example, whereas previously, transitions from conflict and repression were usually achieved through pragmatic bargains brokered between political elites often entailing de facto impunity, the expansion of international criminal law caused these elites to demand and enact a growing number of amnesty laws to shield themselves from prosecution.[9]

Concurrent to the growing legalism creating incentives for the enactment of new amnesty laws, the emergence of international legal obligations for states to investigate, prosecute, and punish serious human rights violations resulted in international attitudes toward amnesty laws shifting. During this period, as is documented in United Nations' reports, perceptions of amnesties as tools for the 'safeguard and promotion of human rights and fundamental freedoms'[10] were replaced with increasing condemnation of amnesty laws as forms of impunity.[11] The anti-impunity critiques, as articulated for example in the 2005 United Nations' *Updated Set of Principles to Combat Impunity* understand impunity as 'the impossibility, de jure

---

* Louise Mallinder, "Amnesties in the Pursuit of Reconciliation, Peacebuilding, and Restorative Justice", in Jennifer Llewellyn and Daniel Philpott, eds., *Restorative Justice, Reconciliation and Peacebuilding*. Oxford: Oxford University Press, 2014, pp. 138–140, 141–142, 151–152, 164. By Permission of Oxford University Press, USA.

or de facto, of bringing the perpetrators of violations to account – whether in criminal, civil, administrative or disciplinary proceedings'. The principles continue that both judicial and non-judicial proceedings should lead to perpetrators of serious crimes under international law 'being accused, arrested, tried and, if found guilty, sentenced to appropriate penalties, and to making reparations to their victims'.[12] Under this approach, holding perpetrators to account is viewed as synonymous with criminal trials, and a state's failure to investigate violations and to ensure that 'those suspected of criminal responsibility are prosecuted, tried and duly punished' by, for example, enacting amnesty laws, is perceived as resulting in impunity, even when the amnesty is 'intended to establish conditions conducive to a peace agreement or to foster national reconciliation'.[13]

The desire to prosecute and punish serious human rights violations is of course understandable; however, this anti-impunity approach has some limitations. For example, it is narrowly focused on primarily Western, legalistic, and formal understandings of justice, accountability, and the rule of law.[14] As this chapter will explore, this overlooks the role that informal or traditional accountability mechanisms can play in combating impunity and delivering more holistic forms of justice.[15] In many parts of the world, informal justice processes[16] are used to respond to both ordinary crime and mass violence. Indeed, the United Nations Development Program estimates that 'informal justice systems usually resolve between 80 and 90 percent of disputes' in many countries.[17] Although the mandates, composition, processes, and outcomes of these mechanisms can vary considerably between communities, they are often permeated by common elements of restorative justice, which are outlined below. As the field of transitional justice has developed, informal approaches to justice have attracted increasing attention as a way of redressing past crimes,[18] and some transitional justice institutions have explicitly embraced restorative justice principles, even while implementing amnesties.[19] However, as will be explored below, supporters of legalistic approaches to combating impunity often view restorative approaches as compromised forms of justice to be pursued where 'full' justice in the form of trials is not possible. This chapter will argue, however, that such narrow approaches to justice fail to acknowledge the full extent to which restorative justice can contribute to peacebuilding and reconciliation.

A second critique of amnesty-as-impunity arguments is that they overlook the considerable diversity that exists among amnesty laws today in terms of the crimes they cover, their implementation processes, and their diverse relationships to transitional accountability mechanisms, including trials, truth commissions, and vetting programs.[20] In particular, although amnesty laws bar criminal proceedings against certain categories of crimes or offenders, no amnesty laws to date have prohibited offenders participating in restorative justice processes; indeed, some require it. As this chapter will explore, understanding how amnesties can coexist with or even be integrated into restorative justice mechanisms can cast light on how victims, offenders, communities, and wider societies can engage with amnesty laws in ways that seek to deliver truth, accountability, reparations, and the articulation of non-violent social norms. . . .

Restoring Relationships: Exploring the Nexus between Peacebuilding, Reconciliation and Transitional Justice

From the mid-1990s, theoretical and empirical inquiries into conflict began to emphasize the role that unequal relations can play in the onset of conflict, the ways in which rupturing relationships within and between communities can be a central objective of combatant factions, and ways in which fractured relationships can undermine the durability of peace and reconciliation programs.[21] These insights contributed to the emergence of what Philpott describes as a new 'ethic of political reconciliation', which situated reconciliation as both a process and outcome that is central to transitional justice.[22] Philpott defines this ethic as

> a concept of justice that involves the will to restore victims, perpetrators, citizens, and the governments of states who have been involved in political injustices to a condition of right relationship within a political order or between political orders – a condition characterized by human rights, democracy, the rule of law, and respect for international law, by widespread recognition of the legitimacy of these values, and by accompanying virtues.[23]

This definition illustrates how under the newly evolving ethic of political reconciliation, national reconciliation policies moved from being primarily negative measures, whereby states refrained from delving into their violent pasts, to processes in which states committed themselves to more positive obligations to investigate political injustices, to repair the harms that they created, and to work toward a more just society. Thus, the recognition of the causes, nature, and long-term impacts of conflict shifted scholars and practitioners toward understandings of reconciliation as the longer-term restoration of relationships. In this way, the concept of reconciliation has deepened and come to share an emphasis on rebuilding relationships with restorative understandings of justice. However, within both concepts, 'restoring' social relationships does not imply restoring the status quo ante, but rather establishing conditions whereby each individual's 'rights to equal dignity, respect and concern' are respected in society.[24] The evolution within the concept of reconciliation has meant that rather than being in tension with transitional justice, sustainable reconciliation has become a central objective of many transitional justice institutions, most notably, the South African Truth and Reconciliation Commission,[25] as well as a key element of peacebuilding programs....

Restorative Theories of Transitional Justice

Around the world, restorative justice has been practiced in diverse forms by many communities since ancient times. However, the label of restorative justice has been applied to a variety of settings with the result that restorative justice 'is often used as a catchall phrase to refer to any alternative practice that does not look like mainstream justice practices'.[26] Due to the array of mechanisms that have been described as restorative, no widely accepted definition of the concept has yet developed and there is no clear consensus on restorative justice principles, either in relation to ordinary crime or mass violence.[27]

Although restorative principles are contested, several elements of restorative justice appear to be broadly accepted in the literature. First, in contrast to criminal justice approaches that focus on crime and punishment, restorative justice primarily views crime as 'a violation of people and relationships'.[28] As a result, rather than privileging the illegality of the action, restorative approaches emphasize the 'harms' caused by the offenders' actions, both to individual victims and the wider community.[29] Second, the notion that restorative justice processes should aim primarily to repair the harm rather than punish the perpetrators appears largely uncontested.[30] Indeed, restorative theories argue that causing harm creates 'responsibilities' for offenders to right their wrongs.[31] Third, the focus on encouraging offenders to fulfil their responsibilities in repairing such damage emanates not just from the urge to 'restore' victims but also from an acceptance that the aim of restorative justice should also be to reintegrate the offenders rather than 'alienate and isolate' them from society.[32] Breaking cycles of recidivism is, from a restorative perspective, not just in the interests of individual offenders, but also has obvious benefits for the community and society to which they return.

In this way, the outcomes of restorative justice processes are 'forward looking' as they seek to address the 'implication of a wrong in the future', rather than punishing the offender 'for what she did in the past'.[33] Finally, throughout the process of identifying the harms and the necessary remedies, restorative justice processes are generally geared toward encouraging the involvement of all stakeholders, including the direct victims, the offenders, the families of the victims and offenders, and their wider communities.[34] This inclusive approach recognizes that all these persons, including the offenders themselves, can suffer harm as a result of the offenders' actions. It therefore encourages a version of justice wherein the participants are encouraged to work collaboratively to develop remedies that are acceptable to all parties. This more inclusive approach contributes to the identification of harms and remedies that are not commonly discussed in formal justice processes, encourages healing and responsibility among all the participants, and envisages a sufficiently broad understanding of harm to include structural injustices that affect people and communities beyond the immediate participants.[35]. . .

Some theorists argue that restorative justice has the potential to offer a complete framework to address mass atrocity. This approach has been cogently reasoned by Llewellyn, who argues that restoration is not simply one of the goals of justice (along with retribution, deterrence, incapacitation, rehabilitation, and expression of social norms), 'nor is it a theory about a *kind* or *type* of justice appropriate only in certain circumstances. Restorative justice is, rather, a comprehensive theory about the meaning of justice' (emphasis in original).[36] Under this approach, harms or crimes are viewed as creating inequalities in the relationships between victims and offenders. Consequently, justice is viewed as a process that seeks to respond to wrongdoing through the restoration of relationships between 'the victim(s), wrongdoer and the respective communities' so that 'each party enjoys equal dignity, respect and concern'.[37] As noted above, the restorative goal of rebuilding relationships can be interpreted as a central tenet of both reconciliation and peacebuilding.

In contrast to restorative processes, where prosecution and punishment seek to isolate the offender, although they may 'prevent further harm to relationships where there is a continuing risk of harm – that is where the perpetrator is not willing or able to restore the relationships', but they will do little to restore ruptured relationships.[38] As a result, Llewellyn argues if justice is understood as the restoration of relationships, prosecution and punishment 'are only able to serve the interests of justice in part'.[39] In contrast, amnesty laws that aim to deliver peace may also contribute to delivering restorative justice and reconciliation, where they are designed to encourage offenders to take responsibility for their actions and engage with accountability through participation in restorative justice processes. In this way, by encouraging offender participation, amnesty laws can potentially contribute to creating the conditions for the restoration of relationships. . . .

Designing Amnesties on Restorative Principles

. . . The transitional amnesty process in South Africa began life as the product of an elite pact agreed to in the final stages of the transitional negotiations, but its ultimate shape was determined in the legislation to establish the TRC, which was promulgated by the democratically elected transitional government following public consultations. The enacted law created the Amnesty Committee of the TRC, which was empowered to grant amnesty for civil and criminal liability to individual offenders who fully disclosed their political offenses,[40] with offenders who did not apply for amnesty or did not comply with the conditions remaining liable for prosecution. The conditional and individualized nature of this process introduced elements of accountability, reconciliation, and restorative justice into the process that was originally the product of political compromise. This was recognized by the TRC in its final report, when responding to criticism of the amnesty as a denial of justice, the TRC argued that amnesty could be viewed as a form of justice if justice is conceived, not as retribution, but as restoration.[41] Although the extent to which the South African amnesty process was conducted according to restorative principles has rightly been critiqued by several authors,[42] the framing of the amnesty within the restorative framework transformed a contentious transitional compromise into a process that delivered greater truth and accountability. . . .

Conclusion

. . . Amnesty laws are a constant feature of peacebuilding and reconciliation endeavors in many parts of the world, and despite the growth of international criminal law in recent decades, amnesties are likely to continue to play a role in transitions from war to peace. This role will vary from country to country depending on the balance of power in the transition, the nature of the criminality, and societies' perceptions of justice. In all contexts, however, designing amnesty laws in accordance with restorative principles can offer a way to move from impunity for conflict-related crimes toward more inclusive and holistic approaches that seek to repair the multiplicity of harms suffered by diverse stakeholders and to help societies move toward more just forms of governance.

Notes

1. The author would like to thank Jennifer Llewellyn, Daniel Philpott, Kieran McEvoy, Leslie Vinjamuri and Aaron Boesenecker for their thoughts and comments on the earlier drafts of this chapter. She would also like to thank the participants at the authors' workshop, University of Notre Dame, 17 September 2010, and participants at the Reconciliation, Peacebuilding and Restorative Justice conference, New York, 10 November 2011, for their feedback on this chapter.
2. For a historical overview of the use of amnesties, see Fania Domb, 'Treatment of War Crimes in Peace Settlements – Prosecution or Amnesty'? in *War Crimes in International Law*, ed Yoram Dinstein and Mala Tabory (Hague: Martinus Nijhoff Publishers, 1996), 305; Robert Parker, 'Fighting the Siren's Song: The Problem of Amnesty in Historical and Contemporary Perspective', *Acta Juridica Hungaria* 42, no 1–2 (2001): 69–89.
3. For an analysis of the motivations for introducing amnesty laws see Louise Mallinder, *Amnesty, Human Rights and Political Transitions: Bridging the Peace and Justice Divide (Studies in International Law)* (Oxford: Hart Publishing, 2008), 39–70.
4. Leslie Vinjamuri and Aaron Boesenecker, *Accountability and Peace Agreements: Mapping Trends from 1980 to 2006* (Geneva: Centre for Humanitarian Dialogue, 2007), 5.
5. See, e.g., Diane F Orentlicher, 'Rule-of-Law Tools for Post-Conflict States; Amnesties', Office of the United Nations High Commissioner for Human Rights (Geneva) HR/PUB/09/1.
6. Cesare P R Romano, 'The Proliferation of International Judicial Bodies: The Pieces of the Puzzle', *New York University Journal of International Law and Politics* 31 (1998): 709–51.
7. Kieran McEvoy, 'Beyond Legalism: Towards a Thicker Understanding of Transitional Justice', *Journal of Law and Society* 34, no 4 (2008): 411–40.
8. See, e.g., Kai Ambos and Otto Triffterer, eds, *Commentary on the Rome Statute of the International Criminal Court: Observers' Notes, Article by Article* (Baden-Baden: Aufl edn Nomos Verlagsgesellschaft, 1999), 1295; Laura A Dickinson, 'The Promise of Hybrid

Courts', *American Journal of International Law* 97, no 2 (2003): 295; Roy S K Lee, ed, *The International Criminal Court: The Making of the Rome Statute – Issues, Negotiations, Results* (Hague: Kluwer Law International, 1999), 657; Cesare Romano, André Nollkaemper and Jann K Kleffner, eds, *Internationalized Criminal Courts and Tribunals: Sierra Leone, East Timor, Kosovo, and Cambodia* (Oxford: International Courts and Tribunals Series, Oxford University Press, 2004), 491; William A Schabas, *The UN International Criminal Tribunals: The Former Yugoslavia, Rwanda and Sierra Leone* (Cambridge: Cambridge University Press, 2006); William A Schabas, *An Introduction to the International Criminal Court*, 3rd ed (Cambridge: Cambridge University Press, 2007).

9. Louise Mallinder, 'Amnesties' Challenge to the Global Accountability Norm? Interpreting Regional and International Trends in Amnesty Enactment', in *Amnesty in the Age of Human Rights Accountability: Comparative and International Perspectives*, ed Leigh A Payne and Francesca Lessa (Cambridge: Cambridge University Press, 2012).
10. UN Sub-Commission on Prevention of Discrimination and Protection of Minorities, Resolution 1983/34. The administration of justice and the human rights of detainees. UN Doc E/CN.4/ Sub.2/RES/1983/34 (6 September 1983).
11. These criticisms are most evident in the reports of human rights organisations; see, e.g., Amnesty International, '"We Cry for Justice": Impunity Persists 10 Years on in Timor-Leste', AI Index ASA 57/001/2009; Sara Darehshori, 'Selling Justice Short: Why Accountability Matters for Peace', Human Rights Watch, New York: July 2009.
12. UNCHR, Updated Set of Principles for the Protection and Promotion of Human Rights through Action to Combat Impunity. Commission on Human Rights, 2005.
13. UNCHR, Updated Set of Principles, Principles 1 and 24.
14. See, e.g., Payam Akhavan, 'Are International Criminal Tribunals a Disincentive to Peace? Reconciling Judicial Romanticism with Political Realism', *Human Rights Quarterly* 31, no 3 (2009): 624.
15. For an analysis of the concept of accountability within transitional justice, see Louise Mallinder and Kieran McEvoy, 'Rethinking Amnesties: Atrocity, Accountability and Impunity in Post-Conflict Societies', *Contemporary Social Science: The Journal of the Academy of Social Science* 6, no 1 (2011): 107–28.
16. Within the scholarly literature, a range of terminology is used to describe these processes, including traditional justice, local justice, informal justice, customary justice, indigenous justice and restorative justice. Each of these terms has its strengths and limitations, but it is beyond the scope of the chapter to analyse these debates. Instead, 'informal justice' has been selected as the most appropriate here to contrast these processes with formal prosecutions, although the author acknowledges this term is not unproblematic.
17. Ewa Wojkowska, *Doing Justice: How Informal Justice Systems Can Contribute* (UNDP 2006), 5.
18. E.g., in his August 2004 report on *The Rule of Law and Transitional Justice in Conflict and Post-Conflict Societies*, the UN secretary-general proclaimed that 'due regard must be given to indigenous and informal traditions for administering justice or settling disputes, to help them to continue their often vital role and to do so in conformity with both international standards and local tradition'. See UNSC, *Report of the Secretary-General: The Rule of Law and Transitional Justice in Conflict and Post-Conflict States*, UNDocS/2004/ 616 (August 23, 2004), para 36.
19. E.g., in its final report, the South African Truth and Reconciliation Commission expressly characterised its work as a form of restorative justice. See Truth and Reconciliation

Commission of South Africa Report, vol 1, ch 5, para 82 ('TRC Report'). See also e.g., Erin K Baines, 'The Haunting of Alice: Local Approaches to Justice and Reconciliation in Northern Uganda', *International Journal of Transitional Justice* 1, no 1 (2007): 97; Patrick Burgess, 'A New Approach to Restorative Justice: East Timor's Community Reconciliation Process', in *Transitional Justice in the Twenty-First Century: Beyond Truth Versus Justice*, ed Naomi Roht-Arriaza (Cambridge: Cambridge University Press, 2006), 176; Sinclair Dinnen, Anita Jowitt and Tess Newton Cain, *A Kind of Mending: Restorative Justice in the Pacific Islands* (Canberra: Pandanus Books, 2003); Carola Eyber and Alastair Ager, 'Conselho: Psychological Healing in Displaced Communities in Angola', *Lancet* 306 (2002): 871; Paulo Granjo, 'The Homecomer: Postwar Cleansing Rituals in Mozambique', *Armed Forces & Society* 33, no 3 (2007): 382; Alcinda Honwana, 'Children of War: Understanding War and War Cleansing in Mozambique and Angola', in *Civilians in War*, ed Simon Chesterman (Boulder, CO: Lynne Rienner Publishers, 2001), 1137; Pat Howley, *Breaking Spears and Mending Hearts: Peacemakers and Restorative Justice in Bougainville* (London: Zed Books, 2002), 222; Victor Igreja, *Gamba Spirits and the Homines Aperti: Socio-Cultural Approaches to Deal with the Legacies of the Civil War in Gorongosa, Mozambique* (paper presented at the Building a Future on Peace and Justice conference, Nuremberg, 25–27 June 2007) available at http://www.peace-justice-conference.info/download/WS10-Igreja%20report.pdf; Justice and Reconciliation Project, 'The Cooling of Hearts: Community Truth-Telling in Acholi-Land', Liu Institute for Global Issues and Gulu District NGO Forum (Vancouver, July 2007); Coel Kirkby, 'Rwanda's Gacaca Courts: A Preliminary Critique', *Journal of African Law* 50, no 2 (2006): 94; Andre Le Sage, 'Stateless Justice in Somalia: Formal and Informal Rule of Law Initiatives', Centre for Humanitarian Dialogue (Geneva, July 2005), 1; Kieran McEvoy and Anna Eriksson, 'Restorative Justice in Transition: Ownership, Leadership and "Bottom Up" Human Rights', in *Handbook of Restorative Justice*, ed Dennis Sullivan and Larry Tifft (Routledge, Abingdon: Routledge International Handbooks, 2006), 321; Agnes Nindorera, '*Ubushingantahe* as a Base for Political Transformation in Burundi', http://www.ksg.harvard.edu/wappp/research/working/ bc_nindorera.pdf; Josiah Osamba, 'Peace Building and Transformation from Below: Indigenous Approaches to Conflict Resolution and Reconciliation among the Pastoral Societies in the Borderlands of Eastern Africa', *African Journal on Conflict Resolution* 2, no 1 (2001): 71; A S J Park, 'Community-Based Restorative Transitional Justice in Sierra Leone', *Contemporary Justice Review* 13, no 1 (2010): 95; Jessica Raper, 'The *Gacaca* Experiment: Rwanda's Restorative Dispute Resolution Response to the 1994 Genocide', *Pepperdine Dispute Resolution Law Journal* 5, no 1 (2005): 1; Thomas Harlacher and others, *Traditional Ways of Coping in Acholi* (Kampala, Uganda: Caritas Kampala, 2006), 160; Lars Waldorf, 'Rwanda's Failing Experiment in Restorative Justice', in *Handbook of Restorative Justice: A Global Perspective*, ed Dennis Sullivan and Larry Tifft (Routledge, London: Routledge International Handbooks, 2006), 422; Spencer Zifcak, 'Restorative Justice in Timor-Leste: The Truth and Reconciliation Commission', *Development Bulletin* 68 (2005): 51.
20. Louise Mallinder, 'Can Amnesties and International Justice Be Reconciled'? *International Journal of Transitional Justice* 1, no 2 (2007): 208–30. Louise Mallinder, 'Beyond the Courts? The Complex Relationship of Trials and Amnesty', in *International Criminal Law*, ed William A Schabas (Cheltenham: Edward Elgar Publishing Ltd, 2011); Mallinder, *Amnesty, Human Rights and Political Transitions*, 165–95.
21. See, e.g., Mary Kaldor, *New and Old Wars: Organized Violence in a Global Era*, 2nd ed (Cambridge: Polity Press, 2006); Dinka Corkalo and others, 'Neighbors Again?

Intercommunity Relations after Ethnic Cleansing', in *My Neighbor, My Enemy: Justice and Community in the Aftermath of Mass Atrocity*, ed Eric Stover and Harvey M Weinstein (Cambridge: Cambridge University Press, 2004), 143.
22. Philpott, *Just and Unjust Peace*.
23. Philpott, *Just and Unjust Peace*.
24. Jennifer J Llewellyn, 'Restorative Justice in Transitions and Beyond: The Justice Potential of Truth Telling Mechanisms for Post-Peace Accord Societies', in *Telling the Truths: Truth Telling and Peace Building in Post-Conflict Societies*, ed Tristan Anne Borer (Notre Dame, IN: University of Notre Dame Press, 2006), 91–92.
25. Article 3(1) of the Promotion of National Unity and Reconciliation Act 1995 provided that 'The objectives of the Commission shall be to promote national unity and reconciliation in a spirit of understanding which transcends the conflicts and divisions of the past'.
26. Llewellyn, 'Restorative Justice in Transitions and Beyond', 91.
27. An omission which, as noted elsewhere in this collection, this project has set out to address.
28. Howard Zehr, 'Doing Justice, Healing Trauma: The Role of Restorative Justice in Peacebuilding', *South Asian Journal of Peacebuilding* 1, no 1 (2008).
29. Miriam J Aukerman, 'Extraordinary Evil, Ordinary Crime: A Framework for Understanding Transitional Justice', *Harvard Human Rights Journal* 15 (2002): 39–97, 78.
30. Stephan Parmentier, Kris Vanspauwen and Elmar Weitekamp, 'Dealing with the Legacy of Mass Violence: Changing Lenses to Restorative Justice', in *Supranational Criminology: Towards a Criminology of International Crimes*, ed Smeulers Alette and Haveman Roelof (Antwerp: Intersentia, 2008), 335–56, 344.
31. Zehr, 'Doing Justice, Healing Trauma'.
32. Parmentier, Vanspauwen and Weitekamp, 'Dealing with the Legacy of Mass Violence', 344.
33. Llewellyn, 'Restorative Justice in Transitions and Beyond', 96.
34. Llewellyn, 'Restorative Justice in Transitions and Beyond', 91.
35. See, e.g., Rama Mani, 'Rebuilding an Inclusive Political Community after War', *Security Dialogue* 36, no 4 (2005): 511.
36. Llewellyn, 'Restorative Justice in Transitions and Beyond', 91.
37. Jennifer Llewellyn, 'Justice to the Extent Possible: The Relationship between the International Criminal Court and Domestic Truth Commissions', in *La Voie Vers La Cour Pénale Internationale: Tous Les Chemins Mènent à Rome*, ed Hélène Dumont and Anne-Marie Boisvert (Montreal: Journees Maximilien-Caron, 2003), 334.
38. Llewellyn, 'Justice to the Extent Possible', 334.
39. Llewellyn, 'Justice to the Extent Possible', 334.
40. Promotion of National Unity and Reconciliation Act 1995, sec. 20(1).
41. Truth and Reconciliation Commission of South Africa Report, vol 1, ch 5, para 82 ('TRC Report').
42. See e.g., Graeme Simpson and Paul Van Zyl, 'South Africa's Truth and Reconciliation Commission', *Temps Modernes* 585 (1995): 394; Hugo Van der Merwe and Audrey R Chapman, 'Did the TRC Deliver'? in *Truth and Reconciliation in South Africa: Did the TRC Deliver?* ed Audrey R Chapman and Hugo Van der Merwe (Philadelphia: Pennsylvania Studies in Human Rights, University of Pennsylvania Press, 2008), 241.

CASE STUDY

Chris Cuneen*, 'When Does Transitional Justice Begin and End? Colonised Peoples, Liberal Democracies and Restorative Justice'

Introduction

There are overlaps between restorative and transitional justice with their emphasis on inclusion, non-adversarial approaches, and values such as 'truth, accountability, reparation, reconciliation and participation' (Clamp and Doak 2012: 341, also Cunneen 2006). This chapter explores the relationship between these justice paradigms specifically in the context of Indigenous peoples in the settler colonial states of Canada, the US, Australia and New Zealand. While these states may, to varying degrees, be associated with restorative justice, they are not normally considered within a transitional justice framework. This chapter argues there is some value in challenging this assumption, and that indeed settler colonial states might be seen as 'transitional societies' in their need to confront and remedy past injustices arising from their own colonial histories (Balint *et al.* 2014; Cunneen 2008).

When Ruti Teitel's (2000) important book *Transitional Justice* was published, I was struck at the time by some of the unarticulated assumptions that underpinned the ideas behind transitional justice, in particular that transitional processes involved a movement to a Western liberal-democratic ideal. In 'established democracies', adherence to the rule of law was taken as a given. The need for transitional justice was something that was required 'out there' in the wider world of genocidal conflicts, faltering military dictatorships, post-communist and post-fascist regimes and failed states. The subliminal message was clear: liberal democracies represented the ideal of justice, the place to which Others would be *transitioned*, perhaps through a concentrated period of tutelage. There was an assumption that democratic societies had either resolved the conflicts and injustices of their own past, or that these past injustices were inconsequential enough to be safely ignored and buried.

The 1990s and early 2000s was also a period of growing demand within the settler colonial states of the US, Canada, Australia and New Zealand for various forms of reparations, restitution, recognition and compensation. These demands, by both Indigenous peoples and, in the case of the US, African Americans, were for a variety of historical events, policies and practices from lynching to mass murder and genocide, from broken treaties to stolen and abused children, and from fraudulently used trust funds to slavery, forced labour and systematic racial discrimination. They had common elements: the various injustices had their genesis in the experience of being colonised; the colonial states that had profited from various forms of exploitation were today well-established liberal democracies; and, further, the contemporary social, economic and political marginalisation, particularly of Indigenous peoples, was argued to have its derivation in colonial oppression. These arguments for reparations, compensation and the recognition of Indigenous peoples' inherent sovereignty, and the political and legal strategies that were developed to progress these claims, can be seen to largely parallel Teitel's (2000) identification of the elements of transitional justice, that is, criminal, administrative and historical investigations of past wrongdoing, processes for reparations (including acknowledgement and compensation) and transitional constitutionalism.

The same period also saw the inexorable rise of restorative justice. By 2002 restorative justice was established on the United Nations agenda when the Economic and Social Council adopted the *Basic Principles on the Use of Restorative Justice Programs in Criminal Matters*. Restorative justice increasingly

---

* Chris Cunneen, "When Does Transitional Justice Begin and End? Colonized Peoples, Liberal Democracies and Restorative Justice", in Kerry Clamp, ed., *Restorative Justice in Transitional Settings*. © 2016 Routledge, pp. 190–210, reproduced by permission of Taylor & Francis Books UK.

appeared to offer a plausible strategy to a range of crime control problems, from local domestic issues like juvenile offending to international crimes and human rights abuses in transitional societies (Cunneen and Hoyle 2010). The South African Truth and Reconciliation Commission (TRC), for example, was identified not as an instrument within a political settlement, but rather as an example of traditional African restorative justice in action. In the West, the TRC was seen as providing reparative and restorative justice for post-apartheid South Africa, but reparative and restorative approaches for Indigenous peoples and formerly enslaved peoples at home was met politically with far more limited acceptance, if any. While the language of restorative justice was not ruled out completely in relation to some historical injustices, for the most part restorative justice was understood in the settler colonial states as a domestic and localised crime control strategy, particularly for juvenile offenders. Further, the idea that there could be a legitimate need for transitional justice processes in the settler colonial states appeared almost perverse. Settler state governments frequently and firmly argued that their existing laws and legal processes were adequate to respond to the claims for the redress of past wrongs, such as the forced removal of Indigenous children and subsequent residential school abuses. One result of this was that Indigenous peoples were forced into decades of slow, expensive and often futile litigation.

In this chapter I propose to argue four general points. First, settler colonialism involved substantial and systematic violence against Indigenous peoples. Second, the various forms of systematic racial discrimination were both historical injustices in their own right, and have led to the profound immiseration of Indigenous peoples within contemporary settler societies. Third, where states have been moved to consider a reparative approach to these injustices, these responses have been limited, begrudging, and only developed after years of adversarial litigation by Indigenous peoples. Finally, past historical injustices have a direct link to perhaps the most pressing human rights issues facing contemporary Indigenous peoples: that is, their contemporary over-representation in settler state criminal justice systems. The final section of this chapter opens up a new way of considering the link between restorative and transitional justice, and their connection to Indigenous concepts of justice, particularly through healing. Indigenous healing approaches have application to both criminal justice, and to broader problems of changing and challenging the effects of colonialism. Indigenous justice, through the concept of healing, has potential to challenge the contemporary problem of high levels of criminalisation *and* provide an important part of the reparative process for historical injustice. Indigenous justice is thus necessarily a decolonising strategy, bridging notions of both restorative and transitional justice.

Liberal Democracies and the Return of the Colonised

In 1955 Aimé Césaire wrote the *Discourse on Colonialism*, where he articulated the decivilising effect that colonialism has on the coloniser: 'We must study how colonisation works to *decivilise* the coloniser, to *brutalise* him in the true sense of the word, to degrade him, to awaken him to buried instincts, to covetousness, violence, race hatred, and moral relativism . . .' (Césaire 2000: 35). For Césaire, the rise of fascism in Europe during the course of the twentieth century was not an aberration, but the application to Europe of 'colonialist procedures' that had hitherto only been applied against the colonised (Césaire 2000: 36). While Césaire was not specifically concerned with Indigenous peoples in Anglo-settler societies, his argument on the decivilising effects of colonialism nevertheless holds true. There is indeed a blindness to and silencing of the Indigenous past. There is a disavowal of both the ongoing effects of colonisation found in the contemporary marginalisation of colonised peoples, and Indigenous demands for a response to historical injustices. Martin writes that, by neglecting colonialism, 'Anglo-white society [can] re-write history as if these events had never occurred . . . what emerges is a sense of triumphalism among the dominant population which is so seamless, pervasive, and pronounced' (Martin 2014: 238).

Settler colonialism requires violence, or its threat, to achieve its outcomes. 'People do not hand over their land, resources, children, and futures without a fight. . . . In employing the force necessary to accomplish its expansionist goals, a colonising regime institutionalises violence' (Dunbar-Ortiz 2014: 8). Settler colonialism was a process of invasion, settlement and nation-building which fundamentally altered the lives of those original peoples and tribal nations living in the occupied territories. It was a particular type of colonialism where the primary economic objective was securing the land and where sovereignty was asserted usually on the basis of 'discovery'. As Wolfe (2006) has argued, settler colonialism was a form of the colonial experience whereby Indigenous peoples had to be either eliminated or contained and controlled in order to make land available as private property for the settlers who had come to stay. The substantial loss of land for Indigenous peoples in Australia, New Zealand, Canada and the US contributed directly to the contemporary material conditions of socio-economic disadvantage. Further, many argue that settler colonialism was fundamentally genocidal, either directly through extermination in the violence of the initial colonial onslaught, or later through processes of forced assimilation designed to bring about the destruction of Indigenous societies and cultures (Dunbar-Ortiz 2014; Stannard 1992). By their very presence, Indigenous people threaten assertions of colonial sovereignty and rights to land. As Bignall and Svirksy (2012: 8) argue, colonial sovereignty functions

> as a part of a fundamentally circular and self-validating performance that grounds the legitimacy of settler-state rule on nothing more than the axiomatic negation of Native peoples' authority to determine . . . for themselves the normative principles by which they will be governed.

Or, in the words of Watson (2009: 45), the claim of colonial sovereignty is the 'originary violence' at the foundation of settler states that today 'retain a vested interest in maintaining the founding order of things'.

The imposition of colonial systems of law (including criminal, civil, property and constitutional law) was core to the assertion of sovereignty. Colonial law was a tool *both* for legitimising the use of force *and* in imposing a range of cultural, social and institutional values and processes. Importantly, colonial law imposed criminal and penological concepts that were foreign to Indigenous peoples. As Quince (2007: 341) notes in relation to New Zealand, there were fundamental differences between colonial and Indigenous concepts of law: individual responsibility compared to collective responsibility for wrong-doing; the removal of the victim from the judicial process; the concept of the state as the injured party rather than the collective group; the separation of the criminal process from the community; the distinction between civil and criminal law; and differences in the justifications for, and types of, punishment (for example, imprisonment compared to restitution and reparation). Although Indigenous nations differed between themselves in cultural values and law, in general they were often in opposition to the values represented by colonial criminal law.

The justificatory logic of the coloniser's 'civilising mission' rested on foundational beliefs of racial superiority, and provided an overarching basis to governmental law and policy towards Indigenous people in settler states throughout the eighteenth, nineteenth and twentieth centuries. Racism was a precondition for the colonial genocides and the systematic abuse of human rights. The suspension of the rule of law and the use of violence against Indigenous people was contextualised and legitimated within racialised constructions of Indigenous people as inferior human beings. Racialised and gendered constructions of Indigenous people also facilitated legalised and institutionalised discrimination, irrespective of whether they were designed to eradicate, protect or assimilate the 'Native'. Furthermore, legal protections could be suspended and otherwise unlawful behaviour by the colonialists could be ignored in the higher interest of the betterment, protection or control of colonised peoples.

Indigenous law was viewed disparagingly by British colonialists: it became defined as 'customary' law and was regarded as distinctly inferior to colonial law. The delegitimisation of Indigenous law was part of the 'civilising' process designed to bring the superior political and legal institutions of the West to the native, and the imposition of colonial systems of law was integral to the civilising process. The colonising impact of settler law had a number of consequences. First, it meant the continued subjection of Indigenous peoples to legal processes that were systemically racist, built on the denial of the legitimacy of Indigenous law. Second, it led to equating *justice* with the law of the colonising power. Settler colonial states continue to choose whether and which Indigenous laws can be recognised. Yet it is clear that many Indigenous peoples see state criminal justice systems as oppressive, and insist on Indigenous law as a rightful alternative to an imposed system of law (for example, Black 2010; Jackson 1994).

The laws of the coloniser were also always applied ambiguously, anomalously, strategically (Shenhav 2012). Colonised peoples were 'both within the reach of the law and yet outside its protection' (Anghie 1999: 103). Criminal law and penalty reflected different cultural understandings of Indigenous people compared to non-Indigenous people. For example, ideas of modernity and the development of modes of punishment that disavowed corporal punishment and public execution were seen as inapplicable to Indigenous people because of their perceived racial and cultural characteristics, and were utilised on Indigenous people long after their demise for non-Indigenous offenders. Thus a genealogy of crime and punishment in settler societies must consider the symbiotic links between punishment and race, or what has been referred to elsewhere as a penal/colonial complex (Cunneen et al. 2013).

In summary then, the 'return of the colonised' exposes fundamental questions about the claims of sovereign power, and about the foundations, nature and legitimacy of law in settler societies. While governments and courts can proclaim unitary and indivisible visions of sovereign power in settler societies, Indigenous peoples have long challenged the validity of these claims, and laid bare the foundational violence upon which these claims to sovereignty rest. Such questions go to the heart of transitional justice, particularly in relation to the need for inclusive national-building and constitutional change which respects principles of non-discrimination and self-determination.

Historical Injustices and Reparations

There were specific historical injustices against Indigenous people that require appropriate state responses in the context of both restorative and transitional justice. I explore two examples in more detail below. However at the outset it is important to note that claims concerning historical injustices and human rights abuses against Indigenous peoples are multi-layered. At the highest level is the claim that particular colonial practices against Indigenous people constituted genocide. Below genocide are claims of mass murder, racism, ethnocide (or cultural genocide), slavery, forced labour, forced removals and relocations, the denial of property rights, and the denial of civil and political rights. The claims of genocide against Indigenous people in the settler colonies of North America and Australia have been controversial (Alvarez 2014; Van Krieken 2004). However there seems little doubt that genocide is the appropriate description for specific colonial laws and practices at particular times and places and targeted at specific tribal nations (Dunbar-Ortiz 2014; Moses 2000). More broadly, the concept of ethnocide or cultural genocide captures the aggressive attempt to 'civilise' Indigenous peoples through a range of state-endorsed laws, policies and practices.

For the purposes of this chapter, I want to concentrate on two specific and long-term historical injustices: first, the forced removal of Indigenous children from their families and communities, and their placement in institutions and residential schools, and, second, government fraud and corruption in relation to the management of Indigenous peoples' finances and property. As I argue further below, in line with transitional justice, both have been the subject of demands for apologies, compensation and reparations by Indigenous people. Both arose directly from government *policies* aimed at regulation and assimilation of Indigenous peoples and also bear a direct responsibility in bringing about the contemporary immiseration of Indigenous people. Further, and this is particularly important to the relationship between restorative justice and criminal justice, both can be seen to directly contribute to crime and victimisation. In other words, they demonstrate the contemporary *criminogenic* effects of colonial policies.

Residential Schools and the Stolen Generations

One process for 'civilising' Indigenous people was through the focus on children: their removal and placement in institutions, their instruction in English and prohibitions on Indigenous languages and cultures. Various policies designed to implement these outcomes were introduced in Australia, Canada and the US. The Canadian residential school system lasted for more than a century from the 1870s to the 1980s. The policy was 'violent in its intention to "kill the Indian" in the child. . . . The system was, even as a concept, abusive' (Milloy 1999: xv). The policy relied on a church–state partnership, with the Department of Indian Affairs providing the funding, setting the standards and exercising legal control over the children who were wards, and various Christian churches operating a nationwide network of schools (Milloy 1999). Authorities would frequently take children to schools far from their home communities as part of a strategy to alienate them from their families and tribal culture. In 1920, under the Indian Act, it became mandatory for every Indian child to attend a residential school and illegal for them to attend any other educational institution. More than 150,000 First Nations, Métis and Inuit children were placed in these schools. There are an estimated 80,000 former students still living (TRCC 2012a: 2).

In the US the main period of the Indian residential school movement was from the 1860s to the 1980s. The number of American Indian children in the boarding schools reached a peak in the 1970s. As in Canada, Indian children were removed from their culture, language and identity. More than 100,000 Native American children were forced to attend these residential schools (Smith 2004: 89). Conditions in the schools were harsh and abusive. Investigations revealed many cases of sexual, physical and mental abuse occurring in these schools, with documented cases of sexual abuse at reservation schools continuing until the end of the 1980s (Smith 2004, 2007).

By the late nineteenth and early twentieth centuries, most states of Australia developed a systematic policy of Aboriginal child removal utilising both church and state-run institutions (NISATSIC 1997: 25–149). Removal policies rested on specific assumptions about race, 'blood' and racial hygiene. Law was fundamental to the categorisation and separation of individuals within racialised boundaries. According to Social Darwinist ideas, 'full blood' Aboriginal people were bound to die out because of their inferiority. However, the concern for the state was the apparently rapidly growing population of 'mixed blood' children. It was these children that became the target of intervention. By permanently removing them from their families and communities it was believed that this group of children would, over generations, eventually be biologically absorbed into the non-Indigenous population. Their Aboriginality would be 'bred' out. Eugenicist arguments required a proactive state to manage, cleanse and maintain the 'white' population. It was estimated that about one in ten Indigenous children were removed from their families (NISATSIC 1997).

Long-Term Outcomes of Indigenous Child Removal

In Canada, the US and Australia, authorities saw the removal process as essential to eradicating Indigenous cultures. The system in all three countries was characterised by 'denial of identity through attacks on language and spiritual beliefs, frequent lack of basic care, the failure to ensure safety of children from physical and sexual abuse, [and] the failure to ensure education' (RCAP 1996: 187). It is important to recognise the contemporary multiple effects of policies of child removal. These have been well documented in various inquiries and reports. In Australia, a 1997 federal inquiry found that basic legal safeguards that protected non-Indigenous families were cast aside when it came to the removal of Indigenous children (NISATSIC 1997). Unlawful practices under the Aboriginal child removal policies included deprivation of liberty, deprivation of parental rights, abuses of power, and breach of guardianship duties. In relation to international human rights, the main obligations imposed on Australia and breached by a policy of forced removals, particularly after 1948, were the prohibitions on racial discrimination and genocide (NISATSIC 1997).

In Australia, twice as many Indigenous people who were removed as children have reported being arrested; and those who were removed have reported significantly poorer health (NISATSIC 1997: 15). Almost one in ten boys and more than one in ten girls reported that they were sexually abused in children's institutions; and three in ten girls reported sexual abuse in foster placements (NISATSIC 1997: 163). There has also been a range of complex trauma-related psychological and psychiatric effects that have been intergenerational. These relate to issues such as poorer educational and employment outcomes, loss of parenting skills, unresolved grief and trauma, violence, depression, mental illness, and other behavioural problems including alcohol and other substance abuse. A large-scale survey in Western Australia of Aboriginal people who had been forcibly removed found that one-third had also had their children removed (NISATSIC 1997: 226). The links between early childhood removal and later juvenile and adult criminalisation were clearly articulated in the reports of the Royal Commission into Aboriginal Deaths in Custody (see, for example, Wootten 1989).

The Manitoba Justice Inquiry found that, in Canada, residential schools laid the foundation for the prevalence of domestic abuse and violence against Aboriginal women and children. Generations of children grew up without a nurturing family life (Hamilton and Sinclair 1991). The Canadian Truth and Reconciliation Commission noted that, 'while some former students had positive experiences at residential schools, many suffered emotional, physical and sexual abuse, and others died while attending these schools. The unresolved trauma suffered by former students has been passed on from generation to generation' (TRCC 2012a: 2). A sense of worthlessness was instilled in many students, which resulted in low self-esteem and self-abuse through high rates of alcoholism, substance abuse, and suicide (TRCC 2012b: 5–8).

In the US, inquiries dating back to 1920s considered the effects of the Indian Residential Schools. In 1928 a Brookings Institution report found the schools were a 'menace to both health and education'. Malnutrition, grossly inadequate care, and routine institutionalisation were all documented (Meriam 1928). The report found that the work by children in the boarding schools would violate child labour laws in most states (Meriam 1928). Forty years later the Kennedy Report (Committee on Labour and Public Welfare 1969) reiterated serious deficiencies: the school environment was 'sterile, impersonal and rigid' with an emphasis on discipline and punishment, teachers and administrators still saw their role as 'civilising the native', and Indian boarding schools were 'emotionally and culturally destructive' (Committee on Labour and Public Welfare 1969: 100–3). The Boarding School Healing Project (BSHP 2008: 3–7) noted both the human rights abuses in these schools and the continuing effects which include increased physical, sexual and emotional violence in Indigenous communities; increased rates of suicide and substance abuse; loss of language and cultural traditions; increased depression and post-traumatic stress disorder; and increased child abuse.

Seemingly indicative of a restorative justice approach, the long-term harm caused by the forced removal of Indigenous children and their treatment in institutions has been recognised through formal apologies in Canada and Australia. However, it is important to recognise that it was only after years of litigation by Indigenous peoples that these settler states were forced into recognition of the harms caused by removals. It was after class actions, and to avoid ongoing litigation, that the Canadian government agreed to the Indian Residential Schools Settlement Agreement[1] in 2006, with the federal government and the churches involved agreeing to pay individual and collective compensation to residential school survivors. A Truth and Reconciliation Commission was also established.

In both the US and Australia, lawsuits filed by Indigenous people for abuse which occurred in institutions have met with only limited success, and there have been no federal reparation packages in either country. In Australia the federal government refused to consider monetary compensation even before the Australian Human Rights Commission inquiry into the 'stolen generations' was completed (NISATSIC 1997). The recommended Reparations Tribunal was never established, and it was to take another ten years, and a change in federal government, before an apology was issued. In the US, Congress apologised to Native Americans for the 'official depredations, ill-conceived policies . . . [and] for the many instances of violence, maltreatment and neglect' (Public Law 111–118, sec 8113). However, Congress did not refer explicitly to Indian residential schools, and the apology itself was 'buried in the billions of dollars of spending on new weapons and other items' in the Defense Appropriations Act 2010 (McKinnon 2009). Further, the apology explicitly noted that it was not intended to support any lawsuit claims against the US government.

Government Fraud, Indigenous Trust Funds and Forced Labour

Settler colonial states were involved in vast frauds against Indigenous people who were under their care and protection. These included such matters as missing trust monies, stolen wages, widespread corruption, mismanagement and bribery. The precondition for this fraudulent activity was the extensive state control over Indigenous people that was instituted as part of colonial policies of protection and wardship in the periods after open warfare. State agents clearly engaged in activities which were defined *at the time* as unlawful (such as breaches of fiduciary or guardianship duties), and in many cases were clearly criminal (acts of fraud).

In the US, fraud, corruption, and bribery were endemic to the Bureau of Indian Affairs (BIA). Local BIA officials had discretionary control over money, goods, trading licences, and supplies provided by the Bureau. 'Substantial portions of the supplies and annuity payments owed to the tribes were routinely siphoned off by traders, in cooperation with corrupt federal Indian agents' (Piecuch and Lutz 2011: 384) and by the 1860s the BIA 'was rife with corruption' (Pierpaoli 2011: 101). Such corruption was publicly acknowledged at the time, the *New York Times* describing, in an editorial on 12 December 1868, 'the dishonesty which pervades the whole Bureau'. A decade later systematic corruption by the BIA was again noted. In commenting on an official investigation of the Bureau, the *New York Times* described it as a 'Disgrace to the Nation' with 'frauds in goods and supplies, frauds in receipts and accounts, frauds in the management of Indian trust funds' (8 January 1878). Over the next century, various US House of Representatives and Congressional reports identified the defrauding and gross mismanagement of Indian trust funds arising from the Dawes Act 1887. In the end it was not a commitment to reparations or restorative justice that drove government policy but adversarial litigation on the part of Indigenous people. In 2009 after a protracted 13-year lawsuit involving some 11 separate appellate court decisions, there was a $3.4 billion settlement to a class action relating to the mismanagement of hundreds of thousands of American Indian trust accounts (Riccardi 2009; also Kidd 2006: 28–35). According to President Obama, the settlement cleared 'the way for reconciliation' (CNN Wire Staff 2012). However, the settlement was tempered by the fact that it was far short of the estimated $46 billion that was owed. Elouise Corbell from the Blackfeet Nation who led the class action noted in relation to the settlement, 'time takes a toll, especially on elders living in abject poverty. Many of them died as we continued our struggle to settle this suit. Many more would not survive long to see a financial gain, if we had not settled now' (quoted in Riccardi 2009). The settlement provided for a $1,000 payment to individual trust account holders, plus allocations for land purchases for tribes and educational scholarships.

In Australia, governments put in place legislative and administrative controls over the employment, working conditions and wages of Indigenous workers. These controls allowed for the non-payment of wages to some Aboriginal workers, the underpayment of wages to others, and the diversion of wages into trust and savings accounts. Legislation set minimum wages. For example, in Queensland the Indigenous wage was less than one-eighth the 'white wage'. The regulation of Aboriginal labour amounted to forced labour in some states. Many Aboriginal workers in Western Australia were not paid wages and were remunerated through rations such as flour, tea, tobacco and clothing until as late as the 1960s (Toussaint 1995: 259). The exploitation of Aboriginal workers in the pastoral industry was often considered as 'unpaid slavery' at the time (Haebich 1992: 150). Australia was clearly in contravention of various International Labour Organisation conventions to which it was a party. In 1930 Australia had signed the Forced Labour Convention that generally prohibited forced labour and working for rations, although the practice of working for rations was to last for decades later.

In addition there were negligent, corrupt and dishonest practices that led to the withholding of moneys from Aboriginal wages that had been paid into savings accounts and trust funds. The defrauding of trust funds and savings accounts was widespread. In 2006 the Australian Senate Standing Committee on Legal and Constitutional Affairs [the Standing Committee] released the report of its inquiry into what had become known as Indigenous 'Stolen Wages'. The inquiry itself was the outcome of many years of Indigenous political agitation around the issue (Kidd 2006). The inquiry defined 'wages' broadly to include wages, savings, entitlements, and other monies due to Indigenous people. The Standing Committee found

> compelling evidence that governments systematically withheld and mismanaged Indigenous wages and entitlements over decades ... there is evidence of Indigenous people being underpaid or not paid at all for their work. These practices were implemented from the late 19th century onwards and, in some cases, were still in place in the 1980s. (Standing Committee 2006: 4)

The inquiry found that Indigenous people had been 'seriously disadvantaged by these practices across generations' (Standing Committee 2006: 4), and subsequently this created a cycle of poverty.

Given the depth of contemporary Indigenous detriment across all social, educational, health and economic indicators (SCRGSP 2014), and the active role played by the state in controlling Aboriginal access to wages and entitlements, the outcome of this colonial process was one of *immiseration*: the forcible imposition and maintenance of structural conditions of extreme poverty. Some of the long-term impacts are captured below:

> Aboriginal people were subject to a disabling system that denied them proper wages, protection from exploitation and abuse, proper living conditions, and adequate education and training. So while other Australians were able to build financial security and an economic future for their families, Aboriginal workers were hindered by these controls. Aboriginal poverty ... today is a direct consequence of this discriminatory treatment. (Standing Committee 2006: 68)

The Elephant in the Room

The above discussion on residential schools and various forms of fraud and misappropriation of Indigenous finances raises several issues. First, it is important to note that where there have been moves towards a more restorative and reparative approach, such as in Canada, this has only occurred after a sustained period of adversarial litigation. Second, where there have been federal inquiries which have recommended a reparations approach to historical injustices such as the 'Stolen Generations' inquiry in Australia (NISATSIC 1997), these have been ignored by government particularly in relation to compensation (Cunneen 2006: 363–65). Third, when governments have moved to provide some monetary compensation, these have often been seen to be woefully inadequate, either because of restricted eligibility criteria, small compensation sums compared to the harms suffered, or because of a 'lottery effect' depending on which state or territory the effected person resided. For example, in Australia compensation schemes for stolen wages and trust funds varied from $2,000, to $4,000 and $25,000 depending on eligibility criteria and whether the person fell within state-based schemes in Western Australia, Queensland or New South Wales. In addition, Indigenous people living outside of those state jurisdictions received no compensation at all (Behrendt et al. 2009: 59–64). Despite Indigenous demands, these responses have fallen far short of what might be expected in any comprehensive restorative justice approach.

It is important to note that in specific contexts Indigenous people may be reluctant to have their claims for compensation framed within a restricted restorative justice paradigm. Understanding the reasons for this reluctance sheds light on the reason why Indigenous people show some scepticism towards narrowly defined approaches to restorative justice.

For example, in the US the BSHP (2008), while certainly not discounting a reparations approach, has noted potential limitations to such a strategy in relation to the survivors of American Indian boarding schools. The limitations include the commodification of harm that essentially relegates colonialism to a problem of the past. Compensation forces a monetary value on past harms, which by its nature implies that the harms are only a matter of the past. Thus colonialism becomes a process relegated to 'history', rather than an ongoing structural relationship existing through a range of manifestations (for example, through high levels of criminalisation and contemporary child welfare removals). Related to the above point is that a reparations process may fail to address structural oppression (see also Balint et al. 2014). The BSHP notes that

> It may be possible that a reparations struggle can be a strategy for bringing attention to the underlying structures and ideologies that give rise to specific human rights violations, but they can also normalize these structures and ideologies by positioning specific atrocities as an exception to the system rather than as an integral part of systemic oppression. (BSHP 2008: 12)

These structural conditions may include capitalist processes that entrench Indigenous poverty and disadvantage. If structural problems are not addressed, Indigenous people receiving reparations may not have the means to change their impoverished conditions: 'cash payments do not generally result in poor people becoming less poor' (BSHP 2008: 12).

More fundamentally, reparations do not challenge the colonial relationship between settler states and Indigenous people: settler state sovereignty can remain unaffected by a reparations process because the broader issue of Indigenous sovereignty is left unaddressed. The inviolability of settler state sovereignty is maintained and, as a result, the colonial relationship between Indigenous people and settler states is further solidified (BSHP 2008: 11, see also Balint et al. 2014: 201). According to Corntassel and Holder (2008), reconciliation and truth commission mechanisms have failed Indigenous people because states have separated these processes from considerations of Indigenous sovereignty and self-determination. They note that, 'If apologies and truth commissions cannot effectively address historic and ongoing injustices committed against Indigenous peoples, then they are fundamentally flawed mechanisms for transforming intergroup relations' (Corntassel and Holder 2008: 466). This linking of the contemporary oppression of Indigenous peoples with the colonial past is a fundamental part of Corntassel and Holder's argument, with Indigenous people 'disproportionately the target of state violence as well as neoliberal reforms' (2008: 466). The indivisibility between the colonial past and the colonial present is also a core argument of this chapter. The problem is that restorative approaches to historical injustices can often fail to recognise this indivisibility between past and present. Colonialism can remain the 'elephant in the room': its contemporary manifestations remain unseen, unacknowledged and unaddressed.

Rethinking the Relationship between Restorative Justice and Indigenous Justice

I have argued in this chapter that the historical injustices of settler colonialism are usually not considered within the framework of transitional justice and, more specifically, that restorative and reparative justice has had a very mixed history in relation to responding to the multiple harms of colonialism. Another way of thinking about restorative justice, however, is in the context of contemporary settler society criminal justice systems. In a nutshell, the argument I propose is that the contemporary over-representation of Indigenous people in criminal justice systems is itself a product of the effects of colonialism, and that restorative justice conceptualised within a context of Indigenous self-determination may offer a pathway out of the mass criminalisation and incarceration of Indigenous peoples in settler societies (see, for example, Cunneen 2014a). Restorative justice, conceived as *Indigenous justice*, may be both a response to historical injustices by recognising the criminogenic effects of colonialism, as well as a more effective way of responding to contemporary criminal justice problems. I return to how we might conceptualise restorative justice as Indigenous justice in more detail below. First though it is important to acknowledge the contemporary criminogenic effects of colonialism, and the current limitations of restorative justice in settler societies in responding to the problem of criminalisation.

Colonialism and Criminalisation

The loss of an economic foundation to land and resources created the social and economic disadvantage among the colonised that we see today. At a general level, settler colonialism is criminogenic to the extent that it actively produces dispossession, marginalisation and cultural dislocation. However, this marginalisation has been exacerbated by specific colonial policies and practices including, among others, the forced removal of Indigenous children from their families and communities, and government controls over Indigenous resources and finances. Over-crowded housing, low incomes, chronic health issues, substance abuse, lower life expectancies, poor educational outcomes, child protection concerns, the psychological and social effects of racism and discrimination – precisely the factors known to be associated with higher levels of violence and offending – can be related in various degrees to the policies of settler colonialism.

As I have argued in this chapter, the relationship between Indigenous people and the colonial settler states exhibits the features of a transitional setting where basic questions of justice, participation, legitimacy and human rights need to be addressed. And these basic questions of justice are particularly revealed in the way criminal justice systems operate in relation to Indigenous people. When the Canadian Royal Commission on Aboriginal Peoples reported in 1996 on criminal justice issues, they introduced their findings by making two core points. First, what Aboriginal people experience is not justice but the injustice of a system that is alien and oppressive. Second, Aboriginal people think of justice differently, reflecting

> distinctive Aboriginal world views and in particular a holistic understanding of peoples' relationships and responsibilities to each other and to their material and spiritual world. . . . Aboriginal conceptions of justice must be understood as part of the fabric of social and political life rather than as a distinct, formal legal process. (RCAP 1996: 3)

These two points capture succinctly Indigenous demands for the recognition of their distinct Indigenous status with all that entails: political rights to self-determination and inherent sovereignty, and cultural and social rights to practise and maintain their distinct cultures free from discrimination.

The Limitations of Existing Restorative Justice Approaches in Settler Societies

The question arises then as to whether we can think of restorative justice, conceived as Indigenous justice, as offering a pathway forward. I argue that we can, but with a number of important caveats. In the first instance, we need a far more radical approach than currently found in state-sponsored restorative justice schemes. As I have argued elsewhere (Cunneen 2012), the limitation for Indigenous people of current restorative justice practice arises in part because of the broader political conditions under which it emerged. Restorative justice developed in settler states at a time of mass imprisonment – when imprisonment rates were progressively reaching historic highs. The rise of restorative justice also occurred concurrent with research identifying that higher imprisonment rates are associated with societies that have higher levels of inequality (Wilkinson and Pickett 2009) and a lesser commitment to social democratic and inclusionary values (Lacey 2008). Among Western democracies, it is those who have most strongly adopted neoliberalism that have the highest imprisonment rates and these include the settler states of the US, Canada, Australia and New Zealand.

Relatedly, *some* of the values associated with restorative justice can be consonant with more punitive law-and-order politics, such as free will, individual responsibility, accountability and a narrowly defined, individualised sense of civic obligation. The promotion of a free-market individualism can downplay the need for social and structural responses to crime, such as reducing unemployment rates, improving educational outcomes, increasing wages, ensuring proper welfare support, and improving housing and urban conditions (Brown 2009). In this context it is perhaps not surprising that state-sponsored restorative justice approaches have not had a great benefit for Indigenous people, despite the claim often made that they are based on Indigenous approaches to justice (Cunneen and Hoyle 2010). Indeed, in the area of juvenile justice, Indigenous over-representation has deepened since the introduction of restorative justice approaches (Cunneen 2014b: 13).

As McCaslin and Breton (2008) articulate it, the fundamental problem with restorative justice from an Indigenous perspective is that colonialism remains as an invisible backdrop to the harms which restorative justice seeks to remedy. While there might be some temporary fixes to problems, there is no broader or deeper decolonising vision that would tackle the structures that lead to social harms in the first place. For McCaslin and Breton (2008: 518), 'decolonization is the only hope, but as yet, it is not on the restorative justice radar'.

An Alternative Vision

It is possible however to see an alternative vision of restorative justice that can resonate with Indigenous justice. Clamp (2014) identifies four core values necessary for restorative justice in transitional settings: engagement, empowerment, reintegration and transformation. The Indigenous approach to *healing* is aligned with these values and is an integral part of Indigenous justice. As a political process of individual and collective change, it is somewhat akin to the Friereian notion of *conscientisation*. It involves shifting the epistemological priority given to Western understandings of crime and control. It begins from a disbelief in the functionality and the legitimacy of state-centred institutional responses: criminalisation and incarceration are seen as destructive of family, community and culture; cause further social disintegration; and do not change the behaviour of offenders. A focus on healing relies on inter-relationality rather than individualism, and the importance of identity and culture in the process of decolonisation. As Archibald notes:

> The experience of being colonised involves loss – of culture, language, land, resources, political autonomy, religious freedom, and, often, personal autonomy. These losses may have a direct relationship to poor health, social and economic status of Indigenous people. Understanding the need for personal and collective healing from this perspective points to a way of healing, one that combines the socio-political work involved in decolonization with the more personal therapeutic healing journey. (Archibald 2006: 49)

Indigenous healing approaches start with the collective experience, with the collective harms and outcomes of colonisation, and draw strength from Indigenous culture. Inevitably, that involves an understanding of the collective harms and outcomes of colonisation, the loss of lands, the disruptions of culture, the changing of traditional roles of men and women, the collective loss and sorrow of the removal of children and relocation of communities. Wanganeen (2008) discusses seven phases to cultural healing which include acknowledgement of ancestral losses, contemporary grief and loss (such as child removal) and future strength through a contemporised traditional culture.

Indigenous healing processes have developed in many of the settler states and focus on a number of different areas. These include residential school survivors, members of the Stolen Generations, people involved in family violence, child protection, alcohol and other drug addictions, and those in various stages of the criminal justice system (for a variety of specific examples, see Archibald 2006: 39–48; ATSISJC 2008: 167–76). At a broader level, these approaches cover three pillars: reclaiming history, cultural interventions and therapeutic healing (ATSISJC 2008: 167). Reclaiming history allows an understanding of the past and present impacts of colonialism. 'Healing from historic trauma brings history and culture together with personal healing on a journey that is both individual and collective in nature' (Archibald 2006: 26). Cultural interventions are focused on recovering and reconnecting with language, culture and ceremony. However,

> culture isn't limited to traditions and the past, it is a living breathing thing. These programs foster identity and pride, dispelling the negative stereotypes that many hold about Indigenous peoples. [By providing] a different way of understanding . . . they are actively creating a new culture of pride and possibilities. (ATSISJC 2008: 174)

The third pillar is therapeutic healing. These might include individual counselling, men's and women's groups, healing circles and traditional ceremonies. They may involve traditional Indigenous counsellors, healers and medicine people, as well as modified or adapted western approaches (see for example, Archibald 2006: 29–30 on developments in postcolonial psychology).

Healing is not simply about addressing individualised offending behaviour. It is fundamentally about addressing trauma. Three types of trauma have been identified: situational trauma caused by discrete events (for example, the contemporary child welfare removal of children); cumulative trauma caused by pervasive distress over time (for example, the long-term effects of racism); and inter-generational trauma which is passed down from one generation to another (for example, the forced relocation of communities, the denigration of Indigenous cultures) (ASTISJC 2008: 153–54). The process of healing is inextricably linked to Indigenous spirituality and culture and to repairing the effects of trauma in its various manifestations (ASTISJC 2008: 152).

The importance of a healing approach is that individual harms and wrongs are placed within a collective context. On the one hand, offenders are dealt with as individuals responsible for their own actions; their pain and the forces that propel them to harmful behaviour towards themselves and others are confronted. However, they are *understood* within a collective context of the experience of Indigenous peoples in a non-indigenous society. What this means in a practical context is that there is a focus on factors such as grief, depression, spiritual healing, loss of culture and educational deficits and a recognition that these needs must be addressed because they are directly related to criminal offending (Gilbert and Wilson 2009: 4). For example, grief and loss, which is experienced by Indigenous people in settler societies at a much higher frequency and much younger age than non-Indigenous people, have been identified as a core issue that healing programs can and need to address (Gilbert and Wilson 2009: 4). Overall the explanatory context for individual behaviour is within the collective experiences of the Indigenous peoples. In this sense Indigenous healing approaches are unique because they seek individual change within a collective context.

Indigenous healing approaches are also Indigenous controlled and are consistent with the principle of Indigenous self-determination. One of the consequences of this is the tension that is created between Indigenous approaches and state-controlled interventions. In the current period we see an institutional emphasis on various behavioural modification programmes put in place as a result of the identification of narrowly defined individualised 'deficits'. Reviewing the international literature on the Indigenous healing movement, Lane et al. (2002: 23) highlight the ways in which the many inter-connected outcomes of Indigenous healing have led to increased emphasis upon the need for a transformation of existing mainstream approaches. As McCaslin and Breton (2008: 518) explain, 'coloniser programming' in the criminal justice system is permeated by a view of Indigenous peoples as the problem and the colonisers as the solution. Unless colonialism is brought 'front and centre and named as the root cause' of Indigenous overrepresentation in the criminal justice system, Indigenous peoples will continue to be oppressed through processes of state criminalisation. Governments favour those approaches that it can closely administer, control and monitor – and these tend to be programmes reliant on expert interventions that further privilege dominant definitions of crime disavow the voices of Indigenous peoples. They also tend to be programmes that are 'off-the-shelf' and are not programmes that are organic to Indigenous people and their communities, or their needs and experiences. While Indigenous people are most likely to be the subjects of these programmes as offenders, they are far less likely to be in control of defining or delivering these professionalised interventions (Cunneen 2014a: 399–401).

In summary, the concept of healing is a fundamental part of Indigenous concepts of justice. Indigenous healing processes have been developed in many of the settler states and they cover a range of issues as outlined above. Healing is focused on addressing trauma, for both individual and collective harms. They are based on principles of Indigenous control and self-determination.

Conclusion

As argued throughout this chapter, there are parallels between transitional justice and Indigenous demands for reparations and compensation for past wrongs, and for constitutional developments that are inclusive of contemporary Indigenous claims for recognition of their rights as peoples. In this sense, settler states can be seen as societies in need of some form of transitional and restorative justice. However, it has been also argued that state-defined restorative justice has failed Indigenous people both as a reparative process for past wrongs, and as a process within criminal justice systems responding to contemporary harms. A key reason for both failures has been the inability to confront the structural conditions of colonialism. However, I do not believe this has to be the case. Restorative justice has a role to play where it is conceived as Indigenous justice, where Indigenous law, culture and politics define the values, processes and practices of restorative justice.

Restorative justice thus conceived can play a fundamental part in the broader struggle of decolonisation, that is, the process towards remedying both past and contemporary injustices. Settler states might then begin the transitional process of resolving their own conflicts and injustices. I do not suggest that this is necessarily an easy task. As McCaslin and Breton (2008: 511) state, 'Healing our communities from the onslaught of imperialism and colonisation in every form – economic, political, social, educational, emotional, religious, cultural, cognitive – is a complex, sometimes confusing, and often over-whelming process'. However, opening up a process of *transitional decolonisation* built on an Indigenous-defined restorative justice would be a welcome start.

Note

1. A $2 billion settlement to redress a reported $11 billion in lawsuits (BSHP 2008: 31).

References

Alvarez, A. (2014) *Native America and the Question of Genocide*. Lanham, MD: Rowman & Littlefield.

Anghie, A. (1999) 'Francisco de Vittoria and the Colonial Origins of International Law', in *Laws of the Postcolonial*, eds P Fitzpatrick and E Darian-Smith. Ann Arbor, MI: University of Michigan Press.

Archibald, L. (2006) *Decolonization and Healing: Indigenous Experiences in the United States, New Zealand Australia and Greenland*. Ottawa: Aboriginal Healing Foundation.

ATSISJC (Aboriginal and Torres Strait Islander Social Justice Commissioner). (2008) *Social Justice Report 2008*. Sydney: Australian Human Rights Commission.

Balint, J, J Evans, and N McMillan. (2014) 'Rethinking Transitional Justice, Redressing Indigenous Harm: A New Conceptual Approach'. *International Journal of Transitional Justice* 8: 194–216.

Behrendt, L, C Cunneen, and T Libesman. (2009) *Indigenous Legal Relations in Australia*. Melbourne: Oxford University Press.

Bignall, S, and M Svirksy. (2012) 'Introduction: Agamben and Colonialism', in *Agamben and Colonialism*, eds M Svirksy and S Bignall. Edinburgh: Edinburgh University Press.

Black, C. (2010) *The Land Is the Source of the Law: A Dialogic Encounter with an Indigenous Jurisprudence*. London: Routledge-Cavendish.

Brown, D. (2009) 'Searching for a Social Democratic Narrative in Criminal Justice'. *Current Issues in Criminal Justice* 20, no 3: 453–56.

BSHP (Boarding School Healing Project). (2008) *Reparations and American Indian Boarding Schools: A Critical Appraisal*. www.boardingschoolhealingproject.org/files/A_Critical_Appraisal_of_Reparations_final.pdf.

Césaire, A. (2000) [1955] *Discourse on Colonialism*. New York: Monthly Review Press.

Clamp, K. (2014) *Restorative Justice in Transition*. Milton Park: Routledge.

Clamp, K, and J Doak. (2012) 'More Than Words: Restorative Justice Concepts in Transitional Settings'. *International Criminal Law Review* 12: 339–60.

CNN Wire Staff. (2012) 'US Finalizes $3.4 Billion Settlement with American Indians'. CNN, http://edition.cnn.com/2012/11/26/politics/american-indian-settlment/.

Committee on Labour and Public Welfare, United States Senate. (1969) *Indian Education: A National Tragedy – A National Challenge*. Washington, DC: US Government Printing Office.

Corntassel, J, and C Holder. (2008) 'Who's Sorry Now? Government Apologies, Truth Commissions, and Indigenous Self-Determination in Australia, Canada, Guatemala and Peru'. *Human Rights Review* 9: 465–89.

Cunneen, C. (2006) 'Exploring the Relationship between Reparations, the Gross Violations of Human Rights, and Restorative Justice', in *The Handbook of Restorative Justice. Global Perspectives*, ed D Sullivan and L Tift (eds). New York: Routledge.

Cunneen, C. (2008) 'State Crime, the Colonial Question and Indigenous Peoples' in *Supranational Criminology: Towards a Criminology of International Crimes*, eds A Smuelers and R Haveman. Antwerp: Intersentia Press.

Cunneen, C. (2012) 'Restorative Justice, Globalization and the Logic of Empire', in *Borders and Transnational Crime: Pre-Crime, Mobility and Serious Harm in an Age of Globalization*, eds J McCulloch and S Pickering. London: Palgrave Macmillan.

Cunneen, C. (2014a) 'Colonial Processes, Indigenous Peoples, and Criminal Justice Systems', in *The Oxford Handbook of Ethnicity, Crime, and Immigration*, eds T Bucerius and M Tonry. Oxford: Oxford University Press.

Cunneen, C. (2014b) 'Youth Justice in Australia', in *Criminology and Criminal Justice, Oxford Handbooks Online*, ed M Tonry. Oxford University Press, New York. http://dx.doi.org/10.1093/oxfordhb/9780199935383.013.62.

Cunneen, C, E Baldry, D Brown, M Brown, M Schwartz and A Steel. (2013) *Penal Culture and Hyperincarceration*. Farnham, UK: Ashgate.

Cunneen, C, and C Hoyle. (2010) *Debating Restorative Justice*. Hart Publishing: Oxford.

Dunbar-Ortiz, R. (2014) *An Indigenous Peoples' History of the United States*. Boston: Beacon Press.

Gilbert, R, and A Wilson. (2009) *Staying Strong on the Outside: Improving the Post Release Experience of Indigenous Young Adults*, Brief No 4, Indigenous Justice Clearinghouse. www.indigenousjustice.gov.au/briefs/brief004.pdf.

Haebich, A. (1992) *For Their Own Good: Aborigines and Government in the South West of Western Australia 1900–1940*. Perth: University of Western Australia Press.

Hamilton, A, and M Sinclair. (1991) *Report of the Aboriginal Justice Inquiry of Manitoba: The Justice System and Aboriginal People, Vol 1*. www.ajic.mb.ca/volumel/toc.html.

Jackson, M. (1994) 'Changing Realities: Unchanging Truths'. *Australian Journal of Law and Society* 115, no 10: 115–29.

Kidd, R. (2006) *Trustees on Trial: Recovering the Stolen Wages*. Canberra: Aboriginal Studies Press.

Lacey, N. (2008) *The Prisoners' Dilemma: Political Economy and Punishment in Contemporary Democracies – the Hamlyn Lectures*. Cambridge: Cambridge University Press.

Lane, P Jr, M Bopp, J Bopp, and J Norris. (2002) *Mapping the Healing Journey: Final Report of a First Nation Research Project on Healing in Canadian Aboriginal Communities*. Ontario: Aboriginal Corrections Policy Unit.

Martin, F A. (2014) 'The Coverage of American Indians and Alaskan Natives in Criminal Justice and Criminology Introductory Textbooks'. *Critical Criminology* 22: 237–56.

McCaslin, W D, and D C Breton. (2008) 'Justice as Healing: Going Outside the Colonisers' Cage', in *Handbook of Critical and Indigenous Methodologies*, eds N Denzin, Y Lincoln and L T Smith. London: Sage Publications.

McKinnon, A D. (2009) 'U.S. Offers an Apology to Native Americans'. *Wall Street Journal*, 22 December 2009. http://blogs.wsj.com/washwire/2009/12/22/us-offers-an-official-apology-to-native-americans/.

Meriam, L. (1928) *The Problem of Indian Administration*. Baltimore: The Johns Hopkins University Press. Extracts available: www.npr.org/templates/story/story.php?storyId=16516865.

Milloy, J. (1999) *A National Crime. The Canadian Government and the Residential School System 1879 to 1986*. Winnipeg: The University of Manitoba Press.

Moses, D. (2000) 'An Antipodean Genocide? The Origins of the Genocidal Moment in the Colonisation of Australia'. *Journal of Genocide Research* 2, no 1: 89–106.

NISATSIC (National Inquiry into the Separation of Aboriginal and Torres Strait Islander Children from Their Families). (1997) *Bringing Them Home*. Sydney: Human Rights and Equal Opportunity Commission.

Piecuch, J, and J Lutz. (2011) 'Indian Ring Scandal', in *The Encyclopaedia of North American Indian Wars, 1607–1890. A Political, Social and Military History*, ed S C Tucker. Santa Barbara, CA: ABC-CLIO.

Pierpaoli, P G (2011) 'Bureau of Indian Affairs', in *The Encyclopaedia of North American Indian Wars, 1607–1890. A Political, Social and Military History*, ed S C Tucker. Santa Barbara, CA: ABC-CLIO.

Quince, K. (2007) 'Maori and the Criminal Justice System in New Zealand', in *The New Zealand Criminal Justice System*, eds J Tolmie and W Brookbanks. Auckland: Lexis Nexis.

RCAP (Royal Commission on Aboriginal Peoples). (1996) *Bridging the Cultural Divide: A Report on Aboriginal People and Criminal Justice in Canada*. Ottawa: Canada Communications Group.

Riccardi, L. (2009) 'U.S. Settles Indian Trust Account Lawsuit', *Los Angeles Times*, 9 December 2009. http://articles.latimes.com/2009/dec/09/nation/la-na-indian-settlement9-2009dec09.

SCRGSP (Steering Committee for the Review of Government Service Provision). (2014) *Overcoming Indigenous Disadvantage: Key Indicators 2014*. Canberra: Productivity Commission.

Senate Standing Committee on Legal and Constitutional Affairs. (2006) *Unfinished Business: Indigenous Stolen Wages*. Canberra: Commonwealth of Australia.

Shenhav, Y. (2012) 'Imperialism, Exceptionalism and the Contemporary World', in *Agamben and Colonialism*, eds M Svirsky and S Bignall. Edinburgh: Edinburgh University Press.

Smith, A. (2004) 'Boarding School Abuses, Human Rights, and Reparations'. *Social Justice* 31, no 4: 89–102.

Smith, A. (2007) *Soul Wound: The Legacy of Native American Schools*. Amnesty International, www.amnestyusa.org/node/87342.

Stannard, D. (1992) *American Holocaust*. New York: Oxford University Press.

Teitel, R. (2000) *Transitional Justice*. New York: Oxford University Press.

Toussaint, S. (1995) 'Western Australia', in *Contested Ground*, ed A McGrath. St Leonards: Allen and Unwin.

TRCC (Truth and Reconciliation Commission of Canada). (2012a) *Backgrounder*. Winnipeg: Truth and Reconciliation Commission of Canada.

TRCC (Truth and Reconciliation Commission of Canada). (2012b) *Interim Report*. Winnipeg: Truth and Reconciliation Commission of Canada.

Van Krieken, R. (2004) 'Rethinking Cultural Genocide: Aboriginal Child Removal and Settler–Colonial State Formation'. *Oceania* 75, no 2: 125–51.

Wanganeen, R. (2008) 'A Loss and Grief Model in Practice', in *Anger and Indigenous Men*, eds A Day, M Nakata and K Howells. Leichhardt, Australia: Federation Press.

Watson, I. (2009) 'In the Northern Territory Intervention: What Is Saved or Rescued and at What Cost'? *Cultural Studies Review* 15, no 2: 45–60.

Wilkinson, R, and K Pickett. (2009) *The Spirit Level*. New York: Bloomsbury Press.

Wolfe, P. (2006) 'Settler Colonialism and the Elimination of the Native'. *Journal of Genocide Research* 8, no 4: 387–409.

Wootten, H. (1989) *Report of the Inquiry into the Death of Malcolm Charles Smith*. Royal Commission into Aboriginal Deaths in Custody, Canberra: Australian Government.

CASE STUDY

Hon Joan Gottschall and Molly Armour*, Rethinking the War on Drugs: What Insights Does Restorative Justice Offer?

It is a typical day in federal court, and I am taking a guilty plea in a drug case.[1] Most prosecutions end in guilty pleas, so such a plea is the usual outcome. Because this is federal court, the quantity of drugs is more than the amount needed for personal use, but the defendant is not a kingpin. He is what in the jargon of drug cases is referred to as 'a mule', the person who carried the drugs from the supplier to the buyer. The buyer was likely an informant or federal agent operating undercover. The federal agents running this sting have kept it going as long as possible in the hope of identifying more suppliers and driving up the quantity of drugs which changes hands, because the defendant's sentence is driven by the quantity of drugs involved. Further, the longer the potential sentence, the more likely the defendant is to provide information in return for a sentencing concession.[2]

Most of the time, the defendant is black or brown. He is unemployed and poor. A large number of federal agents and undercover participants (individuals who receive financial stipends and/or deals on pending cases) investigated the case. The case is prosecuted by assistant United States Attorneys and defended by government-paid appointed counsel. During the pendency of the case, a federal pretrial services officer supervises the defendant, but in preparation for sentencing, a United States probation officer takes over and writes a presentence report, containing some background information, criminal history, and sentencing guideline calculations. The defendant is probably in custody; thus, a number of United States Deputy Marshals escort him to court. As presiding judge, I am on the bench, assisted by a courtroom deputy (my order-enterer and scheduler), a court reporter, and one or two law clerks. Once sentenced, the defendant will be committed to the custody of the Bureau of Prisons, where he will become the charge of the huge employment machine that is the prison-industrial complex.

I doubt that any serious person would disagree that this exercise is futile; if we have made any dent in the availability of drugs, I have seen no evidence of it. It is possible that a major criminal prosecution temporarily diminishes the supply of drugs and raises the price, but that just provokes market wars and violence.[3] Over time, drug prices have fallen.[4] The defendant is fungible; once he is arrested and out of the picture, some other underemployed person will be recruited to do what he has been doing.[5] Indeed, even if the investigation nets someone high up in the supply chain, which it rarely does, he is fungible too. The participants change, but in many poor communities in Chicago, the drug trade is gainful employment, tempting enough so that filling the ranks of the 'disappeared' is not difficult.

Well before Michelle Alexander's book, *The New Jim Crow*,[6] the racial implications of the War on Drugs were obvious. My staff is mostly white, as are most of the law enforcement agents, marshals, pretrial and probation officers, assistant United States Attorneys, and Federal Defenders. We are all living reasonably adequate middle-class lives – putting food on our tables, paying our mortgages – with the incomes we make from doing what we do, a huge part of which is processing drug cases. Conversely, the defendant is not white and is struggling to survive. This impoverished young person of color has probably never had so much attention from middle-class white people as he does on this day in my courtroom, when a dozen of us surround him and he is the center of our attention.

My discomfort with such cases goes beyond their futility and their racial impact. It goes beyond my certainty that *any intervention* in the defendant's life would be better than *this* intervention. It inheres in this: In drug case after drug case, the government argues for draconian sentences for the poor minority youths before me, arguing that if I see their crimes as victimless, I am mistaken. Rather, the government argues, drug crimes injure poor communities, relegating countless people to miserable

---

* Hon. Joan Gottschall and Molly Armour, "Rethinking the War on Drugs: What Insights Does Restorative Justice Offer?" in Murphy and Seng, eds., *Restorative Justice in Practice: A Holistic Approach*. Lake Mary, FL: Vandeplas Publishing, 2015, pp. 89–101. Permission by the Hon. Joan Gottschall.

drug-addled lives, and leading to drug markets on open street corners and violent turf wars, making the streets unsafe for law-abiding persons who want merely to go about their business, go to the store, or go to school.

At some level, the government is right: Drug crimes are often a scourge of poor, minority communities. But the problem with this argument is that the defendant, probably the third generation living through the War on Drugs, is almost always the paradigmatic victim as well as the perpetrator. He may be an addict himself. He grew up in a household with a parent or parents addicted to controlled substances who were periodically incarcerated. His career as a drug dealer may have started when a parent had him carry drugs to a buyer in the hope that he would avoid detection more successfully than an adult or be punished less severely if apprehended. He grew up surrounded by poverty and unemployment, went to poor schools, probably dropped out before graduating from high school, and may be functionally illiterate. He has little or no legitimate employment history. By the time he comes before me, he has lived most of his life in a war zone, having lost numerous friends and relatives to gun violence. His low-level drug dealing has allowed him to pay a little child support for his children, but never to get on his feet or accumulate income. So sure, he made bad choices and did illegal things, but what good choices did he have? How can I see him as responsible, for the community degradation that so powerfully contributed to making him what he is? And how likely is it that this young man can return to his community after imprisonment with any hope of a different future?

Restorative justice principles offer insight into how to reunite former offenders with their communities. From its early roots, to the Truth and Reconciliation hearings in post-apartheid South Africa, the restorative justice process has sought to reunite perpetrators, victims, and the community through truth-telling.[7] It teaches that healing can occur if victims and perpetrators talk to and try to understand each other. But in the context of the American War on Drugs, application of restorative justice principles is complicated. The perpetrator is often himself a victim, and our society is committed to punitive crime policies that thoughtful experts agree are themselves 'criminogenic' – that is, *causing* rather than *preventing* crime.[8] Such policies worsen the perpetrator's future prospects and do real harm to the community from which he comes. Decades of research make clear that whole communities are collateral casualties of the War on Drugs. Restorative justice has something to say in this situation: The policies we are pursuing are undermining reconciliation and healing, not promoting them.

Where are we now? The statistics appear in many places but nowhere in a more jaw-dropping form than in Loïc Wacquant's essay in *Race, Incarceration and American Values*.[9] Between 1975 and 2000, the population behind bars rose from 380,000 to over two million, driven mostly by increased admissions.[10] Michelle Alexander states, 'Drug offenses alone account for two-thirds of the rise in the federal inmate population and more than half of the rise in state prisoners between 1985 and 2000', with approximately a half million people in prison or jail for a drug offense today, compared to an estimated 41,100 in 1980.[11] Jail and prison expenditures jumped from $7 billion in 1980 to $57 billion in 2000, with one million staff, making corrections the third largest employer in the nation behind Manpower and Wal-Mart.[12] Census numbers, which matter for voter apportionment and federal benefits, count prisoners as residents of the mostly white, rural districts where they are incarcerated, not of the minority, urban districts from which they come.[13] Huge federal disbursements are linked to the number of local drug arrests, incentivizing drug arrests in easy-to-make cases at the expense of arrests for more concealed and often more serious drug crime as well as for other significant criminal conduct.[14] The financial lifeblood of many police departments is forfeitures from anyone suspected of possessing drugs; the property owner usually walks away from the seized car or house or boat rather than trying to prove his innocence, and the police department is richer for the value of the property seized.[15] And minority unemployment figures seriously underreport minority employment because prisoners are not counted among the unemployed.[16] Failure to account for the incarcerated as among the unemployed also distorts measured wage inequality by removing low-wage workers from the wage distribution.[17]

Mass-incarceration, Wacquant says, is a misnomer. A better term is 'hyper-incarceration' of 'lower-class black men in the crumbling ghetto'.[18] One of every nine black men between the ages of 20 and 34 is incarcerated, and in 2003 the federal Bureau of Justice Statistics projected that one in three young black men could expect to spend some time behind bars.[19] Moreover, two-thirds of the nation's inmates come from households with incomes less than half the poverty level.[20] In the impoverished and overwhelmingly black North Lawndale neighborhood in Chicago, seventy percent of men between 18 and 45 are ex-offenders.[21] Black men are seven times more likely to go to prison than white men; black women are eight times more likely to go to prison than white women.[22] Wacquant quotes Bruce Western: '[T]he cumulative risk of imprisonment for African-American males without a high school education tripled between 1978 and 1998 to reach the astonishing rate of 59 percent. . . .'[23] Black men born in the late 1960s are more likely to go to prison than to college or the military.[24] One in three African American males in his twenties is under some kind of criminal justice system control.[25] In the words of Glenn Loury, 'Never before has a supposedly free country denied basic liberty to so many of its citizens', drawn from the most disadvantaged parts of society and disproportionately black and brown.[26]

These startling statistics, while worrisome in themselves, also point toward something more alarming. A growing body of evidence strongly indicates that our penal policies are criminogenic, actually *causing* crime. What is the evidence?

(1) The US imprisonment rate far exceeds that of any other Western democracy; indeed, it exceeds that of every other country.[27] Concentrated incarceration in impoverished neighborhoods disrupts family relationships, weakens the social-control capacity of parents, erodes economic strength, and sours attitudes toward society.[28] Going to prison is a bedrock experience of growing up in some communities, such that it has lost its deterrent effect.[29]

(2) Our laws make reintegration into a law-abiding life upon release from imprisonment almost impossible, particularly in light of the meager social and personal resources of the people who go to prison in the first place.[30] Since our society gave up on the rehabilitative ideal decades ago,[31] inmates spend their lengthy sentences with few educational or vocational opportunities and no opportunity to build social capital or improve mental or physical health.[32] Ex-drug offenders are ineligible for student loans, public housing, and welfare.[33] They are subject to heightened scrutiny for years – drug testing, fines and restitution payments, parole reporting – creating numerous occasions for the occurrence of technical violations that send them back to prison.[34]

(3) One out of seven black males is disenfranchised as a result of a criminal conviction, further marginalizing ex-offenders. According to Heather Ann Thompson in a recent article in *The Atlantic*, by 2011 more than 23 percent of African Americans in Florida, 18 percent in Wyoming, and 20 percent in Virginia were barred from voting, thereby potentially changing results in numerous elections.[35]

(4) Residents of neighborhoods targeted in the War on Drugs are arrested at levels that damage the social fabric, destabilize the community, and prevent individuals from functioning as law-abiding citizens.[36] Because of cycles of imprisonment and reimprisonment, with many residents of those neighborhoods are constantly in flux – entering and leaving, going into shelters, families being forced to move in the absence of a breadwinner. Chronic homelessness and transience are often lifetime collateral consequences of imprisonment.[37] Under these circumstances, the quality of social support diminishes, including trust, communication, and access to assistance among neighbors.[38]

(5) Ex-prisoners encounter often insurmountable obstacles in finding work.[39] State laws bar them from countless occupations.[40] Many employers will not hire ex-offenders.[41] They earn less during their lifetimes and find it harder to stay employed.[42] In the words of Bruce Western:

> Incarceration reduces not just the level of wages, it also slows wage growth over the life course and restricts the kinds of jobs that former inmates might find. Incarceration redirects the life path from the usual trajectory of steady jobs with career ladders that normally propels wage growth for young men. Men tangled in the justice system become permanent labor market outsiders, finding only temporary or unreliable jobs that offer little economic stability.[43]

There is little work in the communities from which the ex-prisoners come and little convenient transportation to get them to places where there is work.[44] Few have drivers' licenses and most have accumulated large fines for driving without a license – fines which they will never be able to pay.

(6) Prison acts as a fissure in the lives of both the incarcerated and their families. It removes young people, especially young men, from their communities during the prime years for building foundations for a lifetime of work and social connection.[45] Meaningful participation in the life-stabilizing structures of marriage, children, and career – the very things that cause young men to mature out of criminal involvement – are rendered impossible by imprisonment.[46] Going to prison within one year of a child's birth cuts the rate of marriage by at least one half and doubles the chance of a couple separating in the same year.[47]

(7) Our imprisonment policies have created several generations of 'children of the incarcerated'. These young people grow up without access to at least one parent for a significant portion of their childhoods and are greatly affected both psychologically and socially as a result. A parent's incarceration creates an extremely high risk that his or her child will become a prisoner later in life.[48] By the end of the 1990s, one in ten young black children had a father in jail or prison.[49] Because repeated incarceration is common, especially for drug offenders, multiple separations of parents from their children is the norm.[50] Imprisonment irreparably tears the family fabric in countless ways. Because of the effect of these separations on the way in which parent-child bonds are formed, 'incarceration diminishes the capacity for effective parent-child relationships'.[51] Having an adult family member go to prison elevates the risk of early infant death,[52] increases the risk of juvenile delinquency and being in a gang,[53] and shortens life expectancy.[54] Children of incarcerated parents experience school performance-related issues, depression and anxiety, low self-esteem, and aggressiveness,[55] all of which are aggravated when they see their parents arrested at gunpoint and taken away in handcuffs.[56] Prison visiting rooms are frightening places for children,[57] if a parent-child relationship survives prison at all.[58] Many children are removed from the home or put up for adoption because a parent is imprisoned, severing ties of an entire family and destroying the family's morale.[59] The argument that the removal of a criminally active parent from the home improves the home environment for children has been proven to be untrue.[60]

This evidence overwhelmingly demonstrates that our crime prevention policies as embodied in the War on Drugs actually *create* more crime, destabilize impoverished communities of color, and forge lasting, toxic consequences for us all. An abundance of research makes clear that not only is the defendant himself a victim of our punitive-focused criminal drug laws, but whole communities are also collateral casualties. These 'criminogenic' or crime-causing policies foster a vicious cycle that is overwhelmingly difficult to interrupt.

Thoughtful commentators across the political spectrum believe that this evidence indicates a failure of democracy, and that the communities with so much at stake both in their safety and in the future of their young people must be empowered to have significant input in directing the law enforcement priorities by which they live. William Stuntz's *The Collapse of American Criminal Justice* suggests that when budgetary considerations drive the decisions that make arrests and fill prison beds, those who pay the highest price are those who can be most cheaply caught and convicted, not those whose punishment is most in the public interest.[61] Stuntz insists we need a return to greater control of each neighborhood over its own law-enforcement priorities, injecting more local democracy into the criminal justice system and supplanting our current system where 'poor black neighborhoods see too little of the kinds of policing and criminal punishment that do the most good, and too much of the kinds that do the most harm'.[62]

Todd Clear conceptualizes this differently but ends in a very similar place. Discussing the ideas of Pettit and Braithwaite, Clear observes that before people can justly be punished, they must have had a reasonable capacity to attain their preferred ends within the law – a reasonable chance at a good life.[63] When choosing among punishments, we should prefer those that tend to expand legitimate capacity rather than destroy it, and we should be suspicious of punishments that have, as an unintended consequence, the expansion of inequality. These ideas, Clear says, have as their central value the promotion of community.[64]

The rehabilitative perspective of restorative justice suggests an alternative path forward. Generally speaking, restorative justice focuses on mending individual relationships. Yet the experience of the South African Truth and Reconciliation process makes clear that whole communities can be direct beneficiaries of a restorative-based approach. Indeed, for wounds so large, healing must occur on a community scale, not just an individual scale. As Ernest Drucker points out, the South African experience 'provides a new model of how to rebuild a damaged society without retribution, and how to deal effectively with a history of extreme violence and massive injustice'.[65] Along those lines, he suggests that a formal peace process, modeled after the Truth and Reconciliation hearings, should be convened to restore trust and heal the damage wrought by our policies of hyper-incarceration.[66]

Whether such a radical undertaking is possible or even desirable, it is clear that we need more democracy, more local involvement in setting law-enforcement priorities, and more attention to the kinds of crimes that undermine decent, law-abiding life in poor communities, not just mass arrests of the low-hanging fruit. We need less destruction of the hopes and possibilities of generations of young people and a reform of those laws that permanently disable those who have paid their debt to society from establishing positive, law-abiding lives. Our law-enforcement policies should strengthen communities, not undermine them.

In the aftermath of the events in Ferguson, Missouri, and the related Department of Justice Report, there can no longer be any doubt that poor urban communities frequently feel disconnected from and disserved by their local police forces.[67] Ferguson is a stark demonstration of what the War on Drugs, and related policing strategies, have wrought. It makes clear that democracy has failed these communities. The complex, interwoven issues surrounding mass incarceration do not lend themselves to easy solutions. Nevertheless, no solution is possible without community involvement.[68]

The complex, interwoven issues surrounding mass incarceration do not lend to easy solutions. Yet restorative justice principles offer both a constructive lens and concrete tools to approach these enormous challenges. There are numerous restorative justice-based approaches which might help reverse our current trajectory, such as specialized community courts,[69] community-based policing[70] and prosecution,[71] and utilization of the circle process – that is, a gathering of various stakeholders aimed at facilitating dialogue in an interconnected, interdependent, and equal manner.[72] These rehabilitative approaches – local, collaborative, and focused on problem-solving – offer a more constructive paradigm than our current model. Courts, communities, and other stakeholders should encourage open dialogue, creativity, and experimentation in reaching for less destructive approaches.

The communities from which so many prisoners come endure failing schools, massive unemployment, widespread physical and mental health problems, poverty, and social dysfunction. Mass incarceration is inextricably entangled with these significant social ills. Restorative justice points toward ways of building and strengthening the fabric of these communities, as well as restoring former offenders to a place in their community where they can succeed. There are no easy answers to suggest, but if we are serious about justice and serious about making justice an instrument of healing, not just of destruction, it is time we thought about healing these communities, not making their suffering worse.

Notes

1. The authors thank John Robinson for his invaluable assistance. Bruce Moran and Thomas P Sullivan generously read this paper in draft; their suggestions made it far clearer and more compelling. A shorter version of this paper was presented at the Bellarmine Conference on Restorative Justice at Loyola Marymount University in November 2013.
2. Human Rights Watch, *An Offer You Can't Refuse: How US Federal Prosecutors Force Drug Defendants to Plead Guilty*, http://www.hrw.org/reports/2013/12/05/offer-you-can-t-refuse-0 (posted 5 December 2013).
3. Dan Werb et al., *Effect of Drug Law Enforcement on Drug Market Violence: A Systematic Review*, 22 Intl. J. Drug & Policy 87, 92 (2011).
4. Dan Werb et al., *The Temporal Relationship between Drug Supply Indicators: An Audit of International Government Surveillance Systems*, BMJ Open 1, 6 (19 July 2013).
5. See e.g. Michelle Alexander, *The New Jim Crow: Mass Incarceration in the Age of Colorblindness* 123 (New Press 2010).
6. Alexander, *The New Jim Crow*.
7. David K Androff, *Reconciliation in a Community-Based Restorative Justice Intervention* 39 J. Sociology & Soc. Welfare 73, 74, 81 (2012). The Truth and Reconciliation process popularised modem restorative justice concepts, which had been taking hold in Canada, New Zealand, Australia and the United States since the 1970s.
8. See e.g. Martin H Pritkin, *Is Prison Increasing Crime?* 2008 Wis. L. Rev. 1049 (cataloguing the 'crime-causing, or "criminogenic" effects' of incarceration).
9. Loïc Wacquant, *Forum: Loïc Wacquant*, in *Race, Incarceration and American Values*, ed Glenn C Loury, 57, 57–59 (Cambridge, MA: MIT Press, 2008).
10. Wacquant, Forum, at 57–58.
11. Alexander, *supra* n.5, at 59.
12. Wacquant, *supra* n.9, at 58–59. The past three decades have also seen a rapid rise in private prison expenditures. Cody Mason, *Too Good to Be True: Private Prisons in America*, http://sentencingproject.org/ doc/publications/inc_too_good_to_be_true.pdf. (January 2012) (noting that since the inception of prison privatisation in the 1980s, at least 1.6 million people are now held in privately run prisons, which earn revenue in excess of $2.9 billion a year). With the expansion of prison privatisation, unique policy concerns have emerged, such as how certain private contracts incentivise municipalities to fill prison beds. See, e.g., *Criminal: How Lockup Quotas and 'Low-Crime Taxes' Guarantee Profits for Private Prison Corporations*, http://www.inthepublicinterest.org/sites/default/files/Criminal-Lockup-Quota-Report.pdf (September 2013).
13. Alexander, *supra* n.5, at 188; Heather Ann Thompson, *How Prisons Change the Balance of Power in America*, http://www.theatlantic.com/national/archive/2013/10/how-prisons-change-the-balance-of-power-in-america/280341 (posted October 7, 2013).
14. Alexander, *supra* n.5, at 180; William J Stuntz, *The Collapse of American Criminal Justice* 54 (Cambridge: Harvard University Press, 2011).

15. Alexander, *supra* n.5, at 77–79; Sarah Stillman, *Taken: The Use and Abuse of Civil Forfeiture*, http://www.newyorker.com/reporting/2013/08/12/130812fa_fact_stillman (posted August 12, 2013).
16. Todd R Clear, *Imprisoning Communities: How Mass Incarceration Makes Disadvantaged Neighborhoods Worse* (Oxford: Oxford University Press, 2007), 62–63; Bruce Western, *Punishment and Inequality in America* 91 (New York: Russell Sage Foundation 2006).
17. Western, *supra* n.16, at 89.
18. Wacquant, *supra* n.9, at 59.
19. Sonja B Starr and M Marit Rehavi, *Mandatory Sentencing and Racial Disparity: Assessing the Role of Prosecutors and the Effects of Booker*, 123 *Yale L.J.* 2, 3 (2013) (citing Pew Center on the States, *One in 100: Behind Bars in America 2008* 3, http://www.pewtrusts.org/~/media/legacy/uploadedfiles/pcs_assets/ 2008/one20in20100pdf.pdf (February 2008), and Thomas P Bonczar, *Prevalence of Imprisonment in the U.S. Population, 1974–2001* 1, http://www.bjs.gov/content/pub/pdf/piusp01.pdf (August 2003)).
20. Wacquant, *supra* n.9, at 60.
21. Alexander, *supra* n.5, at 191.
22. Clear, *supra* n.16, at 63.
23. Wacquant, *supra* n.9, at 61 (quoting Western, *supra* n.16, at 26).
24. Western, *supra* n.16, at 189.
25. Ernest Drucker, *A Plague of Prisons: The Epidemiology of Mass Incarceration in America* 157 (New York: New Press 2011) (citing 2007 statistics).
26. Glenn C Loury, *Race, Incarceration and American Values*, in *Race, Incarceration and American Values*, ed Glenn C Loury (Cambridge: MIT Press, 2008), 3, 5–6.
27. Loury, *Race, Incarceration and American Values*, at 4–5; Marc Mauer, *Race to Incarcerate* 10 (New York: New Press, 2006).
28. Drucker, *supra* n.25, at 79–80; Clear, *supra* n.16, at 5; Alexander, *supra* n.5, at 224.
29. Western, *supra* n.16, at 23; Stuntz, *supra* n.14, at 1.
30. Clear, *supra* n.16, at 10, 76–77; Drucker, *supra* n.25, at 140.
31. Western, *supra* n.16, at 172; Clear, *supra* n.16, at 50.
32. Western, *supra* n.16, at 113, 174–75.
33. Alexander, *supra* n.5, at 92, 141–42; Drucker, *supra* n.25, at 130, 137; Clear, *supra* n.16, at 58.
34. Alexander, *supra* n.5, at 150; Clear, *supra* n.16, at 59.
35. Thompson, *supra* n.13 (explaining how the scope of this African American disenfranchisement affected results in numerous elections).
36. Drucker, *supra* n.25, at 106; Clear, *supra* n.16, at 10.
37. Drucker, *supra* n.25, at 133.
38. Drucker, at 79–80, 106; Clear, *supra* n.16, at 73; Western, *supra* n.16, at 36.
39. Alexander, *supra* n.5, at 148–49.
40. Drucker, *supra* n.25, at 135–36; Clear, *supra* n.16, at 58.
41. Western, *supra* n.16, at 21.
42. Clear, *supra* n.16, at 9; Western, *supra* n.16, at 115, 120, 125.
43. Western, *supra* n.16, at 109.
44. Alexander, *supra* n.5, at 147.
45. Clear, *supra* n.16, at 21.
46. Clear, at 61; Western, *supra* n.16, at 20–21, 129.
47. Clear, *supra* n.16, at 98. '[r]educed marriage prospects resulting from a term in prison are a risk factor in recidivism'.

48. Clear, at 6; Drucker, *supra* n.25, at 79–80.
49. Western, *supra* n.16, at 190.
50. Drucker, *supra* n.25, at 149. 'It is crucial that we recognize the frequency and severity of this phenomenon for what it is – mass trauma'.
51. Clear, *supra* n.16, at 99.
52. Drucker, *supra* n.25, at 157.
53. Drucker, *supra* n.25 at 160.
54. Drucker, *supra* n.25 at 37.
55. Drucker, *supra* n.25 at 79–80, 103, 142, 146; Clear, *supra* n.16, at 96.
56. Christopher Wildeman, *Parental Imprisonment, the Prison Boom, and the Concentration of Childhood Disadvantage*, 46 *Demography* 265, 277 (2009).
57. Drucker, *supra* n.25, at 142.
58. Wildeman, *supra* n.56, at 277.
59. Drucker, *supra* n.25, at 146.
60. Clear, *supra* n.16, at 97.
61. Stuntz, *supra* n.14, at 54.
62. Stuntz, *supra* n.14 at 5.
63. Clear, *supra* n.16, at 193–94 (citing Philip Pettit and John Braithwaite, *Not Just Deserts: A Republican Theory of Criminal Justice* [Oxford: Oxford University Press, 1993]).
64. Clear, *supra* n.16, at 193–94.
65. Drucker, *supra* n.25 at 187.
66. Drucker, *supra* n.25 at 187.
67. *See generally*, US Department of Justice, Investigation of the Ferguson Police Department (4 March 2015).
68. See US Department of Justice, 5–6, 86–88, 90, 95, asserting that the lack of trust and divisiveness between the community and police can be restored only through 'diligent, committed collaboration' with the community (at 6).
69. See e.g. Cynthia G Lee et al., *A Community Court Grows in Brooklyn: A Comprehensive Evaluation of the Red Hook Community Justice Center: Final Report* (Nat'l Ctr. for State Courts 2013) (available at http://www.courtinnovation.org/sites/default/files/documents/RH%20Evaluation%20Final%20Report.pdf).
70. See e.g. Caroline G Nicholl, *Community Policing, Community Justice, and Restorative Justice: Exploring the Links for the Delivery of a Balanced Approach to Public Safety* (U.S. Department of Justice, Office of Community Oriented Policing Services 1999) (available at http://www.cops.usdoj.gov/publications/e09990014_web.pdf). Engaging the community is recognised as essential to success in dealing productively with urban crime. For instance, a local police department in Springfield, Massachusetts, has been utilising 'counter-insurgency' techniques learned during the Iraq War by veteran officers with significant success. *60 Minutes*, 'Counterinsurgency Methods Used to Fight Gang Crime' (CBS May 3, 2013) (available at http://www.cbsnews.com/news/counterinsurgency-methods-used-to-fight-gang-crime). This strategy recognises the importance of positive community engagement and involves regular consultation with community members both on the street and in a weekly community meeting.
71. See e.g. Anthony C Thompson, *It Takes a Community to Prosecute*, 77 Notre Dame L. Rev. 321 (2002).
72. Jean Greenwood, *The Circle Process: A Path for Restorative Dialogue* 2 (Saint Paul: University of Minnesota Center for Restorative Justice and Peacemaking 2005).

Glossary

alienation the condition of workers in a capitalist economy, resulting from a lack of control over their labour. Estrangement from one's human potential (Marx).

anafemale/anamale anatomically female/male.

Another Thinking Abdelkebir Khatibi's concept for 'border thinking' (see definition), which raised the importance of alternative methods of thought.

Asian Women's Fund the Asian Women's Fund was established by the government of Japan in 1995. However, the fund was sustained from donations from private citizens, not government monies, and Korean activists opposed its existence. The fund ceased operating in 2007.

Border Thinking a way of thinking externally that looks at alternative theories and experiences of typically marginalised communities rather than those of imperial countries.

bourgeoisie capitalist class that owns the means of production, the ruling class (Marx).

capitalism a socioeconomic system based on the private ownership of the means of production and profit.

Captain Dreyfus In 1994 Captain Alfred Dreyfus, a young French artillery officer of Alsatian and Jewish descent, was unjustly sentenced to life imprisonment for allegedly communicating French military secrets to the German embassy in Paris. The Dreyfus Affair was a political scandal that divided the Third French Republic from 1894 until its resolution in 1906. The affair remains one of the most notable examples of a complex miscarriage of justice and anti-Semitism. Eventually all the accusations against Dreyfus were demonstrated to be baseless. In 1906 Dreyfus was exonerated and reinstated as a major in the French army. He died in 1935.

class struggle the conflict of interests between the workers and the ruling class in a capitalist society (Marx).

Colonial Difference a power-relation strategy where the colonising power employs the use of claimed absolute distance on the part of the colonised nation in order to justify colonial pursuits.

Coloniality of Power a complex and ongoing power structure created by colonising powers that has institutionalised racial, social, political and economic hierarchies that identify who has power and who is disenfranchised.

Comfort Stations Japanese military brothels established by the Japanese government to enhance the soldiers' morale.

Comfort Women women and girls mainly from Korea, China and the Philippines who were forced into sexual slavery by the Imperial Japanese Army in occupied territories before and during World War II. The word is a translation of the Japanese word *ianfu*, which is a euphemism for 'prostitutes'.

commodification under the logic of capitalism, such things as friendship, knowledge, women, and more are understood only in terms of their monetary value. In this way, they are no longer treated as things with intrinsic worth but as commodities. They are valued, that is, only extrinsically in terms of money (Marx).

commodity an 'external object, a thing which through its qualities satisfies human needs of whatever kind' (Marx, *Capital*) and is then exchanged for something else.

commodity fetishism the tendency to attribute to commodities (including money) a power that really inheres only in the labour expended to create commodities (Marx).

communism a system where the major means of production are publicly owned. For Marx, the communal ownership and control of the *means of production* represents the fulfillment of human history where society subscribes to the principle 'from each according to ability, to each according to need' (Marx and Engels, *The Communist Manifesto*).

Compromise of 1850 a set of laws, passed in the midst of fierce wrangling between groups favouring slavery and groups opposing it, that attempted to give something to both sides. As part of the Compromise of 1850, the Fugitive Slave Act was amended and the slave trade in Washington, DC, was abolished. The compromise admitted California to the United States as a 'free' (no slavery) state but allowed some newly acquired territories to decide on slavery for themselves.

conjugal right sexual rights and privileges conferred on spouses by the marriage bond. Carole Pateman suggests that a husband had a kind of special right over his wife, which helps to explain the extremely slow development of legal protections against rape by husbands.

Consent Theory   the idea that individuals as free agents enter into consensual relationships with other free agents to form a social contract that becomes the basis for political governance.

criminogenic   causing or likely to cause criminal behaviour.

cultural difference   a distinction of cultures, between colonised and colonial, created and enforced by imperial powers in order to maintain their power.

cultural injustice   when one's culture's beliefs, values or practices are suppressed by the members (or dominant institutions) of another culture, whether or not that suppression goes along with other kinds of injustice.

decolonisation   a process created in developing countries that aims to deconstruct colonial impacts and claims that capitalism and communism are not the only two ways of thinking. Instead, decolonisation focuses on equality, economic justice and communal thinking.

Decolonisation of Philosophy   a concept that recognises that Eurocentric philosophy is still dominant in developing countries. Decolonisation of Philosophy demands that colonising philosophies are taken down in order to open space for native philosophies.

Double Consciousness   W E B Du Bois's concept for the struggle Black Americans face when trying to unify their Black and American identities.

E Franklin Frazier   Baldwin introduces his nephew to what sociologist E Franklin Frazier (1894–1962) called 'the cities of destruction'. Cities of destruction isolate and impoverish Black Americans and communicate a devastating message: Black lives do not count.

Enlightenment   philosophical movement of the 18th century, especially in France, that proclaimed the triumph of reason and science over custom and superstition.

environmental job blackmail   if workers want to keep their job, they must work under environmentally hazardous conditions.

Foucault, Michel   a French philosopher and historian who became one of the most influential and controversial scholars of the post–World War II period (1924–1986).

Gemeinschaft **(community)**   traditional discourses are based on *Gemeinschaft* (ethics of care, charity and sympathy).

Gesellschaft **(society)**   modern discourses are based on *Gesellschaft* (ethics based on legal and human rights discourse).

hegemony   Gramsci, an Italian intellectual and politician, developed the notion of hegemony as part of his critique of the deterministic economist interpretation of history. Hegemony, to Gramsci, is the 'cultural, moral and ideological' leadership of a group over subaltern groups. This leadership, however, also needs to be economic. It is based on the equilibrium between consent and coercion. Gramsci noted that in Europe, the dominant class, the bourgeoisie, protected some of the interests of the subaltern classes in order to get their support; it was, therefore, hegemonic, because it ruled with the consent of the subordinate masses.

historicism   the concept of historical time as linear or evolutional and its justification of colonisation in the name of speeding up modernisation of those regions that are behind *in history*.

Idees de Droit* and *Regles de Droit   After the French Revolution, the French Constitutionalists claimed that the state was supposed to build *regles de droit* (rules of law) grounded in the *idees de droit* (ideas of the law) and thereby establish the necessary means to enforce the rules using the power of the state, the only modern institution with the legitimate monopoly of coercive force.

inferiority complex   the feeling of inadequacy by the colonised who has lost his native cultural origin and embraced the culture of the coloniser's country produces an inferiority complex in the mind of the Black Subject, who then will try to appropriate and imitate the culture of the coloniser.

internal colonialism   a system of power and suppression where whites in power create internal colonies by exploiting the resources and labour of communities of colour inside their borders.

intersectionality   the complex and cumulative way that the effects of different forms of discrimination (such as racism, sexism and classism) combine, overlap and intersect, especially in the experiences of marginalised people.

labour-power   the abstraction of human labour into something that can be exchanged for money (Marx).

maquiladoras   factories built by US companies in Mexico near the US border to take advantage of much lower labour costs in Mexico. They import certain materials on a tariff-free basis for assembling, processing and manufacturing and then export the assembled, processed and manufactured products, sometimes back to the raw materials' country of origin.

means of production   the tools and raw material used to create a product (Marx).

Miguel Leon-Portilla   an ethno-historian who published *La filosofia Nahuatl* (Nahuatl Philosophy), which claims that the Aztecs or Nahuatl-speaking people had philosophy.

mode of production everything that goes into the production of the necessities of life, including the 'productive forces' (labour, instruments and raw material) and the 'relations of production' (the social structures that regulate the relation between humans in the production of goods). According to Marx and Engels, for individuals, the mode of production is 'a definite form of expressing their life, a definite mode of life on their part. As individuals express their life, so they are. What they are, therefore, coincides with their production, both with what they produce and how they produce'.

modernisation a Western concept that aims to 'modernise' developing countries, like those in Latin America, by democratising them as well as developing their economies. Moroccan philosopher Abdelkebir Khatibi says that decolonisation is the dark side of modernisation.

natural right a right that everyone has by virtue of being human. It cannot be granted nor taken away by any person or political authority.

NIMBY ('not in my backyard') residents of a community who object to the siting of a facility perceived as unpleasant or potentially dangerous in their own neighbourhood, such as a landfill or hazardous waste facility, while raising no such objections to similar developments elsewhere.

Orientalism Edward Said's term for the Western power strategy of creating a distinction between the West as superior and the East as inferior in order to justify colonial pursuits.

Original Position John Rawls's concept of a hypothetical situation as a thought experiment similar to the state of nature of prior political philosophers like Locke. In the Original Position, the parties select principles that will determine the basic structure of the society they will live in.

penal/colonial complex the link between colonialism and the penal system; the effects of colonialism on criminal behaviour and incarceration.

Philosophy of Liberation the philosophical concept that later became decolonisation. It originated first in Argentina and then was employed in other Latin American countries in the 1970s. Philosophy of liberation can be applied to all systems of oppression including but not limited to sexism, racism and colonialism.

pidgin grammatically simplified speech used for communication between people with different languages.

Politics of Recognition a politics that accommodates recognition of different cultural identities.

Proletariat working class that possesses only its labour power (Marx).

Relations of Production the social structures that regulate the relation between humans in the production of goods (Marx).

Saros Saros or Creoles in Nigeria during the 19th century and early 20th century were freed slaves who migrated from Brazil and Cuba to Nigeria in the beginning of the 1830s.

settler colonialism a type of colonialism that functions through the replacement of indigenous populations with an invasive settler society.

Sir Galahad one of the knights of King Arthur's Round Table who achieves the Holy Grail.

Sir Henry Morton Stanley Welsh American journalist and explorer who was famous for his exploration of central Africa and his search for missionary and explorer David Livingstone. Stanley is also known for his work in enabling the plundering of the Congo Basin region in association with King Leopold II of Belgium.

social contract agreement amongst individuals by which, according to the theories of Hobbes, Locke or Rousseau, among others, organised society is brought into being and invested with the right to secure mutual protection and welfare or to regulate the relations amongst its members.

State of Nature in the theories of Hobbes, Locke and Rousseau, amongst others, the hypothetical condition in which people live before they create society and government. Everyone is free and equal in this state, and no one has authority over anyone else.

Stolen Generations term used for Aboriginal children that were forcefully removed from their families between the 1890s and 1970s in Australia. Since the period covers several decades, we speak of 'stolen generations' in the plural.

surplus value the surplus produced over and above what is required to survive, which is translated into profit in capitalism (Marx).

Swaraj self-rule (Gandhi).

Thingification commoditisation, turning humans into things.

toxic colonialism the practice of exporting hazardous waste from developed countries to underdeveloped ones for disposal.

traducer/sufferer perpetrator/victim.

veil W E B Du Bois's idea that a veil prevents white people from seeing Black Americans as Americans, therefore denying them their deserved rights. Du Bois states that while the veil is constantly present, it is not always consciously recognised.

Veil of Ignorance John Rawls's device that prevents individuals in the Original Position from knowing their identities and their social, economic and political characteristics. The function of the veil of ignorance is to push participants towards principles of justice that would be reasonably acceptable and, in some way, beneficial to all. Hence, we would not choose a social arrangement that would solely or primarily benefit the rich if we knew that we ourselves could be poor or if we knew that we ourselves are likely to be poor.

William Lloyd Garrison (1805–1879) American journalistic crusader who published a newspaper, *The Liberator* (1831–1865), and helped lead the successful abolitionist campaign against slavery. Through *The Liberator*, Garrison soon achieved recognition as the most radical of American antislavery advocates.

Yoruba People an ethnic group of southwestern and north-central Nigeria as well as southern and central Benin, together known as Yorubaland.

Index

aboriginal child removal, 343–344; people, 344–348
acequias (irrigation systems), 231–232
"activist mothering," 214
affirmative action, 43, 157, 159, 312
African Americans. *See* blacks
agricultural workers. *See* farmworkers
Algeria, 265–266
alienation, 21, 263
American Indian women, 215–216
amnesty, 321, 325, 327–328; laws, 331–335
Anderson, Carol, 71
Anti-Lynching Bureau, 90
Antilles, 263
Aristotle, x, 319
Asian Women's Fund, 302–306
assimilation, 104, 252, 262, 341, 343
Astell, Mary, 34
atonement, 299, 300, 302–305
Australia, 34, 46, 47, 320, 339, 341, 342, 343–347, 349

Baldus, David C., 114
"Beyond the Hashtags" report, 118
biculturalism, 172
black church, 197–198
black liberation theology, 197
Black Lives Matter. *See* social movements
black suspect-white victim effect, 114
blackness, 71, 99
blacks, 2, 8, 46, 70–73, 85, 110–117, 127–128, 132, 156–160, 184, 187–193, 195–201, 204, 228, 233, 261–264, 312, 313; arrest rates of, 110–111, 114–115; incarceration of, 110–113, 320, 357–358
Blackstone, William, 37
'border thinking', 252
bourgeois, 138, 142, 154, 258
Bureau of Indian Affairs (BIA), 345

Canada, 46, 47, 234, 235, 236, 320, 339, 341, 343, 344, 346, 349
capital, 145, 175, 278, 281, 286; accumulation of, 133, 160, 286
capitalism, 131, 133, 139, 171, 172, 246
capital punishment, 90, 110, 113–114,
Chávez, César, 226, 228, 229
Cherokee Nation v. State of Georgia (1831), 238
chlorine, 166, 169
Chomsky, Noam, 272
Christianity, 91, 99, 138, 259, 280, 283–285
Christianization, 278, 284
citizenship, 22, 29, 35, 60, 61, 71, 84, 86, 91, 129, 150, 254, 280
Ciudad Juárez, 171–172, 179
Civil Rights Act, 160
civil rights, 58, 70, 72, 108, 116, 118, 119, 159, 184, 192, 193, 197–200, 213, 219, 228, 235
civil society, 8, 15, 19, 32–33, 36, 37, 48, 49, 254, 270, 272, 299, 301, 302, 307
class, 26, 61, 73, 102, 128, 131, 132, 133, 139, 149, 150, 171, 173, 177, 178, 180, 183, 189, 191–192, 198–199, 201, 214, 218, 220, 245, 280, 286, 310, 355, 357
Clinton, Bill, 114, 119, 200
colonial: administration, 267, 268, 273, 278–279; education, 280–283; expansion, 101–102, 245; experience, 245, 247, 290, 295, 341; legacy, xi, 276–290, 296–297, 347–348; oppression, xi, 245, 258–261, 274, 339, 342, 346; resistance, 245, 313; rule, ix, 255, 258–261, 276–278, 286–288, 290, 295, 298, 309, 312, 341–343; settler state, 319, 320, 339, 340, 345, 348; status, 188, 308

Comfort Stations, 299, 300, 302, 305
Comfort Women, 2, 247, 298–306
commodification of harm, 347; of land, 285; of women, 299
commodity, 131, 139–143, 285
communism, 138–139
compensation, 299, 301–304, 306, 320, 321, 339, 342, 345, 347, 351
conjugal right, 33
consent, 7, 8, 14–16, 30, 34–38, 48, 51, 69, 270, 285
contract: racial, 2, 8, 40–44; sexual, 2, 8, 32–34, 38, 69; social, 2, 3, 6, 7, 8, 20–23, 25, 26, 32–34, 35, 40, 41, 58, 69; theory of, 28, 32, 35–37, 41–44, 58–67, 69
cooperation: scheme of, 26, 27; social, 25, 27, 28, 58, 132, 179, 220
cost-benefit analysis, 184, 209–210
Crenshaw, Kimberlé, 70
Cuban revolution, 311, 312, 313

death penalty. *See* capital punishment
DDT, 229
decolonization, 251–253, 349, 350
democracy, 6, 7, 24–25, 38, 70, 71, 100, 105, 131, 132, 133, 150, 151, 154, 171, 176, 179, 180, 214, 222, 254, 296, 307, 333, 358, 359
difference principle, 7, 47, 61, 63
discrimination: economic, 156, 159, 192, 204; racial, 8, 109, 113–114, 117, 132, 159, 189, 192, 203–204, 233, 307, 339, 341, 344, 348; sexual, 280, 289, 299, 306, 307
Disraeli, Benjamin, 269
division of labor: sexual, 287, 300
Doctrine of Double Effect, 203–204
double colonization, 277

367

double-self, 92
double-consciousness, 71, 247
drug crimes, 355–356

ecological movement, 196, 200
economic inequality: income and wage differentials and, 157–158; occupational mobility and segmentation and, 158–159; racial practices in the labor market and, 159–160; wealth and, 160
Emancipation Proclamation of 1863, 70, 92, 93, 96
environmental: destruction, 183, 185, 189, 195, 213, 235, 236, 240; hazards, 184, 185, 188, 189, 198, 203, 211, 229, 235, 236, 238, 239; identity, 227, 228, 231, 232, 233; injustice, 132, 198, 211, 226, 227, 235; justice, 183, 184, 188, 189, 213, 218, 226, 233, 235, 238; movement, 179, 184, 185, 188, 189, 197, 198, 212–215, 218–223, 227, 228–233; racism, 2, 184, 185, 188, 189–190, 191, 198, 203–204, 211, 226, 227, 228, 232, 233; reproductive justice, 183, 185, 234, 235–236, 239, 240
European: colonial expansion, 260, 261, 285; colonialism, 8, 245, 246, 255, 267, 278; colonization, 102, 245, 277, 289; culture, 101, 102, 246, 254, 255, 256, 267–268, 270; hegemony, 269, 270, 296; identity, 270; women, 277, 278, 290
exploitation, 102, 131, 132, 139, 155, 164, 188, 190, 195, 228, 274, 286, 307, 339, 346

Fair Labor Relations Act of 1938, 228
farmworkers, 2, 133, 162–166, 174, 175, 178, 193, 226, 227, 228–229, 231–232, 289
Ferguson, Missouri, 115, 118, 119, 127, 359

Fifteenth Amendment, 94
Filmer, Sir Robert, 33
Flaubert, Gustave, 269, 271, 273, 275
food: access, 46, 47, 50, 52, 53, 72; availability, 46, 49, 53, 127, 163, 164; deserts, 8, 9, 46–53; insecurity, 47, 49, 50, 52, 53, 72; security, 46–47, 49, 50
Foucault, Michel, 246, 268, 275
franchise, 84, 94
freedom, 2, 5, 6–8, 10, 12, 15, 16, 20–21, 23, 25, 28–29, 30–35, 38, 49, 58, 60, 62, 63, 65, 70, 71, 72, 73, 78–79, 80–83, 93, 94, 95, 104, 105, 108, 109, 110, 130, 139, 145, 150, 196, 197, 255, 266, 288, 309, 311, 312, 314, 344, 350, 357
Furman statutes, 113–114

Gandhi, M K, 201, 246, 247, 297
Garrison, William Lloyd, 83
gender: distinction, 218, 278, 285, 288, 300, 341; equity, 219, 222, 223; identity, 119, 183, 223, 277, 284; oppression, x, xi, 69, 185, 277, 284, 286–287, 290, 301, 303, 305, 307
general will, 21, 22–24
Goethe, Johann Wolfgang von, 136
Gramsci, Antonio, 270, 272, 275
grassroots activism, 2, 52, 188, 190, 198, 199, 213–223, 226, 228–233
Great Recession, 157, 160
groundwater contamination, 213, 222

health care, 2, 9, 47, 50, 53, 58–59, 61–67, 170, 177, 185, 188–193, 199, 206, 209, 213, 221–223, 228–229, 235–240
hegemony, 227, 269, 270, 290, 296, 308, 309, 310, 313, 314
Hobbes, Thomas, 5, 18–19, 35, 36, 40
housing: audit, 159; segregation, 73, 117, 127, 132, 189, 190, 204, 348
human nature, 147–148

human rights, 175, 178, 179, 254, 255, 298–299, 301, 302–304, 306, 319, 321, 323–328, 331–333, 340–342, 344–345, 347, 348

ICC. *See* International Criminal Court
ideal theory, 8, 40, 43–44
Idées de droit, 302–307
imperialism, ix, 104, 245, 252, 255, 260, 271, 274–275, 293
income: distribution, 7, 29, 31, 47, 58, 59, 61, 63, 66, 132, 133, 148, 162, 172, 183, 189,190, 206, 209–210, 213, 235, 348; racial disparities of, 73, 117, 132, 156–158, 160, 162, 192, 204, 355–357
indigenous people, 34, 174, 184, 185, 196, 213–214, 219, 221, 227, 234–240, 313, 320, 339–351. *See also* American Indian women
inferiority complex, 246, 260
injustice: cultural, 233, 247, 293–296, 319; economic, 27, 29, 47, 53, 147, 171; environmental, 2, 132, 184, 198, 204, 211, 226–227, 229, 233, 235; gender, historical, xi, 8, 43, 51, 51, 70, 221, 339–340, 342, 347–348, 352, 359; political, 22, 71, 211, 294, 333–334; racial, xi, 42–43, 72, 82, 85, 88, 100, 118, 192, 311
International Criminal Court (ICC), 331
intersectionality, 1, 2, 69–70, 185, 245

Japan, 98, 102, 105, 247, 261, 267, 298–306
Jim Crow, 110, 118, 159, 355

Kant, Immanuel, 8, 40, 41–42, 254
King, Martin Luther, Jr., 72, 129, 131, 197
Ku Klux Klan, 84, 87, 93

labor, 13–15, 132, 140–144; abuses, 164–166; cheap, 103–104, 190, 193, 229; child, 154, 344; division of, 300; market, 117, 156–159, 188, 228; power, 131, 141, 143–146; price of, 142–146; slave, 78–79, 145, 188, 339, 342, 345–346; time, 141–142, 144; unions, 102, 168, 175, 179, 193; value of, 48, 142–146; wage, 138, 140, 143–146, 287–289
land: appropriation, 5, 14–15, 16, 48–49, 104, 188, 218, 221, 226, 238, 259, 260, 341, 348, 350; grants, 213; sale of, 232, 285–287; use, 14, 183–184, 189, 198, 203, 210, 213, 219, 221–222, 232–233, 287
language, 263–264, 286, 330, 343–344, 350
law of nature, 10–12, 14, 16
lead poisoning, 184, 191–192, 198
León Portilla, Miguel, 249–252
liberalism, 2, 6, 7, 41–42, 44, 220, 272, 309
libertarianism, 184, 207, 210
liberty. See freedom
locally undesirable land uses (LULUs), 184, 203, 210–211
lynchings, 70, 71, 86–89, 91, 110

maquiladoras, 172, 178, 190, 233
Marable, Manning, 110
Maslow's Hierarchy of Needs, 206
maximin procedure, 60, 62, 64–65, 67
McCleskey v. Kemp, 14
meatpacking industry, 2, 133, 166–168
Memmi, Albert, 2, 276
migrants, 105, 128–129, 133, 164, 166, 172, 177, 178, 180, 228, 281, 315
Mill, John Stuart, 37, 38, 274–275
missionaries, 278, 280–284; and propaganda, 100, 102, 270, 280–281, 283–284
modernity, ix, x, xi, 41, 246, 252, 254, 255, 256, 296, 342
movements. See social movements

NAACP. See National Association for the Advancement of Colored People
NAFTA. See North American Free Trade Agreement
National Association for the Advancement of Colored People (NAACP), 71, 118, 184
national consciousness, 264–266
national struggle, 264
nationalism, 172, 296, 313
Native Americans, 5, 174, 187, 188, 192, 228, 233, 237, 314, 345. See also Indigenous people
New Zealand, 46, 47, 320, 339, 341, 349
Nigeria, 100, 103, 247, 259, 277, 278, 281, 282, 283, 287, 288, 289
NIMBY. See "Not in My Backyard"
North American Free Trade Agreement (NAFTA), 175, 179
Nozick, Robert, 41, 42, 47, 50–52
"Not in My Backyard" (NIMBY), 198, 206, 229
Nuestra América (our America), 308–310, 311, 312, 313–315

Obama, Barack, 117, 119, 121
Occident, the, 44, 267, 268, 269, 273
Occidentalism, 246, 252
Occupational Safety and Health Act (OSHA), 228
Occupational Safety and Health Administration (OSHA), 167
Orient, the, 246, 266–271, 273–274
Orientalism, 245–246, 267–271, 273–275
original position, 2, 6–7, 8, 26–27, 28, 59–67, 206
Orwell, George, 117
OSHA. See Occupational Safety and Health Act and Occupational Safety and Health Administration

paternalism, 228
patriarchy, 32–33, 201, 278–285
peacebuilding, 331–335
pidgin, 262

police: brutality, 2, 72, 111, 112, 115–116, 119, 121, 127–129, 260; and body cameras, 116
pollution, 2, 184, 185, 189, 190, 191, 192, 193, 198, 199, 204, 207, 209, 211, 213, 221, 236, 237, 238, 240
polygamy, 283–284, 289
"postcolonial revenge," 296
poverty, ix, 2, 46, 53, 73, 78, 79, 93, 94, 117, 132, 133, 148, 150, 162, 164, 172, 184, 189, 193, 198–199, 2013, 219, 229, 234–235, 237, 345–347, 356–357, 359; "draft," 178
primary goods, 7, 29–30, 47, 58, 60, 62
private property, 5, 6, 47, 49–52, 138, 204
profit, 102, 104, 131, 133, 144–145, 187, 339
proletariat, 132, 133, 258
prostitution, 33, 99, 299–302, 305–307

racism, 1, 2, 8, 41–42, 70, 71, 73, 116–118, 120–121, 160, 184–185, 188–190, 191–192, 195–201, 203, 204, 211, 214, 218, 226–229, 232–233, 261, 271, 277, 310, 311, 312, 341, 342, 348, 350
rape, 2, 35, 37, 38, 71, 85, 89, 90, 100, 103, 105, 115, 259
rational choice theory, 28
recognition: of state responsibility, 299, 302, 304–305; politics of, 185, 214, 227, 228–230, 233, 279, 312, 314, 333, 339, 344, 349, 351
reconciliation, 295, 326, 331–335, 339, 340, 345, 347, 356
rectification, 42, 51, 52, 211, 294, 302, 304, 306
refugees, 73, 127–130, 178
Règles de droit, 302, 304, 306
reintegration, 325, 327–328, 349, 357
religion, 27, 98, 99, 100, 101, 105, 138, 139, 197, 199, 200, 259, 279, 283–285, 304

reparations, 118, 247, 293, 319, 321, 326–328, 332, 339, 342, 345, 346–347, 351
resistance, 20, 21, 90, 118, 121, 132, 190, 197, 199, 211, 232, 245, 270, 282, 294, 308, 309, 310, 314, 315
restitution, 339, 341, 357. *See also* compensation

Salmonella contamination, 169
Sàró, 281, 282, 283, 286
savage man, 17–18
sex: discrimination, 280–290; industry, 299–300, 305–307
sexual assault, 37
Shakespeare, William, 135–137, 271
slavery, ix, 8, 23, 30, 36, 41, 70, 77, 81–82, 83, 85, 93, 95, 96, 100, 103, 104, 105, 110, 118, 120, 133, 146, 162, 163, 164, 165, 195, 258, 274, 284, 288, 312, 313, 339, 342, 346; sexual, 298–307
social movements: abolitionist, 197; anticolonial, 245, 297; Black Lives Matter, 113, 114, 118–120, 121; civil rights, 69, 72, 118, 184, 197, 200; environmental, 192–193, 195–196, 199, 200; environmental justice, 2, 184, 185, 187–188, 197–198, 212–215, 217, 223, 226–227, 229–233; Indigenous healing, 351; *Indignado*, 175; *Madres de Este de Los Angeles* (MELA), 230–231; Occupy, 2, 132, 170–180; restorative justice, 320; students, 121; victims' rights, 320. *See also* Black Lives Matter

Songen Jigyo, 304–305
sovereignty: colonial, 341–342, 347; food, 178; Indian, 213, 254; Indigenous, 339, 347, 349; national, 279, 290, 313
South African Truth and Reconciliation Commission (TRC), 321, 324–328, 333, 334–335, 340, 356, 359
state of nature, 5, 10–13, 14, 15, 16, 17–19, 20, 21, 23, 26, 32, 35–36, 40, 47, 50
"Stolen Generations," 343, 345–346, 350
suffrage, 86, 87, 105
surplus value, 48
swaraj, 297

Teitel, Ruth, 321, 339
therapeutic healing, 350
toxic: chemicals, 184, 203; colonialism, 190; herbicides, 184, 203; hazards, 204–205, 211; landfill, 184, 227; pesticides, 184, 203; waste, 2, 184, 191, 197–199, 203–211, 219, 226, 237
trade, 100, 101, 104, 172, 178, 191, 283, 287–289; drug, 355; slave, 196; spice, 268
transitional: justice, 2, 319, 320–321, 331–333, 339, 342, 348, 351; contexts, 323, 325–326, 328, 334–335, 339–340, 348, 349, 352
trauma, 344, 350, 351
TRC. *See* South African Truth and Reconciliation Commission
TRCC. *See* Truth and Reconciliation Commission Canada

Truth and Reconciliation Commission Canada (TRCC), 343, 344, 345
truth telling, 247, 293–294

UFW. *See* United Farm Workers
United Farm Workers (UFW), 226, 228–229
UN. *See* United Nations
United Nations (UN), 299, 331, 332, 339
utilitarianism, 28, 40, 41, 59, 184, 207–208, 209, 210

value: exchange, 140–141, 145, 288; surplus, 143–145; use, 139–142, 145, 288
veil, 92; of ignorance, 2, 6, 9, 26, 59, 60, 63, 206
Vico, Giambattista, 269
voluntarism, 35–36, 38
voluntary scheme, 26

"War on Drugs," 320, 355–356, 357, 358, 359
Warren County, NC, 184, 197
white man, 72, 81, 84–85, 87, 89–91, 94, 98, 99, 103, 108, 197, 255, 261–264, 278, 280; supremacy, 8, 71, 102, 110, 195, 196–197, 199, 201
whiteness, 42, 97; religion of, 98
World Bank, 191
World War: 99, 101–103, 105, 209, 245; II, 2, 42, 77, 209, 211, 228, 245, 252, 268, 300, 301

Yorùbá, 278–290

Made in the USA
Middletown, DE
11 December 2021